Literary Reflections

William R. Elkins

Kansas State Teachers College

Jack L. Kendall

University of Oklahoma

John R. Willingham

University of Kansas

Literary Reflections

McGraw-Hill Book Company

New York St. Louis San Francisco
Toronto London Sydney

Literary Reflections

Library of Congress Catalog Card Number 67-16927

19178

3 4 5 6 7 8 9 0 11 WC WC 7 5 4 3 2 1 0 6 9 8

Acknowledgments

W. H. Auden, "The Unknown Citizen" and "Musee des Beaux Arts." Copyright 1940 by W. H. Auden. Reprinted in the U.S. from *The Collected Poetry of W. H. Auden*, by permission of Random House, Inc., and in Canada from *Collected Shorter Poems* by W. H. Auden by permission of Faber and Faber Ltd., London.

James Baldwin, "Faulkner and Desegregation." Reprinted from *Nobody Knows My Name* by James Baldwin. Copyright © 1954, 1956, 1958, 1959, 1960, 1961 by James Baldwin and used with the permission of the publishers, The Dial Press, Inc.

Ambrose Bierce, "Parker Addison, Philosopher." Reprinted from *In the Midst of Life* by Ambrose Bierce, Random House, Inc.

Philip Booth, "Cold-Water Flat" from *Letter from a Distant Land* by Philip Booth. Copyright 1953 by Philip Booth. Reprinted by permission of The Viking Press, Inc.

Ivan Bunin, "The Gentleman from San Francisco." Copyright 1923, 1951 by Alfred A. Knopf, Inc. Reprinted from *The Gentleman from San Francisco and Other Stories*, by Ivan Bunin (Bernard Guilbert Guerney, trans.), by permission of Alfred A. Knopf, Inc.

John Cheever, "Torch Song." Reprinted from *The Enormous Radio and Other Stories* by John Cheever. By permission of the publishers, Funk & Wagnalls, N.Y.

E. E. Cummings, "since feeling is first." Copyright, 1926, by Horace Liveright; renewed, 1954 by E. E. Cummings. "pity this busy monster, manunkind." Copyright, 1944, by E. E. Cummings. Both reprinted from *Poems 1923–1954* by E. E. Cummings by permission of Harcourt, Brace & World, Inc.

T. S. Eliot, "The Love Song of J. Alfred Prufrock" from *Collected Poems 1909–1962* by T. S. Eliot, copyright, 1936, by Harcourt, Brace & World, Inc.; copyright, © 1963, 1964, by T. S. Eliot. Reprinted by permission of the publishers, Harcourt, Brace & World, Inc., and Faber and Faber Ltd., London.

William Faulkner, "Letter to the North," originally published as "Letter to a Northern Editor" © Copyright 1956 by William Faulkner. Reprinted from *Essays, Speeches and Public Letters*, by William Faulkner. "A Rose for Emily." Copyright 1930 and renewed 1957 by William Faulkner. Reprinted from *Collected Stories of William Faulkner*. Both used by permission of Random House, Inc.

Kenneth Fearing, "Dirge" from *Poems Selected and New*. Reprinted by permission of Indiana University Press.

Erich Fromm, excerpt from pp. 20–31, "The Theory of Love," *The Art of Loving* by Erich Fromm. Copyright © 1956 by Erich Fromm. Reprinted by permission of Harper & Row, Publishers.

Robert Frost, "The Death of the Hired Man," "Departmental" and "After Apple-Picking" from *Complete Poems of Robert Frost*. Copyright 1930, 1939 by Holt, Rinehart and Winston, Inc. Copyright 1936, © 1958 by Robert Frost. Copyright © 1964, 1967 by Lesley Frost Ballantine. Reprinted by permission of Holt, Rinehart and Winston, Inc.

Horace Gregory, "The Postman's Bell Is Answered Everywhere" from *Collected Poems* by Horace Gregory. Copyright 1941 by Horace Gregory. Reprinted by permission of Holt, Rinehart and Winston, Inc.

Thomas Hardy, "Channel Firing." Reprinted in the U.S. with permission of The Macmillan Company from *Collected Poems* by Thomas Hardy. Copyright 1925 by The Macmillan Company. Reprinted in Canada from *The Collected Poems of Thomas Hardy* by permission of the Trustees of the Hardy Estate, The Macmillan Co. of Canada Ltd., and Macmillan & Co. Ltd.

Ernest Hemingway, "A Clean, Well-Lighted Place" (Copyright 1933 Charles Scribner's Sons; renewal copyright © 1961 Ernest Hemingway) is reprinted with the permission of Charles Scribner's Sons from *Winner Take Nothing* by Ernest Hemingway.

John Holloway, "Journey Through the Night" from *The Minute and Longer Poems*, Marvell Press, Publishers. Reprinted by permission of David Higham Associates, Ltd., London.

Gerard Manley Hopkins, "God's Grandeur," "To R.B." and "The Caged Skylark" from *Poems of Gerard Manley Hopkins*, Third Edition, edited by W. H. Gardner. Copyright 1948 by Oxford University Press, Inc. Reprinted by permission.

A. E. Housman, "When I Was One and Twenty" and "Terence, This Is Stupid Stuff" from "A Shropshire Lad," Authorized Edition, from *The Collected Poems of A. E. Housman*. Copyright 1939, 1940, © 1959 by Holt, Rinehart and Winston, Inc. Copyright © 1967 by Robert E. Symons. Reprinted in the U.S. by permission of Holt, Rinehart and Winston, Inc., and in Canada by permission of The Society of Authors as literary representatives of the Estate of the late A. E. Housman, and Messrs. Jonathan Cape Ltd., publishers of A. E. Housman's *Collected Poems*.

Morton M. Hunt, "Love as Panacea." From *The Natural History of Love*, by Morton M. Hunt. © Copyright 1959 by Morton M. Hunt. Reprinted by permission of Alfred A. Knopf, Inc.

Robinson Jeffers, "Hurt Hawks." Copyright 1928 and renewed 1956 by Robinson Jeffers. Reprinted from *The Selected Poetry of Robinson Jeffers*, by permission of Random House, Inc.

Soren Kierkegaard, "Despair Is the Sickness Unto Death" reprinted from *The Sickness Unto Death* by Soren Kierkegaard. Translated by Walter Lowrie. Copyright 1941. By permission of Princeton University Press.

D. H. Lawrence, "The Spirit of Place" from *Studies in Classic American Literature* by D. H. Lawrence. Copyright 1923, 1951 by Frieda Lawrence, © 1961 by the Estate of the late Mrs. Frieda Lawrence. All Rights Reserved. "The Horse-Dealer's Daughter" from *The Complete Short Stories* by D. H. Lawrence, Vol. II. Copyright 1922 by Thomas B. Seltzer, Inc., 1950 by Frieda Lawrence. "Love on the Farm." Copyright 1920 by B. W. Huebsch, Inc., 1948 by Frieda Lawrence. "Terra Incognita." Copyright 1933 by Frieda Lawrence. All Rights Reserved. Both from *The Complete Poems of D. H. Lawrence,* Vol. I, edited by Vivian de Sola Pinto and F. Warren Roberts. All selections reprinted by permission of The Viking Press, Inc.

Archibald MacLeish, "Hypocrite Auteur" from *The Collected Poems of Archibald MacLeish.* Reprinted by permission of the publisher, Houghton Mifflin Company.

Bryan MacMahon, "Chestnut and Jet" from the book *The Lion-Tamer and Other Stories* by Bryan MacMahon. Copyright 1949 by Bryan MacMahon, Dutton Paperback Series. Reprinted in the U.S. by permission of E. P. Dutton & Co., Inc., and in Canada by permission of the author and Macmillan & Co. Ltd.

Thomas Mann, "Little Herr Friedemann." Copyright 1936 by Alfred A. Knopf, Inc. Reprinted from *Stories of Three Decades* by Thomas Mann, by permission of Alfred A. Knopf, Inc.

Marianne Moore, "Poetry." Reprinted with permission of The Macmillan Company from *Collected Poems* by Marianne Moore. Copyright Marianne Moore 1935, renewed 1963 by Marianne Moore and T. S. Eliot.

George Orwell, "Shooting an Elephant" from *Shooting an Elephant and Other Essays* by George Orwell, copyright, 1945, 1946, 1949, 1950 by Sonia Brownell Orwell. Reprinted by permission of Harcourt, Brace & World, Inc., and Martin Secker & Warburg Limited (Publishers).

Robert Pack, "A Bird in Search of a Cage" is reprinted with the permission of Charles Scribner's Sons from *The Irony of Joy: Poems by Robert Pack* (Copyright 1954, 1955 Robert Pack), POETS OF TODAY II.

Vance Packard, "The Growing Power of Admen." Copyright © 1957, by The Atlantic Monthly Company, Boston, Mass.

Ezra Pound, "Commission." From Ezra Pound, *Personae.* Copyright 1926 by Ezra Pound. Reprinted by permission of New Directions Publishing Corporation.

John Crowe Ransom, "Bells for John Whiteside's Daughter." Copyright 1924 by Alfred A. Knopf, Inc., and renewed 1952 by John Crowe Ransom. Reprinted from *Selected Poems,* by John Crowe Ransom, by permission of Alfred A. Knopf, Inc.

E. A. Robinson, "Miniver Cheevy" (Copyright 1907 Charles Scribner's Sons; renewal copyright 1935) is reprinted with the permission of Charles Scribner's Sons from *The Town Down the River* by Edwin Arlington Robinson. "Mr. Flood's Party" from *Collected Poems* by Edwin Arlington Robinson. Copyright Edwin Arlington Robinson 1921, renewed 1949 by Ruth Nivison. "Cassandra" from *Man Against the Sky* by Edwin Arlington Robinson. Copyright The Macmillan Company 1916, renewed 1944 by Ruth Nivison. Both reprinted with permission of The Macmillan Company.

Philip Roth, "The Conversion of the Jews" from *Goodbye, Columbus* by Philip Roth. Reprinted by permission of the publisher, Houghton Mifflin Company.

Karl Shapiro, "Drug Store." Copyright 1941 by Karl Shapiro. Reprinted from *Poems 1940–1953*, by Karl Shapiro, by permission of Random House, Inc.

Sophocles, *The Oedipus Rex of Sophocles:* An English version by Dudley Fitts and Robert Fitzgerald, copyright, 1949 by Harcourt, Brace & World, Inc., and reprinted with their permission.

Stephen Spender, "I Think Continually of Those." Copyright 1934 and renewed 1961 by Stephen Spender. Reprinted in the U.S. from *Collected Poems 1928–1953*, by Stephen Spender, by permission of Random House, Inc., and in Canada from *Collected Poems* by Stephen Spender by permission of Faber and Faber Ltd., London.

Edmund Spenser, Sonnet 79 from the *Amoretti* and selection from Book II, Canto VII of *The Faerie Queene*, both from *The Complete Poetical Works of Spenser*, Cambridge Edition of the Poets. Reprinted by permission of the publisher, Houghton Mifflin Company.

James Stephens, "Deirdre." Reprinted in the U.S. with permission of The Macmillan Company from *Songs from the Clay* by James Stephens. Copyright The Macmillan Company 1915, renewed 1943 by James Stephens. Reprinted in Canada from *Collected Poems* by James Stephens by permission of Mrs. Iris Wise, Macmillan & Co. Ltd., and The Macmillan Co. of Canada Ltd.

Wallace Stevens, "Of Modern Poetry." Copyright 1942 by Wallace Stevens. Reprinted from *The Collected Poems of Wallace Stevens*, by permission of Alfred A. Knopf, Inc.

R. L. Stevenson, "Requiem" from *Complete Poems of Robert Louis Stevenson*, Charles Scribner's Sons.

A. C. Swinburne, "The Garden of Proserpine" from *Complete Works of Algernon Charles Swinburne*, William Heinemann Ltd., 1925.

Dylan Thomas, "In My Craft or Sullen Art" from Dylan Thomas, *Collected Poems*. Copyright 1953 by Dylan Thomas. Reprinted in the U.S. by permission of the publisher, New Directions Publishing Corporation, and in Canada by permission of J. M. Dent & Sons Ltd., London, and the Literary Executors of the Dylan Thomas Estate.

Thorstein Veblen, "Pecuniary Canons of Taste" from *The Theory of the Leisure Class* by Thorstein Veblen. All Rights Reserved. Reprinted by permission of The Viking Press, Inc.

Eudora Welty, "Powerhouse." Copyright, 1941 by Eudora Welty. Reprinted from her volume, *A Curtain of Green and Other Stories*, by permission of Harcourt, Brace & World, Inc.

Leslie A. White, "The Symbol: The Origin and Basis of Human Behavior." Reprinted from *The Science of Culture* by Leslie A. White, by permission of Farrar, Straus & Giroux, Inc. Copyright 1949 by Leslie A. White.

Reed Whittemore, "A Projection." Copyright 1956 by Reed Whittemore. Reprinted from *The Yale Review* by permission of the author.

Richard Wilbur, "Junk" © 1961 by Richard Wilbur. Reprinted from his volume, *Advice to a Prophet and Other Poems*, by permission of Harcourt, Brace & World, Inc.

Tennessee Williams, The Glass Menagerie. Copyright 1945 by Tennessee Williams. Reprinted from *Six Modern American Plays*, by permission of Random House, Inc.

For Eileen, Dorothy, and Yvonne

Preface

Literary Reflections *encompasses a vast amount and an unusual variety of literary expression. It disclaims the limitations imposed by separating literature into segments suggested by genres, nationality of authors, or chronology. Instead, our book seeks to relate literature to thematic headings which suggest the most compelling aspects of the human condition. Such a plan, we believe, encourages the student almost immediately to make comparisons of attitudes, the technical possibilities of each literary type, and, equally important, the formal strategies of individual authors. Our text is intended to serve three separate but necessarily overlapping purposes.*

1. *It offers a stimulating insight into the history of ideas.*
2. *It provides a viable means of identifying, comparing, and contrasting modes of expression.*
3. *It challenges the student to come to grips with universally relevant ideas and problems, as they recur in literature, and encourages him to work out, carefully and imaginatively, his own formulations of them.*

To accomplish our objectives, we have arranged the selections in six thematic units. Each unit is internally structured to present 1. essays that introduce in a relatively familiar prose form the thematic emphasis of the unit, 2. short stories as a logical step from the essay to more imaginative writing, 3. a drama (in three units only), placed third because it retains some features of fiction but adds the dimension of visual presentation. 4. selected poetry that carries the student to the most intricate, most compressed, hence most intense form of the literary imagination. In effect, that movement from type to type within each unit will enhance both the understanding of technique and the interest in ideas.

In addition, we have provided brief introductory discussions for each thematic unit to support and guide the student's reading. For each selection we have appended appropriate headnotes, provocative study questions, and suggestions for compositions. All of these devices are intended simply to challenge the student without in any way preempting his critical judgments. The book, then, contains ample materials for a rich encounter with literature and adds, for those who wish it, a framework for purposeful writing about literature. And the thematic organization, keeping faith with each author's general intent and vision, will not hamper the perceptive instructor who chooses his own alignment of selections.

Many colleagues and students have helped the editors to shape this book. For assistance varying from encouragement to strong suggestions, we gratefully acknowledge the generous offices of Professors Charlton Hinman and James A. Gowen, Mrs. Melinda M. Carpenter, Mrs. Karen Lescarboura, and Mr. Donald F. Warders, all of the University of Kansas; and Professor Theodore C. Owen of the Kansas State Teachers College. For generously sharing her editorial expertise we owe much to Yvonne Willingham of The University of Kansas Press.

William R. Elkins
Jack L. Kendall
John R. Willingham

Contents

PART TWO / THE PROTEST AGAINST RESTRAINT

The Essay

The Short Story

Poetry

PART THREE / THE MEANING OF LOVE

The Essay

The Short Story

Drama

Poetry

PART FOUR / THE PROTEST AGAINST MATERIALISM

The Essay

The Short Story

Poetry

PART FIVE / THE SEARCH FOR MODES OF EXPRESSION

The Essay

The Short Story

Poetry

PART SIX / IN VIEW OF DEATH

The Essay

The Short Story

Drama

Poetry

Introduction to Literary Types

Critics and scholars have speculated endlessly from the days of Aristotle about the nature and analysis of literature. Literary Reflections *demonstrates not only the vital relationship between human experience and literary expression but it also directs the reader's attention to the apparently unlimited variety of uses of language in effecting techniques and forms. For any generalization about literature must include statements about the artist's use of words in a certain way to achieve a certain effect. And such statements necessarily must recognize the existence of conventional categories—literary genres or types. In this volume, we encounter four major genres—the essay, the short story, the drama, and the poem. Although the resources of any one of these may be present in the others, we can make some statements which are generally true only for each of the four types.*

THE ESSAY

The term essay, *as the designation for a type of literary composition, first appeared in English toward the end of the sixteenth century. To the Elizabethans the word meant a kind of literary exploration, an attempt (cf. the French verb* essayer, *"to try") to state something—perhaps a serious argument, sometimes a more or less random reflection upon experience. However or whenever it originally appeared, the essay has always involved exposition of an idea. The author may be relatively uninterested in aesthetic effects, but he is always attempting an orderly arrangement of thought. The characteristic mode of the essay, then, is "man thinking" in relatively formal structures. In a well-developed essay, the reader looks for a central idea or thesis, either explicit or implicit. The rest is mainly the arrangement of evidence, of reasons, of illustrations, or whatever amplification the thesis requires. If the author's literary bent permits, he may in addition utilize figurative language, narration, description, or dramatic incident as important elements of his thought, as does George Orwell in "Shooting an Elephant." The "literary essay," distinguished by its conscious display of style and rhetorical virtuosity, does not enjoy in the twentieth century the favor it enjoyed up through the nineteenth century. Far more familiar today is the "article" which we find in newspapers and magazines, with the writer's ideas set forth in relatively familiar terms. The journalist, such as Vance Packard, with his characteristically simple language and short paragraphs, fills for our day the role which brought honor to such men as Richard Steele, Joseph Addison, Jonathan Swift, Thomas Carlyle, Thomas Babington Macaulay, Ralph Waldo Emerson, and James Russell Lowell. Nevertheless such twentieth-century stylists as George Orwell, Virginia Woolf, Loren Eisley, and Alfred Kazin keep alive the tradition of the essay as a creative literary medium. For discriminating readers, the journey with such representatives of "man thinking" (as Emerson called his ideal "American scholar") can be stimulating and fruitful, whether the author presents himself as an analyst of juvenile delinquency, as a professional sociologist probing the difficulties of love in the modern world, as a scientist advancing his hypothesis about life on Mars, or as a "personal essayist" simply detailing his reactions to old china or recalling his memories of a Creole courtyard in old New Orleans.*

THE SHORT STORY

Relatively new as a recognized literary genre, the short story utilizes the mode of narrative. That is, someone recounts for us a plausible, sequential experience. Gertrude Stein may have simplified outrageously the formula for narration: "And after that what changes what changes after that, after that what changes and what changes after that and after that and what changes and after that and what changes after that"; but she emphasized rightly the importance of progression and the relationship of events within imagined time.

The writer of fiction further imposes upon his narrative a deliberate design by the kind of characters he creates, the quality and outcome of the situation in which those characters are involved, and the establishment of a viewpoint toward those characters and their situations. Whether the story is told ostensibly by a character deeply involved in the events of the plot, by an outside observer, or even frankly by the author himself, the method of fiction establishes some meaningful order of events, reveals what of significance the characters did and said, and brings the sequence to a conclusion that implies an attitude toward experience. The order of events may be as straightforward as that outlined by Miss Stein; on the other hand, the narrative may leap backward and forward in time, as it does in Faulkner's "A Rose for Emily," making strategic use of what in the movies is called the "flashback." But even when straight chronological order is violated, fiction creates for us a world more or less like the one we have known: the big difference between fiction and life arises from the writer's prerogative to impose upon his fictional "world" the kind of order and control he desires.

Whereas the essayist restricts his statement to facts, to a report of what he has thought and observed, to his beliefs and an invitation to the reader to accept or at least understand those beliefs, the writer of fiction, particularly in our day, characteristically does not intervene in his narrative with direct, editorial statement. He merely tells his story as artfully as possible and allows the combination of characterization, plot, theme, imagery, dramatic situation, and condensed narrative to imply as much about his world view as it can. Ivan Bunin does not have to state directly his attitude toward the materialistic values of his nameless "gentleman from San Francisco": every juxtaposition of scene and every exchange of dialogue forcibly conveys to us Bunin's judgments. The difference between the "pulp" magazine story or the saccharine tale in a woman's magazine, on the one hand, and the memorable fictional illumination of human experience, on the other, is simply one of insight and artistry, which together distinguish good fiction from escape fiction.

Every student has heard of the pyramid design for plot—in which generating circumstances rise through conflict to denouement *(literally, the "untying of the knot," or the solution). And ordinarily the pyramid design fits the typical short story rather well. In one way or another, the author of a short story quickly establishes a situation containing the seeds of conflict which rises to a point of crisis or "climax" before descending, perhaps very abruptly, to the resolution or* denouement. *Although the sequence of events may not end happily, it must satisfy the reader's sense of appropriateness in terms of the kind of conflict narrated.*

THE DRAMA

Drama, an ancient literary form, was explained by the Greeks with considerable sophistication. Aristotle analyzed the various elements—plot, diction, spectacle—which the dramatist utilizes; and his successors have elaborated endlessly upon theories of the drama. Although much of what we have said about the short story is equally true of the drama (both relate stories, both ask the reader to accept as plausible the sequence of events, and both have a plot design), the writer of fiction tells us in his own way about *certain characters in a certain situation, whereas the dramatist conjures up a world to be created by stage designers and actors and brought to life by actors. In* Antony and Cleopatra, *Shakespeare allows the stage designer much leeway: for act I, scene i, we have only the stark notation: "Alexandria. A room in Cleopatra's Palace." On the other hand, Tennessee Williams provides elaborate "Production Notes" for* The Glass Menagerie; *and his stage directions specify the kind of atmosphere he desires and the aura of character and incident he expects. Shakespeare's poetry is the source of clues to character interpretation, although such clues of course can be refined by an imaginative director. Cleopatra can be made as lascivious as the director wishes; Antony can be portrayed as magnificently or as irresolutely as the production planners desire. Williams, however, indicates the tone and the effect his characters should achieve in their gestures as well as their speeches. In any play the characters are interpreted, with the help of such notes and stage directions as the dramatist provides, by directors and by actors who move on and off a stage, speak to each other or to themselves as the script of the play dictates, and seem with the help of lighting, makeup, stage properties, costumes, and gestures to be real people who undergo a span of experience before an audience. One important distinction between drama and fiction is that those segments of imagined experience selected by the playwright as most important are acted out before an audience; moreover, those segments, whether or not divided into acts and scenes, occupy exactly the same time span spent by the audience in watching those segments. To read a play successfully, we must supply through the imagination the staging, the lighting, the direction, the sound effects, and, with such help as we may get from the stage directions, the movements of the actors. Reading a play may be a relatively poor substitute for watching a performance of it, but the reading can be both exciting and profitable nevertheless. We can pause to consider the possible implications of a character's speech, or we may backtrack as often as we wish in order to fathom the emerging form of the drama. And to the extent that drama forces us to attend to each word a character speaks, it requires something of the close reading that we give to poetry.*

THE POEM

Like the short story and the novel, the poem may relate a narrative. Or, as in Browning's "The Bishop Orders His Tomb at St. Praxed's Church" or Frost's "The Death of the Hired Man," the poem may be a drama in miniature: though it is not intended for a performance, its characters simply speak aloud and reveal a dramatic situation. Although it is the most ancient and exalted literary type, poetry is harder than any of the other types to define. We know that poems look *different: the poet dictates how his work will appear upon the printed page. Its lines, unlike those of prose, tend to be symmetrical, though sentence units are not always completed within the line. Even the poems of an idiosyncratic modern poet like E. E. Cummings, with unconventional uses of typography, have a more formal appearance than any work of prose. But quantitative measures like typography, stanzaic pattern, or meter do not really help much to define poetry. For greeting card "verse" exhibits many of the physical properties of poetry. Qualitative standards, on the other hand, discover for us the presence of poetry. The essential point is that in poetry language is compressed and elevated beyond that of ordinary discourse. Poetry may not always be, as William Wordsworth said, "emotion recollected in tranquillity"; but at least, whether in conventionally metrical or "free" verse or even "prose poems," the conscious ordering of language is all-important. In its compulsion toward rhythmic patterns and selective word sounds, poetry suggests strong relationships to music; in its typical drive to evoke images, poetry suggests comparisons with painting. Perhaps Emerson's witty definition of a poem as a "metre-making argument" comes close enough to a formal definition; but in its combined appeals to emotion and thought through the artful arrangement of words, even the relatively short poem, if it is successful, brings to the reader a sudden illumination of the human condition and a "deliverance" that he cannot obtain through any other literary type. In the twentieth century, poetry probably does not enjoy the prestige it commanded in other ages; on the other hand, more poets write and more experimentation takes place than in any other century.*

PART ONE

The Search for a Place in Society

When we speak of man's search for a place in society, we touch upon that side of man's nature that he almost always conceals from others and often conceals from himself. Obviously, the search for a place is both a search for a physical place and a search for an inner sense of identity. In this dual function, only the physical place manifests itself; yet the search is primarily an inner one. Each man, whether or not he admits it, carries within him an ideal image of himself. This self-image is a primary consideration in his attempts to place himself physically within society. In short, the search for a place becomes an attempt of each man to reconcile that ideal image he has of himself not only with his position in society but, also, with the treatment that society accords him. Consequently, writers have found the inner conflict between the what ought to be *and the* what is *a theme so basic, yet so diverse, that its treatment lends itself to all types of literature.*

D. H. Lawrence's essay "The Spirit of Place" is the first chapter of his book Studies in Classic American Literature. *In this essay, Lawrence considers place as a dominant factor in the development of a national character and a national literature. But, in keeping with the dual function of place, Lawrence has much to say about man's inner search for identity and its control of his actions, and the physical place in which he chooses to exercise his actions. Lawrence says, "Men are only free when they are doing what the deepest self likes." George Orwell's personal narrative "Shooting an Elephant" also deals with the conflict that arises when a man's physical place—in this essay, Orwell's position of authority in an alien society—runs counter to his personal wishes. Although a position of authority seems most attractive to man because it is tangible evidence that he has achieved a place in society, he must decide if he is ready to limit his inner image in line with the dictates of his position.*

Rudyard Kipling fictionalizes the same underlying theme that Orwell deals with firsthand in his narrative. As you read "The Man Who Would Be King," observe how the author reveals the desire of Carnehan and Dravot to find a place of authority in an alien society. Because colonial India is inferior, in their opinions, to white Western civilization, the inner image they hold of their superiority grows to godlike proportions, and their position of authority becomes untenable. The second short story, Thomas Mann's "Little Herr Friedemann," takes another turn within this theme. Herr Friedemann, crippled from birth, has created a world of compromise, suppressing his normal desires in recognition that society cannot accept abnormality. When, however, he forgets the limitations of his place in society, he finds the disparity between the what is *and the* what ought to be *too great to allow a return to the world of compromise.*

Tennessee Williams' play The Glass Menagerie *posits a world in which everyone, except possibly the "gentleman caller," faces an intolerable conflict between his place in a dreamworld and his place in a "real" world he never made or wanted. Even Jim O'Connor, the "gentleman caller," remembers with nostalgia his days of glory in high school; nevertheless, he has come to terms with life, beyond the ability of the Wingfields, by settling for a relatively commonplace existence. But everyone else, particularly the mother, frantically demands an escape hatch into a world made tolerable by some kind of romantically oriented private dream. The conflict (always the essence of drama) arises from the apparent impossibility of compromising those dreams with the demands of economics, custom, or social position as insisted upon by Amanda.*

The Essay

THE essay that follows points up the fact that literary classifications should be flexible enough to accommodate the creative talents of the writer. Lawrence's informal approach to what is generally considered a formal area (literary criticism) in essay writing illustrates that the writer of the essay need not be limited by dictates of form in his attempt to reach his reader. Lawrence disarms his reader with a wide variety of unexpected techniques. We should be alert, however, and weigh carefully our reaction to the following:

1. The conversational, bantering tone
2. The use of charged, colorful, idiosyncratic speech forms more characteristic of the orated diatribe than the essay
3. The highly subjective point of view—Lawrence's experience becomes authority for every man's experience
4. The name-calling, blatantly revealing Lawrence's prejudices in such a way as to suggest that they should rightly be every man's prejudices

The Spirit of Place

D. H. LAWRENCE

We like to think of the old-fashioned American classics as children's books. Just childishness, on our part. The old American art-speech contains an alien quality, which belongs to the American continent and to nowhere else. But, of course, so long as we insist on reading the books as children's tales, we miss all that.

One wonders what the proper high-brow Romans of the third and fourth or later centuries read into the strange utterances of Lucretius or Apuleius or Tertullian, Augustine or Athanasius. The uncanny voice of Iberian Spain, the weirdness of old Carthage, the passion of Libya and North Africa; you may bet the proper old Romans never heard these at all. They read old Latin inference over the top of it, as we read old European inference over the top of Poe or Hawthorne.

It is hard to hear a new voice, as hard as it is to listen to an unknown language. We just don't listen. There is a new voice in the old American classics. The world has declined to hear it, and has babbled about children's stories.

Why?—Out of fear. The world fears a new experience more than it fears anything. Because a new experience displaces so many old experiences. And it is like trying to use muscles that have perhaps never been used, or that have been going stiff for ages. It hurts horribly.

The world doesn't fear a new idea. It can pigeon-hole any idea. But it can't pigeon-hole a real new experience. It can only dodge. The world is a great dodger, and the Americans the greatest. Because they dodge their own very selves.

There is a new feeling in the old American books, far more than there is in the modern American books, which are pretty empty of any feeling, and proud of it. There is a "different" feeling in the old American classics. It is the shifting over from the old psyche to something new, a displacement. And displacements hurt. This hurts. So we try to tie it up, like a cut finger. Put a rag round it.

It is a cut too. Cutting away the old emotions and consciousness. Don't ask what is left.

Art-speech is the only truth. An artist is usually a damned liar, but his art, if it be art, will tell you the truth of his day. And that is all that matters. Away with eternal truth. Truth lives from day to day, and the marvellous Plato of yesterday is chiefly bosh to-day.

The old American artists were hopeless liars. But they were artists, in spite of themselves. Which is more than you can say of most living practitioners.

And you can please yourself, when you read *The Scarlet Letter*, whether you accept what that sugary, blue-eyed little darling of a Hawthorne has to say for himself, false as all darlings are, or whether you read the impeccable truth of his art-speech.

The curious thing about art-speech is that it prevaricates so terribly, I mean it tells such lies. I suppose because we always all the time tell ourselves lies. And out of a pattern of lies art weaves the truth. Like Dostoevsky posing as a sort of Jesus, but most truthfully revealing himself all the while as a little horror.

Truly art is a sort of subterfuge. But thank God for it, we can see through the subterfuge if we choose. Art has two great functions. First, it provides an emotional experience. And then, if we have the courage of our own feelings, it becomes a mine of practical truth. We have had the feelings *ad nauseam*. But we've never dared dig the actual truth out of them, the truth that concerns us, whether it concerns our grandchildren or not.

The artist usually sets out—or used to—to point a moral and adorn a tale. The tale, however, points the other way, as a rule. Two blankly opposing morals, the artist's and the tale's. Never trust the artist. Trust the tale. The proper function of a critic is to save the tale from the artist who created it.

Now we know our business in these studies; saving the American tale from the American artist.

Let us look at this American artist first. How did he ever get to America, to start with? Why isn't he a European still, like his father before him?

Now listen to me, don't listen to him. He'll tell you the lie you expect. Which is partly your fault for expecting it.

He didn't come in search of freedom of worship. England had more freedom of worship in the year 1700 than America had. Won by Englishmen who wanted freedom, and so stopped at home and fought for it. And got it. Freedom of worship? Read the history of New England during the first century of its existence.

Freedom anyhow? The land of the free! This the land of the free! Why, if I say anything that displeases them, the free mob will lynch me, and that's my freedom. Free? Why, I have never been in any country where the individual has such an abject fear of his fellow countrymen. Because, as I say, they are free to lynch him the moment he shows he is not one of them.

No, no, if you're so fond of the truth about Queen Victoria, try a little about yourself.

Those Pilgrim Fathers and their successors never came here for freedom of worship. What did they set up when they got here? Freedom, would you call it?

They didn't come for freedom. Or if they did, they sadly went back on themselves.

All right then, what did they come for? For lots of reasons. Perhaps least of all in search of freedom of any sort: positive freedom, that is.

They came largely to get *away*—that most simple of motives. To get away. Away from what? In the long run, away from themselves. Away from everything. That's why most people have come to America, and still do come. To get away from everything they are and have been.

"Henceforth be masterless."

Which is all very well, but it isn't freedom. Rather the reverse. A hopeless sort of constraint. It is never freedom till you find something you really *positively want to be*. And people in America have always been shouting about the things they are *not*. Unless, of course, they are millionaires, made or in the making.

And after all there is a positive side to the movement. All that vast flood of human life that has flowed over the Atlantic in ships from Europe to America has not flowed over simply on a tide of revulsion from Europe and from the confinements of the European ways of life. This revulsion was, and still is, I believe, the prime motive in emigration. But there was some cause, even for the revulsion.

It seems as if at times man had a frenzy for getting away from any control of any sort. In Europe the old Christianity was the real master. The Church and the true aristocracy bore the responsibility for the working out of the Christian ideals: a little irregularly, maybe, but responsible nevertheless.

Mastery, kingship, fatherhood had their power destroyed at the time of the Renaissance.

And it was precisely at this moment that the great drift over the Atlantic started. What were men drifting away from? The old authority of Europe? Were they breaking the bonds of authority, and escaping to a new more absolute unrestrainedness? Maybe. But there was more to it.

Liberty is all very well, but men cannot live without masters. There is always a master. And men either live in glad obedience to the master they believe in, or they live in a frictional opposition to the master they wish to undermine. In America this frictional opposition has been the vital factor. It has given the Yankee his kick. Only the continual influx of more servile Europeans has provided America with an obedient labouring class. The true obedience never outlasting the first generation.

But there sits the old master, over in Europe. Like a parent. Somewhere deep in every American heart lies a rebellion against the old parenthood of Europe. Yet no American feels he has completely escaped its mastery. Hence the slow, smouldering patience of American opposition. The slow, smouldering, corrosive obedience to the old master Europe, the unwilling subject, the unremitting opposition.

Whatever else you are, be masterless.

> "Ca Ca Caliban
> Get a new master, be a new man."

Escaped slaves, we might say, people the republics of Liberia or Haiti. Liberia enough! Are we to look at America in the same way? A vast republic of escaped slaves. When you consider the hordes from eastern Europe, you might well say it: a vast republic of escaped slaves. But one dare not say this of the Pilgrim Fathers, and the great old body of idealist Americans, the modern Americans tortured with thought. A vast republic of escaped slaves. Look out, America! And a minority of earnest, self-tortured people.

The masterless.

"Ca Ca Caliban
Get a new master, be a new man."

What did the Pilgrim Fathers come for, then, when they came so gruesomely over the black sea? Oh, it was in a black spirit. A black revulsion from Europe, from the old authority of Europe, from kings and bishops and popes. And more. When you look into it, more. They were black, masterful men, they wanted something else. No kings, no bishops maybe. Even no God Almighty. But also, no more of this new "humanity" which followed the Renaissance. None of this new liberty which was to be so pretty in Europe. Something grimmer, by no means free-and-easy.

America has never been easy, and is not easy to-day. Americans have always been at a certain tension. Their liberty is a thing of sheer will, sheer tension: a liberty of THOU SHALT NOT. And it has been so from the first. The land of THOU SHALT NOT. Only the first commandment is: THOU SHALT NOT PRESUME TO BE A MASTER. Hence democracy.

"We are the masterless." That is what the American Eagle shrieks. It's a Hen-Eagle.

The Spaniards refused the post-Renaissance liberty of Europe. And the Spaniards filled most of America. The Yankees, too, refused, refused the post-Renaissance humanism of Europe. First and foremost, they hated masters. But under that, they hated the flowing ease of humour in Europe. At the bottom of the American soul was always a dark suspense, at the bottom of the Spanish-American soul the same. And this dark suspense hated and hates the old European spontaneity, watches it collapse with satisfaction.

Every continent has its own great spirit of place. Every people is polarized in some particular locality, which is home, the homeland. Different places on the face of the earth have different vital effluence, different vibration, different chemical exhalation, different polarity with different stars: call it what you like. But the spirit of place is a great reality. The Nile valley produced not only the corn, but the terrific religions of Egypt. China produces the Chinese, and will go on doing so. The Chinese in San Francisco will in time cease to be Chinese, for America is a great melting-pot.

There was a tremendous polarity in Italy, in the city of Rome. And this seems to have died. For even places die. The Island of Great Britain had a wonderful terrestrial magnetism or polarity of its own, which made the British people. For the moment, this polarity seems to be breaking. Can England die? And what if England dies?

Men are less free than they imagine; ah, far less free. The freest are perhaps least free.

Men are free when they are in a living homeland, not when they are straying and breaking away. Men are free when they are obeying some deep, inward voice of religious belief. Obeying from within. Men are free when they belong to a living, organic, *believing* community, active in fulfilling some unfulfilled, perhaps unrealized purpose. Not when they are escaping to some wild west. The most unfree souls go west, and shout of freedom. Men are freest when they are most unconscious of freedom. The shout is a rattling of chains, always was.

Men are not free when they are doing just what they like. The moment you can do just what you like, there is nothing you care about doing. Men are only free when they are doing what the deepest self likes.

And there is getting down to the deepest self! It takes some diving.

Because the deepest self is way down, and the conscious self is an obstinate monkey. But of one thing we may be sure. If one wants to be free, one has to give up the illusion of doing what one likes, and seek what IT wishes done.

But before you can do what IT likes, you must first break the spell of the old mastery, the old IT.

Perhaps at the Renaissance, when kingship and fatherhood fell, Europe drifted into a very dangerous half-truth: of liberty and equality. Perhaps the men who went to America felt this, and so repudiated the old world together. Went one better than Europe. Liberty in America has meant so far the breaking away from *all* dominion. The true liberty will only begin when Americans discover IT, and proceed possibly to fulfil IT. IT being the deepest *whole* self of man, the self in its wholeness, not idealistic halfness.

That's why the Pilgrim Fathers came to America, then; and that's why we come. Driven by IT. We cannot see that invisible winds carry us, as they carry swarms of locusts, that invisible magnetism brings us as it brings the migrating birds to their unforeknown goal. But it is so. We are not the marvellous choosers and deciders we think we are. IT chooses for us, and decides for us. Unless, of course, we are just escaped slaves, vulgarly cocksure of our ready-made destiny. But if we are living people, in touch with the source, IT drives us and decides us. We are free only so long as we obey. When we run counter, and think we will do as we like, we just flee around like Orestes pursued by the Eumenides.

And still, when the great day begins, when Americans have at last discovered America and their own wholeness, still there will be the vast number of escaped slaves to reckon with, those who have no cocksure, ready-made destinies.

Which will win in America, the escaped slaves, or the new whole men?

The real American day hasn't begun yet. Or at least, not yet sunrise. So far it has been the false dawn. That is, in the progressive American consciousness there has been the one dominant desire, to do away with the old thing. Do away with masters, exalt the will of the people. The will of the people being nothing but a figment, the exalting doesn't count for much. So, in the name of the will of the people, get rid of masters. When you have got rid of masters, you are left with this mere phrase of the will of the people. Then you pause and bethink yourself, and try to recover your own wholeness.

So much for the conscious American motive, and for democracy over here. Democracy in America is just the tool with which the old master of Europe, the European spirit, is undermined. Europe destroyed, potentially, American democracy will evaporate. America will begin.

American consciousness has so far been a false dawn. The negative ideal of democracy. But underneath, and contrary to this open ideal, the first hints and revelations of IT. IT, the American whole soul.

You have got to pull the democratic and idealistic clothes off American utterance, and see what you can of the dusky body of IT underneath.

"Henceforth be masterless."

Henceforth be mastered.

Questions

1. Why does Lawrence say that the world finds it hard to hear a new voice? In what way does he draw a parallel between the "new voice" and a new experience?
2. How does Lawrence view the intent of the artist in respect to the art that he creates?
3. Lawrence sees the story of America's founding as a myth. What theory does he offer to replace the myth? Is his definition of freedom valid?
4. What does he mean by "Henceforth be masterless"?
5. If we separate Lawrence's hysteria from his subject matter, what three main ideas emerge?

Topics for Composition

1. Lawrence's style may obscure many interesting ideas. Write a summary of this essay.
2. The author speaks of a tension in the American idea of freedom. He literally means that Americans constantly work to preserve their concept of freedom. Support this idea by focusing on current events.
3. Investigate the possibilities of complete freedom—the idea of "Henceforth be masterless."

ORWELL'S "Shooting an Elephant," from the viewpoint of form, is an excellent example of narrative technique and descriptive writing. Since both narration and description are indispensable tools for the writer, we should look closely at Orwell's handling of these techniques. The following guidelines should prove helpful:

1. Narration achieves its unity through the writer's ability to select events for their relevance and arrange them in a sequence that will best hold the reader's attention. Observe Orwell's selectivity and his chronological arrangement.
2. The writer of a narrative essay has a responsibility to elements of plot, character, and setting. He will most often emphasize one and subordinate the other two. In this essay, is it the plot, the actual shooting of the elephant? Is it the setting, the picture of lower Burma? Or is it the man, Orwell's inner conflict?
3. The writer of the narrative essay should maintain a consistent point of view. Orwell is both narrator and participant. How does point of view reflect this dual role?

Shooting an Elephant

GEORGE ORWELL

In Moulmein, in lower Burma, I was hated by large numbers of people—the only time in my life that I have been important enough for this to happen to me. I was sub-divisional police officer of the town, and in an aimless, petty kind of way anti-European feeling was very bitter. No one had the guts to raise a riot, but if a European woman went through the bazaars alone somebody would probably spit betel juice over her dress. As a police officer I was an obvious target and was baited whenever it seemed safe to do so. When a nimble Burman tripped me up on the football field and the referee (another Burman) looked the other way, the crowd yelled with hideous laughter. This happened more than once. In the end the sneering yellow faces of young men that met me everywhere, the insults hooted after me when I was at a safe distance, got badly on my nerves. The young Buddhist priests were the worst of all. There were several thousands of them in the town and none of them seemed to have anything to do except stand on street corners and jeer at Europeans.

All this was perplexing and upsetting. For at that time I had already made up my mind that imperialism was an evil thing and the sooner I chucked up my job and got out of it the better. Theoretically—and secretly, of course—I was all for the Burmese and all against their oppressors, the British. As for the job I was doing, I hated it more bitterly than I can perhaps make clear. In a job like that you see the dirty work of Empire at close quarters. The wretched prisoners huddling in the stinking cages of the lock-ups, the grey, cowed faces of the long-term convicts, the scarred buttocks of the men who had been flogged with bamboos—all these oppressed me with an intolerable sense of guilt. But I could get nothing into perspective. I was young and ill-educated and I had had to think out my problems in the utter silence that is imposed on every Englishman in the East. I did not even know that the British Empire is dying, still less did I know that it is a great deal better than the younger empires that are going to supplant it. All I knew was that I was stuck between my hatred of the empire I served and my rage against the evil-spirited little beasts who tried to make my job impossible. With one part of my mind I thought of the British Raj as an unbreakable tyranny, as something clamped down, in *saecula saecu-*

lorum, upon the will of prostrate peoples; with another part I thought that the greatest joy in the world would be to drive a bayonet into a Buddhist priest's guts. Feelings like these are the normal by-products of imperialism; ask any Anglo-Indian official, if you can catch him off duty.

One day something happened which in a roundabout way was enlightening. It was a tiny incident in itself, but it gave me a better glimpse than I had had before of the real nature of imperialism—the real motives for which despotic governments act. Early one morning the sub-inspector at a police station the other end of the town rang me up on the 'phone and said that an elephant was ravaging the bazaar. Would I please come and do something about it? I did not know what I could do, but I wanted to see what was happening and I got on to a pony and started out. I took my rifle, an old .44 Winchester and much too small to kill an elephant, but I thought the noise might be useful *in terrorem*. Various Burmans stopped me on the way and told me about the elephant's doings. It was not, of course, a wild elephant, but a tame one which had gone "must." It had been chained up, as tame elephants always are when their attack of "must" is due, but on the previous night it had broken its chain and escaped. Its mahout, the only person who could manage it when it was in that state, had set out in pursuit, but had taken the wrong direction and was now twelve hours' journey away, and in the morning the elephant had suddenly reappeared in the town. The Burmese population had no weapons and were quite helpless against it. It had already destroyed somebody's bamboo hut, killed a cow and raided some fruit-stalls and devoured the stock; also it had met the municipal rubbish van and, when the driver jumped out and took to his heels, had turned the van over and inflicted violences upon it.

The Burmese sub-inspector and some Indian constables were waiting for me in the quarter where the elephant had been seen. It was a very poor quarter, a labyrinth of squalid bamboo huts, thatched with palm-leaf, winding all over a steep hillside. I remember that it was a cloudy, stuffy morning at the beginning of the rains. We began questioning the people as to where the elephant had gone and, as usual, failed to get any definite information. That is invariably the case in the East; a story always sounds clear enough at a distance, but the nearer you get to the scene of events the vaguer it becomes. Some of the people said that the elephant had gone in one direction, some said that he had gone in another, some professed not even to have heard of any elephant. I had almost made up my mind that the whole story was a pack of lies, when we heard yells a little distance away. There was a loud, scandalized cry of "Go away, child! Go away this instant!" and an old woman with a switch in her hand came round the corner of a hut, violently shooing away a crowd of naked children. Some more women followed, clicking their tongues and exclaiming; evidently there was something that the children ought not to have seen. I rounded the hut and saw a man's dead body sprawling in the mud. He was an Indian, a black Dravidian coolie, almost naked, and he could not have been dead many minutes. The people said that the elephant had come suddenly upon him round the corner of the hut, caught him with its trunk, put its foot on his back and ground him into the earth. This was the rainy season and the ground was soft, and his face had scored a trench a foot deep and a couple of yards long. He was lying on his belly with arms crucified and head sharply twisted to one side. His face was coated with mud, the eyes wide open, the teeth bared and grinning with an expression of unendurable agony. (Never tell me, by the way, that the dead look peaceful. Most of the corpses I have seen looked devilish.) The friction of the great beast's foot had stripped the skin from his back as neatly as one skins a rabbit. As soon as I saw the dead man I sent an orderly to a friend's house nearby to borrow an elephant rifle. I had already sent back the pony, not wanting it to go mad with fright and throw me if it smelt the elephant.

The orderly came back in a few minutes with a rifle and five cartridges, and meanwhile some Burmans had arrived and told us that the elephant was in the paddy fields below, only a few hundred yards away. As I started forward practically the whole population of the quarter flocked out of the houses and followed me. They had seen the rifle and were all shouting excitedly that I was going to shoot the elephant. They had not shown much interest in the elephant when he was merely ravaging their homes, but it was different now that he was going to be shot. It was a bit of fun to them, as it would be to an English crowd; besides they wanted the meat. It made me vaguely uneasy. I had no intention of shooting the elephant—I had merely sent for the rifle to defend myself if necessary—and it is always unnerving to have a crowd following you. I marched down the hill, looking and feeling a fool, with the rifle over my shoulder and an ever-growing army of people jostling at my heels. At the bottom, when you got away from the huts, there was a metalled road and beyond that a miry waste of paddy fields a thousand yards across, not yet ploughed but soggy from the first rains and dotted with coarse grass. The elephant was standing eight yards from the road, his left side towards us. He took not the slightest notice of the crowd's approach. He was tearing up bunches of grass, beating them against his knees to clean them and stuffing them into his mouth.

I had halted on the road. As soon as I saw the elephant I knew with perfect certainty that I ought not to shoot him. It is a serious matter to shoot a working elephant—it is comparable to destroying a huge and costly piece of machinery—and obviously one ought not to do it if it can possibly be avoided. And at that distance, peacefully eating, the elephant looked no more dangerous than a cow. I thought then and I think now that his attack of "must" was already passing off; in which case he would merely wander harmlessly about until the mahout came back and caught him. Moreover, I did not in the least want to shoot him. I decided that I would watch him for a little while to make sure that he did not turn savage again, and then go home.

But at that moment I glanced round at the crowd that had followed me. It was an immense crowd, two thousand at the least and growing every minute. It blocked the road for a long distance on either side. I looked at the sea of yellow faces above the garish clothes—faces all happy and excited over this bit of fun, all certain that the elephant was going to be shot. They were watching me as they would watch a conjurer about to perform a trick. They did not like me, but with the magical rifle in my hands I was momentarily worth watching. And suddenly I realized that I should have to shoot the elephant after all. The people expected it of me and I had got to do it; I could feel their two thousand wills pressing me forward, irresistibly. And it was at this moment, as I stood there with the rifle in my hands, that I first grasped the hollowness, the futility of the white man's dominion in the East. Here was I, the white man with his gun, standing in front of the unarmed native crowd—seemingly the leading actor of the piece; but in reality I was only an absurd puppet pushed to and fro by the will of those yellow faces behind. I perceived in this moment that when the white man turns tyrant it is his own freedom that he destroys. He becomes a sort of hollow, posing dummy, the conventionalized figure of a sahib. For it is the condition of his rule that he shall spend his life in trying to impress the "natives," and so in every crisis he has got to do what the "natives" expect of him. He wears a mask, and his face grows to fit it. I had got to shoot the elephant. I had committed myself to doing it when I sent for the rifle. A sahib has got to act like a sahib; he has got to appear resolute, to know his own mind and do definite things. To come all that way, rifle in hand, with two thousand people marching at my heels, and then to trail feebly away, having done nothing—no, that was impossible. The crowd would laugh at me. And my whole life, every white man's life in the East, was one long struggle not to be laughed at.

But I did not want to shoot the elephant. I watched him beating his bunch of grass against his knees, with that preoccupied grandmotherly air that elephants have. It seemed to me that it would be murder to shoot him. At that age I was not squeamish about killing animals, but I had never shot an elephant and never wanted to. (Somehow it always seems worse to kill a *large* animal.) Besides, there was the beast's owner to be considered. Alive, the elephant was worth at least a hundred pounds; dead, he would only be worth the value of his tusks, five pounds, possibly. But I had got to act quickly. I turned to some experienced-looking Burmans who had been there when we arrived, and asked them how the elephant had been behaving. They all said the same thing: he took no notice of you if you left him alone, but he might charge if you went too close to him.

It was perfectly clear to me what I ought to do. I ought to walk up to within, say, twenty-five yards of the elephant and test his behavior. If he charged, I could shoot; if he took no notice of me, it would be safe to leave him until the mahout came back. But also I knew that I was going to do no such thing. I was a poor shot with a rifle and the ground was soft mud into which one would sink at every step. If the elephant charged and I missed him, I should have about as much chance as a toad under a steam-roller. But even then I was not thinking particularly of my own skin, only of the watchful yellow faces behind. For at that moment, with the crowd watching me, I was not afraid in the ordinary sense, as I would have been if I had been alone. A white man mustn't be frightened in front of "natives"; and so, in general, he isn't frightened. The sole thought in my mind was that if anything went wrong those two thousand Burmans would see me pursued, caught, trampled on and reduced to a grinning corpse like that Indian up the hill. And if that happened it was quite probable that some of them would laugh. That would never do. There was only one alternative. I shoved the cartridges into the magazine and lay down on the road to get a better aim.

The crowd grew very still, and a deep, low, happy sigh, as of people who see the theatre curtain go up at last, breathed from innumerable throats. They were going to have their bit of fun after all. The rifle was a beautiful German thing with cross-hair sights. I did not then know that in shooting an elephant one would shoot to cut an imaginary bar running from ear-hole to ear-hole. I ought, therefore, as the elephant was sideways on, to have aimed straight at his ear-hole; actually I aimed several inches in front of this, thinking the brain would be further forward.

When I pulled the trigger I did not hear the bang or feel the kick—one never does when a shot goes home—but I heard the devilish roar of glee that went up from the crowd. In that instant, in too short a time, one would have thought, even for the bullet to get there, a mysterious, terrible change had come over the elephant. He neither stirred nor fell, but every line of his body had altered. He looked suddenly stricken, shrunken, immensely old, as though the frightful impact of the bullet had paralysed him without knocking him down. At last, after what seemed a long time—it might have been five seconds, I dare say—he sagged flabbily to his knees. His mouth slobbered. An enormous senility seemed to have settled upon him. One could have imagined him thousands of years old. I fired again into the same spot. At the second shot he did not collapse but climbed with desperate slowness to his feet and stood weakly upright, with legs sagging and head drooping. I fired a third time. That was the shot that did for him. You could see the agony of it jolt his whole body and knock the last remnant of strength from his legs. But in falling he seemed for a moment to rise, for as his hind legs collapsed beneath him he seemed to tower upward like a huge rock toppling, his trunk reaching skywards like a tree. He trumpeted, for the first and only time. And then down he came, his belly towards me, with a crash that seemed to shake the ground even where I lay.

I got up. The Burmans were already racing past me across the mud. It was obvious that the elephant would never rise again, but he was not dead. He was breathing very rhythmically with long rattling gasps, his great mound of a side painfully rising and falling. His mouth was wide open—I could see far down into caverns of pale pink throat. I waited a long time for him to die, but his breathing did not weaken. Finally I fired my two remaining shots into the spot where I thought his heart must be. The thick blood welled out of him like red velvet, but still he did not die. His body did not even jerk when the shots hit him, the tortured breathing continued without a pause. He was dying, very slowly and in great agony, but in some world remote from me where not even a bullet could damage him further. I felt that I had got to put an end to that dreadful noise. It seemed dreadful to see the great beast lying there, powerless to move and yet powerless to die, and not even to be able to finish him. I sent back for my small rifle and poured shot after shot into his heart and down his throat. They seemed to make no impression. The tortured gasps continued as steadily as the ticking of a clock.

In the end I could not stand it any longer and went away. I heard later that it took him half an hour to die. Burmans were bringing dahs and baskets even before I left, and I was told they had stripped his body almost to the bones by the afternoon.

Afterwards, of course, there were endless discussions about the shooting of the elephant. The owner was furious, but he was only an Indian and could do nothing. Besides, legally I had done the right thing, for a mad elephant has to be killed, like a mad dog, if its owner fails to control it. Among the Europeans opinion was divided. The older men said I was right, the younger men said it was a damn shame to shoot an elephant for killing a coolie, because an elephant was worth more than any damn Coringhee coolie. And afterwards I was very glad that the coolie had been killed; it put me legally in the right and it gave me a sufficient pretext for shooting the elephant. I often wondered whether any of the others grasped that I had done it solely to avoid looking a fool.

Questions

1. What statement of Orwell's comes closest to stating his actual problem? What is the universal application of his predicament?
2. Orwell constantly refers to his personal feelings about government and imperialism. How do these feelings support his inner conflict?
3. What descriptive passages are added to the sequence of events? In what way does his description contribute to the impact of the essay?
4. Were Orwell's actions justified? How would you classify his attitude in the final paragraph?

Topics for Composition

1. Everyone at some time has had to assume authority. Select an incident in which you had authority over others. Write a narrative essay describing the limitations placed on your personal wishes by your position of

authority. Pay close attention to selectivity and arrangement of the events. Give attention also to descriptive detail.

2. Describe an event that you witnessed or a scene that you came upon suddenly and that has remained vividly in your mind. Orwell's description of the man trampled by the elephant can serve as an excellent model for your attention to relevant detail.
3. Write an essay in answer to the question: "How individual can an individual be?"

The Short Story

Like the narrative essayist, the short story writer combines elements of plot, character, and setting in proportions that best suit his theme; hence, the structure of a short story may provide important insights about the overall effect the writer wished to create. Note the following aspects of Kipling's structural technique:

1. His story is actually two stories, each having its narrator and individual point of view. Observe the way in which the two stories aid us to understand the differences in character between Carnehan and Dravot.
2. Setting is important in both the narrator's story and Carnehan and Dravot's story. Note the way in which the setting in the narrator's story contributes to the credibility of the other story.
3. Point of view and details of setting may be merged to create a special atmosphere. Note the way Kipling achieves this merging and its effect on the atmosphere.

The Man Who Would Be King

RUDYARD KIPLING

Brother to a Prince and fellow to a beggar if he be found worthy.

The Law, as quoted, lays down a fair conduct of life, and one not easy to follow. I have been fellow to a beggar again and again under circumstances which prevented either of us finding out whether the other was worthy. I have still to be brother to a Prince, though I once came near to kinship with what might have been a veritable King and was promised the reversion of a Kingdom—army, law-courts, revenue and policy all complete. But, to-day, I greatly fear that my King is dead, and if I want a crown I must go hunt it for myself.

The beginning of everything was in a railway train upon the road to Mhow from Ajmir. There had been a Deficit in the Budget, which necessitated travelling, not Second-class, which is only half as dear as First-class, but by Intermediate, which is very awful indeed. There are no cushions in the Intermediate class, and the population are either Intermediate, which is Eurasian, or native, which for a long night journey is nasty, or Loafer, which is amusing though intoxicated. Intermediates do not buy from refreshment-rooms. They carry their food in bundles and pots, and buy sweets from the native sweetmeat-sellers, and drink the roadside water. That is why in hot weather Intermediates are taken out of the carriages dead, and in all weathers are most properly looked down upon.

My particular Intermediate happened to be empty till I reached Nasirabad, when a big black-browed gentleman in shirt-sleeves entered, and, following the custom of Intermediates, passed the time of day. He was a wanderer and a vagabond like myself, but with an educated taste for whiskey. He told tales of things he had seen and done, of out-of-the-way corners of the Empire into which he had penetrated, and of adventures in which he risked his life for a few days' food.

"If India was filled with men like you and me, not knowing more than the crows where they'd get their next day's rations, it isn't seventy millions of revenue the land would be paying—it's seven hundred millions," said he; and as I looked at his mouth and chin I was disposed to agree with him.

We talked politics—the politics of Loaferdom that sees things from the underside where the lath and plaster is not smoothed off—and we talked postal arrangements because my friend wanted to send a telegram back from the next station to Ajmir, the turning-off place from the Bombay to the Mhow line as you travel westward. My friend had no money beyond eight annas which he wanted for dinner, and I had no money at all, owing to the hitch in the Budget before mentioned. Further, I was going into a wilderness where, though I should resume touch with the Treasury, there were no telegraph offices. I was, therefore, unable to help him in any way.

"We might threaten a Station-master, and make him send a wire on tick," said my friend, "but that'd mean enquiries for you and for me, and *I've* got my hands full these days. Did you say you were traveling back along this line within many days?"

"Within ten," I said.

"Can't you make it eight?" said he. "Mine is rather urgent business."

"I can send your telegram within ten days if that will serve you," I said.

"I couldn't trust the wire to fetch him now I think of it. It's this way. He leaves Delhi on the 23rd for Bombay. That means he'll be running through Ajmir about the night of the 23rd."

"But I'm going into the Indian Desert," I explained.

"Well *and* good," said he. "You'll be changing at Marwar Junction to get into Jodhpore territory—you must do that—and he'll be coming through Marwar Junction in the early morning of the 24th by the Bombay Mail. Can you be at Marwar Junction on that time? 'Twon't be inconveniencing you because I know that there's precious few pickings to be got out of these Central India States—even though you pretend to be correspondent of the *Backwoodsman*."

"Have you ever tried that trick?" I asked.

"Again and again, but the Residents find you out and then you get escorted to the Border before you've time to get your knife into them. But about my friend here. I *must* give him a word o' mouth to tell him what's come to me or else he won't know where to go. I would take it more than kind of you if you was to come out of Central India in time to catch him at Marwar Junction, and say to him: 'He has gone South for the week.' He'll know what that means. He's a big man with a red beard, and a great swell he is. You'll find him sleeping like a gentleman with all his luggage round him in a Second-class apartment. But don't you be afraid. Slip down the window and say: 'He has gone South for the week,' and he'll tumble. It's only cutting your time of stay in those parts by two days. I ask you as a stranger—going to the West," he said with emphasis.

"Where have *you* come from?" said I.

"From the East," said he, "and I am hoping that you will give him the message on the Square—for the sake of my Mother as well as your own."

Englishmen are not usually softened by appeals to the memory of their mothers; but for certain reasons, which will be fully apparent, I saw fit to agree.

"It's more than a little matter," said he, "and that's why I asked you to do it—and now I know that I can depend on you doing it. A Second-class carriage at Marwar Junction, and a red-haired man asleep in it. You'll be sure to remember. I get out at the next station, and I must hold on there till he comes or sends me what I want."

"I'll give the message if I catch him," I said, "and for the sake of your Mother as well as mine I'll give you a word of advice. Don't try to run the Central India States just now as the correspondent of the *Backwoodsman*. There's a real one knocking about here, and it might lead to trouble."

"Thank you," said he simply, "and when will the swine be gone? I can't starve because he's ruining my work. I wanted to get hold of the Degumber Rajah down here about his father's widow, and give him a jump."

"What did he do to his father's widow, then?"

"Filled her up with red pepper and slippered her to death as she hung from a beam. I found that out myself and I'm the only man that would dare going into the State to get hush-money for it. They'll try to poison me, same as they did in Chortumna when I went on the loot there. But you'll give the man at Marwar Junction my message?"

He got out at a little roadside station, and I reflected. I had heard, more than once, of men personating correspondents of newspapers and bleeding small Native States with threats of exposure, but I had never met any of the caste before. They lead a hard life, and generally die with great suddenness. The Native States have a wholesome horror of English newspapers, which may throw light on their peculiar methods of government, and do their best to choke correspondents with champagne, or drive them out of their mind with four-in-hand barouches. They do not understand that nobody cares a straw for the internal administration of Native States so long as oppression and crime are kept within decent limits, and the ruler is not drugged, drunk, or diseased from one end of the year to the other. They are the dark places of the earth, full of unimaginable cruelty, touching the Railway and the Telegraph on one side, and, on the other, the days of Harun-al-Raschid. When I left the train I did business with divers Kings, and in eight days passed through many changes of life. Sometimes I wore dress-clothes and consorted with Princes and Politicals, drinking from crystal and eating from silver. Sometimes I lay out upon the ground and devoured what I could get, from a plate made of leaves, and drank the running water, and slept under the same rug as my servant. It was all in the day's work.

Then I headed for the Great Indian Desert upon the proper date, as I had promised, and the night Mail set me down at Marwar Junction, where a funny little, happy-go-lucky, native-managed railway runs to Jodhpore. The Bombay Mail from Delhi makes a short halt at Marwar. She arrived as I got in, and I had just time to hurry to her platform and go down the carriages. There was only one Second-class on the train. I slipped the window and looked down upon a flaming red beard, half covered by a railway rug. That was my man, fast asleep, and I dug him gently in the ribs. He woke with a grunt and I saw his face in the light of the lamps. It was a great and shining face.

"Tickets again?" said he.

"No," said I. "I am to tell you that he is gone South for the week. He has gone South for the week!"

The train had begun to move out. The red man rubbed his eyes. "He has gone South for the week," he repeated. "Now that's just like his impudence. Did he say that I was to give you anything? 'Cause I won't."

"He didn't," I said and dropped away, and watched the red lights die out in the dark. It was horribly cold because the wind was blowing off the sands. I climbed into my own train—not an Intermediate carriage this time—and went to sleep.

If the man with the beard had given me a rupee I should have kept it as a memento of a rather curious affair. But the consciousness of having done my duty was my only reward.

Later on I reflected that two gentlemen like my friends could not do any good if they foregathered and personated correspondents of newspapers, and might, if they black-mailed one of the little rat-trap states of Central India or Southern Rajputana, get themselves into serious difficulties. I therefore took some trouble to describe them as accurately as I could remember to people who would be interested in deporting them: and succeeded, so I was later informed, in having them headed back from the Degumber borders.

Then I became respectable, and returned to an Office where there were no Kings and no incidents outside the daily manufacture of a newspaper. A newspaper office seems to attract every conceivable sort of person, to the prejudice of discipline. Zenana-mission ladies arrive, and beg that the Editor will instantly abandon all his duties to describe a Christian prize-giving in a back-slum of a perfectly inaccessible village; Colonels who have been overpassed for command sit down and sketch the outline of a series of ten, twelve, or twenty-four leading articles on Seniority *versus* Selection; missionaries wish to know why they have not been permitted to escape from their regular vehicles of abuse and swear at a brother-missionary under special patronage of the editorial We; stranded theatrical companies troop up to explain that they cannot pay for their advertisements, but on their return from New Zealand or Tahiti will do so with interest; inventors of patent punkah-pulling machines, carriage couplings and unbreakable swords and axle-trees call with specifications in their pockets and hours at their disposal; tea-companies enter and elaborate their prospectuses with the office pens; secretaries of ball-committees clamour to have the glories of their last dance more fully described; strange ladies rustle in and say:

"I want a hundred lady's cards printed *at once,* please," which is manifestly part of an Editor's duty; and every dissolute ruffian that ever tramped the Grand Trunk Road makes it his business to ask for employment as a proof-reader. And, all the time, the telephone-bell is ringing madly, and Kings are being killed on the Continent, and Empires are saying—"You're another," and Mister Gladstone is calling down brimstone upon the British Dominions, and the little black copyboys are whining, "*kaa-pi chay-ha-yeh*" (copy wanted) like tired bees, and most of the paper is as blank as Modred's shield.

But that is the amusing part of the year. There are six other months when none ever come to call, and the thermometer walks inch by inch up to the top of the glass, and the office is darkened to just above reading-light, and the press-machines are red-hot to touch, and nobody writes anything but accounts of amusements in the Hill-stations or obituary notices. Then the telephone becomes a tinkling terror, because it tells you of the sudden deaths of men and women that you knew intimately, and the prickly heat covers you with a garment, and you sit down and write: "A slight increase of sickness is reported from the Khuda Janta Khan District. The outbreak is purely sporadic in its nature, and, thanks to the energetic efforts of the District authorities, is now almost at an end. It is, however, with deep regret we record the death," etc.

Then the sickness really breaks out, and the less recording and reporting the better for the peace of the subscribers. But the Empires and the Kings continue to divert themselves as selfishly as before, and the Foreman thinks that a daily paper really ought to come out once in twenty-four hours, and all the people at the Hill-stations in the middle of their amusements say: "Good gracious! Why can't the paper be sparkling? I'm sure there's plenty going on up here."

That is the dark half of the moon, and, as the advertisements say, "must be experienced to be appreciated."

It was in that season, and a remarkably evil season, that the paper began running the last issue of the week on Saturday night, which is to say Sunday morning, after the custom of a London paper. This was a great convenience, for immediately after the paper was put to bed, the dawn would lower the thermometer from 96° to almost 84° for half an hour, and in that chill—you have no idea how cold is 84° on the grass until you begin to pray for it—a very tired man could get off to sleep ere the heat roused him.

One Saturday night it was my pleasant duty to put the paper to bed alone. A King or courtier or a courtesan or a Community was going to die or get a new Constitution, or do something that was important on the other side of the world, and the paper was to be held open till the latest possible minute in order to catch the telegram.

It was a pitchy black night, as stifling as a June night can be, and the *loo*, the red-hot wind from the westward, was booming among the tinder-dry trees and pretending that the rain was on its heels. Now and again a spot of almost boiling water would fall on the dust with the flop of a frog, but all our weary world knew that was only pretence. It was a shade cooler in the press-room than the office, so I sat there, while the type ticked and clicked, and the night-jars hooted at the windows, and the all but naked compositors wiped the sweat from their foreheads, and called for water. The thing that was keeping us back, whatever it was, would not come off, though the *loo* dropped and the last type was set, and the whole round earth stood still in the choking heat, with its finger on its lip, to wait the event. I drowsed, and wondered whether the telegraph was a blessing, and whether this dying man, or struggling people, might be aware of the inconvenience the delay was causing. There was no special reason beyond the heat and worry to make tension, but, as the clock-hands crept up to three o'clock and the machines spun their fly-wheels two and three times to see that all was in order, before I said the word that would set them off, I could have shrieked aloud.

Then the roar and rattle of the wheels shivered the quiet into little bits. I rose to go away, but two men in white clothes stood in front of me. The first one said: "It's him!" The second said: "So it is!" And they both laughed almost as loudly as the machinery roared, and mopped their foreheads. "We seed there was a light burning across the road and we were sleeping in that ditch there for coolness, and I said to my friend here, The office is open. Let's come along and speak to him as turned us back from the Degumber State," said the smaller of the two. He was the man I had met in the Mhow train, and his fellow was the red-bearded man of Marwar Junction. There was no mistaking the eyebrows of the one or the beard of the other.

I was not pleased, because I wished to go to sleep, not to squabble with loafers. "What do you want?" I asked.

"Half an hour's talk with you, cool and comfortable, in the office," said the red-bearded man. "We'd *like* some drink—the Contrack doesn't begin yet, Peachey, so you needn't look—but what we really want is advice. We don't want money. We ask you as a favour, because we found out you did us a bad turn about Degumber State."

I led from the press-room to the stifling office with the maps on the walls, and the red-haired man rubbed his hands. "That's something like," said he. "This was the proper shop to come to. Now, Sir, let me introduce to you Brother Peachey Carnehan, that's him, and Brother Daniel Dravot, that is *me*, and the less said about our professions the better, for we have been most things in our time. Soldier, sailor, compositor, photographer, proof-reader, street-preacher, and correspondents of the *Backwoodsman* when we thought the paper wanted one. Carnehan is sober, and so am I. Look at us first, and see that's sure. It will save you cutting into my talk. We'll take one of your cigars apiece, and you shall see us light up."

I watched the test. The men were absolutely sober, so I gave them each a tepid whiskey and soda.

"Well *and* good," said Carnehan of the eyebrows, wiping the froth from his moustache. "Let me talk now, Dan. We have been all over India, mostly on foot. We have been boiler-fitters, engine-drivers, petty contractors, and all that, and we have decided that India isn't big enough for such as us."

They certainly were too big for the office. Dravot's beard seemed to fill half the room and Carnehan's shoulders the other half, as they sat on the big table. Carnehan continued: "The country isn't half worked out because they that governs it won't let you touch it. They spend all their blessed time in governing it, and you can't lift a spade, nor chip a rock, nor look for oil, nor anything like that without all the Government saying—'Leave it alone, and let us govern.' Therefore, such *as* it is, we will let it alone, and go away to some other place where a man isn't crowded and can come to his own. We are not little men, and there is nothing that we are afraid of except Drink, and we have signed a Contrack on that. *Therefore*, we are going away to be Kings."

"Kings in our own right," muttered Dravot.

"Yes, of course," I said. "You've been tramping in the sun, and it's a very warm night, and hadn't you better sleep over the notion? Come to-morrow."

"Neither drunk nor sunstruck," said Dravot. "We have slept over the notion half a year, and require to see Books and Atlases, and we have decided that there is only one place now in the world that two strong men can Sar-a-*whack*. They call it Kafiristan. By my reckoning it's the top right-hand corner of Afghanistan, not more than three hundred miles from Peshawar. They have two-and-thirty heathen idols there, and we'll be the thirty-third and fourth. It's a mountaineous country, and the women of those parts are very beautiful."

"But that is provided against in the Contrack," said Carnehan. "Neither Woman nor Liqu-or, Daniel."

"And that's all we know, except that no one has gone there, and they fight, and in any place where they fight a man who knows how to drill men can always be a King. We shall go to those parts and say to any King we find—'D'you want to vanquish your foes?' and we will show him how to drill men; for that we know better than anything else. Then we will subvert that King and seize his Throne and establish a Dy-nasty."

"You'll be cut to pieces before you're fifty miles across the Border," I said. "You have to travel through Afghanistan to get to that country. It's one mass of mountains and peaks and glaciers, and no Englishman has been through it. The people are utter brutes, and even if you reached them you couldn't do anything."

"That's more like," said Carnehan. "If you could think us a little more mad we would be more pleased. We have come to you to know about this country, to read a book about it, and to be shown maps. We want you to tell us that we are fools and to show us your books." He turned to the book-cases.

"Are you at all in earnest?" I said.

"A little," said Dravot sweetly. "As big a map as you have got, even if it's all blank where Kafiristan is, and any books you've got. We can read, though we aren't very educated."

I uncased the big thirty-two-miles-to-the-inch map of India, and two smaller Frontier maps, hauled down volume INF-KAN of the *Encyclopædia Britannica*, and the men consulted them.

"See here!" said Dravot, his thumb on the map. "Up to Jagdallak, Peachey and me know the road. We was there with Roberts' Army. We'll have to turn off to the right at Jagdallak through Laghmann territory. Then we get among the hills—fourteen thousand feet—fifteen thousand—it will be cold work there, but it don't look very far on the map."

I handed him Wood on the *Sources of the Oxus*. Carnehan was deep in the *Encyclopædia*.

"They're a mixed lot," said Dravot reflectively; "and it won't help us to know the names of their tribes. The more tribes the more they'll fight, and the better for us. From Jagdallak to Ashang. H'mm!"

"But all the information about the country is as sketchy and inaccurate as can be," I protested. "No one knows anything about it really. Here's the file of the *United Services' Institute*. Read what Bellew says."

"Blow Bellew!" said Carnehan. "Dan, they're a stinkin' lot of heathens, but this book here says they think they're related to us English."

I smoked while the men pored over *Raverty*, *Wood*, the maps, and the *Encyclopædia*.

"There is no use your waiting," said Dravot politely. "It's about four o'clock now. We'll go before six o'clock if you want to sleep, and we won't steal any of the papers. Don't you sit up. We're two harmless lunatics, and if you come to-morrow evening down to the Serai we'll say good-bye to you."

"You *are* two fools," I answered. "You'll be turned back at the Frontier or cut up the minute you set foot in Afghanistan. Do you want any money or a recommendation down-country? I can help you to the chance of work next week."

"Next week we shall be hard at work ourselves, thank you," said Dravot. "It isn't so easy being a King as it looks. When we've got our Kingdom in going order we'll let you know, and you can come up and help us to govern it."

"Would two lunatics make a Contrack like that?" said Carnehan, with subdued pride, showing me a greasy half-sheet of notepaper on which was written the following. I copied it, then and there, as a curiosity—

This Contract between me and you persuing witnesseth in the name of God—Amen and so forth.

(*One*) *That me and you will settle this matter together;* i.e., *to be Kings of Kafiristan.*

(*Two*) *That you and me will not, while this matter is being settled, look at any Liquor, nor any Woman black, white, or brown, so as to get mixed up with one or the other harmful.*

(*Three*) *That we conduct ourselves with Dignity and Discretion, and if one of us gets into trouble the other will stay by him.*

Signed by you and me this day.
Peachey Taliaferro Carnehan.
Daniel Dravot.
Both Gentlemen at Large.

"There was no need for the last article," said Carnehan, blushing modestly; "but it looks regular. Now you know the sort of men that loafers are—we *are* loafers, Dan, until we get out of India—and *do* you think that we would sign a Contrack like that unless we was in earnest? We have kept away from the two things that make life worth having."

"You won't enjoy your lives much longer if you are going to try this idiotic adventure. Don't set the office on fire," I said, "and go away before nine o'clock."

I left them still poring over the maps and making notes on the back of the "Contrack." "Be sure to come down to the Serai tomorrow," were their parting words.

The Kumharsen Serai is the great four-square sink of humanity where the strings of camels and horses from the North load and unload. All the nationalities of Central Asia may be found there, and most of the folk of India proper. Balkh and Bokhara there meet Bengal and Bombay, and try to draw eye-teeth. You can buy ponies, turquoises, Persian pussy-cats, saddle-bags, fat-tailed sheep and musk in the Kumharsen Serai, and get many strange things for nothing. In the afternoon I went down to see whether my friends intended to keep their word or were lying there drunk.

A priest attired in fragments of ribbons and rags stalked up to me, gravely twisting a child's paper whirligig. Behind him was his servant bending under the load of a crate of mud toys. The two were loading up two camels, and the inhabitants of the Serai watched them with shrieks of laughter.

"The priest is mad," said a horse-dealer to me. "He is going up to Kabul to sell toys to the Amir. He will either be raised to honour or have his head cut off. He came in here this morning and has been behaving madly ever since."

"The witless are under the protection of God," stammered a flat-cheeked Usbeg in broken Hindi. "They foretell future events."

"Would they could have foretold that my caravan would have been cut up by the Shinwaris almost within shadow of the Pass!" grunted the Eusufzai agent of a Rajputana trading-house whose goods had been diverted into the hands of other robbers just across the Border, and whose misfortunes were the laughing-stock of the bazar. "Ohé, priest, whence come you and whither do you go?"

"From Roum have I come," shouted the priest, waving his whirligig; "from Roum, blown by the breath of a hundred devils across the sea! O thieves, robbers, liars, the blessing of Pir Khan on pigs, dogs, and perjurers! Who will take the Protected of God to the North to sell charms that are never still to the Amir? The camels shall not gall, the sons shall not fall sick, and the wives shall remain faithful while they are away, of the men who give me place in their caravan. Who will assist me to slipper the King of the Roos with a golden slipper with a silver heel? The protection of Pir Khan be upon his labours!" He spread out the skirts of his gaberdine and pirouetted between the lines of tethered horses.

"There starts a caravan from Peshawar to Kabul in twenty days, *Huzrut*," said the Eusufzai trader. "My camels go therewith. Do thou also go and bring us good-luck."

"I will go even now!" shouted the priest. "I will depart upon my winged camels, and be at Peshawar in a day! Ho! Hazar Mir Khan," he yelled to his servant, "drive out the camels, but let me first mount my own."

He leaped on the back of his beast as it knelt, and, turning round to me, cried: "Come thou also, Sahib, a little along the road, and I will sell thee a charm—an amulet that shall make thee King of Kafiristan."

Then the light broke upon me, and I followed the two camels out of the Serai till we reached open road and the priest halted.

"What d'you think o' that?" said he in English. "Carnehan can't talk their patter, so I've made him my servant. He makes a handsome servant. 'Tisn't for nothing that I've been knocking about the country for fourteen years. Didn't I do that talk neat? We'll hitch on to a caravan at Peshawar till we get to Jagdallak, and then we'll see if we can get donkeys for our camels, and strike into Kafiristan. Whirligigs for the Amir, O Lor! Put your hand under the camel-bags and tell me what you feel."

I felt the butt of a Martini, and another and another.

"Twenty of 'em," said Dravot placidly. "Twenty of 'em and ammunition to correspond, under the whirligigs and the mud dolls."

"Heaven help you if you are caught with those things!" I said. "A Martini is worth her weight in silver among the Pathans."

"Fifteen hundred rupees of capital—every rupee we could beg, borrow, or steal—are invested on these two camels," said Dravot. "We won't get caught. We're going through the Khaiber with a regular caravan. Who'd touch a poor mad priest?"

"Have you got everything you want?" I asked, overcome with astonishment.

"Not yet, but we shall soon. Give us a memento of your kindness,

Brother. You did me a service, yesterday, and that time in Marwar. Half my Kingdom shall you have, as the saying is." I slipped a small charm compass from my watch chain and handed it up to the priest.

"Good-bye," said Dravot, giving me a hand cautiously. "It's the last time we'll shake hands with an Englishman these many days. Shake hands with him, Carnehan," he cried, as the second camel passed me.

Carnehan leaned down and shook hands. Then the camels passed away along the dusty road, and I was left alone to wonder. My eye could detect no failure in the disguises. The scene in the Serai proved that they were complete to the native mind. There was just the chance, therefore, that Carnehan and Dravot would be able to wander through Afghanistan without detection. But, beyond, they would find death—certain and awful death.

Ten days later a native correspondent giving me the news of the day from Peshawar, wound up his letter with: "There has been much laughter here on account of a certain mad priest who is going in his estimation to sell petty gauds and insignificant trinkets which he ascribes as great charms to H. H. the Amir of Bokhara. He passed through Peshawar and associated himself to the Second Summer caravan that goes to Kabul. The merchants are pleased because through superstition they imagine that such mad fellows bring good-fortune."

The two, then, were beyond the Border. I would have prayed for them, but, that night, a real King died in Europe, and demanded an obituary notice.

The wheel of the world swings through the same phases again and again. Summer passed and winter thereafter, and came and passed again. The daily paper continued and I with it, and upon the third summer there fell a hot night, a night-issue, and a strained waiting for something to be telegraphed from the other side of the world, exactly as had happened before. A few great men had died in the past two years, the machines worked with more clatter, and some of the trees in the Office garden were a few feet taller. But that was all the difference.

I passed over to the press-room, and went through just such a scene as I have already described. The nervous tension was stronger than it had been two years before, and I felt the heat more acutely. At three o'clock I cried, "Print off," and turned to go, when there crept to my chair what was left of a man. He was bent into a circle, his head was sunk between his shoulders, and he moved his feet one over the other like a bear. I could hardly see whether he walked or crawled—this rag-wrapped, whining cripple who addressed me by name, crying that he was come back. "Can you give me a drink?" he whimpered. "For the Lord's sake, give me a drink!"

I went back to the office, the man following with groans of pain, and I turned up the lamp.

"Don't you know me?" he gasped, dropping into a chair, and he turned his drawn face, surmounted by a shock of gray hair, to the light.

I looked at him intently. Once before had I seen eyebrows that met over the nose in an inch-broad black band, but for the life of me I could not tell where.

"I don't know you," I said, handing him the whiskey. "What can I do for you?"

He took a gulp of the spirit raw, and shivered in spite of the suffocating heat.

"I've come back," he repeated; "and I was the King of Kafiristan—me and Dravot—crowned Kings we was! In this office we settled it—you setting there and giving us the books. I am Peachey—Peachey Taliaferro Carnehan, and you've been setting here ever since—O Lord!"

I was more than a little astonished, and expressed my feelings accordingly.

"It's true," said Carnehan, with a dry cackle, nursing his feet, which were wrapped in rags. "True as gospel. Kings we were, with crowns upon our heads—me and Dravot—poor Dan—oh, poor, poor Dan, that would never take advice, not though I begged of him!"

"Take the whiskey," I said, "and take your own time. Tell me all you can recollect of everything from beginning to end. You got across the border on your camels, Dravot dressed as a mad priest and you his servant. Do you remember that?"

"I ain't mad—yet, but I shall be that way soon. Of course I remember. Keep looking at me, or maybe my words will go all to pieces. Keep looking at me in my eyes and don't say anything."

I leaned forward and looked into his face as steadily as I could. He dropped one hand upon the table and I grasped it by the wrist. It was twisted like a bird's claw, and upon the back was a ragged, red, diamond-shaped scar.

"No, don't look there. Look at *me*," said Carnehan. "That comes afterwards, but for the Lord's sake don't distrack me. We left with that caravan, me and Dravot playing all sorts of antics to amuse the people we were with. Dravot use to make us laugh in the evenings when all the people was cooking their dinners—cooking their dinners, and . . . what did they do then? They lit little fires with sparks that went into Dravot's beard, and we all laughed—fit to die. Little red fires they was, going into Dravot's big red beard—so funny." His eyes left mine and he smiled foolishly.

"You went as far as Jagdallak with that caravan," I said at a venture, "after you had lit those fires. To Jagdallak, where you turned off to try to get into Kafiristan."

"No, we didn't neither. What are you talking about? We turned off before Jagdallak, because we heard the roads was good. But they wasn't good enough for our two camels—mine and Dravot's. When we left the caravan, Dravot took off all his clothes and mine too, and said we would be heathen, because the Kafirs didn't allow Mohammedans to talk to them. So we dressed betwixt and between, and such a sight as Daniel Dravot I never saw yet nor expect to see again. He burned half his beard, and slung a sheep-skin over his shoulder, and shaved his head into patterns. He shaved mine, too, and made me wear outrageous things to look like a heathen. That was in a most mountaineous country, and our camels couldn't go along any more because of the mountains. They were tall and black, and coming home I saw them fight like wild goats—there are lots of goats in Kafiristan. And these mountains, they never keep still, no more than the goats. Always fighting they are, and don't let you sleep at night."

"Take some more whiskey," I said very slowly. "What did you and Daniel Dravot do when the camels could go no further because of the rough roads that led into Kafiristan?"

"What did which do? There was a party called Peachey Taliaferro Carnehan that was with Dravot. Shall I tell you about him? He died out there in the cold. Slap from the bridge fell old Peachey, turning and twisting in the air like a penny whirligig that you can sell to the Amir.—No; they was two for three ha'pence, those whirligigs, or I am much mistaken and woeful sore. . . . And then these camels were no use, and Peachey said to Dravot—'For the Lord's sake let's get out of this before our heads are chopped off,' and with that they killed the camels all among the mountains, not having anything in particular to eat, but first they took off the boxes with the guns and the ammunition, till two men came along driving four mules. Dravot up and dances in front of them, singing—'Sell me four mules.' Says the first man—'If you are rich enough to buy, you are rich enough to rob'; but before ever he could put his hand to his knife, Dravot breaks his neck over his knee, and the other party runs away. So Carnehan loaded the mules with the rifles that was taken off the camels, and together we starts forward into those bitter cold mountaineous parts, and never a road broader than the back of your hand."

He paused for a moment, while I asked him if he could remember the nature of the country through which he had journeyed.

"I am telling you as straight as I can, but my head isn't as good as it might be. They drove nails through it to make me hear better how Dravot died. The country was mountainous and the mules were most contrary, and the inhabitants was dispersed and solitary. They went up and up, and down and down, and that other party, Carnehan, was imploring of Dravot not to sing and whistle so loud, for fear of bringing down the tremenjus avalanches. But Dravot says that if a King couldn't sing it wasn't worth being King, and whacked the mules over the rump, and never took no heed for ten cold days. We came to a big level valley all among the mountains, and the mules were near dead, so we killed them, not having anything in special for them or us to eat. We sat upon the boxes, and played odd and even with the cartridges that was jolted out.

"Then ten men with bows and arrows ran down that valley, chasing twenty men with bows and arrows, and the row was tremenjus. They was fair men—fairer than you or me—with yellow hair and remarkable well built. Says Dravot, unpacking the guns—'This is the beginning of the business. We'll fight for the ten men,' and with that he fires two rifles at the twenty men, and drops one of them at two hundred yards from the rock where he was sitting. The other men began to run, but Carnehan and Dravot sits on the boxes picking them off at all ranges, up and down the valley. Then we goes up to the ten men that had run across the snow too, and they fires a footy little arrow at us. Dravot he shoots above their heads and they all falls down flat. Then he walks over them and kicks them, and then he lifts them up and shakes hands all round to make them friendly like. He calls them and gives them the boxes to carry, and waves his hand for all the world as though he was King already. They takes the boxes and him across the valley and up the hill into a pine wood on the top, where there was half a dozen big stone idols. Dravot he goes to the biggest—a fellow they call Imbra—and lays a rifle and a cartridge at his feet, rubbing his nose respectful with his own nose, patting him on the head, and saluting in front of it. He turns round to the men and nods his head, and says—'That's all right. I'm in the know too, and all these old jim-jams are my friends.' Then he opens his mouth and points down it, and when the first man brings him food, he says—'No;' and when the second man brings him food he says—'No;' but when one of the old priests and the boss of the village brings him food, he says—'Yes;' very haughty, and eats it slow. That was how we came to our first village, without any trouble, just as though we had tumbled from the skies. But we tumbled from one of those damned rope-bridges, you see and—you couldn't expect a man to laugh much after that?"

"Take some more whiskey and go on," I said. "That was the first village you came into. How did you get to be King?"

"I wasn't King," said Carnehan. "Dravot he was the King, and a handsome man he looked with the gold crown on his head and all. Him and the other party stayed in that village, and every morning Dravot sat by the side of old Imbra, and the people came and worshipped. That was Dravot's order. Then a lot of men came into the valley, and Carnehan and Dravot picks them off with the rifles before they knew where they was, and runs down into the valley and up again the other side and finds another village, same as the first one, and the people all falls down flat on their faces, and Dravot says—'Now what is the trouble between you two villages?' and the people points to a woman, as fair as you or me, that was carried off, and Dravot takes her back to the first village and counts up the dead—eight there was. For each dead man Dravot pours a little milk on the ground and waves his arms like a whirligig and 'That's all right,' says he. Then he and Carnehan takes the big boss of each village by the arm and walks them down into the valley, and shows them how to scratch a line with a spear right down the valley, and gives each a sod of turf from both sides of the line. Then all the people comes down and shouts like the devil and all, and Dravot says—'Go and dig the land, and be fruitful and multiply,' which they did, though they didn't understand. Then we asks the names of things in their lingo—bread and water and fire and idols and such, and Dravot leads the priest of each village up to the idol, and says he must sit there and judge the people, and if anything goes wrong he is to be shot.

"Next week they was all turning up the land in the valley as quiet as bees and much prettier, and the priests heard all the complaints and told Dravot in dumb show what it was about. 'That's just the beginning,' says Dravot. 'They think we're Gods.' He and Carnehan picks out twenty good men and shows them how to click off a rifle, and form fours, and advance in line, and they was very pleased to do so, and clever to see the hang of it. Then he takes out his pipe and his baccy-pouch and leaves one at one village, and one at the other, and off we two goes to see what was to be done in the next valley. That was all rock, and there was a little village there, and Carnehan says—'Send 'em to the old valley to plant,' and takes 'em there and gives 'em some land that wasn't took before. They were a poor lot, and we blooded 'em with a kid before letting 'em into the new Kingdom. That was to impress the people, and then they settled down quiet, and Carnehan went back to Dravot who had got into another valley, all snow and ice and most mountaineous. There was no people there and the Army got afraid, so Dravot shoots one of them, and goes on till he finds some people in a village, and the Army explains that unless the people wants to be killed they had better not shoot their little matchlocks; for they had matchlocks. We makes friends with the priest and I stays there alone with two of the Army, teaching the men how to drill, and a thundering big Chief comes across the snow with kettle-drums and horns twanging, because he heard there was a new God kicking about. Carnehan sights for the brown of the men half a mile across the snow and wings one of them. Then he sends a message to the Chief that, unless he wished to be killed, he must come and shake hands with me and leave his arms behind. The Chief comes alone first, and Carnehan shakes hands with him and whirls his arms about, same as Dravot used, and very much surprised that Chief was, and strokes my eyebrows. Then Carnehan goes alone to the Chief, and asks him in dumb show if he had an enemy he hated. 'I have,' says the Chief. So Carnehan weeds out the pick of his men, and sets the two of the Army to show them drill and at the end of two weeks the men can manœuvre about as well as Volunteers. So he marches with the Chief to a great big plain on the top of a mountain, and the Chief's men rushes into a village and takes it; we three Martinis firing into the brown of the enemy. So we took that village too, and I gives the Chief a rag from my coat and says, 'Occupy till I come;' which was scriptural. By way of a reminder, when me and the Army was eighteen hundred yards away, I drops a bullet near him standing on the snow, and all the people falls flat on their faces. Then I sends a letter to Dravot wherever he be by land or by sea."

At the risk of throwing the creature out of train I interrupted—"How could you write a letter up yonder?"

"The letter?—Oh!—The letter! Keep looking at me between the eyes, please. It was a string-talk letter, that we'd learned the way of it from a blind beggar in the Punjab."

I remember that there had once come to the office a blind man with a knotted twig and a piece of string which he wound round the twig according to some cipher of his own. He could, after the lapse of days or hours, repeat the sentence which he had reeled up. He had reduced the alphabet to eleven primitive sounds; and tried to teach me his method, but I could not understand.

"I sent that letter to Dravot," said Carnehan; "and told him to come back because this Kingdom was growing too big for me to handle, and then I struck for the first valley, to see how the priests were working. They called the village we took along with the Chief, Bashkai, and the first village we took, Er-Heb. The priests at Er-Heb was doing all right, but they had a lot of pending cases about land to show me, and some men from another village had been firing arrows at night. I went out and looked for that village, and fired four rounds at it from a thousand yards. That used all the cartridges I cared to spend, and I waited for Dravot, who had been away two or three months, and I kept my people quiet."

"One morning I heard the devil's own noise of drums and horns, and Dan Dravot marches down the hill with his Army and a tail of hundreds of men, and, which was the most amazing, a great gold crown on his head. 'My Gord, Carnehan,' says Daniel, 'this is a tremenjus business, and we've got the whole country as far as it's worth having. I am the son of Alexander by Queen Semiramis, and you're my younger brother and a God too! It's the biggest thing we've ever seen. I've been marching and fighting for six weeks with the Army, and every footy little village for fifty miles has come in rejoiceful; and more than that, I've got the key of the whole show, as you'll see, and I've got a crown for you! I told 'em to make two of 'em at a place called Shu, where the gold lies in the rock like suet in mutton. Gold I've seen, and turquoise I've kicked out of the cliffs, and there's garnets in the sands of the river, and here's a chunk of amber that a man brought me. Call up all the priests and, here, take your crown.'"

"One of the men opens a black hair bag, and I slips the crown on. It was too small and too heavy, but I wore it for the glory. Hammered gold it was—five pound weight, like a hoop of a barrel."

"'Peachey,' says Dravot, 'we don't want to fight no more. The Craft's the trick so help me!' and he brings forward that same Chief that I left at Bashkai—Billy Fish we called him afterwards, because he was so like Billy Fish that drove the big tank-engine at Mach on the Bolan in the old days. 'Shake hands with him,' says Dravot, and I shook hands and nearly dropped, for Billy Fish gave me the Grip. I said nothing, but tried him with the Fellow Craft Grip. He answers, all right, and I tried the Master's Grip, but that was a slip. 'A Fellow Craft he is!' I says to Dan. 'Does he know the word?'—'He does,' says Dan, 'and all the priests know. It's a miracle. The Chiefs and the priests can work a Fellow Craft Lodge in a way that's very like ours, and they've cut the marks on the rocks, but they don't know the Third Degree, and they've come to find out. It's Gord's Truth. I've known these long years that the Afghans knew up to the Fellow Craft Degree, but this is a miracle. A God and a Grand-Master of the Craft am I, and a Lodge in the Third Degree I will open, and we'll raise the head priests and the Chiefs of the villages.' "

" 'It's against all the law,' I says, 'holding a Lodge without warrant from any one; and you know we never held office in any Lodge.' "

" 'It's a master-stroke o' policy,' says Dravot. 'It means running the country as easy as a four-wheeled bogie on a down grade. We can't stop to enquire now, or they'll turn against us. I've forty Chiefs at my heel, and passed and raised according to their merit they shall be. Billet these men on the villages, and see that we run up a Lodge of some kind. The temple of Imbra will do for the Lodge-room. The women must make aprons as you show them. I'll hold a levee of Chiefs to-night and Lodge to-morrow.' "

"I was fair run off my legs, but I wasn't such a fool as not to see what a pull this Craft business gave us. I showed the priests' families how to make aprons of the degrees, but for Dravot's apron the blue border and marks was made of turquoise lumps on white hide, not cloth. We took a great square stone in the temple for the Master's chair, and little stones for the officers' chairs, and painted the black pavement with white squares, and did what we could to make things regular."

"At the levee which was held that night on the hillside with big bonfires, Dravot gives out that him and me were Gods and sons of Alexander, and Past Grand-Masters in the Craft, and was come to make Kafiristan a country where every man should eat in peace and drink in quiet, and specially obey us. Then the Chiefs come round to shake hands, and they were so hairy and white and fair it was just shaking hands with old friends. We gave them names according as they was like men we had known in India—Billy Fish, Holly

Dilworth, Pikky Kergan, that was Bazar-master when I was at Mhow, and so on, and so on."

"*The* most amazing miracles was at Lodge next night. One of the old priests was watching us continuous, and I felt uneasy, for I knew we'd have to fudge the Ritual, and I didn't know what the men knew. The old priest was a stranger come in from beyond the village of Bashkai. The minute Dravot puts on the Master's apron that the girls had made for him, the priest fetches a whoop and a howl, and tries to overturn the stone that Dravot was sitting on. 'It's all up now,' I says. 'That comes of meddling with the Craft without warrant!' Dravot never winked an eye, not when ten priests took and tilted over the Grand-Master's chair—which was to say the stone of Imbra. The priest begins rubbing the bottom end of it to clear away the black dirt, and presently he shows all the other priests the Master's Mark, same as was on Dravot's apron, cut into the stone. Not even the priests of the temple of Imbra knew it was there. The old chap falls flat on his face at Dravot's feet and kisses 'em. 'Luck again,' says Dravot, across the Lodge to me, 'they say it's the missing Mark that no one could understand the why of. We're more than safe now.' Then he bangs the butt of his gun for a gavel and says: 'By virtue of the authority vested in me by my own right hand and the help of Peachey, I declare myself Grand-Master of all Freemasonry in Kafiristan in this the Mother Lodge o' the country, and King of Kafiristan equally with Peachey!' At that he puts on his crown and I puts on mine—I was doing Senior Warden—and we opens the Lodge in most ample form. It was a amazing miracle! The priests moved in Lodge through the first two degrees almost without telling, as if the memory was coming back to them. After that, Peachey and Dravot raised such as was worthy—high priests and Chiefs of far-off villages. Billy Fish was the first, and I can tell you we scared the soul out of him. It was not in any way according to Ritual, but it served our turn. We didn't raise more than ten of the biggest men, because we didn't want to make the Degree common. And they was clamouring to be raised."

"'In another six months,' says Dravot, 'we'll hold another Communication, and see how you are working.' Then he asks them about their villages, and learns that they was fighting one against the other, and were sick and tired of it. And when they wasn't doing that they was fighting with the Mohammedans. 'You can fight those when they come into our country,' says Dravot. 'Tell off every tenth man of your tribes for a Frontier guard, and send two hundred at a time to this valley to be drilled. Nobody is going to be shot or speared any more so long as he does well, and I know that you won't cheat me, because you're white people—sons of Alexander—and not like common, black Mohammedans. You are *my* people, and by God," says he, running off into English at the end—'I'll make a damned fine Nation of you, or I'll die in the making!'"

"I can't tell all we did for the next six months, because Dravot did a lot I couldn't see the hang of, and he learned their lingo in a way I never could. My work was to help the people plough, and now and again go out with some of the Army and see what the other villages were doing, and make 'em throw rope-bridges across the ravines which cut up the country horrid. Dravot was very kind to me, but when he walked up and down in the pine wood pulling that bloody red beard of his with both fists I knew he was thinking plans I could not advise about, and I just waited for orders."

"But Dravot never showed me disrespect before the people. They were afraid of me and the Army, but they loved Dan. He was the best of friends with the priests and the Chiefs; but any one could come across the hills with a complaint, and Dravot would hear him out fair, and call four priests together and say what was to be done. He used to call in Billy Fish from Bashkai, and Pikky Kergan from Shu, and an old Chief we called Kafuzelum—it was like enough to his real name—and hold councils with 'em when there was any fighting to be done in small villages. That was his Council of War, and the four priests of Bashkai, Shu, Khawak, and Madora was his Privy Council. Between the lot of 'em they sent me, with forty men and twenty rifles, and sixty men carrying turquoises, into the Ghorband country to buy those hand-made Martini rifles, that come out of the Amir's workshops at Kabul, from one of the Amir's Herati regiments that would have sold the very teeth out of their mouths for turquoises."

"I stayed in Ghorband a month, and gave the Governor there the pick of my baskets for hush-money, and bribed the Colonel of the regiment some more, and, between the two and the tribes-people, we got more than a hundred hand-made Martinis, a hundred good Kohat Jezails that'll throw to six hundred yards, and forty man-loads of very bad ammunition for the rifles. I came back with what I had, and distributed 'em among the men that the Chiefs sent in to me to drill. Dravot was too busy to attend to those things, but the old Army that we first made helped me, and we turned out five hundred men that could drill, and two hundred that knew how to hold arms pretty straight. Even those cork-screwed, hand-made guns was a miracle to them. Dravot talked big about powder-shops and factories, walking up and down in the pine wood when the winter was coming on."

"'I won't make a Nation,' says he. 'I'll make an Empire! These men aren't niggers; they're English! Look at their eyes—look at their mouths. Look at the way they stand up. They sit on chairs in their own houses. They're the Lost Tribes, or something like it, and they've grown to be English. I'll take a census in the spring if the priests don't get frightened. There must be a fair two million of 'em in these hills. The villages are full o' little children. Two million people—two hundred and fifty thousand fighting men—and all English! They only want the rifles and a little drilling. Two hundred and fifty thousand men, ready to cut in on Russia's right flank when she tries for India! Peachey, man,' he says, chewing his beard in great hunks, 'we shall be Emperors—Emperors of the Earth! Rajah Brooke will be a suckling to us. I'll treat with the Viceroy on equal terms. I'll ask him to send me twelve picked English—twelve that I know of—to help us govern a bit. There's Mackray, Sergeant-pensioner at Segowli—many's the good dinner he's given me, and his wife a pair of trousers. There's Donkin, the Warder of Tounghoo Jail; there's hundreds that I could lay my hand on if I was in India. The Viceroy shall do it for me, I'll send a man through in the spring for those men, and I'll write for a dispensation from the Grand Lodge for what I've done as Grand-Master. That—and all the Sniders that'll be thrown out when the native troops in India take up the Martini. They'll be worn smooth, but they'll do for fighting in these hills. Twelve English, a hundred thousand Sniders run through the Amir's country in driblets—I'd be content with twenty thousand in one year—and we'd be an Empire. When everything was shipshape, I'd hand over the crown—this crown I'm wearing now—to Queen Victoria on my knees, and she'd say: 'Rise up, Sir Daniel Dravot.' Oh, it's big! It's big, I tell you! But there's so much to be done in every place—Bashkai, Khawak, Shu, and everywhere else.'"

"'What is it?' I says. 'There are no more men coming in to be drilled this autumn. Look at those fat, black clouds. They're bringing the snow.'"

"'It isn't that,' says Daniel, putting his hand very hard on my shoulder; 'and I don't wish to say anything that's against you, for no other living man would have followed me and made me what I am as you have done. You're a first-class Commander-in-Chief, and the people know you; but–it's a big country, and somehow you can't help me, Peachey, in the way I want to be helped.' "

" 'Go to your blasted priests, then!' I said, and I was sorry when I made that remark, but it did hurt me sore to find Daniel talking so superior when I'd drilled all the men, and done all he told me."

" 'Don't let's quarrel, Peachey,' says Daniel without cursing. 'You're a King too, and the half of this Kingdom is yours; but can't you see, Peachey, we want cleverer men than us now–three or four of 'em, that we can scatter about for our Deputies. It's a hugeous great State, and I can't always tell the right thing to do, and I haven't time for all I want to do, and here's the winter coming on and all.' He put half his beard into his mouth, all red like the gold of his crown."

" 'I'm sorry, Daniel,' says I. 'I've done all I could. I've drilled the men and shown the people how to stack their oats better; and I've brought in those tin-ware rifles from Ghorband–but I know what you're driving at. I take it Kings always feel oppressed that way.' "

" 'There's another thing too,' says Dravot, walking up and down. 'The winter's coming and these people won't be giving much trouble, and if they do we can't move about. I want a wife.' "

" 'For Gord's sake leave the women alone!' I says. 'We've both got all the work we can, though I *am* a fool. Remember the Contrack, and keep clear o' women.' "

" 'The Contrack only lasted till such time as we was Kings; and Kings we have been these months past,' says Dravot, weighing his crown in his hand. 'You go get a wife too, Peachey–a nice, strappin', plump girl that'll keep you warm in the winter. They're prettier than English girls, and we can take the pick of 'em. Boil 'em once or twice in hot water, and they'll come out like chicken and ham.' "

" 'Don't tempt me!' I says. 'I will not have any dealings with a woman not till we are a dam' side more settled than we are now. I've been doing the work o' two men, and you've been doing the work o' three. Let's lie off a bit, and see if we can't get some better tobacco from Afghan country and run in some good liquor; but no women.' "

" 'Who's talking o' *women?*' says Dravot. 'I said *wife*–a queen to breed a King's son for the King. A Queen out of the strongest tribe, that'll make them your blood-brothers, and that'll lie by your side and tell you all the people thinks about you and their own affairs. That's what I want.' "

" 'Do you remember that Bengali woman I kept at Mogul Serai

when I was a plate-layer?' says I. 'A fat lot o' good she was to me. She taught me the lingo and one or two other things; but what happened? She ran away with the Station Master's servant and half my month's pay. Then she turned up at Dadur Junction in tow of a half-caste, and had the impidence to say I was her husband—all among the drivers in the running-shed too!'"

"'We've done with that,' says Dravot, 'these women are whiter than you or me, and a Queen I will have for the winter months.'"

"'For the last time o' asking, Dan, do *not,*' I says. 'It'll only bring us harm. The Bible says that Kings ain't to waste their strength on women, 'specially when they've got a new raw Kingdom to work over.'"

"'For the last time of answering I will,' said Dravot, and he went away through the pine-trees looking like a big red devil, the sun being on his crown and beard and all."

"But getting a wife was not as easy as Dan thought. He put it before the Council, and there was no answer till Billy Fish said he'd better ask the girls. Dravot damned them all round. 'What's wrong with me?' he shouts, standing by the idol Imbra. 'Am I a dog or am I not enough of a man for your wenches? Haven't I put the shadow of my hand over this country? Who stopped the last Afghan raid?' It was me really, but Dravot was too angry to remember. 'Who bought your guns? Who repaired the bridges? Who's the Grand-Master of the sign cut in the stone?' says he, and he thumped his hand on the block that he used to sit on in Lodge, and at Council, which opened like Lodge always. Billy Fish said nothing and no more did the others. 'Keep your hair on, Dan,' said I; 'and ask the girls. That's how it's done at Home, and these people are quite English.'"

"'The marriage of the King is a matter of State,' says Dan, in a white-hot rage, for he could feel, I hope, that he was going against his better mind. He walked out of the Council-room, and the others sat still, looking at the ground."

"'Billy Fish,' says I to the Chief of Bashkai, 'what's the difficulty here? A straight answer to a true friend.'"

"'You know,' says Billy Fish. 'How should a man tell you who knows everything? How can daughters of men marry Gods or Devils? It's not proper.'"

"I remembered something like that in the Bible; but if, after seeing us as long as they had, they still believed we were Gods, it wasn't for me to undeceive them."

"'A God can do anything,' says I. 'If the King is fond of a girl he'll not let her die.'—'She'll have to,' said Billy Fish. 'There are all sorts of Gods and Devils in these mountains, and now and again a girl marries one of them and isn't seen any more. Besides, you two know the Mark cut in the stone. Only the Gods know that. We thought you were men till you showed the sign of the Master.' "

"I wished then that we had explained about the loss of the genuine secrets of a Master-Mason at the first go-off; but I said nothing. All that night there was a blowing of horns in a little dark temple half-way down the hill, and I heard a girl crying fit to die. One of the priests told us that she was being prepared to marry the King."

" 'I'll have no nonsense of that kind,' says Dan. 'I don't want to interfere with your customs, but I'll take my own wife.'—'The girl's a little bit afraid,' says the priest. 'She thinks she's going to die, and they are a-heartening of her up down in the temple.' "

" 'Hearten her very tender, then,' says Dravot, 'or I'll hearten you with the butt of a gun so you'll never want to be heartened again.' He licked his lips, did Dan, and stayed up walking about more than half the night, thinking of the wife that he was going to get in the morning. I wasn't by any means comfortable, for I knew that dealings with a woman in foreign parts, though you was a crowned King twenty times over, could not but be risky. I got up very early in the morning while Dravot was asleep, and I saw the priests talking together in whispers, and the Chiefs talking together too, and they looked at me out of the corners of their eyes."

" 'What is up, Fish?' " I say to the Bashkai man, who was wrapped up in his furs and looking splendid to behold."

" 'I can't rightly say,' says he; 'but if you can make the King drop all this nonsense about marriage, you'll be doing him and me and yourself a great service.' "

" 'That I do believe,' says I. 'But sure, you know, Billy, as well as me, having fought against and for us, that the King and me are nothing more than two of the finest men that God Almighty ever made. Nothing more, I do assure you.' "

" 'That may be,' says Billy Fish, 'and yet I should be sorry if it was.' He sinks his head upon his great fur cloak for a minute and thinks. 'King,' says he, 'be you man or God or Devil, I'll stick by you to-day. I have twenty of my men with me, and they will follow me. We'll go to Bashkai until the storm blows over.' "

"A little snow had fallen in the night, and everything was white except the greasy fat clouds that blew down and down from the north. Dravot came out with his crown on his head, swinging his arms and stamping his feet, and looking more pleased than Punch."

" 'For the last time, drop it, Dan,' says I in a whisper, 'Billy Fish here says that there will be a row.' "

" 'A row among my people!' says Dravot. 'Not much. Peachey, you're a fool not to get a wife too. Where's the girl?' says he with a voice as loud as the braying of a jackass. 'Call up all the Chiefs and priests, and let the Emperor see if his wife suits him.' "

"There was no need to call any one. They were all there leaning on their guns and spears round the clearing in the centre of the pine wood. A lot of priests went down to the little temple to bring up the girl, and the horns blew fit to wake the dead. Billy Fish saunters round and gets as close to Daniel as he could, and behind him stood his twenty men with matchlocks. Not a man of them under six feet. I was next to Dravot, and behind me was twenty men of the regular Army. Up comes the girl, and a strapping wench she was, covered with silver and turquoises but white as death, and looking back every minute at the priests."

" 'She'll do,' said Dan, looking her over. 'What's to be afraid of, lass? Come and kiss me.' He puts his arm round her. She shuts her eyes, gives a bit of a squeak, and down goes her face in the side of Dan's flaming red beard."

" 'The slut's bitten me!' says he, clapping his hand to his neck, and, sure enough, his hand was red with blood. Billy Fish and two of his matchlock-men catches hold of Dan by the shoulders and drags him into the Bashkai lot, while the priests howls in their lingo,—'Neither God nor Devil but a man!' I was all taken aback, for a priest cut at me in front, and the Army began firing into the Bashkai men."

" 'God A'mighty!' says Dan. 'What is the meaning o' this?' "

" 'Come back! Come away!' says Billy Fish. 'Ruin and Mutiny is the matter. We'll break for Bashkai if we can.' "

"I tried to give some sort of orders to my men—the men o' the regular Army—but it was no use, so I fired into the brown of 'em with an English Martini and drilled three beggars in a line. The volley was full of shouting, howling creatures, and every soul shrieking, 'Not a God nor a Devil but only a man!' The Bashkai troops stuck to Billy Fish all they were worth, but their matchlocks wasn't half as good as the Kabul breech-loaders, and four of them dropped. Dan was bellowing like a bull, for he was very wrathy; and Billy Fish had a hard job to prevent him running out at the crowd."

" 'We can't stand,' says Billy Fish. 'Make a run for it down the valley! The whole place is against us.' The matchlock-men ran, and we went down the valley in spite of Dravot. He was swearing horrible and crying out he was a King. The priests rolled great stones on us, and the regular Army fired hard, and there wasn't more than six men, not counting Dan, Billy Fish, and Me, that came down to the bottom of the valley alive."

"Then they stopped firing and the horns in the temple blew again. 'Come away—for Gord's sake come away!' says Billy Fish. 'They'll send runners out to all the villages before ever we get to Bashkai. I can protect you there, but I can't do anything now.' "

"My own notion is that Dan began to go mad in his head from that hour. He stared up and down like a stuck pig. Then he was all for walking back alone and killing the priests with his bare hands; which he could have done. 'An Emperor am I,' says Daniel, 'and next year I shall be a Knight of the Queen.' "

" 'All right, Dan,' says I; 'but come along now while there's time.' "

" 'It's your fault,' says he, 'for not looking after your Army better. There was mutiny in the midst, and you didn't know—you damned engine-driving, plate-laying, missionary's-pass-hunting hound!' He sat upon a rock and called me every foul name he could lay tongue to. I was too heart-sick to care, though it was all his foolishness that brought the smash."

" 'I'm sorry, Dan,' says I, 'but there's no accounting for natives. This business is our Fifty-seven. Maybe we'll make something out of it yet, when we've got to Bashkai.' "

" 'Let's get to Bashkai, then,' says Dan, 'and, by God, when I come back here again I'll sweep the valley so there isn't a bug in a blanket left!' "

"We walked all that day, and all that night Dan was stumping up and down on the snow, chewing his beard and muttering to himself."

" 'There's no hope o' getting clear,' said Billy Fish. 'The priests will have sent runners to the villages to say that you are only men. Why didn't you stick on as Gods till things was more settled? I'm a dead man,' says Billy Fish, and he throws himself down on the snow and begins to pray to his Gods."

"Next morning we was in a cruel bad country—all up and down, no level ground at all, and no food either. The six Bashkai men looked at Billy Fish hungry-way as if they wanted to ask something, but they said never a word. At noon we came to the top of a flat mountain all covered with snow, and when we climbed up into it, behold, there was an Army in position waiting in the middle!"

" 'The runners have been very quick,' says Billy Fish, with a little bit of a laugh. 'They are waiting for us.' "

"Three or four men began to fire from the enemy's side, and a chance shot took Daniel in the calf of the leg. That brought him to his senses. He looks across the snow at the Army, and sees the rifles that we had brought into the country."

" 'We're done for,' says he. 'They are Englishmen, these people,—and it's my blasted nonsense that has brought you to this. Get back, Billy Fish, and take your men away; you've done what you could, and now cut for it. Carnehan,' says he, 'shake hands with me and go along with Billy. Maybe they won't kill you. I'll go and meet 'em alone. It's me that did it. Me, the King!' "

" 'Go!' says I. 'Go to Hell, Dan. I'm with you here. Billy Fish, you clear out, and we two will meet those folk.' "

" 'I'm a Chief,' says Billy Fish, quite quiet. 'I stay with you. My men can go.' "

"The Bashkai fellows didn't wait for a second word but ran off, and Dan and Me and Billy Fish walked across to where the drums were drumming and the horns were horning. It was cold—awful cold. I've got that cold in the back of my head now. There's a lump of it there."

The punkah-coolies had gone to sleep. Two kerosene lamps were blazing in the office, and the perspiration poured down my face and splashed on the blotter as I leaned forward. Carnehan was shivering, and I feared that his mind might go. I wiped my face, took a fresh grip of the piteously mangled hands, and said, "What happened after that?"

The momentary shift of my eyes had broken the clear current.

"What was you pleased to say?" whined Carnehan. "They took them without any sound. Not a little whisper all along the snow, not though the King knocked down the first man that set hand on him—not though old Peachey fired his last cartridge into the brown of 'em. Not a single solitary sound did those swines make. They just closed up tight, and I tell you their furs stunk. There was a man called Billy Fish, a good friend of us all, and they cut his throat, Sir, then and there, like a pig; and the King kicks up the bloody snow and says: 'We've had a dashed fine run for our money. What's coming next?' But Peachey, Peachey Taliaferro, I tell you, Sir, in confidence as betwixt two friends, he lost his head, Sir. No, he didn't neither. The King lost his head, so he did, all along o' one of those cunning rope-bridges. Kindly let me have the paper-cutter, Sir. It tilted this way. They marched him a mile across that snow to a rope-bridge over a ravine with a river at the bottom. You may have seen such. They prodded him behind like an ox. 'Damn your eyes!' says the King. 'D'you suppose I can't die like a gentleman?' He turns to Peachey–Peachey that was crying like a child. 'I've brought you to this, Peachey,' says he. 'Brought you out of your happy life to be killed in Kafiristan where you was late Commander-in-Chief of the Emperor's forces. Say you forgive me, Peachey.'–'I do,' says Peachey. 'Fully and freely do I forgive you, Dan.'–'Shake hands, Peachey,' says he. 'I'm going now.' Out he goes, looking neither right nor left, and when he was plumb in the middle of those dizzy dancing ropes–'Cut, you beggars,' he shouts, and they cut, and old Dan fell, turning round and round and round, twenty thousand miles, for he took half an hour to fall till he struck the water, and I could see his body caught on a rock with the gold crown close beside."

"But do you know what they did to Peachey between two pine-trees? They crucified him, Sir, as Peachey's hands will show. They used wooden pegs for his hands and his feet; and he didn't die. He hung there and screamed, and they took him down next day, and said it was a miracle that he wasn't dead. They took him down–poor old Peachey that hadn't done them any harm–that hadn't done them any——"

He rocked to and fro and wept bitterly, wiping his eyes with the back of his scarred hands and moaning like a child for some ten minutes.

"They was cruel enough to feed him up in the temple, because they said he was more of a God than old Daniel that was a man. Then they turned him out on the snow, and told him to go home, and Peachey came home in about a year, begging along the roads quite safe; for Daniel Dravot he walked before and said: 'Come along, Peachey. It's a big thing we're doing.' The mountains they danced at night, and the mountains they tried to fall on Peachey's head, but Dan he held up his hand, and Peachy came along bent double. He never let go of Dan's hand, and he never let go of Dan's head. They gave it to him as a present in the temple, to remind him not to come again, and though the crown was pure gold, and Peachey was starving, never would Peachey sell the same. You knew Dravot, Sir! You knew Right Worshipful Brother Dravot! Look at him now!"

He fumbled in the mass of rags round his bent waist; brought out a black horsehair bag embroidered with silver thread; and shook therefrom on to my table–the dried, withered head of Daniel

Dravot! The morning sun that had long been paling the lamps struck the red beard and blind sunken eyes; struck, too, a heavy circlet of gold studded with raw turquoises, that Carnehan placed tenderly on the battered temples.

"You be'old now,' said Carnehan, "the Emperor in his 'abit as he lived—the King of Kafiristan with his crown upon his head. Poor old Daniel that was a monarch once!"

I shuddered, for, in spite of defacements manifold, I recognised the head of the man of Marwar Junction. Carnehan rose to go. I attempted to stop him. He was not fit to walk abroad. "Let me take away the whiskey, and give me a little money," he gasped. "I was a King once. I'll go to the Deputy Commissioner and ask to set in the Poorhouse till I get my health. No, thank you, I can't wait till you get a carriage for me. I've urgent private affairs—in the south—at Marwar."

He shambled out of the office and departed in the direction of the Deputy Commissioner's house. That day at noon I had occasion to go down the blinding hot Mall, and I saw a crooked man crawling along the white dust of the roadside, his hat in his hand, quavering dolorously after the fashion of street-singers at Home. There was not a soul in sight, and he was out of all possible earshot of the houses. And he sang through his nose, turning his head from right to left:—

"The Son of Man goes forth to war,
  A golden crown to gain;
His blood-red banner streams afar—
  Who follows in his train?"

I waited to hear no more, but put the poor wretch into my carriage and drove him off to the nearest missionary for eventual transfer to the Asylum. He repeated the hymn twice while he was with me whom he did not in the least recognise, and I left him singing it to the missionary.

Two days later I enquired after his welfare of the Superintendent of the Asylum.

"He was admitted suffering from sun-stroke. He died early yesterday morning," said the Superintendent. "Is it true that he was half an hour bare-headed in the sun at midday?"

"Yes," said I, "but do you happen to know if he had anything upon him by any chance when he died?"

"Not to my knowledge," said the Superintendent.

And there the matter rests.

Questions

1. Kipling not only tells a fascinating story but has many sociological and political statements to make. How does he relate these to the story he tells?
2. What structure does he use in presenting his story? Is it appropriate or could he have used another plan? Specifically, what is the effect of the chronological break in the story?
3. How does the "contrack" prepare us for the events which follow? What clues to the characters of Carnehan and Dravot does the "contrack" scene reveal? How do these clues foreshadow subsequent events?
4. Kipling is an acknowledged master at depicting the atmosphere of colonial India. Which descriptive passages are especially effective?

Topics for Composition

1. Partners are rarely equal in their relationship. Usually, one exerts a dominant influence—one becomes master, so to speak; the other becomes servant. Write an essay showing how the relationship between Carnehan and Dravot, which began as a partnership, actually becomes a master-servant association. Indicate in your essay how the disintegrating partnership foreshadows the conclusion.
2. Carnehan and Dravot establish a kind of "government." Write an essay contrasting the beneficial and the despotic aspects of their "government." You might center your discussion on the thesis that "dictatorships are rarely successful."
3. Compare and contrast Orwell's attitude toward authority with that shown by Kipling's characters. Use both of Kipling's main characters, since they provide contrastive attitudes within his story.
4. From your own experience, narrate an incident where assuming too much authority led to the loss of that authority. Refer to Orwell's essay noting his techniques of chronological arrangement, attention to detail, and revelation of personal attitude.

To more fully understand Mann's investigation into the psychology of human action, we should recognize that the author explicitly and implicitly frees his main character from most of the responsibility for his own actions. Mann primarily accomplishes this by the way in which he portrays the characters who surround Herr Friedemann. As you read this story, give some careful attention to the attendant characters; especially note Mann's portrayal of the following:

1. The nurse, who symbolizes mankind's weaknesses and absorbs the initial responsibility for Friedemann's misfortune
2. The mother and the sisters, whose passive natures contribute to Friedemann's early development
3. Friedemann's classmates and associates, whose compassionate attitudes, paradoxically, increase his isolation
4. Frau von Rinnlingen, whose alien qualities disrupt the tranquillity of Friedemann's existence

Little Herr Friedemann

THOMAS MANN

It was the nurse's fault. When they first suspected, Frau Consul Friedemann had spoken to her very gravely about the need of controlling her weakness. But what good did that do? Or the glass of red wine which she got daily besides the beer which was needed for the milk? For they suddenly discovered that she even sank so low as to drink the methylated spirit which was kept for the spirit lamp. Before they could send her away and get someone to take her place, the mischief was done. One day the mother and sisters came home to find that little Johannes, then about a month old, had fallen from the couch and lay on the floor, uttering an appallingly faint little cry, while the nurse stood beside him quite stupefied.

The doctor came and with firm, gentle hands tested the little creature's contracted and twitching limbs. He made a very serious face. The three girls stood sobbing in a corner and the Frau Consul in the anguish of her heart prayed aloud.

The poor mother, just before the child's birth, had already suffered a crushing blow: her husband, the Dutch Consul, had been snatched away from her by sudden and violent illness, and now she was too broken to cherish any hope that little Johannes would be spared to her. But by the second day the doctor had given her hand an encouraging squeeze and told her that all immediate danger was over. There was no longer any sign that the brain was affected. The facial expression was altered, it had lost the fixed and staring look. . . . Of course, they must see how things went on—and hope for the best, hope for the best.

The grey gabled house in which Johannes Friedemann grew up stood by the north gate of the little old commercial city. The front door led into a large flag-paved entry, out of which a stair with a white wooden balustrade led up into the second storey. The faded wall-paper in the living-room had a landscape pattern, and straight-backed chairs and sofas in dark-red plush stood round the heavy mahogany table.

Often in his childhood Johannes sat here at the window, which always had a fine showing of flowers, on a small footstool at his mother's feet, listening to some fairy-tale she told him, gazing at her smooth grey head, her mild and gentle face, and breathing in the faint scent she exhaled. She showed him the picture of his father, a kindly man with grey side-whiskers—he was now in heaven, she said, and awaiting them there.

Behind the house was a small garden where in summer they spent much of their time, despite the smell of burnt sugar which came over from the refinery close by. There was a gnarled old walnut tree in whose shade little Johannes would sit, on a low wooden stool, cracking walnuts, while Frau Friedemann and her three daughters, now grown women, took refuge from the sun under a grey canvas tent. The mother's gaze often strayed from her embroidery to look with sad and loving eyes at her child.

He was not beautiful, little Johannes, as he crouched on his stool industriously cracking his nuts. In fact, he was a strange sight, with his pigeon breast, humped back, and disproportionately long arms. But his hands and feet were delicately formed, he had soft red-brown eyes like a doe's, a sensitive mouth, and fine, light-brown hair. His head, had it not sat so deep between his shoulders, might almost have been called pretty.

When he was seven he went to school, where time passed swiftly and uniformly. He walked every day, with the strut deformed people often have, past the quaint gabled houses and shops to the old schoolhouse with the vaulted arcades. When he had done his preparation he would read in his books with the lovely title-page illustrations in colour, or else work in the garden, while his sisters kept house for their invalid mother. They went out too, for they belonged to the best society of the town; but unfortunately they had not married, for they had not much money nor any looks to recommend them.

Johannes too was now and then invited out by his schoolmates, but it is not likely that he enjoyed it. He could not take part in their games, and they were always embarrassed in his company, so there was no feeling of good fellowship.

There came a time when he began to hear certain matters talked about, in the courtyard at school. He listened wide-eyed and large-eared, quite silent, to his companions' raving over this or that little girl. Such things, though they entirely engrossed the attention of these others, were not, he felt, for him; they belonged in the same category as the ball games and gymnastics. At times he felt a little sad. But at length he had become quite used to standing on one side and not taking part.

But after all it came about—when he was sixteen—that he felt suddenly drawn to a girl of his own age. She was the sister of a classmate of his, a blonde, hilarious hoyden, and he met her when calling at her brother's house. He felt strangely embarrassed in her neighbourhood; she too was embarrassed and treated him with such artificial cordiality that it made him sad.

One summer afternoon as he was walking by himself on the wall outside the town, he heard a whispering behind a jasmine bush and peeped cautiously through the branches. There she sat on a bench beside a long-legged, red-haired youth of his acquaintance. They had their arms about each other and he was imprinting on her lips a kiss, which she returned amid giggles. Johannes looked, turned round, and went softly away.

His head was sunk deeper than ever between his shoulders, his hands trembled, and a sharp pain shot upwards from his chest to his throat. But he choked it down, straightening himself as well as he could. "Good," said he to himself. "That is over. Never again will I let myself in for any of it. To the others it brings joy and happiness, for me it can only mean sadness and pain. I am done with it. For me that is all over. Never again."

The resolution did him good. He had renounced, renounced forever. He went home, took up a book, or else played on his violin, which despite his deformed chest he had learned to do.

At seventeen Johannes left school to go into business, like everybody else he knew. He was apprenticed to the big lumber firm of Herr Schlievogt down on the river-bank. They were kind and considerate, he on his side was responsive and friendly, time passed with peaceful regularity. But in his twenty-first year his mother died, after a lingering illness.

This was a sore blow for Johannes Friedemann, and the pain of it endured. He cherished this grief, he gave himself up to it as one gives oneself to a great joy, he fed it with a thousand childhood memories; it was the first important event in his life and he made the most of it.

Is not life in and for itself a good, regardless of whether we may call its content "happiness"? Johannes Friedemann felt that it was so, and he loved life. He, who had renounced the greatest joy it can bring us, taught himself with infinite, incredible care to take pleasure in what it had still to offer. A walk in the springtime in the parks surrounding the town; the fragrance of a flower; the song of a bird—might not one feel grateful for such things as these?

And that we need to be taught how to enjoy, yes, that our education is always and only equal to our capacity for enjoyment—he knew that too, and he trained himself. Music he loved, and attended all the concerts that were given in the town. He came to play the violin not so badly himself, no matter what a figure of fun he made when he did it; and took delight in every beautiful soft tone he succeeded in producing. Also, by much reading he came in time to possess a literary taste the like of which did not exist in the place. He kept up with the new books, even the foreign ones; he knew how to savour the seductive rhythm of a lyric or the ultimate flavour of a subtly told tale—yes, one might almost call him a connoisseur.

He learned to understand that to everything belongs its own enjoyment and that it is absurd to distinguish between an experience which is "happy" and one which is not. With a right good will he accepted each emotion as it came, each mood, whether sad or gay. Even he cherished the unfulfilled desires, the longings. He loved them for their own sakes and told himself that with fulfillment the best of them would be past. The vague, sweet, painful yearning and hope of quiet spring evenings—are they not richer in joy than all the fruition the summer can bring? Yes, he was a connoisseur, our little Herr Friedemann.

But of course they did not know that, the people whom he met on the street, who bowed to him with the kindly, compassionate air he knew so well. They could not know that this unhappy cripple, strutting comically along in his light overcoat and shiny top hat—strange to say, he was a little vain—they could not know how tenderly he loved the mild flow of his life, charged with no great emotions, it is true, but full of a quiet and tranquil happiness which was his own creation.

But Herr Friedemann's great preference, his real passion, was for the theatre. He possessed a dramatic sense which was unusually strong; at a telling theatrical effect or the catastrophe of a tragedy his whole small frame would shake with emotion. He had his regular seat in the first row of boxes at the opera-house; was an assiduous frequenter and often took his sisters with him. Since their mother's death they kept house for their brother in the old home which they all owned together.

It was a pity they were unmarried still; but with the decline of hope had come resignation—Friederike, the eldest, was seventeen years further on than Herr Friedemann. She and her sister Henriette were over-tall and thin, whereas Pfiffi, the youngest, was too short and stout. She had a funny way, too, of shaking herself as she talked, and water came in the corners of her mouth.

Little Herr Friedemann did not trouble himself overmuch about his three sisters. But they stuck together loyally and were always of one mind. Whenever an engagement was announced in their circle they with one voice said how very gratifying that was.

Their brother continued to live with them even after he became independent, as he did by leaving Herr Schlievogt's firm and going into business for himself, in an agency of sorts, which was no great tax on his time. His offices were in a couple of rooms on the ground floor of the house so that at mealtimes he had but the pair of stairs to mount—for he suffered now and then from asthma.

His thirtieth birthday fell on a fine warm June day, and after dinner he sat out in the grey canvas tent, with a new head-rest embroidered by Henriette. He had a good cigar in his mouth and a good book in his hand. But sometimes he would put the latter down to listen to the sparrows chirping blithely in the old nut tree and look at the clean gravel path leading up to the house between lawns bright with summer flowers.

Little Herr Friedemann wore no beard, and his face had scarcely changed at all, save that the features were slightly sharper. He wore his fine light-brown hair parted on one side.

Once, as he let the book fall on his knee and looked up into the sunny blue sky, he said to himself: "Well, so that is thirty years. Perhaps there may be ten or even twenty more, God knows. They will mount up without a sound or a stir and pass by like those that are gone; and I look forward to them with peace in my heart."

Now, it happened in July of the same year that a new appointment to the office of District Commandant had set the whole town talking. The stout and jolly gentleman who had for many years occupied the post had been very popular in social circles and they saw him go with great regret. It was in compliance with goodness knows what regulations that Herr von Rinnlingen and no other was sent thither from the capital.

In any case the exchange was not such a bad one. The new Commandant was married but childless. He rented a spacious villa in the southern suburbs of the city and seemed to intend to set up an establishment. There was a report that he was very rich—which received confirmation in the fact that he brought with him four servants, five riding and carriage horses, a landau and a light hunting-cart.

Soon after their arrival the husband and wife left cards on all the best society, and their names were on every tongue. But it was not Herr von Rinnlingen, it was his wife who was the centre of interest. All the men were dazed, for the moment too dazed to pass judgment; but their wives were quite prompt and definite in the view that Gerda von Rinnlingen was not their sort.

"Of course, she comes from the metropolis, her ways would naturally be different," Frau Hagenström, the lawyer's wife, said, in conversation with Henriette Friedemann. "She smokes, and she rides. That is of course. But it is her manners—they are not only free, they are positively brusque, or even worse. You see, no one could call her ugly, one might even say she is pretty; but she has not a trace of feminine charm in her looks or gestures or her laugh—they completely lack everything that makes a man fall in love with a woman. She is not a flirt—and goodness knows I would be the last to disparage her for that. But it is strange to see so young a woman—she is only twenty-four—so entirely wanting in natural charm. I am not expressing myself very well, my dear, but I know what I mean. All the men are simply bewildered. In a few weeks, you will see, they will be disgusted."

"Well," Fräulein Friedemann said, "she certainly has everything she wants."

"Yes," cried Frau Hagenström, "look at her husband! And how does she treat him? You ought to see it—you will see it! I would be the first to approve of a married woman behaving with a certain reserve towards the other sex. But how does she behave to her own husband? She has a way of fixing him with an ice-cold stare and saying 'My dear friend!' with a pitying expression that drives me mad. For when you look at him—upright, correct, gallant, a brilliant officer and a splendidly preserved man of forty! They have been married four years, my dear."

Herr Friedemann was first vouchsafed a glimpse of Frau von Rinnlingen in the main street of the town, among all the rows of shops, at midday, when he was coming from the Bourse, where he had done a little bidding.

He was strolling along beside Herr Stephens, looking tiny and important, as usual. Herr Stephens was in the wholesale trade, a huge stocky man with round side-whiskers and bushy eyebrows. Both of them wore top hats; their overcoats were unbuttoned on account of the heat. They tapped their canes along the pavement and talked of the political situation; but half-way down the street Stephens suddenly said:

"Deuce take it if there isn't the Rinnlingen driving along."

"Good," answered Herr Friedemann in his high, rather sharp voice, looking expectantly ahead. "Because I have never yet set eyes on her. And here we have the yellow cart we hear so much about."

It was in fact the hunting-cart which Frau von Rinnlingen was herself driving today with a pair of thoroughbreds; a groom sat behind her, with folded arms. She wore a loose beige coat and skirt and a small round straw hat with a brown leather band, beneath which her well-waved red-blonde hair, a good, thick crop, was drawn into a knot at the nape of her neck. Her face was oval, with a dead-white skin and faint bluish shadows lurking under the close-set eyes. Her nose was short but well-shaped, with a becoming little saddle of freckles; whether her mouth was as good or no could not be told, for she kept it in continual motion, sucking the lower and biting the upper lip.

Herr Stephens, as the cart came abreast of them, greeted her with a great show of deference; little Herr Friedemann lifted his hat too and looked at her with wide-eyed attention. She lowered her whip, nodded slightly, and drove slowly past, looking at the houses and shop-windows.

After a few paces Herr Stephens said:

"She has been taking a drive and was on her way home."

Little Herr Friedemann made no answer, but stared before him at the pavement. Presently he started, looked at his companion, and asked: "What did you say?"

And Herr Stephens repeated his acute remark.

Three days after that Johannes Friedemann came home at midday from his usual walk. Dinner was at half past twelve, and he would spend the interval in his office at the right of the entrance door. But the maid came across the entry and told him that there were visitors.

"In my office?" he asked.

"No, upstairs with the mistresses."

"Who are they?"

"Herr and Frau Colonel von Rinnlingen."

"Ah," said Johannes Friedemann. "Then I will–"

And he mounted the stairs. He crossed the lobby and laid his hand on the knob of the high white door leading into the "landscape room." And then he drew back, turned round, and slowly returned as he had come. And spoke to himself, for there was no one else there, and said: "No, better not."

He went into his office, sat down at his desk, and took up the paper. But after a little he dropped it again and sat looking to one side out of the window. Thus he sat until the maid came to say that luncheon was ready; then he went up into the dining-room where his sisters were already waiting, and sat down in his chair, in which there were three music-books.

As she ladled the soup Henriette said:

"Johannes, do you know who were here?"

"Well?" he asked.

"The new Commandant and his wife."

"Indeed? That was friendly of them."

"Yes," said Pfiffi, a little water coming in the corners of her mouth. "I found them both very agreeable."

"And we must lose no time in returning the call," said Friederike. "I suggest that we go next Sunday, the day after tomorrow."

"Sunday," Henriette and Pfiffi said.

"You will go with us, Johannes?" asked Friederike.

"Of course he will," said Pfiffi, and gave herself a little shake. Herr Friedemann had not heard her at all; he was eating his soup, with a hushed and troubled air. It was as though he were listening to some strange noise he heard.

Next evening *Lohengrin* was being given at the opera, and everybody in society was present. The small auditorium was crowded, humming with voices and smelling of gas and perfumery. And every eye-glass in the stalls was directed towards box thirteen, next to the stage; for this was the first appearance of Herr and Frau von Rinnlingen and one could give them a good looking-over.

When little Herr Friedemann, in flawless dress clothes and glistening white pigeon-breasted shirt-front, entered his box, which was number thirteen, he started back at the door, making a gesture with his hand towards his brow. His nostrils dilated feverishly. Then he took his seat, which was next to Frau von Rinnlingen's.

She contemplated him for a little while, with her under lip stuck out; then she turned to exchange a few words with her husband, a tall, broad-shouldered gentleman with a brown, good-natured face and turned-up moustaches.

When the overture began and Frau von Rinnlingen leaned over the balustrade Herr Friedemann gave her a quick, searching side glance. She wore a light-coloured evening frock, the only one in the theatre which was slightly low in the neck. Her sleeves were full and her white gloves came up to her elbows. Her figure was statelier than it had looked under the loose coat; her full bosom slowly rose and fell and the knot of red-blonde hair hung low and heavy at the nape of her neck.

Herr Friedemann was pale, much paler than usual, and little beads of perspiration stood on his brow beneath the smoothly parted brown hair. He could see Frau von Rinnlingen's left arm, which lay upon the balustrade. She had taken off her glove and the rounded, dead-white arm and ringless hand, both of them shot with pale blue veins, were directly under his eye—he could not help seeing them.

The fiddles sang, the trombones crashed, Telramund was slain, general jubilation reigned in the orchestra, and little Herr Friedemann sat there motionless and pallid, his head drawn in between his shoulders, his forefinger to his lips and one hand thrust into the opening of his waistcoat.

As the curtain fell, Frau von Rinnlingen got up to leave the box with her husband. Johannes Friedemann saw her without looking, wiped his handkerchief across his brow, then rose suddenly and went as far as the door into the foyer, where he turned, came back to his chair, and sat down in the same posture as before.

When the bell rang and his neighbours re-entered the box he felt Frau von Rinnlingen's eyes upon him, so that finally against his will he raised his head. As their eyes met, hers did not swerve aside; she continued to gaze without embarrassment until he himself, deeply humiliated, was forced to look away. He turned a shade paler and felt a strange, sweet pang of anger and scorn. The music began again.

Towards the end of the act Frau von Rinnlingen chanced to drop her fan; it fell at Herr Friedemann's feet. They both stooped at the same time, but she reached it first and gave a little mocking smile as she said: "Thank you."

Their heads were quite close together and just for a second he got the warm scent of her breast. His face was drawn, his whole body twitched, and his heart thumped so horribly that he lost his breath. He sat without moving for half a minute, then he pushed back his chair, got up quietly, and went out.

He crossed the lobby, pursued by the music; got his top hat from the cloak-room, his light overcoat and his stick, went down the stairs and out of doors.

It was a warm, still evening. In the gas-lit street the gabled houses towered towards a sky where stars were softly beaming. The pavement echoed the steps of a few passers-by. Someone spoke to him, but he heard and saw nothing; his head was bowed and his deformed chest shook with the violence of his breathing. Now and then he murmured to himself:

"My God, my God!"

He was gazing horror-struck within himself, beholding the havoc which had been wrought with his tenderly cherished, scrupulously managed feelings. Suddenly he was quite overpowered by the strength of his tortured longing. Giddy and drunken he leaned against a lamp-post and his quivering lips uttered the one word: "Gerda!"

The stillness was complete. Far and wide not a soul was to be seen. Little Herr Friedemann pulled himself together and went on, up the street in which the opera-house stood and which ran steeply down to the river, then along the main street northwards to his home.

How she had looked at him! She had forced him, actually, to cast down his eyes! She had humiliated him with her glance. But was she not a woman and he a man? And those strange brown eyes of hers—had they not positively glittered with unholy joy?

Again he felt the same surge of sensual, impotent hatred mount up in him; then he relived the moment when her head had touched his, when he had breathed in the fragrance of her body—and for the second time he halted, bent his deformed torso backwards, drew in the air through clenched teeth, and murmured helplessly, desperately, uncontrollably:

"My God, my God!"

Then went on again, slowly, mechanically, through the heavy evening air, through the empty echoing streets until he stood before his own house. He paused a minute in the entry, breathing the cool, dank inside air; then he went into his office.

He sat down at his desk by the open window and stared straight ahead of him at a large yellow rose which somebody had set there in a glass of water. He took it up and smelt it with his eyes closed, then put it down with a gesture of weary sadness. No, no. That was all over. What was even that fragrance to him now? What any of all those things that up to now had been the well-springs of his joy?

He turned away and gazed into the quiet street. At intervals steps passed and the sound died away. The stars stood still and glittered. He felt so weak, so utterly tired to death. His head was quite vacant, and suddenly his despair began to melt into a gentle, pervading melancholy. A few lines of a poem flickered through his head, he heard the *Lohengrin* music in his ears, he saw Frau von Rinnlingen's face and her round white arm on the red velvet —then he fell into a heavy fever-burdened sleep.

Often he was near waking, but feared to do so and managed to sink back into forgetfulness again. But when it had grown quite light, he opened his eyes and looked round him with a wide and painful gaze. He remembered everything, it was as though the anguish had never been intermitted by sleep.

His head was heavy and his eyes burned. But when he had washed up and bathed his head with cologne he felt better and sat down in his place by the still open window. It was early, perhaps only five o'clock. Now and then a baker's boy passed; otherwise there was no one to be seen. In the opposite house the blinds were down. But birds were twittering and the sky was luminously blue. A wonderfully beautiful Sunday morning.

A feeling of comfort and confidence came over little Herr Friedemann. Why had he been distressing himself? Was not everything just as it had been? The attack of yesterday had been a bad one. Granted. But it should be the last. It was not too late, he could still escape destruction. He must avoid every occasion of a fresh seizure; he felt sure he could do this. He felt the strength to conquer and suppress his weakness.

It struck half past seven and Friederike came in with the coffee, setting it on the round table in front of the leather sofa against the rear wall.

"Good morning, Johannes," said she; "here is your breakfast."

"Thanks," said little Herr Friedemann. And then: "Dear Friederike, I am sorry, but you will have to pay your call without me, I do not feel well enough to go. I have slept badly and have a headache – in short, I must ask you – "

"What a pity!" answered Friederike. "You must go another time. But you do look ill. Shall I lend you my menthol pencil?"

"Thanks," said Herr Friedemann. "It will pass." And Friederike went out.

Standing at the table he slowly drank his coffee and ate a croissant. He felt satisfied with himself and proud of his firmness. When he had finished he sat down again by the open window, with a cigar. The food had done him good and he felt happy and hopeful. He took a book and sat reading and smoking and blinking into the sunlight.

Morning had fully come, wagons rattled past, there were many voices and the sound of the bells on passing trams. With and among it all was woven the twittering and chirping; there was a radiant blue sky, a soft mild air.

At ten o'clock he heard his sisters cross the entry; the front door creaked, and he idly noticed that they passed his window. An hour went by. He felt more and more happy.

A sort of hubris mounted in him. What a heavenly air–and how the birds were singing! He felt like taking a little walk. Then suddenly, without any transition, yet accompanied by a terror namelessly sweet came the thought: "Suppose I were to go to her!" And suppressing, as though by actual muscular effort, every warning voice within him, he added with blissful resolution: "I will go to her!"

He changed into his Sunday clothes, took his top hat and his stick, and hurried with quickened breath through the town and into the southern suburbs. Without looking at a soul he kept raising and dropping his head with each eager step, completely rapt in his exalted state until he arrived at the avenue of chestnut trees and the red brick villa with the name of Commandant von Rinnlingen on the gate-post.

But here he was seized by a tremor, his heart throbbed and pounded in his breast. He went across the vestibule and rang at the inside door. The die was cast, there was no retreating now. "Come what come may," thought he, and felt the stillness of death within him.

The door suddenly opened and the maid came toward him across the vestibule; she took his card and hurried away up the red-carpeted stair. Herr Friedemann gazed fixedly at the bright colour until she came back and said that her mistress would like him to come up.

He put down his stick beside the door leading into the salon and stole a look at himself in the glass. His face was pale, the eyes red, his hair was sticking to his brow, the hand that held his top hat kept on shaking.

The maid opened the door and he went in. He found himself in a rather large, half-darkened room, with drawn curtains. At his right was a piano, and about the round table in the centre stood several arm-chairs covered in brown silk. The sofa stood along the left-hand wall, with a landscape painting in a heavy gilt frame hanging above it. The wall-paper too was dark in tone. There was an alcove filled with potted palms.

A minute passed, then Frau von Rinnlingen opened the portières on the right and approached him noiselessly over the thick brown carpet. She wore a simply cut frock of red and black plaid. A ray of light, with motes dancing in it, streamed from the alcove and fell upon her heavy red hair so that it shone like gold. She kept her strange eyes fixed upon him with a searching gaze and as usual stuck out her under lip.

"Good morning, Frau Commandant," began little Herr Friedemann, and looked up at her, for he came only as high as her chest. "I wished to pay you my respects too. When my sisters did so I was unfortunately out . . . I regretted sincerely . . ."

He had no idea at all what else he should say; and there she stood and gazed ruthlessly at him as though she would force him to go on. The blood rushed to his head. "She sees through me," he thought, "she will torture and despise me. Her eyes keep flickering. . . ."

But at last she said, in a very high, clear voice:

"It is kind of you to have come. I have also been sorry not to see you before. Will you please sit down?"

She took her seat close beside him, leaned back, and put her arm along the arm of the chair. He sat bent over, holding his hat between his knees. She went on:

"Did you know that your sisters were here a quarter of an hour ago? They told me you were ill."

"Yes," he answered, "I did not feel well enough to go out, I thought I should not be able to. That is why I am late."

"You do not look very well even now," said she tranquilly, not shifting her gaze. "You are pale and your eyes are inflamed. You are not very strong, perhaps?"

"Oh," said Herr Friedemann, stammering, "I've not much to complain of, as a rule."

"I am ailing a good deal too," she went on, still not turning her eyes from him, "but nobody notices it. I am nervous, and sometimes I have the strangest feelings."

She paused, lowered her chin to her breast, and looked up expectantly at him. He made no reply, simply sat with his dreamy gaze directed upon her. How strangely she spoke, and how her clear and thrilling voice affected him! His heart beat more quietly and he felt as though he were in a dream. She began again:

"I am not wrong in thinking that you left the opera last night before it was over?"

"Yes, madam."

"I was sorry to see that. You listened like a music-lover—though the performance was only tolerable. You are fond of music, I am sure. Do you play the piano?"

"I play the violin, a little," said Herr Friedemann. "That is, really not very much—"

"You play the violin?" she asked, and looked past him consideringly. "But we might play together," she suddenly said. "I can accompany a little. It would be a pleasure to find somebody here—would you come?"

"I am quite at your service—with pleasure," said he, stiffly. He was still as though in a dream. A pause ensued. Then suddenly her expression changed. He saw it alter for one of cruel, though hardly perceptible mockery, and again she fixed him with that same searching, uncannily flickering gaze. His face burned, he knew not where to turn; drawing his head down between his shoulders he stared confusedly at the carpet, while there shot through him once more that strangely sweet and torturing sense of impotent rage.

He made a desperate effort and raised his eyes. She was looking over his head at the door. With the utmost difficulty he fetched out a few words:

"And you are so far not too dissatisfied with your stay in our city?"

"Oh, no," said Frau Rinnlingen indifferently. "No, certainly not; why should I not be satisfied? To be sure, I feel a little hampered, as though everybody's eyes were upon me, but—oh, before I forget it," she went on quickly, "we are entertaining a few people next week, a small, informal company. A little music, perhaps, and conversation. . . . There is a charming garden at the back, it runs down to the river. You and your sisters will be receiving an invitation in due course, but perhaps I may ask you now to give us the pleasure of your company?"

Herr Friedemann was just expressing his gratitude for the invitation when the door-knob was seized energetically from without and the Commandant entered. They both rose and Frau von Rinnlingen introduced the two men to each other. Her husband bowed to them both with equal courtesy. His bronze face glistened with the heat.

He drew off his gloves, addressing Herr Friedemann in a powerful, rather sharp-edged voice. The latter looked up at him with large vacant eyes and had the feeling that he would presently be clapped benevolently on the shoulder. Heels together, inclining from the waist, the Commandant turned to his wife and asked, in a much gentler tone:

"Have you asked Herr Friedemann if he will give us the pleasure of his company at our little party, my love? If you are willing I should like to fix the date for next week and I hope that the weather will remain fine so that we can enjoy ourselves in the garden."

"Just as you say," answered Frau von Rinnlingen, and gazed past him.

Two minutes later Herr Friedemann got up to go. At the door he turned and bowed to her once more, meeting her expressionless gaze still fixed upon him.

He went away, but he did not go back to the town; unconsciously he struck into a path that led away from the avenue towards the old ruined fort by the river, among well-kept lawns and shady avenues with benches.

He walked quickly and absently, with bent head. He felt intolerably hot, as though aware of flames leaping and sinking within him, and his head throbbed with fatigue.

It was as though her gaze still rested on him—not vacantly as it had at the end, but with that flickering cruelty which went with the strange still way she spoke. Did it give her pleasure to put him beside himself, to see him helpless? Looking through and through him like that, could she not feel a little pity?

He had gone along the river-bank under the moss-grown wall; he sat down on a bench within a half-circle of blossoming jasmine. The sweet, heavy scent was all about him, the sun brooded upon the dimpling water.

He was weary, he was worn out; and yet within him all was

tumult and anguish. Were it not better to take one last look and then to go down into that quiet water; after a brief struggle to be free and safe and at peace? Ah, peace, peace—that was what he wanted! Not peace in an empty and soundless void, but a gentle, sunlit peace, full of good, of tranquil thoughts.

All his tender love of life thrilled through him in that moment, all his profound yearning for his vanished "happiness." But then he looked about him into the silent, endlessly indifferent peace of nature, saw how the river went its own way in the sun, how the grasses quivered and the flowers stood up where they blossomed, only to fade and be blown away; saw how all that was bent submissively to the will of life; and there came over him all at once that sense of acquaintance and understanding with the inevitable which can make those who know it superior to the blows of fate.

He remembered the afternoon of his thirtieth birthday and the peaceful happiness with which he, untroubled by fears or hopes, had looked forward to what was left of his life. He had seen no light and no shadow there, only a mild twilight radiance gently declining into the dark. With what a calm and superior smile had he contemplated the years still to come—how long ago was that?

Then this woman had come, she had to come, it was his fate that she should, for she herself was his fate and she alone. He had known it from the first moment. She had come—and though he had tried his best to defend his peace, her coming had roused in him all those forces which from his youth up he had sought to suppress, feeling, as he did, that they spelled torture and destruction. They had seized upon him with frightful, irresistible power and flung him to the earth.

They were his destruction, well he knew it. But why struggle, then, and why torture himself? Let everything take its course. He would go his appointed way, closing his eyes before the yawning void, bowing to his fate, bowing to the overwhelming, anguishingly sweet, irresistible power.

The water glittered, the jasmine gave out its strong, pungent scent, the birds chattered in the tree-tops that gave glimpses among them of a heavy, velvety-blue sky. Little hump-backed Herr Friedemann sat long upon his bench; he sat bent over, holding his head in his hands.

Everybody agreed that the Rinnlingens entertained very well. Some thirty guests sat in the spacious dining-room, at the long, prettily decorated table, and the butler and two hired waiters were already handing round the ices. Dishes clattered, glasses rang, there was a warm aroma of food and perfumes. Here were comfortable merchants with their wives and daughters; most of the officers of the garrison; a few professional men, lawyers and the popular old family doctor—in short, all the best society.

A nephew of the Commandant, on a visit, a student of mathematics, sat deep in conversation with Fräulein Hagenström, whose place was directly opposite Herr Friedemann's, at the lower end of the table. Johannes Friedemann sat there on a rich velvet cushion, beside the unbeautiful wife of the Colonial Director and not far off Frau von Rinnlingen, who had been escorted to table by Consul Stephens. It was astonishing, the change which had taken place in little Herr Friedemann in these few days. Perhaps the incandescent lighting in the room was partly to blame; but his cheeks looked sunken, he made a more crippled impression even than usual, and his inflamed eyes, with their dark rings, glowed with an inexpressibly tragic light. He drank a great deal of wine and now and then addressed a remark to his neighbour.

Frau von Rinnlingen had not so far spoken to him at all; but now she leaned over and called out:

"I have been expecting you in vain these days, you and your fiddle."

He looked vacantly at her for a while before he replied. She wore a light-coloured frock with a low neck that left the white throat bare; a Maréchal Niel rose in full bloom was fastened in her shining hair. Her cheeks were a little flushed, but the same bluish shadows lurked in the corners of her eyes.

Herr Friedemann looked at his plate and forced himself to make some sort of reply; after which the school superintendent's wife asked him if he did not love Beethoven and he had to answer that too. But at this point the Commandant, sitting at the head of the table, caught his wife's eye, tapped on his glass and said:

"Ladies and gentlemen, I suggest that we drink our coffee in the next room. It must be fairly decent out in the garden too, and whoever wants a little fresh air, I am for him."

Lieutenant von Deidesheim made a tactful little joke to cover the ensuing pause, and the table rose in the midst of laughter. Herr Friedemann and his partner were among the last to quit the room; he escorted her through the "old German" smoking-room to the dim and pleasant living-room, where he took his leave.

He was dressed with great care: his evening clothes were irreproachable, his shirt was dazzlingly white, his slender, well-shaped feet were encased in patent-leather pumps, which now and then betrayed the fact that he wore red silk stockings.

He looked out into the corridor and saw a good many people descending the steps into the garden. But he took up a position at the door of the smoking-room, with his cigar and coffee, where he could see into the living-room.

Some of the men stood talking in this room, and at the right of the door a little knot had formed round a small table, the centre of which was the mathematics student, who was eagerly talking. He had made the assertion that one could draw through a given point more than one parallel to a straight line; Frau Hagenström had cried that this was impossible, and he had gone on to prove it so conclusively that his hearers were constrained to behave as though they understood.

At the rear of the room, on the sofa beside the red-shaded lamp, Gerda von Rinnlingen sat in conversation with young Fräulein Stephens. She leaned back among the yellow silk cushions with one knee slung over the other, slowly smoking a cigarette, breathing out the smoke through her nose and sticking out her lower lip. Fräulein Stephens sat stiff as a graven image beside her, answering her questions with an assiduous smile.

Nobody was looking at little Herr Friedemann, so nobody saw that his large eyes were constantly directed upon Frau von Rinnlingen. He sat rather droopingly and looked at her. There was no passion in his gaze nor scarcely any pain. But there was something dull and heavy there, a dead weight of impotent, involuntary adoration.

Some ten minutes went by. Then as though she had been secretly watching him the whole time, Frau von Rinnlingen approached and paused in front of him. He got up as he heard her say:

"Would you care to go into the garden with me, Herr Friedemann?"

He answered:

"With pleasure, madam."

"You have never seen our garden?" she asked him as they went down the steps. "It is fairly large. I hope that there are not too many people in it; I should like to get a breath of fresh air. I got a headache during supper; perhaps the red wine was too strong for me. Let us go this way." They passed through a glass door, the vestibule, and a cool little courtyard, whence they gained the open air by descending a couple more steps.

The scent of all the flower-beds rose into the wonderful, warm, starry night. The garden lay in full moonlight and the guests were strolling up and down the white gravel paths, smoking and talking as they went. A group had gathered round the old fountain, where the much-loved old doctor was making them laugh by sailing paper boats.

With a little nod Frau von Rinnlingen passed them by, and pointed ahead of her, where the fragrant and well-cared-for garden blended into the darker park.

"Shall we go down this middle path?" asked she. At the beginning of it stood two low, squat obelisks.

In the vista at the end of the chestnut alley they could see the river shining green and bright in the moonlight. All about them was darkness and coolness. Here and there side paths branched off, all of them probably curving down to the river. For a long time there was not a sound.

"Down by the water," she said, "there is a pretty spot where I often sit. We could stop and talk a little. See the stars glittering here and there through the trees."

He did not answer, gazing, as they approached it, at the river's shimmering green surface. You could see the other bank and the park along the city wall. They left the alley and came out on the grassy slope down to the river, and she said:

"Here is our place, a little to the right, and there is no one there."

The bench stood facing the water, some six paces away, with its back to the trees. It was warmer here in the open. Crickets chirped among the grass, which at the river's edge gave way to sparse reeds. The moonlit water gave off a soft light.

For a while they both looked in silence. Then he heard her voice; it thrilled him to recognize the same low, gentle, pensive tone of a week ago, which now as then moved him so strangely:

"How long have you had your infirmity, Herr Friedemann? Were you born so?"

He swallowed before he replied, for his throat felt as though he were choking. Then he said, politely and gently:

"No, *gnädige Frau*. It comes from their having let me fall, when I was an infant."

"And how old are you now?" she asked again.

"Thirty years old."

"Thirty years old," she repeated. "And these thirty years were not happy ones?"

Little Herr Friedemann shook his head, his lips quivered.

"No," he said, "that was all lies and my imagination."

"Then you have thought that you were happy?" she asked.

"I have tried to be," he replied, and she responded:

"That was brave of you."

A minute passed. The crickets chirped and behind them the boughs rustled lightly.

"I understand a good deal about unhappiness," she told him. "These summer nights by the water are the best thing for it."

He made no direct answer, but gestured feebly across the water, at the opposite bank, lying peaceful in the darkness.

"I was sitting over there not long ago," he said.

"When you came from me?" she asked. He only nodded.

Then suddenly he started up from his seat, trembling all over; he sobbed and gave vent to a sound, a wail which yet seemed like a release from strain, and sank slowly to the ground before her. He had touched her hand with his as it lay beside him on the bench, and clung to it now, seizing the other as he knelt before her, this little cripple, trembling and shuddering; he buried his face in her lap and stammered between his gasps in a voice which was scarcely human:

"You know, you understand . . . let me . . . I can no longer . . . my God, oh, my God!"

She did not repulse him, neither did she bend her face towards him. She sat erect, leaning a little away, and her close-set eyes, wherein the liquid shimmer of the water seemed to be mirrored, stared beyond him into space.

Then she gave him an abrupt push and uttered a short, scornful laugh. She tore her hands from his burning fingers, clutched his arm, and flung him sidewise upon the ground. Then she sprang up and vanished down the wooded avenue.

He lay there with his face in the grass, stunned, unmanned, shudders coursing swiftly through his frame. He pulled himself together, got up somehow, took two steps, and fell again, close to the water. What were his sensations at this moment? Perhaps he was feeling that same luxury of hate which he had felt before when she had humiliated him with her glance, degenerated now, when he lay before her on the ground and she had treated him like a dog, into an insane rage which must at all costs find expression even against himself—a disgust, perhaps of himself, which filled him with a thirst to destroy himself, to tear himself to pieces, to blot himself utterly out.

On his belly he dragged his body a little further, lifted its upper part, and let it fall into the water. He did not raise his head nor move his legs, which still lay on the bank.

The crickets stopped chirping a moment at the noise of the little splash. Then they went on as before, the boughs lightly rustled, and down the long alley came the faint sound of laughter.

Questions

1. What is the significance of Herr Friedemann's proficiency in artistic endeavors in relation to the search theme?
2. Frau von Rinnlingen's actions appear difficult to understand. How can you explain her motivation in cultivating Friedemann? How can you explain her final rejection?
3. What are the outward manifestations of Friedemann's "image of himself"?
4. From all viewpoints—the author's, Friedemann's, and ours—the story could only end with the death of Friedemann. Explain why.

Topics for Composition

1. Mann's story, among those selections read thus far, probes more deeply into the inner feelings of man. Using question 3 above as your beginning point, write an essay showing how Mann develops and parallels the outward manifestations of the search with the inner image of himself that Friedemann displays.
2. Obviously, Mann's story illustrates a theme that we might classify as "the social outcast." Write an essay dealing with the "social outcast" in our society. In other words, for what reason or reasons are groups and individuals ostracized by society? Your possible range here is broad: select from minority groups, criminals, social misfits, physical and mental defectives, etc.

Drama

THE play is formally conditioned by Williams' concept of a "memory play." With much the same effect achieved by a first person narrator in fiction, Tom Wingfield shares his memory with the audience. Because the play—even his own role within it—unfolds as he remembers it, we can accept the many expressionistic devices Williams has used to make the situation and the emotional impact of the play more immediate for the audience. The music, the titles flashed on a screen, and the symbolic little glass animals (especially the unicorn) all become points of immediacy for the involvement of audience or reader with the dramatic situation of the Wingfields and their "gentleman caller." As you read the play, keep in mind some clearly distinctive features:

1. Although Tom slips back and forth as narrator and character, the narrator is an older and more philosophical figure than the character.
2. As Williams emphasizes in his character description, Amanda Wingfield transcends the "black and white" limitations of a character in melodrama.
3. The photograph of the father has its own dramatic impact upon the central conflict of the play.
4. The word "crippled" occurs at strategic points of the play's unfolding. Although it is always applied to Laura, in another sense it describes the other characters and their world also.
5. Six scenes, rather than the conventional three acts of most twentieth-century plays, give the play some likeness to cinema.

The Glass Menagerie

TENNESSEE WILLIAMS

THE AUTHOR'S PRODUCTION NOTES

Being a "memory play," *The Glass Menagerie* can be presented with unusual freedom of convention. Because of its considerably delicate or tenuous material, atmospheric touches and subtleties of direction play a particularly important part. Expressionism and all other unconventional techniques in drama have only one valid aid, and that is a closer approach to truth. When a play employs unconventional techniques, it is not, or certainly shouldn't be, trying to escape its responsibility of dealing with reality, or interpreting experience, but is actually or should be attempting to find a closer approach, a more penetrating and vivid expression of things as they are. The straight realistic play with its genuine frigidaire and authentic ice-cubes, its characters that speak exactly as its audience speaks, corresponds to the academic landscape and has the same virtue of a photographic likeness. Everyone should know nowadays the unimportance of the photographic in art: that truth, life, or reality is an organic thing which the poetic imagination can represent or suggest, in essence, only through transformation, through changing into other forms than those which were merely present in appearance.

These remarks are not meant as a preface only to this particular play. They have to do with a conception of a new, plastic theatre which must take the place of the exhausted theatre of realistic conventions if the theatre is to resume vitality as a part of our culture.

The Screen Device

There is *only one important difference between the original and acting version of the play* and that is the *omission* in the latter of the device which I tentatively included in my *original* script. This device was the use of a screen on which were projected magic-lantern slides bearing images or titles. I do not regret the omission of this device from the present Broadway production. The extraordinary power of Miss [Laurette] Taylor's performance made it suitable to have the utmost simplicity in the physical production. But I think it may be interesting to some readers to see how this device was conceived. So I am putting it into the published manuscript. These images and legends, projected from behind, were cast on a section of wall between the front-room and dining-room areas, which should be indistinguishable from the rest when not in use.

The purpose of this will probably be apparent. It is to give accent to certain values in each scene. Each scene contains a particular point (or several) which is structurally the most important. In an episodic play, such as this, the basic structure or narrative line may be obscured from the audience; the effect may seem fragmentary rather than architectural. This may not be the fault of the play so much as a lack of attention in the audience. The legend or image upon the screen will strengthen the effect of what is merely allusion in the writing and allow the primary point to be made more simply and lightly than if the entire responsibility were on the spoken lines. Aside from this structural value, I think the screen will have a definite emotional appeal, less definable but just as important. An imaginative producer or director may invent many other uses for this device than those indicated in the present script. In fact the possibilities of the device seem much larger to me than the instance of this play can possibly utilize.

The Music

Another extra-literary accent in this play is provided by the use of music. A single recurring tune, "The Glass Menagerie," is used to give emotional emphasis to suitable passages. This tune is like circus music, not when you are on the grounds or in the immediate vicinity of the parade, but when you are at some distance and very likely thinking of something else. It seems under those circumstances to continue almost interminably and it weaves in and out of your preoccupied consciousness; then it is the lightest, most delicate music in the world and perhaps the saddest. It expresses the surface vivacity of life with the underlying strain of immutable and inexpressible sorrow. When you look at a piece of delicately spun glass you think of two things: how beautiful it is and how easily it can be broken. Both of those ideas should be woven into the recurring tune, which dips in and out of the play as if it were carried on a wind that changes. It serves as a thread of connection and allusion between the narrator with his separate point in time and space and the subject of his story. Between each episode it returns as reference to the emotion, nostalgia, which is the first condition of the play. It is primarily Laura's music and therefore comes out most clearly when the play focuses upon her and the lovely fragility of glass which is her image.

The Lighting

The lighting in the play is not realistic. In keeping with the atmosphere of memory, the stage is dim. Shafts of light are focused on selected areas or actors, sometimes in contradistinction to what is the apparent center. For instance, in the quarrel scene between Tom and Amanda, in which Laura has no active part, the clearest pool of light is on her figure. This is also true of the supper scene, when her silent figure on the sofa should remain the visual center. The light upon Laura should be distinct from the others, having a peculiar pristine clarity such as light used in early religious portraits of female saints or madonnas. A certain correspondence to light in religious paintings, such as El Greco's, where the figures are radiant in atmosphere that is relatively dusky, could be effectively used throughout the play. (It will also permit a more effective use of the screen.) A free, imaginative use of light can be of enormous value in giving a mobile, plastic quality to plays of a more or less static nature.

CHARACTERS

AMANDA WINGFIELD, *the mother*

A little woman of great but confused vitality clinging frantically to another time and place. Her characterization must be carefully created, not copied from type. She is not paranoiac, but her life is paranoia. There is much to admire in Amanda, and as much to love and pity as there is to laugh at. Certainly she has endurance and a kind of heroism, and though her foolishness makes her unwittingly cruel at times, there is tenderness in her slight person.

LAURA WINGFIELD, *her daughter*

Amanda, having failed to establish contact with reality, continues to live vitally in her illusions, but Laura's situation is even graver. A childhood illness has left her crippled, one leg slightly shorter than the other, and held in a brace. This defect need not be more than suggested on the stage. Stemming from this, Laura's separation increases till she is like a piece of her own glass collection, too exquisitely fragile to move from the shelf.

TOM WINGFIELD, *her son*

And the narrator of the play. A poet with a job in a warehouse. His nature is not remorseless, but to escape from a trap he has to act without pity.

JIM O'CONNOR, *the gentleman caller*

A nice, ordinary, young man.

SCENE *An Alley in St. Louis*

PART I. Preparation for a Gentleman Caller.
PART II. The Gentleman calls.

TIME: Now and the Past.

SCENE I

The Wingfield apartment is in the rear of the building, one of those vast hive-like conglomerations of cellular living-units that flower as warty growths in overcrowded urban centers of lower middle-class population and are symptomatic of the impulse of this largest and fundamentally enslaved section of American society to avoid fluidity and differentiation and to exist and function as one interfused mass of automatism.

The apartment faces an alley and is entered by a fire-escape, a structure whose name is a touch of accidental poetic truth, for all of these huge buildings are always burning with the slow and implacable fires of human desperation. The fire-escape is included in the set—that is, the landing of it and steps descending from it.

The scene is memory and is therefore nonrealistic. Memory takes a lot of poetic license. It omits some details; others are exaggerated, according to the emotional value of the articles it touches, for memory is seated predominantly in the heart. The interior is therefore rather dim and poetic.

At the rise of the curtain, the audience is faced with the dark, grim rear wall of the Wingfield tenement. This building, which runs parallel to the footlights, is flanked on both sides by dark, narrow alleys which run into murky canyons of tangled clotheslines, garbage cans and the sinister lattice-work of neighboring fire-escapes. It is up and down these side alleys that exterior entrances and exits are made, during the play. At the end of Tom's *opening commentary, the dark tenement wall slowly reveals (by means of a transparency) the interior of the ground floor Wingfield apartment.*

Downstage is the living room, which also serves as a sleeping room for Laura, *the sofa unfolding to make her bed. Upstage, center, and divided by a wide arch or second proscenium with transparent faded portieres (or second curtain), is the dining room. In an old-fashioned what-not in the living room are seen scores of transparent glass animals. A blown-up photograph of the father hangs on the wall of the living room, facing the audience, to the left of the archway. It is the face of a very handsome young man in a doughboy's First World War cap. He is gallantly smiling, ineluctably smiling, as if to say, "I will be smiling forever."*

The audience hears and sees the opening scene in the dining room through both the transparent fourth wall of the building and the transparent gauze portieres of the dining-room arch. It is during this revealing scene that the fourth wall slowly ascends out of sight. This transparent exterior wall is not brought down again until the very end of the play, during Tom's *final speech.*

The narrator is an undisguised convention of the play. He takes whatever license with dramatic convention as is convenient to his purposes.

Tom *enters dressed as a merchant sailor from alley, stage left, and strolls across the front of the stage to the fire-escape. There he stops and lights a cigarette. He addresses the audience.*

Tom. Yes, I have tricks in my pocket, I have things up my sleeve. But I am the opposite of a stage magician. He gives you illusion that has the appearance of truth. I give you truth in the pleasant disguise of illusion.

To begin with, I turn back time. I reverse it to that quaint period, the thirties, when the huge middle class of America was matriculating in a school for the blind. Their eyes had failed them, or they had failed their eyes, and so they were having their fingers pressed forcibly down on the fiery Braille alphabet of a dissolving economy.

In Spain there was revolution. Here there was only shouting and confusion.

In Spain there was Guernica. Here there were disturbances of labor, sometimes pretty violent, in otherwise peaceful cities such as Chicago, Cleveland, St. Louis . . .

This is the social background of the play.

[*Music*]

The play is memory.

Being a memory play, it is dimly lighted, it is sentimental, it is not realistic.

In memory everything seems to happen to music. That explains the fiddle in the wings.

I am the narrator of the play, and also a character in it.

The other characters are my mother, Amanda, my sister, Laura, and a gentleman caller who appears in the final scenes.

He is the most realistic character in the play, being an emissary from a world of reality that we were somehow set apart from.

But since I have a poet's weakness for symbols, I am using this character also as a symbol; he is the long delayed but always expected something that we live for.

There is a fifth character in the play who doesn't appear except in this larger-than-life-size photograph over the mantel.

This is our father who left us a long time ago.

He was a telephone man who fell in love with long distances; he gave up his job with the telephone company and skipped the light fantastic out of town . . .

The last we heard of him was a picture post-card from Mazatlan, on the Pacific coast of Mexico, containing a message of two words–

"Hello–Good-bye!" and no address.

I think the rest of the play will explain itself. . . .

[Amanda's *voice becomes audible through the portieres*]

[*Legend on screen:* "Où sont les neiges"]

[*He divides the portieres and enters the upstage area.* Amanda *and* Laura *are seated at a drop-leaf table. Eating is indicated by gestures without food or utensils.* Amanda *faces the audience.* Tom *and* Laura *are seated in profile. The interior has lit up softly and through the scrim we see* Amanda *and* Laura *seated at the table in the upstage area.*]

Amanda [*calling*]. Tom?

Tom. Yes, Mother.

Amanda. We can't say grace until you come to the table!

Tom. Coming, Mother. [*He bows slightly and withdraws, reappearing a few moments later in his place at the table*]

Amanda [*to her son*]. Honey, don't *push* with your *fingers.* If you have to push with something, the thing to push with is a crust of bread. And chew–chew! Animals have secretions in their stomachs which enable them to digest food without mastication, but human beings are supposed to chew their food before they swallow it down. Eat food leisurely, son, and really enjoy it. A well-cooked meal has lots of delicate flavors that have to be held in the mouth for appreciation. So chew your food and give your salivary glands a chance to function!

[Tom *deliberately lays his imaginary fork down and pushes his chair back from the table*]

Tom. I haven't enjoyed one bite of this dinner because of your constant directions on how to eat it. It's you that makes me rush through meals with your hawk-like attention to every bite I take. Sickening–spoils my appetite–all this discussion of animal's secretion–salivary glands–mastication!

Amanda [*lightly*]. Temperament like a Metropolitan star! [*He rises and crosses downstage*] You're not excused from the table.

Tom. I'm getting a cigarette.

Amanda. You smoke too much.

[Laura *rises*]

Laura. I'll bring in the blanc mange.

[*He remains standing with his cigarette by the portieres during the following*]

Amanda [*rising*]. No, sister, no, sister—you be the lady this time and I'll be the darky.

Laura. I'm already up.

Amanda. Resume your seat, little sister—I want you to stay fresh and pretty—for gentlemen callers!

Laura. I'm not expecting any gentlemen callers.

Amanda [*crossing out to kitchenette. Airily*]. Sometimes they come when they are least expected! Why I remember one Sunday afternoon in Blue Mountain—

[*Enters kitchenette*]

Tom. I know what's coming!

Laura. Yes. But let her tell it.

Tom. Again?

Laura. She loves to tell it.

[Amanda *returns with bowl of dessert*]

Amanda. One Sunday afternoon in Blue Mountain—your mother received—*seventeen*—gentlemen callers! Why, sometimes there weren't chairs enough to accommodate them all. We had to send the nigger over to bring in folding chairs from the parish house.

Tom [*remaining at portieres*]. How did you entertain those gentlemen callers?

Amanda. I understood the art of conversation.

Tom. I bet you could talk.

Amanda. Girls in those days *knew* how to talk, I can tell you.

Tom. Yes?

[*Image:* Amanda *as a girl on a porch, greeting callers*]

Amanda. They knew how to entertain their gentlemen callers. It wasn't enough for a girl to be possessed of a pretty face and a graceful figure—although I wasn't slighted in either respect. She also needed to have a nimble wit and a tongue to meet all occasions.

Tom. What did you talk about?

Amanda. Things of importance going on in the world! Never anything coarse or common or vulgar. [*She addresses* Tom *as though he were seated in the vacant chair at the table though he remains by portieres. He plays this scene as though he held the book*] My callers were gentlemen—all! Among my callers were some of the most prominent young planters of the Mississippi Delta—planters and sons of planters!

[Tom *motions for music and a spot of light on* Amanda. *Her eyes lift, her face glows, her voice becomes rich and elegiac*]

[*Screen legend:* "Où sont les neiges"]

There was young Champ Laughlin who later became vice-president of the Delta Planters Bank.

Hadley Stevenson who was drowned in Moon Lake and left his widow one hundred and fifty thousand in Government bonds.

There were the Cutrere brothers, Wesley and Bates. Bates was one of my bright particular beaux! He got in a quarrel with that wild Wainwright boy. They shot it out on the floor of Moon Lake Casino. Bates was shot through the stomach. Died in the ambulance on his way to Memphis. His widow was also well-provided for, came into eight or ten thousand acres, that's all. She married him on the rebound—never loved her—carried my picture on him the night he died!

And there was that boy that every girl in the Delta had set her cap for! That beautiful, brilliant young Fitzhugh boy from Greene County!

Tom. What did he leave his widow?

Amanda. He never married! Gracious, you talk as though all of my old admirers had turned up their toes to the daisies!

Tom. Isn't this the first you've mentioned that still survives?

Amanda. That Fitzhugh boy went North and made a fortune—came to be known as the Wolf of Wall Street! He had the Midas touch, whatever he touched turned to gold!

And I could have been Mrs. Duncan J. Fitzhugh, mind you! But—I picked your *father!*

Laura [*rising*]. Mother, let me clear the table.

Amanda. No, dear, you go in front and study your typewriter chart. Or practice your shorthand a little. Stay fresh and pretty!—It's almost time for our gentlemen callers to start arriving. [*She flounces girlishly toward the kitchenette*] How many do you suppose we're going to entertain this afternoon?

[Tom *throws down the paper and jumps up with a groan*]

Laura [*alone in the dining room*]. I don't believe we're going to receive any, Mother.

Amanda [*reappearing, airily*]. What? No one—not one? You must be joking! [Laura *nervously echoes her laugh. She slips in a fugitive manner through the half-opened portieres and draws them gently behind her. A shaft of very clear light is thrown on her face against the faded tapestry of the curtains. Music: "The Glass Menagerie" under faintly. Lightly*] Not one gentleman caller? It can't be true! There must be a flood, there must have been a tornado!

Laura. It isn't a flood, it's not a tornado, Mother. I'm just not popular like you were in Blue Mountain. . . . [Tom *utters another groan.* Laura *glances at him with a faint apologetic smile. Her voice catching a little*] Mother's afraid I'm going to be an old maid.

[*The scene dims out with "Glass Menagerie" music*]

SCENE II

"Laura, Haven't You Ever Liked Some Boy?"

On the dark stage the screen is lighted with the image of blue roses. Gradually Laura's *figure becomes apparent and the screen goes out. The music subsides.*

Laura *is seated in the delicate ivory chair at the small clawfoot table. She wears a dress of soft violet material for a kimono—her hair is tied back from her forehead with a ribbon. She is washing and polishing her collection of glass.*

Amanda *appears on the fire-escape steps. At the sound of her ascent,* Laura *catches her breath, thrusts the bowl of ornaments away and seats herself stiffly before the diagram of the typewriter keyboard as though it held her spellbound. Something has happened to* Amanda. *It is written in her face as she climbs to the landing: a look that is grim and hopeless and a little absurd. She has on one of those cheap or imitation velvety-looking cloth coats with imitation fur collar. Her hat is five or six years old, one of those dreadful cloche hats that were worn in the late twenties and she is clasping an enormous black patent-leather pocketbook with nickel clasps and initials. This is her full-dress outfit, the one she usually wears to the D.A.R. Before entering she looks through the door. She purses her lips, opens her eyes very wide, rolls them upward and shakes her head. Then she slowly lets herself in the door. Seeing her mother's expression* Laura *touches her lips with a nervous gesture.*

Laura. Hello, Mother, I was—[*she makes a nervous gesture toward the chart on the wall.* Amanda *leans against the shut door and stares at* Laura *with a martyred look*]

Amanda. Deception? Deception? [*She slowly removes her hat and gloves, continuing the sweet suffering stare. She lets the hat and gloves fall on the floor—a bit of acting*]

Laura [*shakily*]. How was the D.A.R. meeting? [Amanda *slowly opens her purse and removes a dainty white handkerchief which she shakes out delicately and delicately touches to her lips and nostrils*] Didn't you go to the D.A.R. meeting, Mother?

Amanda [*faintly, almost inaudibly*]. —No.—No. [*Then more forcibly*] I did not have the strength—to go to the D.A.R. It fact, I did not have the courage! I wanted to find a hole in the ground and hide myself in it forever! [*She crosses slowly to the wall and removes the diagram of the typewriter keyboard. She holds it in front of her for a second, staring at it sweetly and sorrowfully—then bites her lips and tears it in two pieces*]

Laura [*faintly*]. Why did you do that, Mother? [Amanda *repeats the same procedure with the chart of the Gregg Alphabet*] Why are you—

Amanda. Why? Why? How old are you, Laura?

Laura. Mother, you know my age.

Amanda. I thought that you were an adult; it seems that I was mistaken. [*She crosses slowly to the sofa and sinks down and stares at Laura*]

Laura. Please don't stare at me, Mother.

[Amanda *closes her eyes and lowers her head. Count ten*]

Amanda. What are we going to do, what is going to become of us, what is the future?

[*Count ten*]

Laura. Has something happened, Mother? [Amanda *draws a long breath and takes out the handkerchief again. Dabbing process*] Mother, has—something happened?

Amanda. I'll be all right in a minute. I'm just bewildered—[*Count five*]—by life. . . .

Laura. Mother, I wish that you would tell me what's happened!

Amanda. As you know, I was supposed to be inducted into my office at the D.A.R. this afternoon. [*Image: a swarm of typewriters*] But I stopped off at Rubicam's Business College to speak to your teachers about your having a cold and ask them what progress they thought you were making down there.

Laura. Oh. . . .

Amanda. I went to the typing instructor and introduced myself as your mother. She didn't know who you were. Wingfield, she said. We don't have any such student enrolled at the school!

I assured her she did, that you have been going to classes since early in January.

"I wonder," she said, "if you could be talking about that terribly shy little girl who dropped out of school after only a few days' attendance?"

"No," I said, "Laura, my daughter, has been going to school every day for the past six weeks!"

"Excuse me," she said. She took the attendance book out and there was your name, unmistakably printed, and all the dates you were absent until they decided that you had dropped out of school.

I still said, "No, there must have been some mistake! There must have been some mix-up in the records!"

And she said, "No—I remember her perfectly now. Her hands shook so that she couldn't hit the right keys! The first time we gave a speed-test, she broke down completely—was sick at the stomach and almost had to be carried into the wash-room! After that morning she never showed up any more. We phoned the house but never got any answer"—while I was working at Famous and Barr, I suppose, demonstrating those—Oh!

I felt so weak I could barely keep on my feet!

I had to sit down while they got me a glass of water!

Fifty dollars' tuition, all of our plans—my hopes and ambitions for you—just gone up the spout, just gone up the spout like that. [Laura *draws a long breath and gets awkwardly to her feet. She crosses to the victrola and winds it up*] What are you doing?

Laura. Oh! [*She releases the handle and returns to her seat*]

Amanda. Laura, where have you been going when you've gone out pretending that you were going to business college?

Laura. I've just been going out walking.

Amanda. That's not true.

Laura. It is. I just went walking.

Amanda. Walking? Walking? In winter? Deliberately courting pneumonia in that light coat? Where did you walk to, Laura?

Laura. All sorts of places—mostly in the park.

Amanda. Even after you'd started catching that cold?

Laura. It was the lesser of two evils, Mother. [*Image: Winter scene in park*] I couldn't go back up. I—threw up—on the floor!

Amanda. From half past seven till after five every day you mean to tell me you walked around in the park, because you wanted to make me think that you were still going to Rubicam's Business College?

Laura. It wasn't as bad as it sounds. I went inside places to get warmed up.

Amanda. Inside where?

Laura. I went in the art museum and the birdhouses at the Zoo. I visited the penguins every day! Sometimes I did without lunch and went to the movies. Lately I've been spending most of my afternoons in the Jewel-box, that big glass house where they raise the tropical flowers.

Amanda. You did all this to deceive me, just for deception? [Laura *looks down*] Why?

Laura. Mother, when you're disappointed, you get that awful suffering look on your face, like the picture of Jesus' mother in the museum!

Amanda. Hush!

Laura. I couldn't face it.

[*Pause. A whisper of strings*]

[*Legend: "The Crust of Humility"*]

Amanda [*hopelessly fingering the huge pocketbook*]. So what are we going to do the rest of our lives? Stay home and watch the parades go by? Amuse ourselves with the glass menagerie, darling? Eternally play those worn-out phonograph records your father left as a painful reminder of him?

We won't have a business career—we've given that up because it gave us nervous indigestion! [*Laughs wearily*] What is there left but dependency all our lives? I know so well what becomes of unmarried women who aren't prepared to occupy a position. I've seen such pitiful cases in the South—barely tolerated spinsters living upon the grudging patronage of sister's husband or brother's wife!—stuck away in some little mouse-trap of a room—encouraged by one in-law to visit another—little birdlike women without any nest—eating the crust of humility all their life!

Is that the future that we've mapped out for ourselves?

I swear it's the only alternative I can think of!

It isn't a very pleasant alternative, is it?

Of course—some girls *do marry.*

[Laura *twists her hands nervously*]

Haven't you ever liked some boy?

Laura. Yes. I liked one once. [*Rises*] I came across his picture a while ago.

Amanda [*with some interest*]. He gave you his picture?

Laura. No, it's in the year-book.

Amanda [*disappointed*]. Oh—a high-school boy.

[*Screen image:* Jim *as high-school hero bearing a silver cup*]

Laura. Yes. His name was Jim. [Laura *lifts the heavy annual from the claw-foot table*] Here he is in *The Pirates of Penzance.*

Amanda [*absently*]. The what?

Laura. The operetta the senior class put on. He had a wonderful voice and we sat across the aisle from each other Mondays, Wednesdays and Fridays in the Aud. Here he is with the silver cup for debating! See his grin?

Amanda [*absently*]. He must have had a jolly disposition.

Laura. He used to call me—Blue Roses.

[*Image: Blue roses*]

Amanda. Why did he call you such a name as that?

Laura. When I had that attack of pleurosis—he asked me what was the matter when I came back. I said pleurosis—he thought that I said Blue Roses! So that's what he always called me after that. Whenever he saw me, he'd holler, "Hello, Blue Roses!" I didn't care for the girl that he went out with. Emily Meisenbach. Emily was the best-dressed girl at Soldan. She never struck me, though, as being sincere . . . It says in the Personal Section—they're engaged. That's—six years ago! They must be married by now.

Amanda. Girls that aren't cut out for business careers usually wind up married to some nice man. [*Gets up with a spark of revival*] Sister, that's what you'll do!

[Laura *utters a startled, doubtful laugh. She reaches quickly for a piece of glass*]

Laura. But, Mother—

Amanda. Yes? [*Crossing to photograph*]

Laura [*in a tone of frightened apology*]. I'm—crippled!

[*Image: screen*]

Amanda. Nonsense! Laura, I've told you never, never to use that word. Why, you're not crippled, you just have a little defect —hardly noticeable, even! When people have some slight disadvantage like that, they cultivate other things to make up for it—develop charm—and vivacity—and—*charm!* That's all you have to do! [*She turns again to the photograph*] One thing your father had *plenty of*—was *charm!*

[Tom *motions to the fiddle in the wings*]

[*The scene fades out with music*]

SCENE III

Legend on screen: "After the fiasco—"

Tom *speaks from the fire-escape landing.*

Tom. After the fiasco at Rubicam's Business College, the idea of getting a gentleman caller for Laura began to play a more and more important part in Mother's calculations.

It became an obsession. Like some archetype of the universal unconscious, the image of the gentleman caller haunted our small apartment. . . .

[*Image: Young man at door with flowers*]

An evening at home rarely passed without some allusion to this image, this spectre, this hope. . . .

Even when he wasn't mentioned, his presence hung in Mother's preoccupied look and in my sister's frightened, apologetic manner —hung like a sentence passed upon the Wingfields!

Mother was a woman of action as well as words.

She began to take logical steps in the planned direction.

Late that winter and in the early spring—realizing that extra money would be needed to properly feather the nest and plume the bird—she conducted a vigorous campaign on the telephone, roping in subscribers to one of those magazines for matrons called *The Home-maker's Companion,* the type of journal that features the serialized sublimations of ladies of letters who think in terms of delicate cup-like breasts, slim, tapering waists, rich, creamy thighs, eyes like wood-smoke in autumn, fingers that soothe and caress like strains of music, bodies as powerful as Etruscan sculpture.

[*Screen image: Glamor magazine cover*]

[Amanda *enters with phone on long extension cord. She is spotted in the dim stage*]

Amanda. Ida Scott? This is Amanda Wingfield! We *missed* you at the D.A.R. last Monday!

I said to myself: She's probably suffering with that sinus condition! How is that sinus condition?

Horrors! Heaven have mercy!—You're a Christian martyr, yes, that's what you are, a Christian martyr!

Well, I just now happened to notice that your subscription to the *Companion's* about to expire! Yes, it expires with the next issue, honey!—just when that wonderful new serial by Bessie Mae Hopper is getting off to such an exciting start. Oh, honey, it's something that you can't miss! You remember how *Gone With the Wind* took everybody by storm? You simply couldn't go out if you hadn't read it. All everybody *talked* was Scarlet O'Hara. Well, this is a book that critics already compare to *Gone With the Wind*. It's the *Gone With the Wind* of the post-World War generation!—What?—Burning?—Oh, honey, don't let them burn, go take a look in the oven and I'll hold the wire! Heavens—I think she's hung up!

[*Dim out*]

[*Legend on screen: "You think I'm in love with Continental Shoemakers?"*]

[*Before the stage is lighted, the violent voices of* Tom *and* Amanda *are heard. They are quarreling behind the portieres. In front of them stands* Laura *with clenched hands and panicky expression. A clear pool of light on her figure throughout this scene*]

Tom. What in Christ's name am I—

Amanda [*shrilly*]. Don't you use that—

Tom. Supposed to do!

Amanda. Expression! Not in my—

Tom. Ohhh!

Amanda. Presence! Have you gone out of your senses?

Tom. I have, that's true, *driven* out!

Amanda. What is the matter with you, you—big—big—IDIOT!

Tom. Look!—I've got *no thing*, no single thing—

Amanda. Lower your voice!

Tom. In my life here that I can call my OWN! Everything is—

Amanda. Stop that shouting!

Tom. Yesterday you confiscated my books! You had the nerve to—

Amanda. I took that horrible novel back to the library—yes! That hideous book by that insane Mr. Lawrence. [Tom *laughs wildly*] I cannot control the output of diseased minds or people who cater to them—[Tom *laughs still more wildly*] *but I won't allow such filth brought into my house!* No, no, no, no, no!

Tom. House, house! Who pays rent on it, who makes a slave of himself to—

Amanda [*fairly screeching*]. Don't you DARE to—

Tom. No, no, *I* mustn't say things! *I've* got to just—

Amanda. Let me tell you—

Tom. I don't want to hear any more! [*He tears the portieres open. The upstage area is lit with a turgid smoky red glow*]

[Amanda's *hair is in metal curlers and she wears a very old bath-*

robe, much too large for her slight figure, a relic of the faithless Mr. Wingfield. An upright typewriter and a wild disarray of manuscripts is on the drop-leaf table. The quarrel was probably precipitated by Amanda's *interruption of his creative labor. A chair lying overthrown on the floor. Their gesticulating shadows are cast on the ceiling by the fiery glow*]

Amanda. You *will* hear more, you–

Tom. No, I won't hear more, I'm going out!

Amanda. You come right back in–

Tom. Out, out, out! Because I'm–

Amanda. Come back here, Tom Wingfield! I'm not through talking to you!

Tom. Oh, go–

Laura [*desperately*]. –Tom!

Amanda. You're going to listen, and no more insolence from you! I'm at the end of my patience!

[*He comes back toward her*]

Tom. What do you think I'm at? Aren't I supposed to have any patience to reach the end of, Mother? I know, I know. It seems unimportant to you, what I'm *doing*–what I *want* to do–having a little *difference* between them! You don't think that–

Amanda. I think you've been doing things that you're ashamed of. That's why you act like this. I don't believe that you go every night to the movies. Nobody goes to the movies night after night. Nobody in their right minds goes to the movies as often as you pretend to. People don't go to the movies at nearly midnight, and movies don't let out at two A.M. Come in stumbling. Muttering to yourself like a maniac! You get three hours' sleep and then go to work. Oh, I can picture the way you're doing down there. Moping, doping, because you're in no condition.

Tom [*wildly*]. No, I'm in no condition!

Amanda. What right have you got to jeopardize your job? Jeopardize the security of us all? How do you think we'd manage if you were–

Tom. Listen! You think I'm crazy *about* the *warehouse?* [*He bends fiercely toward her slight figure*] You think I'm in love with the Continental Shoemakers? You think I want to spend fifty-five *years* down there in that–*celotex interior!* with–*fluorescent–tubes!* Look! I'd rather somebody picked up a crowbar and battered out my brains–than go back mornings! I *go!* Every time you come in yelling that God damn "*Rise and Shine!*" "*Rise and Shine!*" I say to myself, "How *lucky dead* people are!" But I get up. *I go!* For sixty-five dollars a month I give up all that I dream of doing and being *ever!* And you say self—*self's* all I ever think of. Why, listen, if self is what I thought of, Mother, I'd be where he is—GONE! [*Pointing to father's picture*] As far as the system of transportation reaches! [*He starts past her. She grabs his arm*] Don't grab at me, Mother!

Amanda. Where are you going?

Tom. I'm going to the *movies!*

Amanda. I don't believe that lie!

Tom [*crouching toward her, overtowering her tiny figure. She backs away, gasping*]. I'm going to opium dens. Yes, opium dens, dens of vice and criminals' hang-outs, Mother. I've joined the Hogan gang, I'm a hired assassin, I carry a tommy-gun in a violin case! I run a string of cat-houses in the Valley! They call me Killer, Killer Wingfield, I'm leading a double-life, a simple, honest warehouse worker by day, by night a dynamic *czar* of the *underworld, Mother.* I go to gambling casinos, I spin away fortunes on the roulette table! I wear a patch over one eye and a false mustache, sometimes I put on green whiskers. On those occasions they call me—*El Diablo!* Oh, I could tell you things to make you sleepless! My enemies plan to dynamite this place. They're going to blow us all sky-high some night! I'll be glad, very happy, and so will you! You'll go up, up on a broomstick, over Blue Mountain with seventeen gentlemen callers! You ugly—babbling old—*witch.* . . . [*He goes through a series of violent, clumsy movements, seizing his overcoat, lunging to the door, pulling it fiercely open. The women watch him, aghast. His arm catches in the sleeve of the coat as he struggles to pull it on. For a moment he is pinioned by the bulky garment. With an outraged groan he tears the coat off again, splitting the shoulder of it, and hurls it across the room. It strikes against the shelf of* Laura's *glass collection, there is a tinkle of shattering glass.* Laura *cries out as if wounded*]

[*Music. Legend: "The Glass Menagerie"*]

Laura [*shrilly*]. *My glass!*—menagerie. . . . [*She covers her face and turns away*]

[*But* Amanda *is still stunned and stupefied by the "ugly witch" so that she barely notices this occurrence. Now she recovers her speech*]

Amanda [*in an awful voice*]. I won't speak to you—until you apologize! [*She crosses through portieres and draws them together be-*

hind her. Tom *is left with* Laura. Laura *clings weakly to the mantel with her face averted.* Tom *stares at her stupidly for a moment. Then he crosses to shelf. Drops awkwardly on his knees to collect the fallen glass, glancing at* Laura *as if he would speak but couldn't*]

[*"The Glass Menagerie" steals in as the scene dims out*]

SCENE IV

The interior is dark. Faint light in the alley. A deep-voiced bell in a church is tolling the hour of five as the scene commences.

Tom *appears at the top of the alley. After each solemn boom of the bell in the tower, he shakes a little noise-maker or rattle as if to express the tiny spasm of man in contrast to the sustained power and dignity of the Almighty. This and the unsteadiness of his advance make it evident that he has been drinking. As he climbs the few steps to the fire-escape landing, light steals up inside.* Laura *appears in night-dress, observing* Tom's *empty bed in the front room.* Tom *fishes in his pockets for door-key, removing a motley assortment of articles in the search, including a perfect shower of movie-ticket stubs and an empty bottle. At last he finds the key, but just as he is about to insert it, it slips from his fingers. He strikes a match and crouches below the door.*

Tom [*bitterly*]. One crack—and it falls through!

[Laura *opens the door*]

Laura. Tom! Tom, what are you doing?
Tom. Looking for a door-key.
Laura. Where have you been all this time?
Tom. I have been to the movies.
Laura. All this time at the movies?
Tom. There was a very long program. There was a Garbo picture and a Mickey Mouse and a travelogue and a newsreel and a preview of coming attractions. And there was an organ solo and a collection for the milk-fund—simultaneously—which ended up in a terrible fight between a fat lady and an usher!
Laura [*innocently*]. Did you have to stay through everything?
Tom. Of course! And, oh, I forgot! There was a big stage show! The headliner on this stage show was Malvolio the Magician. He performed wonderful tricks, many of them, such as pouring water back and forth between pitchers. First it turned to wine and then

it turned to beer and then it turned to whiskey. I know it was whiskey it finally turned into because he needed somebody to come up out of the audience to help him, and I came up—both shows! It was Kentucky Straight Bourbon. A very generous fellow, he gave souvenirs. [*He pulls from his back pocket a shimmering rainbow-colored scarf.*] He gave me this. This is his magic scarf. You can have it, Laura. You wave it over a canary cage and you get a bowl of gold-fish. You wave it over the gold-fish bowl and they fly away canaries. . . . But the wonderfullest trick of all was the coffin trick. We nailed him into a coffin and he got out of the coffin without removing one nail. [*He has come inside*] There is a trick that would come in handy for me—get me out of this 2 by 4 situation. [*Flops onto bed and starts removing shoes*]

Laura. Tom—Shhh!

Tom. What're you shushing me for?

Laura. You'll wake up Mother.

Tom. Goody, goody! Pay 'er back for all those "Rise an' Shines." [*Lies down, groaning*] You know it don't take much intelligence to get yourself into a nailed-up coffin, Laura. But who in hell ever got himself out of one without removing one nail?

[*As if in answer, the father's grinning photograph lights up*]

[*Scene dims out*]

[*Immediately following: The church bell is heard striking six. At the sixth stroke the alarm clock goes off in* Amanda's *room, and after a few moments we hear her calling: "Rise and Shine! Rise and Shine! Laura, go tell your brother to rise and shine!"*]

Tom [*sitting up slowly*]. I'll rise—but I won't shine.

[*The light increases*]

Amanda. Laura, tell your brother his coffee is ready.

[Laura *slips into front room*]

Laura. Tom!—It's nearly seven. Don't make Mother nervous. [*He stares at her stupidly. Beseechingly*] Tom, speak to Mother this morning. Make up with her, apologize, speak to her!

Tom. She won't to me. It's her that started not speaking.

Laura. If you just say you're sorry she'll start speaking.

Tom. Her not speaking—is that such a tragedy?

Laura. Please—please!

Amanda [*calling from kitchenette*]. Laura, are you going to do what I asked you to do, or do I have to get dressed and go out myself?

Laura. Going, going—soon as I get on my coat! [*She pulls on a shapeless felt hat with nervous, jerky movement, pleadingly glancing at* Tom. *Rushes awkwardly for coat. The coat is one of* Amanda's, *inaccurately made-over, the sleeves too short for* Laura] Butter and what else?

Amanda [*entering upstage*]. Just butter. Tell them to charge it.

Laura. Mother, they make such faces when I do that.

Amanda. Sticks and stones can break our bones, but the expression on Mr. Garfinkel's face won't harm us! Tell your brother his coffee is getting cold.

Laura [*at door*]. Do what I asked you, will you, will you, Tom?

[*He looks sullenly away*]

Amanda. Laura, go now or just don't go at all!

Laura [*rushing out*]. Going—going! [*A second later she cries out.* Tom *springs up and crosses to door.* Amanda *rushes anxiously in.* Tom *opens the door*]

Tom. Laura?

Laura. I'm all right. I slipped, but I'm all right.

Amanda [*peering anxiously after her*]. If anyone breaks a leg on those fire-escape steps, the landlord ought to be sued for every cent he possesses! [*She shuts door. Remembers she isn't speaking and returns to other room*]

[*As* Tom *enters listlessly for his coffee, she turns her back to him and stands rigidly facing the window on the gloomy gray vault of the areaway. Its light on her face with its aged but childish features is cruelly sharp, satirical as a Daumier print*]

[*Music under: "Ave Maria"*]

[Tom *glances sheepishly but sullenly at her averted figure and slumps at the table. The coffee is scalding hot; he sips it and gasps and spits it back in the cup. At his gasp,* Amanda *catches her breath and half turns. Then catches herself and turns back to window.* Tom *blows on his coffee, glancing sidewise at his mother. She clears her throat.* Tom *clears his. He starts to rise. Sinks back down again, scratches his head, clears his throat again.* Amanda *coughs.* Tom *raises his cup in both hands to blow on it, his eyes staring over the rim of it at his mother for several moments. Then he slowly sets the cup down and awkwardly and hesitantly rises from the chair*]

Tom [*hoarsely*]. Mother. I—I apologize, Mother. [Amanda *draws a quick, shuddering breath. Her face works grotesquely. She breaks into childlike tears*] I'm sorry for what I said, for everything that I said, I didn't mean it.

Amanda [*sobbingly*]. My devotion has made me a witch and so I make myself hateful to my children!

Tom. No. you *don't.*

Amanda. I worry so much, don't sleep, it makes me nervous!

Tom [*gently*]. I understand that.

Amanda. I've had to put up a solitary battle all these years. But you're my right-hand bower! Don't fall down, don't fail!

Tom [*gently*]. I try, Mother.

Amanda [*with great enthusiasm*]. Try and you will SUCCEED! [*The notion makes her breathless*] Why, you—you're just *full* of natural endowments! Both of my children—they're *unusual* children! Don't you think I know it? I'm so—*proud!* Happy and—feel I've—so much to be thankful for but—Promise me one thing, Son!

Tom. What, Mother?

Amanda. Promise, son, you'll—never be a drunkard!

Tom [*turns to her grinning*]. I will never be a drunkard, Mother.

Amanda. That's what frightened me so, that you'd be drinking! Eat a bowl of Purina!

Tom. Just coffee, Mother.

Amanda. Shredded wheat biscuit?

Tom. No. No, Mother, just coffee.

Amanda. You can't put in a day's work on an empty stomach. You've got ten minutes—don't gulp! Drinking too-hot liquids makes cancer of the stomach. . . . Put cream in.

Tom. No, thank you.

Amanda. To cool it.

Tom. No! No, thank you, I want it black.

Amanda. I know, but it's not good for you. We have to do all that we can to build ourselves up. In these trying times we live in, all that we have to cling to is—each other. . . . That's why it's so important to—Tom, I—I sent out your sister so I could discuss something with you. If you hadn't spoken I would have spoken to you. [*Sits down*]

Tom [*gently*]. What is it, Mother, that you want to discuss?

Amanda. Laura!

[Tom *puts his cup down slowly*]
[*Legend on screen: "Laura"*]
[*Music: "The Glass Menagerie"*]

Tom. —Oh.—Laura . . .

Amanda [*touching his sleeve*]. You know how Laura is. So quiet but—still water runs deep! She notices things and I think she—

broods about them. [*Tom looks up*] A few days ago I came in and she was crying.

Tom. What about?

Amanda. You.

Tom. Me?

Amanda. She has an idea that you're not happy here.

Tom. What gave her that idea?

Amanda. What gives her any idea? However, you do act strangely. I–I'm not criticizing, understand *that!* I know your ambitions do not lie in the warehouse, that like everybody in the whole wide world–you've had to–make sacrifices, but–Tom–Tom–life's not easy, it calls for–Spartan endurance! There's so many things in my heart that I cannot describe to you! I've never told you but I–*loved* your father. . . .

Tom [*gently*]. I know that, Mother.

Amanda. And you–when I see you taking after his ways! Staying out late–and–well, you *had* been drinking the night you were in that–terrifying condition! Laura says that you hate the apartment and that you go out nights to get away from it! Is that true, Tom?

Tom. No. You say there's so much in your heart that you can't describe to me. That's true of me, too. There's so much in my heart that I can't describe to *you!* So let's respect each other's–

Amanda. But, why–*why*, Tom–are you always so *restless?* Where do you *go* to, nights?

Tom. I–go to the movies.

Amanda. Why do you go to the movies so much, Tom?

Tom. I go to the movies because–I like adventure. Adventure is something I don't have much of at work, so I go to the movies.

Amanda. But, Tom, you go to the movies *entirely too much!*

Tom. I like a lot of adventure.

[Amanda *looks baffled, then hurt. As the familiar inquisition resumes he becomes hard and impatient again.* Amanda *slips back into her querulous attitude toward him*]

[*Image on screen: Sailing vessel with Jolly Roger*]

Amanda. Most young men find adventure in their careers.

Tom. Then most young men are not employed in a warehouse.

Amanda. The world is full of young men employed in warehouses and offices and factories.

Tom. Do all of them find adventure in their careers?

Amanda. They do or they do without it! Not everybody has a craze for adventure.

Tom. Man is by instinct a lover, a hunter, a fighter, and none of those instincts are given much play at the warehouse!

Amanda. Man is by instinct! Don't quote instinct to me! Instinct is something that people have got away from! It belongs to animals! Christian adults don't want it!

Tom. What do Christian adults want, then, Mother?

Amanda. Superior things! Things of the mind and the spirit! Only animals have to satisfy instincts! Surely your aims are somewhat higher than theirs! Than monkeys—pigs—

Tom. I reckon they're not.

Amanda. You're joking. However, that isn't what I wanted to discuss.

Tom [*rising*]. I haven't much time.

Amanda [*pushing his shoulders*]. Sit down.

Tom. You want me to punch in red at the warehouse, Mother?

Amanda. You have five minutes. I want to talk about Laura.

[*Legend: "Plans and provisions"*]

Tom. All right! What about Laura?

Amanda. We have to be making some plans and provisions for her. She's older than you, two years, and nothing has happened. She just drifts along doing nothing. It frightens me terribly how she just drifts along.

Tom. I guess she's the type that people call home girls.

Amanda. There's no such type, and if there is, it's a pity! That is unless the home is hers, with a husband!

Tom. What?

Amanda. Oh, I can see the handwriting on the wall as plain as I see the nose in front of my face! It's terrifying! More and more you remind me of your father! He was out all hours without explanation!—Then *left! Good-bye!* And me with the bag to hold. I saw that letter you got from the Merchant Marine. I know what you're dreaming of. I'm not standing here blindfolded. Very well, then. Then *do* it! But not till there's somebody to take your place.

Tom. What do you mean?

Amanda. I mean that as soon as Laura has got somebody to take care of her, married, a home of her own, independent—why, then you'll be free to go wherever you please, on land, on sea, whichever way the wind blows you! But until that time you've got to look out for your sister. I don't say me because I'm old and don't matter! I say for your sister because she's young and dependent. I put her in business college—a dismal failure! Frightened her so it made her sick at the stomach. I took her over to the Young People's League at the church. Another fiasco. She spoke to nobody, nobody spoke to her. Now all she does is fool with those pieces of glass and play those worn-out records. What kind of a life is that for a girl to lead?

Tom. What can I do about it?

Amanda. Overcome selfishness! Self, self, self is all that you ever think of! [Tom *springs up and crosses to get his coat. It is ugly and bulky. He pulls on a cap with earmuffs*] Where is your muffler? Put your wool muffler on! [*He snatches it angrily from the closet and tosses it around his neck and pulls both ends tight*] Tom! I haven't said what I had in mind to ask you.

Tom. I'm too late to—

Amanda [*catching his arm—very importunately. Then shyly*]. Down at the warehouse, aren't there some—nice young men?

Tom. No!

Amanda. There *must* be—*some* . . .

Tom. Mother—[*Gesture*]

Amanda. Find out one that's clean-living—doesn't drink and—ask him out for sister!

Tom. What?

Amanda. For *sister!* To *meet!* Get *acquainted!*

Tom [*stamping to door*]. Oh, my *go-osh!*

Amanda. Will you? [*He opens door. Imploringly*] Will you? [*He starts down*] Will you? *Will* you, dear?

Tom [*calling back*]. YES!

[Amanda *closes the door hesitantly and with a troubled but faintly hopeful expression*]

[*Screen image: Glamor magazine cover*]

[*Spot* Amanda *at phone*]

Amanda. Ella Cartwright? This is Amanda Wingfield! How are you, honey? How is that kidney condition? [*Count five*] *Horrors!* [*Count five*] You're a Christian martyr, yes, honey, that's what you are, a Christian martyr! Well, I just now happened to notice in my little red book that your subscription to the *Companion* has just run out! I knew that you wouldn't want to miss out on the wonderful serial starting in this new issue. It's by Bessie Mae Hopper, the first thing she's written since *Honeymoon for Three*. Wasn't that a strange and interesting story? Well, this one is even lovelier, I believe. It has a sophisticated, society background. It's all about the horsey set on Long Island!

[*Fade out*]

SCENE V

Legend on screen: "Annunciation." Fade with music.

It is early dusk of a spring evening. Supper has just been finished in the Wingfield apartment. Amanda *and* Laura *in light-colored dresses are removing dishes from the table, in the upstage area, which is shadowy, their movements formalized almost as a dance or ritual, their moving forms as pale and silent as moths.* Tom, *in white shirt and trousers, rises from the table and crosses toward the fire-escape.*

Amanda [*as he passes her*]. Son, will you do me a favor?

Tom. What?

Amanda. Comb your hair! You look so pretty when your hair is combed! [Tom *slouches on sofa with evening paper. Enormous caption "Franco Triumphs"*] There is only one respect in which I would like you to emulate your father.

Tom. What respect is that?

Amanda. The care he always took of his appearance. He never allowed himself to look untidy. [*He throws down the paper and crosses to fire-escape*] Where are you going?

Tom. I'm going out to smoke.

Amanda. You smoke too much. A pack a day at fifteen cents a pack. How much would that amount to in a month? Thirty times fifteen is how much, Tom? Figure it out and you will be astounded at what you could save. Enough to give you a night-school course in accounting at Washington U! Just think what a wonderful thing that would be for you, Son!

[Tom *is unmoved by the thought*]

Tom. I'd rather smoke. [*He steps out on landing, letting the screen door slam*]

Amanda [*sharply*]. I know! That's the tragedy of it. . . . [*Alone, she turns to look at her husband's picture*]

[*Dance music: "All the World Is Waiting for the Sunrise!"*]

Tom [*to the audience*]. Across the alley from us was the Paradise Dance Hall. On evenings in spring the windows and doors were open and the music came outdoors. Sometimes the lights were turned out except for a large glass sphere that hung from the ceiling. It would turn slowly about and filter the dusk with delicate rainbow colors. Then the orchestra played a waltz or a tango, something that had a slow and sensuous rhythm. Couples would come outside, to the relative privacy of the alley. You could see them kissing behind ash-pits and telephone poles. This was the compensation for lives that passed like mine, without any change or adventure. Adventure and change were imminent in this year. They were waiting around the corner for all these kids. Suspended in the mist over Berchtesgaden, caught in the folds of Chamberlain's umbrella—In Spain there was Guernica! But here there was only hot swing music and liquor, dance halls, bars, and movies, and sex that hung in the gloom like a chandelier and flooded the world with brief, deceptive rainbows. . . . All the world was waiting for bombardments!

[Amanda *turns from the picture and comes outside*]

Amanda [*sighing*]. A fire-escape landing's a poor excuse for a porch. [*She spreads a newspaper on a step and sits down, gracefully and demurely as if she were settling into a swing on a Mississippi veranda*] What are you looking at?

Tom. The moon.

Amanda. Is there a moon this evening?

Tom. It's rising over Garfinkel's Delicatessen.

Amanda. So it is! A little silver slipper of a moon. Have you made a wish on it yet?

Tom. Um-hum.

Amanda. What did you wish for?

Tom. That's a secret.

Amanda. A secret, huh? Well, I won't tell mine either. I will be just as mysterious as you.

Tom. I bet I can guess what yours is.

Amanda. Is my head so transparent?

Tom. You're not a sphinx.

Amanda. No, I don't have secrets. I'll tell you what I wished for on the moon. Success and happiness for my precious children! I wish for that whenever there's a moon, and when there isn't a moon I wish for it, too.

Tom. I thought perhaps you wished for a gentleman caller.

Amanda. Why do you say that?

Tom. Don't you remember asking me to fetch one?

Amanda. I remember suggesting that it would be nice for your sister if you brought home some nice young man from the warehouse. I think that I've made that suggestion more than once.

Tom. Yes, you have made it repeatedly.

Amanda. Well?

Tom. We are going to have one.

Amanda. *What?*

Tom. A gentleman caller!

[*The annunciation is celebrated with music*]

[Amanda *rises*]

[*Image on screen: Caller with bouquet*]

Amanda. You mean you have asked some nice young man to come over?

Tom. Yep. I've asked him to dinner.

Amanda. You really did?

Tom. I did!

Amanda. You did, and did he–*accept?*

Tom. He did!

Amanda. Well, well–well, well! That's–lovely!

Tom. I thought that you would be pleased.

Amanda. It's definite, then?

Tom. Very definite.

Amanda. Soon?

Tom. Very soon.

Amanda. For heaven's sake, stop putting on and tell me some things, will you?

Tom. What things do you want me to tell you?

Amanda. *Naturally* I would like to know when he's *coming!*

Tom. He's coming tomorrow.

Amanda. *Tomorrow?*

Tom. Yep. Tomorrow.

Amanda. But, Tom!

Tom. Yes, Mother?

Amanda. Tomorrow gives me no time!

Tom. Time for what?

Amanda. Preparation! Why didn't you phone me at once, as soon as you asked him, the minute that he accepted? Then, don't you see, I could have been getting ready!

Tom. You don't have to make any fuss.

Amanda. Oh, Tom, Tom, Tom, of course I have to make a fuss! I want things nice, not sloppy! Not thrown together. I'll certainly have to do some fast thinking, won't I?

Tom. I don't see why you have to think at all.

Amanda. You just don't know. We can't have a gentleman caller in a pig-sty. All my wedding silver has to be polished, the monogrammed table linen ought to be laundered! The windows have to be washed and fresh curtains put up. And how about clothes? We have to *wear* something, don't we?

Tom. Mother, this boy is no one to make a fuss over!

Amanda. Do you realize he's the first young man we've introduced to your sister? It's terrible, dreadful, disgraceful that poor little sister has never received a single gentleman caller! Tom, come inside! [*She opens the screen door*]

Tom. What for?

Amanda. I want to ask you some things.

Tom. If you're going to make such a fuss, I'll call it off, I'll tell him not to come!

Amanda. You certainly won't do anything of the kind. Nothing offends people worse than broken engagements. It simply means I'll have to work like a Turk! We won't be brilliant, but we will pass inspection. Come on inside. [Tom *follows, groaning*] Sit down.

Tom. Any particular place you would like me to sit?

Amanda. Thank heavens I've got that new sofa! I'm also making payments on a floor lamp I'll have sent out! And put the chintz covers on, they'll brighten things up! Of course I'd hoped to have these walls re-papered. . . . What is the young man's name?

Tom. His name is O'Connor.

Amanda. That, of course, means fish—tomorrow is Friday! I'll have that salmon loaf—with Durkee's dressing! What does he do? He works at the warehouse?

Tom. Of course! How else would I—

Amanda. Tom, he—doesn't drink?

Tom. Why do you ask me that?

Amanda. Your father *did!*

Tom. Don't get started on that!

Amanda. He *does* drink, then?

Tom. Not that I know of!

Amanda. Make sure, be certain! The last thing I want for my daughter's a boy who drinks!

Tom. Aren't you being a little bit premature? Mr. O'Connor has not yet appeared on the scene!

Amanda. But will tomorrow. To meet your sister, and what do I know about his character? Nothing! Old maids are better off than wives of drunkards!

Tom. Oh, my God!

Amanda. Be still!

Tom [*leaning forward to whisper*]. Lots of fellows meet girls whom they don't marry!

Amanda. Oh, talk sensibly, Tom—and don't be sarcastic! [*She has gotten a hairbrush*]

Tom. What are you doing?

Amanda. I'm brushing that cow-lick down! What is this young man's position at the warehouse?

Tom [*submitting grimly to the brush and the interrogation*]. This young man's position is that of a shipping clerk, Mother.

Amanda. Sounds to me like a fairly responsible job, the sort of a job *you* would be in if you just had more *get-up.*

What is his salary? Have you any idea?

Tom. I would judge it to be approximately eighty-five dollars a month.

Amanda. Well—not princely, but—

Tom. Twenty more than I make.

Amanda. Yes, how well I know! But for a family man, eighty-five dollars a month is not much more than you can just get by on. . . .

Tom. Yes, but Mr. O'Connor is not a family man.

Amanda. He might be, mightn't he? Some time in the future?

Tom. I see. Plans and provisions.

Amanda. You are the only young man that I know of who ignores the fact that the future becomes the present, the present the past, and the past turns into everlasting regret if you don't plan for it!

Tom. I will think that over and see what I can make of it.

Amanda. Don't be supercilious with your mother! Tell me some more about this—what do you call him?

Tom. James D. O'Connor. The D. is for Delaney.

Amanda. Irish on *both* sides! *Gracious!* And doesn't drink?

Tom. Shall I call him up and ask him right this minute?

Amanda. The only way to find out about those things is to make discreet inquiries at the proper moment. When I was a girl in Blue Mountain and it was suspected that a young man drank, the girl whose attentions he had been receiving, if any girl was, would sometimes speak to the minister of his church, or rather her father would if her father was living, and sort of feel him out on the young man's character. That is the way such things are discreetly handled to keep a young woman from making a tragic mistake!

Tom. Then how did you happen to make a tragic mistake?

Amanda. That innocent look of your father's had everyone fooled! He *smiled*—the world was *enchanted!* No girl can do worse than put herself at the mercy of a handsome appearance! I hope that Mr. O'Connor is not too good-looking.

Tom. No, he's not too good-looking. He's covered with freckles and hasn't too much of a nose.

Amanda. He's not right-down homely, though?

Tom. Not right-down homely. Just medium homely, I'd say.

Amanda. Character's what to look for in a man.

Tom. That's what I've always said, Mother.

Amanda. You've never said anything of the kind and I suspect you would never give it a thought.

Tom. Don't be so suspicious of me.

Amanda. At least I hope he's the type that's up and coming.

Tom. I think he really goes in for self-improvement.

Amanda. What reason have you to think so?

Tom. He goes to night school.

Amanda [*beaming*]. Splendid! What does he do, I mean study?

Tom. Radio engineering and public speaking!

Amanda. Then he has visions of being advanced in the world! Any young man who studies public speaking is aiming to have an executive job some day! And radio engineering? A thing for the future! Both of these facts are very illuminating. Those are the sort of things that a mother should know concerning any young man who comes to call on her daughter. Seriously or–not.

Tom. One little warning. He doesn't know about Laura. I didn't let on that we had dark ulterior motives. I just said, why don't you come and have dinner with us? He said okay and that was the whole conversation.

Amanda. I bet it was! You're eloquent as an oyster. However, he'll know about Laura when he gets here. When he sees how lovely and sweet and pretty she is, he'll thank his lucky stars he was asked to dinner.

Tom. Mother, you mustn't expect too much of Laura.

Amanda. What do you mean?

Tom. Laura seems all those things to you and me because she's ours and we love her. We don't even notice she's crippled any more.

Amanda. Don't say crippled. You know that I never allow that word to be used!

Tom. But face facts, Mother. She is and–that's not all–

Amanda. What do you mean "not all"?

Tom. Laura is very different from other girls.

Amanda. I think the difference is all to her advantage.

Tom. Not quite all–in the eyes of others–strangers–she's terribly shy and lives in a world of her own and those things make her seem a little peculiar to people outside the house.

Amanda. Don't say peculiar.

Tom. Face the facts. She is.

[*The dance-hall music changes to a tango that has a minor and somewhat ominous tone*]

Amanda. In what way is she peculiar—may I ask?

Tom [*gently*]. She lives in a world of her own—a world of—little glass ornaments, Mother. . . . [*Gets up.* Amanda *remains holding brush, looking at him, troubled*] She plays old phonograph records and—that's about all—[*He glances at himself in the mirror and crosses to door*]

Amanda [*sharply*]. Where are you going?

Tom. I'm going to the movies. [*Out screen door*]

Amanda. Not to the movies, every night to the movies! [*Follows quickly to screen door*] I don't believe you always go to the movies! [*He is gone.* Amanda *looks worriedly after him for a moment. Then vitality and optimism return and she turns from the door. Crossing to portieres*] Laura! Laura! [Laura *answers from kitchenette*]

Laura. Yes, Mother.

Amanda. Let those dishes go and come in front! [Laura *appears with dish towel. Gaily*] Laura, come here and make a wish on the moon!

[*Screen image: Moon*]

Laura [*entering*]. Moon—moon?

Amanda. A little silver slipper of a moon. Look over your left shoulder, Laura, and make a wish! [Laura *looks faintly puzzled as if called out of sleep.* Amanda *seizes her shoulders and turns her at an angle by the door*] Now! Now, darling, *wish!*

Laura. What shall I wish for, Mother?

Amanda [*her voice trembling and her eyes suddenly filling with tears*]. Happiness! Good fortune!

[*The violin rises and the stage dims out*]

[*Curtain*]

SCENE VI

[*Image: High school hero*]

Tom. And so the following evening I brought Jim home to dinner. I had known Jim slightly in high school. In high school Jim was a hero. He had tremendous Irish good nature and vitality with the scrubbed and polished look of white chinaware. He seemed to move in a continual spotlight. He was a star in basketball, captain of the debating club, president of the senior class and the glee club and he sang the male lead in the annual light operas. He was always running or bounding, never just walking. He seemed always at the point of defeating the law of gravity. He was shooting with such velocity through his adolescence that you would logically expect him to arrive at nothing short of the White House by the time he was thirty. But Jim apparently ran into more interference after his graduation from Soldan. His speed had definitely slowed. Six years after he left high school he was holding a job that wasn't much better than mine.

[*Image: Clerk*]

He was the only one at the warehouse with whom I was on friendly terms. I was valuable to him as someone who could remember his former glory, who had seen him win basketball games and the silver cup in debating. He knew of my secret practice of retiring to a cabinet of the wash-room to work on poems when business was slack in the warehouse. He called me Shakespeare. And while the other boys in the warehouse regarded me with suspicious hostility, Jim took a humorous attitude toward me. Gradually his attitude affected the others, their hostility wore off and they also began to smile at me as people smile at an oddly fashioned dog who trots across their path at some distance.

I knew that Jim and Laura had known each other at Soldan, and I had heard Laura speak admiringly of his voice. I didn't know if Jim remembered her or not. In high school Laura had been as unobtrusive as Jim had been astonishing. If he did remember Laura, it was not as my sister, for when I asked him to dinner, he grinned and said, "You know, Shakespeare, I never thought of you as having folks!"

He was about to discover that I did. . . .

[*Light up stage*]

[*Legend on screen: "The accent of a coming foot"*]

[*Friday evening. It is about five o'clock of a late spring evening which comes "scattering poems in the sky." A delicate lemony light is in the Wingfield apartment.* Amanda *has worked like a Turk in preparation for the gentleman caller. The results are astonishing. The new floor lamp with its rose-silk shade is in place, a colored paper lantern conceals the broken light-fixture in the ceiling, new billowing white curtains are at the windows, chintz covers are on chairs and sofa, a pair of new sofa pillows make their initial appearance. Open boxes and tissue paper are scattered on the floor.* Laura *stands in the middle with lifted arms while* Amanda *crouches before her, adjusting the hem of the new dress, devout and ritualistic. The dress is colored and designed by memory. The arrangement of* Laura's *hair is changed: it is softer and more becoming. A fragile, unearthly prettiness has come out in* Laura: *she is like a piece of translucent glass touched by light, given a momentary radiance, not actual, not lasting*]

Amanda [*impatiently*]. Why are you trembling?

Laura. Mother, you've made me so nervous!

Amanda. How have I made you nervous?

Laura. By all this fuss! You make it seem so important!

Amanda. I don't understand you, Laura. You couldn't be satisfied with just sitting home, and yet whenever I try to arrange something for you, you seem to resist it. [*She gets up*] Now take a look at yourself. No, wait! Wait just a moment–I have an idea!

Laura. What is it now?

[Amanda *produces two powder puffs which she wraps in handkerchiefs and stuffs in* Laura's *bosom*]

Laura. Mother, what are you doing?

Amanda. They call them "Gay Deceivers"!

Laura. I won't wear them!

Amanda. You will!

Laura. Why should I?

Amanda. Because, to be painfully honest, your chest is flat.

Laura. You make it seem like we were setting a trap.

Amanda. All pretty girls are a trap, a pretty trap, and men expect them to be. [*Legend: "A pretty trap"*] Now look at yourself, young lady. This is the prettiest you will ever be! I've got to fix myself now! You're going to be surprised by your mother's appearance! [*She crosses through portieres, humming gaily.* Laura *moves slowly to the long mirror and stares solemnly at herself. A wind blows the white curtains inward in a slow, graceful motion and with a faint, sorrowful sighing.*]

Amanda [*off stage*]. It isn't dark enough yet. [*She turns slowly before the mirror with a troubled look*]

[*Legend on screen: "This is my sister: celebrate her with strings!" Music*]

Amanda [*laughing, off*]. I'm going to show you something. I'm going to make a spectacular appearance!

Laura. What is it, Mother?

Amanda. Possess your soul in patience—you will see! Something I've resurrected from that old trunk! Styles haven't changed so terribly much after all. . . . [*She parts the portieres*] Now just look at your mother! [*She wears a girlish frock of yellowed voile with a blue silk sash. She carries a bunch of jonquils—the legend of her youth is nearly revived. Feverishly*] This is the dress in which I led the cotillion. Won the cakewalk twice at Sunset Hill, wore one spring to the Governor's ball in Jackson! See how I sashayed around the ballroom, Laura? [*She raises her skirt and does a mincing step around the room*] I wore it on Sundays for my gentlemen callers! I had it on the day I met your father—I had malaria fever all that spring. The change of climate from East Tennessee to the Delta—weakened resistance—I had a little temperature all the time—not enough to be serious—just enough to make me restless and giddy!—Invitations poured in—parties all over the Delta!—"Stay in bed," said Mother, "you have fever!"—but I just wouldn't.—I took quinine but kept on going, going!—Evenings, dances!—Afternoons, long, long rides! Picnics—lovely! —So lovely, that country in May.—All lacy with dogwood, literally flooded with jonquils!—That was the spring I had the craze for jonquils. Jonquils became an absolute obsession. Mother said, "Honey, there's no more room for jonquils." And still I kept on bringing in more jonquils. Whenever, wherever I saw them, I'd say, "Stop! Stop! I see jonquils!" I made the young men help me gather the jonquils! It was a joke, Amanda and her jonquils! Finally there were no more vases to hold them, every available space was filled with jonquils. No vases to hold them? All right, I'll hold them myself! And then I—[*She stops in front of the picture. Music*] met your father! Malaria fever and jonquils and then —this—boy. . . . [*She switches on the rose-colored lamp*] I hope they get here before it starts to rain. [*She crosses upstage and places the jonquils in bowl on table*] I gave your brother a little extra change so he and Mr. O'Connor could take the service car home.

Laura [*with altered look*]. What did you say his name was?

Amanda. O'Connor.

Laura. What is his first name?

Amanda. I don't remember. Oh, yes, I do. It was—Jim!

[Laura *sways slightly and catches hold of a chair*]

[*Legend on screen: "Not Jim!"*]

Laura [*faintly*]. Not—Jim!

Amanda. Yes, that was it, it was Jim! I've never known a Jim that wasn't nice!

[*Music: Ominous*]

Laura. Are you sure his name is Jim O'Connor?

Amanda. Yes. Why?

Laura. Is he the one that Tom used to know in high school?

Amanda. He didn't say so. I think he just got to know him at the warehouse.

Laura. There was a Jim O'Connor we both knew in high school— [*Then, with effort*] If that is the one that Tom is bringing to dinner—you'll have to excuse me. I won't come to the table.

Amanda. What sort of nonsense is this?

Laura. You asked me once if I'd ever liked a boy. Don't you remember I showed you this boy's picture?

Amanda. You mean the boy you showed me in the year book?

Laura. Yes, that boy.

Amanda. Laura, Laura, were you in love with that boy?

Laura. I don't know, Mother. All I know is I couldn't sit at the table if it was him!

Amanda. It won't be him! It isn't the least bit likely. But whether it is or not, you will come to the table. You will not be excused.

Laura. I'll have to be, Mother.

Amanda. I don't intend to humor your silliness, Laura. I've had too much from you and your brother, both! So just sit down and compose yourself till they come. Tom has forgotten his key so you'll have to let them in, when they arrive.

Laura [*panicky*]. Oh, Mother—*you* answer the door!

Amanda [*lightly*]. I'll be in the kitchen—busy!

Laura. Oh, Mother, please answer the door, don't make me do it!

Amanda [*crossing into kitchenette*]. I've got to fix the dressing for the salmon. Fuss, fuss—silliness!—over a gentleman caller!

[*Door swings shut.* Laura *is left alone*]

[*Legend: "Terror!"*]

[*She utters a low moan and turns off the lamp—sits stiffly on the edge of the sofa, knotting her fingers together*]

[*Legend on screen: "The opening of a door!"*]

[Tom *and* Jim *appear on the fire-escape steps and climb to landing. Hearing their approach,* Laura *rises with a panicky gesture. She retreats to the portieres. The doorbell.* Laura *catches her breath and touches her throat. Low drums*]

Amanda [*calling*]. Laura, sweetheart! The door! [Laura *stares at it without moving*]

Jim. I think we just beat the rain.

Tom. Uh-huh. [*He rings again, nervously.* Jim *whistles and fishes for a cigarette*]

Amanda [*very, very gaily*]. Laura, that is your brother and Mr. O'Connor! Will you let them in, darling?

[Laura *crosses toward kitchenette door*]

Laura [*breathlessly*]. Mother—you go to the door!

[Amanda *steps out of kitchenette and stares furiously at* Laura. *She points imperiously at the door*]

Laura. Please, please!

Amanda [*in a fierce whisper*]. What is the matter with you, you silly thing?

Laura [*desperately*]. Please, you answer it, *please!*

Amanda. I told you I wasn't going to humor you, Laura. Why have you chosen this moment to lose your mind?

Laura. Please, please, please, you go!

Amanda. You'll have to go to the door because I can't!

Laura [*despairingly*]. I can't either!

Amanda. *Why?*

Laura. I'm *sick!*

Amanda. I'm sick, too—of your nonsense! Why can't you and your brother be normal people? Fantastic whim and behavior! [Tom *gives a long ring*] Preposterous goings on! Can you give me one reason—[*Calls out lyrically*] Coming! Just one second!—why you should be afraid to open a door? Now you answer it, Laura!

Laura. Oh, oh, oh . . . [*She returns through the portieres. Darts to the victrola and winds it frantically and turns it on*]

Amanda. Laura Wingfield, you march right to that door!

Laura. Yes—yes, Mother!

[*A faraway, scratchy rendition of "Dardanella" softens the air and gives her strength to move through it. She slips to the door and draws it cautiously open.* Tom *enters with the caller,* Jim O'Connor]

Tom. Laura, this is Jim. Jim, this is my sister, Laura.

Jim [*stepping inside*]. I didn't know that Shakespeare had a sister!

Laura [*retreating stiff and trembling from the door*]. How—how do you do?

Jim [*heartily extending his hand*]. Okay! [Laura *touches it hesitantly with hers*]

Jim. Your hand's *cold,* Laura!

Laura. Yes, well—I've been playing the victrola. . . .

Jim. Must have been playing classical music on it! You ought to play a little hot swing music to warm you up!

Laura. Excuse me—I haven't finished playing the victrola. . . . [*She turns awkwardly and hurries into the front room. She pauses a second by the victrola. Then catches her breath and darts through the portieres like a frightened deer*]

Jim [*grinning*]. What was the matter?

Tom. Oh—with Laura? Laura is—terribly shy.

Jim. Shy, huh? It's unusual to meet a shy girl nowadays. I don't believe you ever mentioned you had a sister.

Tom. Well, now you know. I have one. Here is the *Post Dispatch*. You want a piece of it?

Jim. Uh-huh.

Tom. What piece? The comics?

Jim. Sports! [*Glances at it*] Ole Dizzy Dean is on his bad behavior.

Tom [*disinterest*]. Yeah? [*Lights cigarette and crosses back to fire-escape door*]

Jim. Where are *you* going?

Tom. I'm going out on the terrace.

Jim [*goes after him*]. You know, Shakespeare—I'm going to sell you a bill of goods!

Tom. What goods?

Jim. A course I'm taking.

Tom. Huh?

Jim. In public speaking! You and me, we're not the warehouse type.

Tom. Thanks—that's good news. But what has public speaking got to do with it?

Jim. It fits you for—executive positions!

Tom. Awww.

Jim. I tell you it's done a helluva lot for me.

[*Image: Executive at desk*]

Tom. In what respect?

Jim. In every! Ask yourself what is the difference between you an' me and men in the office down front? Brains?—No!—Ability?—No! Then what? Just one little thing—

Tom. What is that one little thing—

Jim. Primarily it amounts to—social poise! Being able to square up to people and hold your own on any social level!

Amanda [*off stage*]. Tom?

Tom. Yes, Mother?

Amanda. Is that you and Mr. O'Connor?

Tom. Yes, Mother.

Amanda. Ask Mr. O'Connor if he would like to wash his hands.

Jim. Aw, no—no—thank you—I took care of that at the warehouse. Tom—

Tom. Yes?

Jim. Mr. Mendoza was speaking to me about you.

Tom. Favorably?

Jim. What do you think?

Tom. Well—

Jim. You're going to be out of a job if you don't wake up.

Tom. I am waking up—

Jim. You show no signs.

Tom. The signs are interior.

[*Image on screen: The sailing vessel with Jolly Roger again*]

Tom. I'm planning to change. [*He leans over the rail speaking with quiet exhilaration. The incandescent marquees and signs of the first-run movie houses light his face from across the alley. He looks like a voyager*] I'm right at the point of committing myself to a future that doesn't include the warehouse and Mr. Mendoza or even a night-school course in public speaking.

Jim. What are you gassing about?

Tom. I'm tired of the movies.

Jim. Movies!

Tom. Yes, movies! Look at them—[*A wave toward the marvels of Grand Avenue*] All of those glamorous people—having adventures—hogging it all, gobbling the whole thing up! You know what happens? People go to the *movies* instead of *moving!* Hollywood characters are supposed to have all the adventures for everybody in America, while everybody in America sits in a dark room and watches them have them! Yes, until there's a war. That's when adventure becomes available to the masses! *Everyone's* dish, not only Gable's! Then the people in the dark room come out of the dark room to have some adventures themselves—Goody, goody! —It's our turn now, to go to the South Sea Island—to make a safari —to be exotic, far-off!—but I'm not patient. I don't want to wait till then. I'm tired of the *movies* and I am *about* to *move!*

Jim [*incredulously*]. Move?

Tom. Yes.

Jim. When?

Tom. Soon!

Jim. Where? Where?

[*Theme three music seems to answer the question, while* Tom *thinks it over. He searches among his pockets*]

Tom. I'm starting to boil inside. I know I seem dreamy, but inside —well, I'm boiling!—Whenever I pick up a shoe, I shudder a little thinking how short life is and what I am doing!—Whatever that means, I know it doesn't mean shoes—except as something to wear on a traveler's feet! [*Finds paper*] Look—

Jim. What?

Tom. I'm a member.

Jim [*reading*]. The Union of Merchant Seamen.

Tom. I paid my dues this month, instead of the light bill.

Jim. You will regret it when they turn the lights off.

Tom. I won't be here.

Jim. How about your mother?

Tom. I'm like my father. The bastard son of a bastard! See how he grins? And he's been absent going on sixteen years!

Jim. You're just talking, you drip. How does your mother feel about it?

Tom. Shhh!—Here comes Mother! Mother is not acquainted with my plans!

Amanda [*enters portieres*]. Where are you all?

Tom. On the terrace, Mother.

[*They start inside. She advances to them.* Tom *is distinctly shocked at her appearance. Even* Jim *blinks a little. He is making his first contact with girlish Southern vivacity and in spite of the night-school course in public speaking is somewhat thrown off the beam by the unexpected outlay of social charm. Certain responses are attempted by* Jim *but are swept aside by* Amanda's *gay laughter and chatter.* Tom *is embarrassed but after the first shock* Jim *reacts very warmly. Grins and chuckles, is altogether won over*]

[*Image:* Amanda *as a girl*]

Amanda [*coyly smiling, shaking her girlish ringlets*]. Well, well, well, so this is Mr. O'Connor. Introductions entirely unnecessary. I've heard so much about you from my boy. I finally said to him, Tom—good gracious!—why don't you bring this paragon to supper? I'd like to meet this nice young man at the warehouse!—Instead of just hearing him sing your praises so much!

I don't know why my son is so stand-offish—that's not Southern behavior!

Let's sit down and—I think we could stand a little more air in here! Tom, leave the door open. I felt a nice fresh breeze a moment ago. Where has it gone to?

Mmm, so warm already! And not quite summer, even. We're going to burn up when summer really gets started.

However, we're having—we're having a very light supper. I think light things are better fo' this time of year. The same as light clothes are. Light clothes an' light food are what warm weather calls fo'. You know our blood gets so thick during th' winter—it takes a while fo' us to *adjust* ou'selves!—when the season changes . . .

It's come so quick this year. I wasn't prepared. All of a sudden —heavens! Already summer!—I ran to the trunk an' pulled out this light dress—Terribly old! Historical almost! But feels so good—so good an' co-ol, y'know. . . .

Tom. Mother—

Amanda. Yes, honey?

Tom. How about—supper?

Amanda. Honey, you go ask Sister if supper is ready! You know that Sister is in full charge of supper!

Tell her you hungry boys are waiting for it. [*To* Jim] Have you met Laura?

Jim. She—

Amanda. Let you in? Oh, good, you've met already! It's rare for a girl as sweet an' pretty as Laura to be domestic! But Laura is, thank heavens, not only pretty but also very domestic. I'm not at all. I never was a bit. I never could make a thing but angel-food cake. Well, in the South we had so many servants. Gone, gone, gone. All vestige of gracious living! Gone completely! I wasn't prepared for what the future brought me. All of my gentlemen callers were sons of planters and so of course I assumed that I would be married to one and raise my family on a large piece of land with plenty of servants. But man proposes—and woman accepts the proposal!—To vary that old, old saying a little bit—I married no planter! I married a man who worked for the telephone company!—That gallantly smiling gentleman over there! [*Points to the picture*] A telephone man who—fell in love with long-distance!—Now he travels and I don't even know where!— But what am I going on for about my tribulations? Tell me yours —I hope you don't have any! Tom?

Tom [*returning*]. Yes, Mother?

Amanda. Is supper nearly ready?

Tom. It looks to me like supper is on the table.

Amanda. Let me look—[*She rises prettily and looks through portieres*] Oh, lovely!—But where is Sister?

Tom. Laura is not feeling well and she says that she thinks she'd better not come to the table.

Amanda. What?—Nonsense!—Laura? Oh, Laura!

Laura [*off stage, faintly*]. Yes, Mother.

Amanda. You really must come to the table. We won't be seated until you come to the table! Come in, Mr. O'Connor. You sit over there, and I'll—Laura? Laura Wingfield! You're keeping us waiting, honey! We can't say grace until you come to the table!

[*The back door is pushed weakly open and* Laura *comes in. She is obviously quite faint, her lips trembling, her eyes wide and staring. She moves unsteadily toward the table*]

[*Legend: "Terror!"*]

[*Outside a summer storm is coming abruptly. The white curtains billow inward at the windows and there is a sorrowful murmur and deep blue dusk.* Laura *suddenly stumbles—she catches at a chair with a faint moan*]

Tom. Laura!

Amanda. Laura! [*There is a clap of thunder. Legend: "Ah!" Despairingly*] Why, Laura, you *are* sick, darling! Tom, help your sister into the living room, dear! Sit in the living room, Laura—rest on the sofa. Well! [*To the gentleman caller*] Standing over the hot stove made her ill!—I told her that it was just too warm this evening, but—[Tom *comes back in.* Laura *is on the sofa*] Is Laura all right now?

Tom. Yes.

Amanda. What *is* that? Rain? A nice cool rain has come up! [*She gives the gentleman caller a frightened look*] I think we may—have grace—now. . . [Tom *looks at her stupidly*] Tom, honey—you say grace!

Tom. Oh . . . "For these and all thy mercies—" [*They bow their heads,* Amanda *stealing a nervous glance at* Jim. *In the living room* Laura, *stretched on the sofa, clenches her hand to her lips, to hold back a shuddering sob*] God's Holy Name be praised—

[*The scene dims out*]

SCENE VII

A Souvenir.

Half an hour later. Dinner is just being finished in the upstage area which is concealed by the drawn portieres. As the curtain rises Laura *is still huddled upon the sofa, her feet drawn under her,*

her head resting on a pale blue pillow, her eyes wide and mysteriously watchful. The new floor lamp with its shade of rose-colored silk gives a soft, becoming light to her face, bringing out the fragile, unearthly prettiness which usually escapes attention. There is a steady murmur of rain, but it is slackening and stops soon after the scene begins; the air outside becomes pale and luminous as the moon breaks out. A moment after the curtain rises, the lights in both rooms flicker and go out.

Jim. Hey, there, Mr. Light Bulb!

[Amanda *laughs nervously*]

[*Legend: "Suspension of a public service"*]

Amanda. Where was Moses when the lights went out? Ha-ha. Do you know the answer to that one, Mr. O'Connor?

Jim. No, Ma'am, what's the answer?

Amanda. In the dark! [Jim *laughs appreciatively*] Everybody sit still. I'll light the candles. Isn't it lucky we have them on the table? Where's a match? Which of you gentlemen can provide a match?

Jim. Here.

Amanda. Thank you, sir.

Jim. Not at all, Ma'am!

Amanda. I guess the fuse has burnt out. Mr. O'Connor, can you tell a burnt-out fuse? I know I can't and Tom is a total loss when it comes to mechanics. [*Sound: Getting up: Voices recede a little to kitchenette*] Oh, be careful you don't bump into something. We don't want our gentleman caller to break his neck. Now wouldn't that be a fine howdy-do?

Jim. Ha-ha! Where is the fuse-box?

Amanda. Right here next to the stove. Can you see anything?

Jim. Just a minute.

Amanda. Isn't electricity a mysterious thing? Wasn't it Benjamin Franklin who tied a key to a kite? We live in such a mysterious universe, don't we? Some people say that science clears up all the mysteries for us. In my opinion it only creates more!

Have you found it yet?

Jim. No, Ma'am. All these fuses look okay to me.

Amanda. Tom!

Tom. Yes, Mother?

Amanda. That light bill I gave you several days ago. The one I told you we got the notices about?

[*Legend: "Ha!"*]

Tom. Oh.—Yeah.

Amanda. You didn't neglect to pay it by any chance?

Tom. Why, I—

Amanda. Didn't! I might have known it!

Jim. Shakespeare probably wrote a poem on that light bill, Mrs. Wingfield.

Amanda. I might have known better than to trust him with it! There's such a high price for negligence in this world!

Jim. Maybe the poem will win a ten-dollar prize.

Amanda. We'll just have to spend the remainder of the evening in the nineteenth century, before Mr. Edison made the Mazda lamp!

Jim. Candlelight is my favorite kind of light.

Amanda. That shows you're romantic! But that's no excuse for Tom. Well, we got through dinner. Very considerate of them to let us get through dinner before they plunged us into everlasting darkness, wasn't it, Mr. O'Connor?

Jim. Ha-ha!

Amanda. Tom, as a penalty for your carelessness you can help me with the dishes.

Jim. Let me give you a hand.

Amanda. Indeed you will not!

Jim. I ought to be good for something.

Amanda. Good for something? [*Her tone is rhapsodic*] *You?* Why, Mr. O'Connor, nobody, *nobody's* given me this much entertainment in years—as you have!

Jim. Aw, now, Mrs. Wingfield!

Amanda. I'm not exaggerating, not one bit! But Sister is all by her lonesome. You go keep her company in the parlor!

I'll give you this lovely old candelabrum that used to be on the altar at the church of the Heavenly Rest. It was melted a little out of shape when the church burnt down. Lightning struck it one spring. Gypsy Jones was holding a revival at the time and he intimated that the church was destroyed because the Episcopalians gave card parties.

Jim. Ha-ha.

Amanda. And how about you coaxing Sister to drink a little wine? I think it would be good for her! Can you carry both at once?

Jim. Sure. I'm Superman!

Amanda. Now, Thomas, get into this apron!

[*The door of the kitchenette swings closed on* Amanda's *gay laughter; the flickering light approaches the portieres.* Laura *sits up nervously as he enters. Her speech at first is low and breathless from the almost intolerable strain of being alone with a stranger*]

[*The legend: "I don't suppose you remember me at all!"*]

[*In her first speeches in this scene, before* Jim's *warmth overcomes her paralyzing shyness,* Laura's *voice is thin and breathless as though she has just run up a steep flight of stairs.* Jim's *attitude is gently humorous. In playing this scene it should be stressed that while the incident is apparently unimportant, it is to* Laura *the climax of her secret life*]

Jim. Hello, there, Laura.

Laura [*faintly*]. Hello. [*She clears her throat*]

Jim. How are you feeling now? Better?

Laura. Yes. Yes, thank you.

Jim. This is for you. A little dandelion wine. [*He extends it toward her with extravagant gallantry*]

Laura. Thank you.

Jim. Drink it—but don't get drunk! [*He laughs heartily.* Laura *takes the glass uncertainly; laughs shyly*] Where shall I set the candles?

Laura. Oh—oh, anywhere . . .

Jim. How about here on the floor? Any objections?

Laura. No.

Jim. I'll spread a newspaper under to catch the drippings. I like to sit on the floor. Mind if I do?

Laura. Oh, no.

Jim. Give me a pillow?

Laura. What?

Jim. A pillow!

Laura. Oh . . . [*Hands him one quickly*]

Jim. How about you? Don't you like to sit on the floor?

Laura. Oh—yes.

Jim. Why don't you then?

Laura. I—will.

Jim. Take a pillow! [Laura *does. Sits on the other side of the candelabrum.* Jim *crosses his legs and smiles engagingly at her*] I can't hardly see you sitting way over there.

Laura. I can—see you.

Jim. I know, but that's not fair, I'm in the limelight. [Laura *moves her pillow closer*] Good! Now I can see you! Comfortable?

Laura. Yes.

Jim. So am I. Comfortable as a cow! Will you have some gum?

Laura. No, thank you.

Jim. I think that I will indulge, with your permission. [*Musingly unwraps it and holds it up*] Think of the fortune made by the guy that invented the first piece of chewing gum. Amazing, huh? The Wrigley Building is one of the sights of Chicago.—I saw it summer before last when I went up to the Century of Progress. Did you take in the Century of Progress?

Laura. No, I didn't.

Jim. Well, it was quite a wonderful exposition. What impressed me most was the Hall of Science. Gives you an idea of what the future will be in America, even more wonderful than the present time is! [*Pause. Smiling at her*] Your brother tells me you're shy. Is that right, Laura?

Laura. I—don't know.

Jim. I judge you to be an old-fashioned type of girl. Well, I think that's a pretty good type to be. Hope you don't think I'm being too personal—do you?

Laura [*hastily, out of embarrassment*]. I believe I *will* take a piece of gum, if you—don't mind. [*Clearing her throat*] Mr. O'Connor, have you—kept up with your singing?

Jim. Singing? Me?

Laura. Yes. I remember what a beautiful voice you had.

Jim. When did you hear me sing?

[Voice *off stage in the pause*]

Voice [*off stage*].

O blow, ye winds, heigh-ho,
A-roving I will go!
I'm off to my love
With a boxing glove—
Ten thousand miles away!

Jim. You say you've heard me sing?

Laura. Oh, yes! Yes, very often . . . I—don't suppose—you remember me—at all?

Jim [*smiling doubtfully*]. You know I have an idea I've seen you before. I had that idea as soon as you opened the door. It seemed almost like I was about to remember your name. But the name I started to call you—wasn't a name! And so I stopped myself before I said it.

Laura. Wasn't it—Blue Roses?

Jim [*springs up. Grinning*]. Blue Roses!–My gosh, yes–Blue Roses! That's what I had on my tongue when you opened the door! Isn't it funny what tricks your memory plays? I didn't connect you with high school somehow or other. But that's where it was; it was high school. I didn't even know you were Shakespeare's sister! Gosh, I'm sorry.

Laura. I didn't expect you to. You–barely knew me!

Jim. But we did have a speaking acquaintance, huh?

Laura. Yes, we–spoke to each other.

Jim. When did you recognize me?

Laura. Oh, right away!

Jim. Soon as I came in the door?

Laura. When I heard your name I thought it was probably you. I knew that Tom used to know you a little in high school. So when you came in the door–Well, then I was–sure.

Jim. Why didn't you *say* something, then?

Laura [*breathlessly*]. I didn't know what to say, I was–too surprised!

Jim. For goodness' sakes! You know, this sure is funny!

Laura. Yes! Yes, isn't it, though . . . .

Jim. Didn't we have a class in something together?

Laura. Yes, we did.

Jim. What class was that?

Laura. It was–singing–Chorus!

Jim. Aw!

Laura. I sat across the aisle from you in the Aud.

Jim. Aw.

Laura. Mondays, Wednesdays and Fridays.

Jim. Now I remember–you always came in late.

Laura. Yes, it was so hard for me, getting upstairs. I had that brace on my leg–it clumped so loud!

Jim. I never heard any clumping.

Laura [*wincing at the recollection*]. To me it sounded like–thunder!

Jim. Well, well, well, I never even noticed.

Laura. And everybody was seated before I came in. I had to walk in front of all those people. My seat was in the back row. I had to go clumping all the way up the aisle with everyone watching!

Jim. You shouldn't have been self-conscious.

Laura. I know, but I was. It was always such a relief when the singing started.

Jim. Aw, yes, I've placed you now! I used to call you Blue Roses. How was it that I got started calling you that?

Laura. I was out of school a little while with pleurosis. When I came back you asked me what was the matter. I said I had pleurosis—you thought I said Blue Roses. That's what you always called me after that!

Jim. I hope you didn't mind.

Laura. Oh, no—I liked it. You see, I wasn't acquainted with many—people. . . .

Jim. As I remember you sort of stuck by yourself.

Laura. I—I—never have had much luck at—making friends.

Jim. I don't see why you wouldn't.

Laura. Well, I—started out badly.

Jim. You mean being—

Laura. Yes, it sort of—stood between me—

Jim. You shouldn't have let it!

Laura. I know, but it did, and—

Jim. You were shy with people!

Laura. I tried not to be but never could—

Jim. Overcome it?

Laura. No, I—I never could!

Jim. I guess being shy is something you have to work out of kind of gradually.

Laura [*sorrowfully*]. Yes—I guess it—

Jim. Takes time!

Laura. Yes—

Jim. People are not so dreadful when you know them. That's what you have to remember! And everybody has problems, not just you, but practically everybody has got some problems. You think of yourself as having the only problems, as being the only one who is disappointed. But just look around you and you will see lots of people as disappointed as you are. For instance, I hoped when I was going to high school that I would be further along at this time, six years later, than I am now—You remember that wonderful write-up I had in *The Torch?*

Laura. Yes! [*She rises and crosses to table*]

Jim. It said I was bound to succeed in anything I went into! [Laura *returns with the annual*] Holy Jeez! *The Torch!* [*He accepts it reverently. They smile across it with mutual wonder.* Laura *crouches beside him and they begin to turn through it.* Laura's *shyness is dissolving in his warmth*]

Laura. Here you are in *The Pirates of Penzance!*
Jim [*wistfully*]. I sang the baritone lead in that operetta.
Laura [*raptly*]. So—*beautifully!*
Jim [*protesting*]. Aw—
Laura. Yes, yes—beautifully—beautifully!
Jim. You heard me?
Laura. All three times!
Jim. No!
Laura. Yes!
Jim. All three performances?
Laura [*looking down*]. Yes.
Jim. Why?
Laura. I—wanted to ask you to—autograph my program.
Jim. Why didn't you ask me to?
Laura. You were always surrounded by your own friends so much that I never had a chance to.
Jim. You should have just—
Laura. Well, I—thought you might think I was—
Jim. Thought I might think you was—what?
Laura. Oh—
Jim [*with reflective relish*]. I was beleaguered by females in those days.
Laura. You were terribly popular!
Jim. Yeah—
Laura. You had such a—friendly way—
Jim. I was spoiled in high school.
Laura. Everybody—liked you!
Jim. Including you?
Laura. I—yes, I did, too—[*She gently closes the book in her lap*]
Jim. Well, well, well!—Give me that program, Laura. [*She hands it to him. He signs it with a flourish*] There you are—better late than never!
Laura. Oh, I—what a—surprise!
Jim. My signature isn't worth very much right now. But some day —maybe—it will increase in value! Being disappointed is one thing and being discouraged is something else. I am disappointed but I am not discouraged. I'm twenty-three years old. How old are you?
Laura. I'll be twenty-four in June.
Jim. That's not old age!
Laura. No, but—
Jim. You finished high school?

Laura [*with difficulty*]. I didn't go back.

Jim. You mean you dropped out?

Laura. I made bad grades in my final examinations. [*She rises and replaces the book and the program. Her voice strained*] How is—Emily Meisenbach getting along?

Jim. Oh, that kraut-head!

Laura. Why do you call her that?

Jim. That's what she was.

Laura. You're not still—going with her?

Jim. I never see her.

Laura. It said in the Personal Section that you were—engaged!

Jim. I know, but I wasn't impressed by that—propaganda!

Laura. It wasn't—the truth?

Jim. Only in Emily's optimistic opinion!

Laura. Oh—

[*Legend: "What have you done since high school?"*]

[Jim *lights a cigarette and leans indolently back on his elbows smiling at* Laura *with a warmth and charm which lights her inwardly with altar candles. She remains by the table and turns in her hands a piece of glass to cover her tumult*]

Jim [*after several reflective puffs on a cigarette*]. What have you done since high school? [*She seems not to hear him*] Huh? [Laura *looks up*] I said what have you done since high school, Laura?

Laura. Nothing much.

Jim. You must have been doing something these six long years.

Laura. Yes.

Jim. Well, then, such as what?

Laura. I took a business course at business college—

Jim. How did that work out?

Laura. Well, not very—well—I had to drop out, it gave me—indigestion—

[Jim *laughs gently*]

Jim. What are you doing now?

Laura. I don't do anything—much. Oh, please don't think I sit around doing nothing! My glass collection takes up a good deal of time. Glass is something you have to take good care of.

Jim. What did you say—about glass?

Laura. Collection I said—I have one—[*She clears her throat and turns away again, acutely shy*]

Jim [*abruptly*]. You know what I judge to be the trouble with you? Inferiority complex! Know what that is? That's what they call it when someone low-rates himself! I understand it because I had it, too. Although my case was not so aggravated as yours seems to be. I had it until I took up public speaking, developed my voice, and learned that I had an aptitude for science. Before that time I never thought of myself as being outstanding in any way whatsoever! Now I've never made a regular study of it, but I have a friend who says I can analyze people better than doctors that make a profession of it. I don't claim that to be necessarily true, but I can sure guess a person's psychology, Laura! [*Takes out his gum*] Excuse me, Laura. I always take it out when the flavor is gone. I'll use this scrap of paper to wrap it in. I know how it is to get it stuck on a shoe. Yep—that's what I judge to be your principal trouble. A lack of confidence in yourself as a person. You don't have the proper amount of faith in yourself. I'm basing that fact on a number of your remarks and also on certain observations I've made. For instance that clumping you thought was so awful in high school. You say you even dreaded to walk into class. You see what you did? You dropped out of school, you gave up an education because of a clump, which as far as I know was practically non-existent! A little physical defect is what you have. Hardly noticeable even! Magnified thousands of times by imagination! You know what my strong advice to you is? Think of yourself as *superior* in some way!

Laura. In what way would I think?

Jim. Why, man alive, Laura! Just look about you a little. What do you see? A world full of common people! All of 'em born and all of 'em going to die! Which of them has one-tenth of your good points! Or mine! Or anyone else's, as far as that goes—Gosh! Everybody excels in some one thing. Some in many! [*Unconsciously glances at himself in the mirror*] All you've got to do is discover in what! Take me, for instance. [*He adjusts his tie at the mirror*] My interest happens to lie in electro-dynamics. I'm taking a course in radio engineering at night school, Laura, on top of a fairly responsible job at the warehouse. I'm taking that course and studying public speaking.

Laura. Ohhhh.

Jim. Because I believe in the future of television! [*Turning back to her*] I wish to be ready to go up right along with it. Therefore I'm planning to get in on the ground floor. In fact I've already made the right connections and all that remains is for the industry to get under way! Full steam—[*His eyes are starry*] *Knowledge*—Zzzzzp!

Money–Zzzzzzp!–Power! That's the cycle democracy is built on! [*His attitude is convincingly dynamic.* Laura *stares at him, even her shyness eclipsed in her absolute wonder. He suddenly grins*] I guess you think I think a lot of myself!

Laura. No–o-o-o, I–

Jim. Now how about you? Isn't there something you take more interest in than anything else?

Laura. Well, I do–as I said–have my–glass collection–

[*A peal of girlish laughter from the kitchen*]

Jim. I'm not right sure I know what you're talking about. What kind of glass is it?

Laura. Little articles of it, they're ornaments mostly! Most of them are little animals made out of glass, the tiniest little animals in the world. Mother calls them a glass menagerie! Here's an example of one, if you'd like to see it! This is one of the oldest. It's nearly thirteen. [*Music: "The Glass Menagerie." He stretches out his hand*] Oh, be careful–if you breathe, it breaks!

Jim. I'd better not take it. I'm pretty clumsy with things.

Laura. Go on, I trust you with him! [*Places it in his palm*] There now–you're holding him gently! Hold him over the light, he loves the light! You see how the light shines through him?

Jim. It sure does shine!

Laura. I shouldn't be partial, but he is my favorite one.

Jim. What kind of a thing is this one supposed to be?

Laura. Haven't you noticed the single horn on his forehead?

Jim. A unicorn, huh?

Laura. Mmm-hmmm!

Jim. Unicorns, aren't they extinct in the modern world?

Laura. I know!

Jim. Poor little fellow, he must feel sort of lonesome.

Laura [*smiling*]. Well, if he does he doesn't complain about it. He stays on a shelf with some horses that don't have horns and all of them seem to get along nicely together.

Jim. How do you know?

Laura [*lightly*]. I haven't heard any arguments among them!

Jim [*grinning*]. No arguments, huh? Well, that's a pretty good sign! Where shall I set him?

Laura. Put him on the table. They all like a change of scenery once in a while!

Jim [*stretching*]. Well, well, well, well–Look how big my shadow is when I stretch!

Laura. Oh, oh, yes–it stretches across the ceiling!

Jim [*crossing to door*]. I think it's stopped raining. [*Opens fire-escape door*] Where does the music come from?

Laura. From the Paradise Dance Hall across the alley.

Jim. How about cutting the rug a little, Miss Wingfield?

Laura. Oh, I–

Jim. Or is your program filled up? Let me have a look at it. [*Grasps imaginary card*] Why, every dance is taken! I'll just have to scratch some out. [*Waltz music: "La Golondrina"*] Ahhh, a waltz! [*He executes some sweeping turns by himself, then holds his arms toward* Laura]

Laura [*breathlessly*]. I–can't dance!

Jim. There you go, that inferiority stuff!

Laura. I've never danced in my life!

Jim. Come on, try!

Laura. Oh, but I'd step on you!

Jim. I'm not made out of glass.

Laura. How–how–how do we start?

Jim. Just leave it to me. You hold your arms out a little.

Laura. Like this?

Jim. A little bit higher. Right. Now don't tighten up, that's the main thing about it–relax.

Laura [*laughing breathlessly*]. It's hard not to.

Jim. Okay.

Laura. I'm afraid you can't budge me.

Jim. What do you bet I can't? [*He swings her into motion*]

Laura. Goodness, yes, you can!

Jim. Let yourself go, now, Laura, just let yourself go.

Laura. I'm–

Jim. Come on!

Laura. Trying!

Jim. Not so stiff–Easy does it!

Laura. I know but I'm–

Jim. Loosen th' backbone! There now, that's a lot better.

Laura. Am I?

Jim. Lots, lots better! [*He moves her about the room in a clumsy waltz*]

Laura. Oh, my!

Jim. Ha-ha!

Laura. Oh, my goodness!

Jim. Ha-ha-ha! [*They suddenly bump into the table.* Jim *stops*] What did we hit on?

Laura. Table.

Jim. Did something fall off it? I think—

Laura. Yes.

Jim. I hope that it wasn't the little glass horse with the horn!

Laura. Yes.

Jim. Aw, aw, aw. Is it broken?

Laura. Now it is just like all the other horses.

Jim. It's lost its—

Laura. Horn! It doesn't matter. Maybe it's a blessing in disguise.

Jim. You'll never forgive me. I bet that that was your favorite piece of glass.

Laura. I don't have favorites much. It's no tragedy, Freckles. Glass breaks so easily. No matter how careful you are. The traffic jars the shelves and things fall off them.

Jim. Still I'm awfully sorry that I was the cause.

Laura [*smiling*]. I'll just imagine he had an operation. The horn was removed to make him feel less—freakish! [*They both laugh*] Now he will feel more at home with the other horses, the ones that don't have horns . . .

Jim. Ha-ha, that's very funny! [*Suddenly serious*] I'm glad to see that you have a sense of humor.

You know—you're—well—very different! Surprisingly different from anyone else I know! [*His voice becomes soft and hesitant with a genuine feeling*] Do you mind me telling you that? [Laura *is abashed beyond speech*] I mean it in a nice way . . . [Laura *nods shyly, looking away*] You make me feel sort of—I don't know how to put it! I'm usually pretty good at expressing things, but— This is something that I don't know how to say! [Laura *touches her throat and clears it—turns the broken unicorn in her hands. Even softer*] Has anyone ever told you that you were pretty? [*Pause: music.* Laura *looks up slowly, with wonder, and shakes her head*] Well, you are! In a very different way from anyone else. And all the nicer because of the difference too. [*His voice becomes low and husky.* Laura *turns away, nearly faint with the novelty of her emotions*] I wish that you were my sister. I'd teach you to have some confidence in yourself. The different people are not like other people, but being different is nothing to be ashamed of. Because other people are not such wonderful people. They're one hundred times one thousand. You're one times one! They walk all over the earth. You just stay here. They're common as—weeds, but—you—well, you're—*Blue Roses!*

[*Image on screen: Blue roses*]

[*Music changes*]

Laura. But blue is wrong for—roses . . .

Jim. It's right for you!—You're—pretty!

Laura. In what respect am I pretty?

Jim. In all respects—believe me! Your eyes—your hair—are pretty! Your hands are pretty! [*He catches hold of her hand*] You think I'm making this up because I'm invited to dinner and have to be nice. Oh, I could do that! I could put on an act for you, Laura, and say lots of things without being very sincere. But this time I am. I'm talking to you sincerely. I happened to notice you had this inferiority complex that keeps you from feeling comfortable with people. Somebody needs to build your confidence up and make you proud instead of shy and turning away and—blushing—Somebody—ought to—ought to—*kiss* you, Laura! [*His hand slips slowly up her arm to her shoulder. Music swells tumultuously. He suddenly turns her about and kisses her on the lips. When he releases her,* Laura *sinks on the sofa with a bright, dazed look.* Jim *backs away and fishes in his pocket for a cigarette. Legend on screen: "Souvenir"*] Stumble-john! [*He lights the cigarette, avoiding her look. There is a peal of girlish laughter from* Amanda *in the kitchen.* Laura *slowly raises and opens her hand. It still contains the little broken glass animal. She looks at it with a tender, bewildered expression*] Stumble-john! I shouldn't have done that—That was way off the beam. You don't smoke, do you? [*She looks up, smiling, not hearing the question. He sits beside her a little gingerly. She looks at him speechlessly—waiting. He coughs decorously and moves a little farther aside as he considers the situation and senses her feelings, dimly, with perturbation. Gently*] Would you—care for a—mint? [*She doesn't seem to hear him but her look grows brighter even*] Peppermint—Life-Saver? My pocket's a regular drug store—wherever I go . . . [*He pops a mint in his mouth. Then gulps and decides to make a clean breast of it. He speaks slowly and gingerly*] Laura, you know, if I had a sister like you, I'd do the same thing as Tom. I'd bring out fellows and—introduce her to them. The right type of boys of a type to—appreciate her. Only—well—he made a mistake about me. Maybe I've got no call to be saying this. That may not have been the idea in having me over. But what if it was? There's nothing wrong about that. The only trouble is that in my case—I'm not in a situation to—do the right thing.

I can't take down your number and say I'll phone. I can't call up next week and—ask for a date. I thought I had better explain the situation in case you—misunderstood it and—hurt your feelings. . . .

[*Pause. Slowly, very slowly,* Laura's *look changes, her eyes returning slowly from his to the ornament in her palm.* Amanda *utters another gay laugh in the kitchen*]

Laura [*faintly*]. You—won't—call again?

Jim. No, Laura, I can't. [*He rises from the sofa*] As I was just explaining, I've—got strings on me. Laura, I've—been going steady! I go out all the time with a girl named Betty. She's a home-girl like you, and Catholic, and Irish, and in a great many ways we—get along fine. I met her last summer on a moonlight boat trip up the river to Alton, on the *Majestic*. Well—right away from the start it was—love! [*Legend: Love!* Laura *sways slightly forward and grips the arm of the sofa. He fails to notice, now enrapt in his own comfortable being*] Being in love has made a new man of me! [*Leaning stiffly forward, clutching the arm of the sofa,* Laura *struggles visibly with her storm. But* Jim *is oblivious, she is a long way off*] The power of love is really pretty tremendous! Love is something that—changes the whole world, Laura! [*The storm abates a little and* Laura *leans back. He notices her again*] It happened that Betty's aunt took sick, she got a wire and had to go to Centralia. So Tom—when he asked me to dinner—I naturally just accepted the invitation, not knowing that you—that he—that I—[*He stops awkwardly*] Huh—I'm a stumble-john! [*He flops back on the sofa. The holy candles in the altar of* Laura's *face have been snuffed out. There is a look of almost infinite desolation.* Jim *glances at her uneasily*] I wish that you would—say something. [*She bites her lip which was trembling and then bravely smiles. She opens her hand again on the broken glass ornament. Then she gently takes his hand and raises it level with her own. She carefully places the unicorn in the palm of his hand, then pushes his fingers closed upon it*] What are you—doing that for? You want me to have him?—Laura? [*She nods*] What for?

Laura. A—souvenir . . . [*She rises unsteadily and crouches beside the victrola to wind it up*]

[*Legend on screen: "Things have a way of turning out so badly!"*]

[*Or image: "Gentleman caller waving good-bye!—gaily"*]

[*At this moment* Amanda *rushes brightly back in the front room. She bears a pitcher of fruit punch in an old-fashioned cut-glass pitcher and a plate of macaroons. The plate has a gold border and poppies painted on it*]

Amanda. Well, well, well! Isn't the air delightful after the shower?

I've made you children a little liquid refreshment. [*Turns gaily to the gentleman caller*] Jim, do you know that song about lemonade?

> Lemonade, lemonade
> Made in the shade and stirred with a spade—
> Good enough for any old maid!

Jim [*uneasily*]. Ha-ha! No—I never heard it.

Amanda. Why, Laura! You look so serious!

Jim. We were having a serious conversation.

Amanda. Good! Now you're better acquainted!

Jim [*uncertainly*]. Ha-ha! Yes.

Amanda. You modern young people are much more serious-minded than my generation. I was so gay as a girl!

Jim. You haven't changed, Mrs. Wingfield.

Amanda. Tonight I'm rejuvenated! The gaiety of the occasion, Mr. O'Connor! [*She tosses her head with a peal of laughter. Spills lemonade*] Oooo! I'm baptizing myself!

Jim. Here—let me—

Amanda [*setting the pitcher down*]. There now. I discovered we had some maraschino cherries. I dumped them in, juice and all!

Jim. You shouldn't have gone to that trouble, Mrs. Wingfield.

Amanda. Trouble, trouble? Why, it was loads of fun! Didn't you hear me cutting up in the kitchen? I bet your ears were burning! I told Tom how out-done with him I was for keeping you to himself so long a time! He should have brought you over much, much sooner! Well, now that you've found your way, I want you to be a very frequent caller! Not just occasional but all the time. Oh, we're going to have a lot of gay times together! I see them coming! Mmmm, just breathe that air! So fresh, and the moon's so pretty! I'll skip back out—I know where my place is when young folks are having a—serious conversation!

Jim. Oh, don't go out, Mrs. Wingfield. The fact of the matter is I've got to be going.

Amanda. Going, now? You're joking! Why, it's only the shank of the evening, Mr. O'Connor!

Jim. Well, you know how it is.

Amanda. You mean you're a young workingman and have to keep workingmen's hours. We'll let you off early tonight. But only on the condition that next time you stay later. What's the best night for you? Isn't Saturday night the best night for you workingmen?

Jim. I have a couple of time-clocks to punch, Mrs. Wingfield. One at morning, another one at night!

Amanda. My, but you *are* ambitious! You work at night, too?

Jim. No, Ma'am, not work but—Betty! [*He crosses deliberately to pick up his hat. The band at the Paradise Dance Hall goes into a tender waltz*]

Amanda. Betty? Betty? Who's—Betty! [*There is an ominous cracking sound in the sky.*]

Jim. Oh, just a girl. The girl I go steady with! [*He smiles charmingly. The sky falls*]

[*Legend: "The sky falls"*]

Amanda [*a long-drawn exhalation*]. Ohhh . . . Is it a serious romance, Mr. O'Connor?

Jim. We're going to be married the second Sunday in June.

Amanda. Ohhh—how nice! Tom didn't mention that you were engaged to be married.

Jim. The cat's not out of the bag at the warehouse yet. You know how they are. They call you Romeo and stuff like that. [*He stops at the oval mirror to put on his hat. He carefully shapes the brim and the crown to give a discreetly dashing effect*] It's been a wonderful evening, Mrs. Wingfield. I guess this is what they mean by Southern hospitality.

Amanda. It really wasn't anything at all.

Jim. I hope it don't seem like I'm rushing off. But I promised Betty I'd pick her up at the Wabash depot, an' by the time I get my jalopy down there her train'll be in. Some women are pretty upset if you keep 'em waiting.

Amanda. Yes, I know—The tyranny of women! [*Extends her hand*] Good-bye, Mr. O'Connor. I wish you luck—and happiness—and success! All three of them, and so does Laura!—Don't you, Laura?

Laura. Yes!

Jim [*taking her hand*]. Good-bye, Laura. I'm certainly going to treasure that souvenir. And don't you forget the good advice I gave you. [*Raises his voice to a cheery shout*] So long, Shakespeare! Thanks again, ladies—Good night! [*He grins and ducks jauntily out. Still bravely grimacing,* Amanda *closes the door on the gentleman caller. Then she turns back to the room with a puzzled expression. She and* Laura *don't dare to face each other.* Laura *crouches beside the victrola to wind it*]

Amanda [*faintly*]. Things have a way of turning out so badly. I don't believe that I would play the victrola. Well, well—well—Our gentleman caller was engaged to be married! Tom!

Tom [*from back*]. Yes, Mother?

Amanda. Come in here a minute. I want to tell you something awfully funny.

Tom [*enters with macaroon and a glass of the lemonade*]. Has the gentleman caller gotten away already?

Amanda. The gentleman caller has made an early departure. What a wonderful joke you played on us!

Tom. How do you mean?

Amanda. You didn't mention that he was engaged to be married.

Tom. Jim? Engaged?

Amanda. That's what he just informed us.

Tom. I'll be jiggered! I didn't know about that.

Amanda. That seems very peculiar.

Tom. What's peculiar about it?

Amanda. Didn't you call him your best friend down at the warehouse?

Tom. He is, but how did I know?

Amanda. It seems extremely peculiar that you wouldn't know your best friend was going to be married!

Tom. The warehouse is where I work, not where I know things about people!

Amanda. You don't know things anywhere! You live in a dream; you manufacture illusions! [*He crosses to door*] Where are you going?

Tom. I'm going to the movies.

Amanda. That's right, now that you've had us make such fools of ourselves. The effort, the preparations, all the expense! The new floor lamp, the rug, the clothes for Laura! All for what? To entertain some other girl's fiancé! Go to the movies, go! Don't think about us, a mother deserted, an unmarried sister who's crippled and has no job! Don't let anything interfere with your selfish pleasure! Just go, go, go—to the movies!

Tom. All right, I will! The more you shout about my selfishness to me the quicker I'll go, and I won't go to the movies!

Amanda. Go, then! Then go to the moon—you selfish dreamer!

[*Tom smashes his glass on the floor. He plunges out on the fire-escape, slamming the door.* Laura *screams—cut by door. Dance-hall music up.* Tom *goes to the rail and grips it desperately, lifting his face in the chill white moonlight penetrating the narrow abyss of the alley*]

[*Legend on screen: "And so good-bye . . ."*]

[Tom's *closing speech is timed with the interior pantomime.*

The interior scene is played as though viewed through sound-proof glass. Amanda *appears to be making a comforting speech to* Laura *who is huddled upon the sofa. Now that we cannot hear the mother's speech, her silliness is gone and she has dignity and tragic beauty.* Laura's *dark hair hides her face until at the end of the speech she lifts it to smile at her mother.* Amanda's *gestures are slow and graceful, almost dance-like, as she comforts the daughter. At the end of her speech she glances a moment at the father's picture—then withdraws through the portieres. At close of* Tom's *speech,* Laura *blows out the candles, ending the play*]

Tom. I didn't go to the moon, I went much further—for time is the longest distance between two places—Not long after that I was fired for writing a poem on the lid of a shoe-box. I left Saint Louis. I descended the steps of this fire-escape for a last time and followed, from then on, in my father's footsteps, attempting to find in motion what was lost in space—I traveled around a great deal. The cities swept about me like dead leaves, leaves that were brightly colored but torn away from the branches. I would have stopped, but I was pursued by something. It always came upon me unawares, taking me altogether by surprise. Perhaps it was a familiar bit of music. Perhaps it was only a piece of transparent glass—Perhaps I am walking along a street at night, in some strange city, before I have found companions. I pass the lighted window of a shop where perfume is sold. The window is filled with pieces of colored glass, tiny transparent bottles in delicate colors, like bits of a shattered rainbow. Then all at once my sister touches my shoulder. I turn around and look into her eyes. . . . Oh, Laura, Laura, I tried to leave you behind me, but I am more faithful than I intended to be! I reach for a cigarette, I cross the street, I run into the movies or a bar, I buy a drink, I speak to the nearest stranger—anything that can blow your candles out! [Laura *bends over the candles*]—for nowadays the world is lit by lightning! Blow out your candles, Laura—and so good-bye. . . . [*She blows the candles out*]

[*The scene dissolves*]

Questions

1. Why do you think Williams insists upon the importance of his "extraliterary" devices? In answering this question, you are really commenting upon the reader's role as director and stage manager when he reads a play.
2. Comment on the appropriateness of Williams's title. Obviously he emphasizes a major symbol within the play; but does the term "glass menagerie" also apply to the people—Amanda, Laura, Tom, and Jim—within Williams's fictional world?
3. How does Williams manage to secure some sympathy for Amanda? Surely her faults are exposed often and blatantly enough. Does she share some of the fragility of the glass animals, the tenderness of Laura, the dreams of Tom, the realistic bias of Jim?
4. Despite the charged language, the bizarre characters, and the "unrealistic" and "extraliterary" devices, the plot has an almost stark simplicity. Can you offer any rationale for this starkness of plot line?
5. Can you state succinctly just what each character is seeking?
6. If we accept Tom as the poet-dreamer-wanderer and his insight into the pathos of Laura's situation as valid, how can we explain his apparent failure to understand Amanda (as Williams, in his descriptions of the characters, makes clear that he understands her)?
7. What is the role of Mr. Wingfield and his portrait in the play? Why do you think he is always mentioned in comic terms?
8. Do Amanda's speech, her memories of her girlhood, and her manner become something of a parody of a mythical South? And does the Southern background make any difference in the nature of the dramatic conflict (could Amanda just as well have passed her youth in Kansas or Maine?)?

Topics for Composition

1. Compare and contrast the searches for "a place" by Amanda and Tom. Be as specific as you can about their respective goals, and cite specific evidence from the play to illustrate and support your statements.
2. Define "expressionism" and illustrate your extended definition with details from the play.
3. Explain why Amanda avoids using the word "crippled" for Laura until the end of the play. You will want to establish the word's connotation for Amanda and analyze her reasons for not uttering the word until the close.
4. By the time you have finished reading the play, you will have an opinion about the implications of the play beyond mere plot line. Write an argument for your opinion.

Poetry

THE need to belong in and to society encounters many obstacles to its satisfaction and finds expression in many ways, as the poems that follow will amply demonstrate. We shall see, for example, that the matter sometimes presents itself in broad philosophic terms, sometimes in terms of very personal circumstances. It is indeed not easy to generalize about a group of poems that vary as much in perspective as these do; yet many instructive comparisons among them are possible, comparisons that will illuminate both the common theme and various modes of poetic expression. It is admittedly a far cry, for example, from Alexander Pope's reflections on social principles to E. A. Robinson's description of old Mr. Flood conversing drunkenly with himself in the moonlight; and a far cry, perhaps, from either of these to Robert Pack's little fantasy of the bird in search of a cage. Yet all three poems have to do with the human need to have a place in the scheme of things—a stable set of relationships with humanity, or some portion of it. This need, obviously, is partly of an intellectual character, partly of an emotional one; it must be dealt with, by reflective and cultivated persons, both rationally and imaginatively. The very diversity of poems such as these can help us become aware of the dimensions of the problem (which ought to be regarded as a challenge) and of the various resources that we can call upon in facing it. To illustrate: Robinson's portrayal of Mr. Flood, viewed in symbolic perspective, suggests that loneliness is to some extent a universal human condition; we are all more or less vulnerable to the forces within and without that have Mr. Flood talking to himself. Careful reflections upon these symbolic implications might well lead us to such a question as that which Pope attempts to answer in *An Essay on Man:* what is it that mainly holds society together and offers the best hope that universal social harmony will prevail? Pope answers that we are so framed that self-love and social love, rightly viewed, will always seem the same, so that in spite of the often bleak appearance of the world we can be sure that unity and harmony are in the very nature of things. Robert Pack, on the other hand, reminds us that the problem is not so simple, since there must be taken into account a desire for freedom that transcends ordinary selfishness. Thus, comparison leads us to look more deeply into the meaning of each poem and into the ways in which we can clarify in writing our own attitudes toward the subject.

It will be easier, and perhaps more fruitful, to think of comparisons to be made between those poems which are more closely related in subject and method, as well as to draw contrasts between those that are dissimilar. Comparison of poems from different periods will provide useful historical perspective and food for thought about the effect of changing social conditions. The passage from Shakespeare, for example, reflects almost implicit belief in the necessity of a stable, hierarchical social structure; Pope speaks for the so-called Age of Reason, when faith in rational control of the self and society was in the ascendant; Whitman's "Crossing Brooklyn Ferry" voices the later Romantic hope that imaginative sympathy or a mystical sense of the vital unity of all things would provide a sense of free participation that reason could not give; and Arnold's poem marks the decline of Romantic faith and the beginning of a feeling of alienation that has persisted up to the present time. The several contemporary poems, then, will both help us compare our general outlook with those of past eras and enable us to analyze in some depth the special conditions that nowadays affect the search for self-fulfillment through social participation.

It must not be forgotten that these poems can provide not only ideas to be developed or analyzed but also much insight into the nature of language and effective communication. As writers, we would do well to compare carefully the ways in which these poets have achieved perspective, emphasis, and unity of thought and tone.

Troilus and Cressida, I, iii, 75-137

WILLIAM SHAKESPEARE

Troy, yet upon his basis, had been down,[1]
And the great Hector's sword had lacked a master,
But for these instances.[2]
The specialty of rule [3] hath been neglected.
And look how many Grecian tents do stand *5*
Hollow upon this plain, so many hollow factions.
When that the general is not like the hive
To whom the foragers shall all repair,
What honey is expected? Degree being vizarded,[4]
The unworthiest shows as fairly in the mask. *10*

[1] *Ulysses is explaining to the Greeks that they have failed to capture Troy because their leader, Agamemnon, has lost his authority.*
[2] *Reasons.*
[3] *Discipline.*
[4] *Rank being obscured, as by a mask.*

The heavens themselves, the planets and this center,[5]
Observe degree, priority, and place,
Insisture, course, proportion, season, form,
Office and custom, in all line of order.[6]
And therefore is the glorious planet Sol *15*
In noble eminence enthroned and sphered
Amidst the other, whose medicinable eye
Corrects the ill aspécts of planets evil,[7]
And posts like the commandment of a king,
Sans check to good and bad. But when the planets *20*
In evil mixture to disorder wander,
What plagues and what portents, what mutiny,
What raging of the sea, shaking of earth,
Commotion in the winds, frights, changes, horrors,
Divert and crack, rend and deracinate,[8] *25*
The unity and married calm of states
Quite from their fixture! [9] Oh, when degree is shaked,
Which is the ladder to all high designs,
The enterprise is sick! How could communities
Degrees in schools and brotherhoods in cities, *30*
Peaceful commerce from dividable shores,
The primogenitive [10] and due of birth,
Prerogative of age, crowns, scepters, laurels,
But by degree, stand in authentic place?
Take but degree away, untune that string, *35*
And hark what discord follows! Each thing meets
In mere oppugnancy.[11] The bounded waters
Should lift their bosoms higher than the shores,
And make a sop of all this solid globe.
Strength should be lord of imbecility,[12] *40*
And the rude son should strike his father dead.
Force should be right, or rather, right and wrong,
Between whose endless jar justice resides,
Should lose their names, and so should justice too.
Then everything includes itself in power, *45*
Power into will, will into appetite,

[5] *The earth.*
[6] *According to degree of importance. "Insisture": regularity. "Office": function.*
[7] *Controls their positions, upon which their influence depended.*
[8] *Uproot.*
[9] *Established place.*
[10] *The right of the oldest son to inheritance.*
[11] *Complete opposition.*
[12] *Weakness.*

And appetite, a universal wolf,
So doubly seconded with will and power,
Must make perforce a universal prey,
And last eat up himself. Great Agamemnon, *50*
This chaos, when degree is suffocate,
Follows the choking.

1630

Questions

1. What forces, according to Ulysses, come into play when "degree" is neglected?
2. Note the examples of degree mentioned by Ulysses. What kinds of rank or authority are most important in our time?
3. Ulysses urges that hierarchical order is the law of nature. How does our conception of rightful authority differ?
4. Would people feel more secure if various kinds of authority or distinction were more closely defined? Would they be more ambitious, assuming that it was possible to rise to higher "places"? Would they be happier, on the whole?

An Essay on Man, Epistle III, 269-319

ALEXANDER POPE

So drives self-love, through just and through unjust,
To one man's power, ambition, lucre, lust: [1]
The same self-love, in all, becomes the cause
Of what restrains him, government and laws.
For, what one likes if others like as well, *5*
What serves one will, when many wills rebel?
How shall he keep, what, sleeping or awake,
A weaker may surprise, a stronger take?
His safety must his liberty restrain;
All join to guard what each desires to gain. *10*
Forced into virtue thus by self-defence,
Even kings learned justice and benevolence;
Self-love forsook the path it first pursued,
And found the private in the public good.
'Twas then the studious head or generous mind, *15*

[1] *The poet has explained that when reason is obscured by fear, self-love leads to tyranny and conflict, despite the lesson of interdependence taught by nature.*

Follower of God or friend of humankind,
Poet or patriot, rose but to restore
The faith and moral nature gave before;
Re-lumed her ancient light, not kindled new;
If not God's image, yet his shadow drew: *20*
Taught power's due use to people and to kings
Taught nor to slack, nor strain its tender strings;
The less, or greater, set so justly true,
That touching one must strike the other too;
Till jarring interests of themselves create *25*
The according music of a well-mixed state.
Such is the world's great harmony, that springs
From order, union, full consent of things;
Where small and great, where weak and mighty, made
To serve, not suffer, strengthen, not invade– *30*
More powerful each as needful to the rest,
And, in proportion as it blesses, blessed–
Draw to one point, and to one centre bring
Beast, man, or angel, servant, lord, or king.
For forms of government let fools contest; *35*
Whate'er is best administered is best:
For modes of faith let graceless zealots fight;
His can't be wrong whose life is in the right:
In faith and hope the world will disagree,
But all mankind's concern is charity: *40*
All must be false that thwart this one great end
And all of God, that bless mankind or mend.
Man, like the generous vine, supported lives;
The strength he gains is from the embrace he gives.
On their own axis as the planets run, *45*
Yet make at once their circle round the sun;
So two consistent motions act the soul,
And one regards itself, and one the whole.
Thus God and nature linked the general frame,
And bade self-love and social be the same. *50*

1733–1734

Questions

1. Pope's subject here is social love. What is his thesis? What is his argument?
2. Does Pope indicate precisely enough how social love will express itself? Do you find his definition of love adequate?

3. Consider the structure of this passage. What is the function of the paragraphing? Does each paragraph have a new idea to present? Does each paragraph have a special purpose?
4. Are there any features of Pope's style that might be effective in prose writing? Be able to point out at least one.

Stanzas from the Grande Chartreuse[1]

MATTHEW ARNOLD

Through Alpine meadows soft-suffused
With rain, where thick the crocus blows,
Past the dark forges long disused,
The mule-track from Saint Laurent goes.
The bridge is cross'd, and slow we ride, 5
Through forest, up the mountain-side.

The autumnal evening darkens round,
The wind is up, and drives the rain;
While, hark! far down, with strangled sound
Doth the Dead Guier's [2] stream complain, 10
Where that wet smoke, among the woods,
Over his boiling cauldron broods.

Swift rush the spectral vapours white
Past limestone scars with ragged pines,
Showing—then blotting from our sight!— 15
Halt—through the cloud-drift something shines!
High in the valley, wet and drear,
The huts of Courrerie appear.

Strike leftward! cries our guide; and higher
Mounts up the stony forest-way. 20
At last the encircling trees retire;
Look! through the showery twilight grey
What pointed roofs are these advance?—
A palace of the Kings of France?

Approach, for what we seek is here! 25
Alight, and sparely sup, and wait
For rest in this outbuilding near;
Then cross the sward and rach that gate.
Knock; pass the wicket! Thou art come
To the Carthusians' world-famed home. 30

[1] *The Grande Chartreuse was a monastery of the Order of the Carthusians.*
[2] *The Guiers Mort River.*

The silent courts, where night and day
Into their stone-carved basins cold
The splashing icy fountains play—
The humid corridors behold!
Where, ghostlike in the deepening night, *35*
Cowl'd forms brush by in gleaming white.

The chapel, where no organ's peal
Invests the stern and naked prayer—
With penitential cries they kneel
And wrestle; rising then, with bare *40*
And white uplifted faces stand,
Passing the Host [3] from hand to hand;

Each takes, and then his visage wan
Is buried in his cowl once more.
The cells!—the suffering Son of Man *45*
Upon the wall—the knee-worn floor—
And where they sleep, that wooden bed,
Which shall their coffin be, when dead!

The library, where tract and tome
Not to feed priestly pride are there, *50*
To hymn the conquering march of Rome,
Nor yet to amuse, as ours are!
They paint of souls the inner strife,
Their drops of blood, their death in life.

The garden, overgrown—yet mild, *55*
See, fragrant herbs are flowering there!
Strong children of the Alpine wild
Whose culture is the brethren's care;
Of human tasks their only one,
And cheerful works beneath the sun. *60*

Those halls, too, destined to contain
Each its own pilgrim-host of old,
From England, Germany, or Spain—
All are before me! I behold
The House, the Brotherhood austere! *65*
—And what am I, that I am here?

For rigorous teachers seized my youth,
And purged its faith, and trimm'd its fire,
Show'd me the high white star of Truth,
There bade me gaze, and there aspire; *70*

[3] *The consecrated bread used in the Mass.*

Even now their whispers pierce the gloom:
What dost thou in this living tomb?

Forgive me, masters of the mind!
At whose behest I long ago
So much unlearnt, so much resign'd— 75
I come not here to be your foe!
I seek these anchorites,[4] not in ruth,
To curse and to deny your truth;

Not as their friend, or child, I speak!
But as, on some far northern strand, 80
Thinking of his own Gods, a Greek
In pity and mournful awe might stand
Before some fallen Runic [5] stone—
For both were faiths, and both are gone.

Wandering between two worlds, one dead, 85
The other powerless to be born,
With nowhere yet to rest my head,
Like these, on earth I wait forlorn.
Their faith, my tears, the world deride—
I come to shed them at their side. 90

Oh, hide me in your gloom profound,
Ye solemn seats of holy pain!
Take me, cowl'd forms, and fence me round,
Till I possess my soul again;
Till free my thoughts before me roll; 95
Not chafed by hourly false control!

For the world cries your faith is now
But a dead time's exploded dream;
My melancholy, sciolists [6] vow,
Is a pass'd mode, an outworn theme— 100
As if the world had ever had
A faith, or sciolists been sad!

Ah, if it *be* pass'd, take away,
At least, the restlessness, the pain;
Be man henceforth no more a prey 105
To these out-dated stings again!
The nobleness of grief is gone—
Ah, leave us not the fret alone!

[4] *Religious hermits.*
[5] *Marked with the characters of an alphabet used by the people of Northern Europe from about the third to the thirteenth century.*
[6] *Persons of superficial learning.*

But—if you cannot give us ease
Last of the race of them who grieve *110*
Here leave us to die out with these
Last of the people who believe!
Silent, while years engrave the brow;
Silent—the best are silent now.

Achilles [7] ponders in his tent, *115*
The kings of modern thought are dumb;
Silent they are, though not content,
And wait to see the future come.
They have the grief men had of yore,
But they contend and cry no more. *120*

Our fathers water'd with their tears
This sea of time whereon we sail,
Their voices were in all men's ears
Who pass'd within their puissant hail.
Still the same ocean round us raves, *125*
But we stand mute, and watch the waves.

For what avail'd it, all the noise
And outcry of the former men?—
Say, have their sons achieved more joys,
Say, is life lighter now than then? *130*
The sufferers died, they left their pain—
The pangs which tortured them remain.

What helps it now, that Byron bore,
With haughty scorn which mock'd the smart,
Through Europe to the Ætolian shore *135*
The pageant of his bleeding heart?
That thousands counted every groan,
And Europe made his woe her own?

What boots it, Shelley! that the breeze
Carried thy lovely wail away, *140*
Musical through Italian trees
Which fringe thy soft blue Spezzian bay?
Inheritors of thy distress
Have restless hearts one throb the less?

[7] *During the Trojan wars, Achilles, angry because he had been deprived of a captive maiden, refused for a time to take part in the fight. Arnold is here referring to some intellectual leader of his time, perhaps Newman, who had retired for two years of study before becoming a member of the Roman Catholic Church.*

Or are we easier, to have read, *145*
O Obermann![8] the sad, stern page,
Which tells us how thou hidd'st thy head
From the fierce tempest of thine age
In the lone brakes of Fontainebleau,
Or chalets near the Alpine snow? *150*

Ye slumber in your silent grave!–
The world, which for an idle day
Grace to your mood of sadness gave,
Long since hath flung her weeds away.
The eternal trifler breaks your spell; *155*
But we–we learnt your lore too well!

Years hence, perhaps, may dawn an age,
More fortunate, alas! than we,
Which without hardness will be sage,
And gay without frivolity, *160*
Sons of the world, oh, speed those years;
But, while we wait, allow our tears!

Allow them! We admire with awe
The exulting thunder of your race;
You give the universe your law, *165*
You triumph over time and space!
Your pride of life, your tireless powers,
We laud them, but they are not ours.

We are like children rear'd in shade
Beneath some old-world abbey wall, *170*
Forgotten in a forest-glade,
And secret from the eyes of all.
Deep, deep the greenwood round them waves,
Their abbey, and its close of graves!

But, where the road runs near the stream, *175*
Oft through the trees they catch a glance
Of passing troops in the sun's beam–
Pennon, and plume, and flashing lance!
Forth to the world those soldiers fare,
To life, to cities, and to war! *180*

And through the wood, another way,
Faint bugle-notes from far are borne,
Where hunters gather, staghounds bay,
Round some fair forest-lodge at morn.

[8] *Obermann is the hero of a philosophical romance by Etienne Pivert de Senancour (1770–1846).*

Gay dames are there, in sylvan green; 185
Laughter and cries—those notes between!

The banners flashing through the trees
Make their blood dance and chain their eyes;
That bugle-music on the breeze
Arrests them with a charm'd surprise. 190
Banner by turns and bugle woo:
Ye shy recluses, follow too!

O children, what do ye reply?—
'Action and pleasure, will ye roam
Through these secluded dells to cry 195
And call us?—but too late ye come!
Too late for us your call ye blow,
Whose bent was taken long ago.

'Long since we pace this shadow'd nave;
We watch those yellow tapers shine, 200
Emblems of hope over the grave,
In the high altar's depth divine;
The organ carries to our ear
Its accents of another sphere.

'Fenced early in this cloistral round 205
Of reverie, of shade, of prayer,
How should we grow in other ground?
How can we flower in foreign air?
Pass, banners, pass, and bugles, cease,
And leave our desert to its peace!' 210

1855

Questions

1. The first part of this poem is mainly descriptive and is designed to prepare the reader for the reflections that follow. Where does the transition between the two parts occur? Are there elements of the description of the journey and the monastery that seem especially appropriate in view of the speaker's attitude toward the faith of the Carthusian monks?
2. What kind of religious or moral training has the speaker had? What for him is the relationship between faith and truth? What is his attitude toward faith?
3. To whom is the poet speaking in line 109? In the course of the poem the poet refers to several groups of people, each distinguished by its attitude toward the decline of religious faith: the "masters of the mind" (line 73), the people of the "world" (line 97), the sciolists (line 99), the "kings of modern thought" (line 116), "our fathers" (line 121),

the "sons of the world" (line 161), and the group which includes himself. Try to define the general outlook of each of these groups. Do they have counterparts in our own age?

4. What is the unifying element in the passage beginning with line 169 and extending to the end of the poem?
5. Sum up Arnold's assessment of his age. Who are its leaders? What is its principal achievement? What place does the poet find for himself in his world?

Crossing Brooklyn Ferry

WALT WHITMAN

1

Flood-tide below me! I see you face to face!
Clouds of the west—sun there half an hour high—I see you also face to face.

Crowds of men and women attired in the usual costumes, how curious you are to me!
On the ferry-boats the hundreds and hundreds that cross, returning home, are more curious to me than you suppose,
And you that shall cross from shore to shore years hence are more to me, and more in my meditations, than you might suppose. *5*

2

The impalpable sustenance of me from all things at all hours of the day,
The simple, compact, well-join'd scheme, myself disintegrated, every one disintegrated yet part of the scheme.
The similitudes of the past and those of the future,
The glories strung like beads on my smallest sights and hearings, on the walk in the street and the passage over the river,
The current rushing so swiftly and swimming with me far away, *10*
The others that are to follow me, the ties between me and them,
The certainty of others, the life, love, sight, hearing of others.

Others will enter the gates of the ferry and cross from shore to shore,
Others will watch the run of the flood-tide,
Others will see the shipping of Manhattan north and west, and the heights of Brooklyn to the south and east, *15*
Others will see the islands large and small;
Fifty years hence, others will see them as they cross, the sun half an hour high,

A hundred years hence, or ever so many hundred years hence, others will see them,
Will enjoy the sunset, the pouring-in of the flood-tide, the falling-back to the sea of the ebb-tide.

3

It avails not, time nor place—distance avails not, *20*
I am with you, you men and women of a generation, or ever so many generations hence,
Just as you feel when you look on the river and sky, so I felt,
Just as any of you is one of a living crowd, I was one of a crowd,
Just as you are refresh'd by the gladness of the river and the bright flow, I was refresh'd,
Just as you stand and lean on the rail, yet hurry with the swift current, I stood yet was hurried, *25*
Just as you look on the numberless masts of ships and the thick-stemm'd pipes of steamboats, I look'd.

I too many and many a time cross'd the river of old,
Watched the Twelfth-month sea-gulls, saw them high in the air floating with motionless wings, oscillating their bodies,
Saw how the glistening yellow lit up parts of their bodies and left the rest in strong shadow,
Saw the slow-wheeling circles and the gradual edging toward the south, *30*
Saw the reflection of the summer sky in the water,
Had my eyes dazzled by the shimmering track of beams,
Look'd at the fine centrifugal spokes of light round the shape of my head in the sunlit water,
Look'd on the haze on the hills southward and south-westward,
Look'd on the vapor as it flew in fleeces tinged with violet, *35*
Look'd toward the lower bay to notice the vessels arriving,
Saw their approach, saw aboard those that were near me,
Saw the white sails of schooners and sloops, saw the ships at anchor,
The sailors at work in the rigging or out astride the spars,
The round masts, the swinging motion of the hulls, the slender serpentine pennants, *40*
The large and small steamers in motion, the pilots in their pilot-houses,
The white wake left by the passage, the quick tremulous whirl of the wheels,
The flags of all nations, the falling of them at sunset,
The scallop-edged waves in the twilight, the ladled cups, the frolicsome crests and glistening,
The stretch afar growing dimmer and dimmer, the gray walls of the granite storehouses by the docks,

On the river the shadowy group, the big steam-tug closely flank'd on each side by the barges, the hay-boat, the belated lighter,
On the neighboring shore the fires from the foundry chimneys burning high and glaringly into the night,
Casting their flicker of black contrasted with wild red and yellow light over the tops of houses and down into the clefts of streets.

4

These and all else were to me the same as they are to you,
I loved well those cities, loved well the stately and rapid river, *50*
The men and women I saw were all near to me,
Others the same—others who look back on me because I look'd forward to them,
(The time will come, though I stop here to-day and to-night.)

5

What is it then between us?
What is the count of the scores or hundreds of years between us? *55*
Whatever it is, it avails not—distance avails not, and place avails not,
I too lived, Brooklyn of ample hills was mine,
I too walk'd the streets of Manhattan island, and bathed in the waters around it,
I too felt the curious abrupt questionings stir within me,
In the day among crowds of people sometimes they came upon me, *60*
In my walks home late at night or as I lay in my bed they came upon me,
I too had been struck from the float [1] forever held in solution,
I too had receiv'd identity by my body,
That I was I knew was of my body, and what I should be I knew I should be of my body.

6

It is not upon you alone the dark patches fall, *65*
The dark threw its patches down upon me also,
The best I had done seem'd to me blank and suspicious,
My great thoughts as I supposed them, were they not in reality meagre?
Nor is it you alone who know what it is to be evil,
I am he who knew what it was to be evil, *70*
I too knitted the old knot of contrariety,
Blabb'd, blush'd, resented, lied, stole, grudg'd,
Had guile, anger, lust, hot wishes I dared not speak,
Was wayward, vain, greedy, shallow, sly, cowardly, malignant,

[1] *Dissolved substance.*

The wolf, the snake, the hog, not wanting in me, *75*
The cheating look, the frivolous word, the adulterous wish, not wanting,
Refusals, hates, postponements, meanness, laziness, none of these wanting,
Was one with the rest, the days and haps [2] of the rest,
Was call'd my nighest name by clear loud voices of young men as they saw me approaching or passing,
Felt their arms on my neck as I stood, or the negligent leaning of their flesh against me as I sat, *80*
Saw many I loved in the street or ferry-boat or public assembly, yet never told them a word,
Lived the same life with the rest, the same old laughing, gnawing, sleeping,
Play'd the part that still looks back on the actor or actress,
The same old role, the role that is what we make it, as great as we like,
Or as small as we like, or both great and small. *85*

7

Closer yet I approach you,
What thought you have of me now, I had as much of you—I laid in my stores in advance,
I consider'd long and seriously of you before you were born.
Who was to know what should come home to me?
Who knows but I am enjoying this? *90*
Who knows, for all the distance, but I am as good as looking at you now, for all you cannot see me?

8

Ah, what can ever be more stately and admirable to me than mast-hemm'd Manhattan?
River and sunset and scallop-edg'd waves of flood-tide?
The sea-gulls oscillating their bodies, the hay-boat in the twilight, and the belated lighter?

What gods can exceed these that clasp me by the hand, and with voices I love call me promptly and loudly by my nighest name as I approach? *95*

What is more subtle than this which ties me to the woman or man that looks in my face?
Which fuses me into you now, and pours my meaning into you?

We understand then do we not?
What I promis'd without mentioning it, have you not accepted?
What the study could not teach—what the preaching could not accomplish is accomplish'd, is it not? *100*

[2] *Happenings.*

9

Flow on, river! flow with the flood-tide, and ebb with the ebb-tide!
Frolic on, crested and scallop-edg'd waves!
Gorgeous clouds of the sunset! drench with your splendor me, or the men and women generations after me!
Cross from shore to shore, countless crowds of passengers!
Stand up, tall masts of Mannahatta! stand up, beautiful hills of Brooklyn!
Throb, baffled and curious brain! throw out questions and answers!
Suspend here and everywhere, eternal float of solution!
Gaze, loving and thirsting eyes, in the house or street or public assembly!
Sound out, voices of young men! loudly and musically call me by my nighest name!
Live, old life! play the part that looks back on the actor or actress! *110*
Play the old role, the role that is great or small according as one makes it!
Consider, you who peruse me, whether I may not in unknown ways be looking upon you;
Be firm, rail over the river, to support those who lean idly, yet haste with the hasting current;
Fly on, sea-birds! fly sideways, or wheel in large circles high in the air;
Receive the summer sky, you water, and faithfully hold it till all downcast eyes have time to take it from you! *115*
Diverge, fine spokes of light, from the shape of my head, or any one's head, in the sunlit water!
Come on, ships from the lower bay! pass up or down, white-sail'd schooners, sloops, lighters!
Flaunt away, flags of all nations! be duly lower'd at sunset!
Burn high your fires, foundry chimneys! cast black shadows at nightfall! cast red and yellow light over the tops of the houses!
Appearances, now or henceforth, indicate what you are, *120*
You necessary film, continue to envelop the soul,
About my body for me, and your body for you, be hung our divinest aromas,
Thrive, cities—bring your freight, bring your shows, ample and sufficient rivers,
Expand, being than which none else is perhaps more spiritual,
Keep your places, objects than which none else is more lasting. *125*

You have waited, you always wait, you dumb, beautiful ministers,
We receive you with free sense at last, and are insatiate henceforward,
Not you any more shall be able to foil us, or withhold yourselves from us,
We use you,—and do not cast you aside—we plant you permanently within us,
We fathom you not—we love you—there is perfection in you also, *130*
You furnish your parts toward eternity,
Great or small, you furnish your parts toward the soul.

1856–1881

Questions

1. To whom is the poet speaking?
2. What are the bonds that unite the speaker to other people?
3. What are the two principal metaphors used to describe individual existence? What do they mean? How are they related?
4. What is the speaker's view of the relation between the human spirit and the things of nature?
5. Why does the poet use so much repetition in the last part of the poem?

The Death of the Hired Man

ROBERT FROST

Mary sat musing on the lamp-flame at the table
Waiting for Warren. When she heard his step,
She ran on tip-toe down the darkened passage
To meet him in the doorway with the news
And put him on his guard. "Silas is back." 5
She pushed him outward with her through the door
And shut it after her. "Be kind," she said.
She took the market things from Warren's arms
And set them on the porch, then drew him down
To sit beside her on the wooden steps. 10

"When was I ever anything but kind to him?
But I'll not have the fellow back," he said.
"I told him so last haying, didn't I?
'If he left then,' I said, 'that ended it.'
What good is he? Who else will harbor him 15
At his age for the little he can do?
What help he is there's no depending on.
Off he goes always when I need him most.
'He thinks he ought to earn a little pay,
Enough at least to buy tobacco with, 20
So he won't have to beg and be beholden.'
'All right,' I say, 'I can't afford to pay
Any fixed wages, though I wish I could.'
'Someone else can.' 'Then someone else will have to.'
I shouldn't mind his bettering himself 25
If that was what it was. You can be certain,
When he begins like that, there's someone at him
Trying to coax him off with pocket-money,—
In haying time, when any help is scarce.
In winter he comes back to us. I'm done." 30

"Sh! not so loud: he'll hear you," Mary said.

"I want him to: he'll have to soon or late."

"He's worn out. He's asleep beside the stove.
When I came up from Rowe's I found him here,
Huddled against the barn-door fast asleep, 35
A miserable sight, and frightening, too—
You needn't smile—I didn't recognize him—
I wasn't looking for him—and he's changed.
Wait till you see."

"Where did you say he'd been?"

"He didn't say. I dragged him to the house, 40
And gave him tea and tried to make him smoke.
I tried to make him talk about his travels.
Nothing would do: he just kept nodding off."

"What did he say? Did he say anything?"

"But little." 45

"Anything? Mary, confess
He said he'd come to ditch the meadow for me."

"Warren!"

"But did he? I just want to know."

"Of course he did. What would you have him say? 50
Surely you wouldn't grudge the poor old man
Some humble way to save his self-respect.
He added, if you really care to know,
He meant to clear the upper pasture, too.
That sounds like something you have heard before? 55
Warren, I wish you could have heard the way
He jumbled everything. I stopped to look
Two or three times—he made me feel so queer—
To see if he was talking in his sleep.
He ran on Harold Wilson—you remember— 60
The boy you had in haying four years since.
He's finished school, and teaching in his college.
Silas declares you'll have to get him back.
He says they two will make a team for work:
Between them they will lay this farm as smooth! 65
The way he mixed that in with other things.
He thinks young Wilson a likely lad, though daft
On education—you know how they fought
All through July under the blazing sun,

Silas up on the cart to build the load, *70*
Harold along beside to pitch it on."

"Yes, I took care to keep well out of earshot."

"Well, those days trouble Silas like a dream.
You wouldn't think they would. How some things linger!
Harold's young college boy's assurance piqued him. *75*
After so many years he still keeps finding
Good arguments he sees he might have used.
I sympathize. I know just how it feels
To think of the right thing to say too late.
Harold's associated in his mind with Latin. *80*
He asked me what I thought of Harold's saying
He studied Latin like the violin
Because he liked it—that an argument!
He said he couldn't make the boy believe
He could find water with a hazel prong— *85*
Which showed how much good school had ever done him.
He wanted to go over that. But most of all
He thinks if he could have another chance
To teach him how to build a load of hay—"

"I know, that's Silas' one accomplishment. *90*
He bundles every forkful in its place,
And tags and numbers it for future reference,
So he can find and easily dislodge it
In the unloading. Silas does that well.
He takes it out in bunches like big birds' nests. *95*
You never see him standing on the hay
He's trying to lift, straining to lift himself."

"He thinks if he could teach him that, he'd be
Some good perhaps to someone in the world.
He hates to see a boy the fool of books. *100*
Poor Silas, so concerned for other folk,
And nothing to look backward to with pride,
And nothing to look forward to with hope,
So now and never any different."

Part of a moon was falling down the west, *105*
Dragging the whole sky with it to the hills.
Its light poured softly in her lap. She saw it
And spread her apron to it. She put out her hand
Among the harp-like morning-glory strings,
Taut with the dew from garden bed to eaves, *110*
As if she played unheard some tenderness
That wrought on him beside her in the night.

"Warren," she said, "he has come home to die:
You needn't be afraid he'll leave you this time."

"Home," he mocked gently. *115*

"Yes, what else but home?
It all depends on what you mean by home.
Of course he's nothing to us, any more
Than was the hound that came a stranger to us
Out of the woods, worn out upon the trail." *120*

"Home is the place where, when you have to go there,
They have to take you in."

"I should have called it
Something you somehow haven't to deserve."

Warren leaned out and took a step or two, *125*
Picked up a little stick, and brought it back
And broke it in his hand and tossed it by.
"Silas has better claim on us you think
Than on his brother? Thirteen little miles
As the road winds would bring him to his door. *130*
Silas has walked that far no doubt today.
Why doesn't he go there? His brother's rich,
A somebody—director in the bank."

"He never told us that."

"We know it though." *135*
"I think his brother ought to help, of course.
I'll see to that if there is need. He ought of right
To take him in, and might be willing to—
He may be better than appearances.
But have some pity on Silas. Do you think *140*
If he had any pride in claiming kin
Or anything he looked for from his brother,
He'd keep so still about him all this time?"

"I wonder what's between them."

"I can tell you. *145*
Silas is what he is—we wouldn't mind him—
But just the kind that kinsfolk can't abide.
He never did a thing so very bad.
He don't know why he isn't quite as good
As anybody. Worthless though he is, *150*
He won't be made ashamed to please his brother."

"I can't think Si ever hurt anyone."

"No, but he hurt my heart the way he lay
And rolled his old head on that sharp-edged chairback.
He wouldn't let me put him on the lounge. *155*
You must go in and see what you can do.
I made the bed up for him there tonight.
You'll be surprised at him—how much he's broken.
His working days are done; I'm sure of it."

"I'd not be in a hurry to say that." *160*

"I haven't been. Go, look, see for yourself.
But, Warren, please remember how it is:
He's come to help you ditch the meadow.
He has a plan. You mustn't laugh at him.
He may not speak of it, and then he may. *165*
I'll sit and see if that small sailing cloud
Will hit or miss the moon."

It hit the moon.
Then there were three there, making a dim row,
The moon, the little silver cloud, and she. *170*

Warren returned—too soon, it seemed to her,
Slipped to her side, caught up her hand and waited.

"Warren?" she questioned.

"Dead," was all he answered.

1905

Questions

1. Would you say that Silas is a man who has failed to find a place for himself in society? What is his view of the matter? Why does he "run on" about Harold Wilson?
2. What is Warren's view of the relation between the individual and society? To what extent does Mary disagree with him?
3. What is the significance of lines 105-112? Do they have anything to do with social harmony?
4. Does Mary prevail over Warren? How do we know?

Miniver Cheevy

E. A. ROBINSON

Miniver Cheevy, child of scorn,
  Grew lean while he assailed the seasons;
He wept that he was ever born,
  And he had reasons.
Miniver loved the days of old   5
  When swords were bright and steeds were prancing;
The vision of a warrior bold
  Would set him dancing.

Miniver sighed for what was not,
  And dreamed, and rested from his labors;   10
He dreamed of Thebes [1] and Camelot,[2]
  And Priam's [3] neighbors.

Miniver mourned the ripe renown
  That made so many a name so fragrant;
He mourned Romance, now on the town,   15
  And Art, a vagrant.

Miniver loved the Medici,[4]
  Albeit he had never seen one;
He would have sinned incessantly
  Could he have been one.   20

Miniver cursed the commonplace
  And eyed a khaki suit with loathing:
He missed the mediaeval grace
  Of iron clothing.

Miniver scorned the gold he sought,   25
  But sore annoyed was he without it;
Miniver thought, and thought, and thought
  And thought about it.

Miniver Cheevy, born too late,
  Scratched his head and kept on thinking;   30
Miniver coughed, and called it fate,
  And kept on drinking.

1908

[1] *Famous Greek city, the scene of many legendary heroic adventures.*
[2] *The fabulous capital of King Arthur's realm.*
[3] *The king of Troy during the Trojan war.*
[4] *A powerful family in Florence during the Renaissance, noted both for their magnificence and haughty disregard of ordinary moral standards.*

Questions

1. Why does Miniver Cheevy feel that he was born too late? What is his conception of himself?
2. Is Miniver's analysis of his problem correct? Is his temperament wrong for his time? Try to find clues to the poet's view of the matter.
3. What does the diction of the poem reveal about the author's attitude toward Miniver's ambitions? What, for example, is the effect of the phrase "iron clothing"?

Mr. Flood's Party

E. A. ROBINSON

Old Eben Flood, climbing alone one night
Over the hill between the town below
And the forsaken upland hermitage
That held as much as he should ever know
On earth again of home, paused warily. *5*
The road was his with not a native near;
And Eben, having leisure, said aloud,
For no man else in Tilbury Town to hear:

"Well, Mr. Flood, we have the harvest moon
Again, and we may not have many more; *10*
The bird is on the wing, the poet says,[1]
And you and I have said it here before.
Drink to the bird." He raised up to the light
The jug that he had gone so far to fill,
And answered huskily: "Well, Mr. Flood, *15*
Since you propose it, I believe I will."

Alone, as if enduring to the end
A valiant armor of scarred hopes outworn,
He stood there in the middle of the road
Like Roland's ghost [2] winding a silent horn. *20*
Below him, in the town among the trees,
Where friends of other days had honored him,
A phantom salutation of the dead
Rang thinly till old Eben's eyes were dim.

[1] *See the* Rubaiyat of Omar Khayyam, *lines 27–28.*

[2] *Roland is a famous knight of medieval romance. He was ambushed at the pass of Roncevalles and slain after a fierce battle. Not until his forces were almost defeated did he sound his horn to summon Charlemagne and his army to his aid.*

Then, as a mother lays her sleeping child 25
Down tenderly, fearing it may awake,
He set the jug down slowly at his feet
With trembling care, knowing that most things break;
And only when assured that on firm earth
It stood, as the uncertain lives of men 30
Assuredly did not, he paced away,
And with his hand extended paused again:
"Well, Mr. Flood, we have not met like this
In a long time; and many a change has come
To both of us, I fear, since last it was 35
We had a drop together. Welcome home!"
Convivially returning with himself,
Again he raised the jug up to the light;
And with an acquiescent quaver said:
"Well, Mr. Flood, if you insist, I might. 40

"Only a very little, Mr. Flood—
For auld lang syne. No more, sir; that will do."
So, for the time, apparently it did,
And Eben evidently thought so too;
For soon amid the silver loneliness 45
Of night he lifted up his voice and sang,
Secure, with only two moons listening,
Until the whole harmonious landscape rang—

"For auld lang syne." The weary throat gave out,
The last word wavered, and the song was done. 50
He raised again the jug regretfully
And shook his head, and was again alone.
There was not much that was ahead of him,
And there was nothing in the town below—
Where strangers would have shut the many doors 55
That many friends had opened long ago.

1921

Questions

1. What is the poet's attitude toward Mr. Flood? In this connection, what is the effect of lines 16–24?
2. Is this poem more than a character study? What is the fundamental cause of Mr. Flood's loneliness? Is there any solution to the problem raised by the poem?

3. Why does Mr. Flood see two moons? What is the emotional effect of this detail?

Cold-Water Flat

PHILIP BOOTH

Come to conquer
this living labyrinth of rock,
young Theseus [1] of Dubuque
finds he is mazed without a minotaur,
without his Ariadne in the dark. 5

He dreams beyond
his steelwalled fear to fields grown
vertical with corn
and hope. Home to this heroic end:
imprisoned in the city of alone; *10*

here smog obscures
his visionary victor's world
and street sounds dulled
with rain reverberate in airshaft hours
where braver conquerors have been felled. *15*

[1] *The poet alludes repeatedly to the following mythic story of the encounter between the Athenian hero Theseus and a monster called the Minotaur. Minos, the ruler of Crete, whose son had perished in an expedition undertaken while he, as a guest of Aegeus, King of Athens, had conquered Athens and demanded that a tribute of seven Athenian maids and seven youths be sent to him every nine years. When the young people reached Crete, they were placed in an inescapable labyrinth, built by the great inventor Daedalus, there to be devoured by the fabulous Minotaur, who was half human, half bull. When he was old enough, Theseus, who was the son of Aegeus, volunteered to be one of the victims, intending to slay the Minotaur by one means or another. By good fortune, Ariadne, the daughter of Minos, saw Theseus when he and the others were paraded toward the labyrinth, and fell in love with him. She sent for him and promised that she would help him escape from the labyrinth if he would promise to take her to Athens and marry her. Upon his readily agreeing, she gave him a device which she had procured from Daedalus himself, a ball of thread. As he was instructed, Theseus fastened one end of the thread by the inside of the door and unwound the ball as he went boldly into the maze to seek out the Minotaur. He found the monster asleep, fell upon him, and battered him to death with his fists. Then he retraced his steps with the aid of the thread, the other intended victims following him. Once outside, they fled quickly to their ship, taking Ariadne with them, and set sail for Athens.*

Amazed at night,
stalking the seven maids no sword
can save, he is devoured
in passageways of reinforced concrete,
trapped by his beast, and overpowered 20

in sleepless dead-
end dreams. How now, Theseus? How send
word home you are confined
with neither wings nor lover's thread
in the city that a murderer designed? 25

1955

Questions

1. Reconstruct the story upon which this poem is based. Who is "young Theseus of Dubuque"? Why did he leave Dubuque? What has happened to him?
2. What is the general purpose of the comparison between the young man from Dubuque and Theseus? Do any of the details of that comparison have a special significance?

A Bird in Search of a Cage

ROBERT PACK

Said the bird in search of a cage,
This world is even large for wings,
The mindless seasons drive me down
Tormenting me with changing things.

A cage is not escape, but need, 5
And though once in all travel's done,
I'll sing so every bird will know
My wanderings in moon and sun,

And all the crickets will be stilled,
And stilled the summer air and grass, 10
And hushed the secrets of the wind,
For when my final callings pass.

And if a friend should stop to talk,
Reminding me of what is past,
And ask the meaning of my song, *15*
I'd say that only cages last.

1955

Questions

1. This poem, obviously, has something to say about freedom, and it is not, of course, about the nature of birds. What kind of freedom is the poet talking about? What does the cage stand for? Is the poem an allegory?
2. Is there any irony in this poem?
3. What does this poem say about the problem of finding a place in the scheme of things?

A Projection

REED WHITTEMORE

I wish they would hurry up their trip to Mars,
Those rocket gentlemen.
We have been waiting too long; the fictions of little men
And canals,
And of planting and raising flags and opening markets *5*
For beads, cheap watches, perfume and plastic jewelry–
All these begin to be tedious; what we need now
Is the real thing, a thoroughly bang-up voyage
Of discovery.

Led by Admiral Byrd *10*
In the Nina, Pinta and Santa Maria
With a crew of one hundred experts
In physics, geology, war and creative writing,
The expedition should sail with a five-year supply of
Pemmican, Jello, Moxie, *15*
Warm woolen socks and jars of Gramma's preserves.

Think of them out there,
An ocean of space before them, using no compass,
Guiding themselves by speculative equations,
Looking, *20*

Looking into the night and thinking now
There are no days, no seasons, time
Is only on watches,
and landing on Venus
Through some slight error,
Bearing *25*

Proclamations of friendship,
Declarations of interstellar faith,
Acknowledgements of American supremacy,
And advertising matter.
I wonder,
Out in the pitch of space, having worlds enough, *30*
If the walled-up, balled-up self could from its alley
Sally.
I wish they would make provisions for this,
Those rocket gentlemen.

1955

Questions

1. Is this poem a satire on the exploration of space?
2. Does the author indicate why the modern self is in a "walled-up" and "balled-up" state?
3. What is the author's general attitude toward his subject? Is he angry? Bitter? Amused? Is he serious? How can we tell?

Journey through the Night

JOHN HOLLOWAY

At the first hour from dawn
The traveller in the window seat
Rubbed his eyes, woke from a daze,
Brushed his rough hair back with great
Pudgy fingers, gave a yawn, *5*
Cleared the pane's white dewy haze,
Then stared so eagerly, it might
Have been his home place come in sight.

But at the second hour from dawn
The traveller in the window seat
Suddenly turned away from the world

As though he saw some thing too sweet
Or too bitter to be borne;
And when he met my glance, he curled
His body to the wall, and wept *15*
I thought; but it may be he slept.

At the third hour from dawn
The ticket man rolled back the door:
The traveller blurted out that he
Wanted another ticket for *20*
Some other place, somewhere further on;
He spoke shortly, confusedly;
But I saw he did not know,
Now, where in the world to go.

1956

Questions

1. Is "the traveller" really returning to his home place?
2. What might the traveler see that would be too sweet or too bitter to be borne? Could the same thing be both?
3. The first line of each stanza indicates clearly that it is daytime. Why, then, is the poem called "Journey through the Night"?
4. Is this a symbolic journey?

TOPICS FOR COMPOSITION

1. Is Pope's conception of social love adequate to explain all social conduct and feeling? If you think so, write an essay of five or six hundred words defending the thesis that self-love and social love are the same. Use Pope's ideas if you wish, but try to draw upon your own knowledge and experience for illustration. If you disagree with Pope, write an essay explaining why. Other poems in this section may provide material for your argument.
2. Do you think that some young people today feel, like the speaker in "Stanzas from the Grande Chartreuse," that they were born too late or too soon? If so, write an essay entitled "Between Two Worlds." If you are unsympathetic toward this feeling, you might wish to make use of Robinson's "Miniver Cheevy."
3. Write a short essay comparing Walt Whitman's response to life in a large city with that of Philip Booth. Limit your comparison so that you will have only two or three points to make. You might approach the matter by regarding "Cold-Water Flat" as an answer to Whitman, who, after all, addresses himself to people of the future—or simply

by explaining why you are more inclined to agree with one of the poets than the other. If you would like to engage in further analysis, concentrate on the basic reason or reasons for the differences in attitude. You might even wish to dwell on the significance of certain differences in the use of imagery.

4. "Miniver Cheevy" and "Cold-Water Flat" both have to do with the decline of heroism. Have we lost faith in the possibility of heroic living, outside of rather special circumstances such as a war temporarily provides? Think carefully about both of these poems as you consider the question. Write an essay on some point or points that might be raised in a discussion of the matter. For example, you might address yourself to the question, "Are our modern heroes authentic?" and give a tentative answer by examining a typical kind of hero-worship.
5. Miniver Cheevy and Mr. Flood both drink and dream of the past. What are the most important differences between them? Reply in an essay. Be sure to illustrate your statements.
6. Use "Miniver Cheevy" and "Mr. Flood's Party" as the basis for an essay on E. A. Robinson's view of the problem of individual isolation.
7. Use either Warren's or Mary's definition of home ("The Death of the Hired Man," lines 121–122) as the thesis sentence for an essay. If you prefer, write an essay explaining what Warren means and why Mary disagrees with him.
8. Do the ideas expressed in Pope's "An Essay on Man" have any applicability to the problem posed in "The Death of the Hired Man"? Explain your view in an essay.
9. Use a brief commentary on John Holloway's "Journey Through the Night" as a starting point for an essay in which you proceed to elaborate on one or more of the ideas expressed in Reed Whittemore's "A Projection."
10. Drawing upon an interpretation of Robert Pack's "A Bird in Search of a Cage," write an essay on the thesis that "a cage is not escape, but need."

PART TWO

The Protest Against Restraint

When we approach the problem of protest, we recognize that our problem is neither new nor unique; for, certainly, our world is one where protest is constantly with us. Moreover, man's need to protest the restraint that society places on his individuality takes many forms. The protest may be private, concerned only with an issue one man considers vital to his individuality, remaining hidden from all but the most perceptive observer. Or the protest may be public, concerned with a social or political alignment, involving a kindred segment of mankind and, of course, the public view. The following selections, the products of various times and places, show some of the different ways in which man has responded to threats against his individuality.

Since we live during a time when the question of civil rights is a major issue, we would be hard pressed to find a better introductory selection than Henry David Thoreau's "Civil Disobedience." Thoreau's major point, that a good citizen, when oppressed by a bad law, has a duty to break that law, has become the guiding principle of today's civil protests. But equally important to Thoreau's philosophy is the fact that the citizen's protest must remain passive: nowhere in his essay does Thoreau advocate violent overthrow of existing authority. Thoreau's view, radical during his time, is now considered by some as restraining for its insistence on nonviolence. William Faulkner's "Letter to the North" and James Baldwin's "Faulkner and Desegregation" provide a contemporary view of the current civil rights conflict. On the one hand, Faulkner speaks out for restraint, stating that time and the Southern conscience will bring about an end to inequality. On the other hand, James Baldwin, noted Negro essayist and spokesman for his race in the civil rights controversy, says that the time for restraint has passed, pointing to almost two hundred years of stagnation alleviated only by the pressure of protest.

In "A Rose for Emily" William Faulkner takes a different turn within the theme of protest. Here, we encounter a private protest in which Emily simply does not acknowledge a world that has progressed beyond a certain time in her life. Since her world remains the past, she naturally rejects any impingement upon her rights by members of a world she refuses to acknowledge. Rejecting the passage of time, she builds a protest of monstrous horror. "The Conversion of the Jews," by Philip Roth, also concerns an individual protest, by a young Jewish boy, against not only the dogma of his religion, but the insistence by the older generation that he accept the dogma without question. Ozzie's real protest then, as Roth states in the story, is that "what he wanted to know was different."

The Essay

ALTHOUGH this essay is probably longer and more involved than those you will write, we can use its length to advantage to illustrate techniques that are common to effective persuasive writing. As you read, notice the abundant variety of support that Thoreau provides. In particular, observe how he supports his controlling techniques of personal observation, personal experience, and appeal to authority with methods of analogy; cause-to-effect relationship; comparison and contrast; narration; definition; description.

Civil Disobedience

HENRY DAVID THOREAU

I heartily accept the motto,—"That government is best which governs least;" and I should like to see it acted up to more rapidly and systematically. Carried out, it finally amounts to this, which also I believe,—"That government is best which governs not at all;" and when men are prepared for it, that will be the kind of government which they will have. Government is at best but an expedient; but most governments are usually, and all governments are sometimes, inexpedient. The objections which have been brought against a standing army, and they are many and weighty, and deserve to prevail, may also at last be brought against a standing government. The standing army is only an arm of the standing government. The government itself, which is only the mode which the people have chosen to execute their will, is equally liable to be abused and perverted before the people can act through it. Witness the present Mexican war, the work of comparatively a few individuals using the standing government as their tool; for, in the outset, the people would not have consented to this measure.

This American government,—what is it but a tradition, though a recent one, endeavoring to transmit itself unimpaired to posterity, but each instant losing some of its integrity? It has not the vitality and force of a single living man; for a single man can bend it to his will. It is a sort of wooden gun to the people themselves. But it is not the less necessary for this; for the people must have some complicated machinery or other, and hear its din, to satisfy that idea of government which they have. Governments show thus how successfully men can be imposed on, even impose on themselves, for their own advantage. It is excellent, we must all allow. Yet this government never of itself furthered any enterprise, but by the alacrity with which it got out of its way. *It* does not keep the country free. *It* does not settle the West. *It* does not educate. The character inherent in the American people has done all that has been accomplished; it would have done somewhat more, if the government had not sometimes got in its way. For government is an expedient by which men would fain succeed in letting one another alone; and, as has been said, when it is most expedient, the governed are most let alone by it. Trade and commerce, if they were not made of India-rubber, would never manage to bounce over the obstacles which legislators are continually putting in their way; and, if one were to judge these men wholly by the effects of their actions and not partly by their intentions, they would deserve to be classed and punished with those mischievous persons who put obstructions on the railroads.

But, to speak practically and as a citizen, unlike those who call themselves no-government men, I ask for, not at once no government, but *at once* a better government. Let every man make known what kind of government would command his respect, and that will be one step toward obtaining it.

After all, the practical reason why, when the power is once in the hands of the people, a majority are permitted, and for a long period continue, to rule is not because they are most likely to be in the right, nor because this seems fairest to the minority, but because they are physically the strongest. But a government in which the majority rule in all cases cannot be based on justice, even as far as men understand it. Can there be a government in which majorities do not virtually decide right and wrong, but conscience?—in which majorities decide only those questions to which the rule of expediency is applicable? Must the citizen ever for a moment, or in the least degree, resign his conscience to the legislator? Why has every man a conscience, then? I think that we should be men first, and subjects afterward. It is not desirable to cultivate a respect for the law, so much as for the right. The only obligation which I have a right to assume is to do at any time what I think right. It is truly enough said, that a corporation has no conscience; but a corporation of conscientious men is a corporation *with* a conscience. Law never made men a whit more just; and, by means of their respect for it, even the well-disposed are daily made the agents of injustice. A common and natural result of an undue respect for law is, that you may see a file of soldiers, colonel, captain, corporal, privates, powder-monkeys, and all, marching in admirable order over hill and dale to the wars, against their wills, ay, against their common sense and consciences, which makes it very steep marching indeed, and produces a palpitation of the heart. They have no doubt that it is a damnable business in which they are concerned; they are all peaceably inclined. Now, what are they? Men at all? or small movable forts and magazines, at the service of some unscrupulous man in power? Visit the Navy-Yard, and behold a marine, such a man as an American government can make, or such as it can make a man with its black arts,—a mere shadow and reminiscence of humanity, a man laid out alive and standing, and already, as one may say, buried under arms with funeral accompaniments, though it may be,—

> "Not a drum was heard, not a funeral note,
> As his corse to the rampart we hurried;
> Not a soldier discharged his farewell shot
> O'er the grave where our hero we buried."

The mass of men serve the state thus, not as men mainly, but as machines, with their bodies. They are the standing army, and the militia, jailers, constables, posse comitatus, etc. In most cases there is no free exercise whatever of the judgment or of the moral sense; but they put themselves on a level with wood and earth and stones; and wooden men can perhaps be manufactured that will serve the purpose as well. Such command no more respect than men of straw or a lump of dirt. They have the same sort of worth only as horses and dogs. Yet such as these even are commonly esteemed good citizens. Others—as most legislators, politicians, lawyers, ministers, and office-holders—serve the state chiefly with their heads; and, as they rarely make any moral distinctions, they are as likely to serve the Devil, without *intending* it, as God. A very few, as heroes, patriots, martyrs, reformers in the great sense, and *men*, serve the state with their consciences also, and so necessarily resist it for the most part; and they are commonly treated as enemies by it. A wise man will only be useful as a man, and will not submit to be "clay," and "stop a hole to keep the wind away," but leave that office to his dust at least:—

> "I am too high-born to be propertied,
> To be a secondary at control,
> Or useful serving-man and instrument
> To any sovereign state throughout the world."

He who gives himself entirely to his fellowmen appears to them useless and selfish; but he who gives himself partially to them is pronounced a benefactor and philanthropist.

How does it become a man to behave toward this American government to-day? I answer, that he cannot without disgrace be associated with it. I cannot for an instant recognize that political organization as *my* government which is the *slave's* government also.

All men recognize the right of revolution; that is, the right to refuse allegiance to, and to resist, the government, when its tyranny or its inefficiency are great and unendurable. But almost all say that such is not the case now. But such was the case, they think, in the Revolution of '75. If one were to tell me that this was a bad government because it taxed certain foreign commodities brought to its ports, it is most probable that I should not make an ado about it, for I can do without them. All machines have their friction; and possibly this does enough good to counterbalance the evil. At any rate, it is a great evil to make a stir about it. But when the friction comes to have its machine, and oppression and robbery are organized, I say, let us not have such a machine any longer. In other words, when a sixth of the population of a nation which has undertaken to be the refuge of liberty are slaves, and a whole country is unjustly overrun and conquered by a foreign army, and subjected to military law, I think that it is not too soon for honest men to rebel and revolutionize. What makes this duty the more urgent is the fact that the country so overrun is not our own, but ours is the invading army. . . .

> "A drab of state, a cloth-o'-silver slut,
> To have her train borne up, and her soul trail in the dirt."

Practically speaking, the opponents to a reform in Massachusetts are not a hundred thousand politicians at the South, but a hundred thousand merchants and farmers here, who are more interested in commerce and agriculture than they are in humanity, and are not prepared to do justice to the slave and to Mexico, *cost what it may*. I quarrel not with far-off foes, but with those who, near at home, coöperate with, and do the bidding of, those far away, and without whom the latter would be harmless. We are accustomed to say, that the mass of men are unprepared; but improvement is slow, because the few are not materially wiser or better than the many. It is not so important that many should be as good as you, as that there be some absolute goodness somewhere; for that will leaven the whole lump.

There are thousands who are *in opinion* opposed to slavery and to the war, who yet in effect do nothing to put an end to them; who, esteeming themselves children of Washington and Franklin, sit down with their hands in their pockets, and say that they know not what to do, and do nothing; who even postpone the question of freedom to the question of free-trade, and quietly read the prices-current along with the latest advices from Mexico, after dinner, and, it may be, fall asleep over them both. What is the price-current of an honest man and patriot to-day? They hesitate, and they regret, and sometimes they petition; but they do nothing in earnest and with effect. They will wait, well disposed, for others to remedy the evil, that they may no longer have it to regret. At most, they give only a cheap vote, and a feeble countenance and God-speed, to the right, as it goes by them. There are nine hundred and ninety-nine patrons of virtue to one virtuous man. But it is easier to deal with the real possessor of a thing than with the temporary guardian of it.

All voting is a sort of gaming, like checkers or backgammon, with a slight moral tinge to it, a playing with right and wrong, with moral questions; and betting naturally accompanies it. The character of the voters is not staked. I cast my vote, perchance, as I think right; but I am not vitally concerned that that right should prevail. I am willing to leave it to the majority. Its obligation, therefore, never exceeds that of expediency. Even voting *for the right* is *doing* nothing for it. It is only expressing to men feebly your desire that it should prevail. A wise man will not leave the right to the mercy of chance, nor wish it to prevail through the power of the majority. There is but little virtue in the action of masses of men. When the majority shall at length vote for the abolition of slavery, it will be because they are indifferent to slavery, or because there is but little slavery left to be abolished by their vote. *They* will then be the only slaves. Only *his* vote can hasten the abolition of slavery who asserts his own freedom by his vote.

I hear of a convention to be held at Baltimore, or elsewhere, for the selection of a candidate for the Presidency, made up chiefly of editors, and men who are politicians by profession; but I think, what is it to any independent, intelligent, and respectable man what decision they may come to? Shall we not have the advantage of his wisdom and honesty, nevertheless? Can we not count upon some independent votes? Are there not many individuals in the country who do not attend conventions? But no: I find that the respectable man, so called, has immediately drifted from his position, and despairs of his country, when his country has more reason to despair of him. He forthwith adopts one of the candidates thus selected as the only *available* one, thus proving that he is himself *available* for any purposes of the demagogue. His vote is of no more worth than that of any unprincipled foreigner or hireling native, who may have been bought. O for a man who is a *man*, and, as my neighbor says, has a bone in his back which you cannot pass your hand through! Our statistics are at fault: the population has been returned too large. How many *men* are there to a square thousand miles in this country? Hardly one. Does not America offer any inducement for men to settle here? The American has dwindled into an Odd Fellow,—one who may be known by the development of his organ of gregariousness, and a manifest lack of intellect and cheerful self-reliance; whose first and chief concern, on coming into the world, is to see that the Alms-houses are in good repair; and, before yet he has lawfully donned the virile garb, to collect a fund for the support of the widows and orphans that may be; who, in short, ventures to live only by the aid of the Mutual Insurance company, which has promised to bury him decently.

It is not a man's duty, as a matter of course, to devote himself to the eradication of any, even the most enormous wrong; he may still properly have other concerns to engage him; but it is his duty, at least to wash his hands of it, and, if he gives it no thought longer, not to give it practically his support. If I devote myself to other pursuits and contemplations, I must first see, at least, that I do not pursue them sitting upon another man's shoulders. I must get off him first, that he may pursue his contemplations too. See what gross inconsistency is tolerated. I have heard some of my townsmen say, "I should like to have them order me out to help put down an insurrection of the slaves, or to march to Mexico;—see if I would go;" and yet these very men have each, directly by their allegiance, and so indirectly, at least, by their money, furnished a substitute. The soldier is applauded who refuses to serve in an unjust war by those who do not refuse to sustain the unjust government which makes the war; is applauded by those whose own act and authority he disregards and sets at naught; as if the state were penitent to that degree that it hired one to scourge it while it sinned, but not to that degree that it left off sinning for a moment. Thus, under the name of Order and Civil Government, we are all made at last to pay homage to and support our own meanness. After the first blush of sin comes its indifference; and from immoral it becomes, as it were, *un*moral, and not quite unnecessary to that life which we have made.

The broadest and most prevalent error requires the most disinterested virtue to sustain it. The slight reproach to which the virtue of patriotism is commonly liable, the noble are most likely to incur. Those who, while they disapprove of the character and measures of a government, yield to it their allegiance and support are undoubtedly its most conscientious supporters, and so frequently the most serious obstacles to reform. Some are petitioning the state to dissolve the Union, to disregard the requisitions of the President. Why do they not dissolve it themselves,—the union between themselves and the state,—and refuse to pay their quota into its treasury? Do not they stand in the same relation to the state that the state does to the Union? And have not the same reasons prevented the state from resisting the Union which have prevented them from resisting the state?

How can a man be satisfied to entertain an opinion merely, and enjoy *it?* Is there any enjoyment in it, if his opinion is that he is aggrieved? If you are cheated out of a single dollar by your neighbor, you do not rest satisfied with knowing that you are cheated, or with saying that you are cheated, or even with petitioning him to pay you your due; but you take effectual steps at once to obtain the full amount, and see that you are never cheated again. Action from principle, the perception and the performance of right, changes things and relations; it is essentially revolutionary, and does not consist wholly with anything which was. It not only divides states and churches, it divides families; ay, it divides the *individual*, separating the diabolical in him from the divine.

Unjust laws exist: shall we be content to obey them, or shall we endeavor to amend them, and obey them until we have succeeded, or shall we transgress them at once? Men generally, under such a government as this, think that they ought to wait until they have persuaded the majority to alter them. They think that, if they should resist, the remedy would be worse than the evil. But it is the fault of the government itself that the remedy *is* worse than the evil. *It* makes it worse. Why is it not more apt to anticipate and provide for reform? Why does it not cherish its wise minority? Why does it cry and resist before it is hurt? Why does it not encourage its citizens to be on the alert to point out its faults, and *do* better than it would have them? Why does it always crucify Christ, and excommunicate Copernicus and Luther, and pronounce Washington and Franklin rebels?

One would think, that a deliberate and practical denial of its authority was the only offense never contemplated by government; else, why has it not assigned its definite, its suitable and proportionate penalty? If a man who has no property refuses but once to earn nine shillings for the state, he is put in prison for a period unlimited by any law that I know, and determined only by the discretion of those who placed him there; but if he should steal ninety times nine shillings from the state, he is soon permitted to go at large again.

If the injustice is part of the necessary friction of the machine of government, let it go, let it go: perchance it will wear smooth,—certainly the machine will wear out. If the injustice has a spring, or a pulley, or a rope, or a crank, exclusively for itself, then perhaps you may consider whether the remedy will not be worse than the evil; but if it is of such a nature that it requires you to be the agent of injustice to another, then, I say, break the law. Let your life be a counter friction to stop the machine. What I have to do is to see, at any rate, that I do not lend myself to the wrong which I condemn.

As for adopting the ways which the state has provided for remedying the evil, I know not of such ways. They take too much time, and a man's life will be gone. I have other affairs to attend to. I came into this world, not chiefly to make this a good place to live in, but to live in it, be it good or bad. A man has not everything to do, but something; and because he cannot do *everything*, it is not necessary that he should do *something* wrong. It is not my business to be petitioning the Governor or the Legislature any more than it is theirs to petition me; and if they should not hear my petition, what should I do then? But in this case the state has provided no way: its very Constitution is the evil. This may seem to be harsh and stubborn and unconciliatory; but it is to treat with the utmost kindness and consideration the only spirit that can appreciate or deserve it. So is all change for the better, like birth and death, which convulse the body.

I do not hesitate to say, that those who call themselves Abolitionists should at once effectually withdraw their support, both in person and property, from the government of Massachusetts, and not wait till they constitute a majority of one, before they suffer the right to prevail through them. I think that it is enough if they have God on their side, without waiting for that other one. Moreover, any man more right than his neighbors constitutes a majority of one already.

I meet this American government, or its representative, the state government, directly, and face to face, once a year—no more—in the person of its tax-gatherer; this is the only mode in which a man situated as I am necessarily meets it; and it then says distinctly, Recognize me; and the simplest, the most effectual, and, in the present posture of affairs, the indispensablest mode of treating with it on this head, of expressing your little satisfaction with and love for it, is to deny it then. My civil neighbor, the tax-gatherer, is the very man I have to deal with,—for it is, after all, with men and not with parchment that I quarrel,—and he has voluntarily chosen to be an agent of the government. How shall he ever know well what he is and does as an officer of the government, or as a man, until he is obliged to consider whether he shall treat me, his neighbor, for whom he has respect, as a neighbor and well-disposed man, or as a maniac and disturber of the peace, and see if he can get over this obstruction to his neighborliness without a ruder and more impetuous thought or speech corresponding with his action. I know this well, that if one thousand, if one hundred, if ten men whom I could name,—if ten *honest* men only,—ay, if *one* HONEST man, in this State of Massachusetts, *ceasing to hold slaves*, were actually to withdraw from this copartnership, and be locked up in the county jail therefor, it would be the abolition of slavery in America. For it matters not how small the beginning may seem to be: what is once well done is done forever. But we love better to talk about it: that we say is our mission. Reform keeps many scores of newspapers in its service, but not one man. If my esteemed neighbor, the State's ambassador, who will devote his days to the settlement of the question of human rights in the Council Chamber, instead of being threatened with the prisons of Carolina, were to sit down the prisoner of Massachusetts, that State which is so anxious to foist the sin of slavery upon her sister,—though at present she can discover only an act of inhospitality to be the ground of a quarrel with her,—the Legislature would not wholly waive the subject the following winter.

Under a government which imprisons any unjustly, the true place for a just man is also a prison. The proper place to-day, the only place which Massachusetts has provided for her freer and less desponding spirits, is in her prisons, to be put out and locked out of the State by her own act, as they have already put themselves out by their principles. It is there that the fugitive slave, and the Mexican prisoner on parole, and the Indian come to plead the wrongs of his race should find them; on that separate, but more free and honorable ground, where the State places those who are not *with* her, but *against* her,—the only house in a slave State in which a free man can abide with honor. If any think that their influence would be lost there, and their voices no longer afflict the ear of the State, that they would not be as an enemy within its walls, they do not know by how much truth is stronger than error, nor how much more eloquently and effectively he can combat injustice who has experienced a little in his own person. Cast your whole vote, not a strip of paper merely, but your whole influence. A minority is powerless while it conforms to the majority; it is not even a minority then; but it is irresistible when it clogs by its whole weight. If the alternative is to keep all just men in prison, or give up war and slavery, the State will not hesitate which to choose. If a thousand men were not to pay their tax-bills this year, that would not be a violent and bloody measure, as it would be to pay them, and enable the State to commit violence and shed innocent blood. This is, in fact, the definition of a peaceable revolution, if any such is possible. If the tax-gatherer, or any other public officer, asks me, as one has done, "But what shall I do?" my answer is, "If you really wish to do anything, resign your office." When the subject has refused allegiance, and the officer has resigned his office, then the revolution is accomplished. But even suppose blood should flow. Is there not a sort of blood shed when the conscience is wounded? Through this wound a man's real manhood and immortality flow out, and he bleeds to an everlasting death. I see this blood flowing now.

I have contemplated the imprisonment of the offender, rather than the seizure of his goods,—though both will serve the same purpose,—because they who assert the purest right, and consequently are most dangerous to a corrupt State, commonly have not spent much time in accumulating property. To such the State renders comparatively small service, and a slight tax is wont to appear exorbitant, particularly if they are obliged to earn it by special labor with their hands. If there were one who lived wholly without the use of money, the State itself would hesitate to demand it of him. But the rich man—not to make any invidious comparison—is always sold to the institution which makes him rich. Absolutely speaking, the more money, the less virtue; for money comes between a man and his objects, and obtains them for him; and it was certainly no great virtue to obtain it. It puts to rest many questions which he would otherwise be taxed to answer; while the only new question which it puts is the hard but superfluous one, how to spend it. Thus his moral ground is taken from under his feet. The opportunities of living are diminished in proportion as what are called the "means" are increased. The best thing a man can do for his culture when he is rich is to endeavor to carry out those schemes which he entertained when he was poor. Christ answered the Herodians according to their condition. "Show me the tribute-money," said he;—and one took a penny out of his pocket;—if you use money which has the image of Cæsar on it, and which he has made current and valuable, that is, *if you are men of the State*, and gladly enjoy the advantages of Cæsar's government, then pay him back some of his own when he demands it. "Render therefore to Cæsar that which is Cæsar's, and to God those things which are God's,"—leaving them no wiser than before as to which was which; for they did not wish to know. . . .

I have paid no poll-tax for six years. I was put into a jail once on this account, for one night; and, as I stood considering the walls of solid stone, two or three feet thick, the door of wood and iron, a foot thick, and the iron grating which strained the light, I could not help being struck with the foolishness of that institution which treated me as if I were mere flesh and blood and bones, to be locked up. I wondered that it should have concluded at length that this was the best use it could put me to, and had never thought to avail itself of my services in some way. I saw that, if there was a wall of stone between me and my townsmen, there was a still more difficult one to climb or break through before they could get to be as free as I was. I did not for a moment feel confined, and the walls seemed a great waste of stone and mortar. I felt as if I alone of all my townsmen had paid my tax. They plainly did not know how to treat me, but behaved like persons who are underbred. In every threat and in every compliment there was a blunder; for they thought that my chief desire was to stand the other side of that stone wall. I could not but smile to see how industriously they locked the door on my meditations, which followed them out again without let or hindrance, and *they* were really all that was dangerous. As they could not reach me, they had resolved to punish my body; just as boys, if they cannot come at some person against whom they have a spite, will abuse his dog. I saw that the State was half-witted, that it was timid as a lone woman with her silver spoons, and that it did not know its friends from its foes, and I lost all my remaining respect for it, and pitied it.

Thus the State never intentionally confronts a man's sense, intellectual or moral, but only his body, his senses. It is not armed with superior wit or honesty, but with superior physical strength. I was not born to be forced. I will breathe after my own fashion. Let us see who is the strongest. What force has a multitude? They only can force me who obey a higher law than I. They force me to become like themselves. I do not hear of *men* being *forced* to live this way or that by masses of men. What sort of life were that to live? When I meet a government which says to me, "Your money or your life," why should I be in haste to give it my money? It may be in a great strait, and not know what to do: I cannot help that. It must help itself; do as I do. It is not worth the while to snivel about it. I am not responsible for the successful working of the machinery of society. I am not the son of the engineer. I perceive that, when an acorn and a chestnut fall side by side, the one does not remain inert to make way for the other, but both obey their own laws, and spring and grow and flourish as best they can, till one, perchance, overshadows and destroys the other. If a plant cannot live according to its nature, it dies; and so a man. . . .

When I came out of prison,—for some one interfered, and paid that tax,—I did not perceive that great changes had taken place on the common, such as he observed who went in a youth and emerged a tottering and gray-headed man; and yet a change had to my eyes come over the scene,—the town, and State, and country,—greater than any that mere time could effect. I saw yet more distinctly the State in which I lived. I saw to what extent the people among whom I lived could be trusted as good neighbors and friends; that their friendship was for summer weather only; that they did not greatly propose to do right; that they were a distinct race from me by their prejudices and superstitions, as the Chinamen and Malays are; that in their sacrifices to humanity they ran no risks, not even to their property; that after all they were not so noble but they treated the thief as he had treated them, and hoped, by a certain outward observance and a few prayers, and by walking in a particular straight though useless path from time to time, to save their souls. This may be to judge my neighbors harshly; for I believe that many of them are not aware that they have such an institution as the jail in their village.

It was formerly the custom in our village, when a poor debtor came out of jail, for his acquaintances to salute him, looking through their fingers, which were crossed to represent the grating of a jail window, "How do ye do?" My neighbors did not thus salute me, but first looked at me, and then at one another, as if I had returned from a long journey. I was put into jail as I was going to the shoemaker's to get a shoe which was mended. When I was let out the next morning, I proceeded to finish my errand, and, having put on my mended shoe, joined a huckleberry party, who were impatient to put themselves under my conduct; and in half an hour,—for the horse was soon tackled,—was in the midst of a huckleberry field, on one of our highest hills, two miles off, and then the State was nowhere to be seen. . . .

I have never declined paying the highway tax, because I am as desirous of being a good neighbor as I am of being a bad subject; and as for supporting schools, I am doing my part to educate my fellow-countrymen now. It is for no particular item in the tax-bill that I refuse to pay it. I simply wish to refuse allegiance to the State, to withdraw and stand aloof from it effectually. I do not care to trace the course of my dollar, if I could, till it buys a man or a musket to shoot one with,—the dollar is innocent,—but I am concerned to trace the effects of my allegiance. In fact, I quietly declare war with the State, after my fashion, though I will still make what use and get what advantage of her I can, as is usual in such cases.

If others pay the tax which is demanded of me, from a sympathy with the State, they do but what they have already done in their own case, or rather they abet injustice to a greater extent than the State requires. If they pay the tax from a mistaken interest in the individual taxed, to save his property, or prevent his going to jail, it is because they have not considered wisely how far they let their private feelings interfere with the public good.

This, then, is my position at present. But one cannot be too much on his guard in such a case, lest his action be biased by obstinacy or an undue regard for the opinions of men. Let him see that he does only what belongs to himself and to the hour.

I think sometimes, Why, this people mean well, they are only ignorant; they would do better if they knew how: why give your neighbors this pain to treat you as they are not inclined to? But I think again, This is no reason why I should do as they do, or permit others to suffer much greater pain of a different kind. Again, I sometimes say to myself, When many millions of men, without heat, without ill will, without personal feeling of any kind, demand of you a few shillings only, without the possibility, such is their constitution, of retracting or altering their present demand, and without the possibility, on your side, of appeal to any other millions, why expose yourself to this overwhelming brute force? You do not resist cold and hunger, the winds and the waves, thus obstinately; you quietly submit to a thousand similar necessities. You do not put your head into the fire. But just in proportion as I regard this as not wholly a brute force, but partly a human force, and consider that

I have relations to those millions as to so many millions of men, and not of mere brute or inanimate things, I see that appeal is possible, first and instantaneously, from them to the Maker of them, and, secondly, from them to themselves. But if I put my head deliberately into the fire, there is no appeal to fire or to the Maker of fire, and I have only myself to blame. If I could convince myself that I have any right to be satisfied with men as they are, and to treat them accordingly, and not according, in some respects, to my requisitions and expectations of what they and I ought to be, then, like a good Mussulman and fatalist, I should endeavor to be satisfied with things as they are, and say it is the will of God. And, above all, there is this difference between resisting this and a purely brute or natural force, that I can resist this with some effect; but I cannot expect, like Orpheus, to change the nature of the rocks and trees and beasts.

I do not wish to quarrel with any man or nation. I do not wish to split hairs, to make fine distinctions, or set myself up as better than my neighbors. I seek rather, I may say, even an excuse for conforming to the laws of the land. I am but too ready to conform to them. Indeed, I have reason to suspect myself on this head; and each year, as the tax-gatherer comes round, I find myself disposed to review the acts and position of the general and State governments, and the spirit of the people, to discover a pretext for conformity. . . .

I believe that the State will soon be able to take all my work of this sort out of my hands, and then I shall be no better a patriot than my fellow-countrymen. Seen from a lower point of view, the Constitution, with all its faults, is very good; the law and the courts are very repectable; even this State and this American government are, in many respects, very admirable, and rare things, to be thankful for, such as a great many have described them; but seen from a point of view a little higher, they are what I have described them; seen from a higher still, and the highest, who shall say what they are, or that they are worth looking at or thinking of at all?

However, the government does not concern me much, and I shall bestow the fewest possible thoughts on it. It is not many moments that I live under a government, even in this world. If a man is thought-free, fancy-free, imagination-free, that which *is not* never for a long time appearing *to be* to him, unwise rulers or reformers cannot fatally interrupt him.

I know that most men think differently from myself; but those whose lives are by profession devoted to the study of these or kindred subjects content me as little as any. Statesmen and legislators, standing so completely within the institution, never distinctly and nakedly behold it. They speak of moving society, but have no resting-place without it. They may be men of a certain experience and discrimination, and have no doubt invented ingenious and even useful systems, for which we sincerely thank them; but all their wit and usefulness lie within certain not very wide limits. They are wont to forget that the world is not governed by policy and expediency. Webster never goes behind government, and so cannot speak with authority about it. His words are wisdom to those legislators who contemplate no essential reform in the existing government; but for thinkers, and those who legislate for all time, he never once glances at the subject. I know of those whose serene and wise speculations on this theme would soon reveal the limits of his mind's range and hospitality. Yet, compared with the cheap professions of most reformers, and the still cheaper wisdom and eloquence of politicians in general, his are almost the only sensible and valuable words, and we thank Heaven for him. Comparatively, he is always strong, original, and, above all, practical. Still, his quality is not wisdom, but prudence. The lawyer's truth is not Truth, but consistency or a consistent expediency. Truth is always in harmony with herself, and is not concerned chiefly to reveal the justice that may consist with wrong-doing. He well deserves to be called, as he has been called, the Defender of the Constitution. There are really no blows to be given by him but defensive ones. He is not a leader, but a follower. His leaders are the men of '87. "I have never made an effort," he says, "and never propose to make an effort; I have never countenanced an effort, and never mean to countenance an effort, to disturb the arrangement as originally made, by which the various States came into the Union." Still thinking of the sanction which the Constitution gives to slavery, he says, "Because it was a part of the original compact,—let it stand." Notwithstanding his special acuteness and ability, he is unable to take a fact out of its merely political relations, and behold it as it lies absolutely to be disposed of by the intellect,—what, for instance, it behooves a man to do here in America to-day with regard to slavery,—but ventures, or is driven, to make some such desperate answer as the following, while professing to speak absolutely, and as a private man,—from which what new and singular code of social duties might be inferred? "The manner," says he, "in which the governments of those States where slavery exists are to regulate it is for their own consideration, under their responsibility to their constituents, to the general laws of propriety, humanity, and justice, and to God. Associations formed elsewhere, springing from a feeling of humanity, or any other cause, have nothing whatever to do with it. They have never received any encouragement from me, and they never will." [1]

They who know of no purer sources of truth, who have traced up its stream no higher, stand, and wisely stand, by the Bible and the Constitution, and drink at it there with reverence and humility; but they who behold where it comes trickling into this lake or that pool, gird up their loins once more, and continue their pilgrimage toward its fountain-head.

No man with a genius for legislation has appeared in America. They are rare in the history of the world. There are orators, politicians, and eloquent men, by the thousand; but the speaker has not yet opened his mouth to speak who is capable of settling the much-vexed questions of the day. We love eloquence for its own sake, and not for any truth which it may utter, or any heroism it may inspire. Our legislators have not yet learned the comparative value of free-trade and of freedom, of union, and of rectitude, to a nation. They have no genius or talent for comparatively humble questions of taxation and finance, commerce and manufactures and agriculture. If we were left solely to the wordy wit of legislators in Congress for our guidance, uncorrected by the seasonable experience and the effectual complaints of the people, America would not long retain her rank among the nations. For eighteen hundred years, though perchance I have no right to say it, the New Testament has been written; yet where is the legislator who has wisdom and practical talent enough to avail himself of the light which it sheds on the science of legislation?

The authority of government, even such as I am willing to submit to,—for I will cheerfully obey those who know and can do better than I, and in many things even those who neither know nor can do so well,—is still an impure one: to be strictly just, it must have the sanction and consent of the governed. It can have no pure right over my person and property but what I concede to it. The progress from an absolute to a limited monarchy, from a limited monarchy to a democracy, is a progress toward a true respect for the individual. Even the Chinese philosopher was wise enough to regard the individual as the basis of the empire. Is a democracy, such as we know it, the last improvement possible in government? Is it not possible

[1] *These extracts have been inserted since the lecture was read.*

to take a step further towards recognizing and organizing the rights of man? There will never be a really free and enlightened State until the State comes to recognize the individual as a higher and independent power, from which all its own power and authority are derived, and treats him accordingly. I please myself with imagining a State at last which can afford to be just to all men, and to treat the individual with respect as a neighbor; which even would not think it inconsistent with its own repose if a few were to live aloof from it, not meddling with it, nor embraced by it, who fulfilled all the duties of neighbors and fellowmen. A State which bore this kind of fruit, and suffered it to drop off as fast as it ripened, would prepare the way for a still more perfect and glorious State, which also I have imagined, but not yet anywhere seen.

Questions

1. Paraphrase Thoreau's concept of "This American government" in the second paragraph. How accurate is his appraisal of government's function?
2. What is Thoreau's position on majority rule?
3. How does Thoreau see his obligation to government? Summarize the arguments he uses to support his position.
4. Explain Thoreau's paradoxical statement, "He who gives himself entirely to his fellowmen appears to them useless and selfish; but he who gives himself partially to them is pronounced a benefactor and a philanthropist."
5. What does Thoreau think about the average citizen as a force in government? Briefly summarize his examples—voting, selection of officials, military service, eradication of unjust laws.
6. Summarize Thoreau's arguments for "passive resistance." What was his personal experience in implementing his position?
7. Is the concluding paragraph consistent with the rest of the essay? Is it consistent with an ideal concept of man? An ideal concept of democratic government?

Topics for Composition

1. Using selected comments from "Civil Disobedience," write an essay applying Thoreau's position to the present-day American scene.
2. Refute Thoreau's essay as impractical and irresponsible in view of man's obligation to mankind.
3. Referring directly to the essay, support or refute the position that Thoreau advocates anarchy.

4. Write a composition, based on personal experience, in which you describe the details of a protest against, or a desire to protest, restraint by governmental authority. Support the validity of your position as you saw it.

WILLIAM Faulkner's essay and James Baldwin's that follows it must be read as companion pieces since Baldwin's is a direct response to Faulkner's. Both essays illustrate some techniques used in persuasive writing. Considering both essays, we should assess the relative force of the following appeals:

1. Each author's appeal to personal authority in the opening paragraph of his essay
2. Faulkner's avowed aim to stand as mediator between two extremes; Baldwin's complete rejection of the "middle of the road"
3. Faulkner's use of supporting quotations from members of the Negro community; Baldwin's use of supporting quotations from Faulkner's essay
4. Faulkner's attack upon the Northerner's limited knowledge; Baldwin's attack upon Faulkner's limited knowledge

Letter to the North

WILLIAM FAULKNER

My family has lived for generations in one same small section of north Mississippi. My great-grandfather held slaves and went to Virginia in command of a Mississippi infantry regiment in 1861. I state this simply as credentials for the sincerity and factualness of what I will try to say.

From the beginning of this present phase of the race problem in the South, I have been on record as opposing the forces in my native country which would keep the condition out of which this present evil and trouble has grown. Now I must go on record as opposing the forces outside the South which would use legal or police compulsion to eradicate that evil overnight. I was against compulsory segregation. I am just as strongly against compulsory integration. Firstly of course from principle. Secondly because I don't believe compulsion will work.

There are more Southerners than I who believe as I do and have taken the same stand I have taken, at the same price of contumely and insult and threat from other Southerners which we foresaw and were willing to accept because we believed we were helping our native land which we love, to accept a new condition which it must accept whether it wants to or not. That is, by still being Southerners, yet not being a part of the general majority Southern point of view; by being present yet detached, committed and attainted neither by Citizens' Council nor NAACP; by being in the middle, being in a position to say to any incipient irrevocability: "Wait, wait now, stop and consider first."

But where will we go, if that middle becomes untenable? If we have to vacate it in order to keep from being trampled? Apart from the legal aspect, apart even from the simple incontrovertible immorality of discrimination by race, there was another simply human quantity which drew us to the Negro's side: the simple human instinct to champion the underdog.

But if we, the (comparative) handful of Southerners I have tried to postulate, are compelled by the simple threat of being trampled if we don't get out of the way, to vacate that middle where we could have worked to help the Negro improve his condition—compelled to move for the reason that no middle any longer exists—we will have to make a new choice. And this time the underdog will not be the Negro, since he, the Negro, will now be a segment of the topdog, and so the underdog will be that white embattled minority who are our blood and kin. These non-Southern forces will now say, "Go then. We don't want you because we won't need you again." My reply to that is, "Are you sure you won't?"

So I would say to the NAACP and all the organizations who would compel immediate and unconditional integration: "Go slow now. Stop now for a time, a moment. You have the power now; you can afford to withhold for a moment the use of it as a force. You have done a good job, you have jolted your opponent off-balance and he is now vulnerable. But stop there for a moment; don't give him the advantage of a chance to cloud the issue by that purely automatic sentimental appeal to that same universal human instinct for automatic sympathy for the underdog simply because he is under."

And I would say this too. The rest of the United States knows next to nothing about the South. The present idea and picture which they hold of a people decadent and even obsolete through inbreeding and illiteracy—the inbreeding a result of the illiteracy and the isolation—as to be a kind of species of juvenile delinquents with a folklore of blood and violence, yet who, like juvenile delinquents, can be controlled by firmness once they are brought to believe that the police mean business, is as baseless and illusory as that one a generation ago of (oh yes, we subscribed to it too) columned porticoes and magnolias. The rest of the United States assumes that this condition in the South is so simple and so uncomplex that it can be changed tomorrow by the simple will of the national majority backed by legal edict. In fact, the North does not even recognize what it has seen in its own newspapers.

I have at hand an editorial from the New York *Times* of February 10th on the rioting at the University of Alabama because of the admission of Miss Lucy, a Negro. The editorial said: "This is the first time that force and violence have become part of the question." That is not correct. To all Southerners, no matter which side of the question of racial equality they supported, the first implication, and —to the Southerner—even promise, of force and violence was the Supreme Court decision itself. After that, by any standards at all and following as inevitably as night and day, was the case of the three white teen-agers, members of a field trip group from a Mississippi high school (and, as teen-agers do, probably wearing the bright particolored blazers or jackets blazoned across the back with the name of the school) who were stabbed in passing on a Washington street by Negroes they had never seen before and who apparently had never seen them before either; and that of the Till boy and the two Mississippi juries which freed the defendants from both charges; and of the Mississippi garage attendant killed by a white man because, according to the white man, the Negro filled the tank of the white man's car full of gasoline when all the white man wanted was two dollars' worth.

This problem is far beyond a mere legal one. It is even far beyond the moral one it is and still was a hundred years ago in 1860, when many Southerners, including Robert Lee, recognized it as a moral one at the very instant when they in turn elected to champion the underdog because that underdog was blood and kin and home. The Northerner is not even aware yet of what that war really proved. He assumes that is merely proved to the Southerner that he was wrong. It didn't do that because the Southerner already knew he was wrong and accepted that gambit even when he knew it was the fatal one. What that war should have done, but failed to do, was to prove to the North that the South will go to any length, even that fatal and already doomed one, before it will accept alteration of its racial condition by mere force of law or economic threat.

Since I went on record as being opposed to compulsory racial inequality, I have received many letters. A few of them approved. But most of them were in opposition. And a few of these were from Southern Negroes, the only difference being that they were polite and courteous instead of being threats and insults, saying in effect: "Please, Mr. Faulkner, stop talking and be quiet. You are a good man and you think you are helping us. But you are not helping us. You are doing us harm. You are playing into the hands of the NAACP so that they are using you to make trouble for our race that we don't want. Please hush, you look after your white folks' trouble and let us take care of ours." This one in particular was a long one, from a woman who was writing for and in the name of the pastor and the entire congregation of her church. It went on to say that the Till boy got exactly what he asked for, coming down there with his Chicago ideas, and that all his mother wanted was to make money out of the role of her bereavement. Which sounds exactly like the white people in the South who justified and even defended the crime by declining to find that it was one.

We have had many violent inexcusable personal crimes of race against race in the South, but since 1919 the major examples of communal race tension have been more prevalent in the North, like the Negro family who were refused acceptance in the white residential district in Chicago, and the Korean-American who suffered for the same reason in Anaheim, Calif. Maybe it is because our solidarity is not racial, but instead is the majority white segregationist plus the Negro minority like my correspondent above, who prefer peace to equality. But suppose the line of demarcation should become one of the race; the white minority like myself compelled to join the white segregation majority no matter how much we oppose the principle of inequality; the Negro minority who want peace compelled to join the Negro majority who advocate force, no matter how much that minority wanted only peace?

So the Northerner, the liberal, does not know the South. He can't know it from his distance. He assumes that he is dealing with a simple legal theory and a simple moral idea. He is not. He is dealing with a fact: the fact of an emotional condition of such fierce unanimity as to scorn the fact that it is a minority and which will go to any length and against any odds at this moment to justify and, if necessary, defend that condition and its right to it.

So I would say to all the organizations and groups which would force integration on the South by legal process: "Stop now for a moment. You have shown the Southerner what you can do and what you will do if necessary; give him a space in which to get his breath and assimilate that knowledge; to look about and see that (1) Nobody is going to force integration on him from the outside; (2) That he himself faces an obsolescence in his own land which only he can cure; a moral condition which not only must be cured but a physical condition which has got to be cured if he, the white Southerner, is to have any peace, is not to be faced with another legal process or maneuver every year, year after year, for the rest of his life."

Faulkner and Desegregation

JAMES BALDWIN

Any real change implies the breakup of the world as one has always known it, the loss of all that gave one an identity, the end of safety. And at such a moment, unable to see and not daring to imagine what the future will now bring forth, one clings to what one knew, or thought one knew; to what one possessed or dreamed that one possessed. Yet, it is only when a man is able, without bitterness or self-pity, to surrender a dream he has long cherished or a privilege he has long possessed that he is set free—he has set himself free—for higher dreams, for greater privileges. All men have gone through this, go through it, each according to his degree, throughout their lives. It is one of the irreducible facts of life. And remembering this, especially since I am a Negro, affords me almost my only means of understanding what is happening in the minds and hearts of white Southerners today.

For the arguments with which the bulk of relatively articulate white Southerners of good will have met the necessity of desegregation have no value whatever as arguments, being almost entirely and helplessly dishonest, when not, indeed, insane. After more than two hundred years in slavery and ninety years of quasi-freedom, it is hard to think very highly of William Faulkner's advice to "go slow."

"They don't mean go slow," Thurgood Marshall is reported to have said, "they mean don't go." Nor is the squire of Oxford very persuasive when he suggests that white Southerners, left to their own devices, will realize that their own social structure looks silly to the rest of the world and correct it of their own accord. It has looked silly, to use Faulkner's rather strange adjective, for a long time; so far from trying to correct it, Southerners, who seem to be characterized by a species of defiance most perverse when it is most despairing, have clung to it, at incalculable cost to themselves, as the only conceivable and as an absolutely sacrosanct way of life. They have never seriously conceded that their social structure was mad. They have insisted, on the contrary, that everyone who criticized it was mad.

Faulkner goes further. He concedes the madness and moral wrongness of the South but at the same time he raises it to the level of a mystique which makes it somehow unjust to discuss Southern society in the same terms in which one would discuss any other society. "Our position is wrong and untenable," says Faulkner, "but it is not wise to keep an emotional people off balance." This, if it means anything, can only mean that this "emotional people" have been swept "off balance" by the pressure of recent events, that is, the Supreme Court decision outlawing segregation. When the pressure is taken off—and not an instant before—this "emotional people" will presumably find themselves once again on balance and will then be able to free themselves of an "obsolescence in [their] own land" in their own way and, of course, in their own time. The question left begging is what, in their history to date, affords any evidence that they have any desire or capacity to do this. And it is, I suppose, impertinent to ask just what Negroes are supposed to do while the South works out what, in Faulkner's rhetoric, becomes something very closely resembling a high and noble tragedy.

The sad truth is that whatever modifications have been effected in the social structure of the South since the Reconstruction, and any alleviations of the Negro's lot within it, are due to great and incessant pressure, very little of it indeed from within the South. That the North has been guilty of Pharisaism in its dealing with the South does not negate the fact that much of this pressure has come from the North. That some—not nearly as many as Faulkner would like to believe—Southern Negroes prefer, or are afraid of changing, the status quo does not negate the fact that it is the Southern Negro himself who, year upon year, and generation upon generation, has kept the Southern waters troubled. As far as the Negro's life in the South is concerned, the NAACP is the only organization which has struggled, with admirable single-mindedness and skill, to raise him to the level of a citizen. For this reason alone, and quite apart from the individual heroism of many of its Southern members, it cannot be equated, as Faulkner equates it, with the pathological Citizen's Council. One organization is working within the law and the other is working against and outside it. Faulkner's threat to leave the "middle of the road" where he has, presumably, all these years, been working for the benefit of Negroes, reduces itself to a more or less up-to-date version of the Southern threat to secede from the Union.

Faulkner—among so many others!—is so plaintive concerning this "middle of the road" from which "extremist" elements of both races are driving him that it does not seem unfair to ask just what he has been doing there until now. Where is the evidence of the struggle he has been carrying on there on behalf of the Negro? Why, if he and his enlightened confreres in the South have been boring from within to destroy segregation, do they react with such panic when the walls show any signs of falling? Why—and how—does one move from the middle of the road where one was aiding Negroes into the streets—to shoot them?

Now it is easy enough to state flatly that Faulkner's middle of the road does not—cannot—exist and that he is guilty of great emotional and intellectual dishonesty in pretending that it does. I think this is why he clings to his fantasy. It is easy enough to accuse him of hypocrisy when he speaks of man being "indestructible because of his simple will to freedom." But he is not being hypocritical; he means it. It is only that Man is one thing—a rather unlucky abstraction in this case—and the Negroes he has always known, so fatally tied up in his mind with his grandfather's slaves, are quite another. He is at his best, and is perfectly sincere, when he declares, in *Harpers*, "To live anywhere in the world today and be against equality because of race or color is like living in Alaska and being against snow. We have already got snow. And as with the Alaskan, merely to live in armistice with it is not enough. Like the Alaskan, we had better use it." And though this seems to be flatly opposed to his statement (in an interview printed in *The Reporter*) that, if it came to a contest between the federal government and Mississippi, he would fight for Mississippi, "even if it meant going out into the streets and shooting Negroes," he means that, too. Faulkner means everything he says, means them all at once, and with very nearly the same intensity. This is why his statements demand our attention. He has perhaps never before more concretely expressed what it means to be a Southerner.

What seems to define the Southerner, in his own mind at any rate, is his relationship to the North, that is to the rest of the Republic, a relationship which can at the very best be described as uneasy. It is apparently very difficult to be at once a Southerner and an American; so difficult that many of the South's most independent minds are forced into the American exile; which is not, of course, without its aggravating, circular effect on the interior and public life of the South. A Bostonian, say, who leaves Boston is not regarded by the citizenry he has abandoned with the same venomous distrust as is the Southerner who leaves the South. The citizenry of Boston do not consider that they have been abandoned, much less betrayed. It is only the American Southerner who seems to be fighting, in his own entrails, a peculiar, ghastly, and perpetual war with all the rest of the country. ("Didn't you say," demanded a Southern woman of Robert Penn Warren, "that you was born down here, used to live right near here?" And when he agreed that this was so: "Yes . . . but you never said where you living now!")

The difficulty, perhaps, is that the Southerner clings to two entirely antithetical doctrines, two legends, two histories. Like all other Americans, he must subscribe, and is to some extent controlled by the beliefs and the principles expressed in the Constitution; at the same time, these beliefs and principles seem determined to destroy the South. He is, on the one hand, the proud citizen of a free society and, on the other, is committed to a society which has not yet dared to free itself of the necessity of naked and brutal oppression. He is part of a country which boasts that it has never lost a war; but he is also the representative of a conquered nation. I have not seen a single statement of Faulkner's concerning desegregation which does not inform us that his family has lived in the same part of Mississippi for generations, that his great-grandfather owned slaves, and that his ancestors fought and died in the Civil War. And so compelling is the image of ruin, gallantry and death thus evoked that it demands a positive effort of the imagination to remember that slaveholding Southerners were not the only people who perished in that war. Negroes and Northerners were also blown to bits. American history, as opposed to Southern history, proves that Southerners were not the only slaveholders, Negroes were not even the only slaves. And the segregation which Faulkner sanctifies by references to Shiloh, Chickamauga, and Gettysburg does not extend back that far, is in fact scarcely as old as the century. The "racial condition" which Faulkner will not have changed by "mere force of law or economic threat" was imposed by precisely these means. The Southern tradition, which is, after all, all that Faulkner is talking about, is not a tradition at all: when Faulkner evokes it, he is simply evoking a legend which contains an accusation. And that accusation, stated far more simply than it should be, is that the North, in winning the war, left the South only one means of asserting its identity and that means was the Negro.

"My people owned slaves," says Faulkner, "and the very obligation we have to take care of these people is morally bad." "This problem is . . . far beyond the moral one it is and still was a hundred years ago, in 1860, when many Southerners, including Robert Lee, recognized it as a moral one at the very instant they in turn elected to champion the underdog because that underdog was blood and kin and home." But the North escaped scot-free. For one thing, in freeing the slave, it established a moral superiority over the South which the South has not learned to live with until today; and this despite—or possibly because of—the fact that this moral superiority was bought, after all, rather cheaply. The North was no better prepared than the South, as it turned out, to make citizens of former slaves, but it was able, as the South was not, to wash its hands of the matter. Men who knew that slavery was wrong were forced, nevertheless, to fight to perpetuate it because they were unable to turn against "blood and kin and home." And when blood and kin and home were defeated, they found themselves, more than ever, committed: committed, in effect, to a way of life which was as unjust and crippling as it was inescapable. In sum, the North, by freeing the slaves of their masters, robbed the masters of any possibility of freeing themselves of the slaves.

When Faulkner speaks, then, of the "middle of the road," he is simply speaking of the hope—which was always unrealistic and is now all but smashed—that the white Southerner, with no coercion from the rest of the nation, will lift himself above his ancient, crippling bitterness and refuse to add to his already intolerable burden of blood-guiltiness. But this hope would seem to be absolutely dependent on a social and psychological stasis which simply does not exist. "Things have been getting better," Faulkner tells us, "for a long time. Only six Negroes were killed by whites in Mississippi last year, according to police figures." Faulkner surely knows how little consolation this offers a Negro and he also knows something about "police figures" in the Deep South. And he knows, too, that murder is not the worst thing that can happen to a man, black or white. But murder may be the worst thing a man can do. Faulkner is not trying to save Negroes, who are, in his view, already saved; who, having refused to be destroyed by terror, are far stronger than the terrified white populace; and who have, moreover, fatally, from his point of view, the weight of the federal government behind them. He is trying to save "whatever good remains in those white people." The time he pleads for is the time in which the Southerner will come to terms with himself, will cease fleeing from his conscience, and achieve, in the words of Robert Penn Warren, "moral identity." And he surely believes, with Warren, that "Then in a country where moral identity is hard to come by, the South, because it has had to deal concretely with a moral problem, may offer some leadership. And we need any we can get. If we are to break out of the national rhythm, the rhythm between complacency and panic."

But the time Faulkner asks for does not exist—and he is not the only Southerner who knows it. There is never time in the future in which we will work out our salvation. The challenge is in the moment, the time is always now.

Questions

1. List Faulkner's main points. Place Baldwin's reply beside each point on the list. Which argument appears stronger?
2. How appropriate is Faulkner's letter in view of recent events in the North? Does a consideration of recent Northern racial troubles alter the force of Baldwin's indictment of white Southerners?
3. Which of the two writers seems more objective? What does your answer imply about point of view when writing about racial problems?
4. Considered together, do the two essays offer an impasse or are there points where compromise might be effected? Explain.

Topics for Composition

1. Using your knowledge of current events, write an essay showing that the views expressed by both Faulkner and Baldwin are too restricted to cover current issues.
2. Using one of the above essays and Thoreau's "Civil Disobedience," discuss the writer of the modern essay as a follower/non-follower of Thoreau's theory.
3. Using Faulkner's essay as your model, write a "letter" on a current controversial problem.

The Short Story

In presenting a conflict between the past and the present (Emily and the town), Faulkner deftly elicits a response of mingled pity and horror by the way in which he combines point of view, foreshadowing, chronology, and symbol. We should note:

1. The point of view: the narrator is an anonymous townsman whose very absence of involvement points up the town's part in Emily's fall.
2. The use of foreshadowing: Emily's deteriorating character, Homer's disappearance, are aptly foreshadowed if we are sensitive to seemingly unimportant details.
3. The use of multiple flashbacks: Faulkner's time shifts contribute to an overall atmosphere of distortion.
4. The use of symbols that keep step with the decaying atmosphere surrounding Emily.

A Rose for Emily

WILLIAM FAULKNER

I

When Miss Emily Grierson died, our whole town went to her funeral: the men through a sort of respectful affection for a fallen monument, the women mostly out of curiosity to see the inside of her house, which no one save an old man-servant—a combined gardener and cook—had seen in at least ten years.

It was a big, squarish frame house that had once been white, decorated with cupolas and spires and scrolled balconies in the heavily lightsome style of the seventies, set on what had once been our most select street. But garages and cotton gins had encroached and obliterated even the august names of that neighborhood; only Miss Emily's house was left, lifting its stubborn and coquettish decay above the cotton wagons and the gasoline pumps—an eyesore among eyesores. And now Miss Emily had gone to join the representatives of those august names where they lay in the cedar-bemused cemetery among the ranked and anonymous graves of Union and Confederate soldiers who fell at the battle of Jefferson.

Alive, Miss Emily had been a tradition, a duty, and a care; a sort of hereditary obligation upon the town, dating from that day in 1894 when Colonel Sartoris, the mayor—he who fathered the edict that no Negro woman should appear on the streets without an apron—remitted her taxes, the dispensation dating from the death of her father on into perpetuity. Not that Miss Emily would have accepted charity. Colonel Sartoris invented an involved tale to the effect that Miss Emily's father had loaned money to the town, which the town, as a matter of business, preferred this way of repaying. Only a man of Colonel Sartoris' generation and thought could have invented it, and only a woman could have believed it.

When the next generation, with its more modern ideas, became mayors and aldermen, this arrangement created some little dissatisfaction. On the first of the year they mailed her a tax notice. February came, and there was no reply. They wrote her a formal letter, asking her to call at the sheriff's office at her convenience. A week later the mayor wrote her himself, offering to call or to send his car for her, and received in reply a note on paper of an archaic shape, in a thin, flowing calligraphy in faded ink, to the effect that she no longer went out at all. The tax notice was also enclosed, without comment.

They called a special meeting of the Board of Aldermen. A deputation waited upon her, knocked at the door through which no visitor had passed since she ceased giving china-painting lessons eight or ten years earlier. They were admitted by the old Negro into a dim hall from which a stairway mounted into still more shadow. It smelled of dust and disuse—a close, dank smell. The Negro led them into the parlor. It was furnished in heavy, leather-covered furniture. When the Negro opened the blinds of one window, they could see that the leather was cracked; and when they sat down, a faint dust rose sluggishly about their thighs, spinning with slow motes in the single sun-ray. On a tarnished gilt easel before the fireplace stood a crayon portrait of Miss Emily's father.

They rose when she entered—a small, fat woman in black, with a thin gold chain descending to her waist and vanishing into her belt, leaning on an ebony cane with a tarnished gold head. Her skeleton was small and spare; perhaps that was why what would have been merely plumpness in another was obesity in her. She looked bloated, like a body long submerged in motionless water, and of that pallid hue. Her eyes, lost in the fatty ridges of her face, looked like two small pieces of coal pressed into a lump of dough as they moved from one face to another while the visitors stated their errand.

She did not ask them to sit. She just stood in the door and listened quietly until the spokesman came to a stumbling halt. Then they could hear the invisible watch ticking at the end of the gold chain.

Her voice was dry and cold. "I have no taxes in Jefferson. Colonel Sartoris explained it to me. Perhaps one of you can gain access to the city records and satisfy yourselves."

"But we have. We are the city authorities, Miss Emily. Didn't you get a notice from the sheriff, signed by him?"

"I received a paper, yes," Miss Emily said. "Perhaps he considers himself the sheriff . . . I have no taxes in Jefferson."

"But there is nothing on the books to show that, you see. We must go by the—"

"See Colonel Sartoris. I have no taxes in Jefferson."

"But, Miss Emily—"

"See Colonel Sartoris." (Colonel Sartoris had been dead almost ten years.) "I have no taxes in Jefferson. Tobe!" The Negro appeared. "Show these gentlemen out."

II

So she vanquished them, horse and foot, just as she had vanquished their fathers thirty years before about the smell. That was two years after her father's death and a short time after her sweetheart—the one we believed would marry her—had deserted her. After her father's death she went out very little; after her sweetheart went away, people hardly saw her at all. A few of the ladies had the temerity to call, but were not received, and the only sign of life about the place was the Negro man—a young man then—going in and out with a market basket.

"Just as if a man—any man—could keep a kitchen properly," the ladies said; so they were not surprised when the smell developed. It was another link between the gross, teeming world and the high and mighty Griersons.

A neighbor, a woman, complained to the mayor, Judge Stevens, eighty years old.

"But what will you have me do about it, madam?" he said.

"Why, send her word to stop it," the woman said. "Isn't there a law?"

"I'm sure that won't be necessary," Judge Stevens said. "It's probably just a snake or a rat that nigger of hers killed in the yard. I'll speak to him about it."

The next day he received two more complaints, one from a man who came in diffident deprecation. "We really must do something about it, Judge. I'd be the last one in the world to bother Miss Emily, but we've got to do something." That night the Board of Aldermen met—three graybeards and one younger man, a member of the rising generation.

"It's simple enough," he said. "Send her word to have her place cleaned up. Give her a certain time to do it in, and if she don't . . .

"Dammit, sir," Judge Stevens said, "will you accuse a lady to her face of smelling bad?"

So the next night, after midnight, four men crossed Miss Emily's lawn and slunk about the house like burglars, sniffing along the base of the brickwork and at the cellar openings while one of them performed a regular sowing motion with his hand out of a sack slung from his shoulder. They broke open the cellar door and sprinkled lime there, and in all the outbuildings. As they recrossed the lawn, a window that had been dark was lighted and Miss Emily sat in it, the light behind her, and her upright torso motionless as that of an idol. They crept quietly across the lawn and into the shadow of the locusts that lined the street. After a week or two the smell went away.

That was when people had begun to feel really sorry for her. People in our town, remembering how old lady Wyatt, her great-aunt, had gone completely crazy at last, believed that the Griersons held themselves a little too high for what they really were. None of the young men were quite good enough for Miss Emily and such. We had long thought of them as a tableau, Miss Emily a slender figure in white in the background, her father a spraddled silhouette in the foreground, his back to her and clutching a horsewhip, the two of them framed by the back-flung front door. So when she got to be thirty and was still single, we were not pleased exactly, but vindicated; even with insanity in the family she wouldn't have turned down all of her chances if they had really materialized.

When her father died, it got about that the house was all that was left to her; and in a way, people were glad. At last they could pity Miss Emily. Being left alone, and a pauper, she had become humanized. Now she too would know the old thrill and the old despair of a penny more or less.

The day after his death all the ladies prepared to call at the house and offer condolence and aid, as is our custom. Miss Emily met them at the door, dressed as usual and with no trace of grief on her face.

She told them that her father was not dead. She did that for three days, with the ministers calling on her, and the doctors, trying to persuade her to let them dispose of the body. Just as they were about to resort to law and force, she broke down, and they buried her father quickly.

We did not say she was crazy then. We believed she had to do that. We remembered all the young men her father had driven away, and we knew that with nothing left, she would have to cling to that which had robbed her, as people will.

III

She was sick for a long time. When we saw her again, her hair was cut short, making her look like a girl, with a vague resemblance to those angels in colored church windows–sort of tragic and serene.

The town had just let the contracts for paving the sidewalks, and in the summer after her father's death they began the work. The construction company came with niggers and mules and machinery, and a foreman named Homer Barron, a Yankee–a big, dark, ready man, with a big voice and eyes lighter than his face. The little boys would follow in groups to hear him cuss the niggers, and the niggers singing in time to the rise and fall of picks. Pretty soon he knew everybody in town. Whenever you heard a lot of laughing anywhere about the square, Homer Barron would be in the center of the group. Presently we began to see him and Miss Emily on Sunday afternoons driving in the yellow-wheeled buggy and the matched team of bays from the livery stable.

At first we were glad that Miss Emily would have an interest, because the ladies all said, "Of course a Grierson would not think seriously of a Northerner, a day laborer." But there were still others, older people, who said that even grief could not cause a real lady to forget *noblesse oblige*–without calling it *noblesse oblige*. They just said, "Poor Emily. Her kinsfolk should come to her." She had some kin in Alabama; but years ago her father had fallen out with them over the estate of old lady Wyatt, the crazy woman, and there was no communication between the two families. They had not even been represented at the funeral.

And as soon as the old people said, "Poor Emily," the whispering began. "Do you suppose it's really so?" they said to one another. "Of course it is. What else could . . ." This behind their hands; rustling of craned silk and satin behind jalousies closed upon the sun of

Sunday afternoon as the thin, swift clop-clop-clop of the matched team passed: "Poor Emily."

She carried her head high enough—even when we believed that she was fallen. It was as if she demanded more than ever the recognition of her dignity as the last Grierson; as if it had wanted that touch of earthiness to reaffirm her imperviousness. Like when she bought the rat poison, the arsenic. That was over a year after they had begun to say "Poor Emily," and while the two female cousins were visiting her.

"I want some poison," she said to the druggist. She was over thirty then, still a slight woman, though thinner than usual, with cold, haughty black eyes in a face the flesh of which was strained across the temples and about the eye-sockets as you imagine a lighthouse-keeper's face ought to look. "I want some poison," she said.

"Yes, Miss Emily. What kind? For rats and such? I'd recom—"

"I want the best you have. I don't care what kind."

The druggist named several. "They'll kill anything up to an elephant. But what you want is—"

"Arsenic," Miss Emily said. "Is that a good one?"

"Is . . . arsenic? Yes, ma'am. But what you want—"

"I want arsenic."

The druggist looked down at her. She looked back at him, erect, her face like a strained flag. "Why, of course," the druggist said. "If that's what you want. But the law requires you to tell what you are going to use it for."

Miss Emily just stared at him, her head tilted back in order to look him eye for eye, until he looked away and went and got the arsenic and wrapped it up. The Negro delivery boy brought her the package; the druggist didn't come back. When she opened the package at home there was written on the box, under the skull and bones: "For rats."

IV

So the next day we all said, "She will kill herself"; and we said it would be the best thing. When she had first begun to be seen with Homer Barron, we had said, "She will marry him." Then we said, "She will persuade him yet," because Homer himself had remarked—he liked men, and it was known that he drank with the younger men in the Elks' Club—that he was not a marrying man. Later we said, "Poor Emily" behind the jalousies as they passed on Sunday afternoon in the glittering buggy, Miss Emily with her head high and Homer Barron with his hat cocked and a cigar in his teeth, reins and whip in a yellow glove.

Then some of the ladies began to say that it was a disgrace to the town and a bad example to the young people. The men did not want to interfere, but at last the ladies forced the Baptist minister—Miss Emily's people were Episcopal—to call upon her. He would never divulge what happened during that interview, but he refused to go back again. The next Sunday they again drove about the streets, and the following day the minister's wife wrote to Miss Emily's relations in Alabama.

So she had blood-kin under her roof again and we sat back to watch developments. At first nothing happened. Then we were sure that they were to be married. We learned that Miss Emily had been to the jeweler's and ordered a man's toilet set in silver, with the letters H. B. on each piece. Two days later we learned that she had bought a complete outfit of men's clothing, including a nightshirt, and we said, "They are married." We were really glad. We were glad because the two female cousins were even more Grierson than Miss Emily had ever been.

So we were not surprised when Homer Barron—the streets had been finished some time since—was gone. We were a little disappointed that there was not a public blowing-off, but we believed that he had gone on to prepare for Miss Emily's coming, or to give her a chance to get rid of the cousins. (By that time it was a cabal, and we were all Miss Emily's allies to help circumvent the cousins.) Sure enough, after another week they departed. And, as we had expected all along, within three days Homer Barron was back in town. A neighbor saw the Negro man admit him at the kitchen door at dusk one evening.

And that was the last we saw of Homer Barron. And of Miss Emily for some time. The Negro man went in and out with the market basket, but the front door remained closed. Now and then we would see her at a window for a moment, as the men did that night when they sprinkled the lime, but for almost six months she did not appear on the streets. Then we knew that this was to be expected too; as if that quality of her father which had thwarted her woman's life so many times had been too virulent and too furious to die.

When we next saw Miss Emily, she had grown fat and her hair was turning gray. During the next few years it grew grayer and grayer until it attained an even pepper-and-salt iron-gray, when it ceased turning. Up to the day of her death at seventy-four it was still that vigorous iron-gray, like the hair of an active man.

From that time on her front door remained closed, save for a period of six or seven years, when she was about forty, during which she gave lessons in china-painting. She fitted up a studio in one of the downstairs rooms, where the daughters and granddaughters of Colonel Sartoris' contemporaries were sent to her with the same regularity and in the same spirit that they were sent to church on Sundays with a twenty-five-cent piece for the collection plate. Meanwhile her taxes had been remitted.

Then the newer generation became the backbone and the spirit of the town, and the painting pupils grew up and fell away and did not send their children to her with boxes of color and tedious brushes and pictures cut from the ladies' magazines. The front door closed upon the last one and remained closed for good. When the town got free postal delivery, Miss Emily alone refused to let them fasten the metal numbers above her door and attach a mailbox to it. She would not listen to them.

Daily, monthly, yearly we watched the Negro grow grayer and more stooped, going in and out with the market basket. Each December we sent her a tax notice, which would be returned by the post office a week later, unclaimed. Now and then we would see her in one of the downstairs windows—she had evidently shut up the top floor of the house—like the carven torso of an idol in a niche, looking or not looking at us, we could never tell which. Thus she passed from generation to generation—dear, inescapable, impervious, tranquil, and perverse.

And so she died. Fell ill in the house filled with dust and shadows, with only a doddering Negro man to wait on her. We did not even know she was sick; we had long since given up trying to get any information from the Negro. He talked to no one, probably not even to her, for his voice had grown harsh and rusty, as if from disuse.

She died in one of the downstairs rooms, in a heavy walnut bed with a curtain, her gray head propped on a pillow yellow and moldy with age and lack of sunlight.

V

The Negro met the first of the ladies at the front door and let them in, with their hushed, sibilant voices and their quick, curious glances, and then he disappeared. He walked right through the house and out the back and was not seen again.

The two female cousins came at once. They held the funeral on the second day, with the town coming to look at Miss Emily beneath a mass of bought flowers, with the crayon face of her father musing profoundly above the bier and the ladies sibilant and macabre; and the very old men—some in their brushed Confederate uniforms—on the porch and the lawn, talking of Miss Emily as if she had been a contemporary of theirs, believing that they had danced with her and courted her perhaps, confusing time with its mathematical progression, as the old do, to whom all the past is not a diminishing road but, instead, a huge meadow which no winter ever quite touches, divided from them now by the narrow bottleneck of the most recent decade of years.

Already we knew that there was one room in that region above stairs which no one had seen in forty years, and which would have to be forced. They waited until Miss Emily was decently in the ground before they opened it.

The violence of breaking down the door seemed to fill this room with pervading dust. A thin, acrid pall as of the tomb seemed to lie everywhere upon this room decked and furnished as for a bridal: upon the valance curtains of faded rose color, upon the rose-shaded lights, upon the dressing table, upon the delicate array of crystal and the man's toilet things backed with tarnished silver, silver so tarnished that the monogram was obscured. Among them lay a collar and tie, as if they had just been removed, which, lifted, left upon the surface a pale crescent in the dust. Upon a chair hung the suit, carefully folded; beneath it the two mute shoes and the discarded socks.

The man himself lay in the bed.

For a long while we just stood there, looking down at the profound and fleshless grin. The body had apparently once lain in the attitude of an embrace, but now the long sleep that outlasts love, that conquers even the grimace of love, had cuckolded him. What was left of him, rotted beneath what was left of the nightshirt, had become inextricable from the bed in which he lay; and upon him and upon the pillow beside him lay that even coating of the patient and biding dust.

Then we noticed that in the second pillow was the indentation of a head. One of us lifted something from it, and leaning forward, that faint and invisible dust dry and acrid in the nostrils, we saw a long strand of iron-gray hair.

Questions

1. What details describing Homer are significant to the outcome of the story?
2. What are the important clues in the relationship between Emily and her father?
3. How does the town's attitude contribute to Emily's actions?
4. Examine Emily's activities after Homer's "disappearance." What do they indicate about Emily's desires to retain the past?
5. What becomes of Tobe? Why?
6. What are the possible meanings we can give to Emily as "fallen monument"?
7. What does Faulkner's title have to do with the story? In other words, in what ways can we read the title, "A Rose for Emily"?

Topics for Composition

1. Place Emily as an individual within the "protest" theme. Write an essay in which you illustrate Emily's instances of rejection of authority and, equally important, an essay in which you propose the reasons for her rejections of authority.
2. At least part of the horror in the story arises from the distorted view we receive of Emily. Part of this distortion arises from the author's tampering with a chronological time sequence. Analyze his chronology and comment upon its effect on the story.
3. Using the story as your beginning point, write an argumentative essay showing that an Emily can no longer exist in modern urban society.

ROTH's "The Conversion of the Jews" clearly spans multiple levels of meaning, ranging from an examination of youthful inquisitiveness to a plea for religious and social ecumenicity. Several aspects of the story help in understanding Roth's movement through his levels of meaning. Note the following:

1. The language used by Ozzie and Itzie in their opening "theological" discussion
2. The contrast presented between Ozzie's inquiring mind and the learned responses of his mother, the Rabbi, and the custodian
3. Ozzie's reaction to the power of his individual protest
4. The impact of unexpected action on the mass mind

The Conversion of the Jews

PHILIP ROTH

"You're a real one for opening your mouth in the first place," Itzie said. "What do you open your mouth all the time for?"

"I didn't bring it up, Itz, I didn't," Ozzie said.

"What do you care about Jesus Christ for anyway?"

"I didn't bring up Jesus Christ. He did. I didn't even know what he was talking about. Jesus is historical, he kept saying. Jesus is historical." Ozzie mimicked the monumental voice of Rabbi Binder.

"Jesus was a person that lived like you and me," Ozzie continued. "That's what Binder said–"

"Yeah? . . . So what! What do I give two cents whether he lived or not. And what do you gotta open your mouth!" Itzie Lieberman favored closed-mouthedness, especially when it came to Ozzie Freedman's questions. Mrs. Freedman had to see Rabbi Binder twice before about Ozzie's questions and this Wednesday at four-thirty would be the third time. Itzie preferred to keep *his* mother in the kitchen; he settled for behind-the-back subleties such as gestures, faces, snarls and other less delicate barnyard noises.

"He was a real person, Jesus, but he wasn't like God, and we don't believe he is God." Slowly, Ozzie was explaining Rabbi Binder's position to Itzie, who had been absent from Hebrew School the previous afternoon.

"The Catholics," Itzie said helpfully, "they believe in Jesus Christ, that he's God." Itzie Lieberman used "the Catholics" in its broadest sense–to include the Protestants.

Ozzie received Itzie's remark with a tiny head bob, as though it were a footnote, and went on. "His mother was Mary, and his father probably was Joseph," Ozzie said. "But the New Testament says his real father was God."

"His *real* father?"

"Yeah," Ozzie said, "that's the big thing, his father's supposed to be God."

"Bull."

"That's what Rabbi Binder says, that it's impossible–"

"Sure it's impossible. That stuff's all bull. To have a baby you gotta get laid," Itzie theologized. "Mary hadda get laid."

"That's what Binder says: 'The only way a woman can have a baby is to have intercourse with a man.' "

"He said *that*, Ozz?" For a moment it appeared that Itzie had put the theological question aside. "He said that, intercourse?" A little curled smile shaped itself in the lower half of Itzie's face like a pink mustache. "What you guys do, Ozz, you laugh or something?"

"I raised my hand."

"Yeah? Whatja say?"

"That's when I asked the question."

Itzie's face lit up. "Whatja ask about—intercourse?"

"No, I asked the question about God, how if He could create the heaven and earth in six days, and make all the animals and the fish and the light in six days—the light especially, that's what always gets me, that He could make the light. Making fish and animals, that's pretty good—"

"That's damn good." Itzie's appreciation was honest but unimaginative: it was as though God had just pitched a one-hitter.

"But making light . . . I mean when you think about it, it's really something," Ozzie said. "Anyway, I asked Binder if He could make all that in six days, and He could *pick* the six days he wanted right out of nowhere, why couldn't He let a woman have a baby without having intercourse."

"You said intercourse, Ozz, to Binder?"

"Yeah."

"Right in class?"

"Yeah."

Itzie smacked the side of his head.

"I mean, no kidding around," Ozzie said, "that'd really be nothing. After all that other stuff, that'd practically be nothing."

Itzie considered a moment. "What'd Binder say?"

"He started all over again explaining how Jesus was historical and how he lived like you and me but he wasn't God. So I said I under*stood* that. What I wanted to know was different."

What Ozzie wanted to know was always different. The first time he had wanted to know how Rabbi Binder could call the Jews "The Chosen People" if the Declaration of Independence claimed all men to be created equal. Rabbi Binder tried to distinguish for him between political equality and spiritual legitimacy, but what Ozzie wanted to know, he insisted vehemently, was different. That was the first time his mother had to come.

Then there was the plane crash. Fifty-eight people had been killed in a plane crash at La Guardia. In studying a casualty list in the newspaper his mother had discovered among the list of those dead eight

Jewish names (his grandmother had nine but she counted Miller as a Jewish name); because of the eight she said the plane crash was "a tragedy." During free-discussion time on Wednesday Ozzie had brought to Rabbi Binder's attention this matter of "some of his relations" always picking out the Jewish names. Rabbi Binder had begun to explain cultural unity and some other things when Ozzie stood up at his seat and said that what he wanted to know was different. Rabbi Binder insisted that he sit down and it was then that Ozzie shouted that he wished all fifty-eight were Jews. That was the second time his mother came.

"And he kept explaining about Jesus being historical, and so I kept asking him. No kidding, Itz, he was trying to make me look stupid."

"So what he finally do?"

"Finally he starts screaming that I was deliberately simple-minded and a wise guy, and that my mother had to come, and this was the last time. And that I'd never get bar-mitzvahed if he could help it. Then, Itz, then he starts talking in the voice like a statue, real slow and deep, and he says that I better think over what I said about the Lord. He told me to go to his office and think it over." Ozzie leaned his body toward Itzie. "Itz, I thought it over for a solid hour, and now I'm convinced God could do it."

Ozzie had planned to confess his latest transgression to his mother as soon as she came home from work. But it was a Friday night in November and already dark, and when Mrs. Freedman came through the door she tossed off her coat, kissed Ozzie quickly on the face, and went to the kitchen table to light the three yellow candles, two for the Sabbath and one for Ozzie's father.

When his mother lit the candles she would move her two arms slowly towards her, dragging them through the air, as though persuading people whose minds were half made up. And her eyes would get glassy with tears. Even when his father was alive Ozzie remembered that her eyes had gotten glassy, so it didn't have anything to do with his dying. It had something to do with lighting the candles.

As she touched the flaming match to the unlit wick of a Sabbath candle, the phone rang, and Ozzie, standing only a foot from it, plucked off the receiver and held it muffled to his chest. When his mother lit candles Ozzie felt there should be no noise; even breathing, if you could manage it, should be softened. Ozzie pressed the phone to his breast and watched his mother dragging whatever she was dragging, and he felt his own eyes get glassy. His mother was a round, tired, gray-haired penguin of a woman whose gray skin had begun to feel the tug of gravity and the weight of her own history. Even when she was dressed up she didn't look like a chosen person. But when she lit candles she looked like something better; like a woman who knew momentarily that God could do anything.

After a few mysterious minutes she was finished. Ozzie hung up the phone and walked to the kitchen table where she was beginning to lay the two places for the four-course Sabbath meal. He told her that she would have to see Rabbi Binder next Wednesday at four-thirty, and then he told her why. For the first time in their life together she hit Ozzie across the face with her hand.

All through the chopped liver and chicken soup part of the dinner Ozzie cried; he didn't have any appetite for the rest.

On Wednesday, in the largest of the three basement classrooms of the synagogue, Rabbi Marvin Binder, a tall, handsome, broad-shouldered man of thirty with thick strong-fibered black hair, removed his watch from his pocket and saw that it was four o'clock. At the rear of the room, Yakov Blotnik, the seventy-one-year-old custodian, slowly polished the large window, mumbling to himself, unaware that it was four o'clock or six o'clock, Monday or Wednesday. To most of the students Yakov Blotnik's mumbling along with his brown curly beard, scythe nose, and two heel-trailing black cats, made of him an object of wonder, a foreigner, a relic, towards whom they were alternately fearful and disrespectful. To Ozzie the mumbling had always seemed a monotonous, curious prayer; what made it curious was that old Blotnik had been mumbling so steadily for so many years, Ozzie suspected he had memorized the prayers and forgotten all about God.

"It is now free-discussion time," Rabbi Binder said. "Feel free to talk about any Jewish matter at all—religion, family, politics, sports—"

There was silence. It was a gusty, clouded November afternoon and it did not seem as though there ever was or could be a thing called baseball. So nobody this week said a word about that hero from the past, Hank Greenberg—which limited free discussion considerably.

And the soul-battering Ozzie Freedman had just received from Rabbi Binder had imposed its limitation. When it was Ozzie's turn to read aloud from the Hebrew book the rabbi had asked him petulantly why he didn't read more rapidly. He was showing no progress. Ozzie said he could read faster but that if he did he was sure not to understand what he was reading. Nevertheless, at the rabbi's repeated suggestion Ozzie tried, and showed a great talent, but in the midst of a long passage he stopped short and said he didn't understand a word he was reading, and started in again at a drag-footed pace. Then came the soul-battering.

Consequently when free-discussion time rolled around none of the students felt too free. The rabbi's invitation was answered only by the mumbling of feeble old Blotnik.

"Isn't there anything at all you would like to discuss?" Rabbi Binder asked again, looking at his watch. "No questions or comments?"

There was a small grumble from the third row. The rabbi requested that Ozzie rise and give the rest of the class the advantage of his thought.

Ozzie rose. "I forget it now," he said, and sat down in his place.

Rabbi Binder advanced a seat towards Ozzie and poised himself on the edge of the desk. It was Itzie's desk and the rabbi's frame only a dagger's-length away from his face snapped him to sitting attention.

"Stand up again, Oscar," Rabbi Binder said calmly, "and try to assemble your thoughts."

Ozzie stood up. All his classmates turned in their seats and watched as he gave an unconvincing scratch to his forehead.

"I can't assemble any," he announced, and plunked himself down.

"Stand up!" Rabbi Binder advanced from Itzie's desk to the one directly in front of Ozzie; when the rabbinical back was turned Itzie gave it five-fingers off the tip of his nose, causing a small titter in the room. Rabbi Binder was too absorbed in squelching Ozzie's nonsense once and for all to bother with titters. "Stand up, Oscar. What's your question about?"

Ozzie pulled a word out of the air. It was the handiest word. "Religion."

"Oh, now you remember?"

"Yes."

"What is it?"

Trapped, Ozzie blurted the first thing that came to him. "Why can't He make anything He wants to make!"

As Rabbi Binder prepared an answer, a final answer, Itzie, ten feet behind him, raised one finger on his left hand, gestured it meaningfully towards the rabbi's back, and brought the house down.

Binder twisted quickly to see what had happened and in the midst of the commotion Ozzie shouted into the rabbi's back what he couldn't have shouted to his face. It was a loud, toneless sound that had the timbre of something stored inside for about six days.

"You don't know! You don't know anything about God!"

The rabbi spun back towards Ozzie. "What?"

"You don't know—you don't—"

"Apologize, Oscar, apologize!" It was a threat.

"You don't—"

Rabbi Binder's hand flicked out at Ozzie's cheek. Perhaps it had only been meant to clamp the boy's mouth shut, but Ozzie ducked and the palm caught him squarely on the nose.

The blood came in a short, red spurt on to Ozzie's shirt front.

The next moment was all confusion. Ozzie screamed, "You bastard, you bastard!" and broke for the classroom door. Rabbi Binder lurched a step backwards, as though his own blood had started flowing violently in the opposite direction, then gave a clumsy lurch forward and bolted out the door after Ozzie. The class followed after the rabbi's huge blue-suited back, and before old Blotnik could turn from his window, the room was empty and everyone was headed full speed up the three flights leading to the roof.

If one should compare the light of day to the life of man: sunrise to birth; sunset—the dropping down over the edge—to death; then as Ozzie Freedman wiggled through the trapdoor of the synagogue roof, his feet kicking backwards bronco-style at Rabbi Binder's outstretched arms—at that moment the day was fifty years old. As a rule, fifty or fifty-five reflects accurately the age of late afternoons in November, for it is in that month, during those hours, that one's awareness of light seems no longer a matter of seeing, but of hearing: light begins clicking away. In fact, as Ozzie locked shut the trapdoor in the rabbi's face, the sharp click of the bolt into the lock might momentarily have been mistaken for the sound of the heavier gray that had just throbbed through the sky.

With all his weight Ozzie kneeled on the locked door; any instant he was certain that Rabbi Binder's shoulder would fling it open, splintering the wood into shrapnel and catapulting his body into the sky. But the door did not move and below him he heard only the rumble of feet, first loud then dim, like thunder rolling away.

A question shot through his brain. "Can this be *me?*" For a thirteen-year-old who had just labeled his religious leader a bastard, twice, it was not an improper question. Louder and louder the question came to him—"Is it me? Is it me?"—until he discovered himself no longer kneeling, but racing crazily toward the edge of the roof, his eyes crying, his throat screaming, and his arms flying everywhich-way as though not his own.

"Is it me? Is it me Me ME ME ME! It has to be me—but is it!"

It is the question a thief must ask himself the night he jimmies open his first window, and it is said to be the question with which bridegrooms quiz themselves before the altar.

In the few wild seconds it took Ozzie's body to propel him to the edge of the roof, his self-examination began to grow fuzzy. Gazing down at the street he became confused as to the problem beneath the question: was it, is-it-me-who-called-Binder-a-Bastard? or, is-it-me-prancing-around-on-the-roof? However, the scene below settled all, for there is an instant in any action when whether it is you or somebody else is academic. The thief crams the money in his pockets and scoots out the window. The bridegroom signs the hotel register for two. And the boy on the roof finds a streetful of people gaping at him, necks stretched backwards, faces up, as though he were the ceiling of the Hayden Planetarium. Suddenly you know it's you.

"Oscar! Oscar Freedman!" A voice rose from the center of the crowd, a voice that, could it have been seen, would have looked like the writing on a scroll. "Oscar Freedman, get down from there. Immediately!" Rabbi Binder was pointing one arm stiffly up at him; and at the end of that arm, one finger aimed menacingly. It was the attitude of a dictator, but one—the eyes confessed all—whose personal valet had spit neatly in his face.

Ozzie didn't answer. Only for a blink's length did he look towards Rabbi Binder. Instead his eyes began to fit together the world beneath him, to sort out people from places, friends from enemies, participants from spectators. In little jagged starlike clusters his friends stood around Rabbi Binder, who was still pointing. The topmost point on a star compounded not of angels but of five adolescent boys was Itzie. What a world it was, with those stars below, Rabbi Binder below . . . Ozzie, who a moment earlier hadn't been able to control his own body, started to feel the meaning of the word control: he felt Peace and he felt Power.

"Oscar Freedman, I'll give you three to come down."

Few dictators give their subjects three to do anything; but, as always, Rabbi Binder only looked dictatorial.

"Are you ready, Oscar?"

Ozzie nodded his head yes, although he had no intention in the world—the lower one or the celestial one he'd just entered—of coming down even if Rabbi Binder should give him a million.

"All right then," said Rabbi Binder. He ran a hand through his black Samson hair as though it were the gesture prescribed for uttering the first digit. Then, with his other hand cutting a circle out of the small piece of sky around him, he spoke. "One!"

There was no thunder. On the contrary, at that moment, as though "one" was the cue for which he had been waiting, the world's least thunderous person appeared on the synagogue steps. He did not so much come out the synagogue door as lean out, onto the darkening air. He clutched at the doorknob with one hand and looked up at the roof.

"Oy!"

Yakov Blotnik's old mind hobbled slowly, as if on crutches, and though he couldn't decide precisely what the boy was doing on the roof, he knew it wasn't good—that is, it wasn't-good-for-the-Jews. For Yakov Blotnik life had fractionated itself simply: things were either good-for-the-Jews or no-good-for-the-Jews.

He smacked his free hand to his in-sucked cheek, gently. "Oy, Gut!" And then quickly as he was able, he jacked down his head and surveyed the street. There was Rabbi Binder (like a man at an auction with only three dollars in his pocket, he had just delivered a shaky "Two!"); there were the students, and that was all. So far it-wasn't-so-bad-for-the-Jews. But the boy had to come down immediately, before anybody saw. The problem: how to get the boy off the roof?

Anybody who has ever had a cat on the roof knows how to get him down. You call the fire department. Or first you call the operator and you ask her for the fire department. And the next thing there is great jamming of brakes and clanging of bells and shouting of instructions. And then the cat is off the roof. You do the same thing to get a boy off the roof.

That is, you do the same thing if you are Yakov Blotnik and you once had a cat on the roof.

When the engines, all four of them, arrived, Rabbi Binder had four times given Ozzie the count of three. The big hook-and-ladder swung around the corner and one of the firemen leaped from it, plunging headlong towards the yellow fire hydrant in front of the synagogue. With a huge wrench he began to unscrew the top nozzle. Rabbi Binder raced over to him and pulled at his shoulder.

"There's no fire . . ."

The fireman mumbled back over his shoulder and, heatedly, continued working at the nozzle.

"But there's no fire, there's no fire . . ." Binder shouted. When the fireman mumbled again, the rabbi grasped his face with both hands and pointed it up at the roof.

To Ozzie it looked as though Rabbi Binder was trying to tug the fireman's head out of his body, like a cork from a bottle. He had to giggle at the picture they made: it was a family portrait–rabbi in black skullcap, fireman in red fire hat, and the little yellow hydrant squatting beside like a kid brother, bareheaded. From the edge of the roof Ozzie waved at the portrait, a one-handed, flapping, mocking wave; in doing it his right foot slipped from under him. Rabbi Binder covered his eyes with his hands.

Firemen work fast. Before Ozzie had even regained his balance, a big, round, yellowed net was being held on the synagogue lawn. The firemen who held it looked up at Ozzie with stern, feelingless faces.

One of the firemen turned his head towards Rabbi Binder. "What, is the kid nuts or something?"

Rabbi Binder unpeeled his hands from his eyes, slowly, painfully, as if they were tape. Then he checked: nothing on the sidewalk, no dents in the net.

"Is he gonna jump, or what?" the fireman shouted.

In a voice not at all like a statue, Rabbi Binder finally answered. "Yes, Yes, I think so . . . He's been threatening to . . ."

Threatening to? Why, the reason he was on the roof, Ozzie remembered, was to get away; he hadn't even thought about jumping. He had just run to get away, and the truth was that he hadn't really headed for the roof as much as he'd been chased there.

"What's his name, the kid?"

"Freedman," Rabbi Binder answered. "Oscar Freedman."

The fireman looked up at Ozzie. "What is it with you, Oscar? You gonna jump, or what?"

Ozzie did not answer. Frankly, the question had just arisen.

"Look, Oscar, if you're gonna jump, jump–and if you're not gonna jump, don't jump. But don't waste our time, willya?"

Ozzie looked at the fireman and then at Rabbi Binder. He wanted to see Rabbi Binder cover his eyes one more time.

"I'm going to jump."

And then he scampered around the edge of the roof to the corner, where there was no net below, and he flapped his arms at his sides, swishing the air and smacking his palms to his trousers on the downbeat. He began screaming like some kind of engine, "Wheeeee . . . wheeeee," and leaning way out over the edge with the upper half of his body. The firemen whipped around to cover the ground with the net. Rabbi Binder mumbled a few words to Somebody and covered his eyes. Everything happened quickly, jerkily, as in a silent movie. The crowd, which had arrived with the fire engines, gave out a long, Fourth-of-July fireworks oooh-aahhh. In the excitement no one had paid the crowd much heed, except, of course, Yakov Blotnik, who swung from the doorknob counting heads. "Fier und tsvansik . . . finf und tsvantsik . . . Oy, Gut!" It wasn't like this with the cat.

Rabbi Binder peeked through his fingers, checked the sidewalk and net. Empty. But there was Ozzie racing to the other corner. The firemen raced with him but were unable to keep up. Whenever Oscar wanted to he might jump and splatter himself upon the sidewalk, and by the time the firemen scooted to the spot all they could do with their net would be to cover the mess.

"Wheeeee . . . wheeeee . . ."

"Hey, Oscar," the winded fireman yelled, "What the hell is this, a game or something?"

"Wheeeee . . . wheeeee . . ."

"Hey, Oscar–"

But he was off now to the other corner, flapping his wings fiercely. Rabbi Binder couldn't take it any longer–the fire engines from nowhere, the screaming suicidal boy, the net. He fell to his knees, exhausted, and with his hands curled together in front of his chest like a little dome, he pleaded, "Oscar, stop it, Oscar. Don't jump, Oscar. Please come down . . . Please don't jump."

And further back in the crowd a single voice, a single young voice, shouted a lone word to the boy on the roof.

"Jump!"

It was Itzie. Ozzie momentarily stopped flapping.

"Go ahead, Ozz–jump!" Itzie broke off his point of the star and courageously, with the inspiration not of a wise-guy but of a disciple, stood alone. "Jump, Ozz, jump!"

Still on his knees, his hands still curled, Rabbi Binder twisted his body back. He looked at Itzie, then, agonizingly, back to Ozzie.

"Oscar, DON'T JUMP! PLEASE, DON'T JUMP . . . please please . . ."

"Jump!" This time it wasn't Itzie but another point of the star. By the time Mrs. Freedman arrived to keep her four-thirty appointment with Rabbi Binder, the whole little upside down heaven was shouting and pleading for Ozzie to jump, and Rabbi Binder no longer was pleading with him not to jump, but was crying into the dome of his hands.

Understandably Mrs. Freedman couldn't figure out what her son was doing on the roof. So she asked.

"Ozzie, my Ozzie, what are you doing? My Ozzie, what is it?"

Ozzie stopped wheeeeeing and slowed his arms down to a cruising flap, the kind birds use in soft winds, but he did not answer. He stood against the low, clouded, darkening sky–light clicked down swiftly now, as on a small gear–flapping softly and gazing down at the small bundle of a woman who was his mother.

"What are you doing, Ozzie?" She turned towards the kneeling Rabbi Binder and rushed so close that only a paper-thickness of dusk lay between her stomach and his shoulders.

"What is my baby doing?"

Rabbi Binder gaped up at her but he too was mute. All that moved was the dome of his hands; it shook back and forth like a weak pulse.

"Rabbi, get him down! He'll kill himself. Get him down, my only baby..."

"I can't," Rabbi Binder said, "I can't . . ." and he turned his handsome head towards the crowd of boys behind him. "It's them. Listen to them."

And for the first time Mrs. Freedman saw the crowd of boys, and she heard what they were yelling.

"He's doing it for them. He won't listen to me. It's them." Rabbi Binder spoke like one in a trance.

"For them?"

"Yes."

"Why for them?"

"They want him to . . ."

Mrs. Freedman raised her two arms upward as though she were conducting the sky. "For them he's doing it!" And then in a gesture older than pyramids, older than prophets and floods, her arms came slapping down to her sides. "A martyr I have. Look!" She tilted her head to the roof. Ozzie was still flapping softly. "My martyr."

"Oscar, come down, *please*," Rabbi Binder groaned.

In a startlingly even voice Mrs. Freedman called to the boy on the roof. "Ozzie, come down, Ozzie. Don't be a martyr, my baby."

As though it were a litany, Rabbi Binder repeated her words. "Don't be a martyr, my baby. Don't be a martyr."

"Gawhead, Ozz–*be* a Martin!" It was Itzie. "Be a Martin, be a

Martin," and all the voices joined in singing for Martindom, whatever *it* was. "Be a Martin, be a Martin . . ."

Somehow when you're on a roof the darker it gets the less you can hear. All Ozzie knew was that two groups wanted two new things: his friends were spirited and musical about what they wanted; his mother and the rabbi were even-toned, chanting, about what they didn't want. The rabbi's voice was without tears now and so was his mother's.

The big net stared up at Ozzie like a sightless eye. The big, clouded sky pushed down. From beneath it looked like a gray corrugated board. Suddenly, looking up into that unsympathetic sky, Ozzie realized all the strangeness of what these people, his friends, were asking: they wanted him to jump, to kill himself; they were singing about it now—it made them that happy. And there was an even greater strangeness: Rabbi Binder was on his knees, trembling. If there was a question to be asked now it was not "Is it me?" but rather "Is it us? . . . Is it us?"

Being on the roof, it turned out, was a serious thing. If he jumped would the singing become dancing? Would it? What would jumping stop? Yearningly, Ozzie wished he could rip open the sky, plunge his hands through, and pull out the sun; and on the sun, like a coin, would be stamped JUMP or DON'T JUMP.

Ozzie's knees rocked and sagged a little under him as though they were setting him for a dive. His arms tightened, stiffened, froze, from shoulders to fingernails. He felt as if each part of his body were going to vote as to whether he should kill himself or not—and each part as though it were independent of *him*.

The light took an unexpected click down and the new darkness, like a gag, hushed the friends singing for this and the mother and rabbi chanting for that.

Ozzie stopped counting votes, and in a curiously high voice, like one who wasn't prepared for speech, he spoke.

"Mamma?"

"Yes, Oscar."

"Mamma, get down on your knees, like Rabbi Binder."

"Oscar—"

"Get down on your knees," he said, "or I'll jump."

Ozzie heard a whimper, then a quick rustling, and when he looked down where his mother had stood he saw the top of a head and beneath that a circle of dress. She was kneeling beside Rabbi Binder.

He spoke again. "Everybody kneel." There was the sound of everybody kneeling.

Ozzie looked around. With one hand he pointed towards the synagogue entrance. "Make *him* kneel."

There was a noise, not of kneeling, but of body-and-cloth stretching. Ozzie could hear Rabbi Binder saying in a gruff whisper, ". . . or he'll *kill* himself," and when next he looked there was Yakov Blotnik off the doornob and for the first time in his life upon his knees in the Gentile posture of prayer.

As for the firemen—it is not as difficult as one might imagine to hold a net taut while you are kneeling.

Ozzie looked around again; and then he called to Rabbi Binder.

"Rabbi?"

"Yes, Oscar."

"Rabbi Binder, do you believe in God."

"Yes."

"Do you believe God can do Anything?" Ozzie leaned his head out into the darkness. "Anything?"

"Oscar, I think—"

"Tell me you believe God can do Anything."

There was a second's hesitation. Then: "God can do Anything."

"Tell me you believe God can make a child without intercourse."

"He can."

"Tell me!"

"God," Rabbi Binder admitted, "can make a child without intercourse."

"Mamma, you tell me."

"God can make a child without intercourse," his mother said.

"Make *him* tell me." There was no doubt who *him* was.

In a few moments Ozzie heard an old comical voice say something to the increasing darkness about God.

Next, Ozzie made everybody say it. And then he made them all say they believed in Jesus Christ—first one at a time, then all together.

When the catechizing was through it was the beginning of evening. From the street it sounded as if the boy on the roof might have sighed.

"Ozzie?" A woman's voice dared to speak. "You'll come down now?"

There was no answer, but the woman waited, and when a voice finally did speak it was thin and crying, and exhausted as that of an old man who has just finished pulling the bells.

"Mamma, don't you see—you shouldn't hit me. He shouldn't hit me. You shouldn't hit me about God, Mamma. You should never hit anybody about God—"

"Ozzie, please come down now."

"Promise me, promise me you'll never hit anybody about God."

He had asked only his mother, but for some reason everyone kneeling in the street promised he would never hit anybody about God.

Once again there was silence.

"I can come down now Mamma," the boy on the roof finally said. He turned his head both ways as though checking the traffic lights. "Now I can come down . . ."

And he did, right into the center of the yellow net that glowed in the evening's edge like an overgrown halo.

Questions

1. Part of the design of this story arises from the juxtaposition of the characters. Each of the major characters provides some complementary attitude to each other character. Consider Ozzie, Itzie, Mrs. Freedman, Rabbi Binder, and Yakov Blotnik. What attitude toward religion does each illustrate? How does that attitude react with each other attitude?
2. What point is Roth making about the system of religion? Why is Rabbi Binder's position indicative of the system?
3. Why does Itzie call to Ozzie to jump from the roof? How does Itzie's action and the support it receives reveal the basic dichotomy in the story?
4. What specific statements in the story emphasize Roth's plea for religious ecumenicity?

Topics for Composition

1. Sensitivity and inquisitiveness beyond his years are marks of Ozzie's character. Write an essay showing how Roth manages to maintain the balance between Ozzie's youth and the maturity of his question.
2. This story exemplifies the power of action by a minority. Write an essay illustrating the power of minority action as it is evidenced in America.
3. Roth's story poses the need for greater understanding among religions. Investigate a religion with which you have little familiarity. Write an essay explaining how such an investigation has benefited you.

Poetry

THE poems that follow will widen considerably our sampling of modern thought on the question of social restraint and will perhaps help us to proceed to deeper reflections on the subject. The passage from William Cowper's *The Task* and William Blake's famous "London" both present in general—and metaphorical—terms the problem of the tendency of institutions to become ends instead of means, even to the point where men are merely used rather than served by them. Man can develop fully only in society, Cowper says; but, he adds, when social organization becomes very complex and specialized, individual development is hampered more than it is aided. Identification with special-interest groups tends to rob the individual of perspective and integrity. If one serves such institutions too zealously he ceases to be a whole man; he becomes instead an instrument, and he begins to treat other men as instruments. If this process continues, imagination, sympathy, and even common sense may be destroyed, and all sorts of oppression rationalized. Such is the state that Blake envisions in his powerful lament. To him the great city of London is the symbol of the complete domination of the human spirit by institutions of its own creating. London is a nightmarish place where man languishes in "mind-forg'd manacles," and every face bears "marks of weakness, marks of woe."

Blake's "The Garden of Love" and the two poems by Robert Burns which follow it deal with the effect of subtler forms of restraint and oppression. Both poets are especially concerned over the tendency of common social sanctions to create a puritanical distrust of human nature and a negative attitude toward virtue. Blake bitterly states the general problem in symbolic terms. Burns uses the weapons of wit and humor in his more down-to-earth descriptions of puritanical attitudes. "Address to the Unco Guid" provides an easy, if rather one-sided, approach to the issue. "Tam o' Shanter," with its scapegrace hero and mock moralizing, takes us to more debatable ground. Amusing as this poem is, it is not intended to be merely entertaining; it is written in a philosophical spirit and has broad symbolic implications.

The negative spirit of puritanism (and we must not forget that a more constructive kind of puritanism has been a most important element in modern culture) has assumed many forms in more recent time—some vicious, like the demagoguery that W. B. Yeats protests against in "The Leaders of the Crowd," some seemingly more bland, like the "Greater Community" described in W. H. Auden's "The Unknown Citizen." Yeats believes that not only followers of the crowd but also the leaders are acting out of insecurity and fear. They do not know that truth flourishes only where "the student's lamp has shone" because they are mortally afraid to face themselves in solitude; to them "that lamp is from the tomb," and they struggle to extinguish it as they would resist physical death. Auden describes a more systematic, comfortable kind of demagoguery, justified, as it would seem, by a general content produced by material prosperity and psychological conditioning. No one has complained, the impersonal voice of the poem says; surely, then, nothing is wrong. But it is evident that the contemporary poet agrees with Cowper that too much organization has a dehumanizing and enslaving effect, even if the grosser forms of inhumanity and oppression are eliminated. Robert Frost and Robinson Jeffers clearly think so too. Jeffers, as bitter as Blake, finds in the wild, indomitable hawk a more admirable creature than what man has become; and Frost, writing in the humorous spirit of Burns, broadly hints that our love of system and efficiency has made us almost antlike. Somewhere between these two extremes expressible only in animal imagery lies the truly human range of individual freedom. Obviously, we are still not sure what the right limits are or how they can be maintained.

From *The Task, Book IV*

WILLIAM COWPER

Man in society is like a flower
Blown[1] in its native bed: 'tis there alone *660*
His faculties, expanded in full bloom,
Shine out; there only reach their proper use.
But man, associated and leagued with man
By regal warrant, or self-joined by bond
For interest sake, or swarming into clans *665*
Beneath one head for purposes of war,
Like flowers selected from the rest, and bound
And bundled close to fill some crowded vase,
Fades rapidly, and, by compression marred,
Contracts defilement not to be endured. *670*
Hence chartered boroughs[2] are such public plagues;

[1] *Blossomed.*
[2] *Urban corporations having monopolistic control over property.*

And burghers men immaculate perhaps,
In all their private functions, once combined,
Become a loathsome body, only fit
For dissolution, hurtful to the main. *675*
Hence merchants, unimpeachable of sin
Against the charities of domestic life,
Incorporated, seem at once to lose
Their nature; and, disclaiming all regard
For mercy and the common rights of man, *680*
Build factories with blood, conducting trade
At the sword's point, and dyeing the white robe
Of innocent commercial justice red.
Hence, too, the field of glory, as the world
Misdeems it, dazzled by its bright array, *685*
With all its majesty of thundering pomp,
Enchanting music, and immortal wreaths,
Is but a school where thoughtlessness is taught
On principle, where foppery atones
For folly, gallantry, for every vice. *690*

1785

Questions

1. What is the difference between "man in society" and man associated with man in organizations having special functions? Does Cowper provide a clear conception of society in a healthful state? Is the comparison with flowers a good analogy? Is it a good metaphor?
2. What three kinds of organization does Cowper specifically condemn? Can you offer better instances? Would Cowper condemn unions?

Address to the Unco Guid,[1] *or the Rigidly Righteous*

ROBERT BURNS

My Son, these maxims make a rule,
An' lump them ay thegither:
The Rigid Righteous is a fool,
The Rigid Wise anither:

[1] *Inordinately good.*

The cleanest corn that e'er was dight,[2]
May hae some pyles o' caff[3] *in;*
So ne'er a fellow-creature slight
For random fits o' daffin.[4]

SOLOMON (Ecclesiastes 7:16)

O ye, wha are sae guid yoursel,
Sae pious and sae holy,
Ye've nought to do but mark and tell
Your neebour's fauts and folly;
Whase life is like a weel-gaun[5] mill, *5*
Supplied wi' store o' water;
The heapet happer's[6] ebbing still,
An' still the clap[7] plays clatter!

Hear me, ye venerable core,[8]
As counsel for poor mortals *10*
That frequent pass douce[9] Wisdom's door
For glaikit[10] Folly's portals:
I for their thoughtless, careless sakes,
Would here propone[11] defences,–
Their donsie[12] tricks, their black mistakes, *15*
Their failings and mischances.

Ye see your state wi' theirs compared,
And shudder at the niffer;[13]
But cast a moment's fair regard,
What makes the mighty differ?[14] *20*
Discount what scant occasion gave;
That purity ye pride in;
And (what's aft mair than a' the lave)[15]
Your better art o' hidin'.

Think, when your castigated pulse *25*
Gies now and then a wallop,

[2] *Winnowed.*
[3] *Chaff.*
[4] *Larking, frolicking.*
[5] *Well-going.*
[6] *Heaped hopper.*
[7] *The clapper, which shakes the hopper to keep the grain moving.*
[8] *Corps, group.*
[9] *Sweet.*
[10] *Giddy.*
[11] *Propose.*
[12] *Perverse.*
[13] *Exchange.*
[14] *Difference.*
[15] *Rest.*

What ragings must his veins convulse,
That still eternal gallop!
Wi' wind and tide fair i' your tail,
Right on ye scud your sea-way; *30*
But in the teeth o' baith to sail,
It makes an unco lee-way.

See Social-life and Glee sit down
All joyous and unthinking,
Till, quite transmugrify'd,[16] they're grown *35*
Debauchery and Drinking:
O, would they stay to calculate
Th' eternal consequences,
Or—your more dreaded hell to state—
Damnation of expenses! *40*

Ye high, exalted, virtuous dames,
Tied up in godly laces,
Before ye gie poor Frailty names,
Suppose a change o' cases:
A dear-lov'd lad, convenience snug, *45*
A treach'rous inclination—
But, let me whisper i' your lug,[17]
Ye're aiblins [18] nae temptation.

Then gently scan your brother man,
Still gentler sister woman; *50*
Tho' they may gang a kennin [19] wrang,
To step aside is human:
One point must still be greatly dark,
The moving *why* they do it;
And just as lamely can ye mark *55*
How far perhaps they rue it.

Who made the heart, 'tis He alone
Decidedly can try us:
He knows each chord, its various tone,
Each spring, its various bias: *60*
Then at the balance let's be mute,
We never can adjust it;
What's done we partly may compute,
But know not what's resisted.

1786

16 *Transformed.*
17 *Ear.*
18 *Perhaps.*
19 *A tiny bit.*

Questions

1. What unpleasant traits does the poet see in the "rigidly righteous"?
2. Is the poet denying the moral value of strict regulation of conduct? If so, what basis for judging virtue does he give us?
3. Has the poet displayed in this poem the virtue he preaches?

Tam o' Shanter

ROBERT BURNS

A TALE

Of Brownyis and of Bogillis full is this Buke.[1]
GAWIN DOUGLAS

When chapman billies [2] leave the street,
And drouthy [3] neebors neebors meet,
As market-days are wearing late,
An' folk begin to take the gate; [4]
While we sit bousing at the nappy,[5] *5*
An' gettin fou [6] and unco happy,
We think na on the lang Scots miles,
The mosses, waters, slaps,[7] and stiles,
That lie between us and our hame,
Whare sits our sulky, sullen dame, *10*
Gathering her brows like gathering storm,
Nursing her wrath to keep it warm.

This truth fand [8] honest Tam o' Shanter,
As he frae Ayr ae night did canter:
(Auld Ayr, wham ne'er a town surpasses, *15*
For honest men and bonie lasses.)

O Tam! had'st thou but been sae wise
As taen thy ain wife Kate's advice!
She tauld thee weel thou was a skellum,[9]
A bletherin,[10] blusterin, drunken blellum,[11] *20*
That frae November till October,
Ae market-day thou was na sober;
That ilka melder [12] wi' the miller,
Thou sat as lang as thou had siller; [13]

[1] *"Of Brownyis and of Bogillis": of brownies and of hobgoblins.* [2] *"chapman billies": peddler friends.* [3] *Thirsty.* [4] *"take the gate": take their way, go home.* [5] *"bousing at the nappy": drinking ale.* [6] *Full, drunk.* [7] *Gates.* [8] *Found.* [9] *Good-for-nothing.* [10] *Chattering.* [11] *Blowhard.* [12] *"ilka melder": every grinding.* [13] *Silver, money.*

That ev'ry naig was ca'd [14] a shoe on, *25*
The smith and thee gat roaring fou on;
That at the Lord's house, even on Sunday,
Thou drank wi' Kirkton Jean till Monday.
She prophesied, that, late or soon,
Thou would be found deep drowned in Doon; [15] *30*
Or catched wi' warlocks in the mirk,[16]
By Alloway's auld haunted kirk.[17]

Ah, gentle dames! it gars me greet,[18]
To think how monie counsels sweet,
How monie lengthened sage advices, *35*
The husband frae the wife despises!

But to our tale:—Ae market night,
Tam had got planted unco right,
Fast by an ingle,[19] bleezing finely,
Wi' reaming swats [20] that drank divinely; *40*
And at his elbow, Souter [21] Johnie,
His ancient, trusty, drouthy cronie:
Tam loe'd him like a very brither;
They had been fou for weeks thegither.
The night drave on wi' sangs and clatter; *45*
And ay the ale was growing better:
The landlady and Tam grew gracious
Wi' secret favors, sweet and precious:
The souter tauld his queerest stories;
The landlord's laugh was ready chorus: *50*
The storm without might rair and rustle,
Tam did na mind the storm a whistle.

Care, mad to see a man sae happy,
E'en drowned himsel amang the nappy:
As bees flee hame wi' lades o' treasure, *55*
The minutes winged their way wi' pleasure;
Kings may be blest, but Tam was glorious,
O'er a' the ills o' life victorious!

But pleasures are like poppies spread,
You seize the flow'r, its bloom is shed; *60*
Or like the snow falls in the river,
A moment white—then melts forever;
Or like the borealis race,

[14] *Nailed.* [15] *A small stream in Burns's neighborhood.* [16] *Caught by witches in the dark.* [17] *Church. Burns's father was buried in the churchyard of Alloway Church.* [18] *Makes me weep.* [19] *Fireplace.* [20] *Foaming new ale.* [21] *Cobbler.*

That flit ere you can point their place;
Or like the rainbow's lovely form *65*
Evanishing amid the storm.
Nae man can tether time nor tide;
The hour approaches Tam maun [22] ride–
That hour, o' night's black arch the keystane,[23]
That dreary hour Tam mounts his beast in; *70*
And sic a night he taks the road in,
As ne'er poor sinner was abroad in.

The wind blew as 'twad blawn its last;
The rattling showers rose on the blast;
The speedy gleams the darkness swallowed; *75*
Loud, deep, and lang the thunder bellowed:
That night, a child might understand,
The Deil [24] had business on his hand.

Weel mounted on his gray mare, Meg–
A better never lifted leg– *80*
Tam skelpit [25] on thro' dub [26] and mire,
Despising wind and rain and fire;
Whiles [27] holding fast his guid blue bonnet,
Whiles crooning o'er some auld Scots sonnet,
Whiles glow'ring round wi' prudent cares, *85*
Lest bogles [28] catch him unawares.
Kirk-Alloway was drawing nigh,
Whare ghaists and houlets [29] nightly cry.

By this time he was cross the ford,
Whare in the snaw the chapman smoored; [30] *90*
And past the birks [31] and meikle stane,[32]
Whare drunken Charlie brak's neck-bane;
And thro' the whins,[33] and by the cairn,[34]
Whare hunters fand the murdered bairn: [35]
And near the thorn,[36] aboon the well, *95*
Where Mungo's mither hang'd hersel.
Before him Doon pours all his floods;
The doubling storm roars thro' the woods;
The lightnings flash from pole to pole,
Near and more near the thunders roll; *100*
When, glimmering thro' the groaning trees
Kirk-Alloway seemed in a bleeze:
Thro' ilka bore [37] the beams were glancing,
And loud resounded mirth and dancing.

[22] *Must.* [23] *The keystone of night's black arch, i.e., midnight.* [24] *Devil.* [25] *Clattered.* [26] *Puddle.* [27] *Sometimes.* [28] *Hobgoblins.* [29] *Owls.* [30] *Smothered.* [31] *Birches.* [32] *Great stone.* [33] *Furze.* [34] *Pile of stones.* [35] *Child.* [36] *Thorn tree.* [37] *"ilka bore": every crack.*

Inspiring bold John Barleycorn! 105
What dangers thou canst make us scorn!
Wi' tippenny [38] we fear nae evil;
Wi' usquebae [39] we'll face the devil!
The swats sae reamed [40] in Tammie's noodle,
Fair play, he cared na deils a boddle.[41] 110
But Maggie stood right sair [42] astonished,
Till, by the heel and hand admonished,
She ventured forward on the light;
And, wow! Tam saw an unco sight!

Warlocks and witches in a dance; 115
Nae cotillion brent-new frae France,
But hornpipes, jigs, strathspeys, and reels
Put life and mettle in their heels:
A winnock bunker [43] in the east,
There sat Auld Nick in shape o' beast; 120
A towsie tyke,[44] black, grim, and large,
To gie them music was his charge;
He screwed the pipes and gart them skirl,[45]
Till roof and rafters a' did dirl.[46]
Coffins stood round like open presses, 125
That shawed the dead in their last dresses;
And by some devilish cantraip sleight [47]
Each in its cauld hand held a light,
By which heroic Tam was able
To note upon the haly table 130
A murderer's banes in gibbet airns; [48]
Twa span-lang, wee, unchristened bairns;
A thief, new-cutted frae a rape [49]—
Wi' his last gasp his gab [50] did gape;
Five tomahawks, wi' bluid red-rusted; 135
Five scymitars, wi' murder crusted;
A garter, which a babe had strangled;
A knife, a father's throat had mangled,
Whom his ain son o' life bereft—
The gray hairs yet stack to the heft; 140
Wi' mair o' horrible and awfu',
Which even to name wad be unlawfu'.

As Tammie glowered,[51] amazed and curious,
The mirth and fun grew fast and furious:
The piper loud and louder blew, 145

[38] *Two-penny ale.* [39] *Whisky.* [40] *"swats sae reamed": ale so foamed.* [41] *"Deils a boddle": devil a farthing.* [42] *Sorely.* [43] *"winnock bunker": window seat.* [44] *"towsie tyke": shaggy cur.* [45] *"gart them skirl": made them scream.* [46] *Ring.* [47] *Magic trick.* [48] *"banes in gibbet airns": bones in gibbet irons.* [49] *Rope.* [50] *Mouth.* [51] *Stared.*

The dancers quick and quicker flew;
They reeled, they set, they crossed, they cleekit,[52]
Till ilka carlin swat and reekit,[53]
And coost her duddies to the wark [54]
And linket at it in her sark! [55] *150*

Now Tam, O Tam! had thae been queans,[56]
A' plump and strapping in their teens!
Their sarks, instead o' creeshie flannen,[57]
Been snaw-white seventeen hunder linen! [58]—
Thir breeks [59] o' mine, my only pair, *155*
That ance were plush, o' guid blue hair,
I wad hae gien them aff my hurdies,[60]
For ae blink o' the bonie burdies! [61]

But wither'd beldams, auld and droll,
Rigwoodie [62] hags wad spean [63] a foal, *160*
Louping and flinging on a crummock,[64]
I wonder didna turn thy stomach.

But Tam kend what was what fu' brawlie;[65]
There was ae winsome wench and wawlie,[66]
That night enlisted in the core [67] *165*
Lang after kend on Carrick shore
(For monie a beast to dead she shot,
An' perished monie a bonie boat,
And shook baith meikle corn and bear,[68]
And kept the countryside in fear). *170*
Her cutty sark, [69] o' Paisley harn,[70]
That while a lassie she had worn,
In longitude tho' sorely scanty,
It was her best, and she was vauntie.[71]
Ah! little kend thy reverend grannie, *175*
That sark she coft [72] for her wee Nannie,
Wi' twa pund Scots ('twas a' her riches),
Wad ever graced a dance o' witches!

But here my Muse her wing maun cour,[73]
Sic flights are far beyond her power; *180*
To sing how Nannie lap and flang,

[52] *Clasped each other.* [53] "*ilka carlin swat and reekit*": *each hag sweated and steamed.* [54] "*coost her duddies to the wark*": *threw off her clothes for the work.* [55] "*linket at it in her sark!*": *went at it in her shirt.* [56] *Young wenches.* [57] *Greasy flannel.* [58] "*seventeen-hunder linen*": *fine linen.* [59] *Britches.* [60] *Hips.* [61] *Lasses.* [62] *Withered.* [63] *Wean.* [64] "*Louping and flinging on a crummock*": *jumping and capering on a crooked staff.* [65] *Full well.* [66] *Buxom.* [67] *Company.* [68] *Barley.* [69] *Short shirt.* [70] *Paisley horn is coarse linen made in the town of Paisley.* [71] *Proud.* [72] *Bought.* [73] *Lower.*

(A souple jade she was and strang,)
And how Tam stood like ane bewitched,
And thought his very een enriched;
Even Satan glowered and fidged fu' fain,[74] *185*
And hotched[75] and blew wi' might and main:
Till first ae caper, syne anither,
Tam tint[76] his reason a' thegither,
And roars out, "Weel done, Cutty-sark!"
And in an instant all was dark: *190*
And scarcely had he Maggie rallied,
When out the hellish legion sallied.

As bees bizz out wi' angry fyke,[77]
When plundering herds[78] assail their byke;[79]
As open pussie's[80] mortal foes, *195*
When, pop! she starts before their nose;
As eager runs the market-crowd,
When "Catch the thief!" resounds aloud;
So Maggie runs, the witches follow,
Wi' monie and eldritch[81] skriech and hollo. *200*

Ah, Tam! ah, Tam! thou'll get thy fairin![82]
In hell they'll roast thee like a herrin!
In vain thy Kate awaits thy comin!
Kate soon will be a woefu' woman!
Now, do thy speedy utmost, Meg, *205*
And win the keystane of the brig:[83]
There at them thou thy tail may toss,
A running stream they dare na cross.
But ere the keystane she could make,
The fient[84] a tail she had to shake! *210*
For Nannie, far before the rest,
Hard upon noble Maggie prest,
And flew at Tam wi' furious ettle;[85]
But little wist[86] she Maggie's mettle—
Ae spring brought aff her master hale, *215*
But left behind her ain gray tail:
The carlin claught her by the rump,
And left poor Maggie scarce a stump.

Now, wha this tale o' truth shall read,
Ilk man, and mother's son, take heed: *220*

[74] *"fidged fu' fain": fidgeted with desire.* [75] *Jerked.* [76] *Lost.* [77] *Fuss.* [78] *Herdsmen.* [79] *Hive.* [80] *The hare's.* [81] *Unearthly.* [82] *Present from the fair, i.e., just deserts.* [83] *Bridge.* [84] *Fiend.* [85] *Aim, intent.* [86] *Knew.*

Whene'er to drink you are inclin'd,
Or cutty sarks run in your mind,
Think! ye may buy the joys o'er dear:
Remember Tam o' Shanter's mare.

1792

Questions

1. Can the story of Tam be regarded as a symbolic description of the plight of mankind in general? If so, what does Tam's drunkenness stand for? The ruined church? Tam's escape?
2. What is the tone of lines 59–66?
3. Analyze the poet's attitude toward repressive social forces, paying particular attention to the quality of the humor.

The Garden of Love

WILLIAM BLAKE

I went to the Garden of Love,
And saw what I never had seen:
A chapel was built in the midst,
Where I used to play on the green.

And the gates of this chapel were shut, *5*
And "Thou shalt not" writ over the door;
So I turned to the Garden of Love,
That so many sweet flowers bore:

And I saw it was fillèd with graves,
And tombstones where flowers should be; *10*
And priests in black gowns were walking
their rounds,
And binding with briars my joys and desires.

1801–1803

Question

In this poem Blake is, in the first place, protesting against what he considers to be an unhealthy attitude toward sexual love. Why does he use a garden to symbolize love? The presence of tombstones suggests, of course, fear and death. What general statement about the connection between love, death, and fear does the poet make by means of his symbols? Does the general statement formulated in response to the preceding question mean quite the same or express as much as the poet's symbolic statement? If not, why not?

London

WILLIAM BLAKE

I wander through each chartered [1] street
Near where the chartered Thames does flow,
And mark in every face I meet
Marks of weakness, marks of woe.

In every cry of every man, *5*
In every infant's cry of fear,
In every voice, in every ban,[2]
The mind-forged manacles I hear:

How the chimney-sweeper's cry
Every blackening church appalls, *10*
And the hapless soldier's sigh
Runs in blood down palace walls.

But most, through midnight streets I hear
How the youthful harlot's curse
Blasts [3] the new-born infant's tear, *15*
And blights with plagues the marriage hearse.

1794

[1] *Under the monopolistic control of a corporation.*
[2] *Legal prohibition.*
[3] *Blights.*

Questions

1. Here, as in "The Garden of Love," Blake attacks certain institutions, that is, organizations and established systems that shape and express general social and moral attitudes. What are they in this case? What, for example, is represented by the palace? What is the connection with the suffering suggested by the soldier's sigh?
2. The poet suggests that the basic cause of the various forms of oppression he mentions is a kind of mental enslavement. Where does he make this statement?
3. Why does the poet use the phrase "marriage hearse"? What kind of plague would be associated with the harlot's curse?

The Leaders of the Crowd

WILLIAM BUTLER YEATS

They must to keep their certainty accuse
All that are different of a base intent;
Pull down established honor; hawk for news
Whatever their loose phantasy invent
And murmur it with bated breath, as though 5
The abounding gutter had been Helicon [1]
Or calumny a song. How can they know
Truth flourishes where the student's lamp has shone,
And there alone, that [2] have no solitude?
So the crowd come they care not what may come. 10
They have loud music, hope every day renewed
And heartier loves; that lamp is from the tomb.[3]

1924

[1] *On Mount Helicon in Greece was a spring sacred to the Muses.*
[2] *The antecedent of "that" is "they" in line 7.*
[3] *I.e., the "leaders of the crowd" think so.*

Questions

1. What is the basic motive attributed here to the "leaders of the crowd"? Does the poet have in mind only political demagogues, or social leaders of other kinds as well? Are such leaders as are described here to be found on college campuses?
2. The poet says that truth flourishes only in solitude. Does this imply that all popular opinions are false or that truth can never be generally accepted? Does the poem have a moral?

Commission

EZRA POUND

Go, my songs, to the lonely and the unsatisfied,
Go also to the nerve-wracked, go to the enslaved-by-convention,
Bear to them my contempt for their oppressors.
Go as a great wave of cool water,
Bear my contempt of oppressors. 5

Speak against unconscious oppression,
Speak against the tyranny of the unimaginative,
Speak against bonds.
Go to the bourgeoise who is dying of her ennuis,
Go to the women in suburbs. *10*
Go to the hideously wedded,
Go to them whose failure is concealed,
Go to the unluckily mated,
Go to the bought wife,
Go to the woman entailed.[1] *15*

Go to those who have delicate lust,
Go to those whose delicate desires are thwarted,
Go like a blight upon the dulness of the world;
Go with your edge against this,
Strengthen the subtle cords, *20*
Bring confidence upon the algae and the tentacles of the soul.

Go in a friendly manner,
Go with an open speech.
Be eager to find new evils and new good,
Be against all forms of oppression. *25*
Go to those who are thickened with middle age,
To those who have lost their interest.

Go to the adolescent who are smothered in family—
Oh how hideous it is
To see three generations of one house gathered together! *30*
It is like an old tree with shoots,
And with some branches rotted and falling.

Go out and defy opinion,
Go against this vegetable bondage of the blood.
Be against all sorts of mortmain.[2] *35*

1917

[1] *Treated as a restricted inheritance.*
[2] *Perpetual ownership; the controlling influence of the past.*

Questions

1. What kind of oppression is the poet mainly concerned about? Is it moral restriction? What are the key words in his indictment?

2. Does the poet single out a particular group of people as the main oppressors?
3. Is there any evidence that modern adolescents have been "smothered in family"? Has "song" given them any relief?

Hurt Hawks

ROBINSON JEFFERS

I

The broken pillar of the wing jags from the clotted shoulder,
The wing trails like a banner in defeat,
No more to use the sky forever but live with famine
And pain a few days: cat nor coyote
Will shorten the week of waiting for death, there is game without talons. *5*
He stands under the oak-bush and waits
The lame feet of salvation; at night he remembers freedom
And flies in a dream, the dawns ruin it.
He is strong and pain is worse to the strong, incapacity is worse.
The curs of the day come and torment him *10*
At distance, no one but death the redeemer will humble that head,
The intrepid readiness, the terrible eyes.
The wild God of the world is sometimes merciful to those
That ask mercy, not often to the arrogant.
You do not know him, you communal people, or you have
forgotten him; *15*
Intemperate and savage, the hawk remembers him;
Beautiful and wild, the hawks, and men that are dying, remember him.

II

I'd sooner, except the penalties, kill a man than a hawk; but the great
redtail
Had nothing left but unable misery
From the bone too shattered for mending, the wing that trailed under his
talons when he moved. *20*
We had fed him six weeks, I gave him freedom,
He wandered over the foreland hill and returned in the evening, asking
for death,
Not like a beggar, still eyed with the old
Implacable arrogance. I gave him the lead gift in the twilight.
What fell was relaxed. *25*
Owl-downy, soft feminine feathers; but what

Soared: the fierce rush: the night-herons by the flooded river cried fear
at its rising
Before it was quite unsheathed from reality.

1927

Questions

1. What does Jeffers mean by "the wild God of the world"? Why do men that are dying remember him? Does Jeffers believe in life after death?
2. What kind of mercy does the poet refer to in lines 13–15? Are circumstances really different for those who ask mercy, or is it a matter of the way things look to them?
3. What, according to Jeffers, does being free mean in human terms? Does freedom depend primarily upon circumstances, or rather upon knowledge and attitude? What is the relation between freedom and suffering? Is belief in mercy consistent with the sense of freedom?
4. The subject and intent of this poem pose a problem in the control of tone. Both bluster and sentimentality must be carefully avoided. Has Jeffers succeeded? What features of his style help especially in gaining the intended effect? Does the style change at any point?

Departmental, or, The End of My Ant Jerry

ROBERT FROST

An ant on the table-cloth
Ran into a dormant moth
Of many times her size.
He showed not the least surprise.
His business wasn't with such. *5*
He gave it scarcely a touch,
And was off on his duty run.
Yet if he encountered one
Of the hive's enquiry squad
Whose work is to find out God *10*
And the nature of time and space,
He would put him onto the case.
Ants are a curious race;
One crossing with hurried tread

The body of one of their dead 15
Isn't given a moment's arrest—
Seems not even impressed.
But he no doubt reports to any
With whom he crosses antennae,
And they no doubt report 20
To the higher up at court.
Then word goes forth in Formic: [1]
"Death's come to Jerry McCormic,
Our selfless forager Jerry.
Will the special Janizary 25
Whose office it is to bury
The dead of the commissary
Go bring him home to his people.
Lay him in state on a sepal.
Wrap him for shroud in a petal. 30
Embalm him with ichor of nettle.
This is the word of your Queen."
And presently on the scene
Appears a solemn mortician;
And taking formal position 35
With feelers calmly atwiddle,
Seizes the dead by the middle,
And heaving him high in the air,
Carries him out of there.
No one stands round to stare. 40
It is nobody else's affair.

It couldn't be called ungentle.
But how thoroughly departmental.

1936

[1] *Ant language.*

Questions

1. Frost is implying, it would appear, that the organization and specialization that have characterized modern science and business are extending into the realm of moral activity. What two kinds of moral concerns does he distinguish?
2. Is the current trend toward organization and specialization really having a dehumanizing effect? If you think so, give some examples.
3. This poem is subtitled "The End of My Ant Jerry." Are worker ants males? What is the point of Frost's pun?

The Unknown Citizen

(To JS/07/M378
This Marble Monument
Is Erected by the State)

W. H. AUDEN

He was found by the Bureau of Statistics to be
One against whom there was no official complaint,
And all the reports on his conduct agree
That, in the modern sense of an old-fashioned word, he was a saint,
For in everything he did he served the Greater Community. *5*
Except for the War till the day he retired
He worked in a factory and never got fired,
But satisfied his employers, Fudge Motors Inc.
Yet he wasn't a scab or odd in his views,
For his Union reports that he paid his dues, *10*
(Our report on his Union shows it was sound)
And our Social Psychology workers found
That he was popular with his mates and liked a drink.
The Press are convinced that he bought a paper every day
And that his reactions to advertisements were normal in every way. *15*
Policies taken out in his name prove that he was fully insured,
And his Health-card shows he was once in hospital but left it cured.
Both Producers Research and High-Grade Living declare
He was fully sensible to the advantages of the Instalment Plan
And had everything necessary to the Modern Man, *20*
A phonograph, a radio, a car and a frigidaire.
Our researchers into Public Opinion are content
That he held the proper opinions for the time of year;
When there was peace, he was for peace; when there was war, he went.
He was married and added five children to the population, *25*
Which our Eugenist says was the right number for a parent of his
generation,
And our teachers report that he never interfered with their education.
Was he free? Was he happy? The question is absurd:
Had anything been wrong, we should certainly have heard.

1940

Questions

1. Obviously, the poet thinks that such a man as the unknown citizen is not free. But was the unknown citizen forced to behave in the way he did? What kept him from being free?
2. "Was he happy?" someone asks. Why would he not be? Under what circumstances might he have been happier?
3. What is the difference between the modern and the old-fashioned sense of the word "saint"?
4. What assumption is being satirized in the last two lines of the poem?

TOPICS FOR COMPOSITION

1. Drawing upon Burns's "Address to the Unco Guid" for opinions, write a satirical description of the puritanical character. Or write a description of someone whom you consider to be somewhat puritanical.
2. Express your views on the question of whether virtue is primarily a matter of conduct or of attitude.
3. Defend the thesis that society is still overpuritanical in some important respect. If you prefer, argue that in certain areas of conduct a more puritanical attitude would be beneficial.
4. Using Blake's "The Garden of Love" as a starting point for reflection, write an essay on some aspect of the topic "Sex and Guilt." Try to make an honest appraisal of the problem, if there seems to you to be a problem, and say what you think most needs saying.
5. Advance a general opinion on the question of whether or not legal restraint of private vice is justified. Support your opinion by analyzing a particular problem of this nature.
6. Using Yeats's "The Leaders of the Crowd" as a starting point for reflection, write an essay on good leadership, bad leadership, or the principal difference between the two. Try to get at the heart of the problem of leadership, and limit your consideration of the matter, if you can, to one or two important points. Possible topics: "The Pseudo-Leader"; "Sick Leadership"; "The Loneliness of Leadership"; "Leadership and Compromise."
7. Ezra Pound's "Commission" suggests a number of matters for exploration. What, for example, does he mean by "the tyranny of the unimaginative"? Where does such tyranny operate? Does it ever exist in the home? In the classroom? In school affairs generally? In the world of entertainment? In national affairs? Answer one or more of these questions in an essay.
8. With Pound's poem in mind, write an essay on the topic "The Woman in the Suburbs."
9. Pound's assertion that adolescents may be smothered in family seems prophetic in view of recent "teen-age" unrest. If you feel that you have some insight into the matter, explain how parents may smother their children or why they tend to do so. One might also consider whether parents are not sometimes the victims of their own efforts to mold, control, or protect their children.

10. Write a short essay on the implications of the tree metaphor in Pound's "Commission" (lines 31–32).
11. Using Burns's "Tam o' Shanter" as a point of departure, write an essay satirizing some modern conception of a scapegrace.
12. Analyze the moral implications of Jeffers' "Hurt Hawk." What kind of person would the author (or speaker) of the poem admire? What kind of human relations would he approve of?
13. Write a description of a modern "saint," using the term as it is used in Auden's "The Unknown Citizen."
14. Write a reply to the indictment presented in "The Unknown Citizen"—or propose a partial solution to the problem.
15. After reflecting upon what you have read in this book so far and upon your personal experience, formulate a general statement about the relation between freedom, morality, and happiness. Use the statement as the thesis for an essay developed by the method of exemplification.

PART THREE

The Meaning of Love

The attempts of many writers to define or at least to describe love reflect the universality of interest in this facet of man's makeup as well as the virtual impossibility of arriving at any one definition of so complex an emotion. In treating the spiritual, emotional, or physical aspects of love, or a combination of these, writers have illuminated the elusiveness and complexity of love and accordingly have generated a central, compulsive literary theme.

In the first essay, "Love as Panacea," Morton M. Hunt explores one aspect of love—love as "panacea" in contemporary society. Hunt, in his concern only with the nature and function of love in the twentieth century, in America, assumes that the kind of society in which a man lives controls the kind of love he seeks and experiences. Erich Fromm's "The Theory of Love" refutes the harsh determinism evident in Hunt's essay, asserting, instead, that love is an inherent part of man's being and that he controls the "activity" of love. Whereas Hunt takes an objective view of love in contemporary society, Fromm seeks an individual, highly subjective view of man involved in an act of giving—giving as a requisite to loving.

Turning from the contrasting views of Hunt and Fromm on aspects of love in modern society, we move backward in time for another inquiry into the nature of love, one that touches upon both the harsh aspects of love and the intuitive idealistic concept. Guy de Maupassant's "Love: Pages from a Sportsman's Book" attempts an explanation of love by contrasting a human "drama of passion" with a portrayal of instinctive animal love. "Chestnut and Jet" by Bryan MacMahon interprets still another elemental love force. MacMahon's story pulses with sexual excitement, with those difficult to describe yet fundamental emotions stirred by evidences of physical virility in the communion of love between man and woman. Nora exhibits unashamed pride in love's physical fulfillment, while the attitude of the old maid, the widow, and many of the "watchers" contrasts sharply with Nora's attitude. D. H. Lawrence's "The Horse Dealer's Daughter" offers a variation on the love theme that is not too far removed from that with which we see Hunt take issue in his essay. Love, Lawrence would probably agree, may not be a panacea; but it can be a healing influence on blighted lives. His story shows two people, Mabel and Dr. Ferguson, who only begin to "live" after they find the meaning of love.

William Shakespeare's great play Antony and Cleopatra *might well be called the "tragedy of love"* par excellence. *Its great historical personages and the extravagance of its poetry amplify the theme that Dryden, in his version of the play, emphasized in the title,* All for Love; or, the World Well Lost. *For, indeed, when they must choose, Shakespeare's Roman general and Egyptian queen choose, royally and movingly, to forsake the world rather than compromise their love. Love, in this play, turns out to be stronger than the claims of empire, of honor, of duty, of expediency.*

The Essay

SINCE Hunt assumes that the kind of society in which a man lives controls the kind of love he seeks and experiences, we should note the way in which this assumption largely dictates the form of this essay. We might view the structure of this essay in the following way:

1. A cause-to-effect pattern is used to sustain the primary assumption.
2. The pattern supports an emerging definition of love as panacea in our time.
3. The cause-to-effect pattern and the subsequent definition of love as panacea lead to a conclusion that assesses the merit of the system posited by the assumption.

Love as Panacea

MORTON M. HUNT

Whatever ethical values and practical purposes love may happen to encompass in modern life, however, men and women do not hunger for it primarily on their account; love itself is the goal, the thing beyond price, the good in itself. Other rationalistic and materialistic eras have treated it lightly and considered it nothing more than the agreeable sensations and the sporting pleasure accompanying the sexual drive; our own era makes of it a high, noble, and essential human relationship. One might reasonably suspect, therefore, that there is in it today a value and purpose above all values and purposes —the fulfilment of a major human need that happens to be greater in certain eras of history than in others.

To some extent, the need is one created by civilization itself. The primitive man lived in the most intimate continual contact with all the members of his village; he was linked to scores of his clan-relatives by a web of powerful loyalties and affections; he was rarely restricted to a single sexual partner or severely penalized for sexual adventures. He could not know the feelings and the hungers that made Athenian men endlessly discuss the importance of friendship and love, or caused medieval courtiers and ladies to spend days at a time in conferences concerning the meaning and the rules of love.

But with the coming of industrialization and the growth of the modern city, love achieved in the Victorian period an unprecedented significance. And since these changes were further accentuated in the present century, the sexual revolution had to fail in its attempt to deromanticize love. The impersonality of urban life and the shrinking size of the family produced that central paradox of modern life to which David Riesman several years ago gave a memorable label—the lonely crowd. And to the lonely, love seemed the cure for pain, the harbor for wandering souls. No Greek youth, pleasantly loitering all day with the ever-present gathering of men in the Athenian agora, no knight, constantly surrounded by friends and retainers or lingering for years in the intimate society of his liege-lord's castle, could have known anything like the feelings of the modern bachelor (or career girl) returning at evening to a rented room or tiny apartment, an anonymous cell in a vast prison where one can weep and be unheard, can die and remain undiscovered for days.

The physical isolation and rootlessness of modern life, however, is only half of the reason love has assumed such great significance. The other half lies in the fact that our society, more so than most others, conditions us from earliest childhood to measure and rate ourselves by the amount of love we receive. According to Freudian theory and the observations of a number of students of child development, the typical middle-class technique of controlling and training the child is to give him love when he is good or does something well, and to deny him love when he is bad or does something poorly. This ever-present threat, though highly useful in socializing the child, makes him chronically insecure about love and obsessed by the task of keeping it. It is the key to his personal worth, and he interprets every gain as a reward for goodness, and every loss of love—including the death of a parent—as due to his own badness.[1]

In the context of a competitive society, the child thus rapidly comes to identify success in general with personal worth, and to gauge his own success and worth by the degree to which he is liked and loved by others. He has as yet no access to a career or to social prestige, and all the more, therefore, he measures his own merit by popularity (a thin-spread form of love) or, as an alternative, by the intensity and overpowering quality of his youthful love feelings. Everyone knows how the thirst-stricken man in the desert interprets every shadow as an oasis, and clinical psychologists have

[1] *Freud:* Group Psychology, *pp. 74–5; J. C. Flugel:* Man, Morals, and Society, pp. 55–7; *Talcott Parsons:* Essays in Sociological Theory, p. 257; *and many others.*

fewer emotions

real self

found that when poor children are shown coins, they later recall the coins as being much larger than they really are; rich children do not make the same error. Similarly, the teen-ager, unsure of his own merit and his eventual status in our fluid society, needs love more than he ever did as a child, and so is able to see rare beauty and infinite charm in a giggling dumpling of a bobby-soxer. The jaunty step, new-minted optimism, and smug contentment of the adolescent in love mean that he has found two things to be of great value—his beloved, and himself.

By the time he starts to earn a living or attains the social status of a college man with its attendant career expectations, he is achieving at least some small degree of real success; his image of himself therefore somewhat improves and the intensity of his need to bolster his ego through an idealized love object somewhat decreases. It is not only experience that introduces some realism into love during courtship, but actually a decreased need to have love be a form of magic, solving all one's problems. But it still has enough of them to solve, for at the very time the youth has these first successes, he has also left home and begun to sense in full the isolation so typical of contemporary life.

Meanwhile, what of the girl? She, too, has finished school or is in college, yet her career expectations are nothing like the boy's. She is already aware that she will probably never have a career, make her mark, or seem important to any but a very few people; the result is—and there are a number of serious studies to prove what everyone intuitively recognizes—that girls are more romantic than men, both at the courtship level and after marriage. The young female's addiction to movies and the married woman's equal addiction to soap opera clearly indicate that her romantic needs are greater than those of men in our culture; or as Groucho Marx once put it, a wife is a person who doesn't think she goes dancing enough.

But this difference in need between young men and young women is actually minor; after all, it is these self-same young men who marry the young women. For our own time is one in which a variety of well-known social forces, plus the rapidity of social change itself, conspire to create psychic insecurity in the adolescent and the adult alike. And so love has come to have somewhat the character of a panacea, a medicine curative of career discontent, anemia of the ego, loneliness, over-all anxiety, and lack of purpose. These and other by-products of industrialization are rapidly appearing in many new areas of the world, and it therefore makes sense that in the very same areas, modern love is now beginning to exercise its immense appeal.

In America itself, meanwhile, the use of love as panacea seems to be on the increase. Parents thrust their children into dancing-classes and parties even before puberty, and the young begin to date at twelve and thirteen, when masculinity and feminity are still only uncomfortable and unjustifiable poses. All too soon, they become anxious to "go steady," and tend to do so earlier and more fixedly than used to be the case. Going steady evidently is reassuring in that it signifies they have been accepted by someone; unfortunately it reduces the utility of the dating pattern itself, since it limits the chances for the wider testing of personalities and possible meanings of love.

But having been in the love competition since the age of twelve, the young people are ready ever earlier to marry and attain still greater security. And this represents not just a breakdown of the Victorian pattern of long engagement and late marriage, for the shift is continuing; since 1930, for instance, the average age at first marriage has dropped a year and a half for men and a year for women. *The Reader's Digest* of August 1957 expressed the popular viewpoint on all this, seeing it through a roseate haze of optimism:

> The girl of 19 and the boy of 21 who walk down the aisle today, however, often are far different from the wild, eloping kids of a generation ago. Usually they have tested their affection and loyalty for each other during three or four years . . . [and] acquired an intimate knowledge and a deep tolerance of each other's habits, reactions and attitudes. Thus, marriage poses no overwhelming problems of adjustment.

To test, however, means little unless one has some comparisons by which to measure the results; in any case, to be really valid, much of the testing would have to be done in the period of more mature, secure personal development. Despite the benign cheerfulness of the *Digest* and the wedding-loving American public, the census data show that a girl who marries under twenty is three times as likely to be divorced as one who marries between twenty-two and twenty-four. The hunger for love and marriage, like the hunger for food, is necessary and healthful—and can likewise become exaggerated to a pathological degree.

Similarly, under the pressure of insecurity the healthful interaction of personalities in love can become an actual disease. There is good evidence to show that, normally, people tend to fall in love with other people whose emotional needs complement their own (in this sense, at least, the adage is correct that says opposites attract). The achievement-oriented man or woman tends to pick a partner who is relatively quiescent and passive, the parent-like and care-taking person tends to love and marry someone who is dependent and clinging, and so on. These choices, needless to say, are often unconscious; people frequently think they want someone like themselves, and yet choose otherwise.[2] This is thought to be a normal basis for love, yet a mere exaggeration of it produces what psychoanalysts and marriage counselors call "neurotic marriage," which often involves pain and symptom formation of a kind sufficient to ruin health and destroy careers. But the people involved in such a marriage, though suffering, may be completely unable to do without each other or to cut themselves off from what they think of as love. A typical case from the files of Family Service of Highland Park (Illinois) involves an exhausted, ailing man over whose face flickered a nervous desperate smile, and who told his story to the marriage counselor as follows:

> I had a premonition before I married Lucille that this is the way my marriage would turn out. I guess I was flattered that she chose me instead of some of the other guys. It was pretty tough competition. . . . I was just a nobody—and still am. In fact, if you listen to Lucille, I'm not only a nobody but a complete flop—as husband and as a man. . . . If I don't ask for a raise at work, she ridicules me. If I should happen to get a raise, she says it isn't enough and it proves I'm a sucker. . . . I've lost my last five jobs because she called me so often at work, talking endlessly and telling me off. She has thrown everything at me that she can lift. . . . We haven't lived as man and wife for twelve years.

His wife, a vigorous, voluble woman, frequently tearful but nevertheless in blooming health, came in separately and told her side of it:

> Joe is a poor excuse of a man. He won't stand up to his boss and demand a raise. He won't argue with a clerk who overcharges him. . . . At times when I look at him, I get so mad I just can't control myself. Generally I just don't try. I just let him have it. . . . I wanted a strong, successful man I could lean on, depend on. What did I do instead? When I get after Joe, he gets a smile on his face that looks like the smile of Christ. . . . It's that damned smile that causes me just to throw whatever I can lay my hands on.

[2] *Robert F. Winch:* Mate-Selection, *especially Ch. 6.*

But when the counselor asked each one individually whether it might not be better to break up, their answers were remarkably similar. Joe, clearly horrified at the suggestion, replied with an air of explaining the obvious:

> Oh, I *couldn't* leave Lucille. I love her very much. I decided one night to leave and I did. But I couldn't sleep for thinking about her, wondering what she was doing and if she was all right. I was scared to come home because I knew she would be furious that I had left—and she was, but *I had to come home.*

Lucille, too, was aghast at the idea:

> What would I *do* if I left him? I would be absolutely *lost.* I have thought of it often enough, but when I try to imagine what it would be like without him, I know I just couldn't go on without him. I would miss him, strange as it may seem. I just couldn't get along without him.[3]

In rather more eloquent terms the same pattern was brilliantly portrayed by Eugene O'Neill in *A Touch of the Poet.* The "poet" of the title is only a low-born Irishman who held a commission and fought under Wellington in the Napoleonic wars, but was cashiered for amatory indiscretion. He has moved to the United States and spent his years pretending to be an English gentleman. While he drinks, dresses like a lord, and rides a fine horse, his withered little wife runs the failing inn that is their sole support, but she adores his swaggering gallantry, accepts his roaring abuse without a whimper, and ardently defends the ruinous relationship to her daughter in several throbbing speeches about the glory of love. The sad truth, known to playwright and marriage counselor alike, is that a human being may cherish his disease, cling to the source of his pain and self-destruction, and call the whole thing love; more than that, it may *feel* like love to him or her, and which of us can prove to him that it does not?

The panacea, in other words, may itself produce an addiction that is no better than the ills it is supposed to cure. Infidelity is the prime case in point. As we have seen, it was acceptable, normal, and even required in many other times and places; in our own, however, where faithful monogamy is the professed ideal and the general practice, infidelity is often a symptom of some pressure or need over

[3] *Case reported by Martha Winch, executive director, Family Service of Highland Park, in Winch, ibid., pp. 314–16.*

and above the ordinary.[4] This may be one meaning of Kinsey's revelation that men of the upper educational levels tend to increase their extramarital activities in their late thirties. Many professional and business men either reach a career plateau at that time, or see clearly that their potential success in life has fairly distinct boundaries. Roughly thirty per cent of them try infidelity, as against half that many, in their early twenties; like whiskey, it alleviates the feelings of one's limitations and induces an illusion of general well-being, but it similarly involves multiple dangers and after-effects.

Even without reference to the Kinsey data or career-satisfaction studies, most psychiatrists and marriage counselors have long considered neurotic drives the most important ones behind both male and female infidelity. Behind this lies the Freudian theory of the development of love from the selfish infantile level to the mature and giving level, but there is also statistical evidence to support it; in one careful study of a sizable group of female psychiatric patients and a comparable group of normal women, six times as many of the abnormal women had had extramarital affairs. And if one may judge from the case histories reported by marriage counselors, many of the men and women who believe they have found real love outside their marriages have actually chosen highly inappropriate persons with whom they are unlikely to be better off than they have been. In the more successfully treated cases, therapy typically results in a revival of love and sexual enjoyment with the marriage partner, and a simultaneous fading of the glamour and intensity of the outside love affair.[5]

And thus once again, as so often in the past, love is a thing of paradoxes. In a society which is not only mechanized and impersonal, but in which religious and philosophic goals have lost much of their power, love meets the emotional needs of the individual, gives him a sense of security, and provides him with much of the impetus and inspiration to effort. But at the same time modern love has assumed in the lives of many people the role of a cure-all, or at least an ano-

[4] *Fidelity still is the general practice, though many have supposed that the Kinsey data prove the contrary. Kinsey concluded that half of all American husbands are unfaithful at some time or other, but his figures show that many of these have had only one or a few scattered episodes, a very different phenomenon, psychologically speaking, from repeated, habitual, or practiced infidelity.*

[5] *For the typical psychoanalytic view of infidelity as neurosis or immaturity, see Abraham N. Franzblau:* The Road to Sexual Maturity; *for the comparative study of normal and abnormal women, see Carney Landis* et al.: Sex in Development, *especially p. 97; and for case histories treated successfully, see Emily Mudd* et al., *editors:* Marriage Counseling, A Casebook, *Ch. 6.*

dyne. The immature, the discontented, the lonely, and the neurotic all dose themselves with love; like most panaceas, it seems for a while to lessen their ills, but rarely cures them, and if its analgesic powers later fail, the ailments may be beyond healing.

Questions

1. Within the controlling pattern of cause and effect, Hunt makes use of other, subordinate, patterns (e.g., comparison and contrast, analogy, illustration, or example). Locate the beginnings and ends of each of these subordinate patterns. What does the structure of the essay gain from their use? In other words, how do they assist in supporting the thesis, the dominant pattern of cause and effect, and the conclusion?
2. What assumptions does Hunt ask us to accept? In your opinion, are these assumptions valid?
3. Consider carefully the language of the essay. Do you find much jargon? Can you identify the potential audience for this essay by its language or diction?

Topics for Composition

1. Compare Hunt's view of love in the modern world with the view expressed in any of the poems of this unit.
2. Classify the kinds of popularity prevalent on high school and college campuses. Be sure to define and illustrate adequately each kind.
3. Analyze the kind of romantic love that prevails upon your campus (or at American colleges generally, if you prefer). Try especially to provide concrete illustrations of the prevalent campus notions about what love is or what love ought to be.

In "The Theory of Love," Fromm naturally finds it necessary to first define love. And, as writers of extended definition often find, one definition leads to many more. Fromm's definition shows both its depth and variety in the following ways:

1. The definition of love as activity leads to a definition of activity which in turn leads to definitions of giving, care, responsibility, respect, and knowledge.
2. Each term shows a variety in methods of defining. Note Fromm's use of synonym, example, analogy, and negation.

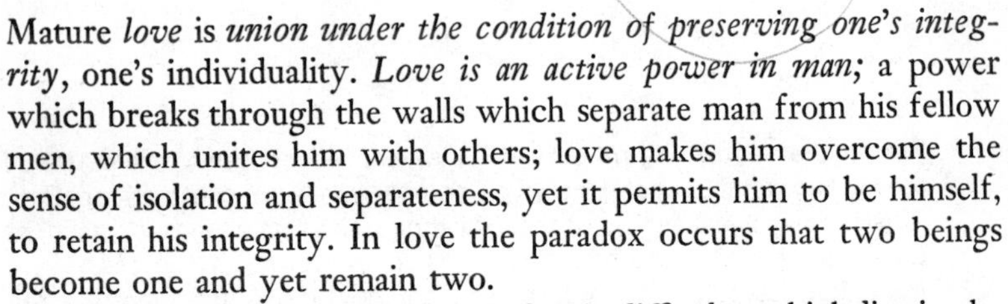

The Theory of Love

ERICH FROMM

Mature *love* is *union under the condition of preserving one's integrity*, one's individuality. *Love is an active power in man;* a power which breaks through the walls which separate man from his fellow men, which unites him with others; love makes him overcome the sense of isolation and separateness, yet it permits him to be himself, to retain his integrity. In love the paradox occurs that two beings become one and yet remain two.

If we say love is an activity, we face a difficulty which lies in the ambiguous meaning of the word "activity." By "activity," in the modern usage of the word, is usually meant an action which brings about a change in an existing situation by means of an expenditure of energy. Thus a man is considered active if he does business, studies medicine, works on an endless belt, builds a table, or is engaged in sports. Common to all these activities is that they are directed toward an outside goal to be achieved. What is *not* taken into account is the *motivation* of activity. Take for instance a man driven to incessant work by a sense of deep insecurity and loneliness; or another one driven by ambition, or greed for money. In all these cases the person is the slave of a passion, and his activity is in reality a "passivity" because he is driven; he is the sufferer, not the "actor." On the other hand, a man sitting quiet and contemplating, with no purpose or aim except that of experiencing himself and his oneness with the world, is considered to be "passive," because he is not "doing" anything. In reality, this attitude of concentrated meditation is the highest activity there is, an activity of the soul, which is possible only under the condition of inner freedom and independence. One concept of activity, the modern one, refers to the use of energy for the achievement of external aims; the other concept of activity refers to the use of man's inherent powers, regardless of whether any external change is brought about. The latter concept of activity has been formulated most clearly by Spinoza. He differentiates among the affects between active and passive affects, "actions" and "passions." In the exercise of an active affect, man is free, he is the master of his affect; in the exercise of a passive affect, man is driven, the object of motivations of which he himself is not aware. Thus Spinoza arrives at the statement that virtue and power are one and the same.[1] Envy, jealousy, ambition, any kind of greed are passions; love is an action, the practice of a human power, which can be practiced only in freedom and never as the result of a compulsion.

Love is an activity, not a passive affect; it is a "standing in," not a "falling for." In the most general way, the active character of love can be described by stating that love is primarily *giving*, not receiving.

What is giving? Simple as the answer to this question seems to be, it is actually full of ambiguities and complexities. The most widespread misunderstanding is that which assumes that giving is "giving up" something, being deprived of, sacrificing. The person whose character has not developed beyond the stage of the receptive, exploitative, or hoarding orientation, experiences the act of giving in this way. The marketing character is willing to give, but only in exchange for receiving; giving without receiving for him is being cheated. People whose main orientation is a non-productive one feel giving as an impoverishment. Most individuals of this type therefore refuse to give. Some make a virtue out of giving in the sense of a sacrifice. They feel that just because it is painful to give, one *should* give; the virtue of giving to them lies in the very act of acceptance of the sacrifice. For them, the norm that it is better to give than to receive means that it is better to suffer deprivation than to experience joy.

For the productive character, giving has an entirely different meaning. Giving is the highest expression of potency. In the very act of giving, I experience my strength, my wealth, my power. This experience of heightened vitality and potency fills me with joy. I experience myself as overflowing, spending, alive, hence as joyous. Giving is more joyous than receiving, not because it is a deprivation, but because in the act of giving lies the expression of my aliveness. . . .

In the sphere of material things giving means being rich. Not he who *has* much is rich, but he who *gives* much. The hoarder who is anxiously worried about losing something is, psychologically speaking, the poor, impoverished man, regardless of how much he has. Whoever is capable of giving of himself is rich. He experiences himself as one who can confer of himself to others. Only one who is deprived of all that goes beyond the barest necessities for subsistence would be incapable of enjoying the act of giving material things. But daily experience shows that what a person considers the

[1] *Spinoza,* Ethics *IV, Def. 8.*

minimal necessities depends as much on his character as it depends on his actual possessions. It is well known that the poor are more willing to give than the rich. Nevertheless, poverty beyond a certain point may make it impossible to give, and is so degrading, not only because of the suffering it causes directly, but because of the fact that it deprives the poor of the joy of giving.

The most important sphere of giving, however, is not that of material things, but lies in the specifically human realm. What does one person give to another? He gives of himself, of the most precious he has, he gives of his life. This does not necessarily mean that he sacrifices his life for the other—but that he gives him of that which is alive in him; he gives him of his joy, of his interest, of his understanding, of his knowledge, of his humor, of his sadness—of all expressions and manifestations of that which is alive in him. In thus giving of his life, he enriches the other person, he enhances the other's sense of aliveness by enhancing his own sense of aliveness. He does not give in order to receive; giving is in itself exquisite joy. But in giving he cannot help bringing something to life in the other person, and this which is brought to life reflects back to him; in truly giving, he cannot help receiving that which is given back to him. Giving implies to make the other person a giver also and they both share in the joy of what they have brought to life. In the act of giving something is born, and both persons involved are grateful for the life that is born for both of them. Specifically with regard to love this means: love is a power which produces love; impotence is the inability to produce love. This thought has been beautifully expressed by Marx: "Assume," he says, "*man* as *man*, and his relation to the world as a human one, and you can exchange love only for love, confidence for confidence, etc. If you wish to enjoy art, you must be an artistically trained person; if you wish to have influence on other people, you must be a person who has a really stimulating and furthering influence on other people. Every one of your relationships to man and to nature must be a definite expression of your *real, individual* life corresponding to the object of your will. If you love without calling forth love, that is, if your love as such does not produce love, if by means of an *expression of life* as a loving person you do not make of yourself a *loved person*, then your love is impotent, a misfortune." [2] But not only in love does giving mean

[2] *"Nationalökonomie und Philosophie," 1844, published in Karl Marx'* Die Frühschriften, *Alfred Kröner Verlag, Stuttgart, 1953, pp. 300, 301. (My translation, E. F.)*

receiving. The teacher is taught by his students, the actor is stimulated by his audience, the psychoanalyst is cured by his patient—provided they do not treat each other as objects, but are related to each other genuinely and productively.

It is hardly necessary to stress the fact that the ability to love as an act of giving depends on the character development of the person. It presupposes the attainment of a predominantly productive orientation; in this orientation the person has overcome dependency, narcissistic omnipotence, the wish to exploit others, or to hoard, and has acquired faith in his own human powers, courage to rely on his powers in the attainment of his goals. To the degree that these qualities are lacking, he is afraid of giving himself—hence of loving.

Beyond the element of giving, the active character of love becomes evident in the fact that it always implies certain basic elements, common to all forms of love. These are *care*, *responsibility*, *respect* and *knowledge*.

That love implies *care* is most evident in a mother's love for her child. No assurance of her love would strike us as sincere if we saw her lacking in care for the infant, if she neglected to feed it, to bathe it, to give it physical comfort; and we are impressed by her love if we see her caring for the child. It is not different even with the love for animals or flowers. If a woman told us that she loved flowers, and we saw that she forgot to water them, we would not believe in her "love" for flowers. *Love is the active concern for the life and the growth of that which we love.* Where this active concern is lacking, there is no love. This element of love has been beautifully described in the book of Jonah. God has told Jonah to go to Nineveh to warn its inhabitants that they will be punished unless they mend their evil ways. Jonah runs away from his mission because he is afraid that the people of Nineveh will repent and that God will forgive them. He is a man with a strong sense of order and law, but without love. However, in his attempt to escape, he finds himself in the belly of a whale, symbolizing the state of isolation and imprisonment which his lack of love and solidarity has brought upon him. God saves him, and Jonah goes to Nineveh. He preaches to the inhabitants as God has told him, and the very thing he was afraid of happens. The men of Nineveh repent their sins, mend their ways, and God forgives them and decides not to destroy the city. Jonah is intensely angry and disappointed; he wanted "justice" to be done, not mercy. At last he finds some comfort in the shade of a tree which God made to grow for him to protect him from the sun. But when God makes the tree wilt, Jonah is depressed and angrily complains to God. God answers: "Thou hast had pity on the gourd for the which thou hast not labored neither madest it grow; which came up in a night, and perished in a night. And should I not spare Nineveh, that great city, wherein are more than sixscore thousand people that cannot discern between their right hand and their left hand; and also much cattle?" God's answer to Jonah is to be understood symbolically. God explains to Jonah that the essence of love is to "labor" for something and "to make something grow," that love and labor are inseparable. One loves that for which one labors, and one labors for that which one loves.

Care and concern imply another aspect of love; that of *responsibility*. Today responsibility is often meant to denote duty, something imposed upon one from the outside. But responsibility, in its true sense, is an entirely voluntary act; it is my response to the needs, expressed or unexpressed, of another human being. To be "responsible" means to be able and ready to "respond." Jonah did not feel responsible to the inhabitants of Nineveh. He, like Cain, could ask: "Am I my brother's keeper?" The loving person responds. The life of his brother is not his brother's business alone, but his own. He feels responsible for his fellow men, as he feels responsible for himself. This responsibility, in the case of the mother and her infant, refers mainly to the care for physical needs. In the love between adults it refers mainly to the psychic needs of the other person.

Responsibility could easily deteriorate into domination and possessiveness, were it not for a third component of love, *respect*. Respect is not fear and awe; it denotes, in accordance with the root of the word (*respicere* = to look at), the ability to see a person as he is, to be aware of his unique individuality. Respect means the concern that the other person should grow and unfold as he is. Respect, thus, implies the absence of exploitation. I want the loved person to grow and unfold for his own sake, and in his own ways, and not for the purpose of serving me. If I love the other person, I feel one with him or her, but with him *as he is*, not as I need him to be as an object for my use. It is clear that respect is possible only if *I* have achieved independence; if I can stand and walk without needing crutches, without having to dominate and exploit anyone else. Respect exists only on the basis of freedom: "l'amour est l'enfant de la liberté" as an old French song says; love is the child of freedom, never that of domination.

To respect a person is not possible without *knowing* him; care and responsibility would be blind if they were not guided by knowledge. Knowledge would be empty if it were not motivated by concern. There are many layers of knowledge; the knowledge which is an aspect of love is one which does not stay at the periphery, but penetrates to the core. It is possible only when I can transcend the concern for myself and see the other person in his own terms. I may know, for instance, that a person is angry, even if he does not show it overtly; but I may know him more deeply than that; then I know that he is anxious, and worried; that he feels lonely, that he feels guilty. Then I know that his anger is only the manifestation of something deeper, and I see him as anxious and embarrassed, that is, as the suffering person, rather than as the angry one.

Knowledge has one more, and a more fundamental, relation to the problem of love. The basic need to fuse with another person so as to transcend the prison of one's separateness is closely related to another specifically human desire, that to know the "secret of man." While life in its merely biological aspects is a miracle and a secret, man in his human aspects is an unfathomable secret to himself—and to his fellow man. We know ourselves, and yet even with all the efforts we may make, we do not know ourselves. We know our fellow man, and yet we do not know him, because we are not a thing, and our fellow man is not a thing. The further we reach into the depth of our being, or someone else's being, the more the goal of knowledge eludes us. Yet we cannot help desiring to penetrate into the secret of man's soul, into the innermost nucleus which is "he."

There is one way, a desperate one, to know the secret: it is that of complete power over another person; the power which makes him do what we want, feel what we want, think what we want; which transforms him into a thing, our thing, our possession. The ultimate degree of this attempt to know lies in the extremes of sadism, the desire and ability to make a human being suffer; to torture him, to force him to betray his secret in his suffering. In this craving for penetrating man's secret, his and hence our own, lies an essential motivation for the depth and intensity of cruelty and destructiveness. In a very succinct way this idea has been expressed by Isaac Babel. He quotes a fellow officer in the Russian civil war, who has just stamped his former master to death, as saying: "With shooting—I'll put it this way—with shooting you only get rid of a chap. . . . With shooting you'll never get at the soul, to where it is in a fellow and how it shows itself. But I don't spare myself, and

I've more than once trampled an enemy for over an hour. You see, I want to get to know what life really is, what life's like down our way."[3]

In children we often see this path to knowledge quite overtly. The child takes something apart, breaks it up in order to know it; or it takes an animal apart; cruelly tears off the wings of a butterfly in order to know it, to force its secret. The cruelty itself is motivated by something deeper: the wish to know the secret of things and of life.

The other path to knowing "the secret" is love. Love is active penetration of the other person, in which my desire to know is stilled by union. In the act of fusion I know you, I know myself, I know everybody—and I "know" nothing. I know in the only way knowledge of that which is alive is possible for man—by experience of union—not by any knowledge our thought can give. Sadism is motivated by the wish to know the secret, yet I remain as ignorant as I was before. I have torn the other being apart limb from limb, yet all I have done is to destroy him. Love is the only way of knowledge, which in the act of union answers my quest. In the act of loving, of giving myself, in the act of penetrating the other person, I find myself, I discover myself, I discover us both, I discover man.

Questions

1. Fromm makes an initial distinction between passions and actions. What other words does he use that are synonymous with "passions" and "actions"?
2. How is the act of giving related to character development? What assumption would Fromm make about a person incapable of loving?
3. Fromm supports his definition of love by assigning certain basic charteristics. How does each support his definition? Is his list complete, or would you add other characteristics?

Topics for Composition

1. Using both Hunt's essay and Fromm's essay discuss the influence that society has upon one's attitude toward love.
2. Write your own view of the meaning of love. Carefully define your terms, using Fromm's essay as a model.

[3] *I. Babel,* The Collected Stories, *Criterion Books, New York, 1955.*

The Short Story

In this story, two seemingly unrelated events are subtly united to provide a statement on the nature of love. As you read this story, keep in mind the connection between the story of the duck hunt and the author's opening comment on the newspaper account of the "drama of passion." Specifically, observe de Maupassant's use of the following:

1. The contrast between the narrator and his cousin in thought, in action, in dress
2. The involved description of the forest, the marsh, the frozen channels
3. The paradox between the narrator's statements about his horror at killing and his participation in the hunt

Love: Pages from a Sportsman's Book

GUY DE MAUPASSANT

I have just read a drama of passion among the general news items in one of the daily papers. He first killed her and then committed suicide, showing that he must have loved her. What matter who the actors were? Their love alone interests me—not because it moves or surprises me, or because it softens me or makes me think, but because it recalls to my mind a remembrance of my youth, a strange recollection of a hunting adventure where love appeared to me as the cross appeared in the sky to the early Christians.

I was born with all the instincts and the senses of primitive man, tempered by the reasoning power and the feelings of a civilized being. I am passionately fond of shooting, and the sight of the wounded animal, with blood on its feathers and on my hands, affects my heart so that it almost stops beating.

That year the cold weather set in suddenly toward the end of autumn, and I was invited by one of my cousins, Karl de Rauville, to go with him duck shooting on the marshes, at daybreak.

My cousin, a jolly fellow of forty, with red hair, very stout and bearded, a country gentleman, an amiable semi-brute, with a happy disposition and endowed with that Gallic wit which makes even mediocrity agreeable, lived in a house, half farmhouse, half château, situated in a broad valley through which a river ran. The hills right and left were covered with woods, old seignorial woods where magnificent trees still remained, and where the rarest feathered game in that part of France was to be found. Eagles were shot there occasionally, and birds of passage, those which rarely come into our over-populated part of the country, almost infallibly stopped amid these branches, which were centuries old, as if they knew or recognized a little corner of an ancient forest which had remained there to serve them as a shelter during their brief nocturnal halt.

In the valley there were large meadows watered by trenches and separated by hedges; farther on, the river, which up to that point had been canalized, expanded into a vast marsh. That marsh, which was the best shooting ground I ever saw, was my cousin's chief care; he kept it like a park. Among the rushes that covered it and made it a living, rustling, noisy spot, narrow passages had been made, through which flat-bottomed boats, impelled and steered by poles, passed along silently over the stagnant water, brushed up against the reeds, and made the swift fish take refuge among the weeds, and frightened the wild fowl, whose pointed, black heads disappeared suddenly as they dived.

I am passionately fond of the water, of the sea, although it is too vast, too restless, too impossible to hold; of the rivers which are so beautiful, but which pass on, flow away, and are gone; and, above all, of the marshes, where the whole unknown existence of aquatic animals palpitates. The marsh is an entire world to itself on this earth, a different world, which has its own life, its settled inhabitants, and its passing travelers, its voices, its noises, and, above all, its mystery. Nothing is more disturbing, nothing more disquieting, more terrifying occasionally, than a fen. Why should this terror hang over these low plains covered with water? Is it the vague rustling of the rushes, the strange will-o'-the-wisps, the profound silence which envelops them on calm nights, or is it the strange mists which hang over the rushes like a shroud? Or else is it the imperceptible plashing, so slight and so gentle, and sometimes more terrifying than the cannon of men or the thunders of skies, which make these marshes resemble the lands of one's dreams, fearsome countries concealing an unknown and dangerous secret?

No, something else belongs to it, another mystery, more profound and graver, floats amid these thick mists, perhaps the mystery of creation itself! For was it not in stagnant and muddy water, amid the heavy humidity of moist land under the heat of the sun, that the first germ of life stirred, vibrated and expanded to the day?

I arrived at my cousin's in the evening. It was freezing hard enough to split stones.

In the large room whose sideboards, walls, and ceiling were covered with stuffed birds with extended wings, or perched on branches to which they were nailed, hawks, herons, owls, nightjars, buzzards, tercels, vultures, falcons, my cousin, who himself resembled some strange animal from a cold country, dressed in a sealskin jacket, told me during dinner what preparations he had made for that same night.

We were to start at half-past three in the morning, so as to arrive at the place which he had chosen for our watching place at about half-past four. On that spot a hut had been built of pieces of ice, so as to shelter us somewhat from the terrible wind which precedes daybreak, that wind which is so cold that it lacerates the flesh as if with a saw, cuts it like the blade of a knife, and wounds it as with a poisoned dart, twists it like a pair of pincers, and burns it like fire.

My cousin rubbed his hands: "I have never known such a frost," he said. "It is already twelve degrees below zero at six o'clock in the evening."

I threw myself on my bed immediately after we had finished our meal, and I went to sleep by the light of a bright fire burning in the grate.

At three o'clock he woke me. In my turn, I put on a sheepskin, and found my Cousin Karl covered with a bearskin. After having swallowed two cups of scalding coffee apiece, followed by two glasses of brandy, we started, accompanied by a gamekeeper and our dogs, Pongeon and Pierrot.

From the first moment that I got outside I felt chilled to the very marrow. It was one of those nights on which the earth seems dead with cold. The frozen air becomes resistant and palpable, such pain does it cause; no breath of wind moves it, it is fixed and motionless; it bites, pierces through you, dries and kills the trees, the plants, the insects, the small birds themselves, that fall from the branches on to the hard ground, and become hard themselves under the grip of the cold.

The moon, which was in her last quarter and was inclining to one side, seemed to be fainting in the midst of space, and so weak that she was unable to take her departure, and thus remained up yonder, also overcome and paralyzed by the severity of the weather. She shed a cold, mournful light over the world, that dying and wan light which she gives us every month, at the end of her resurrection.

Karl and I went side by side, our backs bent, our hands in our pockets, and our guns under our arms. Our boots, which were wrapped in wool so that we might be able to walk without slipping on the frozen river, made no sound, and I looked at the white vapor of our dogs' breath.

We were soon on the edge of the marsh, and we went into one of those lanes of dry rushes which ran through this low forest.

Our elbows, which touched the long, ribbon-like leaves, made a slight noise, and I was seized, as I had never been before, by the powerful, singular emotion which marshes cause in me. This marsh was dead, dead from cold, for we were walking on it, amid its population of dried rushes.

Suddenly, at the turn of one of the lanes, I perceived the ice hut which had been constructed to shelter us. I went in, and as we had nearly an hour to wait before the wandering birds would awake, I rolled myself up in my rug in order to try and get warm.

Then, lying on my back, I began to look at the misshapen moon, which had four horns through the semi-transparent walls of this polar house.

But the frost of the frozen marshes, the cold of these walls, the cold from the firmament penetrated me so terribly that I began to cough.

My cousin Karl became uneasy. "It will be bad if we do not kill much to-day," he said. "I do not want you to catch cold; we will light a fire." And he told the gamekeeper to cut some rushes.

We made a pile in the middle of our hut, which had a hole in the middle of the roof to let out the smoke, and when the red flames rose up, the clear crystal chunks began to melt gently, imperceptibly, as if these stones of ice were sweating. Karl, who had remained outside, called to me: "Come and look here!" I went out of the hut, and remained struck with astonishment. Our hut, in the shape of a cone, looked like an enormous diamond with a heart of fire, which had been suddenly planted there in the midst of the frozen water of the marsh. And inside we saw two fantastic forms, those of our dogs, who were warming themselves at the fire.

But a peculiar cry, a lost, wandering cry, passed over our heads, and the light from our hearth showed us the wild birds. Nothing moves one so much as the first clamor of life which one does not see, and which is passing through the sombre air so quickly and so far off, before the first streak of the winter's day appears on the horizon. It seems to me at this glacial hour of dawn, as if that passing cry which is carried away by the wings of a bird is the sigh of the soul of the world!

"Put out the fire," said Karl. "It is getting daylight."

The sky was, in fact, beginning to grow pale, and the flights of duck made long, rapid streaks on the sky, which were soon obliterated.

A stream of light burst out into the night. Karl had fired, and the two dogs ran forward.

And then, almost every minute, first he, then I, aimed rapidly as soon as the shadow of a flying flock appeared above the rushes. And Pierrot and Plongeon, out of breath but happy, retrieved the bleeding birds, whose eyes, occasionally, still looked at us.

The sun had risen; it was a bright day with a blue sky, and we were thinking of taking our departure, when two birds with extended necks and outstretched wings glided rapidly over our heads. I fired and one of them fell almost at my feet. It was a teal, with a silver breast, and then, in the blue space above me, I heard a voice, the voice of a bird. It was a short, repeated, heartrending lament; and the bird, the little animal that had been spared, began to circle round in the blue sky, above our heads, looking at its dead companion which I was holding in my hand.

Karl was on his knees, his gun to his shoulder, watching it eagerly, until it should be within gunshot. "You have killed the duck," he said, "and the drake will not fly away."

He certainly did not fly away; he circled over our heads continually and continued his cries. Never had any groans of suffering pained me so much as that desolate appeal, as that lamentable reproach of this poor bird which was lost in space.

Occasionally he would fly off, under the menace of the gun which followed his flight, and seemed ready to continue his flight alone; but, as he could not make up his mind to this, he soon returned to find his mate.

"Leave her on the ground," Karl said to me; "he will come within gunshot by and by." And he did indeed come near us, careless of danger, infatuated by his animal love, by his affection for that other animal which I had just killed.

Karl fired, and it was as if somebody had cut the string which held the bird suspended. I saw something black descend, and I heard the noise of a fall among the rushes. And Pierrot brought it to me.

I put them—they were already cold—into the same game bag, and I returned to Paris that evening.

Questions

1. In the opening paragraph the narrator tells us, "love appeared to me as the cross appeared in the sky to the early Christians." How may we connect this statement of initiation into the truth of love with his earlier remarks about the drama of passion?
2. What is the importance of "amiable semi-brute" as it applies to the character of the narrator's cousin? As it reveals the character of the narrator himself? As it applies to the overall contrast in the story?
3. Additional contrasts are symbolically supplied to bring out a sense of initiation and progression from ignorance (darkness) to knowledge (light). Identify the way in which each contrast contributes to the theme and to the structural progression in the story.
4. How does the author bring his story full circle? What are the possible meanings we can attach to "drama of passion"?

Topics for Composition

1. Contrast the character of the narrator and that of his cousin. Develop your contrast to support the central theme of the story.
2. Expand and apply to this story Rousseau's statement: "a new situation . . . the habit of living together gave birth to the sweetest sentiments the human species is acquainted with. . . ."
3. Using the author's statement—"No, something else belongs to it, another mystery . . . perhaps the mystery of creation itself. . . ."—trace the author's implications as his story comments on the progress of civilization.
4. Accepting de Maupassant's story as a revelation of a basic truth, write an essay based on this story and Hunt's essay, in which you reveal society's changing attitude toward love. Of course, you may prefer to show that society's attitude has not changed.

IN "Chestnut and Jet," MacMahon presents a vivid portrayal of Joe and Nora Morrissey in a story that provides little dialogue by which we may assess each of the main characters. Instead, the author uses:

1. Nora's reactions to the comments of her neighbors
2. Nora's attitude as she watches Joe from a distance
3. Joe's mannerisms when he "parades" his animal before the townspeople

Chestnut and Jet

BRYAN MACMAHON

When April came, Joe Morrissey the farmer took down the nail-box from the top of the dresser and rummaged in it to discover the sire-horse's ribbons and rosettes. When at last he found them, they were in sorry over-winter trim. Each year it was the same. Each year he had to ask the milliner in town to make him a new set so that his stallion should look his best as he paraded the town on market day.

The black stallion was taken from the drudgery of the spring work and petted. Jack Donnell the young-old groom gladly abandoned the ploughing of furzy uplands and began to give the horse his April delicacies: porridge and new milk and beaten eggs and oats. There was also a mash, the ingredients of which he kept a tight-fisted secret. Dandruff-brush and curry-comb were unearthed and plied. Gradually the camouflaged splendour and dignity and terror of the animal emerged. Out in the farmyard the as yet white sunlight caught him in swaths on flank and haunch and chest and heliographed his power to the awakening countryside. The horse sloughed winter, welcomed summer, and trumpeted the indignities of his spring. He seemed to find the touch of the cobbles intolerable. He began to whistle and bell. His challenge was the blending of a cluster of four handbells in four different tones mingled with the far-away whistle of a railway engine. This extraordinary noise was the overture of his chaotic blood: making the noise his nostrils were two pouches lined with a terrifying red velvet.

Out in the farmyard the black farmer walked round and round the black stallion. Joe Morrissey was smiling as he watched the cajolings and wheedlings and bullyings of the groom. As day followed day the farmer began to reflect the animal. The man's gait grew to have something of the strut in it. Watching him covertly from the kitchen window, his wife Nora broke into a warm smile as she measured the capers of her man. She threw back her chestnut head as her nose emitted a hiss of humorous tolerance. Her hands automatically kneaded dough while her smiling eyes were busy loving her man. Suddenly she was aware that her daughter Nonie was nuzzling at her dress.

"Mam!" The chestnut child of five was her mother's image.

"Well?"

Out of a crinkling face: "Can I go to town a Wednesday with my Dad?"

"No, my little filly. Not Wednesday. Some other day, maybe."

"Mam!"

"Well, child?"

"I'm not a filly. I'm a lev-er-et."

The woman shook out the scarf of her red rich laughter. "In the spring a filly, in the winter a leveret. Isn't that fair?"

"That's fair . . . an' Mam!"

"Well, Nonie girl?"

"If you go to town a Wednesday with my Dad will you bring me back Queen cakes?"

"I will, of course. I'll bring you back a big white bag of Queen cakes. Isn't that fair, Nonie?"

"That's fair, Mam."

Wednesday was market-day in town. That was the day the stallion stood at Treanor's Yard. Joe Morrissey had the terra-cotta-coloured posters posted on the walls of the fair green and on the pillars of the weighbridge. "Royal Splendour," they bragged, "by Royal Musician out of Splendid Stream. . . . This sire is getting extra well . . . his stock is well known . . . terms . . . groom's fees . . . no responsibility . . . particulars from . . ."

Each Wednesday morning Jack Donnell and another groom danced the great jet Irish Draught up the long street of the town. About midday Joe Morrissey and his wife drummed into town in the tub-trap. Nora Morrissey generally shopped at a store on the outskirts; rarely did she penetrate into the town proper. Her husband saw to it that everything was right in Treanor's Yard. He stood a few drinks to the farmers who had brought their mares. In the evening he himself paraded the stallion down the street and then handed the animal over to the grooms who had been walking some distance behind him. Afterwards he sat into the trap with his wife and returned home. Speaking through the hoof-beats he told his wife how the day had gone with him, with whom he had been drinking, what price one of the stallion's foals had made. His wife listened with tranquillity and understanding.

Mary Sullivan was a neighbour of the Morrissey's. She came into Morrissey's one evening when the man of the house was out. Crouching over the open hearth, Mary whined more to herself than to Nora Morrissey: "Your husband, your grand black husband. God bless you, Big Joe! God in his infinite goodness saw fit to make Mary Sullivan an ould maid. I was in town a Wednesday when he led the sire-horse down the length of the main street. An' all the people came out of their houses to see the grand man and the grand stallion."

Minnie McNaughton was another neighbour. She was a labouring man's widow. She was childless. Speaking to Nora Morrissey, she said: "Fine and fine for you, Mrs. Morrissey. God loves the ground you walk on. I was inside in town on market day getting my commands and I heard the townspeople giving the height of splendour to your upstanding man. God spare him long to you and to your lovely children. When he passes down the street on Wednesday, gentle and simple stand up to see the grand man and the grand stallion. Fine and fine for you, Mrs. Morrissey. Fine again for you. . . ." The woman's voice grumbled on in lonely envy.

Gradually this became Nora Morrissey's problem–to picture her husband and the stallion through alien eyes. But try as she would, her eyes remained unalterably her own. In this effort of imagination she apprehended herself shaking her head suddenly as if to clear her head after a blow. The full consciousness of her antic inevitably flooding her, she would begin to upbraid herself for her foolishness. And to crown her discomfiture there was her little chestnut daughter at the table's head tossing her head and smiling as she mimicked her chestnut mother. On the instant their two laughters were blended in the sunny kitchen.

When next market day came Nora Morrissey went into the centre of the town. The market was a busy one and the streets were thronged. The woman bore herself over-bravely, as if expecting battle and experiencing sharp disappointment in its failure to come upon her. She went in and out of shops on the thinnest pretexts. She offered an excellent pretence of interest in the affairs of acquaintances she met on the pavements. But always she took care to stand where her eyes could command the higher end of the street. There she expected the man and the stallion to appear above the swirl of the people. As evening came an access of excitement compelled her to throw back her Paisley shawl from her forehead and display the light mahogany depths of her hair and the clean-cut outlines of her features. As time passed without her husband's appearance, an insane impatience began to have its way with her: What was keeping him? Will the people have gone home? What on earth am I doing here? The whole side of the country will hear about me. What's delaying you, Joe Morrissey? What's delaying you, I say?

Then the two black dancers were out above at the street's end. Excitement tightened in the woman's chest. Now man and horse had moved well on to the stage of the town. Nora appreciated the strangeness of the as yet silent hooves whose tappeta-tappeta would presently carry their rhythm into her blood. Dark stallion and dark man were now dancing into audibility. Now she could see the ribbons and the rosettes. The animal seemed endowed with a deeper darkness than the man. There was a contrast in the lead of tubular white web which the farmer was holding lightly in his guiding hand and also in the pipe-clayed surcingle which circled the stallion's belly. The surcingle bisected the arc in the animal's back—to the rear of the white band was the treasured violence of the haunches. Man and stallion were completely confident, completely arrogant, completely male.

Nora Morrissey suddenly remembered the town and swung to view it. True for the tellers, the whole place had come out to see the man and the stallion. An old man displaying the last cheap remnants of vigour; a rusty old woman finding herself being revolved like an old locomotive on a turntable; a shop assistant remembering hills and the beat of the tide; a motor mechanic dreaming himself white as a hound's tooth; a hobbledehoy finding a decade of years flung unbearably at his bewildered head; a butcher pausing in the analysis of a belch to recall roses and the scent of roses; six canker-eared corner-boys disinterring bones of buried manhood—the whole spring-throttled town was out to see the jet stallion and the jet man.

As they drew near her Nora Morrissey found herself instinctively withdrawing towards the wall of the shops. She made as if to cover her face with her shawl. Then, as a flame grows tall in a windless moment, she straightened herself, and throwing the shawl back from her hair and face she came out to the pavement's edge and began to glory in their coming. Lifting her head she made ready to greet her Emperor. Slow enough he was in seeing her. His face was as yet rigid with a high urban pride; his air was that of one who had delivered himself up to the reverence of the people. His set mouth disdained domesticities. For a terrifying moment she thought he would fail to see her. Then, being a woman, she made an unwarranted movement of her shawl. His processional eyes rested on her, abandoned her, recaptured her—then his face blazed up into recognition and dear emotion. The woman came close to sobbing in the sweetness of this public statement of ownership. For a moment the farmer relaxed his strain on the lead. Sensing this the horse raised his head and rang his great cluster of bells.

Questions

1. MacMahon's story is rich in imagery, especially in his use of color. What instances can you find where his use of color contributes to the mood of the moment?
2. What statements in the story appear "poetical" in their wording? Why are these statements appropriate to the author's purpose?
3. What does Nora's correction of her daughter's use of leveret indicate about her attitude toward life?
4. Why does MacMahon reveal the attitudes of Mary Sullivan and Minnie McNaughton?
5. As an obvious "love story," MacMahon's work also reveals other perhaps attendant emotions. Where do we see pride, envy, humility?
6. How deeply has the author relied on characterization? What, for instance, can you say about Nora as a person? What about Joe? Can you come to some conclusion about MacMahon's method?

Topics for Composition

1. MacMahon's story obviously illustrates the value of the exact word. Write an essay describing a moment of deep feeling (love, pride, envy, etc.). Base your essay not on the action of the moment but on a careful selection of descriptive words.
2. Using the characterization of Nora and that of the boy in de Maupassant's story, write an essay comparing the techniques used by each author to achieve an initiation.
3. Certainly love is not a panacea in MacMahon's story. Write a refutation of Hunt's essay based on this story.
4. Use, as the central statement for an analysis of MacMahon's theme, Hobbes's equation: "Love of one singularly, with desire to be singularly beloved, equals 'the passion of love.'"

EVEN though Lawrence's story bears an unlikely title for a love story, we have already noted in the introduction that the "birth" of love and a rebirth of "life" are central to this story. We should watch, therefore, the manner in which Lawrence prepares an atmosphere conducive to such a rebirth.

1. He creates a family situation that is obviously dissolving.
2. He heightens the atmosphere of dissolution by emphasizing the

callous indifference of the family members to each other and their situation.

3. He describes the family members as being in a "stupor," as having "glazed hopeless eyes."
4. Finally, he details the tedium and boredom that lead Mabel to the edge of life.

The Horse Dealer's Daughter

D. H. LAWRENCE

"Well, Mabel, and what are you going to do with yourself?" asked Joe, with foolish flippancy. He felt quite safe himself. Without listening for an answer, he turned aside, worked a grain of tobacco to the tip of his tongue, and spat it out. He did not care about anything, since he felt safe himself.

The three brothers and the sister sat round the desolate breakfast-table, attempting some sort of desultory consultation. The morning's post had given the final tap to the family fortunes, and all was over. The dreary dining-room itself, with its heavy mahogany furniture, looked as if it were waiting to be done away with.

But the consultation amounted to nothing. There was a strange air of ineffectuality about the three men, as they sprawled at table, smoking and reflecting vaguely on their own condition. The girl was alone, a rather short, sullen-looking young woman of twenty-seven. She did not share the same life as her brothers. She would have been good-looking save for the impressive fixity of her face, 'bull-dog', as her brothers called it.

There was a confused tramping of horses' feet outside. The three men all sprawled round in their chairs to watch. Beyond the dark holly bushes that separated the strip of lawn from the high-road, they could see a cavalcade of shire horses swinging out of their own yard, being taken for exercise. This was the last time. These were the last horses that would go through their hands. The young men watched with critical, callous look. They were all frightened at the collapse of their lives, and the sense of disaster in which they were involved left them no inner freedom.

Yet they were three fine, well-set fellows enough. Joe, the eldest, was a man of thirty-three, broad and handsome in a hot, flushed way. His face was red, he twisted his black moustache over a thick finger, his eyes were shallow and restless. He had a sensual way of uncovering his teeth when he laughed, and his bearing was stupid. Now he watched the horses with a glazed look of helplessness in his eyes, a certain stupor of downfall.

The great draught-horses swung past. They were tied head to tail, four of them, and they heaved along to where a lane branched off from the high-road, planting their great hoofs floutingly in the fine black mud, swinging their great rounded haunches sumptuously, and trotting a few sudden steps as they were led into the lane, round the corner. Every movement showed a massive, slumbrous strength, and a stupidity which held them in subjection. The groom at the head looked back, jerking the leading rope. And the cavalcade moved out of sight up the lane, the tail of the last horse, bobbed up tight and stiff, held out taunt from the swinging great haunches as they rocked behind the hedges in a motion-like sleep.

Joe watched with glazed hopeless eyes. The horses were almost like his own body to him. He felt he was done for now. Luckily he was engaged to a woman as old as himself, and therefore her father, who was steward of a neighbouring estate, would provide him with a job. He would marry and go into harness. His life was over, he would be a subject animal now.

He turned uneasily aside, the retreating steps of the horses echoing in his ears. Then, with foolish restlessness, he reached for the scraps of bacon-rind from the plates, and making a faint whistling sound, flung them to the terrier that lay against the fender. He watched the dog swallow them, and waited till the creature looked into his eyes. Then a faint grin came on his face, and in a high, foolish voice he said:

"You won't get much more bacon, shall you, you little b——?"

The dog faintly and dismally wagged its tail, then lowered its haunches, circled round, and lay down again.

There was another helpless silence at the table. Joe sprawled uneasily in his seat, not willing to go till the family conclave was dissolved. Fred Henry, the second brother, was erect, clean-limbed, alert. He had watched the passing of the horses with more *sang-froid*. If he was an animal, like Joe, he was an animal which controls, not one which is controlled. He was master of any horse, and he carried himself with a well-tempered air of mastery. But he was not master of the situations of life. He pushed his coarse brown moustache upwards, off his lip, and glanced irritably as his sister, who sat impassive and inscrutable.

"You'll go and stop with Lucy for a bit, shan't you?" he asked. The girl did not answer.

"I don't see what else you can do," persisted Fred Henry.

"Go as a skivvy," Joe interpolated laconically.

The girl did not move a muscle.

"If I was her, I should go in for training for a nurse," said Malcolm, the youngest of them all. He was the baby of the family, a young man of twenty-two, with a fresh, jaunty *museau.*

But Mabel did not take any notice of him. They had talked at her and round her for so many years, that she hardly heard them at all.

The marble clock on the mantelpiece softly chimed the half-hour, the dog rose uneasily from the hearth-rug and looked at the party at the breakfast-table. But still they sat on in ineffectual conclave.

"Oh, all right," said Joe suddenly, apropos of nothing. "I'll get a move on."

He pushed back his chair, straddled his knees with a downward jerk, to get them free, in horsey fashion, and went to the fire. Still he did not go out of the room; he was curious to know what the others would do or say. He began to charge his pipe, looking down at the dog and saying in a high, affected voice:

"Going wi' me? Going wi' me are ter? Tha'rt goin' further than tha counts on just now, dost hear?"

The dog faintly wagged its tail, the man stuck out his jaw and covered his pipe with his hands, and puffed intently, losing himself in the tobacco, looking down all the while at the dog with an absent brown eye. The dog looked up at him in mournful distrust. Joe stood with his knees stuck out, in real horsey fashion.

"Have you had a letter from Lucy?" Fred Henry asked of his sister.

"Last week," came the neutral reply.

"And what does she say?"

There was no answer.

"Does she *ask* you to go and stop there?" persisted Fred Henry.

"She says I can if I like."

"Well, then, you'd better. Tell her you'll come on Monday."

This was received in silence.

"That's what you'll do then, is it?" said Fred Henry, in some exasperation.

But she made no answer. There was a silence of futility and irritation in the room. Malcolm grinned fatuously.

"You'll have to make up your mind between now and next

Wednesday," said Joe loudly, "or else find yourself lodgings on the kerbstone."

The face of the young woman darkened, but she sat on immutable.

"Here's Jack Ferguson!" exclaimed Malcolm, who was looking aimlessly out of the window.

"Where?" exclaimed Joe loudly.

"Just gone past."

"Coming in?"

Malcolm craned his neck to see the gate.

"Yes," he said.

There was a silence. Mabel sat on like one condemned, at the head of the table. Then a whistle was heard from the kitchen. The dog got up and barked sharply. Joe opened the door and shouted:

"Come on."

After a moment a young man entered. He was muffled up in overcoat and a purple woollen scarf, and his tweed cap, which he did not remove, was pulled down on his head. He was of medium height, his face was rather long and pale, his eyes looked tired.

"Hello, Jack! Well, Jack!" exclaimed Malcolm and Joe. Fred Henry merely said: "Jack."

"What's doing?" asked the newcomer, evidently addressing Fred Henry.

"Same. We've got to be out by Wednesday. Got a cold?"

"I have—got it bad, too."

"Why don't you stop in?"

"*Me* stop in? When I can't stand on my legs, perhaps I shall have a chance." The young man spoke huskily. He had a slight Scotch accent.

"It's a knock-out, isn't it," said Joe, boisterously, "if a doctor goes around croaking with a cold. Looks bad for the patients, doesn't it?"

The young doctor looked at him slowly.

"Anything the matter with *you*, then?" he asked sarcastically.

"Not as I know of. Damn your eyes, I hope not. Why?"

"I thought you were very concerned about the patients, wondered if you might be one yourself."

"Damn it, no, I've never been patient to no flaming doctor, and hope I never shall be," returned Joe.

At this point Mabel rose from the table, and they all seemed to become aware of her existence. She began putting the dishes together. The young doctor looked at her, but did not address her. He had not greeted her. She went out of the room with the tray, her face impassive and unchanged.

"When are you off then, all of you?" asked the doctor.

"I'm catching the eleven-forty," replied Malcolm. "Are you goin' down wi' th' trap, Joe?"

"Yes, I've told you I'm going down wi' th' trap, haven't I?"

"We'd better be getting her in then. So long, Jack, if I don't see you before I go," said Malcolm, shaking hands.

He went out, followed by Joe, who seemed to have his tail between his legs.

"Well, this is the devil's own," exclaimed the doctor, when he was left along with Fred Henry. "Going before Wednesday, are you?"

"That's the orders," replied the other.

"Where, to Northampton?"

"That's it."

"The devil!" exclaimed Ferguson, with quiet chagrin.

And there was silence between the two.

"All settled up, are you?" asked Ferguson.

"About."

There was another pause.

"Well, I shall miss yer, Freddy, boy," said the young doctor.

"And I shall miss thee, Jack," returned the other.

"Miss you like hell," mused the doctor.

Fred Henry turned aside. There was nothing to say. Mabel came in again, to finish clearing the table.

"What are *you* going to do, then, Miss Pervin?" asked Ferguson. "Going to your sister's, are you?"

Mabel looked at him with her steady, dangerous eyes, that always made him uncomfortable, unsettling his superficial ease.

"No," she said.

"Well, what in the name of fortune *are* you going to do? Say what you mean to do," cried Fred Henry, with futile intensity.

But she only averted her head, and continued her work. She folded the white table-cloth, and put on the chenille cloth.

"The sulkiest bitch that ever trod!" muttered her brother.

But she finished her task with perfectly impassive face, the young doctor watching her interestedly all the while. Then she went out.

Fred Henry stared after her, clenching his lips, his blue eyes fixing in sharp antagonism, as he made a grimace of sour exasperation.

"You could bray her into bits, and that's all you'd get out of her," he said, in a small, narrowed tone.

The doctor smiled faintly.

"What's she *going* to do, then?" he asked.

"Strike me if *I* know!" returned the other.

There was a pause. Then the doctor stirred.

"I'll be seeing you to-night, shall I?" he said to his friend.

"Ay—where's it to be? Are we going over to Jessdale?"

"I don't know. I've got such a cold on me. I'll come round to the 'Moon and Stars', anyway."

"Let Lizzie and May miss their night for once, eh?"

"That's it—if I feel as I do now."

"All's one——"

The two young men went through the passage and down to the back door together. The house was large, but it was servantless now, and desolate. At the back was a small bricked house-yard and beyond that a big square, gravelled fine and red, and having stables on two sides. Sloping, dank, winter-dark fields stretched away on the open sides.

But the stables were empty. Joseph Pervin, the father of the family, had been a man of no education, who had become a fairly large horse dealer. The stables had been full of horses, there was a great turmoil and come-and-go of horses and of dealers and grooms. Then the kitchen was full of servants. But of late things had declined. The old man had married a second time, to retrieve his fortunes. Now he was dead and everything was gone to the dogs, there was nothing but debt and threatening.

For months, Mabel had been servantless in the big house, keeping the home together in penury for her ineffectual brothers. She had kept house for ten years. But previously it was with unstinted means. Then, however brutal and coarse everything was, the sense of money had kept her proud, confident. The men might be foul-mouthed, the women in the kitchen might have bad reputations, her brothers might have illegitimate children. But so long as there was money, the girl felt herself established, and brutally proud, reserved.

No company came to the house, save dealers and coarse men. Mabel had no associates of her own sex, after her sister went away. But she did not mind. She went regularly to church, she attended to her father. And she lived in the memory of her mother, who had died when she was fourteen, and whom she had loved. She had loved her father, too, in a different way, depending upon him, and feeling secure in him, until at the age of fifty-four he married again. And then she had set hard against him. Now he had died and left them all hopelessly in debt.

She had suffered badly during the period of poverty. Nothing, however, could shake the curious, sullen, animal pride that dominated each member of the family. Now, for Mabel, the end had come. Still she would not cast about her. She would follow her own way just the same. She would always hold the keys of her own situation. Mindless and persistent, she endured from day to day. Why should she think? Why should she answer anybody? It was enough that this was the end, and there was no way out. She need not pass any more darkly along the main street of the small town, avoiding every eye. She need not demean herself any more, going into the shops and buying the cheapest food. This was at an end. She thought of nobody, not even of herself. Mindless and persistent, she seemed in a sort of ecstasy to be coming nearer to her fulfilment, her own glorification, approaching her dead mother, who was glorified.

In the afternoon she took a little bag, with shears and sponge and a small scrubbing-brush, and went out. It was a grey, wintry day, with saddened, dark green fields and an atmosphere blackened by the smoke of foundries not far off. She went quickly, darkly along the causeway, heeding nobody, through the town to the churchyard.

There she always felt secure, as if no one could see her, although as a matter of fact she was exposed to the stare of everyone who passed along under the churchyard wall. Nevertheless, once under the shadow of the great looming church, among the graves, she felt immune from the world, reserved within the thick churchyard wall as in another country.

Carefully she clipped the grass from the grave, and arranged the pinky white, small chrysanthemums in the tin cross. When this was done, she took an empty jar from a neighbouring grave, brought water, and carefully, most scrupulously sponged the marble headstone and the coping-stone.

It gave her sincere satisfaction to do this. She felt in immediate contact with the world of her mother. She took minute pains, went through the park in a state bordering on pure happiness, as if in performing this task she came into a subtle, intimate connection with her mother. For the life she followed here in the world was far less real than the world of death she inherited from her mother.

The doctor's house was just by the church. Ferguson, being a mere hired assistant, was slave to the country-side. As he hurried now to attend to the out-patients in the surgery, glancing across the graveyard with his quick eye, he saw the girl at her task at the grave. She seemed so intent and remote, it was like looking into another world. Some mystical element was touched in him. He slowed down as he walked, watching her as if spellbound.

She lifted her eyes, feeling him looking. Their eyes met. And each looked again at once, each feeling, in some way, found out by the other. He lifted his cap and passed on down the road. There remained distinct in his consciousness, like a vision, the memory of her face, lifted from the tombstone in the churchyard, and looking at him with slow, large, portentous eyes. It *was* portentous, her face. It seemed to mesmerize him. There was a heavy power in her eyes which laid hold of his whole being, as if he had drunk some powerful drug. He had been feeling weak and done before. Now the life came back into him, he felt delivered from his own fretted, daily self.

He finished his duties at the surgery as quickly as might be, hastily filling up the bottles of the waiting people with cheap drugs. Then, in perpetual haste, he set off again to visit several cases in another part of his round, before tea-time. At all times he preferred to walk if he could, but particularly when he was not well. He fancied the motion restored him.

The afternoon was falling. It was grey, deadened, and wintry, with a slow, moist, heavy coldness sinking in and deadening all the faculties. But why should he think or notice? He hastily climbed the hill and turned across the dark green fields, following the black cinder-track. In the distance, across a shallow dip in the country, the small town was clustered like smouldering ash, a tower, a spire, a heap of low, raw, extinct houses. And on the nearest fringe of the town, sloping into the dip, was Oldmeadow, the Pervins' house. He could see the stables and the outbuildings distinctly, as they lay towards him on the slope. Well, he would not go there many more times! Another resource would be lost to him, another place gone: the only company he cared for in the alien, ugly little town he was losing. Nothing but work, drudgery, constant hastening from dwelling to dwelling among the colliers and the iron-workers. It wore him out, but at the same time he had a craving for it. It was a stimulant to him to be in the homes of the working people, moving, as it were, through the innermost body of their life. His nerves were excited and gratified. He could come so near, into the very lives of the rough, inarticulate, powerfully emotional men and women. He grumbled, he said he hated the hellish hole. But as a matter of fact it excited him, the contact with the rough, strongly-feeling people was a stimulant applied direct to his nerves.

Below Oldmeadow, in the green, shallow, soddened hollow of fields, lay a square, deep pond. Roving across the landscape, the doctor's quick eye detected a figure in black passing through the gate of the field, down towards the pond. He looked again. It would be Mabel Pervin. His mind suddenly became alive and attentive.

Why was she going down there? He pulled up on the path on the slope above, and stood staring. He could just make sure of the small black figure moving in the hollow of the failing day. He seemed to see her in the midst of such obscurity, that he was like a clairvoyant, seeing rather with the mind's eye than with ordinary sight. Yet he could see her positively enough, whilst he kept his eye attentive. He felt, if he looked away from her, in the thick, ugly falling dusk, he would lose her altogether.

He followed her minutely as she moved, direct and intent, like something transmitted rather than stirring in voluntary activity, straight down the field towards the pond. There she stood on the bank for a moment. She never raised her head. Then she waded slowly into the water.

He stood motionless as the small black figure walked slowly and deliberately towards the centre of the pond, very slowly, gradually moving deeper into the motionless water, and still moving forward as the water got up to her breast. Then he could see her no more in the dusk of the dead afternoon.

"There!" he exclaimed. "Would you believe it?"

And he hastened straight down, running over the wet, soddened fields, pushing through the hedges, down into the depression of callous wintry obscurity. It took him several minutes to come to the pond. He stood on the bank, breathing heavily. He could see nothing. His eyes seemed to penetrate the dead water. Yes, perhaps that was the dark shadow of her black clothing beneath the surface of the water.

He slowly ventured into the pond. The bottom was deep, soft clay, he sank in, and the water clasped dead cold round his legs. As he stirred he could smell the cold, rotten clay that fouled up into the water. It was objectionable in his lungs. Still, repelled and yet not heeding, he moved deeper into the pond. The cold water rose over his thighs, over his loins, upon his abdomen. The lower part of his body was all sunk in the hideous cold element. And the bottom was so deeply soft and uncertain, he was afraid of pitching with his mouth underneath. He could not swim, and was afraid.

He crouched a little, spreading his hands under the water and moving them round, trying to feel for her. The dead cold pond swayed upon his chest. He moved again, a little deeper, and again, with his hands underneath, he felt all around under the water. And he touched her clothing. But it evaded his fingers. He made a desperate effort to grasp it.

And so doing he lost his balance and went under, horribly, suffocating in the foul earthy water, struggling madly for a few moments. At last, after what seemed an eternity, he got his footing, rose again into the air and looked around. He gasped, and knew he was in the world. Then he looked at the water. She had risen near him. He grasped her clothing, and drawing her nearer, turned to take his way to land again.

He went very slowly, carefully, absorbed in the slow progress. He rose higher, climbing out of the pond. The water was now only about his legs; he was thankful, full of relief to be out of the clutches of the pond. He lifted her and staggered on to the bank, out of the horror of wet, grey clay.

He laid her down on the bank. She was quite unconscious and running with water. He made the water come from her mouth, he worked to restore her. He did not have to work very long before he could feel the breathing begin again in her; she was breathing naturally. He worked a little longer. He could feel her live beneath his hands; she was coming back. He wiped her face, wrapped her in his overcoat, looked round into the dim, dark grey world, then lifted her and staggered down the bank and across the fields.

It seemed an unthinkably long way, and his burden so heavy he felt he would never get to the house. But at last he was in the stable-yard, and then in the house-yard. He opened the door and went into the house. In the kitchen he laid her down on the hearth-rug and called. The house was empty. But the fire was burning in the grate.

Then again he kneeled to attend to her. She was breathing regularly, her eyes were wide open and as if conscious, but there seemed something missing in her look. She was conscious in herself, but unconscious of her surroundings.

He ran upstairs, took blankets from a bed, and put them before the fire to warm. Then he removed her saturated, earthy-smelling clothing, rubbed her dry with a towel, and wrapped her naked in the blankets. Then he went into the dining-room, to look for spirits. There was a little whiskey. He drank a gulp himself, and put some into her mouth.

The effect was instantaneous. She looked full into his face, as if she had been seeing him for some time, and yet had only just become conscious of him.

"Dr. Ferguson?" she said.

"What?" he answered.

He was divesting himself of his coat, intending to find some dry clothing upstairs. He could not bear the smell of the dead, clayey water, and he was mortally afraid for his own health.

"What did I do?" she asked.

"Walked into the pond," he replied. He had begun to shudder like one sick, and could hardly attend to her. Her eyes remained full on him, he seemed to be going dark in his mind, looking back at her helplessly. The shuddering became quieter in him, his life came back to him, dark and unknowing, but strong again.

"Was I out of my mind?" she asked, while her eyes were fixed on him all the time.

"Maybe, for the moment," he replied. He felt quiet, because his strength had come back. The strange fretful strain had left him.

"Am I out of my mind now?" she asked.

"Are you?" he reflected a moment. "No," he answered truthfully, "I don't see that you are." He turned his face aside. He was afraid now, because he felt dazed, and felt dimly that her power was stronger than his, in this issue. And she continued to look at him fixedly all the time. "Can you tell me where I shall find some dry things to put on?" he asked.

"Did you dive into the pond for me?" she asked.

"No," he answered. "I walked in. But I went in overhead as well."

There was silence for a moment. He hesitated. He very much wanted to go upstairs to get into dry clothing. But there was another desire in him. And she seemed to hold him. His will seemed to have gone to sleep, and left him, standing there slack before her. But he felt warm inside himself. He did not shudder at all, though his clothes were sodden on him.

"Why did you?" she asked.

"Because I didn't want you to do such a foolish thing," he said.

"It wasn't foolish," she said, still gazing at him as she lay on the floor, with a sofa cushion under her head. "It was the right thing to do. *I* knew best, then."

"I'll go and shift these wet things," he said. But still he had not the power to move out of her presence, until she sent him. It was as if she had the life of his body in her hands, and he could not extricate himself. Or perhaps he did not want to.

Suddenly she sat up. Then she became aware of her own immediate condition. She felt the blankets about her, she knew her own limbs. For a moment it seemed as if her reason were going. She looked round, with wild eye, as if seeking something. He stood still with fear. She saw her clothing lying scattered.

"Who undressed me?" she asked, her eyes resting full and inevitable on his face.

"I did," he replied, "to bring you round."

For some moments she sat and gazed at him awfully, her lips parted.

"Do you love me, then?" she asked.

He only stood and stared at her, fascinated. His soul seemed to melt.

She shuffled forward on her knees, and put her arms round him, round his legs, as he stood there, pressing her breasts against his knees and thighs, clutching him with strange, convulsive certainty, pressing his thighs against her, drawing him to her face, her throat, as she looked up at him with flaring, humble eyes of transfiguration, triumphant in first possession.

"You love me," she murmured, in strange transport, yearning and triumphant and confident. "You love me. I know you love me, I know."

And she was passionately kissing his knees, through the wet clothing, passionately and indiscriminately kissing his knees, his legs, as if unaware of everything.

He looked down at the tangled wet hair, the wild, bare, animal shoulders. He was amazed, bewildered, and afraid. He had never thought of loving her. He had never wanted to love her. When he rescued her and restored her, he was a doctor, and she was a patient. He had had no single personal thought of her. Nay, this introduction of the personal element was very distasteful to him, a violation of his professional honour. It was horrible to have her there embracing his knees. It was horrible. He revolted from it, violently. And yet—and yet—he had not the power to break away.

She looked at him again, with the same supplication of powerful love, and that same transcendent, frightening light of triumph. In view of the delicate flame which seemed to come from her face like a light, he was powerless. And yet he had never intended to love her. He had never intended. And something stubborn in him could not give way.

"You love me," she repeated, in a murmur of deep, rhapsodic assurance. "You love me."

Her hands were drawing him, drawing him down to her. He was afraid, even a little horrified. For he had, really, no intention of loving her. Yet her hands were drawing him towards her. He put out his hand quickly to steady himself, and grasped her bare shoulder. A flame seemed to burn the hand that grasped her soft shoulder. He had no intention of loving her: his whole will was against his yielding. It was horrible. And yet wonderful was the touch of her shoulders, beautiful the shining of her face. Was she perhaps mad? He had a horror of yielding to her. Yet something in him ached also.

He had been staring away at the door, away from her. But his hand remained on her shoulder. She had gone suddenly very still. He looked down at her. Her eyes were now wide with fear, with doubt, the light was dying from her face, a shadow of terrible greyness was returning. He could not bear the touch of her eyes' question upon him, and the look of death behind the question.

With an inward groan he gave way, and let his heart yield towards her. A sudden gentle smile came on his face. And her eyes, which never left his face, slowly, slowly filled with tears. He watched the strange water rise in her eyes, like some slow fountain coming up. And his heart seemed to burn and melt away in his breast.

He could not bear to look at her any more. He dropped on his knees and caught her head with his arms and pressed her face against his throat. She was very still. His heart, which seemed to have broken, was burning with a kind of agony in his breast. And he felt her slow, hot tears wetting his throat. But he could not move.

He felt the hot tears wet his neck and the hollows of his neck, and he remained motionless, suspended through one of man's eternities. Only now it had become indispensable to him to have her face pressed close to him; he could never let her go again. He could never let her head go away from the close clutch of his arm. He wanted to remain like that for ever, with his heart hurting him in a pain that was also life to him. Without knowing, he was looking down on her damp, soft brown hair.

Then, as it were suddenly, he smelt the horrid stagnant smell of that water. And at the same moment she drew away from him and looked at him. Her eyes were wistful and unfathomable. He was afraid of them, and he fell to kissing her, not knowing what he was doing. He wanted her eyes not to have that terrible, wistful, unfathomable look.

When she turned her face to him again, a faint delicate flush was glowing, and there was again dawning that terrible shining of joy in her eyes, which really terrified him, and yet which he now wanted to see, because he feared the look of doubt still more.

"You love me?" she said, rather faltering.

"Yes." The word cost him a painful effort. Not because it wasn't true. But because it was too newly true, the *saying* seemed to tear open again his newly-torn heart. And he hardly wanted it to be true, even now.

She lifted her face to him, and he bent forward and kissed her on the mouth, gently, with the one kiss that is an eternal pledge. And as he kissed her his heart strained again in his breast. He never intended to love her. But now it was over. He had crossed over the gulf to her, and all that he had left behind had shrivelled and become void.

After the kiss, her eyes again slowly filled with tears. She sat still, away from him, with her face drooped aside, and her hands folded in her lap. The tears fell very slowly. There was complete silence. He too sat there motionless and silent on the hearth-rug. The strange pain of his heart that was broken seemed to consume him. That he should love her? That this was love! That he should be ripped open in this way! Him, a doctor! How they would all jeer if they knew! It was agony to him to think they might know.

In the curious naked pain of the thought he looked again to her. She was sitting there drooped into a muse. He saw a tear fall, and his heart flared hot. He saw for the first time that one of her shoulders was quite uncovered, one arm bare, he could see one of her small breasts; dimly, because it had become almost dark in the room.

"Why are you crying?" he asked, in an altered voice.

She looked up at him, and behind her tears the consciousness of her situation for the first time brought a dark look of shame to her eyes.

"I'm not crying, really," she said, watching him, half frightened.

He reached his hand, and softly closed it on her bare arm.

"I love you! I love you!" he said in a soft, low vibrating voice, unlike himself.

She shrank, and dropped her head. The soft, penetrating grip of his hand on her arm distressed her. She looked up at him.

"I want to go," she said. "I want to go and get you some dry things."

"Why?" he said. "I'm all right."

"But I want to go," she said. "And I want you to change your things."

He released her arm, and she wrapped herself in the blanket, looking at him rather frightened. And still she did not rise.

"Kiss me," she said wistfully.

He kissed her, but briefly, half in anger.

Then, after a second, she rose nervously, all mixed up in the blanket. He watched her in her confusion as she tried to extricate herself and wrap herself up so that she could walk. He watched her relentlessly, as she knew. And as she went, the blanket trailing, and as he saw a glimpse of her feet and her white leg, he tried to remember her as she was when he had wrapped her in the blanket. But then he didn't want to remember, because she had been nothing to him then, and his nature revolted from remembering her as she was when she was nothing to him.

A tumbling, muffled noise from within the dark house startled him. Then he heard her voice: "There are clothes." He rose and went to the foot of the stairs, and gathered up the garments she had thrown down. Then he came back to the fire, to rub himself down and dress. He grinned at his own appearance when he had finished.

The fire was sinking, so he put on coal. The house was now quite dark, save for the light of a street-lamp that shone in faintly from beyond the holly trees. He lit the gas with matches he found on the mantelpiece. Then he emptied the pockets of his own clothes, and threw all his wet things in a heap into the scullery. After which he gathered up her sodden clothes, gently, and put them in a separate heap on the coppertop in the scullery.

It was six o'clock on the clock. His own watch had stopped. He ought to go back to the surgery. He waited, and still she did not come down. So he went to the foot of the stairs and called:

"I shall have to go."

Almost immediately he heard her coming down. She had on her best dress of black voile, and her hair was tidy, but still damp. She looked at him—and in spite of herself, smiled.

"I don't like you in those clothes," she said.

"Do I look a sight?" he answered.

They were shy of one another.

"I'll make you some tea," she said.

"No, I must go."

"Must you?" And she looked at him again with the wide, strained, doubtful eyes, And again, from the pain of his breast, he knew how he loved her. He went and bent to kiss her, gently, passionately, with his heart's painful kiss.

"And my hair smells so horrible," she murmured in distraction. "And I'm so awful, I'm so awful! Oh no, I'm too awful." And she broke into bitter, heart-broken sobbing. "You can't want to love me, I'm horrible."

"Don't be silly, don't be silly," he said, trying to comfort her, kissing her, holding her in his arms. "I want you, I want to marry you, we're going to be married, quickly, quickly–to-morrow if I can."

But she only sobbed terribly, and cried:

"I feel awful. I feel awful. I feel I'm horrible to you."

"No, I want you, I want you," was all he answered, blindly, with that terrible intonation which frightened her almost more than her horror lest he should *not* want her.

Questions

1. How are the descriptions of the horses and the animals used in the beginning of the story? Specifically, why is Mabel's face described as "bulldog"?
2. Point out lines in the beginning of the story that reflect the lifelessness of the family grouping. What other descriptive details add to the atmosphere of futility?
3. What do we know of Mabel's life since the death of her parents?
4. Can we speculate at what time in her life Mabel ceased to "live"?
5. What are the symbolic implications of the episode at the pond?
6. How does the episode at the pond serve as a structural and thematic divider in the story?
7. Can we say that Mabel is the sole protagonist in the story?
8. Explain the transformations in character of both Mabel and Dr. Ferguson.

Topics for Composition

1. Expand your answer to question 6 into an essay. Accept the pond episode as a central structural and thematic guide and support your thesis by referring to descriptive details that control the atmosphere before and after the pond episode. Also use those details that reveal the characters of Mabel and Dr. Ferguson before and after the pond episode.
2. Love brings knowledge of self to Mabel and Dr. Ferguson. Write an essay supporting this thesis.
3. In this unit, three short stories have treated the nature of love. Write an essay comparing and contrasting the methods used in the three stories. Expand your thesis statement to include the fact that the three authors had varying purposes. Support the varied treatments as they exhibit these purposes.

Drama

SHAKESPEARE's play elicits either rhapsody or condemnation from the critics. The structure of the play and the dramatic effect of the contest between Antony and Cleopatra, on the one hand, and the powers of the Roman Empire, on the other, have been severely questioned or enthusiastically justified. Admittedly, the poetry of the play, particularly the exchanges between Antony and Cleopatra on the quality of their love, or Enobarbus' description of their first meeting, is magnificent. From one viewpoint, the rapid alternation of scenes in widely separated parts of the Roman Empire seems to violate the principles of sound dramatic structure. However, Shakespeare sharpens by frequent fluctuation of locale and characters the audience's understanding of the conflict between the values of Rome and those of Egypt. To evaluate questions about the play's form, one might consider these suggestions:

1. The play abounds in contrasting references to Antony's glorious military past and his present softness and equivocal judgment. Likewise, the irresistible charm and the wanton sensuality of Cleopatra are contrasted.
2. Various characters–Philo, Canidius, Enobarbus, even a common soldier–serve to focus our attention upon the issues of the plot, but Enobarbus seems to offer the most reliable viewpoint for understanding the complex struggle within Antony between the rival claims of love and duty.
3. The rapid alternation of scenes not only gives a kind of epic quality to the events but also posits a clearly and dramatically powerful dialectic of honor and love. These rival claims of empire and passion upon Antony are evident not only to him, but also to the warrior-politicians of Rome, to Cleopatra and her train, and even to Antony's loyal supporters. The dimensions of the dialectic are personified by Octavius Caesar and Octavia, on one hand, and by Antony and the Egyptian queen, on the other.

The Tragedy of Antony and Cleopatra

WILLIAM SHAKESPEARE

Characters

MARK ANTONY
OCTAVIUS CAESAR
M. AEMILIUS LEPIDUS } *triumvirs*

SEXTUS POMPEIUS

DOMITIUS ENOBARBUS
VENTIDIUS
EROS
SCARUS
DERCETAS
DEMETRIUS
PHILO
} *friends to Antony*

CANIDIUS, *lieutenant-general to Antony*

MAECENAS
AGRIPPA
DOLABELLA
PROCULEIUS
THIDIAS
GALLUS
} *friends to Caesar*

TAURUS, *lieutenant-general to Caesar*

MENAS
MENECRATES
VARRIUS
} *friends to Pompey*

SILIUS, *a Roman officer under Ventidius*

A SCHOOLMASTER, *ambassador from Antony to Caesar*

ALEXAS
MARDIAN
SELEUCUS
DIOMEDES
} *attendants on Cleopatra*

A SOOTHSAYER

A CLOWN

CLEOPATRA, *Queen of Egypt*

OCTAVIA, *sister to Caesar and wife to Antony*

CHARMIAN
IRAS
} *attendants on Cleopatra*

OFFICERS, SOLDIERS, MESSENGERS, ATTENDANTS

SCENE *In several parts of the Roman Empire*

ACT I

SCENE I. *Alexandria. A room in Cleopatra's palace.*

[*Enter Demetrius and Philo.*]

Philo. Nay, but this dotage of our general's
O'erflows the measure. Those his goodly eyes,

That o'er the files and musters* of the war
Have glowed like plated Mars, now bend, now turn
The office and devotion of their view 5
Upon a tawny front.* His captain's heart,
Which in the scuffles of great fights hath burst
The buckles on his breast, reneges all temper*
And is become the bellows and the fan
To cool a gypsy's lust

[*Flourish. Enter Antony, Cleopatra, her Ladies, the Train with Eunuchs fanning her.*]

Look where they come! 10
Take but good note, and you shall see in him
The triple pillar of the world* transformed
Into a strumpet's fool. Behold and see.

Cleopatra. If it be love indeed, tell me how much.
Antony. There's beggary in the love that can be reckoned. 15
Cleopatra. I'll set a bourn* how far to be beloved.
Antony. Then must thou needs find out new heaven, new earth.

[*Enter a Messenger.*]

Messenger. News, my good lord, from Rome.
Antony. Grates me! The sum.*
Cleopatra. Nay, hear them, Antony.
Fulvia* perchance is angry, or who knows 20
If the scarce-bearded Caesar have not sent
His powerful mandate to you: "Do this, or this.
Take in that kingdom, and enfranchise that.
Perform't, or else we damn thee."
Antony. How, my love?
Cleopatra. Perchance? Nay, and most like. 25
You must not stay here longer, your dismission
Is come from Caesar; therefore hear it, Antony.

3. *files and musters: arrangements of soldiers.*
6. *tawny front: Shakespeare thinks of Cleopatra as quite dark, although she was of Greek descent.*
8. *reneges all temper: declines all moderation or balance.*
12. *the triple pillar of the world: Antony, Octavius Caesar, and Lepidus are the Triumvirs of the Roman world.*
16. *bourn: limit.*
18. *Grates me! The sum.: It annoys me! Be brief.*
20. *Fulvia: Antony's domineering Roman wife.*

Where's Fulvia's process? Caesar's I would say? Both?
Call in the messengers. As I am Egypt's Queen,
Thou blushest, Antony, and that blood of thine 30
Is Caesar's homager.* Else so thy cheek pays shame
When shrill-tongued Fulvia scolds. The messengers!

Antony. Let Rome in Tiber melt and the wide arch
Of the ranged empire fall! Here is my space.
Kingdoms are clay. Our dungy earth alike 35
Feeds beast as man. The nobleness of life
Is to do thus, when such a mutual pair [*Embracing.*]
And such a twain can do't, in which I bind,
On pain of punishment, the world to weet*
We stand up peerless.

Cleopatra. Excellent falsehood! 40
Why, did he marry Fulvia and not love her?
I'll seem the fool I am not. Antony
Will be himself.

Antony. But stirred by Cleopatra.
Now, for the love of Love and her soft hours,
Let's not confound the time with conference harsh. 45
There's not a minute of our lives should stretch
Without some pleasure now. What sport tonight?

Cleopatra. Hear the ambassadors.

Antony. Fie, wrangling queen!
Whom everything becomes—to chide, to laugh,
To weep; whose every passion fully strives 50
To make itself, in thee, fair and admired!
No messenger but thine, and all alone
Tonight we'll wander through the streets and note
The qualities of people. Come, my queen.
Last night you did desire it. Speak not to us. 55

[*Exeunt Antony and Cleopatra with their Train.*]

Demetrius. Is Caesar with Antonius prized so slight?

Philo. Sir, sometimes when he is not Antony,
He comes too short of that great property*
Which still should go with Antony.

Demetrius. I am full sorry

31. *Caesar's homager: pays homage to Caesar's authority.*
39. *weet: know.*
58. *property: personality.*

That he approves* the common liar, who 60
Thus speaks of him at Rome. But I will hope
Of better deeds tomorrow. Rest you happy! [*Exeunt.*]

SCENE II. *Another room in Cleopatra's palace.*

[*Enter Charmian, Iras, Alexas, Mardian the Eunuch, a Soothsayer, and others.*]

Charmian. Lord Alexas, sweet Alexas, most anything Alexas, almost most absolute Alexas, where's the soothsayer that you praised so to the Queen? O that I knew this husband which, you say, must charge his horns with garlands! * 5

Alexas. Soothsayer!

Soothsayer. Your will?

Charmian. Is this the man? Is't you, sir, that know things?

Soothsayer. In nature's infinite book of secrecy
A little I can read.

Alexas. Show him your hand. 10

[*Enter Enobarbus.*]

Enobarbus. Bring in the banquet quickly, wine enough
Cleopatra's health to drink.

Charmian. Good sir, give me good fortune.

Soothsayer. I make not, but foresee.

Charmian. Pray then, foresee me one. 15

Soothsayer. You shall be yet far fairer than you are.

Charmian. He means in flesh.*

Iras. No, you shall paint when you are old.

Charmian. Wrinkles forbid!

Alexas. Vex not his prescience, be attentive. 20

Charmian. Hush!

Soothsayer. You shall be more beloving than beloved.

Charmian. I had rather heat my liver with drinking.*

Alexas. Nay, hear him.

60. *approves: gives proof to.*

4–5. *husband . . . garlands: a husband who wears his horns (the sign of a cuckold, a man with an unfaithful wife) proudly. There is also the suggestion that the husband will be a dumb animal led to the sacrifice.*

17. *in flesh: in weight.*

23. *heat . . . drinking: heat up the liver (supposedly the seat of the passion of love (with drinking rather than with unrequited love.*

Charmian. Good now, some excellent fortune! Let me be married to three kings in a forenoon and widow them all. Let me have a child at fifty, to whom Herod of Jewry may do homage. Find me to marry me with Octavius Caesar, and companion me with my mistress. 25

Soothsayer. You shall outlive the lady whom you serve. 30

Charmian. O excellent! I love long life better than figs.

Soothsayer. You have seen and proved a fairer former fortune
Than that which is to approach.

Charmian. Then belike my children shall have no names.
Prithee, how many boys and wenches must I have? 35

Soothsayer. If every of your wishes had a womb,
And fertile every wish, a million.

Charmian. Out, fool! I forgive thee for a witch.

Alexas. You think none but your sheets are privy to your wishes. 40

Charmian. Nay, come, tell Iras hers.

Alexas. We'll know all our fortunes.

Enobarbus. Mine, and most of our fortunes tonight shall be—drunk to bed.

Iras. There's a palm* presages chastity, if nothing else. 45

Charmian. E'en as the o'erflowing Nilus presageth famine.

Iras. Go, you wild bedfellow, you cannot soothsay.

Charmian. Nay, if an oily palm be not a fruitful prognostication,* I cannot scratch mine ear. Prithee tell her but a workaday fortune. 50

Soothsayer. Your fortunes are alike.

Iras. But how, but how? Give me particulars.

Soothsayer. I have said.

Iras. Am I not an inch of fortune better than she?

Charmian. Well, if you were but an inch of fortune better than I, where would you choose it? 55

Iras. Not in my husband's nose.

Charmian. Our worser thoughts Heavens mend! Alexas—come, his fortune, his fortune! O, let him marry a woman that cannot go, sweet Isis, I beseech thee! And let her die too, and give him a worse! And let worse follow worse till the worst of all follow him laughing 60

45. *palm: Iras holds out her hand for the soothsayer to examine.*
48–49. *fruitful prognostication: a sign of fertility.*

to his grave, fiftyfold a cuckold! Good Isis, hear me this prayer, though thou deny me a matter of more weight. Good Isis, I beseech thee. 65

Iras. Amen, dear goddess, hear that prayer of the people! For as it is a heartbreaking to see a handsome man loose-wived,* so it is a deadly sorrow to behold a foul knave uncuckolded. Therefore, dear Isis, deep decorum, and fortune him accordingly. 70

Charmian. Amen.

Alexas. Lo, now, if it lay in their hands to make me a cuckold, they would make themselves whores but they'd do't.

Enobarbus. Hush, here comes Antony.

[*Enter Cleopatra.*]

Charmian. Not he, the Queen. 75

Cleopatra. Saw you my lord?

Enobarbus. No, lady.

Cleopatra. Was he not here?

Charmian. No, madam.

Cleopatra. He was disposed to mirth, but on the sudden
A Roman thought hath struck him. Enobarbus!

Enobarbus. Madam? 80

Cleopatra. Seek him, and bring him hither. Where's Alexas?

Alexas. Here, at your service. My lord approaches.

[*Enter Antony with a Messenger and Attendants.*]

Cleopatra. We will not look upon him. Go with us.

[*Exeunt all but Antony, Messenger, and Attendants.*]

Messenger. Fulvia thy wife first came into the field.

Antony. Against my brother Lucius? 85

Messenger. Ay.
But soon that war had end, and the time's state*
Made friends of them, jointing their force 'gainst Caesar,
Whose better issue in the war from Italy
Upon the first encounter drave* them.

Antony. Well, what worst? 90

67–68. *loose-wived: married to a loose (unfaithful) wife.*
87. *time's state: circumstances of the time.*
90. *drave: drove.*

Messenger. The nature of bad news infects the teller.
Antony. When it concerns the fool or coward. On.
Things that are past are done, with me. 'Tis thus—
Who tells me true, though in his tale lie death,
I hear him as he flattered.
Messenger. Labienus— *95*
This is stiff news—hath with his Parthian force
Extended Asia from Euphrates,
His conquering banner shook from Syria
To Lydia and to Ionia,
Whilst—
Antony. Antony, thou wouldst say.
Messenger. O, my lord. *100*
Antony. Speak to me home, mince not the general tongue.*
Name Cleopatra as she is called in Rome.
Rail thou in Fulvia's phrase, and taunt my faults
With such full license as both truth and malice
Have power to utter. O, then we bring forth weeds *105*
When our quick minds lie still, and our ills told us
Is as our earing.* Fare thee well awhile.
Messenger. At your noble pleasure. [*Exit Messenger.*]
Antony. From Sicyon, ho, the news! Speak there!
1. *Attendant.* The man from Sicyon—is there such an one? *110*
2. *Attendant.* He stays upon your will.
Antony. Let him appear.
These strong Egyptian fetters I must break,
Or lose myself in dotage.

[*Enter another Messenger.*]

What are you?

Messenger. Fulvia thy wife is dead.
Antony. Where died she?
Messenger. In Sicyon. *115*
Her length of sickness, with what else more serious
Importeth thee to know, this bears. [*Gives a letter.*]
Antony. Forbear me. [*Exit Messenger.*]
There's a great spirit gone! Thus did I desire it.
What our contempts doth often hurl from us,

101. *general tongue: what everyone says.*
107. *earing: cultivation.*

We wish it ours again. The present pleasure, *120*
By revolution lowering, does become
The opposite of itself. She's good, being gone.
The hand could pluck her back that shoved her on.
I must from this enchanting queen break off.
Ten thousand harms, more than the ills I know, *125*
My idleness doth hatch. Ho now, Enobarbus!

[*Enter Enobarbus.*]

Enobarbus. What's your pleasure, sir?
Antony. I must with haste from hence.
Enobarbus. Why, then we kill all our women. We see *130*
how mortal an unkindness is to them. If they suffer our
departure, death's the word.
Antony. I must be gone.
Enobarbus. Under a compelling occasion let women die.
It were pity to cast them away for nothing, though *135*
between them and a great cause they should be esteemed
nothing. Cleopatra, catching but the least noise of this,
dies instantly. I have seen her die twenty times upon far
poorer moment. I do think there is mettle in death,
which commits some loving act upon her, she hath such *140*
a celerity in dying.
Antony. She is cunning past man's thought.
Enobarbus. Alack, sir, no. Her passions are made of nothing but the finest part of pure love. We cannot call her
winds and waters sighs and tears. They are greater *145*
storms and tempests than almanacs can report. This cannot be cunning in her. If it be, she makes a shower of
rain as well as Jove.
Antony. Would I had never seen her!
Enobarbus. O, sir, you had then left unseen a wonderful *150*
piece of work, which not to have been blest withal
would have discredited your travel.
Antony. Fulvia is dead.
Enobarbus. Sir?
Antony. Fulvia is dead. 155
Enobarbus. Fulvia?
Antony. Dead.
Enobarbus. Why, sir, give the gods a thankful sacrifice.

When it pleaseth their deities to take the wife of a man from him, it shows to man the tailors of the earth, comforting therein, that when old robes are worn out, there are members to make new. If there were no more women but Fulvia, then had you indeed a cut, and the case to be lamented. This grief is crowned with consolation. Your old smock brings forth a new petticoat. And indeed the tears live in an onion that should water this sorrow. *160* *165*

Antony. The business she hath broached in the state
Cannot endure my absence.

Enobarbus. And the business you have broached here cannot be without you, especially that of Cleopatra's, which wholly depends on your abode. *170*

Antony. No more light answers. Let our officers
Have notice what we purpose. I shall break
The cause of our expedience* to the Queen
And get her leave to part. For not alone *175*
The death of Fulvia, with more urgent touches,
Do strongly speak to us, but the letters too
Of many our contriving* friends in Rome
Petition us at home. Sextus Pompeius*
Hath given the dare to Caesar and commands *180*
The empire of the sea. Our slippery people,
Whose love is never linked to the deserver
Till his deserts are past, begin to throw
Pompey the Great and all his dignities
Upon his son, who, high in name and power, *185*
Higher than both in blood and life, stands up
For the main soldier. Whose quality, going on,
The sides o' the world may danger. Much is breeding
Which, like the courser's hair,* hath yet but life
And not a serpent's poison. Say our pleasure, *190*
To such whose place is under us, requires
Our quick remove from hence.

Enobarbus. I shall do't. [*Exeunt.*]

174. *expedience: haste.*
178. *contriving: plotting in my behalf.*
179. *Sextus Pompeius: son of Pompey the Great, who was now threatening Roman control of the sea from Sicily.*
189. *courser's hair: A horse's hair placed in water was thought to become a live organism.*

SCENE III. *Another room in Cleopatra's palace.*

[*Enter Cleopatra, Charmian, Alexas, and Iras.*]

Cleopatra. Where is he?
Charmian. I did not see him since.
Cleopatra. See where he is, who's with him, what he does.
I did not send you. If you find him sad,
Say I am dancing; if in mirth, report
That I am sudden sick. Quick, and return. [*Exit Alexas.*] 5
Charmian. Madam, methinks if you did love him dearly,
You do not hold the method to enforce
The like from him.
Cleopatra. What should I do I do not?
Charmian. In each thing give him way, cross him in nothing.
Cleopatra. Thou teachest like a fool the way to lose him! 10
Charmian. Tempt him not so too far. I wish, forbear.
In time we hate that which we often fear.

[*Enter Antony.*]

But here comes Antony.
Cleopatra. I am sick and sullen.
Antony. I am sorry to give breathing to my purpose—
Cleopatra. Help me away, dear Charmian! I shall fall. 15
It cannot be thus long, the sides of nature*
Will not sustain it.
Antony. Now, my dearest queen—
Cleopatra. Pray you stand farther from me.
Antony. What's the matter?
Cleopatra. I know by that same eye there's some good news.
What says the married woman? You may go. 20
Would she had never given you leave to come!
Let her not say 'tis I that keep you here.
I have no power upon you, hers you are.
Antony. The gods best know—
Cleopatra. O, never was there queen
So mightily betrayed! Yet at the first 25
I saw the treasons planted.
Antony. Cleopatra—

16. *sides of nature: bodily strength.*

Cleopatra. Why should I think you can be mine and true,
Though you in swearing shake the throned gods,
Who have been false to Fulvia? Riotous madness,
To be entangled with those mouth-made vows *30*
Which break themselves in swearing!
Antony. Most sweet queen—
Cleopatra. Nay, pray you seek no color* for your going,
But bid farewell and go. When you sued staying,
Then was the time for words. No going then.
Eternity was in our lips and eyes, *35*
Bliss in our brows' bent, none our parts so poor
But was a race of heaven.* They are so still,
Or thou, the greatest soldier of the world,
Art turned the greatest liar.
Antony. How now, lady!
Cleopatra. I would I had thy inches. Thou shouldst know *40*
There were a heart in Egypt.
Antony. Hear me, Queen.
The strong necessity of time commands
Our services awhile, but my full heart
Remains in use with you. Our Italy
Shines o'er with civil swords.* Sextus Pompeius *45*
Makes his approaches to the port of Rome.
Equality of two domestic powers
Breed scrupulous faction.* The hated, grown to strength,
Are newly grown to love. The condemned Pompey,
Rich in his father's honor, creeps apace *50*
Into the hearts of such as have not thrived
Upon the present state, whose numbers threaten,
And quietness, grown sick of rest, would purge
By any desperate change. My more particular,*
And that which most with you should safe* my going, *55*
Is Fulvia's death.
Cleopatra. Though age from folly could not give me freedom,
It does from childishness. Can Fulvia die?

32. *color: excuse.*
37. *But . . . of heaven: belonged to heavenly creatures.*
45. *swords: metonomy for "war."*
48. *scrupulous faction: trivial conflict.*
54. *more particular: more personal reason.*
55. *safe: make safe.*

Antony. She's dead, my queen.
Look here, and at thy sovereign leisure read 60
The garboils* she awaked. At the last, best.
See when and where she died.
Cleopatra. O most false love!
Where be the sacred vials* thou shouldst fill
With sorrowful water? Now I see, I see,
In Fulvia's death, how mine received shall be. 65
Antony. Quarrel no more, but be prepared to know
The purposes I bear, which are, or cease,
As you shall give the advice. By the fire
That quickens Nilus' slime, I go from hence
Thy soldier, servant, making peace or war 70
As thou affect'st.*
Cleopatra. Cut my lace, Charmian, come!
But let it be, I am quickly ill, and well,
So Antony loves.
Antony. My precious queen, forbear,
And give true evidence to his love, which stands
An honorable trial.
Cleopatra. So Fulvia told me. 75
I prithee, turn aside and weep for her,
Then bid adieu to me, and say the tears
Belong to Egypt. Good now, play one scene
Of excellent dissembling, and let it look
Like perfect honor.
Antony. You'll heat my blood. No more! 80
Cleopatra. You can do better yet, but this is meetly,*
Antony. Now by my sword–
Cleopatra. And target.* Still he mends,
But this is not the best. Look, prithee, Charmian,
How this Herculean* Roman does become
The carriage of his chafe. 85
Antony. I'll leave you, lady.
Cleopatra. Courteous lord, one word.
Sir, you and I must part, but that's not it.

61. *garboils: commotions.*
63. *vials: bottles of tears.*
71. *affect'st: choosest.*
81. *meetly: proper.*
82. *target: shield.*
84. *Herculean: Antony was supposed to be descended from Hercules.*

Sir, you and I have loved, but there's not it.
That you know well. Something it is I would—
O, my oblivion is a very Antony, *90*
And I am all forgotten.

Antony. But that your royalty
Holds idleness your subject, I should take you
For idleness itself.

Cleopatra. 'Tis sweating labor
To bear such idleness so near the heart
As Cleopatra this. But, sir, forgive me, *95*
Since my becomings kill me when they do not
Eye well to you. Your honor calls you hence.
Therefore be deaf to my unpitied folly,
And all the gods go with you! Upon your sword
Sit laurel victory! And smooth success *100*
Be strewed before your feet!

Antony. Let us go. Come,
Our separation so abides and flies
That thou residing here go'st yet with me,
And I hence fleeting here remain with thee.
Away! [*Exeunt.*] *105*

SCENE IV. *Rome. Caesar's house.*

[*Enter Octavius Caesar, reading a letter, Lepidus, and their Train.*]

Caesar. You may see, Lepidus, and henceforth know,
It is not Caesar's natural vice to hate
Our great competitor. From Alexandria
This is the news. He fishes, drinks, and wastes
The lamps of night in revel, is not more manlike *5*
Than Cleopatra, nor the queen of Ptolemy*
More womanly than he. Hardly gave audience,* or
Vouchsafed to think he had partners. You shall find there
A man who is the abstract of all faults
That all men follow.

Lepidus. I must not think there are *10*
Evils enow* to darken all his goodness.
His faults, in him, seem as the spots of heaven,

6. *Ptolemy: Ptolemy XII of Egypt, Cleopatra's dead husband.*
7. *audience: to Caesar's messengers from Rome.*
11. *enow: enough.*

More fiery by night's blackness, hereditary
Rather than purchased,* what he cannot change
Than what he chooses. *15*

Caesar. You are too indulgent. Let's grant it is not
Amiss to tumble on the bed of Ptolemy,
To give a kingdom for a mirth, to sit
And keep the turn of tippling with a slave,
To reel the streets at noon, and stand the buffet *20*
With knaves that smell of sweat. Say this becomes him–
As his composure must be rare indeed
Whom these things cannot blemish–yet must Antony
No way excuse his foils when we do bear
So great weight in his lightness. If he filled *25*
His vacancy* with his voluptuousness,
Full surfeits* and the dryness of his bones
Call on him for't. But to confound* such time
That drums him from his sport and speaks as loud
As his own state and ours, 'tis to be chid *30*
As we rate* boys who, being mature in knowledge,
Pawn their experience to their present pleasure
And so rebel to judgment.*

[*Enter a Messenger.*]

Lepidus. Here's more news.

Messenger. Thy biddings have been done, and every hour,
Most noble Caesar, shalt thou have report *35*
How 'tis abroad. Pompey is strong at sea,
And it appears he is beloved of those
That only have feared Caesar. To the ports
The discontents repair, and men's reports
Give him much wronged.

Caesar. I should have known no less. *40*
It hath been taught us from the primal state
That he which is was wished until he were,

14. *purchased: acquired.*
18. *a mirth: mere pleasure.*
26. *His vacancy: his spare time.*
27. *surfeits: physical suffering.*
28. *confound: waste.*
31. *rate: scold.*
33. *to judgment: against common sense.*

And the ebbed man, ne'er loved till ne'er worth love,
Comes deared by being lacked. This common body,*
Like to a vagabond flag upon the stream, 45
Goes to and back, lackeying the varying tide,
To rot itself with motion.

Messenger. Caesar, I bring thee word.
Menecrates and Menas, famous pirates,
Make the sea serve them, which they ear and wound
With keels of every kind. Many hot inroads 50
They make in Italy. The borders maritime
Lack blood* to think on't, and flush* youth revolt.
No vessel can peep forth but 'tis as soon
Taken as seen, for Pompey's name strikes more
Than could his war resisted.

Caesar. Antony, 55
Leave thy lascivious wassails. When thou once
Wast beaten from Modena, where thou slew'st
Hirtius and Pansa, consuls, at thy heel
Did famine follow, whom thou fought'st against,
Though daintily brought up, with patience more 60
Than savages could suffer. Thou didst drink
The stale of horses and the gilded puddle
Which beasts would cough at. Thy palate then did deign
The roughest berry on the rudest hedge.
Yea, like the stag when snow the pasture sheets, 65
The barks of trees thou browsed. On the Alps
It is reported thou didst eat strange flesh,
Which some did die to look on. And all this–
It wounds thine honor that I speak it now–
Was borne so like a soldier that thy cheek 70
So much as lanked* not.

Lepidus. 'Tis pity of him.

Caesar. Let his shames quickly
Drive him to Rome. 'Tis time we twain
Did show ourselves i' the field, and to that end
Assemble we immediate council. Pompey 75
Thrives in our idleness.

44. *This common body: the common people.*
52. *Lack blood: turn pale.*
52. *flush: vigorous.*
71. *lanked: grew thin.*

Lepidus. Tomorrow, Caesar,
I shall be furnished to inform you rightly
Both what by sea and land I can be able
To front* this present time.
Caesar. Till which encounter,
It is my business too. Farewell. *80*
Lepidus. Farewell, my lord. What you shall know meantime
Of stirs abroad, I shall beseech you, sir,
To let me be partaker.
Caesar. Doubt not, sir.
I knew it for my bond.* [*Exeunt.*]

SCENE V. *Alexandria. Cleopatra's palace.*

[*Enter Cleopatra, Charmian, Iras, and Mardian.*]

Cleopatra. Charmian!
Charmian. Madam?
Cleopatra. Ha, ha.
Give me to drink mandragora.*
Charmian. Why, madam?
Cleopatra. That I might sleep out this great gap of time *5*
My Antony is away.
Charmian. You think of him too much.
Cleopatra. O, 'tis treason!
Charmian. Madam, I trust not so.
Cleopatra. Thou, eunuch Mardian!
Mardian. What's your Highness' pleasure?
Cleopatra. Not now to hear thee sing. I take no pleasure
In aught an eunuch has. 'Tis well for thee *10*
That, being unseminared,* thy freer thoughts
May not fly forth of Egypt. Hast thou affections?
Mardian. Yes, gracious madam.
Cleopatra. Indeed?
Mardian. Not in deed, madam, for I can do nothing *15*
But what indeed is honest to be done.
Yet have I fierce affections, and think
What Venus did with Mars.

79. *front: cope with.*
84. *bond: duty.*
4. *mandragora: mandrake (to induce sleep).*
11. *unseminared: emasculated.*

Cleopatra. O Charmian,
Where think'st thou he is now? Stands he, or sits he?
Or does he walk? Or is he on his horse? *20*
O happy horse, to bear the weight of Antony!
Do bravely, horse! For wot'st thou whom thou mov'st?
The demi-Atlas of this earth, the arm
And burgonet* of men. He's speaking now,
Or murmuring, "Where's my serpent of old Nile?" *25*
For so he calls me. Now I feed myself
With most delicious poison. Think on me,
That am with Phoebus'* amorous pinches black
And wrinkled deep in time? Broad-fronted* Caesar,*
When thou wast here above the ground, I was *30*
A morsel for a monarch. And great Pompey
Would stand and make his eyes grow in my brow.
There would he anchor his aspect, and die
With looking on his life.

[*Enter Alexas.*]

Alexas. Sovereign of Egypt, hail!
Cleopatra. How much unlike art thou Mark Antony! *35*
Yet, coming from him, that great medicine hath
With his tinct gilded thee.
How goes it with my brave Mark Antony?
Alexas. Last thing he did, dear Queen,
He kissed—the last of many doubled kisses— *40*
This orient pearl. His speech sticks in my heart.
Cleopatra. Mine ear must pluck it thence.
Alexas. "Good friend," quoth he,
"Say the firm Roman to great Egypt sends
This treasure of an oyster. At whose foot,
To mend the petty present, I will piece *45*
Her opulent throne with kingdoms. All the East,
Say thou, shall call her mistress." So he nodded,
And soberly did mount an arm-gaunt* steed,
Who neighed so high that what I would have spoke
Was beastly dumbed by him.
Cleopatra. What, was he sad or merry? *50*

24. *burgonet: shield.*
28. *Phoebus: the sun god.*
29. *Broad-fronted: with wide forehead.*
29. *Caesar: Julius Caesar, who had been Cleopatra's lover.*
48. *arm-gaunt: made tough by armed service.*

Alexas. Like to the time o' the year between the extremes
Of hot and cold, he was nor sad nor merry.
Cleopatra. O well-divided disposition! Note him,
Note him, good Charmian, 'tis the man, but note him.
He was not sad, for he would shine on those 55
That make their looks by his. He was not merry,
Which seemed to tell them his remembrance lay
In Egypt with his joy. But between both.
O heavenly mingle! Be'st thou sad or merry,
The violence of either thee becomes, 60
So does it no man else. Met'st thou my posts?*
Alexas. Ay, madam, twenty several messengers.
Why do you send so thick?
Cleopatra. Who's born that day
When I forget to send to Antony
Shall die a beggar. Ink and paper, Charmian. 65
Welcome, my good Alexas. Did I, Charmian,
Ever love Caesar so?
Charmian. O that brave Caesar!
Cleopatra. Be choked with such another emphasis!
Say "the brave Antony."
Charmian. The valiant Caesar!
Cleopatra. By Isis, I will give thee bloody teeth 70
If thou with Caesar paragon again
My man of men.
Charmian. By your most gracious pardon,
I sing but after you.
Cleopatra. My salad days,
When I was green in judgment, cold in blood,
To say as I said then! But come, away, 75
Get me ink and paper.
He shall have every day a several greeting,
Or I'll unpeople Egypt. [*Exeunt.*]

ACT II

SCENE I. *Messina. Pompey's house.*

[*Enter Pompey, Menecrates, and Menas, in warlike manner.*]

Pompey. If the great gods be just, they shall assist
The deeds of justest men.

61. *posts: messengers.*

Menecrates. Know, worthy Pompey,
That what they do delay, they not deny.
Pompey. Whiles we are suitors to their throne, decays
The thing we sue for.
Menecrates. We, ignorant of ourselves, 5
Beg often our own harms, which the wise powers
Deny us for our good. So find we profit
By losing of our prayers.
Pompey. I shall do well.
The people love me, and the sea is mine.
My powers are crescent,* and my auguring hope 10
Says it will come to the full. Mark Antony
In Egypt sits at dinner, and will make
No wars withoutdoors. Caesar gets money where
He loses hearts. Lepidus flatters both,
Of both is flattered, but he neither loves, 15
Nor either cares for him.
Menas. Caesar and Lepidus
Are in the field. A mighty strength they carry.
Pompey. Where have you this? 'Tis false.
Menas. From Silvius, sir.
Pompey. He dreams. I know they are in Rome together,
Looking for Antony. But all the charms of love, 20
Salt* Cleopatra, soften thy waned lip!
Let witchcraft join with beauty, lust with both!
Tie up the libertine in a field of feasts,
Keep his brain fuming. Epicurean cooks
Sharpen with cloyless sauce his appetite, 25
That sleep and feeding may prorogue* his honor
Even till a Lethe'd* dullness!

[*Enter Varrius.*]

How now, Varrius?
Varrius. This is most certain that I shall deliver.
Mark Antony is every hour in Rome
Expected. Since he went from Egypt 'tis 30
A space for farther travel.

10. *crescent: growing (as does the moon).*
21. *Salt: lustful.*
26. *prorogue: postpone.*
27. *Lethe'd: pertaining to Lethe, the river of forgetfulness in the under world.*

Pompey. I could have given less matter
A better ear. Menas, I did not think
This amorous surfeiter would have donned his helm
For such a petty war. His soldiership
Is twice the other twain. But let us rear 35
The higher our opinion, that our stirring
Can from the lap of Egypt's widow pluck
The ne'er-lust-wearied Antony.
Menas. I cannot hope
Caesar and Antony shall well greet together.
His wife that's dead did trespasses to Caesar, 40
His brother warred upon him—although I think
Not moved by Antony.
Pompey. I know not, Menas,
How lesser enmities may give way to greater.
Were't not that we stand up against them all,
'Twere pregnant* they should square* between themselves, 45
For they have entertained cause enough
To draw their swords. But how the fear of us
May cement their divisions and bind up
The petty difference, we yet not know.
Be't as our gods will have't! It only stands 50
Our lives upon to use our strongest hands.*
Come, Menas. [*Exeunt.*]

SCENE II. *Rome. The house of Lepidus.*

[*Enter Enobarbus and Lepidus.*]

Lepidus. Good Enobarbus, 'tis a worthy deed,
And shall become you well, to entreat your captain
To soft and gentle speech.
Enobarbus I shall entreat him
To answer like himself. If Caesar move him,
Let Antony look over Caesar's head 5
And speak as loud as Mars. By Jupiter,
Were I the wearer of Antonius' beard,
I would not shave't today!

45. *pregnant: probable.*
45. *square: quarrel.*
50–51. *It . . . hands.: Our lives depend upon our using our greatest physical power.*

Lepidus. 'Tis not a time
For private stomaching.*
Enobarbus. Every time
Serves for the matter that is then born in't. *10*
Lepidus. But small to greater matters must give way.
Enobarbus. Not if the small come first.
Lepidus. Your speech is passion,
But pray you stir no embers up. Here comes
The noble Antony.

[*Enter Antony and Ventidius.*]

Enobarbus. And yonder, Caesar.

[*Enter Caesar, Maecenas, and Agrippa.*]

Antony. If we compose* well here, to Parthia. *15*
Hark, Ventidius.
Caesar. I do not know,
Maecenas. Ask Agrippa.
Lepidus. Noble friends,
That which combined us was most great, and let not
A leaner action rend us. What's amiss,
May it be gently heard. When we debate *20*
Our trivial difference loud, we do commit
Murder in healing wounds. Then, noble partners,
The rather for I earnestly beseech,
Touch you the sourest points with sweetest terms,
Nor curstness* grow to the matter.
Antony. 'Tis spoken well. *25*
Were we before our armies, and to fight,
I should do thus. [*Flourish.*]
Caesar. Welcome to Rome.
Antony. Thank you.
Caesar. Sit.
Antony. Sit, sir.
Caesar. Nay then.
[*They sit.*]
Antony. I learn you take things ill which are not so,
Or being, concern you not.

9. *stomaching: resentment.*
15. *compose: come to an agreement.*
25. *curstness: bad temper.*

Caesar. I must be laughed at 30
If, or for nothing or a little, I
Should say myself offended, and with you
Chiefly i' the world—more laughed at that I should
Once name you derogately, when to sound your name
It not concerned me.

Antony. My being in Egypt, Caesar, 35
What was't to you?

Caesar. No more than my residing here at Rome
Might be to you in Egypt. Yet if you there
Did practice on my state, your being in Egypt
Might be my question.

Antony. How intend you "practiced"? 40

Caesar. You may be pleased to catch at mine intent
By what did here befall me. Your wife and brother
Made wars upon me, and their contestation
Was theme for you. You were the word of war.

Antony. You do mistake your business. My brother never
Did urge me* in his act. I did inquire it,
And have my learning from some true reports
That drew their swords with you. Did he not rather
Discredit my authority with yours,
And make the wars alike against my stomach,* 50
Having alike your cause? Of this my letters
Before did satisfy you. If you'll patch a quarrel,*
As matter whole you have to make it with,
It must not be with this.

Caesar. You praise yourself
By laying defects of judgment to me, but 55
You patched up your excuses.

Antony. Not so, not so.
I know you could not lack, I am certain on't,
Very necessity of this thought, that I,
Your partner in the cause 'gainst which he fought,
Could not with grateful eyes attend those wars 60
Which fronted mine own peace. As for my wife,
I would you had her spirit in such another;
The third o' the world is yours, which with a snaffle*

46. *urge me: make war in my name.*
50. *stomach: inclination.*
52. *patch a quarrel: make a quarrel out of pieces.*
63. *snaffle: bridle bit.*

You may pace easy, but not such a wife.
Enobarbus. Would we had all such wives, that the men 65
might go to wars with the women.
Antony. So much uncurbable, her garboils,* Caesar,
Made out of her impatience, which not wanted
Shrewdness of policy too, I grieving grant
Did you too much disquiet. For that you must 70
But say I could not help it.
Caesar. I wrote to you
When rioting in Alexandria. You
Did pocket up my letters, and with taunts
Did gibe my missive* out of audience.
Antony. Sir,
He fell upon me, ere admitted, then. 75
Three kings I had newly feasted, and did want
Of what I was i' the morning; but next day
I told him of myself, which was as much
As to have asked him pardon. Let this fellow
Be nothing of our strife. If we contend, 80
Out of our question wipe him.
Caesar. You have broken
The article of your oath, which you shall never
Have tongue to charge me with.
Lepidus. Soft, Caesar.
Antony. No,
Lepidus. Let him speak.
The honor is sacred which he talks on now, 85
Supposing that I lacked it. But on, Caesar,
The article of my oath—
Caesar. To lend me arms and aid when I required them,
The which you both denied.
Antony. Neglected rather,
And then when poisoned hours had bound me up 90
From mine own knowledge. As nearly as I may,
I'll play the penitent to you. But mine honesty
Shall not make poor my greatness, nor my power
Work without it. Truth is, that Fulvia,
To have me out of Egypt, made wars here, 95
For which myself, the ignorant motive, do

67. *garboils: disturbances.*
74. *missive: messenger.*

So far ask pardon as befits mine honor
To stoop in such a case.
Lepidus. 'Tis noble spoken.
Maecenas. If it might please you to enforce no further
The griefs between ye, to forget them quite, *100*
Were to remember that the present need
Speaks to atone* you.
Lepidus. Worthily spoken, Maecenas.
Enobarbus. Or, if you borrow one another's love for the instant, you may, when you hear no more words of Pompey, return it again. You shall have time to wrangle *105* in when you have nothing else to do.
Antony. Thou art a soldier only. Speak no more.
Enobarbus. That truth should be silent I had almost forgot.
Antony. You wrong this presence; therefore speak no more.
Enobarbus. Go to, then, your considerate stone.* *110*
Caesar. I do not much dislike the matter, but
The manner, of his speech. For't cannot be
We shall remain in friendship, our conditions*
So diff'ring in their acts. Yet if I knew
What hoop should hold us staunch, from edge to edge *115*
O' the world I would pursue it.
Agrippa. Give me leave, Caesar.
Caesar. Speak, Agrippa.
Agrippa. Thou hast a sister by the mother's side,
Admired Octavia. Great Mark Antony
Is now a widower.
Caesar. Say not so, Agrippa. *120*
If Cleopatra heard you, your reproof
Were well deserved of rashness.
Antony. I am not married, Caesar. Let me hear
Agrippa further speak.
Agrippa. To hold you in perpetual amity, *125*
To make you brothers, and to knit your hearts
With an unslipping knot, take Antony
Octavia to his wife, whose beauty claims
No worse a husband than the best of men,
Whose virtue and whose general graces speak *130*

102. *atone: reconcile.*
110. *your considerate stone: I'll be as dumb as a stone.*
113. *conditions: natures.*

That which none else can utter. By this marriage
All little jealousies, which now seem great,
And all great fears, which now impart their dangers,
Would then be nothing. Truths would be tales,
Where now half-tales be truths. Her love to both 135
Would each to other, and all loves to both,
Draw after her. Pardon what I have spoke,
For 'tis a studied, not a present, thought,
By duty ruminated.

Antony. Will Caesar speak?

Caesar. Not till he hears how Antony is touched 140
With what is spoke already.

Antony. What power is in Agrippa,
If I would say, "Agrippa, be it so,"
To make this good?

Caesar. The power of Caesar, and
His power unto Octavia.

Antony. May I never
To this good purpose, that so fairly shows, 145
Dream of impediment. Let me have thy hand.
Further this act of grace, and from this hour
The heart of brothers govern in our loves
And sway our great designs.

Caesar. There is my hand.
A sister I bequeath you, whom no brother 150
Did ever love so dearly. Let her live
To join our kingdoms and our hearts, and never
Fly off our loves again!

Lepidus. Happily, amen.

Antony. I did not think to draw my sword 'gainst Pompey,
For he hath laid strange courtesies and great 155
Of late upon me. I must thank him only,
Lest my remembrance suffer ill report,
At heel of that, defy him.

Lepidus. Time calls upon's.
Of us must Pompey presently* be sought,
Or else he seeks out us.

Antony. Where lies he? 160

Caesar. About the Mount Mesena.

Antony. What is his strength by land?

159. *presently: immediately.*

Caesar. Great and increasing. But by sea
He is an absolute master.
Antony. So is the fame.*
Would we had spoke together! Haste we for it. 165
Yet, ere we put ourselves in arms, dispatch we
The business we have talked of.
Caesar. With most gladness,
And do invite you to my sister's view,
Whither straight I'll lead you.
Antony. Let us, Lepidus,
Not lack your company.
Lepidus. Noble Antony, 170
Not sickness should detain me.

[*Flourish. Exeunt Caesar, Antony and Lepidus.*]

Maecenas. Welcome from Egypt, sir.
Enobarbus. Half the heart of Caesar, worthy Maecenas!
My honorable friend Agrippa!
Agrippa. Good Enobarbus! 175
Maecenas. We have cause to be glad that matters are so well digested. You stayed well by't in Egypt.
Enobarbus. Aye, sir, we did sleep day out of countenance, and made the night light with drinking.
Maecenas. Eight wild boars roasted whole at a breakfast, 180 and but twelve persons there. Is this true?
Enobarbus. This was but as a fly by an eagle. We had much more monstrous matter of feast which worthily deserved noting.
Maecenas. She's a most triumphant lady, if report be square* to her. 185
Enobarbus. When she first met Mark Antony, she pursed* up his heart, upon the river of Cydnus.*
Agrippa. There she appeared indeed, or my reporter devised well for her. 190
Enobarbus. I will tell you.
The barge she sat in, like a burnished throne,

164. *fame: report.*
185. *square: fair.*
187. *pursed: pocketed (as if she had put his heart in her purse).*
188. *Cydnus: a river that runs by Tarsus.*

Burned on the water. The poop was beaten gold,
Purple the sails, and so perfumed that
The winds were lovesick with them. The oars were silver, *195*
Which to the tune of flutes kept stroke, and made
The water which they beat to follow faster,
As amorous of their strokes. For her own person,
It beggared all description. She did lie
In her pavilion, cloth-of-gold of tissue, *200*
O'erpicturing that Venus where we see
The fancy outwork nature. On each side her
Stood pretty dimpled boys, like smiling Cupids,
With divers-colored fans, whose wind did seem
To glow the delicate cheeks which they did cool, *205*
And what they undid did.

Agrippa. O, rare for Antony!

Enobarbus. Her gentlewomen, like the Nereides,*
So many mermaids, tended her i' the eyes,*
And made their bends adornings. At the helm
A seeming mermaid steers. The silken tackle *210*
Swell with the touches of those flower-soft hands,
That yarely* frame the office. From the barge
A strange invisible perfume hits the sense
Of the adjacent wharfs. The city cast
Her people out upon her. And Antony, *215*
Enthroned i' the market place, did sit alone,
Whistling to the air, which, but for vacancy,
Had gone to gaze on Cleopatra too,
And made a gap in nature.

Agrippa. Rare Egyptian!

Enobarbus. Upon her landing, Antony sent to her, *220*
Invited her to supper. She replied,
It should be better he became her guest,
Which she entreated. Our courteous Antony,
Whom ne'er the word of "No" woman heard speak,
Being barbered ten times o'er, goes to the feast, *225*
And for his ordinary* pays his heart
For what his eyes eat only.

Agrippa. Royal wench!

207. *Nereides: sea nymphs.*
208. *tended . . . eyes: watched to anticipate her every whim.*
212. *yarely: skillfully (in the manner of a good sailor).*
226. *ordinary: public meal at a tavern.*

She made great Caesar lay his sword to bed.
He ploughed her, and she cropped.

Enobarbus. I saw her once
Hop forty paces through the public street. 230
And having lost her breath, she spoke, and panted,
That she did make defect perfection
And, breathless, power breathe forth.

Maecenas. Now Antony must leave her utterly.

Enobarbus. Never! He will not. 235
Age cannot wither her, nor custom stale
Her infinite variety. Other women cloy
The appetites they feed, but she makes hungry
Where most she satisfies. For vilest things
Become themselves in her, that the holy priests 240
Bless her when she is riggish.*

Maecenas. If beauty, wisdom, modesty, can settle
The heart of Antony, Octavia is
A blessed lottery* to him.

Agrippa. Let us go.
Good Enobarbus, make yourself my guest 245
Whilst you abide here.

Enobarbus. Humbly, sir, I thank you. [*Exeunt.*]

SCENE III. *Rome. Caesar's house.*

[*Enter Antony, Caesar, Octavia between them.*]

Antony. The world and my great office will sometimes
Divide me from your bosom.

Octavia. All which time
Before the gods my knee shall bow my prayers
To them for you.

Antony. Good night, sir. My Octavia,
Read not my blemishes in the world's report. 5
I have not kept my square,* but that to come
Shall all be done by the rule. Good night, dear lady.

Octavia. Good night, sir.

Caesar. Good night.

[*Exeunt Caesar and Octavia.*]

241. *riggish: wanton.*
244. *lottery: prize.*
6. *kept . . . square: regulated my life by the carpenter's ruler (i.e., lived uprightly).*

[*Enter Soothsayer.*]

Antony. Now, sirrah,* you do wish yourself in Egypt? *10*
Soothsayer. Would I had never come from thence, nor
you thither!
Antony. If you can, your reason?
Soothsayer. I see it in my motion, have it not in my tongue,
But yet hie you to Egypt again.
Antony. Say to me, *15*
Whose fortunes shall rise hither, Caesar's or mine?
Soothsayer. Caesar's.
Therefore, O Antony, stay not by his side.
Thy demon,* that thy spirit which keeps thee, is
Noble, courageous, high, unmatchable, *20*
Where Caesar's is not. But near him thy angel
Becomes a fear, as being o'erpowered. Therefore
Make space enough between you.
Antony. Speak this no more.
Soothsayer. To none but thee, no more but when to thee.
If thou dost play with him at any game, *25*
Thou art sure to lose. And of that natural luck
He beats thee 'gainst the odds. Thy luster thickens
When he shines by. I say again, thy spirit
Is all afraid to govern thee near him,
But he away, 'tis noble.
Antony. Get thee gone. *30*
Say to Ventidius I would speak with him.
[*Exit Soothsayer.*]
He shall to Parthia. Be it art or hap,*
He hath spoken true. The very dice obey him,
And in our sports my better cunning faints
Under his chance. If we draw lots, he speeds.* *35*
His cocks do win the battle still of mine
When it is all to naught, and his quails ever
Beat mine, inhooped,* at odds. I will to Egypt.
And though I make this marriage for my peace,
I' the East my pleasure lies.

10. *sirrah: a form of "sir" but reserved for inferiors.*
19. *demon: guardian spirit.*
32. *hap: chance.*
35. *speeds: wins.*
38. *inhooped: The quails fought with hoops until one was driven out.*

[*Enter Ventidius.*]

O, come, Ventidius, 40
You must to Parthia. Your commission's ready.
Follow me, and receive't. [*Exeunt.*]

SCENE IV. *Rome. A street.*

[*Enter Lepidus, Maecenas, and Agrippa.*]

Lepidus. Trouble yourselves no further. Pray you, hasten
Your generals after.
Agrippa. Sir, Mark Antony
Will e'en but kiss Octavia, and we'll follow.
Lepidus. Till I shall see you in your soldier's dress,
Which will become you both, farewell.
Maecenas. We shall, 5
As I conceive the journey, be at the Mount
Before you, Lepidus.
Lepidus. Your way is shorter.
My purposes do draw me much about.
You'll win two days upon me.
Both. Sir, good success.
Lepidus. Farewell. [*Exeunt.*] 10

SCENE V. *Alexandria. Cleopatra's palace.*

[*Enter Cleopatra, Charmian, Iras, and Alexas.*]

Cleopatra. Give me some music! Music, moody food
Of us that trade in love.
Omnes. The music, ho!

[*Enter Mardian the Eunuch.*]

Cleopatra. Let it alone, let's to billiards. Come, Charmian.
Charmian. My arm is sore. Best play with Mardian.
Cleopatra. As well a woman with an eunuch played 5
As with a woman. Come, you'll play with me, sir?
Mardian. As well as I can, madam.
Cleopatra. And when good will is showed, though't come too short,
The actor may plead pardon. I'll none now.
Give me mine angle, we'll to the river. There, 10

My music playing far off, I will betray
Tawny-finned fishes. My bended hook shall pierce
Their slimy jaws, and as I draw them up,
I'll think them every one an Antony,
And say, "Ah, ha! You're caught!"

Charmian. 'Twas merry when 15
You wagered on your angling, when your diver
Did hang a salt fish on his hook, which he
With fervency drew up.

Cleopatra. That time—O times!—
I laughed him out of patience, and that night
I laughed him into patience. And next morn, 20
Ere the ninth hour I drunk him to his bed,
Then put my tires* and mantles on him whilst
I wore his sword Philippan.*

[*Enter a Messenger.*]

O, from Italy!
Ram thou thy fruitful tidings in mine ears,
That long time have been barren.

Messenger. Madam, madam— 25

Cleopatra. Antony's dead! If thou say so, villain,
Thou kill'st thy mistress. But well and free,
If thou so yield him, there is gold and here
My bluest veins to kiss, a hand that kings
Have lipped, and trembled kissing. 30

Messenger. First, madam, he is well.

Cleopatra. Why, there's more gold.
But, sirrah, mark, we use
To say the dead are well. Bring it to that,
The gold I give thee will I melt and pour
Down thy ill-uttering throat. 35

Messenger. Good madam, hear me.

Cleopatra. Well, go to, I will.
But there's no goodness in thy face if Antony
Be free and healthful. So tart a favor*
To trumpet such good tidings? If not well,

22. *tires: headdresses.*
23. *Philippan: the sword with which he had won victory over Brutus and Cassius at Philippi.*
38. *So . . . favor: so sour a face.*

Thou shouldst come like a Fury crowned with snakes, *40*
Not like a formal man.*
Messenger. Will't please you hear me?
Cleopatra. I have a mind to strike thee ere thou speak'st.
Yet, if thou say Antony lives, is well,
Or friends with Caesar, or not captive to him,
I'll set thee in a shower of gold, and hail *45*
Rich pearls upon thee.
Messenger. Madam, he's well.
Cleopatra. Well said.
Messenger. And friends with Caesar.
Cleopatra. Thou'rt an honest man.
Messenger. Caesar and he are greater friends than ever.
Cleopatra. Make thee a fortune from me.
Messenger. But yet, madam—
Cleopatra. I do not like "but yet." It does allay *50*
The good precedence.* Fie upon "but yet"!
"But yet" is as a jailer to bring forth
Some monstrous malefactor. Prithee, friend,
Pour out the pack of matter to mine ear,
The good and bad together. He's friends with Caesar, *55*
In state of health, thou say'st, and thou say'st, free.
Messenger. Free, madam? No. I made no such report.
He's bound unto Octavia.
Cleopatra. For what good turn?
Messenger. For the best turn i' the bed.
Cleopatra. I am pale, Charmian.
Messenger. Madam, he's married to Octavia. *60*
Cleopatra. The most infectious pestilence upon thee!
[*Strikes him down.*]
Messenger. Good madam, patience.
Cleopatra. What say you?
[*Strikes him.*]
Hence,
Horrible villain! Or I'll spurn thine eyes
Like balls before me. I'll unhair thy head.
[*She hales him up and down.*]
Thou shalt be whipped with wire and stewed in brine, *65*
Smarting in lingering pickle.

41. *formal man: in normal human form.*
50–51. *allay . . . precedence: ruin the good that has preceded it.*

Messenger. Gracious madam,
I that do bring the news made not the match.
Cleopatra. Say 'tis not so, a province I will give thee,
And make thy fortunes proud. The blow thou hadst
Shall make thy peace for moving me to rage, 70
And I will boot* thee with what gift beside
Thy modesty can beg.
Messenger. He's married, madam.
Cleopatra. Rogue, thou hast lived too long. [*Draws a knife.*]
Messenger. Nay, then I'll run.
What mean you madam? I have made no fault. [*Exit.*]
Charmian. Good madam, keep yourself within yourself. 75
The man is innocent.
Cleopatra. Some innocents 'scape not the thunderbolt.
Melt Egypt into Nile! And kindly creatures
Turn all to serpents! Call the slave again.
Though I am mad, I will not bite him. Call! 80
Charmian. He is afeard to come.
Cleopatra. I will not hurt him.
[*Exit Charmian.*]
These hands do lack nobility, that they strike
A meaner than myself, since I myself
Have given myself the cause.

[*Enter Charmian and the Messenger again.*]

Come hither, sir.
Though it be honest, it is never good 85
To bring bad news. Give to a gracious message
An host of tongues, but let ill tidings tell
Themselves when they be felt.
Messenger. I have done my duty.
Cleopatra. Is he married?
I cannot hate thee worser than I do 90
If thou again say "Yes."
Messenger. He's married, madam.
Cleopatra. The gods confound thee! Dost thou hold there still?
Messenger. Should I lie, madam?
Cleopatra. O, I would thou didst,
So half my Egypt were submerged and made

71. *boot: reward.*

A cistern for scaled snakes! Go, get thee hence. 95
Hadst thou Narcissus in thy face, to me
Thou wouldst appear most ugly. He is married?

Messenger. I crave your Highness' pardon.

Cleopatra. He is married?

Messenger. Take no offense that I would not offend you.
To punish me for what you make me do 100
Seems much unequal. He's married to Octavia.

Cleopatra. O, that his fault should make a knave of thee,
That art not what thou'rt sure of! Get thee hence,
The merchandise which thou hast brought from Rome
Are all too dear for me. Lie they upon thy hand, 105
And be undone by 'em! [*Exit Messenger.*]

Charmian. Good your Highness, patience.

Cleopatra. In praising Antony I have dispraised Caesar.

Charmian. Many times, madam.

Cleopatra. I am paid for't now.
Lead me from hence,
I faint. O Iras, Charmian! 'Tis no matter. 110
Go to the fellow, good Alexas. Bid him
Report the feature of Octavia—her years,
Her inclination, let him not leave out
The color of her hair. Bring me word quickly.
[*Exit Alexas.*]
Let him forever go!—Let him not!—Charmian, 115
Though he be painted one way like a Gorgon,*
The other way's a Mars. [*To Mardian.*] Bid you Alexas
Bring me word how tall she is. Pity me, Charmian,
But do not speak to me. Lead me to my chamber. [*Exeunt.*]

SCENE VI. *Near Misenum.*

[*Flourish. Enter Pompey and Menas at one door, with Drum and Trumpet; at another, Caesar, Lepidus, Antony, Enobarbus, Maecenas, Agrippa, with Soldiers marching.*]

Pompey. Your hostages I have, so have you mine,
And we shall talk before we fight.

Caesar. Most meet*

116. *Gorgon: Medusa, whose hideous face turned all who beheld it to stone.*
2. *meet: proper.*

That first we come to words, and therefore have we
Our written purposes before us sent,
Which if thou hast considered, let us know 5
If 'twill tie up thy discontented sword
And carry back to Sicily much tall youth
That else must perish here.

Pompey. To you all three,
The senators alone of this great world,
Chief factors for the gods. I do not know 10
Wherefore my father should revengers want,
Having a son and friends, since Julius Caesar,
Who at Philippi the good Brutus ghosted,
There saw you laboring for him. What was't
That moved pale Cassius to conspire? And what 15
Made all-honored, honest, Roman Brutus,
With the armed rest, courtiers of beauteous freedom,
To drench the Capitol, but that they would
Have one man but a man? And that is it
Hath made me rig my navy, at whose burden 20
The angered ocean foams, with which I meant
To scourge the ingratitude that despiteful Rome
Cast on my noble father.

Caesar. Take your time.

Antony. Thou canst not fear us, Pompey, with thy sails.
We'll speak with thee at sea. At land thou know'st 25
How much we do o'ercount thee.

Pompey. At land indeed.
Thou dost o'ercount me of my father's house.
But since the cuckoo builds not for himself,
Remain in't as thou mayst.

Lepidus. Be pleased to tell us,
For this is from the present, how you take 30
The offers we have sent you.

Caesar. There's the point.

Antony. Which do not be entreated to, but weigh
What it is worth embraced.*

Caesar. And what may follow,
To try a larger fortune.

Pompey. You have made me offer
Of Sicily, Sardinia, and I must 35

33. *embraced: accepted.*

Rid all the sea of pirates. Then, to send
Measures of wheat to Rome. This 'greed upon,
To part with unhacked edges and bear back
Our targes* undinted.

Omnes. That's our offer.

Pompey. Know then
I came before you here a man prepared 40
To take this offer, but Mark Antony
Put me to some impatience. Though I lose
The praise of it by telling, you must know,
When Caesar and your brother were at blows,
Your mother came to Sicily and did find 45
Her welcome friendly.

Antony. I have heard it, Pompey,
And am well studied* for a liberal thanks,
Which I do owe you.

Pompey. Let me have your hand.
I did not think, sir, to have met you here.

Antony. The beds i' the East are soft, and thanks to
you, 50
That called me timelier than my purpose hither,
For I have gained by't.

Caesar. Since I saw you last
There's a change upon you.

Pompey. Well, I know not
What counts* harsh fortune casts upon my face,
But in my bosom shall she never come 55
To make my heart her vassal.

Lepidus. Well met here.

Pompey. I hope so, Lepidus. Thus we are agreed.
I crave our composition* may be written,
And sealed between us.

Caesar. That's the next to do.

Pompey. We'll feast each other ere we part, and let's 60
Draw lots who shall begin.

Antony. That will I, Pompey.

Pompey. No, Antony, take the lot.
But, first or last, your fine Egyptian cookery

39. *targes: shields.*
47. *studied: prepared.*
54. *counts: accounts.*
58. *composition: agreement.*

Shall have the fame. I have heard that Julius Caesar
Grew fat with feasting there.

Antony. You have heard much. 65

Pompey. I have fair meanings, sir.

Antony. And fair words to them.

Pompey. Then so much have I heard,
And I have heard Apollodorus carried—

Enobarbus. No more of that. He did so.

Pompey. What, I pray you?

Enobarbus. A certain queen to Caesar in a mattress. 70

Pompey. I know thee now. How farest thou, soldier?

Enobarbus. Well,
And well am like to do, for I perceive
Four feasts are toward.

Pompey. Let me shake thy hand.
I never hated thee. I have seen thee fight
When I have envied thy behavior.

Enobarbus. Sir, 75
I never loved you much, but I ha' praised ye
When you have well deserved ten times as much
As I have said you did.

Pompey. Enjoy thy plainness,
It nothing ill becomes thee.
Aboard my galley I invite you all. 80
Will you lead, lords?

Omnes. Show us the way, sir.

Pompey. Come.

[*Exeunt all but Enobarbus and Menas.*]

Menas. [*Aside.*] Thy father, Pompey, would ne'er have made this treaty.—You and I have known,* sir.

Enobarbus. At sea, I think.

Menas. We have, sir. 85

Enobarbus. You have done well by water.

Menas. And you by land.

Enobarbus. I will praise any man that will praise me, though it cannot be denied what I have done by land.

Menas. Nor what I have done by water. 90

Enobarbus. Yes, something you can deny for your own safety. You have been a great thief by sea.

Menas. And you by land.

83. *known: met.*

Enobarbus. There I deny my land service. But give me your hand, Menas. If our eyes had authority, here they might take two thieves kissing. *95*

Menas. All men's faces are true, whatsome'er their hands are.

Enobarbus. But there is never a fair woman has a true face.

Menas. No slander, they steal hearts. *100*

Enobarbus. We came hither to fight with you.

Menas. For my part, I am sorry it is turned to a drinking. Pompey doth this day laugh away his fortune.

Enobarbus. If he do, sure he cannot weep't back again.

Menas. Y' have said, sir. We looked not for Mark Antony here. Pray you, is he married to Cleopatra? *105*

Enobarbus. Caesar's sister is called Octavia.

Menas. True, sir, she was the wife of Caius Marcellus.

Enobarbus. But she is now the wife of Marcus Antonius.

Menas. Pray ye, sir? *110*

Enobarbus. 'Tis true.

Menas. Then is Caesar and he forever knit together.

Enobarbus. If I were bound to divine of this unity, I would not prophesy so.

Menas. I think the policy of that purpose made more in the marriage than the love of the parties. *115*

Enobarbus. I think so too. But you shall find the band that seems to tie their friendship together will be the very strangler of their amity. Octavia is of a holy, cold, and still conversation.* *120*

Menas. Who would not have his wife so?

Enobarbus. Not he that himself is not so, which is Mark Antony. He will to his Egyptian dish again. Then shall the sighs of Octavia blow the fire up in Caesar, and, as I said before, that which is the strength of their amity shall prove the immediate author of their variance. Antony will use his affection where it is. He married but his occasion* here. *125*

Menas. And thus it may be. Come, sir, will you aboard? I have a health for you. *130*

Enobarbus. I shall take it, sir. We have used our throats in Egypt.

Menas. Come, let's away. [*Exeunt.*]

120. *still conversation: quiet way of life.*
128. *occasion: immediate need.*

SCENE VII. *On Pompey's galley, off Misenum.*

[*Music plays. Enter two or three Servants, with a banquet.*]

1. *Servant.* Here they'll be, man. Some o' their plants* are ill-rooted already. The least wind i' the world will blow them down.
2. *Servant.* Lepidus is high-colored.
1. *Servant.* They have made him drink alms-drink.* *5*
2. *Servant.* As they pinch one another by the disposition, he cries out "No more," reconciles them to his entreaty, and himself to the drink.
1. *Servant.* But it raises the greater war between him and his discretion. *10*
2. *Servant.* Why, this it is to have a name in great men's fellowship. I had as lief have a reed that will do me no service as a partisan* I could not heave.
1. *Servant.* To be called into a huge sphere and not to be seen to move in't, are the holes where eyes should be, *15* which pitifully disaster* the cheeks.

[*A sennet sounded. Enter Caesar, Antony, Pompey, Lepidus, Agrippa, Maecenas, Enobarbus, Menas, with other Captains.*]

Antony. Thus do they, sir. They take the flow o' the Nile
By certain scales i' the pyramid. They know
By the height, the lowness, or the mean, if dearth
Or foison* follow. The higher Nilus swells, *20*
The more it promises. As it ebbs, the seedsman
Upon the slime and ooze scatters his grain,
And shortly comes to harvest.
Lepidus. You've strange serpents there.
Antony. Ay, Lepidus. *25*
Lepidus. Your serpent of Egypt is bred now of your mud by the operation of your sun. So is your crocodile.
Antony. They are so.
Pompey. Sit—and some wine! A health to Lepidus!

1. *plants: feet.*
5. *alms-drink: the leavings given to beggars.*
13. *partisan: sword.*
16. *disaster: unstar.*
20. *foison: plenty.*

Lepidus. I am not so well as I should be, but I'll ne'er out.* 30
Enobarbus. Not till you have slept. I fear me you'll be in* till then.
Lepidus. Nay, certainly, I have heard the Ptolemies' pyramises* are very goodly things. Without contradiction I have heard that. 35
Menas. [*Aside to Pompey.*] Pompey, a word.
Pompey. [*Aside to Menas.*] Say in mine ear. What is't?
Menas. [*Aside to Pompey.*] Forsake thy seat, I do beseech thee, captain,
And hear me speak a word.
Pompey. [*Aside to Menas.*] Forbear me till anon.
[*Menas whispers in's ear.*]
This wine for Lepidus!
Lepidus. What manner o' thing is your crocodile? 40
Antony. It is shaped, sir, like itself, and it is as broad as it hath breadth. It is just so high as it is, and moves with its own organs. It lives by that which nourisheth it, and the elements* once out of it, it transmigrates.*
Lepidus. What color is it of? 45
Antony. Of its own color too.
Lepidus. 'Tis a strange serpent.
Antony. 'Tis so, and the tears of it are wet.
Caesar. Will this description satisfy him?
Antony. With the health that Pompey gives him, else he is a very epicure. 50
Pompey. [*Aside to Menas.*] Go hang, sir, hang! Tell me of that? Away!
Do as I bid you.—Where's this cup I called for?
Menas. [*Aside to Pompey.*] If for the sake of merit thou wilt hear me,
Rise from thy stool.
Pompey. [*Aside to Menas.*] I think thou'rt mad.
[*Rises and walks aside.*]
The matter? 55
Menas. I have ever held my cap off to thy fortunes.

30. *out: stop drinking.*
31. *in: drunk.*
33–34. *pyramises: Lepidus's drunken pronunciation of "pyramides," the common plural of "pyramid" in Shakespeare's time.*
44. *elements: life.*
44. *transmigrates: passes into the body of another.*

Pompey. Thou hast served me with much faith. What's else to say?—
Be jolly, lords.
Antony. These quicksands, Lepidus,
Keep off them, for you sink.
Menas. Wilt thou be lord of all the world?
Pompey. What say'st thou? *60*
Menas. Wilt thou be lord of the whole world? That's twice.
Pompey. How should that be?
Menas. But entertain it,
And though thou think me poor, I am the man
Will give thee all the world.
Pompey. Hast thou drunk well?
Menas. No, Pompey, I have kept me from the cup. *65*
Thou art, if thou darest be, the earthly Jove.
Whate'er the ocean pales,* or sky inclips,*
Is thine, if thou wilt ha't.
Pompey. Show me which way.
Menas. These three world-sharers, these competitors,
Are in thy vessel. Let me cut the cable, *70*
And when we are put off, fall to their throats.
All there is thine.
Pompey. Ah, this thou shouldst have done,
And not have spoke on't. In me 'tis villainy,
In thee 't had been good service. Thou must know,
'Tis not my profit that does lead mine honor; *75*
Mine honor, it. Repent that e'er thy tongue
Hath so betrayed thine act. Being done unknown,
I should have found it afterwards well done,
But must condemn it now. Desist, and drink.
Menas. [*Aside.*] For this, *80*
I'll never follow thy palled* fortunes more.
Who seeks, and will not take when once 'tis offered,
Shall never find it more.
Pompey. This health to Lepidus!
Antony. Bear him ashore. I'll pledge it for him, Pompey.
Enobarbus. Here's to thee, Menas.
Menas. Enobarbus, welcome. *85*

67. *pales: encloses.*
67. *inclips: embraces.*
81. *palled: dwindled.*

Pompey. Fill till the cup be hid.
Enobarbus. There's a strong fellow, Menas.

[*Points to the Servant who carries off Lepidus.*]

Menas. Why?
Enobarbus. 'A bears the third part of the world, man, see'st not? *90*
Menas. The third part then is drunk. Would it were all,
That it might go on wheels!*
Enobarbus. Drink thou, increase the reels!*
Menas. Come.
Pompey. This is not yet an Alexandrian feast. *95*
Antony. It ripens towards it. Strike the vessels,* ho!
Here's to Caesar!
Caesar. I could well forbear't.
It's monstrous labor when I wash my brain
And it grows fouler.
Antony. Be a child o' the time.
Caesar. Possess it, I'll make answer. *100*
But I had rather fast from all four days
Than drink so much in one.
Enobarbus. [*To Antony.*] Ha, my brave emperor!
Shall we dance now the Egyptian Bacchanals*
And celebrate our drink?
Pompey. Let's ha't, good soldier.
Antony. Come, let's all take hands *105*
Till that the conquering wine hath steeped our sense
In soft and delicate Lethe.
Enobarbus. All take hands.
Make battery to our ears with the loud music,
The while I'll place you. Then the boy shall sing.
The holding* every man shall bear as loud *110*
As his strong sides can volley.

[*Music plays. Enobarbus places them hand in hand.*]

The Song

Come, thou monarch of the vine,
Plumpy Bacchus with pink eyne!

92. *on wheels: fast.*
93. *reels: whirls.*
96. *Strike the vessels: Open the casks.*
103. *Bacchanals: dances in honor of Bacchus, the god of wine.*
110. *holding: refrain.*

In thy fats* our cares be drowned,
With thy grapes our hairs be crowned. 115
Cup us till the world go round,
Cup us till the world go round!

Caesar. What would you more? Pompey, good night. Good brother,
Let me request you off. Our graver business
Frowns at this levity. Gentle lords, let's part. 120
You see we have burnt our cheeks. Strong Enobarb
Is weaker than the wine, and mine own tongue
Splits what it speaks. The wild disguise* hath almost
Anticked* us all. What needs more words? Good night.
Good Antony, your hand.
Pompey. I'll try you on the shore. 125
Antony. And shall, sir.—Give's your hand.
Pompey. O Antony,
You have my father's house—but what? We are friends!
Come, down into the boat.
Enobarbus. Take heed you fall not.
[*Exeunt all but Enobarbus and Menas.*]
Menas, I'll not on shore.
Menas. No, to my cabin.
These drums! These trumpets, flutes! What! 130
Let Neptune hear we bid a loud farewell
To these great fellows. Sound and be hanged, sound out!
[*Sound a flourish, with drums.*]
Enobarbus. Hoo! says 'a. There's my cap.
Menas. Hoo! Noble captain, come. [*Exeunt.*]

ACT III

SCENE I. *A plain in Syria.*

[*Enter Ventidius as it were in triumph, with Silius and other Romans, officers and soldiers, the dead body of Pacorus borne before him.*]

Ventidius. Now, darting* Parthia, art thou struck, and now

114. *fats: vats or casks.*
123. *disguise: drunken revelry.*
124. *Anticked: made clowns of.*
1. *darting: fast and effective with bows.*

Pleased fortune does of Marcus Crassus'* death
Make me revenger. Bear the King's son's body
Before our army. Thy Pacorus, Orodes,
Pays this for Marcus Crassus.

Silius. Noble Ventidius, 5
Whilst yet with Parthian blood thy sword is warm,
The fugitive Parthians follow. Spur through Media,
Mesopotamia, and the shelters whither
The routed fly. So thy grand captain, Antony,
Shall set thee on triumphant chariots and 10
Put garlands on thy head.

Ventidius. O Silius, Silius,
I have done enough. A lower place, note well,
May make too great an act.* For learn this, Silius,
Better to leave undone than by our deed
Acquire too high a fame when him we serve's away. 15
Caesar and Antony have ever won
More in their officer than person. Sossius,
One of my place in Syria, his lieutenant,
For quick accumulation of renown,
Which he achieved by the minute, lost his favor. 20
Who does i' the wars more than his captain can
Becomes his captain's captain, and ambition,
The soldier's virtue, rather makes choice of loss
Than gain which darkens him.
I could do more to do Antonius good, 25
But 'twould offend him. And in his offense
Should my performance perish.

Silius. Thou hast, Ventidius, that
Without the which a soldier and his sword
Grants scarce distinction. Thou wilt write to Antony?

Ventidius. I'll humbly signify what in his name, 30
That magical word of war, we have effected,
How with his banners and his well-paid ranks
The ne'er-yet-beaten horse of Parthia
We have jaded* out o' the field.

2. *Marcus Crassus: a member of the first triumvirate with Pompey and Julius Caesar, who had been defeated and killed by the Parthians under King Orodes in 53 B.C.*

12–13. *A lower place . . . act.: A subordinate can sometimes do too well for his own good.*

34. *jaded: driven like jades (worn-out nags).*

Silius. Where is he now?
Ventidius. He purposeth to Athens, whither, with what haste 35
The weight we must convey with's will permit,
We shall appear before him. On, there! Pass along!
[*Exeunt.*]

SCENE II. *Rome. Caesar's house.*

[*Enter Agrippa at one door, Enobarbus at another.*]

Agrippa. What, are the brothers parted?
Enobarbus. They have dispatched with Pompey. He is gone,
The other three are sealing.* Octavia weeps
To part from Rome, Caesar is sad, and Lepidus
Since Pompey's feast, as Menas says, is troubled 5
With the green sickness.*
Agrippa. 'Tis a noble Lepidus.
Enobarbus. A very fine one. O, how he loves Caesar!
Agrippa. Nay, but how dearly he adores Mark Antony!
Enobarbus. Caesar? Why, he's the Jupiter of men.
Agrippa. What's Antony? The god of Jupiter. 10
Enobarbus. Spake you of Caesar? Hoo! The nonpareil!
Agrippa. O Antony! O thou Arabian bird! *
Enobarbus. Would you praise Caesar, say "Caesar." Go no further.
Agrippa. Indeed he plied them both with excellent praises.
Enobarbus. But he loves Caesar best, yet he loves Antony. 15
Hoo! Hearts, tongues, figures, scribes, bards, poets, cannot
Think, speak, cast, write, sing, number—hoo!—
His love to Antony. But as for Caesar,
Kneel down, kneel down, and wonder!
Agrippa. Both he loves.
Enobarbus. They are his shards,* and he their beetle. [*Trumpet within.*] So— 20
This is to horse. Adieu, noble Agrippa.
Agrippa. Good fortune, worthy soldier, and farewell!

[*Enter Caesar, Antony, Lepidus, and Octavia.*]

Antony. No further, sir.

3. *sealing: making new agreements (applying their seals).*
6. *green sickness: a common complaint of young girls.*
12. *Arabian bird: the phoenix, of which there is only one.*
20. *shards: beetle-wings.*

Caesar. You take from me a great part of myself.
Use me well in't. Sister, prove such a wife 25
As my thoughts make thee, and as my farthest band
Shall pass on thy approof. Most noble Antony,
Let not the piece of virtue which is set
Betwixt us as the cement of our love
To keep it builded, be the ram to batter 30
The fortress of it. For better might we
Have loved without this mean,* if on both parts
This be not cherished.
Antony. Make me not offended
In your distrust.
Caesar. I have said.
Antony. You shall not find,
Though you be therein curious, the least cause 35
For what you seem to fear. So the gods keep you
And make the hearts of Romans serve your ends!
We will here part.
Caesar. Farewell, my dearest sister, fare thee well.
The elements be kind to thee, and make 40
Thy spirits all of comfort! Fare thee well.
Octavia. My noble brother!
Antony. The April's in her eyes. It is love's spring,
And these the showers to bring it on. Be cheerful.
Octavia. Sir, look well to my husband's house, and—
Caesar. What, 45
Octavia?
Octavia. I'll tell you in your ear.
Antony. Her tongue will not obey her heart, nor can
Her heart inform her tongue, the swan's down-feather
That stands upon the swell at full of tide,
And neither way inclines.* 50
Enobarbus [*Aside to Agrippa.*] Will Caesar weep?
Agrippa [*Aside to Enobarbus.*] He has a cloud in's face.
Enobarbus [*Aside to Agrippa.*] He were the worse for that, were he a horse.*
So is he, being a man.

32. *mean: means.*
48–50. *the swan's . . . inclines: Her love for brother and husband is equally balanced.*
52. *horse: Horses with black or dark faces were supposed to be ill-tempered.*

Agrippa [*Aside to Enobarbus.*] Why, Enobarbus,
When Antony found Julius Caesar dead,
He cried almost to roaring, and he wept *55*
When at Philippi he found Brutus slain.
Enobarbus [*Aside to Agrippa.*] That year indeed he was troubled with a rheum.
What willingly he did confound* he wailed,
Believe't, till I wept too.
Caesar. No, sweet Octavia,
You shall hear from me still. The time shall not *60*
Outgo my thinking on you.
Antony. Come, sir, come.
I'll wrestle with you in my strength of love.
Look, here I have you, thus I let you go,
And give you to the gods.
Caesar. Adieu, be happy!
Lepidus. Let all the number of the stars give light *65*
To thy fair way!
Caesar. Farewell, farewell! [*Kisses Octavia.*]
Antony. Farewell!
[*Trumpets sound. Exeunt.*]

SCENE III. *Alexandria. Cleopatra's palace.*

[*Enter Cleopatra, Charmian, Iras, and Alexas.*]

Cleopatra. Where is the fellow?
Alexas. Half afeard to come.
Cleopatra. Go to, go to!
[*Enter the Messenger.*]
Come hither, sir.
Alexas. Good Majesty,
Herod of Jewry dare not look upon you
But when you are well pleased.
Cleopatra. That Herod's head
I'll have! But how, when Antony is gone *5*
Through whom I might command it? Come thou near.
Messenger. Most gracious Majesty!
Cleopatra. Didst thou behold Octavia?
Messenger. Ay, dread Queen.
Cleopatra. Where? *10*

58. *confound: destroy.*

Messenger. Madam, in Rome.
I looked her in the face, and saw her led
Between her brother and Mark Antony.
Cleopatra. Is she as tall as me?
Messenger. She is not, madam.
Cleopatra. Didst hear her speak? Is she shrill-tongued or low? *15*
Messenger. Madam, I heard her speak. She is low-voiced.
Cleopatra. That's not so good! He cannot like her long.
Charmian. Like her? O, Isis! 'Tis impossible.
Cleopatra. I think so, Charmian. Dull of tongue, and dwarfish!
What majesty is in her gait? Remember, *20*
If e'er thou look'dst on majesty.
Messenger. She creeps.
Her motion and her station are as one.
She shows a body rather than a life,
A statue than a breather.
Cleopatra. Is this certain?
Messenger. Or I have no observance.
Charmian. Three in Egypt *25*
Cannot make better note.
Cleopatra. He's very knowing,
I do perceive't. There's nothing in her yet.
The fellow has good judgment.
Charmian. Excellent.
Cleopatra. Guess at her years, I prithee.
Messenger. Madam,
She was a widow—
Cleopatra. Widow? Charmian, hark! *30*
Messenger. And I do think she's thirty.
Cleopatra. Bear'st thou her face in mind? Is't long or round?
Messenger. Round even to faultiness.
Cleopatra. For the most part, too, they are foolish that are so.
Her hair, what color? *35*
Messenger. Brown, madam, and her forehead
As low as she would wish it.
Cleopatra. There's gold for thee.
Thou must not take my former sharpness ill.
I will employ thee back again. I find thee

Most fit for business. Go, make thee ready. 40
Our letters are prepared. [*Exit Messenger.*]
Charmian. A proper man.
Cleopatra. Indeed he is so. I repent me much
That so I harried him. Why, methinks, by him,
This creature's no such thing.
Charmian. Nothing, madam.
Cleopatra. The man hath seen some majesty, and should know. 45
Charmian. Hath he seen majesty? Isis else defend,
And serving you so long!
Cleopatra. I have one thing more to ask him yet, good Charmian.
But 'tis no matter. Thou shalt bring him to me
Where I will write. All may be well enough. 50
Charmian. I warrant you, madam. [*Exeunt.*]

SCENE IV. *Athens. Antony's house.*

[*Enter Antony and Octavia.*]

Antony. Nay, nay, Octavia, not only that
That were excusable, that and thousands more
Of semblable* import—but he hath waged
New wars 'gainst Pompey, made his will, and read it
To public ear, 5
Spoke scantly* of me. When perforce he could not
But pay me terms of honor, cold and sickly
He vented them, most narrow measure lent me.
When the best hint was given him, he not took't,
Or did it from his teeth.*
Octavia. O, my good lord, 10
Believe not all. Or if you must believe,
Stomach not all. A more unhappy lady,
If this division chance, ne'er stood between,
Praying for both parts.
The good gods will mock me presently 15
When I shall pray, "O, bless my lord and husband!"
Undo that prayer, by crying out as loud,

3. *semblable: similar.*
6. *scantly: slightingly.*
10. *from his teeth: i.e., not from his heart but grudgingly.*

"O, bless my brother!" Husband win, win brother,
Prays, and destroys the prayer—no midway
'Twixt these extremes at all. 20

Antony. Gentle Octavia,
Let your best love draw to that point which seeks
Best to preserve it. If I lose mine honor,
I lose myself. Better I were not yours
Than yours so branchless.* But, as you requested,
Yourself shall go between 's. The meantime, lady, 25
I'll raise the preparation of a war
Shall stain your brother. Make your soonest haste,
So your desires are yours.

Octavia. Thanks to my lord.
The Jove of power make me most weak, most weak,
Your reconciler! Wars 'twixt you twain would be 30
As if the world should cleave, and that slain men
Should solder up the rift.

Antony. When it appears to you where this begins,
Turn your displeasure that way, for our faults
Can never be so equal that your love 35
Can equally move with them. Provide your going,
Choose your own company, and command what cost
Your heart has mind to. [*Exeunt.*]

SCENE V. *The same. Another room in Antony's house.*

[*Enter Enobarbus and Eros.*]

Enobarbus. How now, friend Eros?
Eros. There's strange news come, sir.
Enobarbus. What, man?
Eros. Caesar and Lepidus have made wars upon Pompey.
Enobarbus. This is old. What is the success?* 5
Eros. Caesar, having made use of him in the wars 'gainst Pompey, presently denied him rivality,* would not let him partake in the glory of the action. And not resting here, accuses him of letters he had formerly wrote to Pompey, upon his own appeal, seizes him. So the poor 10 third is up* till death enlarge his confine.

24. *branchless: lopped of honors.*
5. *success: upshot or result.*
7. *rivality: partnership.*
11. *up: imprisoned.*

Enobarbus. Then, world, thou hast a pair of chaps,* no more,
And throw between them all the food thou hast,
They'll grind the one the other. Where's Antony?
Eros. He's walking in the garden—thus, and spurns *15*
The rush that lies before him, cries "Fool Lepidus!"
And threats the throat of that his officer
That murdered Pompey.
Enobarbus. Our great navy's rigged.
Eros. For Italy and Caesar. More, Domitius.
My lord desires you presently. My news *20*
I might have told hereafter.
Enobarbus. 'Twill be naught.
But let it be. Bring me to Antony.
Eros. Come, sir. [*Exeunt.*]

SCENE VI. *Rome. Caesar's house.*

[*Enter Agrippa, Maecenas, and Caesar.*]

Caesar. Contemning* Rome, he has done all this and more
In Alexandria. Here's the manner of't:
I' the market place, on a tribunal silvered,
Cleopatra and himself in chairs of gold
Were publicly enthroned. At the feet sat *5*
Caesarion, whom they call my father's son,
And all the unlawful issue that their lust
Since then hath made between them. Unto her
He gave the stablishment* of Egypt, made her
Of lower Syria, Cyprus, Lydia, *10*
Absolute queen.
Maecenas. This in the public eye?
Caesar. I' the common showplace, where they exercise.
His sons he there proclaimed the kings of kings.
Great Media, Parthia, and Armenia
He gave to Alexander. To Ptolemy he assigned *15*
Syria, Cilicia, and Phoenicia. She
In the habiliments of the goddess Isis
That day appeared, and oft before gave audience,

12. *chaps: jaws (i.e., Octavius and Antony).*
1. *Contemning: scorning.*
9. *stablishment: rule.*

As 'tis reported, so.
Maecenas. Let Rome be thus
Informed.
Agrippa. Who, queasy with his insolence 20
Already, will their good thoughts call from him.
Caesar. The people know it, and have now received
His accusations.
Agrippa. Who does he accuse?
Caesar. Caesar. And that, having in Sicily
Sextus Pompeius spoiled, we had not rated him 25
His part o' the isle. Then does he say he lent me
Some shipping unrestored. Lastly, he frets
That Lepidus of the triumvirate
Should be deposed, and, being, that we detain
All his revenue.
Agrippa. Sir, this should be answered. 30
Caesar. 'Tis done already, and the messenger gone.
I have told him Lepidus was grown too cruel,
That he his high authority abused
And did deserve his change. For what I have conquered,
I grant him part, but then in his Armenia, 35
And other of his conquered kingdoms, I
Demand the like.
Maecenas. He'll never yield to that.
Caesar. Nor must not then be yielded to in this.

[*Enter Octavia with her Train.*]

Octavia. Hail, Caesar, and my lord! Hail, most dear Caesar!
Caesar. That ever I should call thee castaway! 40
Octavia. You have not called me so, nor have you cause.
Caesar. Why have you stol'n upon us thus? You come not
Like Caesar's sister. The wife of Antony
Should have an army for an usher, and
The neighs of horse to tell of her approach 45
Long ere she did appear. The trees by the way
Should have borne men, and expectation fainted,
Longing for what it had not. Nay, the dust
Should have ascended to the roof of heaven,
Raised by your populous troops. But you are come 50

A market maid to Rome, and have prevented*
The ostentation* of our love, which left unshown
Is often left unloved. We should have met you
By sea and land, supplying every stage
With an augmented greeting.
Octavia. Good my lord, 55
To come thus was I not constrained, but did it
On my free will. My lord, Mark Antony,
Hearing that you prepared for war, acquainted
My grieved ear withal, whereon I begged
His pardon for return.
Caesar. Which soon he granted, 60
Being an abstract* 'tween his lust and him.
Octavia. Do not say so, my lord.
Caesar. I have eyes upon him,
And his affairs come to me on the wind.
Where is he now?
Octavia. My lord, in Athens.
Caesar. No, my most wronged sister, Cleopatra 65
Hath nodded him to her. He hath given his empire
Up to a whore, who now are levying
The kings o' the earth for war. He hath assembled
Bocchus, the king of Libya; Archelaus,
Of Cappadocia; Philadelphos, king 70
Of Paphlagonia; the Thracian king, Adallas;
King Mauchus of Arabia; King of Pont;
Herod of Jewry; Mithridates, king
Of Comagene; Polemon and Amyntas,
The kings of Mede and Lycaonia, with a 75
More larger list of sceptres.
Octavia. Ay me, most wretched,
That have my heart parted betwixt two friends
That do afflict each other!
Caesar. Welcome hither.
Your letters did withhold our breaking forth,
Till we perceived both how you were wrong led 80
And we in negligent danger.* Cheer your heart!

51. *prevented: come ahead of.*
52. *ostentation: high ceremony.*
61. *abstract: obstacle.*
81. *negligent danger: danger through our negligence.*

Be you not troubled with the time, which drives
O'er your content these strong necessities,
But let determined things to destiny
Hold unbewailed their way. Welcome to Rome, *85*
Nothing more dear to me! You are abused
Beyond the mark of thought. And the high gods,
To do you justice, makes his* ministers
Of us and those that love you. Best of comfort,
And ever welcome to us!

Agrippa. Welcome, lady. *90*

Maecenas. Welcome, dear madam.
Each heart in Rome does love and pity you.
Only the adulterous Antony, most large*
In his abominations, turns you off
And gives his potent regiment* to a trull* *95*
That noises it against us.

Octavia. Is it so, sir?

Caesar. Most certain. Sister, welcome. Pray you,
Be ever known to patience. My dear'st sister! [*Exeunt.*]

SCENE VII. *Near Actium. Antony's camp.*

[*Enter Cleopatra and Enobarbus.*]

Cleopatra. I will be even with thee, doubt it not.

Enobarbus. But why, why, why?

Cleopatra. Thou hast forspoke* my being in these wars,
And say'st it is not fit.

Enobarbus. Well, is it, is it?

Cleopatra. If not denounced* against us, why should not we *5*
Be there in person?

Enobarbus. [*aside*] Well, I could reply.
If we should serve with horse and mares together,
The horse were merely lost, the mares would bear
A soldier and his horse.

Cleopatra. What is't you say?

88. *his: their.*
93. *large: free.*
95. *regiment: rule or authority.*
95. *trull: whore.*
3. *forspoke: spoken against.*
5. *denounced: proclaimed (i.e., if war has not been proclaimed against her).*

Enobarbus. Your presence needs must puzzle Antony, 10
Take from his heart, take from his brain, from's time,
What should not then be spared. He is already
Traduced for levity, and 'tis said in Rome
That Photinus, an eunuch, and your maids
Manage this war.
Cleopatra. Sink Rome, and their tongues rot 15
That speak against us! A charge we bear i' the war,
And as the president of my kingdom will
Appear there for a man. Speak not against it.
I will not stay behind!

Enobarbus. Nay, I have done.
Here comes the Emperor.

[*Enter Antony and Canidius.*]

Antony. Is it not strange, Canidius. 20
That from Tarentum and Brundusium
He could so quickly cut the Ionian sea
And take in Toryne? You have heard on't, sweet?
Cleopatra. Celerity is never more admired
Than by the negligent.
Antony. A good rebuke, 25
Which might have well becomed the best of men,
To taunt at slackness. Canidius, we
Will fight with him by sea.
Cleopatra. By sea, what else?
Canidius. Why will my lord do so?
Antony. For that he dares us to't.
Enobarbus. So hath my lord dared him to single fight. 30
Canidius. Ay, and to wage this battle at Pharsalia,
Where Caesar fought with Pompey. But these offers,
Which serve not for his vantage, he shakes off,
And so should you.
Enobarbus. Your ships are not well manned,
Your mariners are muleters, reapers, people 35
Ingrossed by swift impress. In Caesar's fleet
Are those that often have 'gainst Pompey fought.
Their ships are yare, yours heavy. No disgrace
Shall fall you for refusing him at sea,

Being prepared for land.
Antony. By sea, by sea! 40
Enobarbus. Most worthy sir, you therein throw away
The absolute soldiership you have by land,
Distract your army, which doth most consist
Of war-marked footmen, leave unexecuted
Your own renownèd knowledge, quite forgo 45
The way which promises assurance, and
Give up yourself merely to chance and hazard
From firm security.
Antony. I'll fight at sea.
Cleopatra. I have sixty sails, Caesar none better.
Antony. Our overplus of shipping will we burn, 50
And with the rest full-manned, from the head of Actium
Beat the approaching Caesar. But if we fail,
We then can do't at land.

[*Enter a Messenger.*]

Thy business?
Messenger. The news is true, my lord. He is descried.
Caesar has taken Toryne. 55
Antony. Can he be there in person? 'Tis impossible!
Strange that his power should be. Canidius,
Our nineteen legions thou shalt hold by land
And our twelve thousand horse. We'll to our ship.
Away, my Thetis!

[*Enter a Soldier.*]

How now, worthy soldier? 60
Soldier. O noble Emperor, do not fight by sea!
Trust not to rotten planks. Do you misdoubt
This sword and these my wounds? Let the Egyptians
And the Phoenicians go a-ducking. We
Have used to conquer standing on the earth 65
And fighting foot to foot.
Antony. Well, well. Away!

[*Exit Antony, Cleopatra, and Enobarbus.*]

Soldier. By Hercules, I think I am i' the right.
Canidius. Soldier, thou art. But his whole action grows

Not in the power on't. So our leader 's led,
And we are women's men.

Soldier. You keep by land 70
The legions and the horse whole, do you not?

Canidius. Marcus Octavius, Marcus Justeius,
Publicola, and Caelius are for sea.
But we keep whole by land. This speed of Caesar's
Carries beyond belief.

Soldier. While he was yet in Rome, 75
His power went out in such distractions as
Beguiled all spies.

Canidius. Who's his lieutenant, hear you?

Soldier. They say, one Taurus.

Canidius. Well I know the man.

[*Enter a Messenger.*]

Messenger. The Emperor calls Canidius.

Canidius. With news the time's with labor and throws
forth 80
Each minute some. [*Exeunt.*]

SCENE VIII. *A plain near Actium.*

[*Enter Caesar, with his Army, marching.*]

Caesar. Taurus!

Taurus. My lord?

Caesar. Strike not by land, keep whole. Provoke not battle
Till we have done at sea. Do not exceed
The prescript of this scroll. Our fortune lies 5
Upon this jump.* [*Exeunt.*]

SCENE IX. *Another part of the plain.*

[*Enter Antony and Enobarbus.*]

Antony. Set we our squadrons on yond side o' the hill
In eye of Caesar's battle, from which place
We may the number of the ships behold,
And so proceed accordingly. [*Exeunt.*]

6. *jump: hazard.*

SCENE X. *Another part of the plain.*

[*Canidius marcheth with his land army one way over the stage, and Taurus, the lieutenant of Caesar, the other way. After their going in is heard the noise of a sea-fight. Alarum. Enter Enobarbus.*]

Enobarbus. Naught, naught, all naught! I can behold no longer.
The Antoniad, the Egyptian admiral,*
With all their sixty, fly and turn the rudder.
To see't mine eyes are blasted.

[*Enter Scarus.*]

Scarus. Gods and goddesses,
All the whole synod of them!
Enobarbus. What's thy passion? 5
Scarus. The greater cantle* of the world is lost
With very ignorance. We have kissed away
Kingdoms and provinces.
Enobarbus. How appears the fight?
Scarus. On our side like the tokened pestilence,
Where death is sure. Yon ribaudred nag* of Egypt– 10
Whom leprosy o'ertake!–i' the midst o' the fight,
When vantage like a pair of twins appeared,
Both as the same or rather ours the elder*–
The breeze* upon her, like a cow in June!–
Hoists sails and flies. 15
Enobarbus. That I beheld.
Mine eyes did sicken at the sight, and could not
Endure a further view.
Scarus. She once being loofed,*
The noble ruin of her magic, Antony.
Claps on his sea wing, and like a doting mallard, 20
Leaving the fight in height, flies after her.
I never saw an action of such shame.
Experience, manhood, honor, ne'er before

2. *admiral: leading or most important ship of a fleet.*
6. *cantle: portion.*
10. *ribaudred nag: wanton jade.*
13. *elder: dominant.*
14. *breeze: gadfly.*
18. *loofed: Her ship turned to the wind in flight.*

Did violate so itself.
Enobarbus. Alack, alack!

[*Enter Canidius.*]

Canidius. Our fortune on the sea is out of breath 25
And sinks most lamentably. Had our general
Been what he knew himself, it had gone well.
O, he has given example for our flight
Most grossly by his own!
Enobarbus. Ay, are you thereabouts?
Why then, good night indeed. 30
Canidius. Toward Peloponnesus are they fled.
Scarus. 'Tis easy to't, and there I will attend
What further comes.
Canidius. To Caesar will I render
My legions and my horse. Six kings already
Show me the way of yielding.
Enobarbus. I'll yet follow 35
The wounded chance* of Antony, though my reason
Sits in the wind against me. [*Exeunt.*]

SCENE XI. *Alexandria. Cleopatra's palace.*

[*Enter Antony with Attendants.*]

Antony. Hark! The land bids me tread no more upon't
It is ashamed to bear me! Friends, come hither.
I am so lated in the world that I
Have lost my way forever. I have a ship
Laden with gold. Take that, divide it. Fly, 5
And make your peace with Caesar.
Omnes. Fly? Not we!
Antony. I have fled myself, and have instructed cowards
To run and show their shoulders. Friends, be gone.
I have myself resolved upon a course
Which has no need of you. Be gone. 10
My treasure 's in the harbor. Take it! O,
I followed that I blush to look upon,
My very hairs do mutiny, for the white
Reprove the brown for rashness, and they them
For fear and doting. Friends, be gone. You shall 15

36. *chance: fortunes.*

Have letters from me to some friends that will
Sweep your way for you. Pray you look not sad
Nor make replies of loathness. Take the hint
Which my despair proclaims. Let that be left
Which leaves itself. To the seaside straightway! *20*
I will possess you of that ship and treasure.
Leave me, I pray, a little. Pray you now.
Nay, do so, for indeed I have lost command.
Therefore I pray you. I'll see you by and by. [*Sits down.*]

[*Enter Cleopatra led by Charmian and Eros, Iras following.*]

Eros. Nay, gentle madam, to him, comfort him. *25*
Iras. Do, most dear Queen.
Charmian. Do? Why, what else?
Cleopatra. Let me sit down. O, Juno!
Antony. No, no, no, no, no.
Eros. See you here, sir? *30*
Antony. O fie, fie, fie!
Charmian. Madam!
Iras. Madam, O good Empress!
Eros. Sir, sir!
Antony. Yes, my lord, yes. He* at Philippi kept *35*
His sword e'en like a dancer,* while I struck
The lean and wrinkled Cassius, and 'twas I
That the mad Brutus ended. He alone
Dealt on lieutenantry* and no practice had
In the brave squares* of war. Yet now–No matter *40*
Cleopatra. Ah, stand by!
Eros. The Queen, my lord, the Queen.
Iras. Go to him, madam, speak to him.
He is unqualitied* with very shame.
Cleopatra. Well then, sustain me. O! *45*
Eros. Most noble, sir, arise. The Queen approaches.
Her head's declined, and death will seize her, but
Your comfort makes the rescue.
Antony. I have offended reputation,
A most unnoble swerving.

35. *He: Octavius Caesar.*
36. *like a dancer: i.e., for show.*
39. *dealt on lieutenantry: left the fighting to his subordinates.*
40. *squares: squadrons.*
44. *unqualitied: unmanned.*

Eros. Sir, the Queen. 50
Antony. O, whither hast thou led me, Egypt? See
How I convey my shame out of thine eyes
By looking back what I have left behind
'Stroyed in dishonor.
Cleopatra. O my lord, my lord,
Forgive my fearful sails! I little thought 55
You would have followed.
Antony. Egypt, thou knew'st too well
My heart was to thy rudder tied by the strings,
And thou shouldst tow me after. O'er my spirit
Thy full supremacy thou know'st, and that
Thy beck might from the bidding of the gods 60
Command me.
Cleopatra. O, my pardon!
Antony. Now I must
To the young man send humble treaties, dodge
And palter in the shifts of lowness,* who
With half the bulk o' the world played as I pleased,
Making and marring fortunes. You did know 65
How much you were my conqueror, and that
My sword, made weak by my affection, would
Obey it on all cause.
Cleopatra. Pardon, pardon!
Antony. Fall not a tear, I say. One of them rates
All that is won and lost. Give me a kiss. 70
Even this repays me. We sent our schoolmaster.
Is 'a come back? Love, I am full of lead.*
Some wine, within there, and our viands! Fortune knows
We scorn her most when most she offers blows. [*Exeunt.*]

SCENE XII. *Egypt. Caesar's camp.*

[*Enter Caesar, Agrippa, Dolabella, Thidias, with others.*]

Caesar. Let him appear that's come from Antony.
Know you him?
Dolabella. Caesar, 'tis his schoolmaster.
An argument that he is plucked, when hither

62–63. *dodge . . . lowness: make the kind of evasions and dodges required for a person in my fallen state.*
72. *lead: sorrow.*

He sends so poor a pinion of his wing,
Which had superfluous kings for messengers *5*
Not many moons gone by.

[*Enter Ambassador from Antony.*]

Caesar. Approach and speak.
Ambassador. Such as I am, I come from Antony.
I was of late as petty to his ends
As is the morn-dew on the myrtle leaf
To his grand sea.
Caesar. Be't so. Declare thine office. *10*
Ambassador. Lord of his fortunes he salutes thee, and
Requires* to live in Egypt, which not granted,
He lessons his requests, and to thee sues
To let him breathe between the heavens and earth,
A private man in Athens. This for him. *15*
Next, Cleopatra does confess thy greatness,
Submits her to thy might, and of thee craves
The circle* of the Ptolemies for her heirs,
Now hazarded to thy grace.
Caesar. For Antony,
I have no ears to his request. The Queen *20*
Of audience nor desire shall fail, so she
From Egypt drive her all-disgraced friend,
Or take his life there. This if she perform,
She shall not sue unheard. So to them both.
Ambassador. Fortune pursue thee!
Caesar. Bring him through the bands.* *25*
[*Exit Ambassador.*]
[*To Thidias.*] To try thy eloquence, now 'tis time.
Dispatch.
From Antony win Cleopatra. Promise,
And in our name, what she requires. Add more,
From thine invention, offers. Women are not
In their best fortunes strong, but want will perjure *30*
The ne'er-touched Vestal. Try thy cunning, Thidias.
Make thine own edict for thy pains, which we
Will answer as a law.

12. *requires: requests.*
18. *circle: crown.*
25. *bands: troops.*

Thidias. Caesar, I go.
Caesar. Observe how Antony becomes* his flaw,
And what thou think'st his very action speaks 35
In every power that moves.*
Thidias. Caesar, I shall. [*Exeunt.*]

SCENE XIII. *Alexandria. Cleopatra's palace.*

[*Enter Cleopatra, Enobarbus, Charmian, and Iras.*]

Cleopatra. What shall we do, Enobarbus?
Enobarbus. Think, and die.
Cleopatra. Is Antony or we in fault for this?
Enobarbus. Antony only, that would make his will
Lord of his reason. What though you fled
From that great face of war, whose several ranges* 5
Frighted each other? Why should he follow?
The itch of his affection should not then
Have nicked* his captainship, at such a point,
When half to half the world opposed, he being
The mered question.* 'Twas a shame no less 10
Than was his loss, to course* your flying flags
And leave his navy gazing.
Cleopatra. Prithee, peace!

[*Enter the Ambassador, with Antony.*]

Antony. Is that his answer?
Ambassador. Ay, my lord.
Antony. The Queen shall then have courtesy, so she 15
Will yield us up.
Ambassador. He says so.
Antony. Let her know't.
To the boy Caesar send this grizzled head,
And he will fill thy wishes to the brim
With principalities.
Cleopatra. That head, my lord?

34. *becomes: adjusts to.*
35–36. *And . . . moves: and your impression of his state of mind by every move he makes.*
5. *ranges: arrangements of troops or ships.*
8. *nicked: marred.*
10. *mered question: sole matter.*
11. *course: chase after.*

Antony. To him again! Tell him he wears the rose 20
Of youth upon him, from which the world should note
Something particular. His coin, ships, legions
May be a coward's, whose ministers would prevail
Under the service of a child as soon
As i' the command of Caesar. I dare him therefore 25
To lay his gay comparisons* apart
And answer me declined, sword against sword,
Ourselves alone. I'll write it. Follow me.
[*Exeunt Antony and Ambassador.*]
Enobarbus. [*aside.*] Yes, like enough! High-battled* Caesar will
Unstate his happiness and be staged to the show 30
Against a sworder! I see men's judgments are
A parcel of their fortunes, and things outward
Do draw the inward quality after them
To suffer all alike. That he should dream,
Knowing all measures,* the full Caesar will 35
Answer his emptiness! Caesar, thou hast subdued
His judgment too.

[*Enter a Servant.*]

Servant. A messenger from Caesar.
Cleopatra. What, no more ceremony? See, my women,
Against the blown rose may they stop their nose
That kneeled unto the buds. Admit him, sir. 40
[*Exit Servant.*]
Enobarbus. [*aside.*] Mine honesty and I begin to square.*
The loyalty well held to fools does make
Our faith mere folly. Yet he that can endure
To follow with allegiance a fall'n lord
Does conquer him that did his master conquer, 45
And earns a place i' the story.

[*Enter Thidias.*]

Cleopatra. Caesar's will?
Thidias. Hear it apart.

26. *gay comparisons: youthful advantages.*
29. *High-battled: leader of a great army.*
35. *Knowing all measures: being such an experienced judge of men and experience.*
41. *square: quarrel.*

Cleopatra. None but friends. Say boldly.
Thidias. So, haply,* are they friends to Antony.
Enobarbus. He needs as many, sir, as Caesar has,
Or needs not us. If Caesar please, our master 50
Will leap to be his friend. For us, you know,
Whose he is we are, and that is Caesar's.
Thidias. So.
Thus then, thou most renowned, Caesar entreats
Not to consider in what case thou stand'st
Further than he is Caesar.
Cleopatra. Go on. Right royal. 55
Thidias. He knows that you embrace not Antony
As you did love, but as you feared him.
Cleopatra. O!
Thidias. The scars upon your honor therefore he
Does pity, as constrained blemishes,
Not as deserved.
Cleopatra. He is a god, and knows 60
What is most right. Mine honor was not yielded,
But conquered merely.
Enobarbus. [*Aside.*] To be sure of that,
I will ask Antony. Sir, sir, thou art so leaky
That we must leave thee to thy sinking, for
Thy dearest quit thee. [*Exit Enobarbus.*]
Thidias. Shall I say to Caesar 65
What you require of him? For he partly begs
To be desired to give. It much would please him
That of his fortunes you should make a staff
To lean upon. But it would warm his spirits
To hear from me you had left Antony, 70
And put yourself under his shroud,*
The universal landlord.
Cleopatra. What's your name?
Thidias. My name is Thidias.
Cleopatra. Most kind messenger,
Say to great Caesar this in deputation:*
I kiss his conquering hand. Tell him I am prompt 75
To lay my crown at's feet, and there to kneel.
Tell him, from his all-obeying* breath, I hear

48. *haply: perhaps.*
71. *shroud: protection.*
74. *in deputation: as my representative.*
77. *all-obeying: obeyed by all.*

The doom of Egypt.
Thidias. 'Tis your noblest course.
Wisdom and fortune combating together,
If that the former dare but what it can, 80
No chance may shake it. Give me grace to lay
My duty on your hand.
Cleopatra. Your Caesar's father oft,
When he hath mused of taking kingdoms in,
Bestowed his lips on that unworthy place,
As it rained kisses.

[*Enter Antony and Enobarbus.*]

Antony. Favors? By Jove that thunders! 85
What are thou, fellow?
Thidias. One that but performs
The bidding of the fullest man, and worthiest
To have command obeyed.
Enobarbus. [*Aside.*] You will be whipped.
Antony. Approach, there! Ah, you kite! Now, gods and devils!
Authority melts from me. Of late, when I cried "Ho!" 90
Like boys unto a muss,* kings would start forth,
And cry "Your will?" Have you no ears? I am
Antony yet.

[*Enter Servants.*]

Take hence this Jack* and whip him.
Enobarbus. [*Aside.*] 'Tis better playing with a lion's whelp
Than with an old one dying.
Antony. Moon and stars! 95
Whip him. Were't twenty of the greatest tributaries
That do acknowledge Caesar, should I find them
So saucy with the hand of she here—what's her name
Since she was Cleopatra? Whip him, fellows,
Till like a boy you see him cringe his face 100
And whine aloud for mercy. Take him hence.
Thidias. Mark Antony—
Antony Tug him away. Being whipped,
Bring him again. This Jack of Caesar's shall

91. *muss: a game involving a scramble.*
93. *Jack: impudent fellow.*

Bear us an errand to him. [*Exeunt Servants with Thidias.*]
You were half blasted ere I knew you. Ha! *105*
Have I my pillow left unpressed in Rome,
Forborne the getting of a lawful race,
And by a gem of women, to be abused
By one that looks on feeders?*
Cleopatra. Good my lord–
Antony. You have been a boggler* ever. *110*
But when we in our viciousness grow hard–
O misery on't!–the wise gods seel* our eyes,
In our own filth drop our clear judgments, make us
Adore our errors, laugh at's while we strut
To our confusion.
Cleopatra. O, is't come to this? *115*
Antony. I found you as a morsel, cold upon
Dead Caesar's trencher.* Nay, you were a fragment*
Of Gneius Pompey's, besides what hotter hours,
Unregistered in vulgar fame, you have
Luxuriously* picked out. For I am sure, *120*
Though you can guess what temperance should be,
You know not what it is.
Cleopatra. Wherefore is this?
Antony. To let a fellow that will take rewards
And say "God quit you!" be familiar with
My playfellow, your hand, this kingly seal *125*
And plighter of high hearts! O, that I were
Upon the hill of Basan to outroar
The horned herd!* For I have savage cause,
And to proclaim it civilly were like
A haltered neck which does the hangman thank *130*
For being yare* about him.

[*Enter Servants with Thidias.*]

Is he whipped?

109. *feeders: servants.*
110. *boggler: shifty creature.*
112. *seel: sew up.*
117. *trencher: plate.*
117. *fragment: leftover morsel.*
120. *Luxuriously: lustfully.*
126–128. *O . . . herd: See Psalm 68 (as phrased in the Prayer Book). Antony likens himself to the other horned bulls of Bashan and thus suggests that he too has been a cuckold.*
131. *yare: quick or skillful.*

1. *Servant.* Soundly, my lord.
Antony. Cried he? And begged 'a pardon?
1. *Servant.* He did ask favor.
Antony. If that thy father live, let him repent
Thou wast not made his daughter. And be thou sorry *135*
To follow Caesar in his triumph, since
Thou hast been whipped for following him. Henceforth
The white hand of a lady fever thee,
Shake thou to look on't. Get thee back to Caesar,
Tell him thy entertainment. Look thou say *140*
He makes me angry with him. For he seems
Proud and disdainful, harping on what I am,
Not what he knew I was. He makes me angry,
And at this time most easy 'tis to do't,
When my good stars, that were my former guides, *145*
Have empty left their orbs* and shot their fires
Into the abysm of hell. If he mislike
My speech and what is done, tell him he has
Hipparchus,* my enfranched bondman, whom
He may at pleasure whip, or hang, or torture, *150*
As he shall like, to quit* me. Urge it thou.
Hence with thy stripes, be gone! [*Exit Thidias.*]
Cleopatra. Have you done yet?
Antony. Alack, our terrene moon*
Is now eclipsed, and it portends alone
The fall of Antony!
Cleopatra. I must stay his time.* *155*
Antony. To flatter Caesar, would you mingle eyes
With one that ties his points?*
Cleopatra. Not know me yet?
Antony. Cold-hearted toward me?
Cleopatra. Ah, dear, if I be so,
From my cold heart let heaven engender hail,
And poison it in the source, and the first stone *160*
Drop in my neck. As it determines,* so
Dissolve my life! The next, Caesarion smite!
Till by degrees the memory of my womb,

146. *orbs: spheres.*
149. *Hipparchus had defected to Caesar.*
151. *quit: requite or repay.*
153. *terrene moon: earthly moon (i.e., Cleopatra).*
155. *stay . . . time: wait until he is himself again.*
157. *one . . . points: the servant or valet who ties his laces.*
161. *determines: terminates or dissolves.*

Together with my brave Egyptians all,
By the discandying* of this pelleted storm, *165*
Lie graveless, till the flies and gnats of Nile
Have buried them for prey!

Antony. I am satisfied.
Caesar sits down in Alexandria, where
I will oppose his fate. Our force by land
Hath nobly held. Our severed navy too *170*
Have knit again, and fleet, threatening most sea-like.
Where hast thou been, my heart? Dost thou hear, lady?
If from the field I shall return once more
To kiss these lips, I will appear in blood.
I and my sword will earn our chronicle. *175*
There's hope in't yet.

Cleopatra. That's my brave lord!

Antony. I will be treble-sinewed, hearted, breathed,
And fight maliciously. For when mine hours
Were nice* and lucky, men did ransom lives *180*
Of me for jests, but now I'll set my teeth
And send to darkness all that stop me. Come,
Let's have one other gaudy night. Call to me
All my sad captains, fill our bowls once more.
Let's mock the midnight bell.

Cleopatra. It is my birthday. *185*
I had thought t' have held it poor. But since my lord
Is Antony again, I will be Cleopatra.

Antony. We will yet do well.

Cleopatra. Call all his noble captains to my lord.

Antony. Do so, we'll speak to them. And tonight I'll force *190*
The wine peep through their scars. Come on, my queen,
There's sap in't yet! The next time I do fight,
I'll make death love me, for I will contend
Even with his pestilent scythe.

[*Exeunt all but Enobarbus.*]

Enobarbus. Now he'll outstare the lightning. To be furious *195*
Is to be frighted out of fear, and in that mood
The dove will peck the estridge.* And I see still

165. *discandying: melting.*
180. *nice: choosy or particular.*
197. *estridge: hawk.*

A diminution in our captain's brain
Restores his heart. When valor preys on reason,
It eats the sword it fights with. I will seek 200
Some way to leave him. [*Exit.*]

ACT IV

SCENE I. *Before Alexandria. Caesar's camp.*

[*Enter Caesar, Agrippa, and Maecenas, with their Army, Caesar reading a letter.*]

Caesar. He calls me boy, and chides as he had power
To beat me out of Egypt. My messenger
He hath whipped with rods, dares me to personal combat,
Caesar to Antony. Let the old ruffian know
I have many other ways to die, meantime 5
Laugh at his challenge.
Maecenas. Caesar needs must think,
When one so great begins to rage, he's hunted
Even to falling. Give him no breath, but now
Make boot* of his distraction. Never anger
Make good guard for itself.
Caesar. Let our best heads 10
Know that to-morrow the last of many battles
We mean to fight. Within our files* there are,
Of those that served Mark Antony but late,
Enough to fetch him in.* See it done,
And feast the army. We have store to do't, 15
And they have earned the waste. Poor Antony!
[*Exeunt.*]

SCENE II. *Alexandria. Cleopatra's palace.*

[*Enter Antony, Cleopatra, Enobarbus, Charmian, Iras, Alexas, with others.*]

Antony. He will not fight with me, Domitius?
Enobarbus. No.
Antony. Why should he not?

9. *make boot: take advantage.*
12. *files: military units.*
14. *fetch him in: capture him.*

Enobarbus. He thinks, being twenty times of better fortune,
He is twenty men to one.
Antony. Tomorrow, soldier,
By sea and land I'll fight. Or I will live, 5
Or bathe my dying honor in the blood
Shall make it live again. Woo't thou fight well?
Enobarbus. I'll strike, and cry "Take all!"*
Antony. Well said. Come on.
Call forth my household servants. Let's tonight
Be bounteous at our meal.

[*Enter three or four Servitors.*]

Give me thy hand. 10
Thou hast been rightly honest—so hast thou—
And thou—and thou—and thou. You have served me well,
And kings have been your fellows.
Cleopatra. [*Aside to Enobarbus.*] What means this?
Enobarbus. [*Aside to Cleopatra.*] 'Tis one of those odd tricks which sorrow shoots
Out of the mind.
Antony. And thou are honest too. 15
I wish I could be made so many men,
And all of you clapped up together in
An Antony, that I might do you service
So good as you have done.
Servitors. The gods forbid!
Antony. Well, my good fellows, wait on me tonight. 20
Scant not my cups, and make as much of me
As when mine empire was your fellow too,
And suffered my command.
Cleopatra. [*Aside to Enobarbus.*] What does he mean?
Enobarbus. [*Aside to Cleopatra.*] To make his followers weep.
Antony. Tend me tonight.
May be it is the period* of your duty. 25
Haply you shall not see me more, or if,
A mangled shadow. Perchance tomorrow
You'll serve another master. I look on you
As one that takes his leave. Mine honest friends,

8. *"Take all": Let the winner take all.*
25. *period: end.*

I turn you not away, but like a master 30
Married to your good service, stay till death.
Tend me tonight two hours. I ask no more,
And the gods yield you for't!
Enobarbus. What mean you, sir,
To give them this discomfort? Look, they weep,
And I, an ass, am onion-eyed. For shame, 35
Transform us not to women.
Antony. Ho, ho, ho!
Now the witch take me if I meant it thus!
Grace grow where those drops fall! My hearty friends,
You take me in too dolorous sense.
For I spake to you for your comfort, did desire you 40
To burn this night with torches. Know, my hearts,
I hope well of tomorrow, and will lead you
Where rather I'll expect victorious life
Than death and honor. Let's to supper, come,
And drown consideration. [*Exeunt.*] 45

SCENE III. *Alexandria. Before Cleopatra's palace.*

[*Enter a Company of Soldiers.*]

1. *Soldier.* Brother, good night. Tomorrow is the day.
2. *Soldier.* It will determine one way. Fare you well.
Heard you of nothing strange about the streets?
1. *Soldier.* Nothing. What news?
2. *Soldier.* Belike* 'tis but a rumor. Good night to you. 5
1. *Soldier.* Well, sir, good night.

[*Enter two other Soldiers.*]

2. *Soldier.* Soldiers, have careful watch.
3. *Soldier.* And you. Good night, good night.

[*They place themselves in every corner of the stage.*]

4. *Soldier.* Here we. And if tomorrow
Our navy thrive, I have an absolute hope
Our landmen will stand up.
3. *Soldier.* 'Tis a brave army, 10
And full of purpose.

[*Music of the hautboys is under the stage.*]

5. *Belike: probably.*

2. *Soldier.* Peace! What noise?
1. *Soldier.* List, list!
2. *Soldier.* Hark!
1. *Soldier.* Music i' the air.
3. *Soldier.* Under the earth.
4. *Soldier.* It signs well, does it not?
3. *Soldier.* No.
1. *Soldier.* Peace, I say!
What should this mean?
2. *Soldier.* 'Tis the god Hercules,* whom Antony loved, *15*
Now leaves him.
1. *Soldier.* Walk. Let's see if other watchmen
Do hear what we do.
2. *Soldier.* How now, masters?
Omnes. [*Speaking together.*] How now?
How now? Do you hear this?
1. *Soldier.* Ay. Is't not strange?
3. *Soldier.* Do you hear, masters? Do you hear?
1. *Soldier.* Follow the noise so far as we have quarter.* *20*
Let's see how it will give off.
Omnes. Content. 'Tis strange. [*Exeunt.*]

SCENE IV. *Alexandria. A room in Cleopatra's palace.*

[*Enter Antony and Cleopatra, Charmian and others attending.*]

Antony. Eros! Mine armor, Eros!
Cleopatra. Sleep a little.
Antony. No, my chuck.* Eros, come. Mine armor, Eros!

[*Enter Eros with armor.*]

Come, good fellow, put mine iron* on.
If fortune be not ours today, it is
Because we brave her. Come.
Cleopatra. Nay, I'll help too. *5*
What's this for?
Antony. Ah, let be, let be! Thou art
The armorer of my heart. False, false. This, this.

15. *Hercules: Supposedly Antony's ancestor.*
20. *so . . . quarter: as far as the area of our watch goes.*
2. *chuck: chick (a term of endearment).*
3. *iron: armor.*

Cleopatra. Sooth, la, I'll help. Thus it must be.
Antony. Well, well,
We shall thrive now. Seest thou, my good fellow?
Go, put on thy defenses.
Eros. Briefly, sir. *10*
Cleopatra. Is not this buckled well?
Antony. Rarely, rarely.
He that unbuckles this, till we do please
To doff't for our repose, shall hear a storm.
Thou fumblest, Eros, and my queen's a squire
More tight* at this than thou. Dispatch. O love, *15*
That thou couldst see my wars today, and knew'st
The royal occupation! Thou shouldst see
A workman* in't.

[*Enter an armed Soldier.*]

Good morrow to thee, welcome.
Thou look'st like him that knows a warlike charge.
To business that we love we rise betime* *20*
And go to't with delight.
Soldier. A thousand, sir,
Early though't be, have on their riveted trim,*
And at the port* expect you.

[*Shout. Trumpets flourish. Enter Captains and Soldiers.*]

Captain. The morn is fair. Good morrow, General.
Omnes. Good morrow, General.
Antony. 'Tis well blown,* lads. *25*
This morning, like the spirit of a youth
That means to be of note, begins betimes.
So, so. Come, give me that. This way. Well said.
Fare thee well, dame. Whate'er becomes of me,
This is a soldier's kiss. Rebukable *30*
And worthy shameful check it were to stand
On more mechanic compliment.* I'll leave thee

15. *tight: skillful.*
18. *workman: master, artisan.*
20. *betime: early.*
22. *riveted trim: armor.*
23. *port: gate.*
25. *'Tis well blown: The morning has begun.*
32. *mechanic compliment: ordinary leave-taking.*

Now like a man of steel. You that will fight,
Follow me close. I'll bring you to't. Adieu.

[*Exeunt Antony, Eros, Captains, and Soldiers.*]

Charmian. Please you retire to your chamber?
Cleopatra. Lead me. 45
He goes forth gallantly. That he and Caesar might
Determine this great war in single fight!
Then Antony—but now—Well, on. [*Exeunt.*]

SCENE V. *Alexandria. Antony's camp.*

[*Trumpets sound. Enter Antony and Eros, a Soldier meeting them.*]

Soldier. The gods make this a happy day to Antony!
Antony. Would thou and those thy scars had once prevailed
To make me fight at land!
Soldier. Hadst thou done so,
The kings that have revolted and the soldier
That has this morning left thee would have still 5
Followed thy heels.
Antony. Who's gone this morning?
Soldier. Who?
One ever near thee. Call for Enobarbus,
He shall not hear thee, or from Caesar's camp
Say "I am none of thine."
Antony. What sayest thou?
Soldier. Sir,
He is with Caesar.
Eros. Sir, his chests and treasure 10
He has not with him.
Antony. Is he gone?
Soldier. Most certain.
Antony. Go, Eros, send his treasure after. Do it.
Detain no jot, I charge thee. Write to him—
I will subscribe* gentle adieus and greetings.
Say that I wish he never find more cause 15
To change a master. O, my fortunes have
Corrupted honest men! Dispatch. Enobarbus!

[*Exeunt.*]

14. *subscribe: sign.*

SCENE VI. *Alexandria. Antony's camp.*

[*Flourish. Enter Agrippa, Caesar, with Enobarbus, and Dolabella.*]

Caesar. Go forth, Agrippa, and begin the fight.
Our will is Antony be took alive.
Make it so known.
Agrippa. Caesar, I shall. [*Exit.*]
Caesar. The time of universal peace is near. 5
Prove this a prosperous day, the three-nooked* world
Shall bear the olive freely.

[*Enter a Messenger.*]

Messenger. Antony
Is come into the field.
Caesar. Go charge Agrippa
Plant those that have revolted in the van,
That Antony may seem to spend his fury 10
Upon himself. [*Exeunt all but Enobarbus.*]
Enobarbus. Alexas did revolt and went to Jewry on
Affairs of Antony. There did dissuade
Great Herod to incline himself to Caesar
And leave his master Antony. For this pains 15
Caesar hath hanged him. Canidius and the rest
That fell away have entertainment,* but
No honorable trust. I have done ill,
Of which I do accuse myself so sorely
That I will joy no more.

[*Enter a Soldier of Caesar's.*]

Soldier. Enobarbus, Antony 20
Hath after thee sent all thy treasure, with
His bounty overplus. The messenger
Came on my guard, and at thy tent is now
Unloading of his mules.
Enobarbus. I give it you.
Soldier. Mock not, Enobarbus. 25
I tell you true. Best you safed* the bringer
Out of the host. I must attend mine office,

6. *three-nooked: tri-cornered.*
17. *entertainment: employment.*
26. *safed: led safely.*

Or would have done't myself. Your emperor
Continues still a Jove. [*Exit.*]

Enobarbus. I am alone the villain of the earth, 30
And feel I am so most. O Antony,
Thou mine of bounty, how wouldst thou have paid
My better service, when my turpitude
Thou dost so crown with gold! This blows* my heart.
If swift thought* break it not, a swifter mean 35
Shall outstrike thought. But thought will do't, I feel.
I fight against thee? No, I will go seek
Some ditch wherein to die. The foul'st best fits
My latter part of life. [*Exit.*]

SCENE VII. *Field of battle between the camps.*

[*Alarum. Drums and Trumpets. Enter Agrippa and Soldiers.*]

Agrippa. Retire. We have engaged ourselves too far.
Caesar himself has work, and our oppression*
Exceeds what we expected. [*Exeunt.*]

[*Alarums. Enter Antony, and Scarus wounded.*]

Scarus. O my brave Emperor, this is fought indeed!
Had we done so at first, we had droven them home 5
With clouts* about their heads.

Thou bleed'st apace.

Scarus. I had a wound here that was like a T,
But now 'tis made an H.* [*Sound retreat afar.*]

Antony. They do retire.

Scarus. We'll beat 'em into bench-holes.* I have yet
Room for six scotches* more. 10

[*Enter Eros.*]

Eros. They are beaten, sir, and our advantage serves
For a fair victory.

34. *blows: swells to bursting.*
35. *thought: melancholy.*
2. *oppression: difficulty.*
6. *clouts: cloths (bandages).*
8. *H: a pun (in Shakespeare's time the word "ache" and the name of the letter were often pronounced alike).*
9. *bench-holes: the holes of privies.*
10. *scotches: gashes.*

Scarus. Let us score their backs
And snatch 'em up, as we take hares, behind.
'Tis sport to maul a runner.
Antony. I will reward thee
Once for thy sprightly comfort, and tenfold *15*
For thy good valor. Come thee on.
Scarus. I'll halt* after. [*Exeunt.*]

SCENE VIII. *Under the walls of Alexandria.*

[*Alarum. Enter Antony again in a march; Scarus, with others.*]

Antony. We have beat him to his camp. Run one before
And let the Queen know of our gests.* Tomorrow,
Before the sun shall see's, we'll spill the blood
That has today escaped. I thank you all,
For doughty-handed are you, and have fought *5*
Not as you served the cause but as't had been
Each man's like mine. You have shown all Hectors.*
Enter the city, clip* your wives, your friends,
Tell them your feats, whilst they with joyful tears
Wash the congealment from your wounds, and kiss *10*
The honored gashes whole.

[*Enter Cleopatra, attended.*]

[*To Scarus.*] Give me thy hand.
To this great fairy* I'll commend thy acts,
Make her thanks bless thee. O thou day o' the world,
Chain mine armed neck. Leap thou, attire and all,
Through proof of harness to my heart, and there *15*
Ride on the pants triumphing.
Cleopatra. Lord of lords!
O infinite virtue, com'st thou smiling from
The world's great snare* uncaught?
Antony. My nightingale,

16. *halt: limp.*
2. *gests: deeds.*
7. *Hectors: i.e., champions like the great Trojan warrior against the Greeks.*
8. *clip: hug.*
12. *fairy: enchantress.*
18. *world's great snare: death.*

We have beat them to their beds. What, girl! Though gray
Do something mingle with our younger brown, yet ha' we 20
A brain that nourishes our nerves, and can
Get goal for goal of youth. Behold this man.
Commend unto his lips thy favoring hand.—
Kiss it, my warrior.—He hath fought today
As if a god in hate of mankind had 25
Destroyed in such a shape.

Cleopatra. I'll give thee, friend,
An armor all of gold. It was a king's.

Antony. He has deserved it, were it carbuncled*
Like holy Phoebus' car. Give me thy hand.
Through Alexandria make a jolly march, 30
Bear our hacked targets like the men that owe* them.
Had our great palace the capacity
To camp this host, we all would sup together
And drink carouses to the next day's fate,
Which promises royal peril. Trumpeters, 35
With brazen din blast you the city's ear,
Make mingle with our rattling tabourines,*
That heaven and earth may strike their sounds together,
Applauding our approach. [*Exeunt.*]

SCENE IX. *Caesar's camp.*

[*Enter a Sentry and his Company. Enobarbus follows.*]

Sentry. If we be not relieved within this hour,
We must return to the court of guard.* The night
Is shiny, and they say we shall embattle
By the second hour i' the morn.

1. *Watchman.* This last day was
A shrewd* one to's.

Enobarbus. O, bear me witness, night— 5

2. *Watchman.* What man is this?

1. *Watchman.* Stand close, and list him.

28. *carbuncled: set with jewels.*
31. *owe: own.*
37. *tabourines: military drums.*
2. *court of guard: guardroom.*
5. *shrewd: evil.*

Enobarbus. Be witness to me, O thou blessed moon,
When men revolted shall upon record
Bear hateful memory, poor Enobarbus did
Before thy face repent!

Sentry. Enobarbus!

2\. *Watchman.* Peace! *10*
Hark further.

Enobarbus. O sovereign mistress of true melancholy,*
The poisonous damp of night disponge upon me,
That life, a very rebel to my will,
May hang no longer on me. Throw my heart *15*
Against the flint and hardness of my fault,
Which, being dried with grief, will break to powder,
And finish all foul thoughts. O Antony,
Nobler than my revolt is infamous,
Forgive me in thine own particular,* *20*
But let the world rank me in register
A master-leaver* and a fugitive.
O Antony! O Antony! [*Dies.*]

1\. *Watchman.* Let's speak
To him.

Sentry. Let's hear him, for the things he speaks
May concern Caesar.

2\. *Watchman.* Let's do so. But he sleeps. *25*

Sentry. Swoons rather, for so bad a prayer as his
Was never yet for sleep.

1\. *Watchman.* Go we to him.

2\. *Watchman.* Awake, sir, awake. Speak to us.

1\. *Watchman.* Hear you, sir?

Sentry. The hand of death hath raught* him.
[*Drums afar off.*]
Hark! the drums
Demurely* wake the sleepers. Let us bear him *30*
To the court of guard. He is of note. One hour
Is fully out.

2\. *Watchman.* Come on then,
He may recover yet. [*Exeunt with the body.*]

12\. *O . . . melancholy: Enobarbus is addressing the moon.*
20\. *in . . . particular: as far as you individually are concerned.*
22\. *master-leaver: a runaway servant or apprentice.*
29\. *raught: reached or taken.*
30\. *Demurely: soberly.*

SCENE X. *Between the two camps.*

[*Enter Antony and Scarus, with their Army.*]

Antony. Their preparation is today by sea.
We please them not by land.
Scarus. For both, my lord.
Antony. I would they'd fight i' the fire or i' the air.
We'd fight there too. But this it is. Our foot
Upon the hills adjoining to the city 5
Shall stay with us. Order for sea is given,
They have put forth the haven,
Where their appointment* we may best discover
And look on their endeavor. [*Exeunt.*]

SCENE XI. *Between the two camps.*

[*Enter Caesar and his Army.*]

Caesar. But being charged,* we will be still by land,
Which, as I take't, we shall, for his best force
Is forth to man his galleys. To the vales,
And hold our best advantage. [*Exeunt.*]

SCENE XII. *Hills adjoining Alexandria.*

[*Enter Antony and Scarus.*]

Antony. Yet they are not joined. Where yond pine does stand
I shall discover all. I'll bring thee word
Straight how 'tis like to go. [*Exit.*]
Scarus. Swallows have built
In Cleopatra's sails their nests. The augurers*
Say they know not, they cannot tell, look grimly, 5
And dare not speak their knowledge. Antony
Is valiant, and dejected, and by starts
His fretted* fortunes give him hope and fear
Of what he has, and has not.
[*Alarum afar off, as at a sea fight.*]

[*Enter Antony.*]

8. *appointment: arrangement.*
1. *But . . . charged: unless we are charged.*
4. *augurers: interpreters of omens.*
8. *fretted: mixed.*

Antony. All is lost!
This foul Egyptian hath betrayed me. *10*
My fleet hath yielded to the foe, and yonder
They cast their caps up and carouse together
Like friends long lost. Triple-turned whore!* 'Tis thou
Hast sold me to this novice, and my heart
Makes only wars on thee. Bid them all fly, *15*
For when I am revenged upon my charm,*
I have done all. Bid them all fly. Begone! [*Exit Scarus.*]
O sun, thy uprise shall I see no more.
Fortune and Antony part here, even here
Do we shake hands. All come to this? The hearts *20*
That spanieled me at heels, to whom I gave
Their wishes, do discandy, melt their sweets
On blossoming Caesar, and this pine is barked,
That overtopped them all. Betrayed I am.
O this false soul of Egypt! This grave charm,* *25*
Whose eye becked forth my wars, and called them home,
Whose bosom was my crownet,* my chief end,
Like a right gypsy hath at fast and loose*
Beguiled me to the very heart of loss.
What, Eros, Eros!

[*Enter Cleopatra.*]

Ah, thou spell! Avaunt! *30*
Cleopatra. Why is my lord enraged against his love?
Antony. Vanish, or I shall give thee thy deserving
And blemish Caesar's triumph. Let him take thee
And hoist thee up to the shouting plebeians.
Follow his chariot, like the greatest spot *35*
Of all thy sex. Most monster-like be shown
For poor'st diminitives, for dolts.* And let
Patient Octavia plough thy visage up
With her prepared nails. [*Exit Cleopatra.*]
'Tis well thou'rt gone,

13. *Triple-turned whore: the faithless mistress of three—Pompey, Julius Caesar, and Antony.*
16. *charm: charmer.*
25. *grave charm: deadly enchantress.*
27. *crownet: coronet.*
28. *fast and loose: a cheating game.*
37. *diminitives . . . dolts: weaklings and fools (i.e., common people).*

If it be well to live. But better 'twere 40
Thou fell'st into my fury, for one death
Might have prevented many. Eros, ho!
The shirt of Nessus* is upon me. Teach me,
Alcides,* thou mine ancestor, thy rage.
Let me lodge Lichas* on the horns o' the moon, 45
And with those hands that grasped the heaviest club
Subdue my worthiest self. The witch shall die.
To the young Roman boy she hath sold me, and I fall
Under this plot. She dies for't. Eros, ho! [*Exit.*]

SCENE XIII. *Alexandria. Cleopatra's palace.*

[*Enter Cleopatra, Charmian, Iras, and Mardian.*]

Cleopatra. Help me, my women! O, he's more mad
Than Telamon* for his shield. The boar of Thessaly*
Was never so embossed.
Charmian. To the monument!
There lock yourself, and send him word you are dead.
The soul and body rive* not more in parting 5
Than greatness going off.
Cleopatra. To the monument!
Mardian, go tell him I have slain myself.
Say that the last I spoke was "Antony,"
And word it, prithee, piteously. Hence, Mardian,
And bring me how he takes my death. To the monument! 10
[*Exeunt.*]

SCENE XIV. *Cleopatra's palace. Another room.*

[*Enter Antony and Eros.*]

Antony. Eros, thou yet behold'st me?
Eros. Ay, noble lord.

43. *shirt of Nessus: The bloody shirt that poisoned Hercules and so tortured him that he destroyed himself.*
44. *Alcides: Hercules.*
45. *Lichas: The page of Hercules who brought him the shirt of Nessus and who was thrown into the sea by the infuriated Hercules.*
2. *boar of Thessaly: the boar sent by the goddess Diana to ravage the kingdom of Caledon as a punishment for the lack of sacrifices.*
2. *Telamon: Ajax, who went mad when the shield of Achilles was given to Ulysses and killed himself.*
5. *rive: break apart.*

Antony. Sometime we see a cloud that's dragonish,
A vapor sometime like a bear or lion,
A towered citadel, a pendant rock,
A forked mountain, or blue promontory 5
With trees upon't that nod unto the world
And mock our eyes with air. Thou hast seen these signs,
They are black Vesper's pageants.*
Eros. Ay, my lord.
Antony. That which is now a horse, even with a thought
The rack dislimns,* and makes it indistinct 10
As water is in water.
Eros. It does, my lord.
Antony. My good knave Eros, now thy captain is
Even such a body. Here I am Antony,
Yet cannot hold this visible shape, my knave.
I made these wars for Egypt, and the Queen, 15
Whose heart I thought I had, for she had mine,
Which, whilst it was mine, had annexed unto't
A million more, now lost—she, Eros, has
Packed cards* with Caesar, and false-played my glory
Unto an enemy's triumph. 20
Nay, weep not, gentle Eros, there is left us
Ourselves to end ourselves.

[*Enter Mardian.*]

O, thy vile lady!
She has robbed me of my sword.
Mardian. No, Antony.
My mistress loved thee and her fortunes mingled
With thine entirely.
Antony. Hence, saucy eunuch, peace! 25
She hath betrayed me and shall die the death.
Mardian. Death of one person can be paid but once,
And that she has discharged. What thou wouldst do
Is done unto thy hand. The last she spake
Was "Antony! Most noble Antony!" 30
Then in the midst a tearing groan did break
The name of Antony. It was divided

8. *black Vesper's pageants: sights celebrating the coming of night.*
10. *rack dislimns: The shifting cloud erases.*
19. *Packed cards: cheated with the deck of cards.*

Between her heart and lips. She rendered life,
Thy name so buried in her.

Antony. Dead, then?

Mardian. Dead.

Antony. Unarm, Eros. The long day's task is done, *35*
And we must sleep. [*To Mardian.*] That thou depart'st hence safe
Does pay thy labor richly. Go. [*Exit Mardian.*]
Off, pluck off.
The sevenfold shield of Ajax* cannot keep
The battery* from my heart. O, cleave, my sides!
Heart, once be stronger than thy continent,* *40*
Crack thy frail case! Apace, Eros, apace.
No more a soldier. Bruised pieces, go.
You have been nobly borne. From me awhile.
[*Exit Eros.*]
I will o'ertake thee, Cleopatra, and
Weep for my pardon. So it must be, for now *45*
All length* is torture. Since the torch is out,
Lie down, and stray no farther. Now all labor
Mars what it does. Yea, very force entangles
Itself with strength. Seal then, and all is done.
Eros!–I come, my queen.–Eros!–Stay for me. *50*
Where souls do couch on flowers, we'll hand in hand,
And with our sprightly port make the ghosts gaze.
Dido and her Aeneas* shall want troops,
And all the haunt be ours. Come, Eros, Eros!

[*Enter Eros.*]

Eros. What would my lord?

Antony. Since Cleopatra died *55*
I have lived in such dishonor that the gods
Detest my baseness. I, that with my sword
Quartered the world and o'er green Neptune's back
With ships made cities, condemn myself to lack

38. *sevenfold . . . Ajax: The shield of Ajax with its seven thicknesses of hide stopped the lance of Hector.*
39. *battery: the assault of grief upon his heart.*
40. *continent: the body which contains the heart.*
46. *length: extension of life.*
49. *seal: conclude, as with a legal document.*
53. *Dido . . . Aeneas: another famous pair of lovers.*

The courage of a woman—less noble mind 60
Than she which by her death our Caesar tells
"I am conqueror of myself." Thou art sworn, Eros,
That when the exigent* should come, which now
Is come indeed, when I should see behind me
The inevitable prosecution* of 65
Disgrace and horror, that, on my command,
Thou then wouldst kill me. Do't, the time is come.
Thou strikest not me, 'tis Caesar thou defeat'st.
Put color in thy cheek.

Eros. The gods withhold me!
Shall I do that which all the Parthian darts, 70
Though enemy, lost aim and could not?

Antony. Eros.
Wouldst thou be windowed* in great Rome and see
Thy master thus with pleached* arms, bending down
His corrigible* neck, his face subdued
To penetrative shame, whilst the wheeled seat 75
Of fortunate Caesar, drawn before him, branded
His baseness that ensued?

Eros. I would not see't.

Antony. Come then. For with a wound I must be cured.
Draw that thy honest sword, which thou hast worn
Most useful for thy country.

Eros. O sir, pardon me. 80

Antony. When I did make thee free, sworest thou not then
To do this when I bade thee? Do it at once,
Or thy precedent* services are all
But accidents unpurposed. Draw, and come.

Eros. Turn from me then that noble countenance 85
Wherein the worship of the whole world lies.

Antony. Lo thee! [*Turns from him.*]

Eros. My sword is drawn.

Antony. Then let it do at once
The thing why thou hast drawn it.

63. *exigent: crisis.*
65. *prosecution: pursuit.*
72. *windowed: looking from a window.*
73. *pleached: folded.*
74. *corrigible: submissive.*
83. *precedent: former.*

Eros. My dear master,
My captain, and my emperor, let me say, 90
Before I strike this bloody stroke, farewell.
Antony. 'Tis said, man, and farewell.
Eros. Farewell, great chief. Shall I strike now?
Antony. Now, Eros.
Eros. Why, there then! Thus I do escape the sorrow
Of Antony's death. [*Kills himself.*]
Antony. Thrice nobler than myself! 95
Thou teachest me, O valiant Eros, what
I should, and thou couldst not. My queen and Eros
Have by their grave instruction got upon me
A nobleness in record. But I will be
A bridegroom in my death, and run into't 100
As to a lover's bed. Come then, and, Eros,
Thy master dies thy scholar. To do thus
[*Falls on his sword.*]
I learned of thee. How? Not dead? Not dead?
The guard, ho! O, dispatch me!

[*Enter Dercetas and a Company of the Guard.*]

1. *Guardsman.* What's the noise?
Antony. I have done my work ill, friends. O, make an end 105
Of what I have begun.
2. *Guardsman.* The star is fallen.
1. *Guardsman.* And time is at his period.
Omnes. Alas, and woe!
Antony. Let him that loves me strike me dead.
1. *Guardsman.* Not I.
2. *Guardsman.* Nor I.
3. *Guardsman.* Nor any one. [*Exeunt the Guardsmen.*] 110
Dercetas. Thy death and fortunes bid thy followers fly.
This sword but shown to Caesar, with this tidings,
Shall enter* me with him.

[*Enter Diomedes.*]

Diomedes. Where's Antony?
Dercetas. There, Diomed, there.
Diomedes. Lives he?

113. *enter: commend.*

Wilt thou not answer, man? [*Exit Dercetas.*] *115*

Antony. Art thou there, Diomed? Draw thy sword, and give me
Sufficing strokes for death.

Diomedes. Most absolute lord,
My mistress Cleopatra sent me to thee.

Antony. When did she send thee?

Diomedes. Now, my lord.

Antony. Where is she?

Diomedes. Locked in her monument. She had a prophesying fear *120*
Of what hath come to pass. For when she saw
—Which never shall be found—you did suspect
She had disposed* with Caesar, and that* your rage
Would not be purged, she sent you word she was dead;
But, fearing since how it might work, hath sent *125*
Me to proclaim the truth, and I am come,
I dread, too late.

Antony. Too late, good Diomed. Call my guard, I prithee.

Diomedes. What ho! The Emperor's guard! The guard, what ho!
Come, your lord calls! *130*

[*Enter four or five of the Guard of Antony.*]

Antony. Bear me, good friends, where Cleopatra bides.
'Tis the last service that I shall command you.

1. *Guardsman.* Woe, woe are we, sir, you may not live to wear
All your true followers out.

Omnes. Most heavy day!

Antony. Nay, good my fellows, do not please sharp Fate *135*
To grace it with your sorrows. Bid that welcome
Which comes to punish us, and we punish it,
Seeming to bear it lightly. Take me up.
I have led you oft. Carry me now, good friends,
And have my thanks for all. *140*

[*Exeunt, bearing Antony.*]

123. *disposed: come to terms.*
123. *that: because.*

SCENE XV. *Cleopatra's palace. A Monument.*

[*Enter Cleopatra and her Maids aloft, with Charmian and Iras.*]

Cleopatra. O Charmian, I will never go from hence.
Charmian. Be comforted, dear madam.
Cleopatra. No, I will not.
All strange and terrible events are welcome,
But comforts we despise. Our size of sorrow,
Proportioned to our cause, must be as great 5
As that which makes it.

[*Enter, below, Diomed.*]

How now? Is he dead?
Diomedes. His death's upon him, but not dead.
Look out o' the other side your monument.
His guard have brought him thither.

[*Enter, below, Antony and the Guard, bearing him.*]

Cleopatra. O sun,
Burn the great sphere thou movest in. Darkling* stand 10
The varying shore o' the world! O Antony,
Antony, Antony! Help, Charmian, help, Iras, help!
Help, friends below, let's draw him hither.
Antony. Peace!
Not Caesar's valor hath o'erthrown Antony,
But Antony's hath triumphed on itself. 15
Cleopatra. So it should be, that none but Antony
Should conquer Antony, but woe 'tis so!
Antony. I am dying, Egypt, dying, only
I here importune death awhile, until
Of many thousand kisses the poor last 20
I lay upon thy lips.
Cleopatra. I dare not, dear.
Dear my lord, pardon. I dare not,
Lest I be taken. Not the imperious show
Of the full-fortuned Caesar ever shall
Be brooched* with me. If knife, drugs, serpents, have 25
Edge, sting, or operation, I am safe.

10. *Darkling: in the dark.*
25. *brooched: adorned.*

Your wife Octavia, with her modest eyes
And still conclusion,* shall acquire no honor
Demuring* upon me. But come, come, Antony!
Help me, my women—we must draw thee up. 30
Assist, good friends.

Antony. O, quick, or I am gone.

Cleopatra. Here's sport indeed! How heavy weighs my lord!
Our strength is all gone into heaviness.*
That makes the weight. Had I great Juno's power,
The strong-winged Mercury should fetch thee up 35
And set thee by Jove's side. Yet come a little—
Wishers were ever fools. O, come, come, come.
[*They heave Antony aloft to Cleopatra.*]
And welcome, welcome! Die where thou hast lived.
Quicken with kissing. Had my lips that power,
Thus would I wear them out.

Omnes. A heavy sight! 40

Antony. I am dying, Egypt, dying.
Give me some wine, and let me speak a little.

Cleopatra. No, let me speak, and let me rail so high
That the false huswife* Fortune break her wheel,
Provoked by my offense.

Antony. One word, sweet queen. 45
Of Caesar seek your honor, with your safety. O!

Cleopatra. They do not go together.

Antony. Gentle, hear me.
None about Caesar trust but Proculeius.

Cleopatra. My resolution and my hands I'll trust,
None about Caesar. 50

Antony. The miserable change now at my end
Lament nor sorrow at, but please your thoughts
In feeding them with those my former fortunes,
Wherein I lived the greatest prince o' the world,
The noblest, and do now not basely die, 55
Not cowardly put off my helmet to
My countryman—a Roman by a Roman

28. *still conclusion: silent censure.*
29. *Demuring: looking innocently.*
33. *heaviness: both grief and dead weight.*
44. *huswife: an older form of "hussy" (now "housewife").*

Valiantly vanquished. Now my spirit is going,
I can no more.
Cleopatra. Noblest of men, woo't die?
Hast thou no care of me? Shall I abide *60*
In this dull world, which in thy absence is
No better than a sty? O, see, my women, [*Antony dies.*]
The crown o' the earth doth melt. My lord!
O, withered is the garland* of war!
The soldier's pole* is fall'n. Young boys and girls *65*
Are level now with men. The odds* is gone,
And there is nothing left remarkable
Beneath the visiting moon. [*Faints.*]
Charmian. O, quietness, lady!
Iras. She's dead too, our sovereign.
Charmian. Lady!
Iras. Madam!
Charmian. O madam, madam, madam!
Iras. Royal Egypt! *70*
Empress! [*Cleopatra stirs.*]
Charmian. Peace, peace, Iras!
Cleopatra. No more but e'en a woman, and commanded
By such poor passion as the maid that milks
And does the meanest chares.* It were for me *75*
To throw my sceptre at the injurious gods,
To tell them that this world did equal theirs
Till they had stol'n our jewel. All's but naught.
Patience is sottish,* and impatience does
Become a dog that's mad. Then is it sin *80*
To rush into the secret house of death
Ere death dare come to us? How do you, women?
What, what! Good cheer! Why, how now, Charmian?
My noble girls! Ah, women, women, look!
Our lamp is spent, it's out! Good sirs,* take heart. *85*
We'll bury him, and then, what's brave, what's noble,
Let's do it after the high Roman fashion,
And make death proud to take us. Come, away.

64. *garland: flower.*
65. *pole: Maypole.*
66. *odds: distinction between great and little.*
75. *chares: chores.*
79. *sottish: foolish.*
85. *sirs: the women.*

This case of that huge spirit now is cold.
Ah, women, women! Come, we have no friend 90
But resolution, and the briefest end.

[*Exeunt, those aloft bearing off Antony's body.*]

ACT V

SCENE I. *Alexandria. Caesar's camp.*

[*Enter Caesar, Agrippa, Dolabella, Maecenas, Gallus, Proculeius, and others, his Council of War.*]

Caesar. Go to him, Dolabella, bid him yield.
Being so frustrate, tell him he mocks*
The pauses* that he makes.
Dolabella. Caesar, I shall. [*Exit.*]

[*Enter Dercetas, with the sword of Antony.*]

Caesar. Wherefore is that? And what art thou that darest
Appear thus to us?
Dercetes. I am called Dercetas. 5
Mark Antony I served, who best was worthy
Best to be served. Whilst he stood up and spoke,
He was my master, and I wore my life
To spend upon his haters. If thou please
To take me to thee, as I was to him 10
I'll be to Caesar. If thou pleasest not,
I yield thee up my life.
Caesar. What is't thou say'st?
Dercetas. I say, O Caesar, Antony is dead.
Caesar. The breaking of so great a thing should make
A greater crack. The round world 15
Should have shook lions into civil streets
And citizens to their dens. The death of Antony
Is not a single doom. In the name lay
A moiety* of the world.
Dercetas. He is dead, Caesar,
Not by a public minister of justice, 20

2. *mocks: makes ridiculous.*
3. *pauses: delays.*
19. *moiety: half.*

Nor by a hired knife, but that self* hand
Which writ his honor in the acts it did
Hath, with the courage which the heart did lend it,
Splitted the heart. This is his sword.
I robbed his wound of it. Behold it stained 25
With his most noble blood.

Caesar. Look you sad, friends?
The gods rebuke me, but it is tidings
To wash the eyes of kings.

Agrippa. And strange it is
That nature must compel us to lament
Our most persisted deeds.

Maecenas. His taints and honors 30
Waged equal* with him.

Agrippa. A rarer spirit never
Did steer humanity. But you, gods, will give us
Some faults to make us men. Caesar is touched.

Maecenas. When such a spacious mirror's set before him,
He needs must see himself.

Caesar. O Antony, 35
I have followed thee to this! But we do lance
Diseases in our bodies. I must perforce
Have shown to thee such a declining day
Or look on thine. We could not stall* together
In the whole world. But yet let me lament 40
With tears as sovereign* as the blood of hearts
That thou, my brother, my competitor
In top of all design,* my mate in empire,
Friend and companion in the front of war,
The arm of mine own body, and the heart 45
Where mine his thoughts did kindle—that our stars,
Unreconcilable, should divide
Our equalness to this. Hear me, good friends—

[*Enter an Egyptian.*]

But I will tell you at some meeter season.
The business of this man looks out of him. 50

21. *self: same.*
31. *Waged equal: were an equal match.*
39. *stall: dwell.*
41. *sovereign: strong.*
42–43. *my competitor . . . design: my associate in the greatest enterprises.*

We'll hear him what he says. Whence are you?
Egyptian. A poor Egyptian yet. The Queen my mistress,
Confined in all she has, her monument,
Of thy intents desires instruction,
That she preparedly may frame herself 55
To the way she's forced to.
Caesar. Bid her have good heart.
She soon shall know of us, by some of ours,
How honorable and how kindly we
Determine for her. For Caesar cannot live
To be ungentle.
Egyptian. So the gods preserve thee! [*Exit.*] 60
Caesar. Come hither, Proculeius. Go and say
We purpose her no shame. Give her what comforts
The quality of her passion* shall require,
Lest, in her greatness, by some mortal stroke
She do defeat us. For her life in Rome 65
Would be eternal in our triumph. Go,
And with your speediest bring us what she says
And how you find of her.
Proculeius. Caesar, I shall [*Exit.*].
Caesar. Gallus, go you along. [*Exit Gallus.*] Where's Dolabella,
To second Proculeius?
Omnes. Dolabella! 70
Caesar. Let him alone, for I remember now
How he's employed. He shall in time be ready.
Go with me to my tent, where you shall see
How hardly I was drawn into this war,
How calm and gentle I proceeded still 75
In all my writings. Go with me, and see
What I can show in this. [*Exeunt.*]

SCENE II. *Alexandria. A room in the Monument.*

[*Enter Cleopatra, Charmian, Iras, and Mardian.*]

Cleopatra. My desolation does begin to make
A better life. 'Tis paltry to be Caesar.
Not being Fortune, he's but Fortune's knave,*

63. *passion: emotion.*
3. *knave: servant.*

A minister* of her will. And it is great
To do that thing that ends all other deeds, 5
Which shackles accidents and bolts up change,
Which sleeps, and never palates more the dung,
The beggar's nurse and Caesar's.

[*Enter, to the gates of the monument, Proculeius.*]

Proculeius. Caesar sends greeting to the Queen of Egypt,
And bids thee study on what fair demands 10
Thou mean'st to have him grant thee.
Cleopatra. What's thy name?
Proculeius. My name is Proculeius.
Cleopatra. Antony
Did tell me of you, bade me trust you, but
I do not greatly care to be deceived,*
That have no use for trusting. If your master 15
Would have a queen his beggar, you must tell him
That majesty, to keep decorum, must
No less beg than a kingdom. If he please
To give me conquered Egypt for my son,
He gives me so much of mine own as I 20
Will kneel to him with thanks.
Proculeius. Be of good cheer.
Y'are fall'n into a princely hand; fear nothing.
Make your full reference* freely to my lord,
Who is so full of grace that it flows over
On all that need. Let me report to him 25
Your sweet dependency, and you shall find
A conqueror that will pray in aid for kindness,*
Where he for grace is kneeled to.
Cleopatra. Pray you, tell him
I am his fortune's vassal, and I send him
The greatness he has got.* I hourly learn 30
A doctrine of obedience, and would gladly
Look him i' the face.
Proculeius. This I'll report, dear lady.

4. *minister: underling.*
14. *to be deceived: whether I am deceived or not.*
23. *reference: request.*
27. *pray . . . kindness: ask your help in suggesting kindnesses he can do for you.*
29–30. *I . . . got: I acknowledge the superiority he has won.*

Have comfort, for I know your plight is pitied
Of him that caused it.

[*Enter Gallus and Roman Soldiers into the monument.*]

Gallus. You see how easily she may be surprised. 35
[*They seize Cleopatra.*]
Guard her till Caesar come. [*Exit.*]
Iras. Royal Queen!
Charmian. O Cleopatra! Thou art taken, Queen.
Cleopatra. Quick, quick, good hands! [*Draws a dagger.*]
Proculeius. Hold, worthy lady, hold!
[*Disarms her.*]
Do not yourself such wrong, who are in this 40
Relieved, but not betrayed.
Cleopatra. What, of death too,
That rids our dogs of languish?*
Proculeius. Cleopatra,
Do not abuse my master's bounty by
The undoing of yourself. Let the world see
His nobleness well acted, which your death 45
Will never let come forth.
Cleopatra. Where art thou, death?
Come hither, come! Come, come, and take a queen
Worth many babes and beggars!
Proculeius. O, temperance, lady!
Cleopatra. Sir, I will eat no meat. I'll not drink, sir.
If idle talk will once be necessary, 50
I'll not sleep neither. This mortal house I'll ruin,
Do Caesar what he can. Know, sir, that I
Will not wait pinioned at your master's court,
Nor once be chastised with the sober eye
Of dull Octavia. Shall they hoist me up 55
And show me to the shouting varletry*
Of censuring Rome? Rather a ditch in Egypt
Be gentle grave unto me! Rather on Nilus' mud
Lay me stark naked, and let the waterflies
Blow me into abhorring!* Rather make 60
My country's high pyramides my gibbet

42. *languish: misery produced by sickness or injury.*
56. *varletry: mob.*
60. *Blow . . . abhorring: cause me to swell until my body is loathsome.*

And hang me up in chains!
Proculeius. You do extend
These thoughts of horror further than you shall
Find cause in Caesar.

[*Enter Dolabella.*]

Dolabella. Proculeius,
What thou hast done thy master Caesar knows, 65
And he hath sent me for thee. For the Queen,
I'll take her to my guard.
Proculeius. So, Dolabella,
It shall content me best. Be gentle to her.
[*To Cleopatra.*] To Caesar I will speak what you shall please,
If you'll employ me to him.
Cleopatra. Say, I would die. 70
[*Exeunt Proculeius with Soldiers.*]
Dolabella. Most noble Empress, you have heard of me?
Cleopatra. I cannot tell.
Dolabella. Assuredly you know me.
Cleopatra. No matter, sir, what I have heard or known.
You laugh when boys or women tell their dreams—
Is't not your trick?
Dolabella. I understand not, madam. 75
Cleopatra. I dreamt there was an Emperor Antony.
O, such another sleep, that I might see
But such another man!
Dolabella. If it might please ye—
Cleopatra. His face was as the heavens, and therein stuck
A sun and moon, which kept their course and lighted 80
The little O,* the earth.
Dolabella. Most sovereign creature—
Cleopatra. His legs bestrid the ocean. His reared arm
Crested the world. His voice was propertied
As all the tuned spheres,* and that to friends.
But when he meant to quail* and shake the orb, 85
He was as rattling thunder. For his bounty,
There was no winter in't, an autumn 'twas

81. *O: a circle.*
83–84. *was . . . spheres: made music like the turning spheres.*
85. *quail: overpower.*

That grew the more by reaping. His delights
Were dolphin-like, they showed his back above
The element they lived in. In his livery *90*
Walked crowns and crownets,* realms and islands were
As plates* dropped from his pocket.

Dolabella. Cleopatra—

Cleopatra. Think you there was, or might be, such a man
As this I dreamt of?

Dolabella. Gentle madam, no.

Cleopatra. You lie, up to the hearing of the gods. *95*
But if there be nor ever were one such,
It's past the size of dreaming.* Nature wants stuff
To vie strange forms with fancy, yet to imagine
An Antony were nature's piece 'gainst fancy,
Condemning shadows quiet.*

Dolabella. Hear me, good madam. *100*
Your loss is as yourself, great, and you bear it
As answering to the weight. Would I might never
O'ertake pursued success but I do feel,*
By the rebound of yours, a grief that smites
My very heart at root.

Cleopatra. I thank you, sir. *105*
Know you what Caesar means to do with me?

Dolabella. I am loath to tell you what I would you knew.

Cleopatra. Nay, pray you, sir—

Dolabella. Though he be honorable—

Cleopatra. He'll lead me, then, in triumph?

Dolabella. Madam, he will. I know't. *110*

Flourish and shouts within: "Make way there! Caesar!"
Then enter Caesar, with Proculeius, Gallus, Maecenas,
and others of his Train.

Caesar. Which is the Queen of Egypt?

Dolabella. It is the Emperor, madam. [*Cleopatra kneels.*]

91. *crowns and crownets: kings and princes.*
92. *plates: silver coins.*
97. *It's . . . dreaming: Dreams cannot reach the reality.*
97–100. *Nature . . . quite: Nature cannot compete with the fancy (imagination) in the invention of unusual forms (creatures), but in Antony Nature outdid herself by surpassing anything the imagination could have produced.*
102–103. *Would . . . feel: May I never achieve any goal if I do not feel.*

Caesar. Arise! You shall not kneel.
I pray you rise, rise, Egypt.
Cleopatra. Sir, the gods 115
Will have it thus. My master and my lord
I must obey.
Caesar. Take to you no hard thoughts.
The record of what injuries you did us,
Though written in our flesh, we shall remember
As things but done by chance.
Cleopatra Sole sir o' the world, 120
I cannot project* mine own cause so well
To make it clear, but do confess I have
Been laden with like frailties which before
Have often shamed our sex.
Caesar. Cleopatra, know
We will extenuate rather than enforce.* 125
If you apply* yourself to our intents,
Which towards you are most gentle, you shall find
A benefit in this change. But if you seek
To lay on me a cruelty by taking
Antony's course, you shall bereave yourself 130
Of my good purposes and put your children
To that destruction which I'll guard them from
If thereon you rely. I'll take my leave.
Cleopatra. And may, through all the world. 'Tis yours, and we,
Your scutcheons* and your signs of conquest, shall 135
Hang in what place you please. Here, my good lord.
Caesar. You shall advise me in all for Cleopatra.
Cleopatra. This is the brief* of money, plate, and jewels
I am possessed of. 'Tis exactly valued,
Not petty things admitted. Where's Seleucus?
[*Enter Seleucus.*] 140
Seleucus. Here, madam.
Cleopatra. This is my treasurer. Let him speak, my lord,
Upon his peril, that I have reserved
To myself nothing. Speak the truth, Seleucus.

121. *project: set forth.*
125. *enforce: emphasize.*
126. *apply: submit.*
135. *scutcheons: shields with military trappings; symbols of conquest.*
138. *brief: summary.*

Seleucus. Madam, 145
I had rather seal my lips than to my peril
Speak that which is not.
Cleopatra. What have I kept back?
Seleucus. Enough to purchase what you have made known.
Caesar. Nay, blush not, Cleopatra. I approve
Your wisdom in the deed.
Cleopatra. See, Caesar! O, behold 150
How pomp is followed! Mine will now be yours,
And should we shift estates,* yours would be mine.
The ingratitude of this Seleucus does
Even make me wild. O slave, of no more trust
Than love that's hired! What, goest thou back? Thou shalt 155
Go back, I warrant thee, but I'll catch thine eyes,
Though they had wings. Slave, soulless villain, dog!
O rarely base!
Caesar. Good Queen, let us entreat you.
Cleopatra. O Caesar, what a wounding shame is this,
That thou vouchsafing here to visit me, 160
Doing the honor of thy lordliness
To one so meek, that mine own servant should
Parcel* the sum of my disgraces by
Addition of his envy! Say, good Caesar,
That I some lady trifles have reserved, 165
Immoment toys, things of such dignity
As we greet modern friends withal. And say
Some nobler token I have kept apart
For Livia and Octavia, to induce
Their meditation. Must I be unfolded 170
With one that I have bred? The gods! It smites me
Beneath the fall I have. [*To Seleucus.*] Prithee go hence,
Or I shall show the cinders* of my spirits
Through the ashes of my chance.* Wert thou a man,
Thou wouldst have mercy on me.
Caesar. Forbear, Seleucus. 175
[*Exit Seleucus.*]

152. *estates: positions.*
163. *Parcel: add to.*
173. *cinders: concealed fire.*
174. *chance: fortune.*

Cleopatra. Be it known that we, the greatest, are misthought*
For things that others do, and when we fall,
We answer others' merits* in our name,
Are therefore to be pitied.

Caesar. Cleopatra,
Not what you have reserved, nor what acknowledged, *180*
Put we i' the roll of conquest. Still be 't yours,
Bestow it at your pleasure, and believe
Caesar's no merchant, to make prize* with you
Of things that merchants sold. Therefore be cheered,
Make not your thoughts your prison.* No, dear Queen, *185*
For we intend so to dispose you as
Yourself shall give us counsel. Feed and sleep.
Our care and pity is so much upon you
That we remain your friend. And so adieu.

Cleopatra. My master, and my lord!

Caesar. Not so. Adieu. *190*

[*Flourish. Exeunt Caesar and his Train.*]

Cleopatra. He words me, girls, he words me, that I should not
Be noble to myself! But hark thee, Charmian.

[*Whispers to Charmian.*]

Iras. Finish, good lady. The bright day is done,
And we are for the dark.

Cleopatra. Hie* thee again.
I have spoke already, and it is provided. *195*
Go put it to the haste.*

Charmian. Madam, I will.

[*Enter Dolabella.*]

Dolabella. Where is the Queen?

Charmian. Behold, sir. [*Exit.*]

Cleopatra. Dolabella!

Dolabella. Madam, as thereto sworn, by your command,
Which my love makes religion to obey,

176. *misthought: misjudged.*
178. *We . . . merits: We take on in our name the misdeeds of others.*
183. *make prize: quibble about value.*
185. *Make . . . prisons: Do not let your imagination convince you that you are a prisoner.*
194. *Hie: hasten.*
196. *put . . . haste: hurry it up.*

I tell you this. Caesar through Syria *200*
Intends his journey, and within three days
You with your children will he send before.
Make your best use of this. I have performed
Your pleasure and my promise.

Cleopatra. Dolabella,
I shall remain your debtor.

Dolabella. I your servant. *205*
Adieu, good Queen. I must attend on Caesar.

Cleopatra. Farewell, and thanks. [*Exit Dolabella.*]
Now, Iras, what think'st thou?
Thou, an Egyptian puppet, shalt be shown
In Rome as well as I. Mechanic slaves*
With greasy aprons, rules, and hammers shall *210*
Uplift us to the view. In their thick breaths,
Rank of gross diet, shall we be enclouded,
And forced to drink their vapor.

Iras. The gods forbid!

Cleopatra. Nay, 'tis most certain, Iras. Saucy lictors*
Will catch at us like strumpets, and scald* rhymers *215*
Ballad us out o' tune. The quick comedians
Extemporally will stage us, and present
Our Alexandrian revels. Antony
Shall be brought drunken forth, and I shall see
Some squeaking Cleopatra* boy my greatness *220*
I' the posture of a whore.

Iras. O the good gods!

Cleopatra. Nay, that's certain.

Iras. I'll never see't! For I am sure my nails
Are stronger than mine eyes.

Cleopatra. Why, that's the way
To fool their preparation, and to conquer *225*
Their most absurd intents.

[*Enter Charmian.*]

208. *puppet: i.e., in a puppet show.*
209. *Mechanic slaves: laborers.*
214. *lictors: officers of the law.*
215. *scald: scurvy.*
220. *squeaking Cleopatra: in Shakespeare's day young boys with high voices played all female roles.*

Now, Charmian!
Show me, my women, like a queen. Go fetch
My best attires. I am again for Cydnus,
To meet Mark Antony. Sirrah Iras, go.
Now, noble Charmian, we'll dispatch indeed, *230*
And when thou hast done this chare,* I'll give thee leave
To play till doomsday. Bring our crown and all.
[*Exit Iras. A noise within.*]
Wherefore's this noise?

[*Enter a Guardsman.*]

Guardsman. Here is a rural fellow
That will not be denied your Highness' presence.
He brings you figs. *235*

Cleopatra. Let him come in. [*Exit Guardsman.*]
What poor an instrument
May do a noble deed! He brings me liberty.
My resolution's placed, and I have nothing
Of woman in me. Now from head to foot
I am marble-constant. Now the fleeting moon *240*
No planet is of mine.

[*Enter Guardsman, and Clown* with basket.*]

Guardsman. This is the man.

Cleopatra. Avoid,* and leave him. [*Exit Guardsman.*]
Hast thou the pretty worm* of Nilus there,
That kills and pains not?

Clown. Truly, I have him. But I would not be the party *245*
that should desire you to touch him, for his biting is
immortal.* Those that do die of it do seldom or never
recover.

Cleopatra. Rememberest thou any that have died on't?

Clown. Very many, men and women too. I heard of one *250*
of them no longer than yesterday—a very honest woman,
but something given to lie, as a woman should not do
but in the way of honesty—how she died of the biting
of it, what pain she felt. Truly, she makes a very good
report o' the worm. But he that will believe all that they *255*

231. *chare: chore.*
241. *Clown: rural fellow.*
242. *Avoid: Go.*
243. *worm: snake.*
247. *immortal: deadly.*

say shall never be saved by half that they do. But this is most fallible, the worm's an odd worm.

Cleopatra. Get thee hence. Farewell.

Clown. I wish you all joy of the worm.

[*Sets down his basket.*]

Cleopatra. Farewell.

Clown. You must think this, look you, that the worm will do his kind.*

Cleopatra. Ay, ay. Farewell.

Clown. Look you, the worm is not to be trusted but in the keeping of wise people, for indeed there is no goodness in the worm. *265*

Cleopatra. Take thou no care. It shall be heeded.

Clown. Very good. Give it nothing, I pray you, for it is not worth the feeding.

Cleopatra. Will it eat me?

Clown. You must not think I am so simple but I know the devil himself will not eat a woman. I know that a woman is a dish for the gods, if the devil dress* her not. But truly, these same whoreson* devils do the gods great harm in their women, for in every ten that they make, the devils mar five. *270*

Cleopatra. Well, get thee gone. Farewell.

Clown. Yes, forsooth. I wish you joy o' the worm. [*Exit.*]

[*Enter Iras with a robe, crown, etc.*]

Cleopatra. Give me my robe, put on my crown. I have
Immortal longings in me. Now no more *280*
The juice of Egypt's grape shall moist this lip.
Yare, yare,* good Iras, quick. Methinks I hear
Antony call. I see him rouse himself
To praise my noble act. I hear him mock
The luck of Caesar, which the gods give men *285*
To excuse their after wrath. Husband, I come.
Now to that name my courage prove my title!
I am fire and air. My other elements*
I give to baser life. So, have you done?
Come then, and take the last warmth of my lips. *290*

262. *kind: what his nature requires.*
273. *dress: prepare.*
274. *whoreson: bastard.*
282. *yare: nimbly.*
288. *My other elements: earth and water.*

Farewell, kind Charmian. Iras, long farewell.
[*Kisses them. Iras falls and dies.*]
Have I the aspic* in my lips? Dost fall?
If thou and nature can so gently part,
The stroke of death is as a lover's pinch,
Which hurts, and is desired. Dost thou lie still? *295*
If thus thou vanishes, thou tell'st the world
It is not worth leave-taking.

Charmian. Dissolve, thick cloud, and rain, that I may say
The gods themselves do weep!

Cleopatra. This proves me base.
If she first meet the curled Antony, *300*
He'll make demand of her, and spend that kiss
Which is my heaven to have. Come, thou mortal wretch,

[*To an asp, which she applies to her breast.*]

With thy sharp teeth this knot intrinsicate*
Of life at once untie. Poor venomous fool,
Be angry, and dispatch.* O, couldst thou speak, *305*
That I might hear thee call great Caesar ass
Unpolicied!*

Charmian. O Eastern star!

Cleopatra. Peace, peace!
Dost thou not see my baby at my breast,
That sucks the nurse asleep?

Charmian. O, break! O, break!

Cleopatra. As sweet as balm, as soft as air, as gentle— *310*
O Antony! Nay, I will take thee too.
[*Applies another asp to her arm.*]
What should I stay— [*Dies.*]

Charmian. In this wild world? So, fare thee well.
Now boast thee, death, in thy possession lies
A lass unparalleled. Downy windows, close, *315*
And golden Phoebus never be beheld
Of eyes again so royal! Your crown's awry.
I'll mend it, and then play—

[*Enter the Guard, rushing in.*]

292. *aspic: asp.*
303. *intrinsicate: intricate.*
305. *dispatch: hasten.*
307. *Unpolicied: tricked.*

1. *Guardsman.* Where's the Queen?
Charmian. Speak softly, wake her not.
1. *Guardsman.* Caesar hath sent—
Charmian. Too slow a messenger. 320
[*Applies an asp.*]
O, come apace, dispatch. I partly feel thee.
1. *Guardsman.* Approach, ho! All's not well. Caesar's beguiled.*
2. *Guardsman.* There's Dolabella sent from Caesar. Call him.
1. *Guardsman.* What work is here! Charmian, is this well done?
Charmian. It is well done, and fitting for a princess 325
Descended of so many royal kings.
Ah, soldier! [*Charmian dies.*]

[*Enter Dolabella.*]

Dolabella. How goes it here?
2. *Guardsman.* All dead.
Dolabella. Caesar, thy thoughts
Touch their effects* in this. Thyself art coming
To see performed the dreaded act which thou 330
So sought'st to hinder.

[*Enter Caesar and all his Train.*]

Omnes. A way there, a way for Caesar!
Dolabella. O sir, you are too sure an augurer.
That you did fear is done.
Caesar. Bravest at the last,
She levelled* at our purposes, and being royal,
Took her own way. The manner of their deaths? 335
I do not see them bleed.
Dolabella. Who was last with them?
1. *Guardsman.* A simple countryman that brought her figs. This was his basket.
Caesar. Poisoned, then.
1. *Guardsman.* O Caesar,
This Charmian lived but now, she stood and spake.

322. *beguiled: cheated.*
329. *Touch . . . effects: are realized.*
334. *levelled: guessed correctly.*

I found her trimming up the diadem 340
On her dead mistress. Tremblingly she stood,
And on the sudden dropped.

Caesar. O noble weakness!
If they had swallowed poison, 'twould appear
By external swelling. But she looks like sleep,
As she would catch another Antony 345
In her strong toil* of grace.

Dolabella. Here on her breast
There is a vent* of blood, and something blown.*
The like is on her arm.

1. *Guardsman.* This is an aspic's trail. And these fig leaves
Have slime upon them, such as the aspic leaves 350
Upon the caves of Nile.

Caesar. Most probable
That so she died, for her physician tells me
She hath pursued conclusions* infinite
Of easy ways to die. Take up her bed,
And bear her women from the monument. 355
She shall be buried by her Antony,
No grave upon the earth shall clip* in it
A pair so famous. High events as these
Strike* those that make them, and their story is
No less in pity than his glory which 360
Brought them to be lamented. Our army shall
In solemn show attend this funeral,
And then to Rome. Come, Dolabella, see
High order in this great solemnity. [*Exeunt.*]

Questions

1. What thematic conflict is established in the opening lines of the play (I, i: in the exchange between Demetrius and Philo)? Does Antony's first appearance immediately after the exchange seem to bear out the judgment made by Demetrius and Philo?

346. *toil: snare.*
347. *vent: discharge.*
347. *blown: swollen.*
353. *conclusions: experiments.*
357. *clip: clasp.*
359. *Strike: afflict.*

2. Does there appear to be a difference between Antony and Cleopatra in their estimates of the importance of love? If so, relate the difference to specific lines, phrases, and images in Act I, scene i.
3. In Act I, scene ii, what dramatic purpose do you see in the horseplay among Cleopatra's attendants, Enobarbus, and the Soothsayer? Could this comic scene be considered to foreshadow the tragic catastrophe?
4. What does Cleopatra mean by saying of Antony: "A Roman thought hath struck him" (I, ii, 79)? Does this statement again suggest the conflict mentioned in question 1?
5. Antony sees himself as the strong man who values truth above all. (To the Messenger he says, "Who tells me true, though in his tale lie death, / I hear him as he flattered.") Do you perceive any irony in this statement's following so closely upon the scene of the courtiers with the Soothsayer? Does Antony really want to hear the truth about his political fortunes or about himself? Is the function of the Soothsayer comparable to that of Teiresias in **Oedipus Rex?**
6. In Act I, scene ii, Antony both grieves for the death of Fulvia and tells himself and others that he must break off his affair with Cleopatra. Later, however, when Cleopatra appears (I, iii), he seems to say that the death of Fulvia is really good fortune (11. 59–62), and that he will go or stay as Cleopatra advises (11. 66–70). Do you think these apparent discrepancies of purpose suggest an instability of character in Antony?
7. Note that Octavius Caesar and Pompey seem to agree upon the question of what has happened to Antony in Egypt. Do their estimates seemingly proceed more from logical analysis of the facts, or from hope? Are the terms in which each estimates the military capabilities of Antony significantly different?
8. What evidence do we have that Enobarbus offers the only real clarity of insight into the nature of the chief characters and to the situations of the plot? (Consider, for example, Act II, ii, 103–110.) What reputation does he hold among the other characters? What qualities of Cleopatra does he emphasize in his description of her first meeting with Antony (I, ii, 191–206, 207–219, 220–227, 229–233, 236–241)? Does this description really or only apparently conflict with Enobarbus' attitude toward her in Egypt? What attitude does Enobarbus profess to hold toward love? Toward women in general?
9. What evidence do we have that the Soothsayer's analysis of the relation between Antony and Caesar (II, iii) is correct? Does the Soothsayer function here prophetically?
10. Do you find the rapid shifts of scene a flaw in the play? Or do you think this apparently erratic movement from Egypt to Rome, to Pompey's headquarters, to Athens, etc., is dictated by the nature of the play?
11. Cleopatra had carried on an amorous affair with Julius Caesar when he was in Egypt. What references to that intrigue do you find in the play? And how is a difference between it and the love of Antony and Cleopatra made clear?
12. To what extent would you say that the notion of love in this play is

controlled by the kind of society mirrored in the play? (You will want to remember Morton M. Hunt's central thesis, and you must keep in mind that Shakespeare is reflecting the attitudes of Elizabethan England rather than those of ancient Rome or Egypt.)

13. It is often said that the one required ingredient of a tragedy is the recognition scene, in which the tragic hero gains insight into himself, his motives, his situation, and accepts the consequences that these have brought about. Does this "recognition" occur separately for Antony and Cleopatra? What do you identify as Antony's "recognition scene"? Does this "recognition" illuminate the "meaning" of the play for the reader?
14. Find, list, and classify kinds of imagery imbedded in the poetry. For example, consider the references to death and dying, or to earth as a garden. What do such patterns of imagery contribute to the theme of the play?
15. To what extent does the ultimate fate of Antony and Cleopatra fit Aristotle's requirements for the tragic catastrophe? Do you think they accept that fate as justifiable? Does their death seem meaningful to them?

Topics for Composition

A word of warning about essay topics for a complex work like **Antony and Cleopatra** is in order. Generally, the broader the topic, the more diffuse and vague is the resulting theme; generalization succeeds generalization, and one often finds that he is only repeating the critical clichés that have been floating about for years, or that he is laboring the obvious. Neither situation is worth the paper, handwriting, or typing that went into the theme. But a clearly focused, restricted topic can produce original thought and, at best, a genuine understanding of the literary art.

1. Analyze the complexities of Enobarbus' view of Cleopatra. You may wish to give some attention to the shifts in that view.
2. Explain in logical order the reasons for the desertion of Antony by Enobarbus. You may need to arrange chronologically the stages of Enobarbus' change.
3. By a consideration of every mention of the word "death" in the play, analyze the attitudes toward death, and thus, toward life that exist in the world of **Antony and Cleopatra.** (For example, can the loyalties of servants to masters be understood in terms of an attitude toward death?)
4. Explain why you think (or do not think) that Antony becomes an Egyptian, as Cleopatra becomes a Roman. This topic presumably would require you to provide extended definitions and supporting comparisons and contrasts.
5. If your memory of **Julius Caesar** is fresh enough, consider whether Antony in that play is the same Antony as in **Antony and Cleopatra.** If you think that he has changed, analyze the nature of the change. A thorough consideration of this topic obviously requires references to the text of **Julius Caesar.**

6. Consider the recurring imagery of the passing of a day. How does that imagery help to illuminate the meaning of the experience of Antony and Cleopatra? Classify the image patterns and relate them to the play's obvious comment upon life and death.
7. Trace the development of Cleopatra from "strumpet" to great queen through the play. (Does the development lend itself to a chronological pattern of treatment? Or does each stage of the development have to be amplified by analysis of her changing motives and the changing fortunes of the great couple?)
8. Although you can always assume that your reader knows the surface of the play, you cannot assume that he understands as much as you. Therefore, for a person who is puzzled about the seemingly paradoxical character of Antony, explain why he marries Octavia although he presumably loves Cleopatra.
9. From a purely dramatic viewpoint, justify the death scenes of the two protagonists. In your essay, you may want to consider the responsibilities they have for the fortunes of others, and the effect created by a stage littered with corpses.

Poetry

EVERYONE knows that for many centuries love and poetry have been almost inseparable. What is not so well known is that the finest love poetry offers much more than the lyrical expression of romantic emotion. Poets have thought deeply about the relation between love and the purpose of life, and the many meanings that love can have are illuminated by a great variety of reflective poems.

Two of the main preoccupations of reflective love poetry have been the choice between physical and spiritual love and the possibility of escaping that choice by reconciling the two forms. The group of poems that follow can be regarded as an excited conversation on these matters. Edmund Spenser, we see, wishes to link love of physical beauty, which must yield to time, with love of virtue and—finally—of God, the unchanging source of all beauty. In doing so, he draws upon an ancient philosophical concept. The seventeenth-century poet William Cartwright names and defines that concept in "No Platonic Love." But Cartwright also repudiates the Platonic ideal, declaring that the pursuit of such "thin love" is a waste of time. Thus a more complex issue is defined: which kind of love, physical or spiritual, or a combination of the two, makes the most of time? And which is the better test of love, duration or intensity? The whole question receives almost classic expression in Andrew Marvell's "To His Coy Mistress," where ironic treatment of the old *carpe diem* (seize the day) theme leads the poet to a fierce desire to believe in love as a life-giving, world-making force working against the inexplicable natural process that shrinks each man's world to the size of a tomb.

As we might expect, most of our poetic reflections on this problem are highly suggestive rather than explicit and circumstantial; they direct our vision by means of images, metaphors, and symbols that are both thought-provoking and charged with emotion. Shakespeare uses the contrasting metaphors of the guiding star and the court jester to affirm the union of true love with the unchanging order of the mind. e.e. cummings makes syntax stand for intellectualizing in his witty and passionate assertion that to mix philosophy with love is to weaken love and fail to make the most of "Spring." "And death I think is no parenthesis" is his version of the sardonic remark, "The grave's a fine and private place, / But none, I think, do there embrace." The irresolute, alienated modern lover in T. S. Eliot's ironic love song also borrows one of Marvell's metaphors, laughing bitterly at himself as he does so. Remembering the lines

"Let us roll all our strength and all / Our sweetness up into one ball," J. Alfred Prufrock asks:

> And would it have been worth it, after all
> After the cups, the marmalade, the tea,
> Among the porcelain, among some talk of you and me,
> Would it have been worth while
> To have bitten off the matter with a smile,
> To have squeezed the universe into a ball
> To roll it toward some overwhelming question,
> To say: "I am Lazarus, come from the dead,
> Come back to tell you all. . . .

No, he replies to himself, he is not even Prince Hamlet, who at least found the courage of desperation. In sharp contrast is John Donne's bold metaphorical response to similar questions. The exultant lover in "The Anniversary" is scarcely content to compare himself to a prince, and does so casually and parenthetically; for a moment, at least, he feels almost godlike as, secure in the possession of all-suffering love, he serenely envisions "all kings, and all their favorites" drawing to their destruction. Even more startling and impressive is his light-hearted treatment of the rather gruesome thought of two corpses buried together:

> Two graves must hide thine and my corpse,
> If one might, death were no divorce.

Here is a triumphant response to the challenge expressed by Marvell's grimly witty lines about the "fine and private place" where none embrace.

With something more like bravado, perhaps, the speaker in Browning's "Love Among the Ruins" measures the value of love in similar terms, putting into the balance a mighty empire with its centuries of glory on the one hand and a brief, heartfelt embrace on the other.

Finally we have the thoughtful and poignant elaboration of the metaphor of the letter in Horace Gregory's "The Postman's Bell Is Answered Everywhere." His poem further illuminates the question, but, of course, offers no final solution, for this is a question which every person must finally resolve for himself.

Amoretti, Sonnet 79

EDMUND SPENSER

Men call you fayre, and you doe credit it,
for that [1] your selfe ye dayly such doe see:
but the trew fayre,[2] that is the gentle wit,[3]
and vertuous mind, is much more praysd of me.
For all the rest, how ever fayre it be, *5*
shall turne to nought and loose that glorious hew:
but onely that is permanent and free
from frayle corruption, that doth flesh ensew.[4]
That is true beautie: that doth argue you
to be divine and borne of heavenly seed: *10*
deriv'd from that fayre Spirit,[5] from whom al true
And perfect beauty did at first proceed.
He onely fayre, and what he fayre hath made,
all other fayre lyke flowres untymely fade.

1595

1 *Because.*
2 *Fairness, beauty.*
3 *Mind, disposition.*
4 *Overtake.*
5 *God.*

Questions

1. Is the poet making a sharp distinction between beauty and goodness, or is goodness merely a higher degree of beauty? What is the relation between love and virtue?
2. Do the last two lines mean that God did not make all things? If not, what is the meaning?

Sonnet 116

WILLIAM SHAKESPEARE

Let me not to the marriage of true minds
Admit impediments: [1] Love is not love
Which alters when it alteration finds,

Or bends [2] with the remover [3] to remove.
Oh, no! it is an ever-fixéd mark 5
That looks on tempests and is never shaken;
It is the star to every wandering bark,
Whose worth's unknown, although his height [4] be taken.
Love's not Time's fool,[5] though rosy lips and cheeks
Within his bending sickle's compass come; [6] 10
Love alters not with his brief hours and weeks,
But bears it out even to the edge of doom.[7]
If this be error and upon me proved,
I never writ, nor no man ever loved.

1609

[1] *"Impediments" is taken from the Marriage Ceremony in* The Book of Common Prayer: *"If either of you know any impediment, why ye may not be lawfully joined together in Matrimony."*
[2] *Inclines.*
[3] *Restless, changeful persons.*
[4] *Altitude (for navigational purposes).*
[5] *Court jester.*
[6] *Come within the reach of Time's curved scythe.*
[7] *To the Last Judgment.*

Questions

1. Shakespeare is saying, of course, that true love is unaffected by changes in the physical appearance of the loved one. Does he also mean that true love endures even though the loved one is inconstant? Is such faithfulness understandable? What would be the point of it? (In a marriage of two true minds, of course, this kind of alteration would not be a consideration.)
2. What do the principal metaphors of the poem suggest about the relation between love and the whole conduct or meaning of life?

Love Is a Sickness

SAMUEL DANIEL

Love is a sickness full of woes,
All remedies refusing;
A plant that with most cutting grows,

Most barren with best using.
Why so? 5
More we enjoy it, more it dies;
If not enjoyed, it sighing cries
Heigh ho!

Love is a torment of the mind,
A tempest everlasting; 10
And Jove hath made it of a kind
Not well, nor full, nor fasting.
Why so?
More we enjoy it, more it dies;
If not enjoyed, it sighing cries 15
Heigh ho!

1615

Questions

1. What kind of love is this poet talking about?
2. Why, according to the poet, is love always a source of misery?
3. Why, apart from the fact that it causes distress, does the poet call love a sickness?

The Anniversary

JOHN DONNE

All kings, and all their favorites,
All glory of honors, beauties, wits,
The sun itself, which makes times,[1] as they pass,
Is elder by a year, now, than it was
When thou and I first one another saw: 5
All other things to their destruction draw,
Only our love hath no decay;
This, no tomorrow hath, nor yesterday,
Running it never runs from us away,
But truly keeps his first, last, everlasting day. 10

Two graves must hide thine and my corse,
If one might, death were no divorce.

[1] *Seasons.*

Alas! as well as other princes, we
(Who prince enough in one another be)
Must leave at last in death, these eyes, and ears, 15
Oft fed with true oaths, and with sweet salt tears;
But souls where nothing dwells but love
(All other thoughts being inmates [2]) then shall prove [3]
This, or a love increasèd there above,
When bodies to their graves, souls from their graves remove. 20

And then we shall be throughly [4] blest,
But we no more than all the rest;
Here upon earth, we are kings, and none but we
Can be such kings, nor of such subjects be.
Who is so safe as we? where none can do 25
Treason to us, except one of us two.
True and false fears let us refrain,
Let us love nobly, and live, and add again
Years and years unto years, till we attain
To write threescore: this is the second of our reign.

1633

[2] *Temporary lodgers.*
[3] *Experience.*
[4] *Thoroughly.*

Questions

1. Why is the speaker sure that his love is immortal?
2. Why will the lovers, while they remain on earth, be better off even than kings?
3. What will the lovers lose by death? How important is the loss to their relationship with each other? In this connection, what is the significance of the contradictory phrase "sweet salt tears"? Will death change the lovers' status relative to others? Why?
4. Question 3 and the related questions will have suggested what the true fears are that the speaker refers to in line 26. What are the "false fears"?

Song

JOHN DONNE

Go and catch a falling star.
Get with child a mandrake [1] root,

Tell me where all past years are,
  Or who cleft the devil's foot;
Teach me to hear mermaids singing, *5*
Or to keep off envy's stinging,
    And find
    What wind
Serves to advance an honest mind.

If thou be'st born to strange sights, *10*
  Things invisible to see,
Ride ten thousand days and nights
  Till age snow white hairs on thee;
Thou, when thou return'st, wilt tell me
All strange wonders that befell thee, *15*
    And swear
    No where
Lives a woman true, and fair.

If thou find'st one, let me know;
  Such a pilgrimage were sweet. *20*
Yet do not; I would not go,
  Though at next door we might meet.
Though she were true when you met her,
And last, till you write your letter,
    Yet she *25*
    Will be
False, ere I come, to two, or three.

1633

[1] *The mandrake root is forked like the lower part of the human body and was supposed to shriek when it was pulled up.*

Questions

1. Here the poet teases the reader. What means does he use? What is the general effect?
2. Does the poet really believe that there can be no such thing as a woman who is both beautiful and faithful in love? What is the tone of the whole poem? Is it, for example, facetious? Bitter? Gaily cynical? Wryly humorous? Ambivalent?

No Platonic Love

WILLIAM CARTWRIGHT

Tell me no more of minds embracing minds,
    And hearts exchanged for hearts;
That spirits meet, as winds do winds,
    And mix their subt'lest parts;
That two unbodied essences may kiss, *5*
And then like Angels, twist and feel one Bliss.[1]

I was that silly thing that once was wrought [2]
    To practice this thin love;
I climb'd from sex to soul, from soul to thought; [3]
    But thinking there to move,[4] *10*
Headlong I rolled from thought to soul, and then
From soul I lighted at the sex again.

As some strict down-looked men pretend to fast,
    Who yet in closets eat;
So lovers who profess they spirits taste, *15*
    Feed yet on grosser meat;
I know they boast they souls to souls convey,
Howe'r they meet, the body is the way.

Come, I will undeceive thee: they that tread
    Those vain aerial ways, *20*
Are like young heirs and alchemists misled
    To waste their wealth and days,
For searching thus to be for ever rich,
They only find a med'cine for the itch.

1635

[1] *I.e., a pure, impersonal happiness.*
[2] *Persuaded.*
[3] *In Platonic love the search for beauty is supposed to lead from the sensual to the ideal, or purely abstract. "Soul" here may be taken to mean something like imagination.*
[4] *To move in a higher sphere or orbit, so to speak.*

Questions

1. In the first stanza, Cartwright illustrates the language of spiritual love, but not quite fairly. What are the elements that make for parody?

2. Does "thinking," in the tenth line, have the same sense as "thought," in the ninth? What is the effect of the repetition of the word?
3. What is the "itch" that motivates Platonic lovers? How does the "medicine" work?

To His Coy Mistress

ANDREW MARVELL

Had we but world enough, and time,
This coyness, lady, were no crime.
We would sit down and think which way
To walk, and pass our long love's day.
Thou by the Indian Ganges' side *5*
Should'st rubies find; I by the tide
Of Humber would complain.[1] I would
Love you ten years before the Flood,
And you should, if you please, refuse
Till the conversion of the Jews.[2] *10*
My vegetable love should grow
Vaster than empires, and more slow.
An hundred years should go to praise
Thine eyes, and on thy forehead gaze,
Two hundred to adore each breast, *15*
But thirty thousand to the rest.
An age at least to every part,
And the last age should show your heart.
For, lady, you deserve this state,[3]
Nor would I love at lower rate. *20*
But at my back I always hear
Time's winged chariot hurrying near;
And yonder all before us lie
Deserts of vast eternity.
Thy beauty shall no more be found, *25*
Nor in thy marble vault shall sound
My echoing song; then worms shall try
That long preserved virginity,
And your quaint honor turn to dust,
And into ashes all my lust. *30*

[1] *Sing plaintive songs of love. The Humber is in England.*
[2] *Popularly supposed to take place just before the end of the world.*
[3] *Dignified treatment.*

The grave's a fine and private place,
But none, I think, do there embrace.
Now therefore, while the youthful hue
Sits on thy skin like morning dew,
And while thy willing soul transpires *35*
At every pore with instant fires,
Now let us sport us while we may;
And now, like am'rous birds of prey,
Rather at once our time devour,
Than languish in his slow-chapped power, *40*
Let us roll all our strength, and all
Our sweetness, up into one ball;
And tear our pleasures with rough strife
Thorough the iron gates of life.
Thus, though we cannot make our sun *45*
Stand still, yet we will make him run.

1681

Questions

1. Is this poem a satire? If so, what is being satirized?
2. Does the tone change? If it does, why?
3. Do you consider the metaphors of the last part of the poem to be appropriate for a love poem? Does the way the speaker talks about love suggest an attitude toward life in general? Is his attitude toward love—or life—one that can be found in our own time? Does this poem describe a search for personal values?

Love Among the Ruins

ROBERT BROWNING

I

Where the quiet-coloured end of evening smiles
Miles and miles
On the solitary pastures where our sheep
Half-asleep
Tinkle homeward thro' the twilight, stray or stop *5*
As they crop—
Was the site once of a city great and gay,
(So they say)
Of our country's very capital,[1] its prince

[1] *It does not matter what the country or ancient city is.*

Ages since 10
Held his court in, gathered councils, wielding far
Peace or war.

II

Now,—the country does not even boast a tree
As you see,
To distinguish slopes of verdure, certain rills 15
From the hills
Intersect and give a name to (else they run
Into one)
Where the domed and daring palace shot its spires
Up like fires 20
O'er the hundred-gated circuit of a wall
Bounding all,
Made of marble, men might march on nor be pressed,
Twelve abreast.

III

And such plenty and perfection, see, of grass 25
Never was!
Such a carpet as, this summer-time, o'erspreads
And embeds
Every vestige of the city, guessed alone,
Stock or stone— 30
Where a multitude of men breathed joy and woe
Long ago;
Lust of glory pricked their hearts up, dread of shame
Struck them tame;
And that glory and that shame alike, the gold 35
Bought and sold.

IV

Now,—the single little turret that remains
On the plains,
By the caper overrooted, by the gourd
Overscored, 40
While the patching houseleek's head of blossom winks
Through the chinks—
Marks the basement whence a tower in ancient time
Sprang sublime,
And a burning ring, all round, the chariots traced 45
As they raced,
And the monarch and his minions and his dames
Viewed the games.

V

And I know, while thus the quiet-coloured eve
Smiles to leave 50
To their folding, all our many-tinkling fleece
In such peace,
And the slopes and rills in undistinguished grey
Melt away—
That a girl with eager eyes and yellow hair 55
Waits me there
In the turret whence the charioteers caught soul
For the goal,
When the king looked, where she looks now, breathless, dumb
Till I come. 60

VI

But he looked upon the city, every side,
Far and wide,
All the mountains topped with temples, all the glades'
Colonnades,
All the causeys, bridges, aqueducts,—and then, 65
All the men!
When I do come, she will speak not, she will stand,
Either hand
On my shoulder, give her eyes the first embrace
Of my face, 70
Ere we rush, ere we extinguish sight and speech
Each on each.

VII

In one year they sent a million fighters forth
South and north,
And they built their gods a brazen pillar high 75
As the sky,
Yet reserved a thousand chariots in full force—
Gold, of course.
Oh, heart! oh, blood that freezes, blood that burns!
Earth's returns 80
For whole centuries of folly, noise and sin!
Shut them in,
With their triumphs and their glories and the rest!
Love is best.

1855

Questions

1. Half of each stanza describes the present scene, the other half the scene of the past. What is the main point of contrast? Does the extended description of the pastoral landscape serve merely to emphasize the fact that the great city has been obliterated, or does it have something to do with the quality of the love that the speaker cherishes so?
2. What is the effect of the image of the girl waiting in the little turret where the great tower once stood?
3. Why does the speaker make a point of emphasizing the magnificence of the great city? Why does he not dwell more on its sordidness?
4. Why is it significant that the lovers "extinguish sight and speech"?
5. Is the reader supposed to agree with the speaker, or does the poem ask for a judgment on him?

When I Was One-and-Twenty

A. E. HOUSMAN

When I was one-and-twenty
  I heard a wise man say,
"Give crowns and pounds and guineas
  But not your heart away;
Give pearls away and rubies   *5*
  But keep your fancy free."
But I was one-and-twenty,
  No use to talk to me.

When I was one-and-twenty
  I heard him say again,   *10*
"The heart out of the bosom
  Was never given in vain;
'Tis paid with sighs a-plenty
  And sold for endless rue."
And I am two-and-twenty,   *15*
  And oh, 'tis true, 'tis true.

1896

Questions

1. Why is the phrase "When I was one-and-twenty" repeated twice? What are the connotations of "one-and-twenty"?

2. The first fourteen lines of the poem obviously make fun of the cock-sureness of youth. What is the effect of the last two lines?
3. Does the poet take love seriously?

Love on the Farm

D. H. LAWRENCE

What large, dark hands are those at the window
Grasping in the golden light
Which weaves its way through the evening wind
    At my heart's delight?

Ah, only the leaves! But in the west   *5*
I see a redness suddenly come
Into the evening's anxious breast—
    'Tis the wound of love goes home!

The woodbine creeps abroad
Calling low to her lover: *10*
  The sun-lit flirt who all the day
  Has poised above her lips in play
  And stolen kisses, shallow and gay
  Of pollen, now has gone away—
  She woos the moth with her sweet, low word;   *15*
And when above her his moth-wings hover
Then her bright breast she will uncover
And yield her honey-drop to her lover.

Into the yellow, evening glow
Saunters a man from the farm below;   *20*
Leans, and looks in at the low-built shed
Where the swallow has hung her marriage bed.
  The bird lies warm against the wall.
  She glances quick her startled eyes
  Towards him, then she turns away   *25*
  Her small head, making warm display
  Of red upon the throat. Her terrors sway
  Her out of the nest's warm, busy ball,
  Whose plaintive cry is heard as she flies
  In one blue stoop from out the sties   *30*
  Into the twilight's empty hall.
Oh, water-hen, beside the rushes
Hide your quaintly scarlet blushes,

Still your quick tail, lie still as dead,
Till the distance folds over his ominous tread! *35*

The rabbit presses back her ears,
Turns back her liquid, anguished eyes
And crouches low; then with wild spring
Spurts from the terror of *his* oncoming;
To be choked back, the wire ring *40*
Her frantic effort throttling:
  Piteous brown ball of quivering fears!
Ah, soon in his large, hard hands she dies,
And swings all loose from the swing of his walk!
Yet calm and kindly are his eyes *45*
And ready to open in brown surprise
Should I not answer to his talk
Or should he my tears surmise.

I hear his hand on the latch, and rise from my chair
Watching the door open; he flashes bare *50*
His strong teeth in a smile, and flashes his eyes
In a smile like triumph upon me; then careless-wise
He flings the rabbit soft on the table board
And comes towards me: ah! the uplifted sword
Of his hand against my bosom! and oh, the broad *55*
Blade of his glance that asks me to applaud
His coming! With his hand he turns my face to him
And caresses me with his fingers that still smell grim
Of the rabbit's fur! God, I am caught in a snare!
I know not what fine wire is round my throat; *60*
I only know I let him finger there
My pulse of life, and let him nose like a stoat
Who sniffs with joy before he drinks the blood.

And down his mouth comes to my mouth! and down
His bright dark eyes come over me, like a hood *65*
Upon my mind! his lips meet mine, and a flood
Of sweet fire sweeps across me, so I drown
Against him, die, and find death good.

1913

Questions

1. Why is this poem entitled "Love on the Farm"? Is the poem about a special kind of love?
2. What is the point of the contrast between the third stanza and the fifth?
3. Why is the experience of love described here as being like death? In

what way is life, or being, lost through love? Is personality involved? Why is such love found good?

4. Is it significant that neither the man nor the woman speaks?

The Love Song of J. Alfred Prufrock

T. S. ELIOT

S'io credesse che mia risposta fosse
a persona che mai tornasse al mondo,
questa fiamma staria senza più scosse.
Ma per ciò che giammai di questo fondo
non tornò vivo alcun, s'i'odo il vero,
senza tema d'infamia ti rispondo.[1]

Let us go then, you and I,
When the evening is spread out against the sky
Like a patient etherised upon a table;
Let us go, through certain half-deserted streets,
The muttering retreats *5*
Of restless nights in one-night cheap hotels
And sawdust restaurants with oyster-shells:
Streets that follow like a tedious argument
Of insidious intent
To lead you to an overwhelming question . . . *10*
Oh, do not ask, "What is it?"
Let us go and make our visit.

In the room the women come and go
Talking of Michelangelo.

The yellow fog that rubs its back upon the window-panes, *15*
The yellow smoke that rubs its muzzle on the window-panes
Licked its tongue into the corners of the evening,
Lingered upon the pools that stand in drains,
Let fall upon its back the soot that falls from chimneys,
Slipped by the terrace, made a sudden leap, *20*
And seeing that it was a soft October night,

[1] *"If I thought that my reply would be to one who would ever return to the world, this flame would stay without further movement; but since none has ever returned alive from this depth, if what I hear is true, I answer you without fear of infamy." Dante,* Inferno, *XXVII, 61–66. The speaker is Guido da Montefeltro, who is being punished in hell because in life he gave false counsel.*

Curled once about the house, and fell asleep.

And indeed there will be time
For the yellow smoke that slides along the street,
Rubbing its back upon the window-panes; 25
There will be time, there will be time
To prepare a face to meet the faces that you meet;
There will be time to murder and create,
And time for all the works and days of hands [2]
That lift and drop a question on your plate; 30
Time for you and time for me,
And time yet for a hundred indecisions,
And for a hundred visions and revisions,
Before the taking of a toast and tea.

In the room the women come and go 35
Talking of Michelangelo.

And indeed there will be time
To wonder, "Do I dare?" and, "Do I dare?"
Time to turn back and descend the stair,
With a bald spot in the middle of my hair– 40
[They will say: "How his hair is growing thin!"]
My morning coat, my collar mounting firmly to the chin,
My necktie rich and modest, but asserted by a simple pin–
[They will say: "But how his arms and legs are thin!"]
Do I dare 45
Disturb the universe?
In a minute there is time
For decisions and revisions which a minute will reverse.

For I have known them all already, known them all:–
Have known the evenings, mornings, afternoons, 50
I have measured out my life with coffee spoons;
I know the voices dying with a dying fall [3]
Beneath the music from a farther room.
So how should I presume?

And I have known the eyes already, known them all– 55
The eyes that fix you in a formulated phrase,
And when I am formulated, sprawling on a pin,
When I am pinned and wriggling on the wall,

[2] *This is an allusion to* Works and Days, *a poem about farming by the eighth-century Greek poet, Hesiod. An ironic contrast is intended.*

[3] *Cf.* Twelfth Night, *I, i, 4: "That strain again! It had a dying fall." The comparison is ironic.*

Then how should I begin
To spit out all the butt-ends of my days and ways?
  And how should I presume? *60*

And I have known the arms already, known them all—
Arms that are braceleted and white and bare
[But in the lamplight, downed with light brown hair!]
Is it perfume from a dress
That makes me so digress? *65*
Arms that lie along a table, or wrap about a shawl.
  And should I then presume?
  And how should I begin?

. . . . .

Shall I say, I have gone at dusk through narrow streets
And watched the smoke that rises from the pipes *70*
Of lonely men in shirt-sleeves, leaning out of windows? . . .

I should have been a pair of ragged claws [4]
Scuttling across the floors of silent seas.

. . . . .

And the afternoon, the evening, sleeps so peacefully!
Smoothed by long fingers, *75*
Asleep . . . tired . . . or it malingers,
Stretched on the floor, here beside you and me.
Should I, after tea and cakes and ices,
Have the strength to force the moment to its crisis?
But though I have wept and fasted, wept and prayed, *80*
Though I have seen my head [grown slightly bald] brought in
  upon a platter,[5]
I am no prophet—and here's no great matter;
I have seen the moment of my greatness flicker,
And I have seen the eternal Footman hold my coat, and snicker *85*
And in short, I was afraid.

And would it have been worth it, after all,
After the cups, the marmalade, the tea,
Among the porcelain, among some talk of you and me,
Would it have been worth while, *90*
To have bitten off the matter with a smile,
To have squeezed the universe into a ball
To roll it toward some overwhelming question,
To say: "I am Lazarus, come from the dead,[6]
Come back to tell you all, I shall tell you all!"— *95*

[4] *The image is that of a crab.*
[5] *As was that of John the Baptist. See Mark* 6: 17–28 *and Matthew* 14:3–11.
[6] *See Luke* 16:19–31 *and John* 11:1–44.

If one, settling a pillow by her head,
    Should say: "That is not what I meant at all.
    That is not it, at all."

And would it have been worth it, after all,
Would it have been worth while,
After the sunsets and the dooryards and the sprinkled streets, *100*
After the novels, after the teacups, after the skirts that trail along
    the floor–
And this, and so much more?–
It is impossible to say just what I mean!
But as if a magic lantern threw the nerves in patterns on a screen:
Would it have been worth while *105*
If one, settling a pillow or throwing off a shawl,
And turning toward the window, should say:
    "That is not it at all,
    That is not what I meant, at all."

. . . . .

No! I am not Prince Hamlet, nor was meant to be; *110*
Am an attendant lord, one that will do
To swell a progress,[7] start a scene or two,
Advise the prince; no doubt, an easy tool,
Deferential, glad to be of use,
Politic, cautious, and meticulous; *115*
Full of high sentence,[8] but a bit obtuse;
At times, indeed, almost ridiculous–
Almost, at times, the Fool.

I grow old . . . I grow old . . .
I shall wear the bottoms of my trousers rolled. *120*

Shall I part my hair behind? Do I dare to eat a peach?
I shall wear white flannel trousers, and walk upon the beach.
I have heard the mermaids singing, each to each.

I do not think that they will sing to me.

I have seen them riding seaward on the waves *125*
Combing the white hair of the waves blown back
When the wind blows the water white and black.

We have lingered in the chambers of the sea
By sea-girls wreathed with seaweed red and brown
Till human voices wake us, and we drown. *130*

1917

[7] *A state journey.*
[8] *"Full of high sentence" means sententious.*

Questions

1. About how old is Prufrock? To what social level does he belong? What mainly occupies his time?
2. What opinion does Prufrock have of himself? With whom does he compare or contrast himself? What does he mean when he says, "I have measured out my life with coffee spoons"?
3. What does Prufrock think of his world—that is, the people with whom he associates? What is suggested by the repeated lines, "In the room the women come and go / Talking of Michelangelo"?
4. Do you think that Prufrock is really in love? Why does he fear to speak to the lady? What do you think love means to him?

Deirdre[1]

JAMES STEPHENS

Do not let any woman read this verse!
It is for men, and after them their sons,
And their son's sons!

The time comes when our hearts sink utterly;
When we remember Deirdre, and her tale, *5*
And that her lips are dust.

Once she did tread the earth: men took her hand;
They looked into her eyes and said their say,
And she replied to them.

More than two thousand years it is since she *10*
Was beautiful: she trod the waving grass;
She saw the clouds.

Two thousand years! The grass is still the same;
The clouds as lovely as they were that time
When Deirdre was alive. *15*

[1] *Deirdre is the heroine of an ancient Irish tale,* The Fate of the Sons of Uisnech. *She was the granddaughter of Dall, the storyteller of King Conchobar. When she cried out from the womb of her mother, the druid Cathab predicted that a great evil would come with her when she was born. Although his subjects wanted her to be slain, Conchobar had her brought up in seclusion and kept to be his wife, for she was exceedingly beautiful. However, Deirdre accidentally encountered Noisi, son of Uisnech, fell in love with him, and persuaded him and his two brothers to carry her off, at great risk, to Alba, where the four lived in self-imposed exile. Eventually emissaries of Conchobar tricked them into returning. The three brothers were slain in ambush and Deirdre was taken to Conchobar. Rather than submit to him, she committed suicide.*

But there has been again no woman born
Who was so beautiful; not one so beautiful
Of all the women born.

Let all men go apart and mourn together!
No man can ever love her! Not a man *20*
Can dream to be her lover!

No man can bend before her! No man say—
What could one say to her? There are no words
That one could say to her!

Now she is but a story that is told *25*
Beside the fire! No man can ever be
The friend of that poor queen!

1926

Questions

1. What does Deirdre represent to the poet? Why does he say, "Do not let any woman read this verse!"? Is the kind of desire expressed here common among men? Can you think of other figures of fame comparable to that of Deirdre?
2. Would you call this a kind of romantic love? How would you define the general nature of romantic love?
3. How does the poet convey the tantalizing character of this love-concept?

since feeling is first

E. E. CUMMINGS

since feeling is first
who pays any attention
to the syntax of things
will never wholly kiss you;

wholly to be a fool *5*
while Spring is in the world

my blood approves,
and kisses are a better fate
than wisdom
lady i swear by all flowers. Don't cry *10*

—the best gesture of my brain is less than
your eyelids' flutter which says

we are for each other: then
laugh, leaning back in my arms
for life's not a paragraph *15*

And death i think is no parenthesis

1926

Questions

1. What does the poet mean when he says, "feeling is first"? Is the idea here the same as that expressed in "Love Among the Ruins" ("Love is best")?
2. Why should the lady cry?
3. What is implied by the statement, "life's not a paragraph"? Is the same idea expressed in "death i think is no parenthesis"? What is the connection with "the syntax of things"?

The Postman's Bell Is Answered Everywhere

HORACE GREGORY

God and the devil in these letters,
stored in tin trunks, tossed in wastebaskets,
or ticketed away in office files:
love, hate and business, mimeographed sheets, circulars,
bills of lading, official communiques, *5*
accounts rendered, even the anonymous letter says,
Do not forget.

And in that long list: Dean Swift to Stella,
Walpole to Hannah More, Carlyle to Jane.
And what were Caesar's Gallic Wars other than letters *10*
of credit for future empire?

Do not forget me,
I shall wear laurels to face the world;
you shall remember the head in bronze,
profile on coin. *15*

As the bell rings, here is the morning paper and more letters:

the postdate, 10 P.M.: "It is an effort
for me to write; I have grown older.
I have two daughters and a son and business prospers,
but my hair is white. Why can't we meet for lunch? 20
It has been a long time since we met;
I doubt if you would know me, if you glanced quickly
at my overcoat and hat and saw them vanish
in a crowded street. . . ."

Or at another door, ". . . O you must not forget 25
you held me in your arms, while the small room
trembled in darkness; do you recall the slender, violet
dawn between the trees next morning through the park?
Since I'm a woman, how can I unlearn
the arts of love within a single hour; 30
how can I close my eyes before a mirror,
believe I am not wanted, that hands, lips, breast
are merely deeper shadows behind the door
where all is dark? . . ."

Or, "Forgive me if I intrude, the dream I had 35
last night was of your face; it was a child's face,
wreathed with the sun's hair, or pale in moonlight,
more of a child than woman, it followed me
wherever I looked, pierced everything I saw,
proved that you could not leave me, that I am always 40
at your side. . . ."

Or, "I alone am responsible for my own death" or,
"I am White, Christian, Unmarried, 21," or "I
am happy to accept
Your Invitation," or, "Remember that evening 45
at the Savoy-Plaza,"
or, "It was I who saw the fall of France."

As letters are put aside, another bell
rings in another day; it is, perhaps, not too late to remember
the words that leave you naked in their sight, 50
the warning, "You have not forgotten me;
these lines were written by an unseen hand
twelve hours ago, do not reply at this address, these are the last
words I shall write."

1935

Questions

1. When does communication by mail become necessary? Is this point important in the poem?
2. What is the theme of the three letters quoted at greatest length? What specifically, do they all say? In what tone are they written? Would you call them love letters? In what sense is love involved in them?
3. How important is the theme of the passing of time in this poem? How is it brought in?
4. What is the general meaning of the warning of the symbolic letter in the last part of the poem? Why do the words of the letter "leave you naked in their sight"?

TOPICS FOR COMPOSITION

1. With Spenser's definition of beauty in mind, write a critical essay on the modern ideal of feminine desirability. As a way of "getting into" the subject, consider the following questions. Do people nowadays overvalue physical beauty in women? Is the feminine image still a vital symbol of virtue or moral beauty? How are you, for example, inclined to picture virtue in human form? Does the modern concept of personality involve what might be called "spiritual" qualities? Do the national or international beauty contests provide adequate criteria for the assessment of "true beauty"?
2. Write an essay on the subject of idealism based on love between two persons. Can such love be an adequate basis of moral motivation? Can a person achieve an adequate degree of moral motivation without such love? Do people generally tend to be too idealistic about marriage, or too realistic? Is it old-fashioned to regard marriage as a religious sacrament? Use one of these questions or a similar one as a means of focusing your discussion. If you wish, use references to one or more of the poems of this unit.
3. Are lovers sometimes as perverse as Samuel Daniel asserts? If you think so, analyze this "sickness" in an essay.
4. With John Donne's warning in mind, explain in a short article how one can tell quickly whether or not a woman is likely to be fickle.
5. Platonic love in the religious sense is an outmoded doctrine, but it once was an important source of inspiration. If you are philosophically inclined, try to explain in a short essay why such a relatively sophisticated concept is unacceptable to modern taste.
6. Point out the relevance of Marvell's "To His Coy Mistress" to modern circumstances, and defend or attack the attitude expressed in the poem.
7. Write a third person impressionistic description of a scene similar to that presented in "Love Among the Ruins." Use the ideas of the poem if you wish, but try to imagine how the scene would have struck you in a thoughtful mood.
8. Write a character analysis based either upon Browning's monologue or that of D. H. Lawrence.

9. Explain briefly the problem dramatized in "The Love Song of J. Alfred Prufrock"; then give your answer to the problem.
10. Write a commentary on the meaning and appropriateness of the sea imagery in "The Love Song of J. Alfred Prufrock."
11. Define modern love by describing what you think would be the general modern reaction toward each of several poems of this unit. Does the sentiment expressed in Stephens' "Deirdre," for example, still have appeal, or that in "Love Among the Ruins"?
12. Compare carefully the attitudes of the lovers in two or all three of the following poems: "The Love Song of J. Alfred Prufrock"; "To His Coy Mistress"; "since feeling is first."
13. Reconstruct the situation implied in one of the quotations from letters given in "The Postman's Bell Is Answered Everywhere."
14. Using Horace Gregory's thoughts, or your own, write a theme entitled "The Postman's Bell Is Answered Everywhere."
15. Write an essay on the ideal attitude toward love, drawing freely upon ideas or sentiments expressed in the poems of this unit.
16. Write a careful analysis of the handling of tone in any poem in this section.

PART FOUR

The Protest Against Materialism

Society is often rebuked for its emphasis on material gain, in the caricature of the "status-seeker," for example. Yet a complete rejection of material gain appears impractical. This is the paradox we face: on the one hand, material gain corrupts society; on the other hand, society progresses in proportion to man's ambition. Ambition, in the popular sense, is motivated by a desire for gain, material gain, for the most part. Where do we draw the line? Obviously, the question has no simple answer. But, because proper emphasis on materialistic value creates a dilemma as it touches social, moral, and spiritual behavior, we see that writers have generally taken a position of protest. The selections in this unit represent some varying ways writers have protested materialism's influence on society.

The first essay, "Pecuniary Canons of Taste," taken from Thorstein Veblen's book The Theory of the Leisure Class *(1899), is an economist's view of the effect of a materialistically oriented society on the economy of that society. Veblen examines the theory of "conspicuous waste" as it leads to "pecuniary canons of taste." To simplify, he suggests that objects in a materialistic society acquire value, even so abstract a value as beauty, only in proportion to the money value that society assigns them. The second essay, Vance Packard's "The Growing Power of Admen," first appeared in the* Atlantic Monthly *(1957) and brings into modern focus Veblen's theories on "conspicuous waste" and "pecuniary canons of taste." Packard's central concern, as his title states, is an examination of the advertising industry and the power advertising exerts on today's reading, viewing, and listening public. Like Veblen, Packard senses a danger in a society that becomes obsessed with material acquisition.*

Leo Tolstoi's short story, "Three Arshins of Land," often appears with an alternate title or a subtitle in the form of a question: "How Much Land Does a Man Need?" Tolstoi's subtitle raises not only the question of material value but also provides the word on which the question may turn. As you notice, Tolstoi does not ask how much land a man wants; *instead, he asks how much does he* need. *Here, as you will see in other selections in this unit, it is not wealth that is being castigated but the effect on man when wealth becomes his only goal in life.*

Ivan Bunin's "The Gentleman from San Francisco" again centers our attention on the man of wealth: Tolstoi's question of "needs" and "wants" is evident, but in a somewhat different light. Bunin shows us, with devastating force, a picture of a nameless "gentleman" who confronts the one inevitability of life over which his material wealth (acquired at a distinct cost to humanity) has no power.

The Essay

ALTHOUGH Veblen's vocabulary and sentence structure present difficulties for the average reader, his essay shows a cause-to-effect organizational pattern that aids in understanding his thesis and that allows him room to develop a variety of support methods. As you read this essay, you will find it helpful to refer to the following analysis of Veblen's first three paragraphs:

1. The first and second paragraphs provide a transition from Veblen's discussion of "conspicuous waste" to his new topic.
2. The third paragraph provides the thesis statement.
3. The third paragraph provides a qualification for the thesis statement and indicates the factors that will support the thesis.

Pecuniary Canons of Taste

THORSTEIN VEBLEN

The caution has already been repeated more than once, that while the regulating norm of consumption is in large part the requirement of conspicuous waste, it must not be understood that the motive on which the consumer acts in any given case is this principle in its bald, unsophisticated form. Ordinarily his motive is a wish to conform to established usage, to avoid unfavourable notice and comment, to live up to the accepted canons of decency in the kind, amount, and grade of goods consumed, as well as in the decorous employment of his time and effort. In the common run of cases this sense of prescriptive usage is present in the motives of the consumer and exerts a direct constraining force, especially as regards consumption carried on under the eyes of observers. But a considerable element of prescriptive expensiveness is observable also in consumption that does not in any appreciable degree become known to outsiders—as, for instance, articles of underclothing, some articles of food, kitchen utensils, and other household apparatus designed for service rather than for evidence. In all such useful articles a close scrutiny will discover certain features which add to the cost and enhance the commercial value of the goods in question, but do not proportionately increase the serviceability of these articles for the material purposes which alone they ostensibly are designed to serve.

Under the selective surveillance of the law of conspicuous waste there grows up a code of accredited canons of consumption, the effect of which is to hold the consumer up to a standard of expensiveness and wastefulness in his consumption of goods and in his employment of time and effort. This growth of prescriptive usage has an immediate effect upon economic life, but it has also an indirect and remoter effect upon conduct in other respects as well. Habits of thought with respect to the expression of life in any given direction unavoidably affect the habitual view of what is good and right in life in other directions also. In the organic complex of habits of thought which make up the substance of an individual's conscious life the economic interest does not lie isolated and distinct from all other interests. Something, for instance, has already been said of its relation to the canons of reputability.

The principle of conspicuous waste guides the formation of habits of thought as to what is honest and reputable in life and in commodities. In so doing, this principle will traverse other norms of conduct which do not primarily have to do with the code of pecuniary honour, but which have, directly or incidentally, an economic significance of some magnitude. So the canon of honorific waste may, immediately or remotely, influence the sense of duty, the sense of beauty, the sense of utility, the sense of devotional or ritualistic fitness, and the scientific sense of truth.

It is scarcely necessary to go into a discussion here of the particular points at which, or the particular manner in which, the canon of honorific expenditure habitually traverses the canons of moral conduct. The matter is one which has received large attention and illustration at the hands of those whose office it is to watch and admonish with respect to any departures from the accepted code of morals. In modern communities, where the dominant economic and legal feature of the community's life is the institution of private property, one of the salient features of the code of morals is the sacredness of property. There needs no insistence or illustration to gain assent to the proposition that the habit of holding private property inviolate is traversed by the other habit of seeking wealth for the sake of the good repute to be gained through its conspicuous consumption. Most offences against property, especially offences of an appreciable magnitude, come under this head. It is also a matter of common notoriety and byword that in offences which result in a large accession of property to the offender he does not ordinarily incur the extreme penalty or the extreme obloquy with which his offence would be visited on the ground of the naïve moral code alone. The thief or swindler who has gained great wealth by his delinquency has a better chance than the small thief of escaping the rigorous penalty of the law; and some good repute accrues to him from his increased wealth and from his spending the irregularly acquired possessions in a seemly manner. A well-bred expenditure of his booty especially appeals with great effect to persons of a cultivated sense of the proprieties, and goes far to mitigate the sense of moral turpitude with which his dereliction is viewed by them. It may be noted also—and it is more immediately to the point—that we are all inclined to condone an offence against property in the case of a man whose motive is the worthy one of providing the means of a "decent" manner of life for his wife and children. If it is added that the wife has been "nurtured in the lap of luxury," that is accepted as an additional extenuating circumstance. That is to say, we are prone to condone such an offence where its aim is the honorific one of enabling the offender's wife to perform for him such an amount of vicarious consumption of time and substance as is demanded by the standard of pecuniary decency. In such a case the habit of approving the accustomed degree of conspicuous waste traverses the habit of deprecating violations of ownership, to the extent even of sometimes leaving the award of praise or blame uncertain. This is peculiarly true where the dereliction involves an appreciable predatory or piratical element. . . .

Obviously, the canon of conspicuous waste is accountable for a great portion of what may be called devout consumption; as, *e.g.*, the consumption of sacred edifices, vestments, and other goods of the same class. Even in those modern cults to whose divinities is imputed a predilection for temples not built with hands, the sacred buildings and other properties of the cult are constructed and decorated with some view to a reputable degree of wasteful expenditure. And it needs but little either of observation or introspection—and either will serve the turn—to assure us that the expensive splendour of the house of worship has an appreciable uplifting and mellowing effect upon the worshipper's frame of mind. It will serve to enforce the same fact if we reflect upon the sense of abject shamefulness with which any evidence of indigence or squalor about the sacred place affects all beholders. The accessories of any devout observance should be pecuniarily above reproach. This requirement is imperative, whatever latitude may be allowed with regard to these accessories in point of æsthetic or other serviceability.

It may also be in place to notice that in all communities, especially in neighbourhoods where the standard of pecuniary decency for dwellings is not high, the local sanctuary is more ornate, more conspicuously wasteful in its architecture and decoration, than the dwelling-houses of the congregation. This is true of nearly all denominations and cults, whether Christian or Pagan, but it is true in a peculiar degree of the older and maturer cults. At the same time the sanctuary commonly contributes little if anything to the physical comfort of the members. Indeed, the sacred structure not only serves the physical well-being of the members to but a slight extent, as compared with their humbler dwelling-houses; but it is felt by all men that a right and enlightened sense of the true, the beautiful, and the good demands that in all expenditure on the sanctuary anything that might serve the comfort of the worshipper should be conspicuously absent. If any element of comfort is admitted in the fittings of the sanctuary, it should at least be scrupulously screened and masked under an ostensible austerity. In the most reputable latter-day houses of worship, where no expense is spared, the principle of austerity is carried to the length of making the fittings of the place a means of mortifying the flesh, especially in appearance. There are few persons of delicate tastes in the matter of devout consumption to whom this austerely wasteful discomfort does not appeal as intrinsically right and good. Devout consumption is of the nature of vicarious consumption. This canon of devout austerity is based on the pecuniary reputability of conspicuously wasteful consumption, backed by the principle that vicarious consumption should conspicuously not conduce to the comfort of the vicarious consumer. . . .

These canons of reputability have had a similar, but more far-reaching and more specifically determinable, effect upon the popular sense of beauty or serviceability in consumable goods. The requirements of pecuniary decency have, to a very appreciable extent, influenced the sense of beauty and of utility in articles of use or beauty. Articles are to an extent preferred for use on account of their being conspicuously wasteful; they are felt to be serviceable somewhat in proportion as they are wasteful and ill adapted to their ostensible use.

The utility of articles valued for their beauty depends closely upon the expensiveness of the articles. A homely illustration will bring out this dependence. A hand-wrought silver spoon, of a commercial value of some ten to twenty dollars, is not ordinarily more serviceable—in the first sense of the word—than a machine-made spoon of the same material. It may not even be more serviceable than a machine-made spoon of some "base" metal, such as aluminum, the value of which may be no more than some ten to twenty cents. The former of the two utensils is, in fact, commonly a less effective contrivance for its ostensible purpose than the latter. The objection is of course ready to hand that, in taking this view of the matter, one of the chief uses, if not the chief use, of the costlier spoon is ignored; the hand-wrought spoon gratifies our taste, our sense of the beautiful, while that made by machinery out of the base metal has no useful office beyond a brute efficiency. The facts are no doubt as the objection states them, but it will be evident on reflection that the objection is after all more plausible than conclusive. It appears (1) that while the different materials of which the two spoons are made each possesses beauty and serviceability for the purpose for which it is used, the material of the hand-wrought spoon is some one hundred times more valuable than the baser metal, without very greatly excelling the latter in intrinsic beauty of grain or colour, and without being in any appreciable degree superior in point of mechanical serviceability; (2) if a close inspection should show that the supposed hand-wrought spoon were in reality only a very clever imitation of hand-wrought goods, but an imitation so cleverly wrought as to give the same impression of line and surface to any but a minute examination by a trained eye, the utility of the article, including the gratification which the user derives from its contemplation as an object of beauty, would immediately decline by some eighty or ninety per cent, or even more; (3) if the two spoons are, to a fairly close observer, so nearly identical in appearance that the lighter weight of the spurious article alone betrays it, this identity of form and colour will scarcely add to the value of the machine-made spoon, nor appreciably enhance the gratification of the user's "sense of beauty" in contemplating it, so long as the cheaper spoon is not a novelty, and so long as it can be procured at a nominal cost. . . .

It is at this point, where the beautiful and the honorific meet and blend, that a discrimination between serviceability and wastefulness is most difficult in any concrete case. It frequently happens that an article which serves the honorific purpose of conspicuous waste is at the same time a beautiful object; and the same application of labour to which it owes its utility for the former purpose may, and often does, go to give beauty of form and colour to the article. The question is further complicated by the fact that many objects, as, for instance, the precious stones and metals and some other materials used for adornment and decoration, owe their utility as items of conspicuous waste to an antecedent utility as objects of beauty. Gold, for instance, has a high degree of sensuous beauty; very many if not most of the highly prized works of art are intrinsically beautiful, though often with material qualification; the like is true of some stuffs used for clothing, of some landscapes, and of many other things in less degree. Except for this intrinsic beauty which they possess, these objects would scarcely have been coveted as they are, or have become monopolised objects of pride to their possessors and users. But the utility of these things to the possessor is commonly due less to their intrinsic beauty than to the honour which their possession and consumption confers, or to the obloquy which it wards off. . . .

The generalisation for which the discussion so far affords ground is that any valuable object in order to appeal to our sense of beauty must conform to the requirements of beauty and of expensiveness both. But this is not all. Beyond this the canon of expensiveness also affects our tastes in such a way as to inextricably blend the marks of expensiveness, in our appreciation, with the beautiful features of the object, and to subsume the resultant effect under the head of an appreciation of beauty simply. The marks of expensiveness come to be accepted as beautiful features of the expensive articles. They are pleasing as being marks of honorific costliness, and the pleasure which they afford on this score blends with that afforded by the beautiful form and colour of the object; so that we often declare that an article of apparel, for instance, is "perfectly lovely," when pretty much all that an analysis of the æsthetic value of the article would leave ground for is the declaration that it is pecuniarily honorific.

This blending and confusion of the elements of expensiveness and of beauty is, perhaps, best exemplified in articles of dress and of household furniture. The code of reputability in matters of dress decides what shapes, colours, materials, and general effects in human apparel are for the time to be accepted as suitable; and departures from the code are offensive to our taste, supposedly as being departures from æsthetic truth. The approval with which we look upon fashionable attire is by no means to be accounted pure make-believe. We readily, and for the most part with utter sincerity, find those things pleasing that are in vogue. Shaggy dress-stuffs and pronounced colour effects, for instance, offend us at times when the vogue is goods of a high, glossy finish and neutral colours. A fancy bonnet of this year's model unquestionably appeals to our sensibilities to-day much more forcibly than an equally fancy bonnet of the model of last year; although when viewed in the perspective of a quarter of a century, it would, I apprehend, be a matter of the utmost difficulty to award the palm for intrinsic beauty to the one rather than to the other of these structures. So, again, it may be remarked that, considered simply in their physical juxtaposition with the human form, the high gloss of a gentleman's hat or of a patent-leather shoe has no more of intrinsic beauty than a similarly high gloss on a threadbare sleeve; and yet there is no question but that all well-bred people (in the Occidental civilised communities) instinctively and unaffectedly cleave to the one as a phenomenon of great beauty, and eschew the other as offensive to every sense to which it can appeal. It is extremely doubtful if any one could be induced to wear such a contrivance as the high hat of civilised society, except for some urgent reason based on other than æsthetic grounds. . . .

It is not only with respect to consumable goods—including domestic animals—that the canons of taste have been coloured by the canons of pecuniary reputability. Something to the like effect is to be said for beauty in persons. In order to avoid whatever may be matter of controversy, no weight will be given in this connection to such popular predilection as there may be for the dignified (leisurely) bearing and portly presence that are by vulgar tradition associated with opulence in mature men. These traits are in some measure accepted as elements of personal beauty. But there are certain elements of feminine beauty, on the other hand, which come in under this head, and which are of so concrete and specific a character as to admit of itemised appreciation. It is more or less a rule that in communities which are at the stage of economic development at which women are valued by the upper class for their service, the ideal of female beauty is a robust, large-limbed woman. The ground of appreciation is the physique, while the conformation of the face is of secondary weight only. A well-known instance of this ideal of the early predatory culture is that of the maidens of the Homeric poems. . . .

In modern communities which have reached the higher levels of industrial development, the upper leisure class has accumulated so great a mass of wealth as to place its women above all imputation of vulgarly productive labour. Here the status of women as vicarious consumers is beginning to lose its place in the affections of the body of the people; and as a consequence the ideal of feminine beauty is beginning to change back again from the infirmly delicate, translucent, and hazardously slender, to a woman of the archaic type that does not disown her hands and feet, nor, indeed, the other gross material facts of her person. In the course of economic development the ideal of beauty among the peoples of the Western culture has shifted from the woman of physical presence to the lady, and it is beginning to shift back again to the woman; and all in obedience to the changing conditions of pecuniary emulation. The exigencies of emulation at one time required lusty slaves; at another time they required a conspicuous performance of vicarious leisure and consequently an obvious disability; but the situation is now beginning to outgrow this last requirement, since, under the higher efficiency of modern industry, leisure in women is possible so far down the scale of reputability that it will no longer serve as a definitive mark of the highest pecuniary grade. . . .

On this ground, among objects of use the simple and unadorned article is æsthetically the best. But since the pecuniary canon of reputability rejects the inexpensive in articles appropriated to individual consumption, the satisfaction of our craving for beautiful things must be sought by way of compromise. The canons of beauty must be circumvented by some contrivance which will give evidence of a reputably wasteful expenditure, at the same time that it meets the demands of our critical sense of the useful and the beautiful, or at least meets the demand of some habit which has come to do duty in place of that sense. Such an auxiliary sense of taste is the sense of novelty; and this latter is helped out in its surrogateship by the curiosity with which men view ingenious and puzzling contrivances. Hence it comes that most objects alleged to be beautiful, and doing duty as such, show considerable ingenuity of design and are calculated to puzzle the beholder—to bewilder him with irrelevant suggestions and hints of the improbable—at the same time that they give evidence of an expenditure of labour in excess of what would give them their fullest efficiency for their ostensible economic end. . . .

This process of selective adaptation of designs to the end of conspicuous waste, and the substitution of pecuniary beauty for æsthetic beauty, has been especially effective in the development of architecture. It would be extremely difficult to find a modern civilised residence or public building which can claim anything better than relative inoffensiveness in the eyes of any one who will dissociate the elements of beauty from those of honorific waste. The endless variety of fronts presented by the better class of tenements and apartment houses in our cities is an endless variety of architectural distress and of suggestions of expensive discomfort. Considered as objects of beauty, the dead walls of the sides and back of these structures, left untouched by the hands of the artist, are commonly the best feature of the building. . . .

The position here taken is enforced in a felicitous manner by the place assigned in the economy of consumption to machine products. The point of material difference between machine-made goods and the hand-wrought goods which serve the same purposes is, ordinarily, that the former serve their primary purpose more adequately. They are a more perfect product—show a more perfect adaptation of means to end. This does not save them from disesteem and depreciation, for they fall short under the test of honorific waste. Hand labour is a more wasteful method of production; hence the goods turned out by this method are more serviceable for the purpose of pecuniary reputability; hence the marks of hand labour come to be honorific, and the goods which exhibit these marks take rank as of higher grade than the corresponding machine product. Commonly, if not invariably, the honorific marks of hand labour are certain imperfections and irregularities in the lines of the hand-wrought article, showing where the workman has fallen short in the execution of the design. The ground of the superiority of hand-wrought goods, therefore, is a certain margin of crudeness. This margin must never be so wide as to show bungling workmanship, since that would be evidence of low cost, nor so narrow as to suggest the ideal precision attained only by the machine, for that would be evidence of low cost. . . .

The ceremonial inferiority or uncleanness in consumable goods due to "commonness," or in other words to their slight cost of production, has been taken very seriously by many persons. The objection to machine products is often formulated as an objection to the commonness of such goods. What is common is within the (pecuniary) reach of many people. Its consumption is therefore not honorific, since it does not serve the purpose of a favourable invidious comparison with other consumers. Hence the consumption, or even the sight of such goods, is inseparable from an odious suggestion of the lower levels of human life, and one comes away from their contemplation with a pervading sense of meanness that is extremely distasteful and depressing to a person of sensibility. In persons whose tastes assert themselves imperiously, and who have not the gift, habit, or incentive to discriminate between the grounds of their various judgments of taste, the deliverances of the sense of the honorific coalesce with those of the sense of beauty and of the sense of serviceability—in the manner already spoken of; the resulting composite valuation serves as a judgment of the object's beauty or its serviceability, according as the valuer's bias or interest inclines him to apprehend the object in the one or the other of these aspects. It follows not infrequently that the marks of cheapness or commonness are accepted as definitive marks of artistic unfitness, and a code or schedule of æsthetic proprieties on the one hand, and of æsthetic abominations on the other, is constructed on this basis for guidance in questions of taste. . . .

The position of machine products in the civilised scheme of consumption serves to point out the nature of the relation which subsists between the canon of conspicuous waste and the code of proprieties in consumption. Neither in matters of art and taste proper, nor as regards the current sense of the serviceability of goods, does this canon act as a principle of innovation or initiative. It does not go into the future as a creative principle which makes innovations and adds new items of consumption and new elements of cost. The principle in question is, in a certain sense, a negative rather than a positive law. It is a regulative rather than a creative principle. It very rarely initiates or originates any usage or custom directly. Its action is selective only. Conspicuous wastefulness does not directly afford ground for variation and growth, but conformity to its requirements is a condition to the survival of such innovations as may be made on other grounds. In whatever way usages and customs and methods of expenditure arise, they are all subject to the selective action of this norm of reputability; and the degree in which they conform to its requirements is a test of their fitness to survive in the competition with other similar usages and customs. Other things being equal, the more obviously wasteful usage or method stands the better chance of survival under this law. The law of conspicuous waste does not account for the origin of variations, but only for the persistence of such forms as are fit to survive under its dominance. It acts to conserve the fit, not to originate the acceptable. Its office is to prove all things and to hold fast that which is good for its purpose.

Questions

1. What does the author mean by the "standard of pecuniary decency"?
2. How does he fit religion into his theory? What is the relationship between the dwellings in a given neighborhood and the religious edifice in that neighborhood? On whose authority is this fact offered? Can you support or refute it?
3. What are the methods of support Veblen uses in each of his development areas? How effective are they?
4. How timely are the observations made here? Could a stronger case be presented for some? What would Veblen think of the popular image of the modern woman?
5. Examine the concluding paragraph. Does the author pull together his development areas and make a strong conclusion? Explain.

Topics for Composition

1. Veblen, as we have seen, suggests five areas where habits of thought are controlled by money value. Write an essay, based on your observation and experience, in which you parallel Veblen's method of development by suggesting and supporting three areas in which money value becomes "honorific." Concentrate on specific support for each area.
2. Compare and contrast Veblen's assessment of the ideal of womanliness with the modern viewpoint. For instance, you might begin by listing each of the author's points concerning the ideal of feminine beauty, then elaborate on each point, and present the comparative or contrastive modern view.

While Packard's essay should prove useful in assessing our society's particular materialistic bent, his magazine style may also provide us an opportunity to observe those features that produce clear writing for the mass audience. Note especially:

1. The division of the article into four main parts
2. The last paragraph of each part, which provides a transition to the next part
3. The reliance on and support of a topic statement at the outset of each division
4. The variety of supporting arguments within each division
5. The detailed reference to each supporting topic in the conclusion

The Growing Power of Admen

VANCE PACKARD

1

America's advertising industry is moving into a commanding role in our society. Its executives are becoming masters of our economic destiny, the engineers behind some of our most successful political campaigns, major patrons of our social scientists, dictators of the content of most of the radio and television programs we hear, judges with life-and-death power over most of our mass-circulation magazines. Also, they have become our most powerful taste makers. In 1957 they made millions of Americans suddenly feel somehow inadequate because they did not own high-tailed automobiles.

They have, in short, become major wielders of social control in America in this second half of the twentieth century. Their power to do good or nongood is becoming massive, and many are using their power irresponsibly.

The growth of their power is seen in the amount of money entrusted to them to spend. In 1940 they had at their disposal $2 billion to conduct campaigns of persuasion. Today they have $10 billion. If you divide that figure by the total U.S. population, you come up with a fairly startling statistic. Approximately $60 is now being spent each year on *each* man, woman, and child in America solely to coax him or her to use products the admen are promoting.

This growing power of advertising men derives from the dominant role that selling plays in the dynamics of our economy. In the executive suites of thousands of corporations the main preoccupation is no longer with production problems but rather with selling problems.

The most obvious explanation for this shift of emphasis is the fabulous productivity of our automated factories. Since 1940 our gross national product has soared more than 400 per cent. In 1954 it was predicted that our GNP would hit the long-dreamed-of mark of $400 billion by 1958. Actually it shot past that figure of 1956 and is expected to reach $600 billion within the coming decade.

To absorb this fantastic outpouring of goods we shall have to step up our personal consumption of goods by almost 50 per cent. As the chairman of America's leading advertising agency proclaimed recently: "We have to expand our levels of consumption in the next ten years by an amount nearly equal to the entire growth of the country in the two hundred years from colonial days up to 1940." The big problem we face, he said, is to cut down the "time lag" in the process by which we ordinarily learn to expand our wants and needs, in order to "absorb this production." Advertising men are the experts who can overcome this lag.

The real needs of most of us were satisfied long ago. About 40 per cent of the things we buy today are unnecessary in terms of any real need. Even our wants are pretty well satisfied. It has become a question of creating in our minds new, unrealized wants and needs.

Happily for the marketers, Americans by nature seem to relish learning to want new things. We are a restless people who like continually to hear of new things to do and buy. (Note the recent popularity of bejeweled fly swatters and mousetraps.) Emerson commented on this trait in Americans when he said that they, unlike Europeans, exhibit "an uncalculated, headlong expenditure." This makes them the world's prize consumers.

Recently the president of the Institute for Motivational Research (which conducts psychological studies for marketers) noted with satisfaction "our increasing willingness to give vent to our whims and desires" and offered the opinion that America is "experiencing a revolution in self-indulgence."

A corollary problem of marketers in moving their goods into our homes is that of making us discontented with what we already have, since most of us already own perfectly serviceable automobiles, washing machines, refrigerators, and clothing. We must be persuaded that the old product has become hopelessly inadequate to meet our needs or desired style of living. Advertising men call this "creating psychological obsolescence."

Another development adding to the power, glory, and prosperity of advertising men is the increased standardization of competing products. Perhaps connoisseurs can still detect significant differences in gasolines, whiskeys, cigarettes, beer, tires, cake mixes, and detergents, but most of us no longer can. Reports on blindfold tests conducted with cigarette smokers and whiskey and beer drinkers consistently reveal an inability of people to spot their favorite brand. A few days ago I heard a gathering of advertising men being advised that in blindfold tests people can't even tell the difference between Coca-Cola and Pepsi-Cola!

It used to startle me to hear advertising men make casual statements that in many fields such as gasoline and cigarettes the products are "all the same." Now it becomes apparent why they can be so complacent. It is the advertising man's genius that makes products seem compellingly different in our minds.

A third reason for the increasing influence of admen is the growth of self-service selling at supermarkets, vending machines, and so on. More and more, machines or systems are replacing people at the selling counter. The product maker can no longer rely on word-of-mouth selling by a clerk, merchant, or attendant. Thus the customer must be pre-sold, through advertising, so that he will have the product's image firmly etched in his mind as he enters the market place.

2

In the face of all these crying needs for more effective selling, America's 3300 advertising agencies have come to constitute "a great sociological battering ram," to use a phrase current with admen. Individually, advertising men have become "merchants of discontent."

As advertising men by the tens of thousands bring their wiles to bear to stimulate sales of products, we are seeing a massive straining for greater impact. Some months ago a distiller sent a photographic team to the edges of the Sahara Desert in order to obtain a photograph of a martini-filled glass in a setting which would suggest dryness. The photographers faced a crisis when, in searching the fruit markets of Cairo for a sliver of yellow lemon peel to go with the drink, they discovered that lemons sold in Egypt are green. This problem was solved when they arranged for a yellow lemon to be flown over from Italy.

Advertising men now ponder the advisability of making the "entertainment" portion of their TV sponsored programs a little dull so that the commercials will seem more exciting by contrast. In pictorial presentations one trend has been to the absurdly incongruous, to catch our eye as we search for reading matter amid a jungle of ads. Men sell whiskey while seated sideways on white horses, men with beards sell tonic water, shaggy dogs sell rum, kangaroos sell airline tickets. Meanwhile one advertising man complained: "We are suffering from fatigue of believability."

The advertising agencies, in their straining to become more persuasive, have been spending millions of dollars in research designed to learn more about the consumer. Batten Barton Durstine & Osborn has set up a division which it refers to grandiosely as "The National Panel of Consumer Opinion." It consists of several thousand housewives carefully chosen to constitute a "scale model" of the American female populace. These women can earn merchandise premiums by answering questionnaires about products and about their daily habits. Meanwhile Dr. George Gallup, long a researcher for admen, inaugurated a method of probing the consumer which he called "activation research." He set up a "sample bank" of people which he called "Mirror of America," and began probing the people in order to isolate just what triggers the sale of a product.

The most commotion in advertising circles in recent years, however, has centered on a probing technique called "motivation research," which promises to put deeper impact into sales messages. This "depth approach" to consumers involves the use of psychiatry and the social sciences to get inside the consumers' subconscious in order to discover the "psychological hook" which will impel consumers by the millions to buy a certain product.

Most of the leading advertising agencies now have psychologists, psychiatrists, or both on their payrolls. McCann-Erickson recently spent $3 million on a single monumental study of consumer psychology. A Chicago advertising agency rounded up eight leading social scientists in the Midwest (two psychoanalysts, a cultural anthropologist, a social psychologist, two sociologists, and two professors of social science) and had them spend a twelve-hour day in a hotel room watching television programs in order to glean new insights into the appeal of the sponsored programs and the commercials.

Meanwhile several dozen research firms have sprung up, all promising proficiency in depth research. The most famous, the Institute for Motivational Research, commanded by a psychoanalyst from Austria, Dr. Ernest Dichter, occupies a mountaintop castle on the Hudson. The room where local children observe television programs is equipped with hidden tape recorders, one-way viewing screens, and so on, to catch their reactions. Several hundred residents of the area constitute a "psychopanel." They have been depth-probed and card-indexed as to their hidden anxieties, hostilities, and so forth. If you want to know how much impact a sales message will have on hypochondriacs, for example, Dr. Dichter has a group of bona fide hypochondriacs on call for a trial run.

So far much of the depth-probing of consumers is more hunch

than science, but still most of the nation's largest producers of consumer products have been turning to it in an effort to increase their sales penetration. Giant corporations are raiding each other's customers with campaigns mapped by doctors of psychology.

One of the nation's largest advertising agencies now gives every single product it handles a motivational checkup. The merchandising journal *Tide* predicts that within ten years "few national marketers will launch an advertising campaign or introduce a new product without first conducting a thorough study of consumer motivations."

3

Some of the techniques used to probe consumer motives have been borrowed straight from psychiatric clinics and sociological laboratories: the depth interview (a miniature psychoanalysis without the couch), projective picture and word association tests, galvanometers (lie detectors), hypnosis, and social-layer analysis. When our motives are fathomed the experts then shape and bait psychological hooks which will bring us flopping into their corporate boats.

Among the more common strategies devised to lure us are: building self-images of ourselves into their product (playful gasolines for playful people); reminding us that their product can fill one of our hidden needs (security, self-esteem); playing upon our anxiety feelings; offering us ways, through products, to channel our aggressive feelings; selling us sexual reassurance; encouraging impulse buying; conditioning the young; selling us status symbols; making us style-conscious and then switching styles.

Several of the uses to which the insights are put strike me as constructive, or at least non-objectionable. The technique of gearing appeals to the social class most likely to enjoy your product would seem to be a step toward rationality in marketing. One of the notable cases of ill-considered selling occurred in Chicago when one of the leading brewers developed social pretensions for its brew, which had long been popular with the tavern-type clientele. The brewer's advertising men, in an effort to give the brew more class, began showing it being sipped by fox hunters, concert pianists, and drawing-room socialites. Sales did pick up slightly in the better residential areas but began falling disastrously with old customers. The boys in the taverns found the brew didn't taste right any more, though the formula was unchanged.

Social Research, Inc., looked into this fiasco when it depth-probed several hundred typical beer drinkers for the *Chicago Tribune*. It found that beer drinking in America is accepted as an informal, predominantly middle-class custom. So the brewers' foundation in its ads has recently been stressing the back-fence character of beer drinking.

The recent history of beer marketing reveals another way in which motivational analysts can produce constructive, or at least more rational, results. You may recall that in the mid-fifties many beer producers started to proclaim that their beer was particularly low-caloried and hence relatively non-fattening. The campaign was inspired by the mania for weight reduction which was particularly feverish then. Reportedly there were some impressive gains in sales as a result, but the motivational analysts viewed the low-calorie campaigns for beer with misgivings. Dr. Dichter's depth-probers, in testing the thoughts which sprang into people's minds when they saw the words "low calorie," found people thought of self-deprivation, discomfort. He admonished brewers to play up beer as a pleasure, not a medicine.

Motivational analysts have also performed a constructive service by showing advertising men how to conquer unreasonable prejudice against a product. A classic job in this respect was performed on the prune by Dr. Dichter's institute and advertising men of the prune industry. Prunes simply were not selling, and Dr. Dichter was asked to find why. His depth-probers found the prune, in our society, had become ridden with a host of connotations, all unfortunate. We thought of prunes in terms of dried-up old maids, boardinghouses, constipation, even witches. Under Dr. Dichter's guidance the prune has now been "rediscovered" as the "California wonder fruit," and admen now almost always show it in gay, zestful, youthful, colorful settings. The laxative angle is now mentioned in small type; and the prune industry, at last reports, is showing a hearty revival.

Still another way that the depth approach can perform a valid service is to help people achieve a feeling of self-worth through advertising. A producer of steam shovels found sales lagging. When a motivation study was made of prospective customers, it was discovered that steam-shovel operators play a large role in influencing the decisions of purchasing agents, and shovel operators did not like the shovel in question. A study of the ads that had been used to promote the shovel suggested a clue.

The shovel was always shown at work in all its monumental glory. Its operator was depicted as a barely visible figure inside the distant cab. The operators subconsciously felt their role was belittled. When the advertising men were advised of this source of irritation they began taking their pictures over the shoulder of the operator, with the operator shown as the confident master of the machine. This new approach reportedly brought a marked mellowing in the attitude of operators toward the shovel advertised.

4

Several of the techniques being used on us by certain of the advertising men (and their scientific allies), however, do give cause for concern. These are the techniques designed to catch us when our conscious guard is down. Here are some of the types of operation I have in mind.

1. Appeals designed to play upon our hidden weaknesses. At one of America's largest advertising agencies, staff psychologists have been exploring the subconscious of sample humans in order to find how to shape messages that will have maximum impact with people of high anxiety, body consciousness, hostility, passiveness, and so on.

In Chicago a smaller agency has conducted a psychiatric study of women's menstrual cycle and the emotional states which go with each stage of the cycle in order to learn how to sell cake mixes to women more effectively. The aim was to learn how to incorporate within one ad a double-barreled message which would appeal to women in the high phase of their cycle (creative, sexually excitable, narcissistic, outgoing, loving) and also at the same time to women who happened to be in their low phase (want attention, affection, things done for them). This could be achieved, the agency concluded, by offering the high-phase woman something new and the low-phase woman an easy-does-it meal.

2. Strategies involving the manipulation of children. The agency just mentioned also conducted a study of the psyche of straight-haired small girls to find how best to persuade them and their mothers that the girls might feel doomed to ugliness and unhappiness if they were not somehow provided with curly hair. The agency was trying to promote the use of home permanents on children and used many psychiatric techniques in probing the little girls.

The most inviting opportunity to manipulate children for profit, of course, is via television. Five-year-old children, admen have learned, make mighty fine amplifiers of singing jingles (beer or cigarettes included). They can be taught to sing them endlessly with gusto around the house all day long and, unlike the TV set, they can't be turned off.

3. The use of subthreshold effects to slip messages past our conscious guard. Some advertising men have been investigating, very quietly, the possibility of inserting "flash" sales messages in TV and movie film. The bits of film flash by so fast they are not "seen" by the conscious eye, but are reportedly seen by the subconscious eye. In late 1956 the London *Sunday Times* charged that advertisers had produced a notable rise in ice cream consumption at a cinema in New Jersey during experiments with subthreshold effects. The use of such surreptitious appeals on any substantial basis will raise an ethical question of the most serious nature, particularly if such hidden appeals are used to put across political candidates or points of view.

4. The deliberate sale of products for their status-enhancement value. Automotive advertisers have hammered so long and loud on the theme of bigness that many Americans feel socially insecure in a small or medium-sized car (unless it is their second car or a chic foreign-made car). Although the times cry for more compact cars for our crowded highways and traffic-clogged metropolitan centers, most U.S. car makers stress, in their ads, the luxurious bigness of their cars. A TV commercial for one of the medium-priced cars stressed how Big it was and then, in a bit of theatrics, the announcer exclaimed: "People are getting smart about car buying nowadays!" With that, the screen showed a crowd of "people" chanting, "We're everybody. . . . We want a Big Car and style too."

5. The creation of illogical, irrational loyalties. This occurs most conspicuously in the promotion of gasolines, cigarettes, whiskeys, detergents. The research director of a leading advertising agency which has made a study in depth of cigarette smoking states that 65 per cent of all smokers are absolutely loyal to one brand of cigarette, even to the extent of walking down five flights of stairs to buy their own brand rather than accept another brand offered by a friend. About 20 per cent are relatively loyal. Yet he found in tests where cigarettes were masked that people could identify their brand by only 2 per cent better than chance. He concluded: "They are smoking an image completely."

In the building of images, cylinders of tobacco shreds wrapped in white paper have been invested with a variety of "exciting" personalities, to use one researcher's phrase. One smoke may have an image of elegance, another is daintily feminine, still another has an image of hair-on-your-chest virility. One cigarette company deliberately changed its image to almost a teen-age personality—even though most of the heavy smokers are in the thirty-to-forty age group. The aim reportedly was to recruit more beginner smokers and develop loyalty in them which would pay off on a long-term basis.

6. The exploitation of our deepest sexual sensitivities. According to the Institute for Motivational Research the admen who conceived the cigarette slogan "Like Your Pleasures Big?" were not unaware that the phrase was a *double entendre* with "latent sexual meaning." The same institute counseled motorboat builders that men could be appealed to on the fact that power boats can be used to express a sense of power in "almost a sexual way." A midwestern advertising agency has discovered that men can be persuaded to buy a new car by the implied promise that the new, more powerful car offers them a renewal of potency.

7. The application of the insights of depth-selling to politics. In 1956 many political candidates, including the heads of the ticket, were counseled by admen to present an attractive image to the public. The most popular models were father images and courageous young Davids. At one quite important level the presidential campaign settled into a battle between advertising agencies: Batten Barton Durstine & Osborn for the Republicans and the smaller agency Norman Craig & Kummel for the Democrats.

The advertising man's approach to politics was perhaps best summed up by ad executive Rosser Reeves, who conceived the ceaseless barrage of half-minute spots on TV and radio in 1952 for the GOP. He said, "I think of a man in a voting booth who hesitates between two levers as if he were pausing between competing tubes of toothpaste in a drugstore. The brand that has made the highest penetration on his brain will win his choice."

The Democratic candidate, Adlai Stevenson (who reportedly became very unhappy about some of the strategies conceived for him by admen late in the campaign), voiced his irritation at the symbol manipulators' approach to politics (at least the GOP variety) by saying: "The idea that you can merchandise candidates for high office like breakfast cereal . . . is the ultimate indignity to the democratic process."

To sum up, I feel that while advertising in general is a constructive —and indispensable—force in our economy, its practitioners are becoming uncomfortably powerful and many of them need to exhibit more responsibility in their use of their new power than they have been doing. This particularly applies to their use of the depth approach to consumers.

The responsible leaders of the industry should, I believe, review the current trends in advertising and admonish practitioners to proceed with greater consideration for the public's welfare in certain areas. As a start they might consider the following broad trends which I believe should be viewed uneasily by thoughtful citizens:

Advertising men are pushing us toward conformity and passivity. Americans by the millions respond to their signals. Perhaps the trend to passivity is more serious than the trend to conformity. Max Lerner, in commenting on the implications he saw in some of the depth persuasion activities I described in my book, made one of the most perceptive and disquieting remarks I have encountered concerning the trend in selling. He wrote: "In motivation research . . . the consumer is always passive. He is analyzed, dissected, acted upon, bought and sold. He is a commodity to be trafficked in. The human being as a commodity, that is the disease of our age."

Many of the efforts of the advertising men provoke lasting anxieties. Economist Robert Lekachman recently speculated that we could only guess at the tensions and anxieties generated by the relentless pursuit of the emblems of success being encouraged in our society today.

The advertising men frequently are encouraging irrationality, as when they persuade us to buy products on the basis of images they have skillfully devised rather than on the merits of the physical product inside the package.

They are tending to demean many scientists who have been lured into serving them. Some of the social scientists collaborating with the advertising men maintain their standards of investigation; others strive to please, and often lay before their employers insights into our vulnerabilities which the advertising men do not hesitate to exploit.

Many of them are encouraging an attitude of wastefulness on the part of the public toward the nation's fast-shrinking resources. One conspicuous way they do this is by deliberately striving to make us dissatisfied with the serviceable products we already own.

Finally they often seek to invade the privacy of the mind. They want to know too much about us, and the inner workings of our emotions, for comfort. We should be able to be a little irrational and neurotic at times without having to fear that we thus become vulnerable to outside manipulation.

If advertising is to represent progress rather than regress for man in his struggle for self-mastery, then these considerations must be honestly faced.

Questions

1. Into which of Veblen's theories can we place the "big problem" mentioned in the sixth paragraph?
2. What kind of support does Packard primarily use in his first division? What is the effect of this kind of support?
3. What varied support methods appear in parts 2, 3, and 4? Is any one support method dominant in these parts? Is there a reason?
4. Can you add to the list of techniques in part 3? How strong does Packard make his case for concern in part 4? Can you cite other instances to support his concern?
5. Can you apply Veblen's term "honorific" to any of Packard's points? List and explain.

Topics for Composition

1. "The Growing Power of Admen" and "Pecuniary Canons of Taste" are remarkably similar in purpose. Write an essay showing the modernity of Veblen's ideas as reflected in Packard's essay.
2. Select any advertising medium—radio, television, newspaper, magazine—for analysis of its advertising techniques according to the six points Packard makes in part 4 of his essay. Limit your investigation to one issue of a magazine or newspaper or to one evening's programming on radio or television.
3. Show the variety of advertising approaches used by one product group; for instance, the soap manufacturers, the automobile makers, the tobacco companies, etc.
4. Analyze one product, pointing out those features that are utilitarian and those that are honorific. As part of your analysis, classify the honorific items according to the wants they satisfy.

The Short Story

BECAUSE Tolstoi wrote this story primarily for the uneducated Russian peasant, he wanted to present a moral lesson so straightforward and simple in style that the peasant could not overlook its message. Consequently, Tolstoi relies on the following techniques:

1. He initially contrasts the "simple goodness" of peasant life with the moral pitfalls of urban life.
2. He uses the devil as a controlling force to point out the allegiance between greed and evil.
3. He uses Pakhom's journey as a progression into unknown regions —further from humanity.

Three Arshins of Land

LEO TOLSTOI

I

A woman came from the city, to visit her younger sister in the country. The elder was a city merchant's wife; the younger, a country muzhik's. The two sisters drank tea together and talked. The older sister began to boast—to praise up her life in the city; how she lived roomily and elegantly, and went out, and how she dressed her children, and what rich things she had to eat and drink, and how she went to drive, and to walk, and to the theater.

The younger sister felt affronted, and began to depreciate the life of a merchant, and to set forth the advantages of her own,—that of the peasant.

"I wouldn't exchange my life for yours," says she. "Granted that we live coarsely, still we don't know what fear is. You live more elegantly; but you have to sell a great deal, else you find yourselves entirely sold. And the proverb runs, 'Loss is Gain's bigger brother.' It also happens, to-day you're rich, but to-morrow you're a beggar.[1] But our muzhiks' affairs are more reliable; the muzhik's life is meager, but long; we may not be rich, but we have enough."

The elder sister began to say:—

[1] *Literally, find thyself under the windows.*

"Enough,—I should think so! So do pigs and calves! No fine dresses, no good society. How your goodman[2] works! how you live in the dunghill! and so you will die and it will be the same thing with your children."

"Indeed," said the younger, "our affairs are all right. We live well. We truckle to no one, we stand in fear of no one. But you in the city all live in the midst of temptations: to-day it's all right; but to-morrow up comes some improper person, I fear, to tempt you, and tempts your khozyaïn either to cards, or to wine, or to women. And everything goes to ruin. Isn't it so?"

Pakhom, the "goodman," was listening on the oven, as the women discussed.

"That's true," says he, "the veritable truth. As we peasants[3] from childhood turn up mother earth,[4] so folly stays in our head, and does not depart. Our one trouble is,—so little land. If I only had as much land as I wanted, I shouldn't be afraid of any one—even of the Devil."

The women drank up their tea, talked some more about dresses, put away the dishes, and went to bed.

But the Devil was sitting behind the oven; he heard everything. He was delighted because the peasant woman had induced her husband to boast with her; he had boasted that, if he had land enough, the Devil could not get him!

"All right," he thinks; "you and I'll have to fight it out. I will give you a lot of land. I'll get you through the land."

II

Next the muzhiks lived a lady.[5] She had one hundred and twenty desyatins[6] of land. And she had always lived peaceably with the muzhiks, never taking any advantage of them. But a retired soldier engaged himself as her overseer, and he began to vex the muzhiks with fines. No matter how careful Pakhom was, either his horse would trample down the oats, or his cow would wander into the garden, or his calves would get into the meadows; there was a fine for everything.

[2] Khozyaïn.
[3] Nash brat; *literally, our brother.*
[4] Zemlya-matushka.
[5] Baruinka, *diminutive of* baruinya, *gracious lady.*
[6] *Three hundred and twenty-four acres.*

Pakhom paid the fines, and scolded and beat the domestics. And during the summer Pakhom fell into many a sin on account of this overseer. And still he was glad that he had cattle in his dvor; though fodder was scarce, he was in no apprehension.

During the winter, the rumor spread that the lady was going to sell her land, and that a dvornik from the highway had made arrangements to buy it.

The muzhiks heard it, and groaned.

"Now," think they, "the land will belong to the dvornik; he will make us pay worse fines than the lady did. It is impossible for us to live without this land. All of us around here live on it."

The peasants went to the lady in a body and began to beg her not to sell the land to the dvornik, but to let them have it. They promised to pay a higher price.

The lady agreed. The muzhiks tried to arrange, as a mir, to buy all the land. Once, twice, they collected in meeting, but there was a hitch in affairs. The evil one put them at variance; they were utterly unable to come to any agreement.

And the muzhiks determined to purchase the land individually, according to the ability of each. And the lady agreed to this also.

Pakhom heard that a neighbor had bought twenty desyatins[7] from the lady, and that she had given him a year in which to pay her half of the money. Pakhom was envious.

"They will buy all the land," he said to himself, "and I shall be behind them." He began to reason with his wife.

"The people are buying it up," said he. "We must buy ten desyatins too. Otherwise it will be impossible to live; the overseer was eating us up with fines."

They planned how to buy it. They had laid up a hundred rubles; then they sold a colt and half their bees; and they put their son out as a laborer, and they got some more from their brother-in-law; and thus they collected half of the money.

Pakhom gathered up the money, selected fifteen desyatins of land with forest on it, and went to the lady to make the purchase. He negotiated for fifteen desyatins, struck a bargain, and paid down the earnest-money. They went to the city, ratified the purchase; he paid down half of the money; the remainder he bound himself to pay in two years.

And Pakhom now had his land. Pakhom took seed, and sowed the land that he had bought. In a single year he paid up the debt

[7] *Fifty-four acres.*

to the lady and to his brother-in-law. And Pakhom became a proprietor.[8] He plowed all his land, and sowed it; he made hay on his own land; he cut stakes on his own land; and on his own land he pastured cattle. Pakhom would ride out over his wide fields to plow, or he would take note of his crops, or gaze at his meadows. And yet he was not happy. The grass seemed to him to be wasted, and the flowers flowering in it seemed entirely different. Formerly he used to ride over this land,—the land as land; but now the land began to be absolutely peculiar.

III

Thus Pakhom lived, and enjoyed himself. Everything would have been good, only the muzhiks began to trespass on his grain and meadows. He begged them to refrain, but they would not stop it. Now the cowboys let the cows into the meadow; now the horses escaped from the night-guard into his corn-field.

And Pakhom drove them out, and forgave it, and never went to law; then he got tired of it, and complained to the volost-court.[9] And though he knew that the muzhiks did it from carelessness, and not from malice, he said to himself:—

"It is impossible to overlook it, otherwise they'll always be pasturing their cattle there. We must teach them a lesson."

He thus taught them in court once; he taught them twice: first one was fined, then another. The muzhiks, Pakhom's neighbors, began to harbor spite against him. Once more they began to trespass, and this time on purpose. Some one got into his woodland by night. They cut down a dozen of his lindens for basts. Pakhom went to his grove, saw what had been done, and turned pale. Some one had been there; the linden branches lay scattered about, the stumps stood out. The whole clump had been cut down to the very last; the rascal had cleaned it all out; only one was left standing.

Pakhom fell into a rage. "Akh!" said he to himself, "if I only knew who did that, I would give him a kneading."

He thought and he thought, "Who could it be?"

"No one more likely," said he to himself, "than Semka."[10]

He went to search through Semka's dvor; he found nothing; they

[8] Pomyeshchik.
[9] *The* volost *is a district including several villages.*
[10] *Semka, diminutive of Semyon, Simeon.*

only exchanged some quarrelsome words. And Pakhom felt still more certain that Semyon had done it. He entered a complaint against him. They took it into court and had a long trial. The muzhik was acquitted, for there was no proof against him. Pakhom was still more affronted; he got incensed at the starshina and at the judges.

"You," said he, "are on the side of a pack of thieves. If you were decent men, you wouldn't acquit thieves."

Pakhom quarreled both with the judges and with his neighbors. They began even to threaten him with the "red rooster."[11] Pakhom had come to live on a broader scale on his farm, but with more constraint in the commune.

And about this time the rumor spread that the people were going to new places. And Pakhom said to himself:—

"There is no reason for *me* to go from my land; but if any of our neighbors should go, it would give us more room. I would take their land for myself; I would get it around here: life would be much better, for now it is too confined."

One time Pakhom was sitting at home; a wandering muzhik came along. They let the muzhik have a night's lodging; they gave him something to eat; they entered into conversation with him:—

"Whither, please, is God taking you?"

The muzhik said that he was on his way from down the Volga, where he had been at work. The muzhik related, a word at a time, how the people had gone colonizing there. He related how they had settled there, made a community, and given each *soul* ten desyatins of land. "But the land is such," said he, "that they sowed rye. Such stalks—the horses never saw the like—so thick! five handfuls made a sheaf. One muzhik," said he, "was perfectly poor,—came with his hands alone,—and now he has six horses and two cows."

Pakhom's heart burned within him; he said to himself: "Why remain here in straitened circumstances, when it is possible to live well? I will sell my house and land here; then, with the money I get, I will start anew, and have a complete establishment. But here in these narrow quarters—it's a sin. Only I must find out all about it for myself."

He planned to be gone all summer, and started. From Samara he sailed down the Volga in a steamboat, then he went on foot four hundred versts. He reached the place. It was just so. The muzhiks were living on a generous scale,[12] on farms of ten desyatins each,

[11] *The picturesque Russian metaphor for a conflagration.*
[12] Prostorno, *roomily.*

and they were glad to have accessions to their community. "And any one who has a little money can buy for three rubles as much of the very best land as he wishes, besides his allotment. You can buy just as much as you wish."

Pakhom made a thorough study of it; in the autumn he returned home, and proceeded to sell out everything. He sold his land to advantage, sold his dvor, sold all his cattle, withdrew his name from the community, waited till spring, and moved with his family to the new place.

IV

Pakhom came with his family to the new place, and enrolled himself in a large village. He treated the elders to vodka, arranged all the papers. Pakhom was accepted; he was allotted, as for five persons, fifty desyatins[13] of the land, to be located in different fields, besides the pasturage. Pakhom settled down. He got cattle. He had three times as much land as he had had before, and the land was fertile. Life was tenfold better than what it had been in the old time; he had all the arable land and fodder that he needed. He could keep as many cattle as he liked.

At first, while he was getting settled, and putting his house in order, Pakhom was well pleased; but after he began to feel at home, even this farm seemed to him rather narrow quarters.

The first year Pakhom sowed wheat on his allotment; it came up well. He was anxious to sow wheat; but his allotment seemed to him altogether too small for his ambition.

Wheat is sowed there on grass or fallow land. They sow it one year, two years, and let it lie fallow till the feather-grass comes up again. There are many rival claimants for such land and there's not nearly enough to go round.

Quarrels also arose on account of this; one was richer than another: they all wanted to sow, but the poorer ones had to resort to merchants for loans.

Pakhom was desirous of sowing as much as possible. The next year he went to a merchant and hired land for a year. He sowed more; it came up well, but he had to go a long way from the village, not less than fifteen versts. He saw how muzhik-merchants in the vicinity lived in fine houses, and got rich.

[13] *One hundred and thirty-five acres.*

"That's the thing," said Pakhom to himself. "If only I could buy the land, then I would have a fine house. It would all be in one piece."

And Pakhom began to cogitate how he might get a perpetual title.

Thus Pakhom lived three years. He hired land and sowed more wheat. The years were good, and the wheat grew well, and extra money was laid away.

As life passed, it became every year irksome to Pakhom to buy land with the men, to waste time over it; where the land is pretty good, the muzhiks instantly fly to it and divide it all up. He was always too late to buy cheap, and he had nothing to sow on.

But in the third year, he bought, on shares with a merchant, a pasturage of the muzhiks; and they had already plowed it. The muzhiks had been at law about it, and so the work was lost. "If I owned the land," he thinks, "I should not truckle to any one; and it would not be a sin."

And Pakhom began to inquire where he might buy land in perpetuity. And he struck upon a muzhik. The muzhik had five hundred desyatins[14] for sale; and, as he was anxious to get rid of it, he would sell at a bargain.

Pakhom began to dicker with him. He argued and argued, and finally the muzhik agreed to sell for fifteen hundred rubles, half the money on mortgage. They had already come to an agreement, when a peddler happened along, and asked Pakhom to let him have a little something to eat.

While they were drinking a cup of tea, they entered into conversation.

The peddler related how he was on his way from the distant Bashkirs.

"There," said he, "I bought of the Bashkirs fifteen hundred desyatins of land; and I had to pay only a thousand rubles."

Pakhom began to ask questions. The peddler told his story.

"All I did," said he, "was to satisfy the old men. I distributed some khalats and carpets, worth a hundred rubles, besides a chest of tea; and I gave a little wine to those who drank. And I got it for twenty kopeks a desyatin."—He exhibited the title-deed.—"The land," says he, "is by a little river, and the steppe is all covered with grass."

Pakhom went on asking more questions,—How he managed it, and who?

"The land," said the merchant, "you wouldn't go round it in a

[14] *Thirteen hundred and fifty acres.*

year,—it's all Bashkirian. And the people are as stupid as rams. You could almost get it for nothing."

"Well," said Pakhom to himself, "why should I spend my thousand rubles for five hundred desyatins, and hang a burden of debt around my neck besides? But there, how much I could get for a thousand rubles!"

V

Pakhom asked how he went; and, as soon as he said good-by to the peddler, he determined to go. He left his house in his wife's care, took his man, and started. When they reached the city, he bought a chest of tea, gifts, wine, just as the merchant said. They traveled and traveled; they traveled five hundred versts.[15] On the seventh day they came to the range of the wandering Bashkirs. It was all just as the merchant had said. They all live in the steppe, along a little river, in felt-covered kibitkas. They themselves do not plow and they eat no bread. And their cattle graze along the steppe, and their horses are in droves. Behind the kibitkas the colts are tied, and twice a day they bring the mares to them. They milk the mares, and make kumys out of the milk. The women churn the mares' milk, and make cheese; and all the muzhiks can do is to drink kumys and tea, to eat mutton, and play on their dudkas.[16] All are polite and jolly; they keep festival all summer. The people are very dark, and cannot speak Russian, but are affable.

As soon as the Bashkirs saw Pakhom, they came forth from their kibitkas; they surrounded their guest. The interpreter made his acquaintance. Pakhom told him that he had come to see about land. The Bashkirs were delighted, took him to a fine kibitka, spread rugs down, gave him a down-cushion to sit on, sat round him, and proceeded to treat him to tea and kumys. They slaughtered a ram, and gave him mutton.

Pakhom fetched from his tarantas his gifts, and began to distribute them among the Bashkirs.

Pakhom gave the Bashkirs his gifts, and divided the tea. The Bashkirs were overjoyed. They jabbered and jabbered together, and then commanded the interpreter to speak.

"They bid me tell you," says the interpreter, "that they have

[15] *Three hundred and thirty miles.*
[16] *Reed-pipes.*

taken a fancy to you; and that we have a custom of doing everything possible to gratify a guest, and repay him for his gifts. You have given us gifts. Now tell what you wish from among our possessions, in order that we may give it to you."

"Above all else that you have," says Pakhom, "I would like some of your land. In my country," says he, "there is a scarcity of land. The land is cultivated to death. But you have much land, and good land. I never saw the like."

The interpreter translated for him. The Bashkirs talked and talked. Pakhom could not understand what they were saying; but he saw that they were good-natured, that they were talking at the top of their voices and laughing. Then they relapsed into silence, looked at Pakhom; and the interpreter said:—

"They bid me tell you that, in return for your kindness, they are happy to give you as much land as you wish. Only show us your land—it shall be yours."

They were still talking, and began to dispute angrily. And Pakhom asked what they were quarreling about.

And the interpreter replied:—

"Some say that they ought to ask the head man about the land, and that without his consent it is impossible. And others say that it can be done without the head man."

VI

The Bashkirs were quarreling; suddenly a man came in a foxskin shapka.

They grew silent, and all stood up. And the interpreter said:—

"This is the head man himself."

Instantly Pakhom got out his best khalat, and gave it to the head man, together with five pounds of tea.

The head man accepted it, and sat down in the chief place. And immediately the Bashkirs began to tell him all about it.

The head man listened and listened; nodded his head, in sign of silence for all, and began to speak to Pakhom in Russian.

"Well," said he, "it can be done. Take it wherever you please. There is plenty of land."

"I shall get as much as I want," said Pakhom to himself. "I must secure it immediately, else they'll say it's mine, and then take it away."

"I thank you," says he, "for your kind words. I have seen that you have much land, and I need not very much. Only you must let me know what shall be mine. As soon as possible you must have it measured off and secured to me. God disposes of life and death. You good people make the grant, but the time may come when your children will take it away."

"You are right," says the head man; "it must be secured to you."

Pakhom began to speak:—

"I have heard that a merchant was here with you. You also gave him land, and struck a bargain. I should like to do the same."

The head man understood perfectly.

"This can all be done," says he. "We have a clerk; and we will go to the city, and will all put on our seals."

"And the price will be how much?" asked Pakhom.

"We have one price: one thousand rubles a day."

Pakhom did not understand. "What is this measure, the day? How many desyatins are there in it?"

"We can't reckon it," says he. "But we sell it by the day: all that you can go round in a day—that is yours; and the price of a day is one thousand rubles."

Pakhom was astonished.

"Look here," said he. "What I can go round in a day is a good deal of land!"

The head man laughed.

"It's all yours," said he. "Only one stipulation: if you don't come back within the day to the place from which you started, your money is lost."

"But how," says Pakhom, "can I mark where I am going?"

"Well, we'll stand on the place where it pleases you; we will be standing there; and you shall go and draw the circle, and take with you a hoe, and make a mark wherever you please; at the angle dig a little hole, put some turf in it; and we will go over it, from hole to hole, with the plow. Make your circle as large as you like, only at sunset you must be back at that place from which you set out. All that you encircle is yours."

Pakhom was delighted. They agreed to go out early. They talked it over, drank still more kumys, ate the mutton, and drank some more tea. It approached nightfall. They arranged for Pakhom to sleep in a down-bed, and the Bashkirs went off. They agreed to come together at early dawn the next day, and to go out at sunrise.

VII

Pakhom lay in his down-bed; and there he could not sleep, all on account of thinking of his land.

"I will get hold of a great tract," said he to himself. "I can go over fifty versts in one day. A day now is worth a year. There'll be a good bit of land in a circle of fifty versts. I will sell off the worst parts, or let it to the muzhiks; and I will pick out what I like, and I will settle on it. I will have a two-ox plow, and I will take two men as laborers. I will cultivate fifty desyatins, and I will pasture my cattle on the rest."

Pakhom did not get a wink of sleep all night. Just before dawn he dropped into a doze. He just dropped into a doze and had a dream. He seemed to see himself lying in this very same kibitka, and listening to somebody cackling outside. And it seemed to him that he wanted to see who was laughing; and he got up and went out of the kibitka, and lo! that very same head man of the Bashkirs was sitting in front of the kibitka, and was holding his sides, and roaring and cackling about something.

He went up to him and asked:—

"What are you laughing at?"

And then it seemed to him that it was no longer the head man of the Bashkirs, but the peddler who had come to him and told him about the land.

And as soon as he saw that it was the peddler, he asked:—

"Have you been here long?"

And then it was no longer the peddler, but that muzhik who had come down the Volga so long ago.

And Pakhom saw that it was not the muzhik either, but the Devil himself, with horns and hoofs, sitting and laughing; and before him was lying a man barefooted, in shirt and drawers. And Pakhom looked more attentively to find out who the man was.

And he saw that the dead man was none other than—himself! Pakhom was frightened, and woke up.

He woke up.

"What was I dreaming about?" he asked himself. He looked around, he peered out of the closed door: it was already getting light, day was beginning to dawn.

"The people must be getting up," he thinks; "it's time to start."

Pakhom arose, aroused his man in the tarantas, told him to harness up, and then went to arouse the Bashkirs.

"Time," says he, "to go out on the steppe, to measure it off."

The Bashkirs got up, all collected; and the head man came forth. The Bashkirs again began by drinking kumys; they wished Pakhom to treat them to tea, but he was not inclined to delay.

"If we go . . . it is time to go now," said he.

VIII

The Bashkirs made ready; some got on horseback, some climbed into carts; they started. And Pakhom rode with his man in their tarantas, and took with him a hoe. They rode out into the steppe; the dawn was beginning. They reached a mound—*shikhan* in Bashkirian. They descended from their carts, dismounted from their horses, collected in a crowd. The chief man came to Pakhom, and pointed with his hand.

"Here," says he, "all is ours, as far as you can see. Take what you desire."

Pakhom's eyes burned. The whole region was grassy, flat as the palm of your hand, black as a pot; and where there was a hollow, it was filled with grass as high as one's breast.

The chief man took off his foxskin cap, and laid it on the ground.

"Here," says he, "is the spot. Start from here, come back here. All that you go round shall be yours."

Pakhom took out his money, laid it in the cap; took off his kaftan, stood in his blouse [17] alone; girded himself around the belly with his sash, pulled it tighter; hung round his neck a little bag with bread, put a little flask with water into his belt, tightened his leg-wrappers, took the hoe from his man, and got ready to start.

He pondered and pondered on which side to take it; it was good everywhere.

He said to himself:—

"It's all one; I will go toward the sunrise."

He faced toward the east and paced back and forth, waiting till the sun should show above the horizon.

He said to himself, "I will not lose any time. It's cool, and easier to walk."

As soon as the sunlight gushed out over the horizon, he threw his hoe over his shoulder, and started out on the steppe.

Pakhom proceeded neither slow nor fast. He went about a verst; [18]

[17] Poddyovka, *a sort of half kaftan.*
[18] *Thirty-five hundred feet.*

he halted and he dug a little pit and piled the turf in it, so that it might attract attention.

He went farther. As he went on, he quickened his pace. As he kept going on, he dug other little pits.

Pakhom looked around. The shikhan was still in sight in the sun, and the people were standing on it; the tires on the tarantas wheels glistened. Pakhom conjectured that he has been five versts. He began to get warm; he took off his blouse, threw it over his shoulder, and went on. It grew hot. He looked at the sun.[19] It was already breakfast-time.

"One stage over," thinks Pakhom, "and four of them make a day; it's too early as yet to turn round. Only let me take off my boots."

He sat down and took off his boots, put them in his belt, and went on. It was easy walking. He said to himself, "Let me go five versts farther, then I will swing round to the left. This place is very good; it's a pity to give it up."

The farther he went, the better it became. He still went straight ahead. He looked round—the shikhan was now scarcely visible; and the people, like little ants, made a black spot on it; and something barely glistened.

"Well," said Pakhom, "I have enough in this direction; I must be turning round. I am sweaty enough. I should like a drink."

He halted, dug a pit, filled it with turf, unfastened his flask, took a drink, and turned sharply to the left. He went and went—the grass was deep, and it was hot.

Pakhom began to feel weary; he looked at the sun and saw that it was dinner-time.

"Well," said he, "I must have a rest."

Pakhom halted. He sat down and ate his bread and water, but did not try to lie down. He said to himself:—

"If I lie down, I may fall asleep."

He sat a little while; then he started on again; he found it easy walking; his strength was renewed by his meal, but now it was growing very hot—yes, and the sun began to decline; but still he kept going. He said:—

"Endure it for an hour, and you have an age to live."

He still went on a long distance in this direction. He kept intending to turn to the left, but lo! it was a low land and a moist soil. It was a pity to throw it away! He said to himself:—

"This day has been a good one."

[19] *Russian,* solnuishko, *little sun.*

He still continued straight on. He took in the low land—dug his pit on the farther side of the low land, the hollow, and then turned the second corner.

Pakhom gazed back in the direction of the shikhan. The heat had caused a haziness, there was a quivering in the atmosphere, and through the haziness the people on the shikhan could scarcely be seen.

"Well," said Pakhom, "I have taken long sides—I must make this one shorter."

He started on the third side—he tried to hasten his pace. He looked at the sun—it was already far down the west, and on the third side he had only gone two versts; and back to the starting-point, there were fifteen versts.

"No," he said, "even though the tract should be uneven I must hurry back in a straight line. It wouldn't do to take too much; even as it is, I have already a good deal of land."

Pakhom dug his little pit in all haste, and headed straight for the shikhan.

IX

Pakhom went straight toward the shikhan, and now it began to be heavy work for him. He was bathed in sweat; and his bare legs were cut and torn, and began to fail under him. He felt a desire to rest, but it was impossible; he could not stop till sunset. The sun did not delay, but was sinking lower and lower.

"Akh!" he says to himself, "can I have made a blunder? can I have taken too much? why don't you hurry along faster?"

He gazed at the shikhan—it gleamed in the sun; it was still a long distance to the place, and the sun was now not far from the horizon.

Still Pakhom hurried on; it was hard for him, but he kept quickening his pace, quickening his pace. He walked and walked—it was still always far away. He took to the double-quick. He threw away his blouse, his boots, his flask. He threw away his cap, but he clung to his hoe and helped himself along with it.

"Akh!" he said to himself, "I was too greedy; I have ruined the whole business; I shall not get there before sunset."

And his breath began to fail him all the worse because of his apprehension. Pakhom ran—his shirt and drawers clung to his body by reason of sweat—his mouth was parched. In his breast a pair of blacksmith's bellows, as it were, were working; and in his heart a mill was beating; and his legs were almost breaking down under him.

It became painful for Pakhom. He said to himself:—

"Suppose I should die from the strain?"

He was afraid of dropping dead, and yet he could not stop.

"If after running, I were to stop now, they would call me a fool."

He ran and ran. He was now getting near, and he could hear the Bashkirs shouting—screaming at him; and their screams made his heart pain him more than ever.

Pakhom ran on with the last of his strength, and the sun was still hovering on the horizon's edge; it went into the haze; there was a great glow, red as blood. Now—now it was setting! The sun had nearly set, but now Pakhom was not far from the place. He could see it; and the people on the shikhan gesticulating to him, urging him on. He saw the foxskin cap on the ground, he could even see the money in it. And he saw the head man sitting on the ground, holding his belly with his hands. And Pakhom remembered his dream.

"Much land," he said to himself, "but perhaps God has not willed me to live on it. Okh! I have ruined myself," he thinks. "I shall not get it."

Pakhom looked at the sun, but the sun had gone down under the earth; its body was already hidden, and its last segment had disappeared under the horizon.

Pakhom exerted his last energies, threw himself forward with his body; his legs just kept him from falling.

Just as Pakhom reached the shikhan, it suddenly grew dark. He saw that the sun had gone. Pakhom groaned.

"I have lost my labor," thinks he. He was just about to stop; but as he still heard the Bashkirs all screaming, he remembered that he was below them, and therefore the sun seemed to have set, although it had not set to those on top of the shikhan. Pakhom took a breath and ran up the shikhan. It was still light on the mound. Pakhom ran, and there was the cap. In front of the cap sat the head man, laughing and holding his sides.

Pakhom remembered his dream, groaned "Akh!" his legs gave way under him, and he fell forward, reaching out his arms toward the cap.

"Aï! brave lad!" shouted the head man. "You have got a good piece of land."

Pakhom's man ran to him, attempted to help him to his feet; but from his mouth poured a stream of blood, and he lay dead.

The Bashkirs clucked with their tongues, expressing their sorrow.

Pakhom's man took the hoe, dug a grave for him, made it just long enough, from head to foot,—three arshins,[20]—and buried him.

[20] *About seven feet.*

Questions

1. What indications do we have in the opening section that Tolstoi intended his story for the peasant class?
2. Divide the story into its several parts. What kind of progression is evident in each part in respect to setting and characterization?
3. How fully developed is the character of Pakhom? How does the level of development fit the purpose of the story?
4. What Biblical parallel can we offer for Pakhom's dream?
5. Does Tolstoi make any statements about the responsibility that goes with wealth? Explain why such statements should add to the significance of the story.

Topics for Composition

1. Although Pakhom is not a fully developed character, we can see that the story moves to its climax as Pakhom's greed becomes his single purpose in life. Write an essay showing Tolstoi's reduction of Pakhom's human characteristics as he is converted into a symbol of greed.
2. The author obviously wanted his readers to understand that greed is a tool of the devil. Write an essay showing how the presence and involvement of the devil are kept before the reader.
3. From your knowledge of history and some additional research, parallel Pakhom's greed and subsequent death with the life and fate of any one of the notable tyrants of the past.

In this story, elements of characterization, atmosphere, and structure combine to bring about Bunin's indictment of materialistic man who has lost sight of life's true values. As you read, observe closely Bunin's careful blending of the following:

1. The itinerary of the gentleman that neatly contrasts cultural benefits with materialistic objects
2. The brilliance of the "Atlantida" and the subsequent step-by-step dimming of light as the journey progresses
3. The gentleman's attitude toward his wife, daughter, fellow travelers, and servants
4. The circular structure of the story

The Gentleman from San Francisco

IVAN BUNIN

Alas, alas that great city Babylon, that mighty city!

THE APOCALYPSE

The gentleman from San Francisco—neither at Naples nor at Capri had any one remembered his name—was going to the Old World for two whole years, with wife and daughter, solely for the sake of pleasure.

He was firmly convinced that he was fully entitled to rest, to pleasure, to prolonged and comfortable travel, and to not a little else besides. For such a conviction he had his reasons,—that, in the first place, he was rich, and, in the second, that he was only now beginning to live, despite his eight and fifty years. Until now he had not lived, but had merely existed,—not at all badly, it is true, but, never the less, putting all his hopes on the future. He had laboured with never a pause for rest,—the coolies, whom he had imported by whole thousands, well knew what this meant!—and finally he saw that much had already been accomplished, that he had almost come abreast of those whom he had at one time set out to emulate, and he decided to enjoy breathing space. It was a custom among the class of people to which he belonged to commence their enjoyment of life with a journey to Europe, to India, to Egypt. He, too, proposed to do the same. Of course he desired, first of all, to reward himself for his years of toil; however, he rejoiced on account of his wife and daughter as well. His wife had never been distinguished for any special sensitiveness to new impressions,—but then, all elderly American women are fervid travellers. As for his daughter,—a girl no longer in her first youth, and somewhat sickly,—travel was a downright necessity for her: to say nothing of the benefit to her health, were there no fortuitous encounters during travels? It is while travelling that one may at times sit at table with a *milliardaire*, or scrutinize frescoes by his side.

The itinerary worked out by the gentleman from San Francisco was an extensive one. In December and January he hoped to enjoy the sun of Southern Italy, the monuments of antiquity, the *tarantella*, the serenades of strolling singers, and that which men of his age relish with the utmost *finesse:* the love of little, youthful Neapolitaines, even though it be given not entirely without ulterior motives;

he contemplated spending the Carnival in Nice, in Monte Carlo, whither the very pick of society gravitates at that time,—that very society upon which all the benefits of civilization depend: not merely the cut of tuxedos, but, as well, the stability of thrones, and the declaration of wars, and the prosperity of hotels,—Monte Carlo, where some give themselves up with passion to automobile and sail races; others to roulette; a third group to that which it is the custom to call flirting; a fourth, to trap-shooting, in which the pigeons, released from their cotes, soar up most gracefully above emerald-green swards, against the background of a sea that is the colour of forget-me-nots,—only, in the same minute, to strike against the ground as little, crumpled clods of white. . . . The beginning of March he wanted to devote to Florence; about the time of the Passion of Our Lord to arrive at Rome, in order to hear the *Miserere* there; his plans also embraced Venice, and Paris, and bull-fighting in Seville, and sea-bathing in the British Islands, and Athens, and Constantinople, and Palestine, and Egypt, and even Japan,—of course, be it understood, already on the return trip. . . . And everything went very well at first.

It was the end of November; almost as far as Gibraltar it was necessary to navigate now through an icy murk, now amidst a blizzard of wet snow; but the ship sailed in all safety and even without rolling; the passengers the steamer was carrying proved to be many, and all of them people of note; the ship—the famous *Atlantida*—resembled the most expensive of European hotels, with all conveniences: an all-night bar, Turkish baths, a newspaper of its own,—and life upon it flowed in accordance with a most complicated system of regulations: people got up early, to the sounds of bugles, stridently resounding through the corridors at that dark hour when day was so slowly and inimically dawning over the grayish-green desert of waters, ponderously turbulent in the mist. Putting on their flannel pyjamas, the passengers drank coffee, chocolate, cocoa; then they got into marble baths, did their exercises, inducing an appetite and a sense of well-being, performed their toilet for the day, and went to breakfast. Until eleven one was supposed to promenade the decks vigorously, inhaling the fresh coolness of the ocean, or to play at shuffle-board and other games for the sake of arousing the appetite anew, and, at eleven, to seek sustenance in bouillon and sandwiches; having refreshed themselves, the passengers perused their newspaper with gusto and calmly awaited lunch, a meal still more nourishing and varied than the breakfast. The next two hours were sacred to repose,—the decks were then encumbered with *chaises longues*, upon which the travellers reclined, covered up with plaids, contemplating the cloud-flecked sky and the foaming hummocks flashing by over the side, or else pleasantly dozing off; at five o'clock, refreshed and put in good spirits, they were drenched with strong fragrant tea, served with cookies; at seven they were apprized by bugle signals of a dinner of nine courses. . . . And thereupon the gentleman from San Francisco, in an access of animal spirits, would hurry to his resplendent *cabine de luxe*, to dress.

In the evening the tiers of the *Atlantida* gaped through the dusk as though they were fiery, countless eyes, and a great multitude of servants worked with especial feverishness in the kitchens, sculleries, and wine vaults. The ocean, heaving on the other side of the walls, was awesome; but none gave it a thought, firmly believing it under the sway of the captain,—a red-haired man of monstrous bulk and ponderousness, always seeming sleepy, resembling, in his uniform frock-coat, with its golden chevrons, an enormous idol; it was only very rarely that he left his mysterious quarters to appear in public. A siren on the forecastle howled every minute in hellish sullenness and whined in frenzied malice, but not many of the diners heard the siren,—it was drowned by the strains of a splendid stringed orchestra, playing exquisitely and ceaselessly in the two-tiered hall, decorated with marble, its floors covered with velvet rugs; festively flooded with the lights of crystal lustres and gilded *girandoles*, filled to overflowing with diamond-bedecked ladies in *décoletté* and men in tuxedos, graceful waiters and deferent *maitres d'hôtel*,—among whom one, who took orders for wines exclusively, even walked about with a chain around his neck, like a lord mayor. A tuxedo and perfect linen made the gentleman from San Francisco appear very much younger. Spare, not tall, clumsily but strongly built, groomed until he shone and moderately animated, he sat in the aureate-pearly refulgence of this palatial room, at a table with a bottle of amber Johannesberg, with countless goblets, small and large, of the thinnest glass, with a curly bouquet of curly hyacinths. There was something of the Mongol about his yellowish face with clipped silvery moustache; his large teeth gleamed with gold fillings; his stalwart, bald head glistened like old ivory. Rich, yet in keeping with her years, was the dress of his wife,—a big woman, expansive and calm; elaborate, yet light and diaphanous, with an innocent frankness, was that of his daughter,—tall, slender, with magnificent hair, exquisitely dressed, with breath aromatic from violet cachous and with the tenderest of tiny, rosy pimples about her lips and between her shoulder blades, just the least bit powdered. . . . The dinner lasted for two whole hours, while after dinner there was dancing in the ball room, during which the men,–the gentleman from San Francisco among their number, of course,–with their feet cocked up, determined, upon the basis of the latest political and stock-exchange news, the destinies of nations, smoking Habana cigars and drinking *liqueurs* until they were crimson in the face, seated in the bar, where the waiters were negroes in red jackets, the whites of their eyes resembling hard boiled eggs with the shell off. The ocean, with a dull roar, was moiling in black mountains on the other side of the wall; the snow-gale whistled mightily through the sodden rigging; the whole steamer quivered as it mastered both the gale and the mountains, sundering to either side, as though with a plough, their shifting masses, that again and again boiled up and reared high, with tails of foam; the siren, stifled by the fog, was moaning with a deathly anguish; the lookouts up in their crow's-nest froze from the cold and grew dazed from straining their attention beyond their strength. Like to the grim and sultry depths of the infernal regions, like to their ultimate, their ninth circle, was the womb of the steamer, below the water line,–that womb where dully gurgled the gigantic furnaces, devouring with their incandescent maws mountains of hard coal, cast into them by men stripped to the waist, purple from the flames, and with smarting, filthy sweat pouring over them; whereas here, in the bar, men threw their legs over the arms of their chairs with never a care, sipping cognac and *liqueurs*, and were wafted among clouds of spicy smoke as they indulged in well-turned conversation; in the ball room everything was radiant with light and warmth and joy; the dancing couples were now awhirl in waltzes, now twisting in the tango,–and the music insistently, in some delectably-shameless melancholy, was suppliant always of the one, always of the same thing. . . . There was an ambassador among this brilliant throng,–a lean, modest little old man; there was a great man of riches,–clean-shaven, lanky, of indeterminate years, and with the appearance of a prelate, in his dress-coat of an old-fashioned cut; there was a well-known Spanish writer; there was a world-celebrated beauty, already just the very least trifle faded and of an unenviable morality; there was an exquisite couple in love with each other, whom all watched with curiosity and whose happiness was unconcealed: *he* danced only with *her;* sang–and with great ability –only to *her* accompaniment; and everything they did was carried out so charmingly, that the captain was the only one who knew that this pair was hired by Lloyd's to play at love for a good figure, and that they had been sailing for a long time, now on one ship, now on another.

At Gibraltar everybody was gladdened by the sun,—it seemed to be early spring; a new passenger, whose person aroused the general interest, made his appearance on board the *Atlantida*,—he was the hereditary prince of a certain Asiatic kingdom, travelling incognito; a little man who somehow seemed to be all made of wood, even though he was alert in his movements; broad of face, with narrow eyes, in gold-rimmed spectacles; a trifle unpleasant through the fact that his skin showed through his coarse black moustache like that of a cadaver; on the whole, however, he was charming, unpretentious, and modest. On the Mediterranean Sea there was a whiff of winter again; the billows ran high, and were as multi-coloured as the tail of a peacock; they had snowy-white crests, lashed up—although the sun was sparkling brightly and the sky was perfectly clear—by a *tramontana*, a chill northern wind from beyond the mountains, that was joyously and madly rushing to meet the ship. . . . Then, on the second day, the sky began to pale, the horizon became covered with mist, land was nearing; Ischia, Capri appeared; through the binoculars Naples—lumps of sugar strewn at the foot of some dove-coloured mass—could be seen; while over it and this dove-coloured thing were visible the ridges of distant mountains, vaguely glimmering with the dead whiteness of snows. There was a great number of people on deck; many of the ladies and gentlemen had already put on short, light fur coats, with the fur outside; Chinese boys, never contradictory and never speaking above a whisper, bow-legged striplings with pitch-black queues reaching to their heels and with eye-lashes as long and thick as those of young girls, were already dragging, little by little, sundry plaids, canes, and portmanteaux and grips of alligator hide toward the companion-ways. . . . The daughter of the gentleman from San Francisco was standing beside the prince, who had been, through a fortuitous circumstance, presented to her yesterday evening, and she pretended to be looking intently into the distance, in a direction he was pointing out to her, telling, explaining something or other to her, hurriedly and quietly. On account of his height he seemed a boy by contrast with others,—he was queer and not at all prepossessing of person, with his spectacles, his derby, his English great coat, while his scanty moustache looked just as if it were of horse-hair, and the swarthy, thin skin seemed to be drawn tightly over his face, and somehow had the appearance of being lacquered,—but the young girl was listening to him, without understanding, in her agitation, what he was saying; her heart was thumping from an incomprehensible rapture before his presence and from pride that he was speaking with her, and not some other; everything about him that was different from others,—his lean hands, his clear skin, under which flowed the ancient blood of kings, even his altogether unpretentious, yet somehow distinctively neat, European dress, —everything held a secret, inexplicable charm, evoked a feeling of amorousness. As for the gentleman from San Francisco himself,—he, in a high silk hat, in gray spats over patent-leather shoes, kept on glancing at the famous beauty, who was standing beside him,—a tall blonde of striking figure, her eyes were painted in the latest Parisian fashion; she was holding a diminutive, hunched-up, mangy lap dog on a silver chain and was chattering to it without cease. And the daughter, in some vague embarrassment, tried not to notice her father.

Like all Americans of means, he was very generous on his travels, and, like all of them, believed in the full sincerity and good-will of those who brought him food and drink with such solicitude, who served him from morn till night, forestalling his least wish; of those who guarded his cleanliness and rest, lugged his things around, summoned porters for him, delivered his trunks to hotels. Thus had it been everywhere, thus had it been on the ship, and thus was it to be in Naples as well. Naples grew, and drew nearer; the musicians, the brass of their instruments flashing, had already clustered upon the deck, and suddenly deafened everybody with the triumphant strains of a march; the gigantic captain, in his full dress uniform, appeared upon his stage, and, like a condescending heathen god, waved his hand amiably to the passengers,—and to the gentleman from San Francisco it seemed that it was for him alone that the march so beloved by proud America was thundering, that it was he whom the captain was felicitating upon a safe arrival. And every other passenger felt similarly about himself—or herself. And when the *Atlantida* did finally enter the harbour, had heaved to at the wharf with her many-tiered mass, black with people, and the gang-planks clattered down,—what a multitude of porters and their helpers in caps with gold braid, what a multitude of different *commissionaires*, whistling gamins, and strapping ragamuffins with packets of coloured postal cards in their hands, made a rush toward the gentleman from San Francisco, with offers of their services! And he smiled, with a kindly contemptuousness, at these ragamuffins, as he went toward the automobile of precisely that hotel where there was a possibility of the prince's stopping as well, and drawled through his teeth, now in English, now in Italian:

"Go away! * *Via!*"

Life at Naples at once assumed its wonted, ordered current: in the early morning, breakfast in the sombre dining room with its damp draught from windows opening on some sort of a stony little garden; the sky was usually overcast, holding out but little promise, and there was the usual crowd of guides at the door of the vestibule; then came the first smiles of a warm, rosy sun; there was, from the high hanging balcony, a view of Vesuvius, enveloped to its foot by radiant morning mists, and of silver-and-pearl eddies on the surface of the Bay, and of the delicate contour of Capri against the horizon; one could see tiny burros, harnessed in twos to little carts, running down below over the quay, sticky with mire, and detachments of diminutive soldiers, marching off to somewhere or other to lively and exhilarating music. Next came the procession to the waiting automobile and the slow progress through populous, narrow, and damp corridors of streets, between tall, many-windowed houses; the inspection of lifelessly-clean museums, evenly and pleasantly, yet bleakly, lit, seemingly illuminated by snow; or of cool churches, smelling of wax, which everywhere and always contain the same things: a majestic portal, screened by a heavy curtain of leather, and inside,—silence, empty vastness, unobtrusive little flames of a seven-branched candle-stick glowing redly in the distant depths, on an altar bedecked with laces; a solitary old woman among the dark wooden pews; slippery tombstones underfoot; and somebody's *Descent from the Cross*,—inevitably a celebrated one. At one o'clock there was luncheon upon the mountain of San Martino, where, toward noon, gathered not a few people of the very first quality, and where the daughter of the gentleman from San Francisco had once almost fainted away for joy, because she thought she saw the prince sitting in the hall, although she already knew through the newspapers that he had left for a temporary stay at Rome. At five came tea at the hotel, in the showy salon, so cosy with its rugs and flaming fireplaces; and after that it was already time to get ready for dinner, —and once more came the mighty, compelling reverberation of the gong through all the stories; once more the processions in Indian

* *English in the original. The same applies to the other phrases in this story marked with asterisks.* Trans.

file of ladies in *décoletté*, rustling in their silks upon the staircases and reflected in all the mirrors; once more the palatial dining room, widely and hospitably opened, and the red jackets of the musicians upon their platform, and the black cluster of waiters about the *maitre d'hôtel,* who, with a skill out of the ordinary, was ladling some sort of a thick, roseate soup into plates. . . . The dinners, as everywhere else, were the crowning glory of each day; the guests dressed for them as for a rout, and these dinners were so abundant in edibles, and wines, and mineral waters, and sweets, and fruits, that toward eleven o'clock at night the chambermaids were distributing through all the corridors rubber bags with hot water to warm sundry stomachs.

However, the December of that year proved to be not altogether a successful one for Naples; the porters grew confused when one talked with them of the weather, and merely shrugged their shoulders guiltily, muttering that they could not recall such another year,—although it was not the first year that they had been forced to mutter this, and to urge in extenuation that "something terrible is happening everywhere"; there were unheard of storms and torrents of rain on the Riviera; there was snow in Athens; Etna was also all snowed over and was aglow of nights; tourists were fleeing from Palermo in all directions, escaping from the cold. The morning sun deceived the Neapolitans every day that winter: toward noon the sky became gray and a fine rain began falling, but growing heavier and colder all the time; at such times the palms near the entrance of the hotel glistened as though they were of tin, the town seemed especially dirty and cramped, the museums exceedingly alike; the cigar stumps of the corpulent cabmen, whose rubber-coats flapped in the wind like wings, seemed to have an insufferable stench, while the energetic snapping of their whips over their scrawny-necked nags was patently false; the footgear of the *signori* sweeping the rails of the tramways seemed horrible; the women, splashing through the mud, their black-haired heads bared to the rain, appeared hideously short-legged; as for the dampness, and the stench of putrid fish from the sea foaming at the quay,—they were a matter of course. The gentleman and the lady from San Francisco began quarreling in the morning; their daughter either walked about pale, with a headache, or, coming to life again, went into raptures over everything, and was, at such times both charming and beautiful: beautiful were those tender and complex emotions which had been awakened within her by meeting that homely man through whose veins flowed uncommon blood; for, after all is said and done, perhaps it is of no real importance just what it is, precisely, that awakens a maiden's soul,—whether it be money, or fame, or illustrious ancestry. . . .

Everybody affirmed that things were entirely different in Sorrento, in Capri,—there it was both warmer and sunnier, and the lemons were in blossom, and the customs were more honest, and the wine was more natural. And so the family from San Francisco determined to set out with all its trunks to Capri, and, after seeing it all, after treading the stones where the palace of Tiberius had once stood, after visiting the faery-like caverns of the Azure Grotto, and hearing the bag-pipers of Abruzzi, who for a whole month preceding Christmas wander over the island and sing the praises of the Virgin Mary, they meant to settle in Sorrento.

On the day of departure,—a most memorable one for the family from San Francisco!—there was no sun from the early morning. A heavy fog hid Vesuvius to the very base; this gray fog spread low over the leaden heaving of the sea that was lost to the eye at a distance of a half a mile. Capri was entirely invisible,—as though there had never been such a thing in the world. And the little steamer that set out for it was so tossed from side to side that the family from San Francisco was laid prostrate upon the divans in the sorry general cabin of this tub, their feet wrapped up in plaids, and their eyes closed from nausea. Mrs. suffered,—so she thought,—more than anybody; she was overcome by sea-sickness several times; it seemed to her that she was dying, whereas the stewardess, who always ran up to her with a small basin,—she had been, for many years, day in and day out, rolling on these waves, in freezing weather and in torrid, and yet was still tireless and kind to everybody,—merely laughed. Miss was dreadfully pale and held a slice of lemon between her teeth; now she could not have been cheered even by the hope of a chance encounter with the prince at Sorrento, where he intended to be about Christmas. Mr., who was lying on his back, in roomy overcoat and large cap, never unlocked his jaws all the way over; his face had grown darker and his moustache whiter, and his head ached dreadfully: during the last days, thanks to the bad weather, he had been drinking too heavily of evenings, and had too much admired the "living pictures" in dives of *recherché* libertinage. But the rain kept on lashing against the jarring windows, the water from them running down on the divans; the wind, howling, bent the masts, and at times, aided by the onslaught of a wave, careened the little steamer entirely to one side, and then something in the hold would roll with a rumble.

During the stops, at Castellamare, at Sorrento, things were a trifle more bearable, but even then the rocking was fearful,—the shore, with all its cliffs, gardens, *pigin*,* its pink and white hotels and hazy mountains clad in curly greenery, swayed up and down as if on a swing; boats bumped up against the sides of the ship; sailors and steerage passengers were yelling vehemently; somewhere, as though it had been crushed, a baby was wailing and smothering; a raw wind was blowing in at the door; and, from a swaying boat with a flag of the Hotel Royal, a lisping gamin was screaming, luring travellers: "Kgoya-al! Hôtel Kgoya-al! . . ." And the gentleman from San Francisco, feeling that he was an old man,—which was but proper,—was already thinking with sadness and melancholy of all these Royals, Splendids, Excelsiors, and of these greedy, insignificant mannikins, reeking of garlic, that are called Italians. Once, having opened his eyes and raised himself from the divan, he saw, underneath the craggy steep of the shore, a cluster of stone hovels, mouldy through and through, stuck one on top of another near the very edge of the water, near boats, near all sorts of rags, tins, and brown nets,—hovels so miserable, that, at the recollection that this was that very Italy he had come hither to enjoy, he felt despair. . . . Finally, at twilight, the dark mass of the island began to draw near, seemingly bored through and through by little red lights near its base; the wind became softer, warmer, more fragrant; over the abating waves, as opalescent as black oil, golden pythons flowed from the lanterns on the wharf. . . . Then came the sudden rumble of the anchor, and it fell with a splash into the water; the ferocious yells of the boatmen, vying with one another, floated in from all quarters,—and at once the heart grew lighter, the lights in the general cabin shone more brightly, a desire arose to eat, to drink, to smoke, to be stirring. . . . Ten minutes later the family from San Francisco had descended into a large boat; within fifteen minutes it had set foot upon the stones of the wharf, and had then got into a bright little railway car and to its buzzing started the ascent of the slope, amid the stakes of the vineyards, half-crumbled stone enclosures, and wet, gnarled orange trees, some of them under coverings of straw,—trees with thick, glossy foliage, and aglimmer with the orange fruits; all these objects were sliding downward, past the open windows of the little car, toward the base of the mountain. . . . Sweetly smells the earth of Italy after rain, and her every island has its own, its especial aroma!

The island of Capri was damp and dark on this evening. But now

* *Pino-groves.* Trans.

it came into life for an instant; lights sprang up here and there, as always on the steamer's arrival. At the top of the mountain, where stood the station of the *funicular*, there was another throng of those whose duty lay in receiving fittingly the gentleman from San Francisco. There were other arrivals also, but they merited no attention, —several Russians, who had taken up their abode in Capri,—absent-minded because of their bookish meditations, unkempt, bearded, spectacled, the collars of their old drap overcoats turned up; and a group of long-legged, long-necked, round-headed German youths in Tyrolean costumes, with canvas knapsacks slung over their shoulders, —these latter stood in need of nobody's services, feeling themselves at home everywhere, and were not at all generous in their expenditures. The gentleman from San Francisco, on the other hand, who was calmly keeping aloof from both the one group and the other, was immediately noticed. He and his ladies were bustlingly assisted to get out, some men running ahead of him to show him the way: he was surrounded anew by urchins, and by those robust Caprian wives who carry on their heads the portmanteaux and trunks of respectable travellers. The wooden pattens of these women clattered over a *piazetta,* that seemed to belong to some opera, an electric globe swaying above it in the damp wind; the rabble of urchins burst into sharp, bird-like whistles,—and, as though on a stage, the gentleman from San Francisco proceeded in their midst toward some mediæval arch, underneath houses that had become welded into one mass, beyond which a little echoing street,—with the tuft of a palm above flat roofs on its left, and with blue stars in the black sky overhead,—led slopingly to the grand entrance of the hotel, glittering ahead. . . . And again it seemed that it was in honour of the guests from San Francisco that this damp little town of stone on a craggy little island of the Mediterranean Sea had come to life, that it was they who had made so happy and affable the proprietor of the hotel, that it was they only who had been waited for by the Chinese gong, that now began wailing the summons to dinner through all the stories of the hotel, the instant they had set foot in the vestibule.

The proprietor, a young man of haughty elegance, who had met them with a polite and exquisite bow, for a minute dumbfounded the gentleman from San Francisco: having glanced at him, the gentleman from San Francisco suddenly recalled that just the night before, among the rest of the confusion of images that had beset him in his sleep, he had seen precisely this gentleman,—just like him, down to the least detail: in the same sort of frock with rounded skirts, and with the same pomaded and painstakingly combed head. Startled, he was almost taken aback; but since, from long, long before, there was not even a mustard seed of any sort of so-called mystical emotions left in his soul, his astonishment was dimmed the same instant, passing through a corridor of the hotel, he spoke jestingly to his wife and daughter of this strange coincidence of dream and reality. And only his daughter glanced at him with alarm at that moment: her heart suddenly contracted from sadness, from a feeling of their loneliness upon this foreign, dark island,—a feeling so strong that she almost burst into tears. But still she said nothing of her feelings to her father, —as always.

An exalted personage—Rais XVII,—who had been visiting Capri, had just taken his departure, and the guests from San Francisco were given the same apartments that he had occupied. To them was assigned the handsomest and most expert chambermaid, a Belgian, whose waist was slenderly and firmly corseted, and who wore a little starched cap that looked like a pronged crown; also, the stateliest and most dignified of flunkies, a fiery-eyed Sicilian, swarthy as coal; and the nimblest of bell-boys, the short and stout Luigi,—a fellow who was very fond of a joke, and who had changed many places in his time. And a minute later there was a slight tap at the door of the room of the gentleman from San Francisco,—the French *maitre d'hôtel* had come to find out if the newly arrived guests would dine, and, in the event of an answer in the affirmative,—of which, however, there was no doubt,—to inform them that the *carte de jour* consisted of crawfish, roast beef, asparagus, pheasants, and so forth. The floor was still rocking under the gentleman from San Francisco,—so badly had the atrocious little Italian steamer tossed him about,—but, without hurrying, with his own hands, although somewhat clumsily from being unaccustomed to such things, he shut a window that had banged upon the entrance of the *maitre d'hôtel* and had let in the odours of the distant kitchen and of the wet flowers in the garden, and with a leisurely precision replied that they would dine, that their table must be placed at a distance from the door, at the farthest end of the dining room, that they would drink local wine and champagne,—moderately dry and only slightly chilled. The *maitre d'hôtel concurred* in every word of his, in intonations most varied, having, however, but one significance,—that there was never a doubt, nor could there possibly be any, about the correctness of the wishes of the gentleman from San Francisco, and that everything would be carried out punctiliously. In conclusion he inclined his head, and asked deferentially:

"Will that be all, sir?"

And, having received a long-drawn-out "Yes"* in answer, he added that the *tarantella* would be danced in the vestibule to-day,—the dancers would be Carmella and Giuseppe, known to all Italy, and to "the entire world of tourists."

"I have seen her on post cards," said the gentleman from San Francisco in a voice devoid of all expression. "About this Giuseppe, now,—is he her husband?"

"Her cousin, sir," answered the *maitre d'hôtel*.

And, after a little wait, after considering something, the gentleman from San Francisco dismissed him with a nod.

And then he began his preparations anew, as though for a wedding ceremony: he turned on all the electric lights, filling all the mirrors with reflections of light and glitter, of furniture and opened trunks; he began shaving and washing, ringing the bell every minute, while other impatient rings from his wife's and daughter's rooms floated through the entire corridor and interrupted his. And Luigi, in his red apron, was rushing headlong to answer the bell, with an ease peculiar to many stout men, the while he made grimaces of horror that made the chambermaids, running by with glazed porcelain pails in their hands, laugh till they cried. Having knocked on the door with his knuckles, he asked with an assumed timidity, with a respectfulness that verged on idiocy:

"*Ha sonato, signore?* (Did you ring, sir?)"

And from the other side of the door came an unhurried grating voice, insultingly polite:

"Yes, come in. . . ."*

What were the thoughts, what were the emotions of the gentleman from San Francisco on this evening, that was of such portent to him? He felt nothing exceptional,—for the trouble in this world is just that everything is apparently all too simple! And even if he had sensed within his soul that something was impending, he would, never the less, have thought that this thing would not occur for some time to come,—in any case, not immediately. Besides that, like everyone who has gone through the rocking of a ship, he wanted very much to eat, was anticipating with enjoyment the first spoonful of soup, the first mouthful of wine, and performed the usual routine of dressing even with a certain degree of exhilaration that left no time for reflections.

Having shaved and washed himself, having inserted several artificial teeth properly, he, standing before a mirror, wetted the remnants of his thick, pearly-gray hair and plastered it down around his swarthy-yellow skull, with brushes set in silver; drew a suit of cream-coloured silk underwear over his strong old body, beginning to be full at the waist from excesses in food, and put on silk socks and dancing slippers on his shrivelled splayed feet; sitting down, he put in order his black trousers, drawn high by black silk braces, as well as his snowy-white shirt, with the bosom bulging out; put the links through the glossy cuffs, and began the torturous pursuit of the collar-button underneath the stiffly starched collar. The floor was still swaying beneath him, the tips of his fingers pained him greatly, the collar-button at times nipped hard the flabby skin in the hollow under his Adam's-apple, but he was persistent and finally, his eyes glittering from the exertion, his face all livid from the collar that was choking his throat,—a collar far too tight,—he did contrive to accomplish his task, and sat down in exhaustion in front of the pier glass, reflected in it from head to foot, a reflection that was repeated in all the other mirrors.

"Oh, this is dreadful!" he muttered, letting his strong bald head drop, and without trying to understand, without reflecting, just what, precisely, was dreadful; then, with an accustomed and attentive glance, he inspected his stubby fingers, with gouty hardenings at the joints, and his convex nails of an almond colour, repeating, with conviction: "This is dreadful. . . ."

But at this point the second gong, sonorously, as in some heathen temple, reverberated through the entire house. And, getting up quickly from his seat, the gentleman from San Francisco drew his collar still tighter with the necktie and his stomach by means of the low-cut vest, put on his tuxedo, drew out his cuffs, scrutinized himself once more in the mirror. . . . This Carmella, swarthy, with eyes which she knew well how to use most effectively, resembling a mulatto woman, clad in a dress of many colours, with the colour of orange predominant, must dance exceptionally, he reflected. And, stepping briskly out of his room and walking over the carpet to the next one,—his wife's—he asked, loudly, if they would be ready soon?

"In five minutes, Dad!" a girl's voice, ringing and by now gay, responded from the other side of the door.

"Very well," said the gentleman from San Francisco.

And, leisurely, he walked down red-carpeted corridors and staircases, descending in search of the reading room. The servants he met stood aside and hugged the wall to let him pass, but he kept on his way as though he had never even noticed them. An old woman who was late for dinner, already stooping, with milky hair but *décolettée* in a light-gray gown of silk, was hurrying with all her might, but drolly, in a hen-like manner, and he easily outstripped her. Near the glass doors of the dining room, where all the guests had already assembled, and were beginning their dinner, he stopped before a little table piled with boxes of cigars and Egyptian cigarettes, took a large Manila cigar, and tossed three *lire* upon the little table; upon the closed veranda he glanced, in passing, through the open window: out of the darkness he felt a breath of the balmy air upon him, thought he saw the tip of an ancient palm, that had flung wide across the stars its fronds, which seemed gigantic, heard the distant, even noise of the sea floating in to him. . . . In the reading room,—snug, quiet, and illuminated only above the tables, some gray-haired German was standing, rustling the newspapers,—unkempt, resembling Ibsen, in round silver spectacles and with the astonished eyes of a madman. Having scrutinized him coldly, the gentleman from San Francisco sat down in a deep leather chair in a corner near a green-shaded lamp, put on his *pince nez,* twitching his head because his collar was choking him, and hid himself completely behind the newspaper sheet. He rapidly ran through the headlines of certain items, read a few lines about the never-ceasing Balkan war, with an accustomed gesture turned the newspaper over,—when suddenly the lines flared up before him with a glassy glare, his neck became taut, his eyes bulged out, the *pince nez* flew off his nose. . . . He lunged forward, tried to swallow some air,—and gasped wildly; his lower jaw sank, lighting up his entire mouth with the reflection of the gold fillings; his head dropped back on his shoulder and began to sway; the bosom of his shirt bulged out like a basket,—and his whole body, squirming, his heels catching the carpet, slid downward to the floor, desperately struggling with someone.

Had the German not been in the reading room, the personnel of the hotel would have managed, quickly and adroitly, to hush up this dreadful occurrence; instantly, through back passages, seizing him by the head and feet, they would have rushed off the gentleman from San Francisco as far away as possible,—and never a soul among the guests would have found out what he had been up to. But the German had dashed out of the reading room with a scream,—he had aroused the entire house, the entire dining room. And many jumped up from their meal, overturning their chairs; many, paling, ran toward the reading room. "What—what has happened?" was heard in all languages,—and no one gave a sensible answer, no one comprehended anything, since even up to now men are amazed most of all by death, and will not, under any circumstances, believe in it. The proprietor dashed from one guest to another, trying to detain those who were running away and to pacify them with hasty assurances that this was just a trifling occurrence, a slight fainting spell of a certain gentleman from San Francisco. . . . But no one listened to him; many had seen the waiters and bell-boys tearing off the necktie, the vest, and the rumpled tuxedo off this gentleman, and even, for some reason or other, the dancing slippers off his splayed feet, clad in black silk. But he was still struggling. He was still obdurately wrestling with death; he absolutely refused to yield to her, who had so unexpectedly and churlishly fallen upon him. His head was swaying, he rattled hoarsely, like one with his throat cut; his eyes had rolled up, like a drunkard's. . . . When he was hurriedly carried in and laid upon a bed in room number forty-three,—the smallest, the poorest, the dampest and the coldest, situated at the end of the bottom corridor,—his daughter ran in, with her hair down, in a little dressing gown that had flown open, her bosom, raised up by the corset, uncovered; then his wife, big and ponderous, already dressed for dinner,—her mouth rounded in terror. . . . But by now he had ceased even to bob his head.

A quarter of an hour later everything in the hotel had assumed some semblance of order. But the evening was irreparably spoiled. Some guests, returning to the dining room, finished their dinner, but in silence, with aggrieved countenances, while the proprietor would approach now one group, now another, shrugging his shoulders in polite yet impotent irritation, feeling himself guilty without guilt, assuring everybody that he understood very well "how unpleasant all this was," and pledging his word that he would take "all measures within his power" to remove this unpleasantness. It was necessary to call off the *tarantella*, all unnecessary electric lights were switched off, the majority of the guests withdrew into the bar, and it became so quiet that one heard distinctly the ticking of the clock in the vestibule, whose sole occupant was a parrot, dully muttering something, fussing in his cage before going to sleep, contriving to doze off at last with one claw ludicrously stretched up to the upper perch. . . . The gentleman from San Francisco was lying upon a cheap iron bed, under coarse woolen blankets, upon which the dull light of a single bulb beat down from the ceiling. An ice-bag hung down to his moist and cold forehead. The livid face, already dead, was gradually growing cold; the hoarse rattling, expelled from the open mouth, illuminated by the reflection of gold, was growing fainter.

This was no longer the gentleman from San Francisco rattling,—he no longer existed,—but some other. His wife, his daughter, the doctor and the servants were standing, gazing at him dully. Suddenly, that which they awaited and feared was consummated,—the rattling ceased abruptly. And slowly, slowly, before the eyes of all, a pallor flowed over the face of the man who had died, and his features seemed to grow finer, to become irradiated, with a beauty which had been rightfully his in the long ago. . . .

The proprietor entered. "*Già è morto*," said the doctor to him in a whisper. The proprietor, his face dispassionate, shrugged his shoulders. The wife, down whose cheeks the tears were quietly coursing, walked up to him and timidly said that the deceased ought now to be carried to his own room.

"Oh, no, madam," hastily, correctly, but now without any amiability and not in English, but in French, retorted the proprietor, who was not at all interested now in such trifling sums as the arrivals from San Francisco might leave in his coffers. "That is absolutely impossible, madam," said he, and added in explanation that he valued the apartments occupied by them very much; that, were he to carry out her wishes, everybody in Capri would know it and the tourists would shun those apartments.

The young lady, who had been gazing at him strangely, sat down on a chair, and, stuffing her mouth with a handkerchief, burst into sobs. The wife dried her tears immediately, her face flaring up. She adopted a louder tone, making demands in her own language, and still incredulous of the fact that all respect for them had been completely lost. The proprietor, with a polite dignity, cut her short: if madam was not pleased with the customs of the hotel, he would not venture to detain her; and he firmly announced that the body must be gotten away this very day, at dawn, that the police had already been notified, and one of the police officers would be here very soon and would carry out all the necessary formalities. Was it possible to secure even a common coffin in Capri, madam asks? Regrettably, no,—it was beyond possibility, and no one would be able to make one in time. It would be necessary to have recourse to something else. . . . For instance,—English soda water came in large and long boxes. . . . It was possible to knock the partitions out of such a box. . . .

At night the whole hotel slept. The window in room number forty-three was opened,—it gave out upon a corner of the garden where, near a high stone wall with broken glass upon its crest, a phthisic banana tree was growing; the electric light was switched off; the key was turned in the door, and everybody went away. The dead man remained in the darkness,—the blue stars looked down upon him from the sky, a cricket with a pensive insouciance began his song in the wall. . . . In the dimly lit corridor two chambermaids were seated on a window sill, at some darning. Luigi, in slippers, entered with a pile of clothing in his arms.

"*Pronto?* (All ready?)" he asked solicitously, in a ringing whisper, indicating with his eyes the fearsome door at the end of the corridor. And, he waved his hand airily in that direction. . . . "*Partenza!*" he called out in a whisper, as though he were speeding a train, the usual phrase used in Italian depots at the departure of trains,—and the chambermaids, choking with silent laughter, let their heads sink on each other's shoulder.

Thereupon, hopping softly, he ran up to the very door, gave it the merest tap, and, inclining his head to one side, in a low voice, asked with the utmost deference:

"*Ha sonato signore?*"

And, squeezing his throat, thrusting out his lower jaw, in a grating voice, slowly and sadly, he answered his own question, as though from the other side of the door:

"Yes, come in. . . ." *

And at dawn, when it had become light beyond the window of room number forty-three, and a humid wind had begun to rustle the tattered leaves of the banana tree; when the blue sky of morning had lifted and spread out over the Island of Capri, and the pure and clear-cut summit of Monte Solaro had grown aureate against the sun that was rising beyond the distant blue mountains of Italy; when the stone masons, who were repairing the tourists' paths on the island, had set out to work,—a long box that had formerly been used for soda water was brought to room number forty-three. Soon it became very heavy, and was pressing hard against the knees of the junior porter, who bore it off briskly on a one horse cab over the white paved highway that was sinuously winding to and fro over the slopes of Capri, among the stone walls and the vineyards, ever downwards, to the very sea. The cabby, a puny little man with reddened eyes, in an old, wretched jacket with short sleeves and in trodden-down shoes, was undergoing the after effects of drink,—he had diced the whole night through in a *tratoria*, and kept on lashing his sturdy little horse, tricked out in the Sicilian fashion, with all sorts of little bells livelily jingling upon the bridle with its tufts of coloured wool, and upon the brass points of its high pad; with a yard-long feather stuck in its cropped forelock,—a feather that shook as the horse ran. The cabby kept silent; he was oppressed by his shiftlessness, his vices,—by the fact that he had, that night, lost to the last mite all those coppers with which his pockets had been filled. But the morning was fresh; in air such as this, with the sea all around, under the morning sky, the after effects of drink quickly evaporate, and a man is soon restored to a carefree mood, and the cabby was furthermore consoled by that unexpected sum, the opportunity to earn which had been granted him by some gentleman from San Francisco, whose lifeless head was bobbing from side to side in the box at his back. . . . . The little steamer,—a beetle lying far down below, against the tender and vivid deep-blue with which the Bay of Naples is so densely and highly flooded,—was already blowing its final whistles, that reverberated loudly all over the island, whose every bend, every ridge, every stone, was as distinctly visible from every point as if there were absolutely no such thing as atmosphere. Near the wharf the junior porter was joined by the senior, who was speeding with the daughter and wife of the gentleman from San Francisco in his automobile,—they were pale, with eyes hollow from tears and a sleepless night. And ten minutes later the little steamer was again chugging through the water, again running toward Sorrento, toward Castellamare, carrying away from Capri, for all time, the family from San Francisco. . . . And again peace and quiet resumed their reign upon the island.

Upon this island, two thousand years ago, had lived a man who had become completely enmeshed in his cruel and foul deeds, who had for some reason seized the power over millions of people in his hands, and who, having himself lost his head at the senselessness of this power and from the fear of death by assassination, lurking in ambush behind every corner, had committed cruelties beyond all measure,—and humankind has remembered him for all time; and those who, in their collusion, just as incomprehensively and, in substance, just as cruelly as he, reign at present in power over this world, gather from all over the earth to gaze upon the ruins of that stone villa where he had dwelt on one of the steepest ascents of the island. On this splendid morning all those who had come to Capri for just this purpose were still sleeping in the hotels, although, toward their entrances, were already being led little mouse-gray burros with red saddles, upon which, after awaking and sating themselves with food, Americans and Germans, men and women, young and old, would again clamber up ponderously this day, and after whom would again run the old Caprian beggar women, with sticks in their gnarled hands,—would run over stony paths, and always up-hill, up to the very summit of Mount Tiberio. Set at rest by the fact that the dead old man from San Francisco, who had likewise been planning to go with them but instead of that had only frightened them with a *memento mori*, had already been shipped off to Naples, the travellers slept on heavily, and the quiet of the island was still undisturbed, the shops in the city were still shut. The market place on the *piazetta* alone was carrying on traffic,—in fish and greens; and the people there were all simple folk, among whom, without anything to do, as always, was standing Lorenzo the boatman, famous all over Italy,—a tall old man, a care-free rake and a handsome fellow, who had served more than once as a model to many artists; he had brought, and had already sold for a song, two lobsters that he had caught that night and which were already rustling in the apron of the cook of that very hotel where the family from San Francisco had passed the night, and now he could afford to stand in calm idleness even until the evening, looking about him with a kingly bearing (a little trick of his), consciously picturesque with his tatters, clay pipe, and a red woolen *beretta* drooping over one ear.

And, along the precipices of Monte Solaro, upon the ancient Phœnician road, hewn out of the crags, down its stone steps, two mountaineers of Abruzzi were descending from Anacapri. One had bag-pipes under his leathern mantle,—a large bag made from the skin of a she-goat, with two pipes; the other had something in the nature of wooden Pan's-reeds. They went on,—and all the land, joyous, splendid, sun-flooded, spread out below them: the stony humps of the island, which was lying almost in its entirety at their feet; and that faery-like deep-blue in which it was aswim; and the radiant morning vapours over the sea, toward the east, under the blinding sun, that was now beating down hotly, rising ever higher and higher; and, still in their morning vagueness, the mistily azure massive outlines of Italy, of her mountains near and far, whose beauty human speech is impotent to express. . . . Half way down the pipers slackened their pace: over the path, within a grotto in the craggy side of Monte Solaro, all illumed by the sun, all bathed in its warmth and glow, in snowy-white raiment of gypsum, and in a royal crown, golden-rusty from inclement weathers, stood the Mother of God, meek and gracious, her orbs lifted up to heaven, to the eternal and happy abodes of Her thrice-blessed Son. The pipers bared their heads, put their reeds to their lips,—and there poured forth their naïve and humbly-jubilant praises to the sun, to the morning, to Her, the Immaculate Intercessor for all those who suffer in this evil and beautiful world, and to Him Who had been born of Her womb in a cavern at Bethlehem, in a poor shepherd's shelter in the distant land of Judæa. . . .

Meanwhile, the body of the dead old man from San Francisco was returning to its home, to a grave on the shores of the New World. Having gone through many humiliations, through much human neglect, having wandered for a week from one port warehouse to another, it had finally gotten once more on board that same famous ship upon which but so recently, with so much deference, he had been borne to the Old World. But now he was already being concealed from the quick,—he was lowered in his tarred coffin deep into the black hold. And once more the ship was sailing on and on upon its long sea voyage. In the night time it sailed past the Island of Capri, and, to one watching them from the island, there was something sad about the ship's lights, slowly disappearing over the dark sea. But, upon the ship itself, in its brilliant *salons* resplendent with lustres and marbles, there was a crowded ball that night, as usual.

There was a ball on the second night also, and on the third,—again in the midst of a raging snow storm, whirling over an ocean booming like a funeral mass, and heaving in mountains trapped out in mourning by the silver spindrift. The innumerable fiery eyes of the ship that was retreating into the night and the snow gale were barely visible for the snow to the Devil watching from the crags of Gibraltar, from the stony gateway of two worlds. The Devil was as enormous as a cliff, but the ship was still more enormous than he; many-tiered, many-funnelled, created by the pride of the New Man with an ancient heart. The snow gale smote upon its rigging and wide-throated funnels, hoary from the snow, but the ship was steadfast, firm, majestic—and awesome. Upon its topmost deck were reared, in their solitude among the snowy whirlwinds, those snug, dimly-lit chambers where, plunged in a light and uneasy slumber, was its ponderous guide who resembled a heathen idol, reigning over the entire ship. He heard the pained howlings and the ferocious squealings of the storm-stifled siren, but soothed himself by the proximity of that which, in the final summing up, was incomprehensible even to himself, that which was on the other side of his wall: that large cabin, which had the appearance of being armoured, and was being constantly filled by the mysterious rumbling, quivering, and crisp sputtering of blue flames, flaring up and exploding around the pale-faced operator with a metal half-hoop upon his head. In the very depths, in the under-water womb of the *Atlantida,* were the thirty-thousand-pound masses of boilers and of all sorts of other machinery—dully glittering with steel, hissing out stream and exuding oil and boiling water,—of that kitchen, made red hot from infernal furnaces underneath, wherein was brewing the motion of the ship. Forces, fearful in their concentration, were bubbling, were being transmitted to its very keel, into an endlessly long catacomb, into a tunnel, illuminated by electricity, wherein slowly, with an inexorability that was crushing to the human soul, was revolving within its oily couch the gigantean shaft, exactly like a living monster that had stretched itself out in this tunnel. Meanwhile, amidship the *Atlantida,* its warm and luxurious cabins, its dining halls and ball rooms, poured forth radiance and joyousness, were humming with the voices of a well-dressed gathering, were sweetly odorous with fresh flowers, and the strains of the stringed orchestra were their song. And again excrutiatingly writhed and at intervals came together among this throng, among this glitter of lights, silks, diamonds and bared feminine shoulders, the supple pair of hired lovers: the sinfully-modest, very pretty young woman, with eye-lashes cast down, with a chaste coiffure, and the well-built young man, with black hair that seemed to be pasted on, with his face pale from powder, shod in the most elegant of patent-leather foot-gear, clad in a tight-fitting dress coat with long tails,—an Adonis who resembled a huge leech. And none knew that, already for a long time, this pair had grown wearied of languishing dissemblingly in their blissful torment to the sounds of the shamelessly-sad music,—nor that far, far below, at the bottom of the black hold, stood a tarred coffin, in close proximity to the sombre and sultry depths of the ship that was toilsomely overpowering the darkness, the ocean, the snow storm. . . .

Questions

1. Why is the gentleman nameless?
2. What is achieved by the contrast between the lighted ship and the storm that whirls around it?
3. A sense of well-being is important to the gentleman. What does he consider important to his sense of well-being?
4. Why does the dream have no impact on the gentleman?

5. How clearly developed is the characterization of the wife? Of the daughter? Do they reflect the same attitude toward life as that of the gentleman? Explain.
6. What other characters are also shown to be materialists?
7. How does the story of the tyrant who lived on Capri two thousand years ago fit into Bunin's story? What is the point of the reference to the two Abruzzi mountaineers?

Topics for Composition

1. Write an essay comparing and contrasting Tolstoi's characterization of Pakhom and Bunin's characterization of the gentleman.
2. Refer to Veblen's theory about pecuniary canons of taste and apply his examples to the portrayal of the gentleman.
3. Structure is important in Bunin's story. Trace his circular structural pattern and correlate with it his use of light and dark.
4. Write an essay showing the gentleman's lack of moral principle by examining his attitude toward other people. You might begin with those closest to the gentleman—his wife and daughter—and then proceed to the minor characters.

Poetry

ONE of the fallen angels in Milton's *Paradise Lost* is Mammon, whose name means "wealth." He was, the poet says, the least elevated spirit that fell from heaven,

> for even in Heaven his looks and thoughts
> Were always downward bent, admiring more
> The riches of Heaven's pavement, trodden gold,
> Than aught divine or holy else enjoyed
> In vision beatific. (Book I, 680–684)

Here in a single image Milton defines in poetic fashion the essential evil of materialism—lack of vision. Acceptance of ready-made, highly tangible, easily measurable symbols of status means giving up imagination and initiative, allowing personal development to be sharply restricted, and suffering as a consequence a loss of inner motivation. By envisioning Mammon as originally an inhabitant of heaven, Milton reminds us that freedom from the restrictions of materialism depends finally not upon circumstances but upon individual attitude. There is not necessarily anything wrong with golden pavement. It might be a pleasant convenience and even an appropriate if not very vital symbol of spiritual progress. What is wrong is that Mammon, who represents, of course, a basic tendency in human nature, came to admire the road so much that he no longer looked to see where he was going, which is unfortunate indeed, because he has ended up in hell. In the following selection from Spenser's *The Faerie Queene* we are introduced to the daughter of Mammon, Philotime (meaning "love of wealth and honor"), who also dwells in hell, or, what is the same, in the realm of Pluto, god of the underworld and of wealth. She too has been thrust from heaven, but continues to deceive her worshipers, who still think her golden chain is the only way to get to heaven.

With a comparable witty incisiveness and imaginative power the other poems of this section define some of the effects and describe some of the outward aspects of materialism. Alexander Pope's *Epistle IV* of the *Moral Essays* focuses on a relatively harmless aspect of the materialistic spirit, the abominable taste that so often goes with the love of possessions. He makes his point by describing in detail the country home of an eighteenth-century nobleman, indicating by repeated use of antithesis how perversely culture, sensible economy, and even personal comfort are sacrificed to ostentation. Samuel Johnson probes more deeply into the perversity of materialism, stressing the dangers and the fears to which the lust for money and power exposes its victims: disregard for law and fear of punishment, the multiplication of cares that goes with each advance in status, and the sorry exchange of human dignity and self-possession for advantage in a pointless, never-ending race.

Pope and Johnson show that materialism is opposed to plain good sense. Wordsworth and Gerard Manley Hopkins stress its blighting effect on the imagination. More specifically, they deplore the fact that preoccupation with "getting and spending" has prevented man from seeing in the dynamic splendor of nature the inspiring symbol of creativity that it might be. In his use of nature, they feel, man has confused means and end; inordinate exploitation of nature has obscured the ideal of harmony between man and the rest of God's creation.

Robert Browning turns back to the splendor-loving Renaissance to explore, in a dramatic case study, the relation between materialism, aesthetic sensibility, and spirituality. The Bishop of St. Praxed's, clearly, has been unable to reconcile the love of beautiful things with religious ideals; his imagination has been so warped by the conflict that it leads him, in the final crisis of his life, to identify himself with the things of stone that he has more and more coveted.

"Pity this busy monster, manunkind," "Drug Store," and "Dirge," finally, picture very vividly the symptoms of materialism in our time: the glorification of the scientific reduction of reality to quantitative measurement; the sad dependence of youth upon "drugs"—that is, crude, mass-produced, artificial stimuli; and the desperate, personality-destroying pursuit of silly status symbols. The term "symptoms" is appropriate here, it will be noted, because all three of these poems use the metaphor of illness. Poets have always regarded materialism as a disease—of the eyes and of the heart.

The Faerie Queene, Book II, Canto VII

EDMUND SPENSER

XLIV

A route of people there assembled were,[1]
Of every sort and nation under skye,
Which with great uprore preaced [2] to draw nere
To th' upper part, where was advaunced hye

[1] *Sir Guyon, who represents the virtue of temperance, is being conducted by Mammon through the latter's realm.*
[2] *Pressed.*

A stately siege [3] of soveraine majestye;
And thereon satt a woman gorgeous gay,
And richly cladd in robes of royaltye,
That never earthly prince in such aray
His glory did enhaunce and pompous pryde display.

XLV

Her face right wondrous faire did seeme to bee,
That her broad beauties beam great brightnes threw
Through the dim shade, that all men might it see:
Yet was not that same her owne native hew,
But wrought by art and counterfetted shew,[4]
Thereby more lovers unto her to call;
Nath'lesse [5] most hevenly faire in deed and vew
She by creation was, till she did fall;
Thenceforth she sought for helps to cloke her crime withall.

XLVI

There as in glistring glory she did sitt,
She held a great gold chaine ylincked well,
Whose upper end to highest heven was knitt,
And lower part did reach to lowest hell;
And all that preace [6] did rownd about her swell,
To catchen hold of that long chaine, thereby
To climbe aloft, and others to excell:
That was Ambition, rash desire to sty,[7]
And every linck thereof a step of dignity.

XLVII

Some thought to raise themselves to high degree
By riches and unrighteous reward;
Some by close shouldring, some by flatteree;
Others through friendes, others for base regard;
And all by wrong waies for themselves prepard.
Those that were up themselves, kept others low,
Those that were low themselves, held others hard,
Ne suffred them to ryse or greater grow,
But every one did strive his fellow downe to throw.

XLVIII

Which whenas Guyon saw, he gan inquire,
What meant that preace about that ladies throne,

[3] *Seat, throne.*
[4] *Show.*
[5] *Nevertheless.*
[6] *Throng.*
[7] *Ascend, climb.*

And what she was that did so high aspyre.
Him Mammon answered: 'That goodly one,
Whom all that folke with such contention
Doe flock about, my deare, my daughter is:
Honour and dignitie from her alone
Derived are, and all this worldes blis,
For which ye men doe strive: few gett, but many mis.

XLIX

'And fayre Philotime she rightly hight,[8]
The fairest wight that wonneth [9] under skye,
But that this darksom neather [10] world her light
Doth dim with horror and deformity,
Worthie of heven and hye felicitie,
From whence the gods have her for envy thrust:
But sith [11] thou hast found favour in mine eye,
Thy spouse I will her make, if that thou lust,
That she may thee advance for works and merits just.'

L

'Gramercy, Mammon,' said the gentle knight,
'For so great grace and offred high estate,
But I, that am fraile flesh and earthly wight,
Unworthy match for such immortall mate
My selfe well wote,[12] and mine unequall fate:
And were I not, yet is my trouth yplight,
And love avowd to other lady late,
That to remove the same I have no might:
To chaunge love causelesse [13] is reproch to warlike knight.'

1590

[8] *Is named.*
[9] *Dwells.*
[10] *Nether, lower.*
[11] *Since.*
[12] *Know.*
[13] *Without cause.*

Questions

1. What is the significance of the fact that Philotime has to resort to artifice to enhance her beauty? Remember that she was one of the angels who fell with Satan.
2. What is to be made of the fact that the golden chain of ambition extends from heaven to hell?
3. What would marriage to Philotime mean?

Moral Essays

ALEXANDER POPE

Epistle IV

Of the Use of Riches
To Richard Boyle, Earl of Burlington

At Timon's Villa [1] let us pass a day,
Where all cry out, "What sums are thrown away!" *100*
So proud, so grand; of that stupendous air,
Soft and agreeable come never there.
Greatness, with Timon, dwells in such a draught [2]
As brings all Brobdignag [3] before your thought.
To compass this, his building is a town,
His pond an ocean, his parterre a down:
Who but must laugh, the master when he sees,
A puny insect, shivering at a breeze!
Lo, what huge heaps of littleness around!
The whole, a laboured quarry above ground; *110*
Two cupids squirt before; a lake behind
Improves the keenness of the northern wind.
His gardens next your admiration call,
On every side you look, behold the wall!
No pleasing intricacies intervene,
No artful wildness to perplex the scene;
Grove nods at grove, each alley has a brother,
And half the platform just reflects the other.
The suffering eye inverted nature sees,
Trees cut to statues, statues thick as trees; *120*
With here a fountain, never to be played;
And there a summer-house that knows no shade;
Here Amphitrite [4] sails through myrtle bowers;
There gladiators fight, or die in flowers;
Unwatered see the drooping sea-horse mourn,
And swallows roost in Nilus' dusty urn.
My lord advances with majestic mien,

[1] *"This description is intended to comprise the principles of a false taste of magnificence, and to exemplify what was said before, that nothing but good sense can attain it." (Pope's note.)*
[2] *Dose.*
[3] *The land of the giants in Swift's* Gulliver's Travels.
[4] *The wife of Poseidon, god of the sea.*

Smit with the mighty pleasure, to be seen:
But soft,–by regular approach,–not yet,–
First through the length of yon hot terrace sweat; *130*
And when up ten steep slopes you've dragged your thighs,
Just at his study door he'll bless your eyes.
His study! with what authors is it stored?
In books, not authors, curious is my lord;
To all their dated backs he turns you round:
These Aldus printed, those Du Sueil has bound.
Lo, some are vellum, and the rest as good
For all his lordship knows, but they are wood.
For Locke or Milton 'tis in vain to look, *140*
These shelves admit not any modern book.
And now the chapel's silver bell you hear,
That summons you to all the pride of prayer;
Light quirks of music, broken and uneven,
Make the soul dance upon a jig to Heaven.
On painted ceilings you devoutly stare,
Where sprawl the saints of Verrio [5] or Laguerre,
On gilded clouds in fair expansion lie,
And bring all paradise before your eye.
To rest, the cushion and soft dean invite,
Who never mentions hell to ears polite. *150*
But hark! the chiming clocks to dinner call;
A hundred footsteps scrape the marble hall;
The rich buffet well coloured serpents grace,
And gaping Tritons [6] spew to wash your face.
Is this a dinner? this a genial room?
No, 'tis a temple, and a hecatomb.
A solemn sacrifice, performed in state,
You drink by measure, and to minutes eat.
So quick retires each flying course, you'd swear
Sancho's dread doctor [7] and his wand were there. *160*
Between each act the trembling salvers ring,
From soup to sweet-wine, and God bless the King.
In plenty starving, tantalized in state,
And complaisantly helped to all I hate,
Treated, caressed, and tired, I take my leave,
Sick of his civil pride from morn to eve;

[5] "*Verrio (Antonio) painted many ceilings, etc., at Windsor, Hampton Court, etc., and Laguerre at Blenheim Castle and other places.*" (*Pope's note.*)

[6] *Triton, the son of Poseidon, was shaped like a man from the waist upward, but had the tail of a dolphin.*

[7] "*See Don Quixote,* [*Part II*] *chap. xlvii.*" (*Pope's note.*)

I curse such lavish cost, and little skill,
And swear no day was ever passed so ill.

1731

Questions

1. What does Pope mean by "huge heaps of littleness" (line 109)? Do you know what the word oxymoron means?
2. What is the principal basis of the poet's criticism of Timon's villa?

From *The Vanity of Human Wishes*

In Imitation of the Tenth Satire of Juvenal [1]

SAMUEL JOHNSON

But scarce observed, the knowing and the bold
Fall in the general massacre of gold;
Wide-wasting pest! that rages unconfined,
And crowds with crimes the records of mankind:
For gold his sword the hireling ruffian draws; *25*
For gold the hireling judge distorts the laws;
Wealth heaped on wealth, nor truth nor safety buys,
The dangers gather as the treasures rise.
Let history tell, where rival kings command,
And dubious title shakes the madded land, *30*
When statutes glean the refuse of the sword,
How much more safe the vassal than the lord;
Low skulks the hind [2] beneath the rage of power,
And leaves the wealthy traitor in the Tower; [3]
Untouched his cottage, and his slumbers sound, *35*
Though confiscation's vultures hover round.
The needy traveller, serene and gay,
Walks the wild heath, and sings his toil away.
Does envy seize thee? crush the upbraiding joy,
Increase his riches, and his peace destroy; *40*
New fears in dire vicissitude invade,
The rustling brake alarms, and quivering shade;
Nor light nor darkness bring his pain relief,
One shows the plunder, and one hides the thief.

[1] *Juvenal was a famous Roman satirist.*
[2] *Humble rustic.*
[3] *The Tower of London, where political prisoners were held.*

Yet still one general cry the skies assails, *45*
And gain and grandeur load the tainted gales;
Few know the toiling statesman's fear or care,
The insidious rival and the gaping heir.
Once more, Democritus,[4] arise on earth,
With cheerful wisdom and instructive mirth, *50*
See motley life in modern trappings dressed,
And feed with varied fools the eternal jest:
Thou who couldst laugh where want[5] enchained caprice,
Toil crushed conceit, and man was of a piece;
Where wealth unloved without a mourner died, *55*
And scarce a sycophant was fed by pride;
Where ne'er was known the form of mock debate,
Or seen a new-made mayor's unwieldy state;[6]
Where change of favorites made no change of laws,
And senates heard before they judged a cause; *60*
How wouldst thou shake at Britain's modish tribe,
Dart the quick taunt, and edge the piercing gibe,
Attentive truth and nature to descry,
And pierce each scene with philosophic eye!
To thee were solemn toys or empty show *65*
The robes of pleasure and the veils of woe;
All aid the farce, and all thy mirth maintain,
Whose joys are causeless, or whose griefs are vain.

1748

[4] *Called the "laughing philosopher."*
[5] *Poverty.*
[6] *Pomp.*

Questions

1. Who, according to the poet, is most harmed by the tyranny of wealth?
2. What can be inferred from this poem about the poet's general philosophy of life?

The World Is Too Much With Us

WILLIAM WORDSWORTH

The world is too much with us; late and soon,
Getting and spending, we lay waste our powers:
Little we see in Nature that is ours;

We have given our hearts away, a sordid boon![1]
The sea that bares her bosom to the moon; 5
The winds that will be howling at all hours,
And are up-gathered now like sleeping flowers;
For this, for everything, we are out of tune;
It moves us not.—Great God! I'd rather be
A pagan suckled in a creed outworn. 10
So might I, standing on this pleasant lea,
Have glimpses that would make me less forlorn;
Have sight of Proteus[2] rising from the sea;
Or hear old Triton[3] blow his wreathed horn.

1807

[1] *Gift.*
[2] *Proteus is a sea god. He is supposed to have tended the seals of Poseidon.*
[3] *Triton, the son of Poseidon, god of the sea, was shaped like a man from the waist up, but had the tail of a dolphin. He is usually pictured blowing on a conch shell.*

Questions

1. What does Wordsworth mean by "world" in line 1?
2. What are the "powers" that men have destroyed in themselves? Why does the poet say that men have given their **hearts** away? What kind of relationship between man and the rest of nature does he long for? By what means does he define that relationship?

The Bishop Orders His Tomb at Saint Praxed's Church[1]

[Rome, 15—]

ROBERT BROWNING

Vanity, saith the preacher, vanity![2]
Draw round my bed: is Anselm keeping back?
Nephews—sons mine . . . ah God, I know not! Well—
She, men would have to be your mother once,

[1] *So named in honor of St. Praxedes, a Roman virgin of the second century who gave her wealth to needy Christians.*
[2] *See Ecclesiastes 1:2.*

Old Gandolf[3] envied me, so fair she was! 5
What's done is done, and she is dead beside,
Dead long ago, and I am Bishop since,
And as she died so must we die ourselves,
And thence ye may perceive the world's a dream.
Life, how and what is it? As here I lie 10
In this state-chamber, dying by degrees,
Hours and long hours in the dead night, I ask
"Do I live, am I dead?" Peace, peace seems all.
Saint Praxed's ever was the church for peace;
And so, about this tomb of mine. I fought 15
With tooth and nail to save my niche, ye know:
–Old Gandolf cozened[4] me, despite my care;
Shrewd was that snatch from out the corner South
He graced his carrion with, God curse the same!
Yet still my niche is not so cramped but thence 20
One sees the pulpit o' the epistle-side,
And somewhat of the choir, those silent seats,
And up into the aery dome where live
The angels, and a sunbeam's sure to lurk:
And I shall fill my slab of basalt there, 25
And 'neath my tabernacle[5] take my rest,
With those nine columns round me, two and two,
The odd one at my feet where Anselm stands:
Peach-blossom marble all, the rare, the ripe
As fresh-poured red wine of a mighty pulse. 30
–Old Gandolf with his paltry onion-stone,
Put me where I may look at him! True peach,
Rosy and flawless: how I earned the prize!
Draw close: that conflagration of my church
–What then? So much was saved if aught were missed! 35
My sons, ye would not be my death? Go dig
The white-grape vineyard where the oil-press stood,
Drop water gently till the surface sinks,
And if ye find . . . Ah, God I know not, I! . . .
Bedded in store of rotten fig-leaves soft, 40
And corded up in a tight olive-frail,[6]
Some lump, ah God, of *lapis lazuli*,
Big as a Jew's head cut off at the nape,
Blue as a vein o'er the Madonna's breast . . .

[3] *Gandolf was the Bishop's predecessor in office.*
[4] *Cheated.*
[5] *Stone canopy. The roof is to be supported by the "nine columns," and beneath is to lie the effigy of the Bishop, carved in stone.*
[6] *A basket for holding olives.*

Sons, all have I bequeathed you, villas, all, *45*
That brave Frascati[7] villa with its bath,
So, let the blue lump poise between my knees,
Like God the Father's globe on both his hands
Ye worship in the Jesu Church so gay,
For Gandolf shall not choose but see and burst! *50*
Swift as a weaver's shuttle fleet our years:[8]
Man goeth to the grave, and where is he?
Did I say basalt for my slab, sons? Black–
'Twas ever antique-black[9] I meant! How else
Shall ye contrast my frieze[10] to come beneath? *55*
The bas-relief in bronze ye promised me,
Those Pans and Nymphs ye wot of, and perchance
Some tripod,[11] thyrsus, with a vase or so,
The Saviour at his sermon on the mount,
Saint Praxed in a glory, and one Pan *60*
Ready to twitch the Nymph's last garment off,
And Moses with the tables . . . but I know
Ye mark me not! What do they whisper thee,
Child of my bowels, Anselm? Ah, ye hope
To revel down my villas while I gasp *65*
Bricked o'er with beggar's mouldy travertine[12]
Which Gandolf from his tomb-top chuckles at!
Nay, boys, ye love me–all of jasper, then!
'Tis jasper ye stand pledged to, lest I grieve
My bath must needs be left behind, alas! *70*
One block, pure green as a pistachio-nut,
There's plenty jasper somewhere in the world–
And have I not Saint Praxed's ear to pray
Horses for ye, and brown Greek manuscripts,
And mistresses with great smooth marbly limbs? *75*
–That's if ye carve my epitaph aright,
Choice Latin, picked phrase, Tully's[13] every word,
No gaudy ware like Gandolf's second line–
Tully, my masters? Ulpian[14] serves his need!
And then how I shall lie through centuries, *80*

[7] *A wealthy suburb of Rome.*
[8] *See Job 6:6.*
[9] *I.e., black marble.*
[10] *A band of sculpture.*
[11] *A three-legged stool used by the priestesses of the oracle at Delphi. A thyrsis is a staff carried in processions in honor of Bacchus, the god of wine.*
[12] *Limestone.*
[13] *Cicero, whose full name was Marcus Tullius Cicero. His writing was the model of classical Latin prose style.*
[14] *A late Latin writer whose style was considered inferior.*

And hear the blessed mutter of the mass,
And see God made and eaten all day long,
And feel the steady candle-flame, and taste
Good strong thick stupefying incense-smoke!
For as I lie here, hours of the dead night, *85*
Dying in state and by such slow degrees,
I fold my arms as if they clasp a crook,[15]
And stretch my feet forth straight as stone can point,
And let the bedclothes, for a mortcloth,[16] drop
Into great laps and folds of sculptor's-work: *90*
And as yon tapers dwindle, and strange thoughts
Grow, with a certain humming in my ears,
About the life before I lived this life,
And this life too, popes, cardinals and priests,
Saint Praxed at his sermon on the mount, *95*
Your tall pale mother with her talking eyes,
And new-found agate urns as fresh as day,
And marble's language, Latin pure, discreet,
—Aha, ELUCESCEBAT [17] quoth our friend?
No Tully, said I, Ulpian at the best! *100*
Ever your eyes were as a lizard's quick,
All *lapis,* all, sons! Else I give the Pope
My villas! Will ye ever eat my heart?
Ever your eyes were as a lizard's quick,
They glitter like your mother's for my soul, *105*
Or ye would heighten my impoverished frieze,
Piece out its starved design, and fill my vase
With grapes, and add a vizor [18] and a term,
And to the tripod ye would tie a lynx
That in his struggle throws the thyrsus down, *110*
To comfort me on my entablature
Whereon I am to lie till I must ask
"Do I live, am I dead?" There, leave me, there!
For ye have stabbed me with ingratitude
To death—ye wish it—God, ye wish it! Stone— *115*
Gritstone,[19] a-crumble! Clammy squares which sweat
As if the corpse they keep were oozing through—
And no more *lapis* to delight the world!
Well, go! I bless ye. Fewer tapers there,

[15] *A bishop's staff.*
[16] *The cloth spread over a dead body.*
[17] Elucescebat *means "he was illustrious." The Bishop prefers the Ciceronian* elucebat.
[18] *A vizor is part of a helmet. A term is a statue of Terminus, the Roman god of boundaries.*
[19] *Coarse sandstone.*

But in a row: and, going, turn your backs *120*
—Ay, like departing altar-ministrants,
And leave me in my church, the church for peace,
That I may watch at leisure if he leers—
Old Gandolf, at me, from his onion-stone,
As still he envied me, so fair she was! *125*

1845

Questions

1. Judging from the way he begins, what has been the Bishop's purpose in gathering his sons around him? At what point does he get sidetracked? Does he ever get back to the matter at hand?
2. Explain the irony in lines 14–16.
3. What is the Bishop talking about in lines 34–44? Why does he ask his sons to draw close as he begins to speak of the matter?
4. What is notable about lines 81–84?
5. Can you detect any symbolism in lines 85–90?

God's Grandeur

GERARD MANLEY HOPKINS

The world is charged [1] with the grandeur of God.
It will flame out, like shining from shook foil; [2]
It gathers to a greatness, like the ooze of oil
Crushed.[3] Why do men then now not reck his rod? [4]
Generations have trod, have trod, have trod; *5*
And all is seared with trade; bleared, smeared with toil;
And wears man's smudge and shares man's smell: the soil
Is bare now, nor can foot feel, being shod.

And for all this, nature is never spent;
There lives the dearest freshness deep down things; *10*
And though the last lights off the black West went
Oh, morning, at the brown brink eastward, springs—

[1] *As with electricity.*
[2] *Gold leaf.*
[3] *Like oil oozing from crushed olives, which gathers slowly into a mass before it breaks and flows.*
[4] *"Reck his rod": heed his authority.*

Because the Holy Ghost over the bent
World broods [5] with warm breast and with ah! bright wings.

1918 (Composed 1877)

[5] *Like a dove on its nest. The dove traditionally has been the symbol of the Holy Ghost.*

Questions

1. In what ways is the statement of the first line supported in the remainder of the poem? Can you put in your own words the central impression that Hopkins is trying to convey?
2. Lines 5–8 convey the general idea of contact with nature. What makes the description ironic?
3. Does this poem express the same idea as Wordsworth's "The World Is Too Much with Us"?
4. What do the last two lines mean? In what way do the last two words reflect the meaning of the whole poem?

Cassandra[1]

E. A. ROBINSON

I heard one who said: "Verily,
What word have I for children here?
Your Dollar is your only Word,
The wrath of it your only fear.

"You build it altars tall enough 5
To make you see, but you are blind;
You cannot leave it long enough
To look before you or behind.

"When Reason beckons you to pause,
You laugh and say that you know best; 10
But what it is you know, you keep
As dark as ingots in a chest.

"You laugh and answer, 'We are young;
O leave us now, and let us grow.'–

[1] *Cassandra, the daughter of Priam, King of Troy, was given the gift of prophecy by Apollo as a token of love. Later he turned against her. He could not take away her power to prophesy, for the gifts of the gods can never be revoked, but he made it useless by causing everyone to disbelieve her. Cassandra warned the Trojans in vain that the Greeks were in the wooden horse.*

Not asking how much more of this *15*
Will Time endure or Fate bestow.

"Because a few complacent years
Have made your peril of your pride,
Think you that you are to go on
Forever pampered and untried? *20*

"What lost eclipse of history,
What bivouac of the marching stars,
Has given the sign for you to see
Millenniums and last great wars? [2]

"What unrecorded overthrow *25*
Of all the world has ever known,
Or ever been, has made itself
So plain to you, and you alone?

"Your Dollar, Dove and Eagle make
A Trinity that even you *30*
Rate higher than you rate yourselves;
It pays, it flatters, and it's new.

"And though your very flesh and blood
Be what your Eagle eats and drinks,
You'll praise him for the best of birds, *35*
Not knowing what the Eagle thinks.

"The power is yours, but not the sight;
You see not upon what you tread;
You have the ages for your guide,
But not the wisdom to be led. *40*

"Think you to tread forever down
The merciless old verities?
And are you never to have eyes
To see the world for what it is?

"Are you to pay for what you have *45*
With all you are?"—No other word
We caught, but with a laughing crowd
Moved on. None heeded, and few heard.

1915–1916

[2] *See Revelations 16 and 20.*

Questions

1. To what people or country is this warning addressed?
2. What are the "Dove and Eagle" of line 29? What do they symbolize?

Drug Store

KARL SHAPIRO

I do remember an apothecary,
And hereabouts 'a dwells [1]

It baffles the foreigner like an idiom,
And he is right to adopt it as a form
Less serious than the living-room or bar;
  For it disestablishes the café,
Is a collective, and on basic country. *5*

Not that it praises hygiene and corrupts
The ice-cream parlor and the tobacconist's
Is it a center; but that the attractive symbols
  Watch over puberty and leer
Like rubber bottles waiting for sick-use. *10*

Youth comes to jingle nickels and crack wise;
The baseball scores are his, the magazines
Devoted to lust, the jazz, the Coca-Cola,
  The lending-library of love's latest.
He is the customer; he is heroized. *15*

And every nook and cranny of the flesh
Is spoken to by packages with wiles,
"Buy me, buy me," they whimper and cajole;
  The hectic range of lipstick pouts,
Revealing the wicked and the simple mouth. *20*

With scarcely any evasion in their eye
They smoke, undress their girls,[2] exact a stance;
But only for a moment. The clock goes round;
  Crude fellowships are made and lost;
They slump in booths like rags, not even drunk. *25*

1941

[1] *From* Romeo and Juliet, *V, i, 37–8. Romeo is seeking the apothecary in order to buy poison.*
[2] *With their eyes, that is.*

Questions

1. The drug store as a social center might be thought an improvement over the ice-cream parlor and the tobacconist's. Why? What is the real reason for its having become a center?
2. What use does the poet make of the fact that the "attractive symbols" appear like things intended for sick-use?
3. How is youth, the customer, "heroized"?
4. What is the state of mind of the young people that frequent the drug store?
5. Why does the poet approach his subject in such a detached, disinterested way? What evidence of a deeper, more emotional concern is there? Would the poem have been more effective if he had used strong terms of indignation or pity?

pity this busy monster, manunkind

E. E. CUMMINGS

pity this busy monster, manunkind,

not. Progress is a comfortable disease:
your victim (death and life safely beyond)

plays with the bigness of his littleness
—electrons deify one razorblade *5*
into a mountainrange; lenses extend

unwish through curving wherewhen till unwish
returns on its unself.

A world of made
is not a world of born—pity poor flesh *10*

and trees, poor stars and stones, but never this
fine specimen of hypermagical

ultraomnipotence. We doctors know

a hopeless case if—listen: there's a hell
of a good universe next door; let's go *15*

1944

Questions

1. What kind of materialism is satirized in this poem? Does it have to do with personal ambition? Is a kind of ideal involved?
2. What are the scientific achievements described in lines 4–8? What is the author's attitude toward them? What do the coined terms "unwish" and "unself" mean? What general approach to truth or value can be associated with wishing? Does science have anything to do with the wishful self?
3. In what sense is mankind becoming a "monster"? Look up the word in the dictionary if you are familiar with only one sense.
4. Why is this "a hopeless case"?
5. How does one get to the "universe next door"?

Dirge

KENNETH FEARING

1-2-3 was the number he played but today the number came 3-2-1;
  bought his Carbide at 30 and it went to 29; had the favorite at Bowie
    but the track was slow–

O, executive type, would you like to drive a floating power, knee-action,
    silk-upholstered six? Wed a Hollywood star? Shoot the course
    in 58? Draw to the ace, king, jack? *5*
  O, fellow with a will who won't take no, watch out for three cigarettes
    on the same, single match; O democratic voter born in August under
    Mars, beware of liquidated rails–

Dénouement to dénouement, he took a personal pride in the certain,
    certain way he lived his own, private life, *10*
  but nevertheless, they shut off his gas; nevertheless, the bank foreclosed;
    nevertheless, the landlord called; nevertheless, the radio broke,

And twelve o'clock arrived just once too often,
  just the same he wore one grey tweed suit, bought one straw hat,
    drank one straight Scotch, walked one short step, took one long look,
    drew one deep breath, *15*
  just one too many,

And wow he died as wow he lived,
  going whop to the office and blooie home to sleep and biff got married
    and bam had children and oof got fired,
  zowie did he live and zowie did he die, *20*

With who the hell are you at the corner of his casket, and where the hell we going on the right hand silver knob, and who the hell cares walking second from the end with an American Beauty wreath from why the hell not.

Very much missed by the circulation staff of the New York Evening Post; deeply, deeply mourned by the B.M.T.,[1] *25*

Wham, Mr. Roosevelt; pow, Sears Roebuck; awk, big dipper; bop, summer rain; bong, Mr., bong, Mr., bong, Mr., bong.

1956

[1] *The B.M.T. is a subway system in New York.*

Questions

1. What kind of person does the subject of this poem think he is?
2. Why is so much said about luck in this lament? Why does so much depend on it? Is the fact ironic?
3. Is there any development in the poet's use of such words as "wow," "whop," "pow," and "bop"?
4. What is the effect of the last line? What does the sound mean? Why is the word "bong" appropriate? Why does the poet use only the abbreviation "Mr."?

TOPICS FOR COMPOSITION

1. Using Pope's description of Timon's villa as a model, write an essay on ostentation in modern home or automobile design.
2. Write an analytical description of the type of character represented by Democritus, as he is envisaged in Johnson's "The Vanity of Human Wishes."
3. Write an essay supporting the thesis that many people in our time value nature in nonmaterialistic ways.
4. Write a comparative study of "The World Is Too Much with Us" and "God's Grandeur."
5. Read, or reread, Wordsworth's "Michael." In a commentary of about 500 words, try to explain why Michael's love of his land is not materialistic.
6. Have the atmosphere and tone of the most typical gathering-places of young people changed since Karl Shapiro wrote "Drug Store"? Give your answer in an essay.
7. Write a character analysis of the man described in Fearing's "Dirge."
8. Using the title, "The Man Who Turned to Stone," write a character study of the Bishop of St. Praxed's.

9. With E. A. Robinson's "Cassandra" in mind, refute or support the charge that America still worships the dollar or its power.
10. Write a line-by-line interpretation or paraphrase of e. e. cummings's "pity this busy monster manunkind."
11. Write a commentary on the meaning and usefulness of the coined terms in cummings's poem.
12. Write a commentary on the handling of tone in "Drug Store" or "Dirge."
13. Does modern advertising as a whole present a single image or idea of "the good life"? If you think so, write a description of an average day in the life of the typical successful American as conceived by advertisers.
14. Using an invented name, write on the topic, "The Most Materialistic Person I Have Known."
15. Defend the thesis that a man is what he gets.
16. Write on "The True Worth of Material Possessions." Be sure to provide examples or illustration.
17. Write an essay defining two or three kinds of materialism. The poems of this unit should provide you with some ideas.
18. Write on the topic, "In Defense of 'Materialism.'"

PART FIVE

The Search for Modes of Expression

Because language is always with us, because its acquisition is relatively automatic, and because we use it almost without effort and sometimes almost without thought, we are apt to take it too lightly. What is language? Obviously, the answer is not easily formulated; moreover, the simple question generates additional questions: How is language used? What forms may it take? What is its influence on human behavior? A well-known philosopher of our time offers the following observation:

Language is, without a doubt, the most momentous and at the same time the most mysterious product of the human mind. Between the clearest animal call of love or warning or anger, and a man's least trivial *word*, there lies a whole day of Creation—or in modern phrase, a whole chapter of evolution.—Suzanne Langer, *Philosophy in a New Key*, 83.

Two essays, dealing with the questions posed above, introduce this unit. For, if we are to concern ourselves with a search for modes of expression, we must, indeed, begin with expression itself.

"The Uses of Language" by Irving M. Copi discusses the importance of understanding language in its relation to thought. Copi first classifies three basic functions of language; next, investigates discourse serving multiple functions; and, finally, examines the particular forms of discourse that serve his first two sections. Leslie A. White's "The Symbol: The Origin and Basis of Human Behavior" is a logical extension

and amplification of Copi's essay. By focusing on the symbol, White incorporates Copi's "language" into the broad concept of human behavior. Note, especially, the importance of the language symbol as it acts on human behavior and perpetuates what we consider civilized culture.

As part of the search for modes of expression, Eudora Welty's short story "Powerhouse" shows both experimentation with fictional form and with language itself. Perhaps most indicative of the author's purpose are the statements, "Powerhouse is so monstrous he sends everybody into oblivion," and "Powerhouse has as much as possible done by signals." In these two statements, we have indicators of Miss Welty's theme: can the world accept Powerhouse, or more broadly, any artist, and can we understand the signals of his communicative process? Henry James's "The Real Thing" also deals with art and the technique of its expression. We need to understand, however, that the story says more than its painter-narrator's comment that in art "the real thing could be so much less precious than the unreal." Art, though depicted from the point of view of a painter, serves to illustrate point of view in all artistic endeavors. James, therefore, is examining the artist's individual attitude toward his work; specifically, in this story, that process by which the artist constructs his view of "the real thing."

The Essay

SINCE Copi wrote his discussion for a teaching text, we may add to our knowledge of clear organization by analyzing the somewhat mechanical form the author uses to present his material to the student.

1. The title leads to the thesis statement in the opening sentence.
2. The first division-heading provides a qualification for the thesis and indicates the number of supporting factors.
3. The arrangement of title, thesis statement, and division headings shows the limited scope of the present chapter.

The Uses of Language

IRVING M. COPI

I. THREE BASIC FUNCTIONS OF LANGUAGE

Language is so subtle and complicated an instrument that the multiplicity of its uses is often lost sight of. Here, as in many other situations, there is danger in our tendency to oversimplify things.

A not uncommon complaint of those who take too narrow a view of the legitimate uses of language concerns the way in which words are "wasted" at social functions. "So much talk, and so little said!" sums up this kind of criticism. And more than one person has been heard to remark, "So and so asked me how I felt. What a hypocrite! He doesn't care in the least how I feel!" Such remarks reveal a failure to understand the complex purposes for which language is used. It is shown also in the deplorable conduct of the bore, who, when asked how he feels, actually proceeds to tell about the state of his health—usually at great length and in much detail. But people do not usually talk at parties to instruct each other. And ordinarily the question "How are you?" is a friendly greeting, not a request for a medical report.

One very important use of language is to communicate information. Ordinarily this is accomplished by formulating and affirming (or denying) propositions. Language used to affirm or deny propositions, or to present arguments, is said to be serving the *informative function*. In this context we use the word "information" to include misinformation: false as well as true propositions, incorrect as well as correct arguments. Informative discourse is used to *describe* the world, and to reason about it. Whether the alleged facts that are being described are important or unimportant, general or particular, does not matter; in any case the language used to describe or report them is being used informatively.

We may distinguish two basic uses or functions of language in addition to the informative, and refer to them as the *expressive* and the *directive*. Just as science provides us with the clearest examples of informative discourse, so poetry furnishes us the best examples of language serving an *expressive* function. The following lines of Burns:

> O my Luve's like a red, red rose
> That's newly sprung in June:
> O my Luve's like the melodie
> That's sweetly play'd in tune!

are definitely not intended to inform us of any facts or theories concerning the world. The poet's purpose is to communicate not knowledge but feelings and attitudes. The passage was not written to report any information but to *express* certain emotions that the poet felt very keenly and to evoke feelings of a similar kind in the reader. Language serves the *expressive* function whenever it is used to vent or communicate feelings or emotions.

Not all expressive language is poetry, however. We express sorrow by saying "That's too bad," or "Oh my," and enthusiasm by shouting "Wow!" or "Oh boy!" The lover expresses his delicate passion by murmuring "Darling!" or "Oh baby!" The poet expresses his complex and concentrated emotions in a sonnet or some other verse form. A worshipper may express his feeling of wonder and awe at the vastness and mystery of the universe by reciting the Lord's Prayer or the twenty-third Psalm of David. All these are uses of language not to communicate information but to express emotions, feelings, or attitudes. Expressive discourse *as expressive* is neither true nor false. For a person to apply only the criteria of truth or falsehood, correctness or incorrectness, to expressive discourse like a poem is to miss its point and to lose much of its value. The student whose enjoyment of Keats's sonnet *On first looking into Chapman's Homer* is marred by his historical knowledge that Balboa rather than Cortez discovered the Pacific Ocean is a "poor reader" of poetry. The purpose of the poem is not to teach history, but something else entirely. This is not to say that poetry can have no literal significance. Some poems *do* have an informative content which may be an important ingredient in their total effect. Some poetry may well be "criticism of life," in the words of a great poet. But such poems are more than merely expressive, as we are using the term here. Such poetry may be said to have a "mixed usage," or to serve a multiple function. This notion will be explained further in the following section.

Expression may be analyzed into two components. When a man curses to himself when he is alone, or a poet writes poems which he shows to no one, or a man prays in solitude, his language functions to express or evince his own attitude but does not serve to evoke a similar attitude in anyone else. On the other hand, when an orator seeks to inspire his audience–not to action, but to share enthusiasm; when a lover courts his beloved in poetic language; when the crowd cheers its athletic team; the language used not only evinces the attitudes of the speakers but also is intended to evoke the same attitudes in the hearers. Expressive discourse, then, is used either to *evince* the speaker's feelings or to *evoke* certain feelings on the part of the auditor. Of course it may do both.

Language serves the *directive* function when it is used for the purpose of causing (or preventing) overt action. The clearest examples of directive discourse are commands and requests. When a mother tells her little boy to wash his hands before supper, she does not intend to communicate any information to him or to evince or evoke any particular emotion. Her language is intended to get results, to cause action of the indicated kind. When the same mother asks the grocer to deliver certain goods to her house, she is again using language directively, to motivate or effect *action.* To ask a question is ordinarily to request an answer, and is also to be classified as directive discourse. The difference between a command and a request is a rather subtle one, for almost any command can be translated into a request by adding the word "please," or by suitable changes in tone of voice or in facial expression.

In its nakedly imperative form, directive discourse is neither true nor false. A command such as "Close the window" cannot be either true or false in any literal sense. Whether the command is obeyed or disobeyed does not affect or determine its truth-value, for it has none. We may disagree about whether a command has been obeyed or not; we may disagree about whether a command should be obeyed or not; but we never disagree about whether a command is true or false, for it cannot be either. However, the reasonableness or propriety, the unreasonableness or impropriety of commands are properties somewhat analogous to the truth or falsehood of informative discourse. And questions of the propriety of given commands can be raised and resolved in ways that are strictly within the scope of logic.

II. DISCOURSE SERVING MULTIPLE FUNCTIONS

In the preceding section the examples presented were chemically pure specimens, so to speak, of the three basic kinds of communication. The threefold division proposed is illuminating and valuable, but it cannot be applied mechanically, because almost any ordinary communication will probably exemplify, to a greater or less extent, all three uses of language. Thus a poem, which is primarily expressive discourse, may have a moral and be in effect a command to the reader (or hearer) to lead a certain kind of life, and may also convey a certain amount of information. On the other hand, although a sermon is predominantly directive, seeking to cause certain appropriate action by members of the congregation (whether to abandon their evil ways, or to contribute money to the church, or what not), it may evince and evoke sentiments, thus serving the expressive function, and may also include some information, communicating some factual material. And a scientific treatise, essentially informative, may evince something of the writer's own enthusiasm, thus serving an expressive function, and may also, at least implicitly, serve some directive function or other, perhaps bidding the reader to verify independently the author's conclusion. Most ordinary uses of language are mixed.

It is not always the result of any confusion on the part of the speaker when his language serves mixed or multiple functions. It is rather the case that *effective* communication demands certain combinations of function. Few of us stand to each other in the relation of parent to child or employer to employee. And outside the context of such formal relationships as these, one cannot simply issue an order with any expectation of having it obeyed. Consequently a certain indirection must be employed: a bald command would arouse antagonism or resentment and be self-defeating. One cannot cause action by merely voicing an imperative; it is necessary to use a more subtle method of stimulating the desired action.

Action may be said to have very complex causes. Motivation is more properly to be discussed by a psychologist than a logician, but it is common knowledge that actions are usually caused by both desires and beliefs. A man who *desires* to eat food will not touch what is on his plate unless he *believes* it to be food; and even though he *believes* it to be food he will not touch it unless he *desires* to eat. This fact is relevant to our present discussion because desires are a special type of what we have been calling "attitudes."

Consequently actions may be caused by evoking appropriate attitudes *and* communicating relevant information. Assuming your listeners to be benevolent, you may cause them to contribute to a given charity by informing them of its effectiveness in accomplishing benevolent results. In such a case your use of language is ultimately directive, since its purpose is to cause action. But a naked command would be far less effective in this situation than the informative discourse used. Suppose, on the other hand, that your listeners are already persuaded that the charity in question does accomplish benevolent results. Here again you cannot simply command with any great hope of being obeyed, but you may succeed in causing them to act in the desired fashion by somehow arousing a sufficiently benevolent feeling or emotion in them. The discourse you use to realize your end is expressive discourse; you must make a "moving appeal." Thus your language will have a mixed use, functioning both expressively and directively. Or finally, let us suppose that you are seeking a donation from people who have *neither* a benevolent attitude *nor* a belief that the charity serves a benevolent purpose. Here you must use *both* informative and expressive language. In such a case the language used serves all three functions, being directive, informative, and expressive all at once, not accidentally as a mere mixture that just happens to occur, but essentially, as necessary to successful communication.

Some writers on language have suggested that discourse serves more than these three distinct functions. It is possible, however, to understand any other function as a mixture or combination of two or possibly all three of the basic uses that have been distinguished here. The most important of these others has frequently been called the "ceremonial" use of language. Included within this category are many different kinds of phrases, ranging from relatively trivial words of greeting to the more portentous discourse of the marriage ceremony, phrasings of state documents, and the verbal rituals performed on holy days in houses of worship. But these can all be regarded as mixtures of expressive and directive discourse, rather than some altogether different and unique kind. For example, the usual ceremonial greetings and chit-chat at social gatherings serve the purpose of evincing and evoking goodwill and sociability. Perhaps for some speakers they are intended also to serve the directive purpose of causing their hearers to act in certain definite ways, to patronize the speaker's business, to offer him employment, or to invite him to dinner. At the other extreme, the impressive language of the marriage ceremony is intended to emphasize the solemnity of the occasion (its expressive function), and also to cause the bride and groom to perform in their new roles with heightened appreciation of the seriousness of the marriage contract (its directive function).

III. THE FORMS OF DISCOURSE

Textbooks of grammar commonly define a sentence as the unit of language that expresses a complete thought, and divide sentences into four categories, usually called declarative, interrogative, imperative, and exclamatory. These four categories are not identical with those of assertions, questions, commands, and exclamations. We may be tempted to identify form with function—to think that declarative sentences and informative discourse coincide, and that exclamatory sentences are suitable only for expressive discourse. Regarding questions as requests for answers, we may be led further to think that directive discourse consists exclusively of sentences in the interrogative and imperative moods. Were such identifications possible, it would immensely simplify the problem of communication, for then we should be able to tell the intended use or function of a passage by its form, which is open to direct inspection. Some people apparently do identify form with function, but these are not sensitive readers, for the identification often makes them misunderstand what is said, and they "miss the point" of much that is to be communicated.

It is a mistake to believe that everything in the form of a declarative sentence is informative discourse, to be valued if true and rejected if false. "I had a very nice time at your party," is a declarative sentence, but its function need not be informative at all, but rather ceremonial or expressive, evincing a feeling of friendliness and appreciation. Many poems and prayers are in the form of declarative sentences, despite the fact that their functions are not informative. To regard them as such and to attempt to evaluate them by the criteria of truth or falsehood is to shut oneself off from aesthetic and religious satisfactions. Again, many requests and commands are expressed indirectly—perhaps more gently—by means of declarative sentences. The declarative sentence, "I would like some coffee," should not be taken by a waitress to be a mere report of the psychological fact it apparently asserts about her customer, but as a command or request for action. Were we invariably to judge the truth or falsehood of declarative sentences such as "I'd appreciate some help with this," or "I hope you'll be able to meet me after class at the library," and do no more than register them as information received, we should soon be without friends. These examples should suffice to show that the declarative form is no certain indication of the informative function. Declarative sentences lend themselves to the formulation of every kind of discourse.

It is the same with other forms of sentences. The interrogative sentence, "Do you realize that we're almost late?" is not necessarily a request for information but may be a command to hurry. The interrogative sentence "Isn't it true that Russia and Germany signed a pact in 1939 which precipitated the Second World War?" may not be a question at all but either an oblique way of communicating information or an attempt to express and evoke a feeling of hostility towards Russia, functioning informatively in the first instance and expressively in the second. Even what is grammatically an imperative, as in official documents beginning, "Know all men by these presents that . . . ," may not be a command, but rather informative discourse in what it asserts and expressive discourse in its use of language to evoke the appropriate feelings of solemnity and respect. In spite of its close affinity to the expressive, an exclamatory sentence may serve a quite different function. The exclamation "Good Lord it's late!" may really communicate a command to hurry. And the exclamation, "What a beautiful ring!" uttered by a young lady to her gentleman friend as they pass a jeweler's window, may function ever so much more directively than expressively.

It should be remembered that some discourse is intended to serve two or possibly all three functions of language at once. In such cases each aspect or function of a given passage is subject to its own proper criteria. One having an informative function may have that aspect evaluated as true or false. The same passage as serving a directive function may have that aspect evaluated as proper or improper, right or wrong. And if there is also an expressive function served by the passage in question, that component of it may be evaluated as sincere or insincere, as valuable or otherwise. Properly to evaluate a given passage requires knowledge of the function or functions it is intended to serve.

Truth and falsehood, and the attendant notions of correctness and incorrectness of argument, are more important in the study of logic than the others mentioned. Yet the logician's criteria are to be applied only to informative discourse. Hence, as students of logic, we must be able to differentiate discourse that functions informatively from that which does not. And we must be able further to disentangle the informative function a given passage serves from whatever other functions it may also be serving. To do this "disentangling" we must know what different functions language can serve and be able to tell them apart. The grammatical structure of a passage often serves as a cue to its function, but there is no *necessary* connection between function and grammatical form. Nor is there any strict relation between the function and the *content*—in the sense of what might seem to be *asserted* by a passage. This is very clearly shown by an example of Bloomfield's in his chapter on *Meaning:* "A petulant child, at bed-time, says *I'm hungry*, and his mother, who is up to his tricks, answers by packing him off to bed. This is an example of displaced speech." [1] The child's speech here is neither expressive nor informative, but directive—even though it does not succeed in procuring the wanted diversion. By the function of a passage we mean the *intended* function. But this, unfortunately, is not always easy to determine.

When a passage is quoted in isolation, it is often difficult to say what language function it is primarily intended to serve. The reason for this difficulty is that *context* is extremely important in determining the answer to such a question. What is an imperative or a flat statement of fact, by itself, may in its proper context function expressively, as part of a larger whole whose poetic effect is derived from all its parts in their arrangement. For example, in isolation, the sentence:

Give me my sword.

is an imperative serving the directive function; and the sentence

The King comes here tonight.

[1] *Reprinted from* Language *by Leonard Bloomfield. Copyright, 1933, by Henry Holt and Company, Inc.*

is a declarative sentence serving an informative function. But both are from Shakespeare's *Macbeth*, and in that context contribute to the expressive function served by the larger whole.

It is important also to distinguish between the proposition which a sentence formulates and what the fact of its assertion evinces about the person who speaks or writes it. When a man remarks, "It is raining," the proposition which he asserts is about the weather, not about himself. Yet his assertion gives evidence that *he believes* it to be raining, and this is a fact about the speaker. It also may happen that a person makes a statement which is ostensibly about his beliefs, not for the sake of giving information about himself, but simply as a way of saying something else. To say "I believe that gold is valuable," is ordinarily not to be construed as a psychological or autobiographical report on the beliefs of the speaker, but simply his way of saying *that* gold *is* valuable. Similarly, to voice a command usually evinces the desires of the speaker, and under appropriate circumstances to assert that one has such and such a desire is to give a command. To utter an exclamation of joy gives evidence that the speaker is joyful, although the speaker makes no assertion in the process. On the other hand, to present a psychological report which affirms that the speaker is joyful is to assert a proposition, something quite different from exclaiming joyously.

In subsequent chapters we shall develop certain logical techniques that can be applied quite mechanically to arguments for the purpose of testing their validity. But there is no mechanical test applicable to language in general for the purpose of distinguishing the informative and argumentative from other types of discourse. This requires thought and demands an awareness of and sensitivity to the flexibility of language and the multiplicity of its uses.

Questions

1. What are the three basic functions of language? What methods are used to support each function?
2. Do you agree with the author's definition of a "poor reader" of poetry? How does he support this point?
3. In what way does part 2 complement the discussion in part 1?
4. How are the traditional sentence categories (declarative, interrogative, imperative, and exclamatory) used to discuss the forms of discourse? How does this discussion differ from the grammatical concept you learned in school?

Topics for Composition

1. Select a poem from a previously studied unit. Write an essay analyzing the poem as it fits Copi's definition of "expressive language."
2. Select a poem from a previously studied unit that illustrates "multiple functions." Analyze the poem to reveal each function.
3. Write a short essay in which you attempt to be only informative. Write an analysis of your essay, attempting to uncover expressive and directive uses of language.
4. Select one of the essays from a previously studied unit. Analyze the essay according to the language functions used.
5. Select a previously studied short story. Examine the language functions used by the author and relate them to purpose or effect.

WHITE's opening section serves well as an example of a strong controlled introduction; especially his second paragraph, with its repetitive, transitional use of the word *symbol* in a double function, as a key to the supporting factors and as a strengthener for the thesis statement. Such an examination shows:

1. The use of symbol as an equivalent of human behavior in the topic sentence
2. The use of symbol as an equivalent for each of the three supporting factors
3. A restatement of the topic sentence to conclude the paragraph

The Symbol: The Origin and Basis of Human Behavior

LESLIE A. WHITE

"In the Word was the Beginning . . . the beginning of Man and of Culture."

I

In July, 1939, a celebration was held at Leland Stanford University to commemorate the hundredth anniversary of the discovery that the cell is the basic unit of all living tissue. Today we are beginning to realize and to appreciate the fact that the symbol is the basic unit of all human behavior and civilization.

All human behavior originates in the use of symbols. It was the symbol which transformed our anthropoid ancestors into men and made them human. All civilizations have been generated, and are perpetuated, only by the use of symbols. It is the symbol which transforms an infant of Homo sapiens into a human being; deaf mutes who grow up without the use of symbols are not human beings. All human behavior consists of, or is dependent upon, the use of symbols. Human behavior is symbolic behavior; symbolic behavior is human behavior. The symbol is the universe of humanity.

II

The great Darwin declared in *The Descent of Man* that "there is no fundamental difference between man and the higher mammals in their mental faculties," that the difference between them consists "*solely* in his [man's] almost infinitely larger power of associating together the most diversified sounds and ideas . . . the mental powers of higher animals do not differ *in kind*, though greatly *in degree*, from the corresponding powers of man" (Chs. 3, 18; emphasis ours).

This view of comparative mentality is held by many scholars today. Thus, F. H. Hankins, a prominent sociologist, states that "in spite of his large brain, it cannot be said that man has any mental traits that are peculiar to him . . . All of these human superiorities are merely relative or differences of degree." Professor Ralph Linton, an anthropologist, writes in *The Study of Man:* "The differences between men and animals in all these [behavior] respects are enormous, but they seem to be differences in quantity rather than in quality." "Human and animal behavior can be shown to have so much in common," Linton observes, "that the gap [between them] ceases to be of great importance." Dr. Alexander Goldenweiser, likewise an anthropologist, believes that "In point of sheer psychology, mind as such, man is after all no more than a talented animal" and that "the difference between the mentality here displayed [by a horse and a chimpanzee] and that of man is merely one of degree."

That there are numerous and impressive similarities between the behavior of man and that of ape is fairly obvious; it is quite possible that chimpanzees and gorillas in zoos have noted and appreciated them. Fairly apparent, too, are man's behavioral similarities to many other kinds of animals. Almost as obvious, but not easy to define, is a difference in behavior which distinguishes man from all other living creatures. I say 'obvious' because it is quite apparent to the common man that the non-human animals with which he is familiar do not and cannot enter, and participate in, the world in which he, as a human being, lives. It is impossible for a dog, horse, bird, or even an ape, to have any understanding of the meaning of the sign of the cross to a Christian, or of the fact that black (white among the Chinese) is the color of mourning. No chimpanzee or laboratory rat can appreciate the difference between Holy water and distilled water, or grasp the meaning of *Tuesday*, *3*, or *sin*. No animal save man can distinguish a cousin from an uncle, or a cross cousin from a parallel cousin. Only man can commit the crime of incest or adultery; only he can remember the Sabbath and keep it Holy. It is not, as we well know, that the lower animals can do these things but to a lesser degree than ourselves; they cannot perform these acts of appreciation and distinction *at all*. It is, as Descartes said long ago, "not only that the brutes have less Reason than man, but that they have none at all."

But when the scholar attempts to *define* the mental difference between man and other animals he sometimes encounters difficulties which he cannot surmount and, therefore, ends up by saying that the difference is merely one of degree: man has a bigger mind, "larger power of association," wider range of activities, etc. We have a good example of this in the distinguished physiologist, Anton J. Carlson. After taking note of "man's present achievements in science, in the arts (including oratory), in political and social institutions," and noting "at the same time the apparent paucity of such behavior in other animals," he, as a common man "is tempted to conclude that in these capacities, at least, man has a qualitative superiority over other mammals." But, since, as a scientist, Professor Carlson cannot *define* this qualitative difference between man and other animals, since as a physiologist he cannot explain it, he refuses to admit it—". . . the physiologist does not accept the great development of articulate speech in man as something qualitatively new; . . ." —and suggests helplessly that some day we may find some new "building stone," an "additional lipoid, phosphatid, or potassium ion," in the human brain which will explain it, and concludes by saying that the difference between the mind of man and that of non-man is "probably only one of degree."

The thesis that we shall advance and defend here is that there is a *fundamental* difference between the mind of man and the mind of non-man. This difference is one of kind, not one of degree. And the gap between the two types is of the greatest importance—at least to the science of comparative behavior. Man uses symbols; no other creature does. An organism has the ability to symbol or it does not; there are no intermediate stages.

III

A symbol may be defined as a thing the value or meaning of which is bestowed upon it by those who use it. I say 'thing' because a symbol may have any kind of physical form; it may have the form of a material object, a color, a sound, an odor, a motion of an object, a taste.

The meaning, or value, of a symbol is in no instance derived from or determined by properties intrinsic in its physical form: the color appropriate to mourning may be yellow, green, or any other color; purple need not be the color of royalty; among the Manchu rulers of China it was yellow. The meaning of the word "see" is not intrinsic in its phonetic (or pictorial) properties. "Biting one's thumb at"[1] someone might mean anything. The meanings of symbols are derived from and determined by the organisms who use them; meaning is bestowed by human organisms upon physical things or events which thereupon become symbols. Symbols "have their signification," to use John Locke's phrase, "from the arbitrary imposition of men."

All symbols must have a physical form otherwise they could not enter our experience. This statement is valid regardless of our theory of experiencing. Even the exponents of "Extra-Sensory Perception" who have challenged Locke's dictum that "the knowledge of the existence of any other thing [besides ourselves and God] we can have only by sensation," have been obliged to work with physical rather than ethereal forms. But the meaning of a symbol cannot be discovered by mere sensory examination of its physical form. One cannot tell by looking at an *x* in an algebraic equation what it stands for; one cannot ascertain with the ears alone the symbolic value of the phonetic compound *si;* one cannot tell merely by weighing a pig how much gold he will exchange for; one cannot tell from the

[1] *"Do you bite your thumb at us, sir?"*—Romeo and Juliet, *Act I, Sc. 1.*

wave length of a color whether it stands for courage or cowardice, "stop" or "go"; nor can one discover the spirit in a fetish by any amount of physical or chemical examination. The meaning of a symbol can be grasped only by non-sensory, symbolic means.

The nature of symbolic experience may be easily illustrated. When the Spaniards first encountered the Aztecs, neither could speak the language of the other. How could the Indians discover the meaning of santo, or the significance of the crucifix? How could the Spaniards learn the meaning of *calli*, or appreciate Tlaloc? These meanings and values could not be communicated by sensory experience of physical properties alone. The finest ears will not tell you whether *santo* means "holy" or "hungry." The keenest senses cannot capture the value of holy water. Yet, as we all know, the Spaniards and the Aztecs did discover each other's meanings and appreciate each other's values. But not with sensory means. Each was able to enter the world of the other only by virtue of a faculty for which we have no better name than *symbol.*

But a thing which in one context is a symbol is, in another context, not a symbol but a sign. Thus, a word is a symbol only when one is concerned with the distinction between its meaning and its physical form. This distinction *must* be made when one bestows value upon a sound-combination or when a previously bestowed value is discovered for the first time; it *may* be made at other times for certain purposes. But after value has been bestowed upon, or discovered in, a word, its meaning becomes identified, in use, with its physical form. The word then functions as a sign, rather than as a symbol. Its meaning is then grasped with the senses.

We define a *sign* as a physical thing or event whose function is to indicate some other thing or event. The meaning of a sign may be inherent in its physical form and its context, as in the case of the height of a column of mercury in a thermometer as an indication of temperature, or the return of robins in the spring. Or, the meaning of a sign may be merely identified with its physical form as in the case of a hurricane signal or a quarantine flag. But in either case, the meaning of the sign may be ascertained by sensory means. The fact that a thing may be both a symbol (in one context) and a sign (in another context) has led to confusion and misunderstanding.

Thus Darwin says: "That which distinguishes man from the lower animals is not the understanding of articulate sounds, for as everyone knows, dogs understand many words and sentences," (Ch. III, *The Descent of Man*).

It is perfectly true, of course, that dogs, apes, horses, birds, and perhaps creatures even lower in the evolutionary scale, can be taught to respond in a specific way to a vocal command. Little Gua, the infant chimpanzee in the Kelloggs' experiment, was, for a time, "considerably superior to the child in responding to human words." But it does not follow that no difference exists between the meaning of "words and sentences" to a man and to an ape or dog. Words are both signs and symbols to man; they are merely signs to a dog. Let us analyze the situation of vocal stimulus and response.

A dog may be taught to roll over at the command "Roll over!" A man may be taught to stop at the command "Halt!" The fact that a dog can be taught to roll over in Chinese, or that he can be taught to "go fetch" at the command "roll over" (and, of course, the same is true for a man) shows that there is no necessary and invariable relationship between a particular sound combination and a specific reaction to it. The dog or the man can be taught to respond in a certain manner to *any* arbitrarily selected combination of sounds, for example, a group of nonsense syllables, coined for the occasion. On the other hand, any one of a great number and variety of responses may become evocable by a given stimulus. Thus, so far as the *origin* of the relationship between vocal stimulus and response is concerned, the nature of the relationship, i.e., the meaning of the stimulus, is not determined by properties intrinsic in the stimulus.

But, once the relationship has been established between vocal stimulus and response, the meaning of the stimulus becomes *identified with the sounds;* it is then *as if* the meaning were intrinsic in the sounds themselves. Thus, 'halt' does not have the same meaning as 'hilt' or 'malt,' and these stimuli are distinguished from one another with the auditory mechanism. A dog may be conditioned to respond in a certain way to a sound of a given wave length. Sufficiently alter the pitch of the sound and the response will cease to be forthcoming. The meaning of the stimulus has become identified with its physical form; its value is appreciated with the senses.

Thus in *sign* behavior we see that in *establishing* a relationship between a stimulus and a response the properties intrinsic in the stimulus do not determine the nature of the response. But, *after the relationship has been established* the meaning of the stimulus is *as if* it were *inherent* in its physical form. It does not make any difference what phonetic combination we select to evoke the response of terminating self-locomotion. We may teach a dog, horse, or man to stop at any vocal command we care to choose or devise. But once the relationship has been established between sound and response, the meaning of the stimulus becomes identified with its physical form and is, therefore, perceivable with the senses.

So far we have discovered no difference between the dog and the man; they appear to be exactly alike. And so they are as far as we have gone. But we have not told the whole story yet. No difference between dog and man is discoverable so far as learning to respond appropriately to a vocal stimulus is concerned. But we must not let an impressive similarity conceal an important difference. A porpoise is not yet a fish.

The man differs from the dog—and all other creatures—in that *he can and does play an active role in determining what value the vocal stimulus is to have, and the dog cannot.* The dog does not and cannot play an active part in determining the value of the vocal stimulus. Whether he is to roll over or go fetch at a given stimulus, or whether the stimulus for roll over be one combination of sounds or another is a matter in which the dog has nothing whatever to "say." He plays a purely passive role and can do nothing else. He learns the meaning of a vocal command just as his salivary glands may learn to respond to the sound of a bell. But man plays an active role and thus becomes a creator: let x equal three pounds of coal and it does equal three pounds of coal; let removal of the hat in a house of worship indicate respect and it becomes so. This creative faculty, that of freely, actively, and arbitrarily bestowing value upon things, is one of the most commonplace as well as *the* most important characteristic of man. Children employ it freely in their play: "Let's pretend that this rock is a wolf."

The difference between the behavior of man and other animals then, is that the lower animals may receive new values, may acquire new meanings, but they cannot create and bestow them. Only man can do this. To use a crude analogy, lower animals are like a person who has only the receiving apparatus for wireless messages: he can receive messages but cannot send them. Man can do both. And this difference is one of kind, not of degree: a creature can either "arbitrarily impose signification," can either create and bestow values, or he cannot. There are no intermediate stages. This difference may appear slight, but, as a carpenter once told William James in discussing differences between men, "It's very important." All *human* existence depends upon it and it alone.

The confusion regarding the nature of words and their significance to men and the lower animals is not hard to understand. It arises, first of all, from a failure to distinguish between the two quite different contexts in which words function. The statements, "The meaning of a word cannot be grasped with the senses," and "The meaning of a word can be grasped with the senses," though contradictory, are nevertheless equally true. In the *symbol* context the meaning cannot be perceived with the senses; in the *sign* context it can. This is confusing enough. But the situation has been made worse by using the words 'symbol' and 'sign' to label, not the *different contexts*, but *one and the same thing:* the word. Thus a word is a symbol *and* a sign, two different things. It is like saying that a vase is a *doli* and a *kana*—two different things—because it may function in two contexts, esthetic and commercial.

IV

That man is unique among animal species with respect to mental abilities, that a fundamental difference of kind—not of degree—separates man from all other animals is a fact that has long been appreciated, despite Darwin's pronouncement to the contrary. Long ago, in his *Discourse on Method*, Descartes pointed out that "there are no men so dull and stupid . . . as to be incapable of joining together different words . . . on the other hand, there is no other animal, however perfect . . . which can do the like." John Locke, too, saw clearly that "the power of abstracting is not at all in them [i.e., beasts], and that the having of general ideas is that which puts a perfect distinction between man and brutes, and is an excellency which the faculties of brutes do by no means attain to . . . they have no use of words or any other general signs." The great British anthropologist, E. B. Tylor, remarked upon "the mental gulf that divides the lowest savage from the highest ape . . . A young child can understand what is not proved to have entered the mind of the cleverest dog, elephant, or ape." And, of course, there are many today who recognize the "mental gulf" between man and other species.

Thus, for over a century we have had, side by side, two traditions in comparative psychology. One has declared that man does not differ from other animals in mental abilities except in degree. The other has seen clearly that man is unique in at least one respect, that he possesses an ability that no other animal has. The difficulty of *defining* this difference adequately has kept this question open until the present day. The distinction between *sign* behavior and *symbol* behavior as drawn here may, we hope, contribute to a solution of this problem once and for all.

V

Very little indeed is known of the organic basis of the symbolic faculty: we know next to nothing of the neurology of "symbolling." And very few scientists—anatomists, neurologists or physical anthropologists—appear to be interested in the subject. Some, in fact, seem to be unaware of the existence of such a problem. The duty and task of giving an account of the neural basis of symbolling does not, however, fall within the province of the sociologist or the cultural anthropologist. On the contrary, he should scrupulously exclude it as irrelevant to his problems and interests; to introduce it would bring only confusion. It is enough for the sociologist or cultural anthropologist to take the ability to use symbols, possessed by man alone, as given. The use to which he puts this fact is in no way affected by his, or even the anatomist's, inability to describe the symbolic process in neurological terms. However, it is well for the social scientist to be acquainted with the little that neurologists and anatomists do know about the structural basis of symbolling. We, therefore, review briefly the chief relevant facts here.

The anatomist has not been able to discover why men can use symbols and apes cannot. So far as is known the only difference between the brain of man and the brain of an ape is a quantitative one: ". . . man has no new kinds of brain cells or brain cell connections," as A. J. Carlson has remarked. Nor does man, as distinguished from other animals, possess a specialized "symbol-mechanism." The so-called speech areas of the brain should not be identified with symbolling. The notion that symbolling is identified with, or dependent upon, the ability to utter articulate sounds is not uncommon. Thus, L. L. Bernard lists as "the fourth great organic asset of man . . . his vocal apparatus, . . . characteristic of him alone." But this is an erroneous conception. The great apes have the mechanism necessary for the production of articulate sounds. "It seemingly is well established," write R. M. and A. W. Yerkes in *The Great Apes*, "that the motor mechanism of voice in this ape [chimpanzee] is adequate not only to the production of a considerable variety of sounds, but also to definite articulations similar to those of man." And the physical anthropologist, E. A. Hooton, asserts that "all of the anthropoid apes are vocally and muscularly equipped so that they could have an articulate language if they possessed the requisite intelligence." Furthermore, as Descartes and Locke pointed out long ago, there are birds who do actually utter articulate sounds, who duplicate the sounds of human speech, but who of course are quite incapable of symbolling. The "speech areas" of the brain are merely areas associated with the muscles of the tongue, with the larynx, etc. But, as we know, symbolling is not at all confined to the use of these organs. One may symbol with any part of the body that he can move at will.

To be sure, the symbolic faculty was brought into existence by the natural processes of organic evolution. And we may reasonably believe that the focal point, if not the locus, of this faculty is in the brain, especially the forebrain. Man's brain is much larger than that of an ape, both absolutely and relatively. The brain of the average adult human male is about 1500 c.c. in size; brains of gorillas seldom exceed 500 c.c. Relatively, the human brain weighs about 1/50th of the entire body weight, while that of a gorilla varies from 1/150th to 1/200th part of that weight. And the forebrain especially is large in man as compared with ape. Now in many situations we know that quantitative changes give rise to qualitative differences. Water is transformed into steam by additional quantities of heat. Additional power and speed lift the taxiing airplane from the ground and transform terrestrial locomotion into flight. The difference between wood alcohol and grain alcohol is a qualitative expression of a quantitative difference in the proportions of carbon and hydrogen. Thus a marked growth in size of the brain in man may have brought forth a *new kind* of function.

VI

All culture (civilization) depends upon the symbol. It was the exercise of the symbolic faculty that brought culture into existence and it is the use of symbols that makes the perpetuation of culture possible. Without the symbol there would be no culture, and man would be merely an animal, not a human being.

Articulate speech is the most important form of symbolic expression. Remove speech from culture and what would remain? Let us see.

Without articulate speech we would have no *human* social organization. Families we might have, but this form of organization is not peculiar to man; it is not *per se, human*. But we would have no prohibitions of incest, no rules prescribing exogamy and endogamy, polygamy or monogamy. How could marriage with a cross cousin be prescribed, marriage with a parallel cousin proscribed, without articulate speech? How could rules which prohibit plural mates possessed simultaneously but permit them if possessed one at a time, exist without speech?

Without speech we would have no political, economic, ecclesiastic, or military organization; no codes of etiquette or ethics; no laws; no science, theology, or literature; no games or music, except on an ape level. Rituals and ceremonial paraphernalia would be meaningless without articulate speech. Indeed, without articulate speech we would be all but toolless: we would have only the occasional and insignificant use of the tool such as we find today among the higher apes, for it was articulate speech that transformed the non-progressive tool-using of the ape into the progressive, cumulative tool-using of man, the human being.

In short, without symbolic communication in some form, we would have no culture. "In the Word was the beginning" of culture —and its perpetuation also.

To be sure, with all his culture man is still an animal and strives for the same ends that all other living creatures strive for: the preservation of the individual and the perpetuation of the race. In concrete terms these ends are food, shelter from the elements, defense from enemies, health, and offspring. The fact that man strives for these ends just as all other animals do has, no doubt, led many to declare that there is "no fundamental difference between the behavior of man and of other creatures." But man does differ, not in *ends* but in *means*. Man's means are cultural means: culture is simply the human animal's way of living. And, since these means, culture, are dependent upon a faculty possessed by man alone, the ability to use symbols, the difference between the behavior of man and of all other creatures is not merely great, but basic and fundamental.

VII

The behavior of man is of two distinct kinds: symbolic and nonsymbolic. Man yawns, stretches, coughs, scratches himself, cries out in pain, shrinks with fear, "bristles" with anger, and so on. Nonsymbolic behavior of this sort is not peculiar to man; he shares it not only with the other primates but with many other animal species as well. But man communicates with his fellows with articulate speech, uses amulets, confesses sins, makes laws, observes codes of etiquette, explains his dreams, classifies his relatives in designated categories, and so on. This kind of behavior is unique; only man is capable of it; it is peculiar to man because it consists of, or is dependent upon, the use of symbols. The nonsymbolic behavior of Homo sapiens is the behavior of man the animal; the symbolic behavior is that of man the human being. It is the symbol which has transformed man from a mere animal to a human animal.

Because *human* behavior is symbol behavior and since the behavior of infra-human species is non-symbolic, it follows that we can learn nothing about human behavior from observations upon or experiments with the lower animals. Experiments with rats and apes have indeed been illuminating. They have thrown much light upon mechanisms and processes of behavior among mammals or the higher vertebrates. But they have contributed nothing to an understanding of *human* behavior because the symbol mechanism and all of its consequences are totally lacking among the lower species. And as for neuroses in rats, it is of course interesting to know that rats can be made neurotic. But science probably had a better understanding of psychopathic behavior among human beings before neuroses were produced experimentally in rats than they now have of the neuroses of the rats. Our understanding of human neuroses has helped us to understand those of rats; we have, as a matter of fact, interpreted the latter in terms of *human* pathology. But I cannot see where the neurotic laboratory rats have served to deepen or enlarge our understanding of *human* behavior.

As it was the symbol that made *mankind* human, so it is with each member of the species. A baby is not a *human* being until he begins to symbol. Until the infant begins to talk there is nothing to distinguish his behavior qualitatively from that of a very young ape, as *The Ape and the Child* showed. As a matter of fact, one of the impressive results of this fascinating experiment by Professor and Mrs. Kellogg was the demonstration of how ape-like an infant of Homo sapiens is before he begins to talk. The baby boy acquired exceptional proficiency in climbing in association with the little chimpanzee, and even acquired her "food bark"! The Kelloggs speak of how the little ape became "humanized" during her sojourn in their home. But what the experiment demonstrated so conclusively was the ape's utter inability to learn to talk or even to make *any* progress in this direction—in short, her inability to become "humanized" at all.

The infant of the species *Homo sapiens* becomes human only when and as he exercises his symbol faculty. Only through articulate speech—not necessarily vocal—can he enter the world of human beings and take part in their affairs. The questions asked earlier may be repeated now. How could a growing child know and appreciate such things as social organization, ethics, etiquette, ritual, science, religion, art and games without symbolic communication? The answer is of course that he could know nothing of these things and have no appreciation of them at all.

The question of "wolf children" is relevant here. A belief in instances in which human children have been reared by wolves or other animals has flourished ever since the myth of Romulus and Remus—and long before that time. Despite the fact that accounts of "wolf children" have been shown repeatedly to be erroneous or unsupported by adequate evidence ever since Blumenbach discovered that "Wild Peter" was merely a half-witted boy ejected from his home at the instance of a newly acquired stepmother, this deplorable folk-tale still flourishes in certain "scientific" circles today. But the use to which these lupine wards and "feral men" are put by some sociologists and psychologists is a good one, namely, to show that a member of the species *Homo sapiens* who lives in a world without symbols is not a human being but a brute. To paraphrase Voltaire, one might say that if wolf children did not exist "social science" would have to invent them.

Children who have been cut off from human intercourse for years by blindness and deafness but who have eventually effected communication with their fellows on a symbolic level are exceedingly illuminating. The case of Helen Keller is exceptionally instructive, although those of Laura Bridgman, Marie Heurtin, and others are very valuable also.

Helen Keller was rendered blind and deaf at a very early age by illness. She grew up as a child without symbolic contact with anyone. Descriptions of her at the age of seven, the time at which her teacher, Miss Sullivan, came to her home, disclose no *human* attributes of Helen's behavior at all. She was a headstrong, undisciplined and unruly little animal.

Within a day or so after her arrival at the Keller home, Miss Sullivan taught Helen her first word, spelling it into her hand. But this word was merely a sign, not a symbol. A week later Helen knew several words but, as Miss Sullivan reports, she had "no idea how to use them or that everything has a name." Within three weeks Helen knew eighteen nouns and three verbs. But she was still on the level of signs; she still had no notion "that everything has a name."

Helen confused the word signs for "mug" and "water" because, apparently, both were associated with drinking. Miss Sullivan made a few attempts to clear up this confusion but without success. One morning, however, about a month after Miss Sullivan's arrival, the two went out to the pump in the garden. What happened then is best told in their own words:

> I made Helen hold her mug under the spout while I pumped. As the cold water gushed forth, filling the mug, I spelled 'w-a-t-e-r' into Helen's free hand. The word coming so close upon the sensation of cold water rushing over her hand seemed to startle her. She dropped the mug and stood as one transfixed. A new light came into her face. She spelled 'water' several times. Then she dropped on the ground and asked for its name and pointed to the pump and the trellis, and suddenly turning round she asked for my name . . . *In a few hours she had added thirty new words to her vocabulary.*

But these words were now more than mere signs as they are to a dog and as they had been to Helen up to then. They were *symbols.* Helen had at last grasped and turned the key that admitted her for the first time to a new universe: the world of human beings. Helen describes this marvellous experience herself:

> We walked down the path to the well-house, attracted by the fragrance of the honeysuckle with which it was covered. Someone was drawing water and my teacher placed my hand under the spout. As the cool stream gushed over one hand she spelled into the other the word *water,* first slowly, then rapidly. I stood still, my whole attention fixed upon the motion of her fingers. Suddenly I felt a misty consciousness as of something forgotten—a thrill of returning thought; and somehow *the mystery of language was revealed to me.* I knew then that 'w-a-t-e-r' meant the wonderful cool something that was flowing over my hand. That living word awakened my soul, gave it light, hope, joy, set it free!

Helen was transformed on the instant by this experience. Miss Sullivan had managed to touch Helen's symbol mechanism and set it in motion. Helen, on her part, grasped the external world with this mechanism that had lain dormant and inert all these years, sealed in dark and silent isolation by eyes that could not see and ears that heard not. But now she had crossed the boundary and entered a new land. Henceforth her progress would be rapid.

"I left the well-house," Helen reports, "eager to learn. Everything had a name, and each name gave birth to a new thought. As we returned to the house every object which I touched seemed to quiver with life. That was because I saw everything with the strange new sight that had come to me."

Helen became humanized rapidly. "I see an improvement in Helen from day to day," Miss Sullivan wrote in her diary, "*almost from hour to hour*. Everything must have a name now . . . She drops the signs and pantomime she used before as soon as she has words to supply their place . . . We notice her face grows more expressive each day . . ."

A more eloquent and convincing account of the significance of symbols and of the great gulf between the human mind and that of minds without symbols could hardly be imagined.

VIII

Summary. The natural processes of biologic evolution brought into existence in man, and man alone, a new and distinctive ability: the ability to use symbols. The most important form of symbolic expression is articulate speech. Articulate speech means communication of ideas; communication means preservation—tradition—and preservation means accumulation and progress. The emergence of the faculty of symbolling has resulted in the genesis of a new order of phenomena: an extra-somatic, cultural, order. All civilizations are born of, and are perpetuated by, the use of symbols. A culture, or civilization, is but a particular kind of form which the biologic, life-perpetuating activities of a particular animal, man, assume.

Human behavior is symbolic behavior; if it is not symbolic, it is not human. The infant of the genus Homo becomes a human being only as he is introduced into and participates in that order of phenomena which is culture. And the key to this world and the means of participation in it is—the symbol.

Questions

1. What kind of support does White provide in section 2? How effective is his choice?
2. In section 3, White defines the symbol. What are his methods of

definition? How does he vary his method of support within each definition-framework?

3. Find the point in section 3 at which White completes his definition of symbol and begins to compare and contrast man and dog as primary examples of his definition. Which is the transitional paragraph? Explain its transitional qualities.
4. Outline White's comparison of man and dog with the idea of revealing his comparative and contrastive techniques. What assumptions can you make about technique in writing effective comparison and contrast?
5. How does section 4 function in the overall structure of the essay?
6. Classify White's techniques in sections 5, 6, and 7. What previously used techniques do you find? How has he expanded some?
7. Section 8 provides a neatly organized summary. Do you agree with White's conclusions? Why or why not?

Topics for Composition

1. Write an essay showing how White has expanded Copi's discussion of the expressive function of language.
2. White implies that words function as symbols to stimulate human behavior. Select any word or phrase and show its symbolic effect on behavior. Some good ones might be: Hate, Love, Anger, Wealth, etc.
3. Write a précis of White's essay. Limit your précis to no more than 250 words.

The Short Story

THERE is a deliberate incoherency in Miss Welty's story. In fact, it retains few of the features on which we ordinarily rely in analyzing fiction. We find neither a clearly developed plot nor a characterization that approximates our view of human experience. We should, therefore, approach this story as we approach a musical selection—more ready to react than to understand. For all of its unusual qualities, however, we may find it helpful to consider the following:

1. The kind and intensity of Powerhouse's music
2. The validity of the story of Gypsy's death
3. The other musicians' comments in reply to Powerhouse
4. The function of the café scene

Powerhouse

EUDORA WELTY

Powerhouse is playing!

He's here on tour from the city—"Powerhouse and His Keyboard"—"Powerhouse and His Tasmanians"—think of the things he calls himself! There's no one in the world like him. You can't tell what he is. "Nigger man"?—he looks more Asiatic, monkey, Jewish, Babylonian, Peruvian, fanatic, devil. He has pale gray eyes, heavy lids, maybe horny like a lizard's, but big glowing eyes when they're open. He has African feet of the greatest size, stomping, both together, on each side of the pedals. He's not coal black—beverage colored—looks like a preacher when his mouth is shut, but then it opens—vast and obscene. And his mouth is going every minute: like a monkey's when it looks for something. Improvising, coming on a light and childish melody—*smooch*—he loves it with his mouth.

Is it possible that he could be this! When you have him there performing for you, that's what you feel. You know people on a stage—and people of a darker race—so likely to be marvelous, frightening.

This is a white dance. Powerhouse is not a show-off like the Harlem boys, not drunk, not crazy—he's in a trance; he's a person of joy, a fanatic. He listens as much as he performs, a look of hideous, powerful rapture on his face. Big arched eyebrows that never stop traveling, like a Jew's—wandering-Jew eyebrows. When he plays he beats down piano and seat and wears them away. He is in motion every moment—what could be more obscene? There he is with his great head, fat stomach, and little round piston legs, and long yellow-sectioned strong big fingers, at rest about the size of bananas. Of course you know how he sounds—you've heard him on records—but still you need to see him. He's going all the time, like skating around the skating rink or rowing a boat. It makes everybody crowd around, here in this shadowless steel-trussed hall with the rose-like posters of Nelson Eddy and the testimonial for the mind-reading horse in handwriting magnified five hundred times. Then all quietly he lays his finger on a key with the promise and serenity of a sibyl touching the book.

Powerhouse is so monstrous he sends everybody into oblivion. When any group, any performers, come to town, don't people always come out and hover near, leaning inward about them, to learn what it is? What is it? Listen. Remember how it was with the acrobats. Watch them carefully, hear the least word, especially what they say to one another, in another language—don't let them escape you; it's the only time for hallucination, the last time. They can't stay. They'll be somewhere else this time tomorrow.

Powerhouse has as much as possible done by signals. Everybody, laughing as if to hide a weakness, will sooner or later hand him up a written request. Powerhouse reads each one, studying with a secret face: that is the face which looks like a mask—anybody's; there is a moment when he makes a decision. Then a light slides under his eyelids, and he says, "92!" or some combination of figures—never a name. Before a number the band is all frantic, misbehaving, pushing, like children in a schoolroom, and he is the teacher getting silence. His hands over the keys, he says sternly, "You-all ready? You-all ready to do some serious walking?"—waits—then, STAMP. Quiet. STAMP, for the second time. This is absolute. Then a set of rhythmic kicks against the floor to communicate the tempo. Then, O Lord! say the distended eyes from beyond the boundary of the trumpets, Hello and good-bye, and they are all down the first note like a waterfall.

This note marks the end of any known discipline. Powerhouse seems to abandon them all—he himself seems lost—down in the song, yelling up like somebody in a whirlpool—not guiding them—hailing them only. But he knows, really. He cries out, but he must know exactly. "Mercy! . . . What I say! . . . Yeah!" And then drifting, listening—"Where that skin beater?"—wanting drums, and starting up and pouring it out in the greatest delight and brutality. On the sweet pieces such a leer for everybody! He looks down so benevolently upon all our faces and whispers the lyrics to us. And if you could hear him at this moment on "Marie, the Dawn is Breaking"! He's going up the keyboard with a few fingers in some very derogatory triplet-routine, he gets higher and higher, and then he looks over the end of the piano, as if over a cliff. But not in a show-off way—the song makes him do it.

He loves the way they all play, too—all those next to him. The far section of the band is all studious, wearing glasses, every one—they don't count. Only those playing around Powerhouse are the real ones. He has a bass fiddler from Vicksburg, black as pitch, named Valentine, who plays with his eyes shut and talking to himself, very young: Powerhouse has to keep encouraging him. "Go on, go on, give it up, bring it on out there!" When you heard him like that on records, did you know he was really pleading?

He calls Valentine out to take a solo.

"What you going to play?" Powerhouse looks out kindly from behind the piano; he opens his mouth and shows his tongue, listening.

Valentine looks down, drawing against his instrument, and says without a lip movement, "'Honeysuckle Rose.'"

He has a clarinet player named Little Brother, and loves to listen to anything he does. He'll smile and say, "Beautiful!" Little Brother takes a step forward when he plays and stands at the very front, with the whites of his eyes like fishes swimming. Once when he played a low note, Powerhouse muttered in dirty praise, "He went clear downstairs to get that one!"

After a long time, he holds up the number of fingers to tell the band how many choruses still to go—usually five. He keeps his directions down to signals.

It's a bad night outside. It's a white dance, and nobody dances, except a few straggling jitterbugs and two elderly couples. Everybody just stands around the band and watches Powerhouse. Sometimes they steal glances at one another, as if to say, Of course, you know how it is with *them*—Negroes—band leaders—they would play the same way, giving all they've got, for an audience of one. . . . When somebody, no matter who, gives everything, it makes people feel ashamed for him.

Late at night they play the one waltz they will ever consent to play—by request, "Pagan Love Song." Powerhouse's head rolls and sinks like a weight between his waving shoulders. He groans, and his fingers drag into the keys heavily, holding on to the notes, retrieving. It is a sad song.

"You know what happened to me?" says Powerhouse.

Valentine hums a response, dreaming at the bass.

"I got a telegram my wife is dead," says Powerhouse, with wandering fingers.

"Uh-huh?"

His mouth gathers and forms a barbarous O while his fingers walk up straight, unwillingly, three octaves.

"Gypsy? Why how come her to die, didn't you just phone her up in the night last night long distance?"

"Telegram say—here the words: Your wife is dead." He puts 4/4 over the 3/4.

"Not but four words?" This is the drummer, an unpopular boy named Scoot, a disbelieving maniac.

Powerhouse is shaking his vast cheeks. "What the hell was she trying to do? What was she up to?"

"What name has it got signed, if you got a telegram?" Scoot is spitting away with those wire brushes.

Little Brother, the clarinet player, who cannot now speak, glares and tilts back.

"Uranus Knockwood is the name signed." Powerhouse lifts his eyes open. "Ever heard of him?" A bubble shoots out on his lip like a plate on a counter.

Valentine is beating slowly on with his palm and scratching the strings with his long blue nails. He is fond of a waltz, Powerhouse interrupts him.

"I don't know him. Don't know who he is." Valentine shakes his head with the closed eyes.

"Say it agin."

"Uranus Knockwood."

"That ain't Lenox Avenue."

"It ain't Broadway."

"Ain't ever seen it wrote out in any print, even for horse racing."

"Hell, that's on a star, boy, ain't it?" Crash of the cymbals.

"What the hell was she up to?" Powerhouse shudders. "Tell me, tell me, tell me." He makes triplets, and begins a new chorus. He holds three fingers up.

"You say you got a telegram." This is Valentine, patient and sleepy, beginning again.

Powerhouse is elaborate. "Yas, the time I go out, go way downstairs along a long cor-ri-dor to where they puts us: coming back along the cor-ri-dor: steps out and hands me a telegram: Your wife is dead."

"Gypsy?" The drummer like a spider over his drums.

"Aaaaaaaaa!" shouts Powerhouse, flinging out both powerful arms for three whole beats to flex his muscles, then kneading a dough of bass notes. His eyes glitter. He plays the piano like a drum sometimes —why not?

"Gypsy? Such a dancer?"

"Why you don't hear it straight from your agent? Why it ain't come from headquarters? What you been doing, getting telegrams in the *corridor*, signed nobody?"

They all laugh. End of that chorus.

"What time is it?" Powerhouse calls. "What the hell place is this? Where is my watch and chain?"

"I hang it on you," whimpers Valentine. "It still there."

There it rides on Powerhouse's great stomach, down where he can never see it.

"Sure did hear some clock striking twelve while ago. Must be *midnight*."

"It going to be intermission," Powerhouse declares, lifting up his finger with the signet ring.

He draws the chorus to an end. He pulls a big Northern hotel towel out of the deep pocket in his vast, special-cut tux pants and pushes his forehead into it.

"If she went and killed herself!" he says with a hidden face. "If she up and jumped out that window!" He gets to his feet, turning vaguely, wearing the towel on his head.

"Ha, ha!"

"Sheik, sheik!"

"She wouldn't do that." Little Brother sets down his clarinet like a precious vase, and speaks. He still looks like an East Indian queen, implacable, divine, and full of snakes. "You ain't going to expect people doing what they says over long distance."

"Come on!" roars Powerhouse. He is already at the back door, he has pulled it wide open, and with a wild, gathered-up face is smelling the terrible night.

Powerhouse, Valentine, Scoot and Little Brother step outside into the drenching rain.

"Well, they emptying buckets," says Powerhouse in a mollified voice. On the street he holds his hands out and turns up the blanched palms like sieves.

A hundred dark, ragged, silent, delighted Negroes have come around from under the eaves of the hall, and follow wherever they go.

"Watch out Little Brother don't shrink," says Powerhouse. "You just the right size now, clarinet don't suck you in. You got a dry throat, Little Brother, you in the desert?" He reaches into the pocket and pulls out a paper of mints. "Now hold 'em in your mouth—don't chew 'em. I don't carry around nothing without limit."

"Go in that joint and have beer," says Scoot, who walks ahead.

"Beer? Beer? You know what beer is? What do they say is beer? What's beer? Where I been?"

"Down yonder where it say World Café—that do?" They are in Negrotown now.

Valentine patters over and holds open a screen door warped like a sea shell, bitter in the wet, and they walk in, stained darker with the rain and leaving footprints. Inside, sheltered dry smells stand like screens around a table covered with a red-checkered cloth, in the center of which flies hang onto an obelisk-shaped ketchup bottle. The midnight walls are checkered again with admonishing "Not Responsible" signs and black-figured, smoky calendars. It is a waiting, silent, limp room. There is a burned-out-looking nickelodeon and right beside it a long-necked wall instrument labeled "Business Phone, Don't Keep Talking." Circled phone numbers are written up everywhere. There is a worn-out peacock feather hanging by a thread to an old, thin, pink, exposed light bulb, where it slowly turns around and around, whoever breathes.

A waitress watches.

"Come here, living statue, and get all this big order of beer we fixing to give."

"Never seen you before anywhere." The waitress moves and comes forward and slowly shows little gold leaves and tendrils over her teeth. She shoves up her shoulders and breasts. "How I going to know who you might be? Robbers? Coming in out of the black of night right at midnight, setting down so big at my table?"

"Boogers," says Powerhouse, his eyes opening lazily as in a cave.

The girl screams delicately with pleasure. O Lord, she likes talk and scares.

"Where you going to find enough beer to put out on this here table?"

She runs to the kitchen with bent elbows and sliding steps.

"Here's a million nickels," says Powerhouse, pulling his hand out of his pocket and sprinkling coins out, all but the last one, which he makes vanish like a magician.

Valentine and Scoot take the money over to the nickelodeon, which looks as battered as a slot machine, and read all the names of the records out loud.

"Whose 'Tuxedo Junction'?" asks Powerhouse.

"You know whose."

"Nickelodeon, I request you please to play 'Empty Red Blues' and let Bessie Smith sing."

Silence: they hold it like a measure.

"Bring me all those nickels on back here," says Powerhouse. "Look at that! What you tell me the name of this place?"

"White dance, week night, raining, Alligator, Mississippi, long ways from home."

"Uh-huh."

"Sent for You Yesterday and Here You Come Today" plays.

The waitress, setting the tray of beer down on a back table, comes up taut and apprehensive as a hen. "Says in the kitchen, back there putting their eyes to little hole peeping out, that you is Mr. Powerhouse. . . . They knows from a picture they seen."

"They seeing right tonight, that is him," says Little Brother.

"You him?"

"That is him in the flesh," says Scoot.

"Does you wish to touch him?" asks Valentine. "Because he don't bite."

"You passing through?"

"Now you got everything right."

She waits like a drop, hands languishing together in front.

"Little-Bit, ain't you going to bring the beer?"

She brings it, and goes behind the cash register and smiles, turning different ways. The little fillet of gold in her mouth is gleaming.

"The Mississippi River's here," she says once.

Now all the watching Negroes press in gently and bright-eyed through the door, as many as can get in. One is a little boy in a straw sombrero which has been coated with aluminum paint all over.

Powerhouse, Valentine, Scoot and Little Brother drink beer, and their eyelids come together like curtains. The wall and the rain and the humble beautiful waitress waiting on them and the other Negroes watching enclose them.

"Listen!" whispers Powerhouse, looking into the ketchup bottle and slowly spreading his performer's hands over the damp, wrinkling cloth with the red squares. "Listen how it is. My wife gets missing me. Gypsy. She goes to the window. She looks out and sees you know what. Street. Sign saying Hotel. People walking. Somebody looks up. Old man. She looks down, out the window. Well? . . . *Sssst! Plooey!* What she do? Jump out and bust her brains all over the world."

He opens his eyes.

"That's it," agrees Valentine. "You gets a telegram."

"Sure she misses you," Little Brother adds.

"No, it's night time." How softly he tells them! "Sure. It's the night time. She say, What do I hear? Footsteps walking up the hall? That him? Footsteps go on off. It's not me. I'm in Alligator, Mississippi, she's crazy. Shaking all over. Listens till her ears and all grow out like old music-box horns but still she can't hear a thing. She says, All right! I'll jump out the window then. Got on her nightgown. I know that nightgown, and her thinking there. Says, Ho hum, all right, and jumps out the window. Is she mad at me! Is she crazy! She don't leave *nothing* behind her!"

"Ya! Ha!"

"Brains and insides everywhere, Lord, Lord."

All the watching Negroes stir in their delight, and to their higher delight he says affectionately, "Listen! Rats in here."

"That must be the way, boss."

"Only, naw, Powerhouse, that ain't true. That sound too *bad*."

"Does? I even know who finds her," cries Powerhouse. "That no-good pussyfooted crooning creeper, that creeper that follow around after me, coming up like weeds behind me, following around after me everything I do and messing around on the trail I leave. Bets my numbers, sings my songs, gets close to my agent like a Betsybug; when I going out he just coming in. I got him now! I got my eye on him."

"Know who he is?"

"Why, it's that old Uranus Knockwood!"

"Ya! Ha!"

"Yeah, and he coming now, he going to find Gypsy. There he is, coming around that corner, and Gypsy kadoodling down, oh-oh, watch out! *Sssst! Plooey!* See, there she is in her little old nightgown, and her insides and brains all scattered round."

A sigh fills the room.

"Hush about her brains. Hush about her insides."

"Ya! Ha! You talking about her brains and insides—old Uranus

Knockwood," says Powerhouse, "look down and say Jesus! He say, Look here what I'm walking round in!"

They all burst into halloos of laughter. Powerhouse's face looks like a big hot iron stove.

"Why, he picks her up and carries her off!" he says.

"Ya! Ha!"

"Carries her *back* around the corner. . . ."

"Oh, Powerhouse!"

"You know him."

"Uranus Knockwood!"

"Yeahhh!"

"He take our wives when we gone!"

"He come in when we goes out!"

"Uh-huh!"

"He go out when we comes in!"

"Yeahhh!"

"He standing behind the door!"

"Old Uranus Knockwood."

"You know him."

"Middle-size man."

"Wears a hat."

"That's him."

Everybody in the room moans with pleasure. The little boy in the fine silver hat opens a paper and divides out a jelly roll among his followers.

And out of the breathless ring somebody moves forward like a slave, leading a great logy Negro with bursting eyes, and says, "This here is Sugar-Stick Thompson, that dove down to the bottom of July Creek and pulled up all those drownded white people fall out of a boat. Last summer, pulled up fourteen."

"Hello," says Powerhouse, turning and looking around at them all with his great daring face until they nearly suffocate.

Sugar-Stick, their instrument, cannot speak; he can only look back at the others.

"Can't even swim. Done it by holding his breath," says the fellow with the hero.

Powerhouse looks at him seekingly.

"I his half brother," the fellow puts in.

They step back.

"Gypsy say," Powerhouse rumbles gently again, looking at *them*, " 'What is the use? I'm gonna jump out so far—so far. . . .' *Sssst—!*"

"Don't, boss, don't do it agin," says Little Brother.

"It's awful," says the waitress. "I hates that Mr. Knockwoods. All that the truth?"

"Want to see the telegram I got from him?" Powerhouse's hand goes to the vast pocket.

"Now wait, now wait, boss." They all watch him.

"It must be the real truth," says the waitress, sucking in her lower lip, her luminous eyes turning sadly, seeking the windows.

"No, babe, it ain't the truth." His eyebrows fly up, and he begins to whisper to her out of his vast oven mouth. His hand stays in his pocket. "Truth is something worse, I ain't said what, yet. It's something hasn't come to me, but I ain't saying it won't. And when it does, then want me to tell you?" He sniffs all at once, his eyes come open and turn up, almost too far. He is dreamily smiling.

"Don't, boss, don't, Powerhouse!"

"Oh!" the waitress screams.

"Go on git out of here!" bellows Powerhouse, taking his hand out of his pocket and clapping after her red dress.

The ring of watchers breaks and falls away.

"*Look* at that! Intermission is up," says Powerhouse.

He folds money under a glass, and after they go out, Valentine leans back in and drops a nickel in the nickelodeon behind them, and it lights up and begins to play "The Goona Goo." The feather dangles still.

"Take a telegram!" Powerhouse shouts suddenly up into the rain over the street. "Take a answer. Now what was that name?"

They get a little tired.

"Uranus Knockwood."

"You ought to know."

"Yas? Spell it to me."

They spell it all the ways it could be spelled. It puts them in a wonderful humor.

"Here's the answer. I got it right here. 'What in the hell you talking about? Don't make any difference: I gotcha.' Name signed: Powerhouse."

"That going to reach him, Powerhouse?" Valentine speaks in a maternal voice.

"Yas, yas."

All hushing, following him up the dark street at a distance, like old rained-on black ghosts, the Negroes are afraid they will die laughing.

Powerhouse throws back his vast head into the steaming rain, and a look of hopeful desire seems to blow somehow like a vapor from his own dilated nostrils over his face and bring a mist to his eyes.

"Reach him and come out the other side."

"That's it, Powerhouse, that's it. You got him now."

Powerhouse lets out a long sigh.

"But ain't you going back there to call up Gypsy long distance, the way you did last night in that other place? I seen a telephone. . . . Just to see if she there at home?"

There is a measure of silence. That is one crazy drummer that's going to get his neck broken some day.

"No," growls Powerhouse. "No! How many thousand times tonight I got to say No?"

He holds up his arm in the rain.

"You sure-enough unroll your voice some night, it about reach up yonder to her," says Little Brother, dismayed.

They go on up the street, shaking the rain off and on them like birds.

Back in the dance hall, they play "San" (99). The jitterbugs start up like windmills stationed over the floor, and in their orbits—one circle, another, a long stretch and a zigzag—dance the elderly couples with old smoothness, undisturbed and stately.

When Powerhouse first came back from intermission, no doubt full of beer, they said, he got the band tuned up again in his own way. He didn't strike the piano keys for pitch—he simply opened his mouth and gave falsetto howls—in A, D and so on—they tuned by him. Then he took hold of the piano, as if he saw it for the first time in his life, and tested it for strength, hit it down in the bass, played an octave with his elbow, lifted the top, looked inside, and leaned against it with all his might. He sat down and played it for a few minutes with outrageous force and got it under his power—a bass deep and coarse as a sea net—then produced something glimmering and fragile, and smiled. And who could ever remember any of the things he says? They are just inspired remarks that roll out of his mouth like smoke.

They've requested "Somebody Loves Me," and he's already done twelve or fourteen choruses, piling them up nobody knows how, and it will be a wonder if he ever gets through. Now and then he calls and shouts, " 'Somebody loves me! Somebody loves me, I wonder who!' " His mouth gets to be nothing but a volcano. "I wonder who!"

"Maybe . . ." He uses all his right hand on a trill.

"Maybe . . ." He pulls back his spread fingers, and looks out upon the place where he is. A vast, impersonal and yet furious grimace transfigures his wet face.

". . . Maybe it's you!"

Questions

1. How clearly can we picture the main character? What features are emphasized more than others? Can you offer a reason for this emphasis?
2. How would you classify the music played by Powerhouse's band? Can you detect a merging of tempo from the music described and the story itself? For instance, divide the story into its scenes: the dance hall, the café, the return to the dance hall.
3. What do the onlookers in the café suggest about the position of the artist in society? How important are the onlookers to Powerhouse?
4. Can we believe that Powerhouse's wife, Gypsy, is dead? What can we make of the name, Uranus Knockwood?
5. Powerhouse, Valentine, Scoot, and Little Brother are the four most clearly defined characters in the story. What does each name suggest about the music each prefers? The instruments each plays? The comments each makes?
6. What does the final utterance in the story mean?

Topics for Composition

1. Using White's explanation of the symbol as your basis, write an essay discussing the use of language as symbol in the story, "Powerhouse."
2. Select a limited number of paragraphs in the story and analyze the sentences according to Copi's functions of language. As part of your analysis, comment on the effect of sentence use in relation to the story.
3. Either support or refute the assumption that Gypsy is dead and Uranus Knockwood is involved.

"The Real Thing" depicts one of James's attempts to define the illusive artistic impression of reality; therefore, it is not the Monarchs who should capture our main interest, but, rather, we should follow the painter-narrator as he searches for his concept of reality. James's definition emerges as he places contrasting models before his painter-narrator. Notice the following:

1. The Monarchs, whose appearances seem to be reality itself
2. Miss Churm, whose appearance and actions contradict the artist's view of her
3. Oronte, who, lacking the affinity of either nationality or language, seems least appropriate of all

The Real Thing

HENRY JAMES

I

When the porter's wife (she used to answer the house-bell), announced "A gentleman—with a lady, sir," I had, as I often had in those days, for the wish was father to the thought, an immediate vision of sitters. Sitters my visitors in this case proved to be; but not in the sense I should have preferred. However, there was nothing at first to indicate that they might not have come for a portrait. The gentleman, a man of fifty, very high and very straight, with a moustache slightly grizzled and a dark grey walking-coat admirably fitted, both of which I noted professionally—I don't mean as a barber or yet as a tailor—would have struck me as a celebrity if celebrities often were striking. It was a truth of which I had for some time been conscious that a figure with a good deal of frontage was, as one might say, almost never a public institution. A glance at the lady helped to remind me of this paradoxical law: she also looked too distinguished to be a "personality." Moreover one would scarcely come across two variations together.

Neither of the pair spoke immediately—they only prolonged the preliminary gaze which suggested that each wished to give the other a chance. They were visibly shy; they stood there letting me take them in—which, as I afterwards perceived, was the most practical thing they could have done. In this way their embarrassment served their cause. I had seen people painfully reluctant to mention that they desired anything so gross as to be represented on canvas; but the scruples of my new friends appeared almost insurmountable. Yet the gentleman might have said "I should like a portrait of my wife," and the lady might have said "I should like a portrait of my husband." Perhaps they were not husband and wife—this naturally would make the matter more delicate. Perhaps they wished to be done together—in which case they ought to have brought a third person to break the news.

"We come from Mr. Rivet," the lady said at last, with a dim smile which had the effect of a moist sponge passed over a "sunk" piece of painting, as well as of a vague allusion to vanished beauty. She was as tall and straight, in her degree, as her companion, and with ten years less to carry. She looked as sad as a woman could look whose face was not charged with expression; that is her tinted oval mask showed friction as an exposed surface shows it. The hand of time had played over her freely, but only to simplify. She was slim and stiff, and so well-dressed, in dark blue cloth, with lappets and pockets and buttons, that it was clear she employed the same tailor as her husband. The couple had an indefinable air of prosperous thrift—they evidently got a good deal of luxury for their money. If I was to be one of their luxuries it would behove me to consider my terms.

"Ah, Claude Rivet recommended me?" I inquired; and I added that it was very kind of him, though I could reflect that, as he only painted landscape, this was not a sacrifice.

The lady looked very hard at the gentleman, and the gentleman looked round the room. Then staring at the floor a moment and stroking his moustache, he rested his pleasant eyes on me with the remark: "He said you were the right one."

"I try to be, when people want to sit."

"Yes, we should like to," said the lady anxiously.

"Do you mean together?"

My visitors exchanged a glance. "If you could do anything with *me*, I suppose it would be double," the gentleman stammered.

"Oh yes, there's naturally a higher charge for two figures than for one."

"We should like to make it pay," the husband confessed.

"That's very good of you," I returned, appreciating so unwonted a sympathy—for I supposed he meant pay the artist.

A sense of strangeness seemed to dawn on the lady. "We mean for the illustrations—Mr. Rivet said you might put one in."

"Put one in—an illustration?" I was equally confused.

"Sketch her off, you know," said the gentleman, colouring.

It was only then that I understood the service Claude Rivet had rendered me; he had told them that I worked in black and white, for magazines, for story-books, for sketches of contemporary life, and consequently had frequent employment for models. These things were true, but it was not less true (I may confess it now—whether because the aspiration was to lead to everything or to nothing I leave the reader to guess), that I couldn't get the honours, to say nothing of the emoluments, of a great painter of portraits out of my head. My "illustrations" were my pot-boilers; I looked to a different branch of art (far and away the most interesting it had always seemed to me), to perpetuate my fame. There was no shame in looking to it also to make my fortune; but that fortune was by so much further from being made from the moment my visitors wished to be "done" for nothing. I was disappointed; for in the pictorial sense I had immediately *seen* them. I had seized their type—I had already settled what I would do with it. Something that wouldn't absolutely have pleased them, I afterwards reflected.

"Ah, you're—you're—a—?" I began, as soon as I had mastered my surprise. I couldn't bring out the dingy word "models"; it seemed to fit the case so little.

"We haven't had much practice," said the lady.

"We've got to *do* something, and we've thought that an artist in your line might perhaps make something of us," her husband threw off. He further mentioned that they didn't know many artists and that they had gone first, on the off-chance (he painted views of course, but sometimes put in figures—perhaps I remembered), to Mr. Rivet, whom they had met a few years before at a place in Norfolk where he was sketching.

"We used to sketch a little ourselves," the lady hinted.

"It's very awkward, but we absolutely *must* do something," her husband went on.

"Of course, we're not so *very* young," she admitted, with a wan smile.

With the remark that I might as well know something more about them, the husband had handed me a card extracted from a neat new pocket-book (their appurtenances were all of the freshest) and inscribed with the words "Major Monarch." Impressive as these words were they didn't carry my knowledge much further; but my visitor presently added: "I've left the army, and we've had the misfortune to lose our money. In fact our means are dreadfully small."

"It's an awful bore," said Mrs. Monarch.

They evidently wished to be discreet—to take care not to swagger because they were gentlefolks. I perceived they would have been willing to recognise this as something of a drawback, at the same time that I guessed at an underlying sense—their consolation in adversity—that they *had* their points. They certainly had; but these advantages struck me as preponderantly social; such for instance as would help to make a drawing-room look well. However, a drawing-room was always, or ought to be, a picture.

In consequence of his wife's allusion to their age Major Monarch observed: "Naturally, it's more for the figure that we thought of going in. We can still hold ourselves up." On the instant I saw that the figure was indeed their strong point. His "naturally" didn't sound vain, but it lighted up the question. "*She* has got the best," he continued, nodding at his wife, with a pleasant after-dinner absence of circumlocution. I could only reply, as if we were in fact sitting over our wine, that this didn't prevent his own from being very good; which led him in turn to rejoin: "We thought that if you ever have to do people like us, we might be something like it. *She*, particularly —for a lady in a book, you know."

I was so amused by them that, to get more of it, I did my best to take their point of view; and though it was an embarrassment to find myself appraising physically, as if they were animals on hire or useful blacks, a pair whom I should have expected to meet only in one of the relations in which criticism is tacit, I looked at Mrs. Monarch judicially enough to be able to exclaim, after a moment, with conviction: "Oh yes, a lady in a book!" She was singularly like a bad illustration.

"We'll stand up, if you like," said the Major; and he raised himself before me with a really grand air.

I could take his measure at a glance—he was six feet two and a perfect gentleman. It would have paid any club in process of formation and in want of a stamp to engage him at a salary to stand in the principal window. What struck me immediately was that in coming to me they had rather missed their vocation; they could surely have been turned to better account for advertising purposes. I couldn't of course see the thing in detail, but I could see them make someone's fortune—I don't mean their own. There was something in them for a waistcoat-maker, an hotel-keeper or a soap-vendor. I could imagine "We always use it" pinned on their bosoms with the greatest effect; I had a vision of the promptitude with which they would launch a table d'hôte.

Mrs. Monarch sat still, not from pride but from shyness, and presently her husband said to her: "Get up my dear and show how smart you are." She obeyed, but she had no need to get up to show it. She walked to the end of the studio, and then she came back blushing, with her fluttered eyes on her husband. I was reminded of an incident I had accidentally had a glimpse of in Paris—being with a friend there, a dramatist about to produce a play—when an actress came to him to ask to be intrusted with a part. She went through her paces before him, walked up and down as Mrs. Monarch was doing. Mrs. Monarch did it quite as well, but I abstained from applauding. It was very odd to see such people apply for such poor pay. She looked as if she had ten thousand a year. Her husband had used the word that described her: she was, in the London current jargon, essentially and typically "smart." Her figure was, in the same order of ideas, conspicuously and irreproachably "good." For a woman of her age her waist was surprisingly small; her elbow moreover had the orthodox crook. She held her head at the conventional angle; but why did she come to *me?* She ought to have tried on jackets at a big shop. I feared my visitors were not only destitute, but "artistic"—which would be a great complication. When she sat down again I thanked her, observing that what a draughtsman most valued in his model was the faculty of keeping quiet.

"Oh, *she* can keep quiet," said Major Monarch. Then he added, jocosely: "I've always kept her quiet."

"I'm not a nasty fidget, am I?" Mrs. Monarch appealed to her husband.

He addressed his answer to me. "Perhaps it isn't out of place to mention—because we ought to be quite business-like, oughtn't we?—that when I married her she was known as the Beautiful Statue."

"Oh dear!" said Mrs. Monarch, ruefully.

"Of course I should want a certain amount of expression," I rejoined.

"Of *course!*" they both exclaimed.

"And then I suppose you know that you'll get awfully tired."

"Oh, we *never* get tired!" they eagerly cried.

"Have you had any kind of practice?"

They hesitated—they looked at each other. "We've been photographed, *immensely*," said Mrs. Monarch.

"She means the fellows have asked us," added the Major.

"I see—because you're so good-looking."

"I don't know what they thought, but they were always after us."

"We always got our photographs for nothing," smiled Mrs. Monarch.

"We might have brought some, my dear," her husband remarked.

"I'm not sure we have any left. We've given quantities away," she explained to me.

"With our autographs and that sort of thing," said the Major.

"Are they to be got in the shops?" I inquired, as a harmless pleasantry.

"Oh, yes; *hers*—they used to be."

"Not now," said Mrs. Monarch, with her eyes on the floor.

II

I could fancy the "sort of thing" they put on the presentation-copies of their photographs, and I was sure they wrote a beautiful hand. It was odd how quickly I was sure of everything that concerned them. If they were now so poor as to have to earn shillings and pence, they never had had much of a margin. Their good looks had been their capital, and they had good-humouredly made the most of the career that this resource marked out for them. It was in their faces, the blankness, the deep intellectual repose of the twenty years of country-house visiting which had given them pleasant intonations. I could see the sunny drawing-rooms, sprinkled with periodicals she didn't read, in which Mrs. Monarch had continuously sat; I could see the wet shrubberies in which she had walked, equipped to admiration for either exercise. I could see the rich covers the Major had helped to shoot and the wonderful garments in which, late at night, he repaired to the smoking-room to talk about them. I could imagine their leggings and waterproofs, their knowing tweeds and rugs, their rolls of sticks and cases of tackle and neat umbrellas; and I could evoke the exact appearance of their servants and the compact variety of their luggage on the platforms of country stations.

They gave small tips, but they were liked; they didn't do anything themselves, but they were welcome. They looked so well everywhere; they gratified the general relish for stature, complexion and "form." They knew it without fatuity or vulgarity, and they respected themselves in consequence. They were not superficial; they were thorough and kept themselves up—it had been their line. People with such a taste for activity had to have some line. I could feel how, even in a dull house, they could have been counted upon for cheerfulness. At present something had happened—it didn't matter what, their little income had grown less, it had grown least—and they had to do something for pocket-money. Their friends liked them, but didn't like to support them. There was something about them that represented credit—their clothes, their manners, their type; but if credit is a large empty pocket in which an occasional chink reverberates, the chink at least must be audible. What they wanted of me was to help to make it so. Fortunately they had no children—I soon divined that. They would also perhaps wish our relations to be kept secret: this was why it was "for the figure"—the reproduction of the face would betray them.

I liked them—they were so simple; and I had no objection to them if they would suit. But, somehow, with all their perfections I didn't easily believe in them. After all they were amateurs, and the ruling passion of my life was the detestation of the amateur. Combined with this was another perversity—an innate preference for the represented subject over the real one: the defect of the real one was so apt to be a lack of representation. I liked things that appeared; then one was sure. Whether they *were* or not was a subordinate and almost always a profitless question. There were other considerations, the first of which was that I already had two or three people in use, notably a young person with big feet, in alpaca, from Kilburn, who for a couple of years had come to me regularly for my illustrations and with whom I was still—perhaps ignobly—satisfied. I frankly explained to my visitors how the case stood; but they had taken more precautions than I supposed. They had reasoned out their opportunity, for Claude Rivet had told them of the projected *édition de luxe* of one of the writers of our day—the rarest of the novelists—who, long neglected by the multitudinous vulgar and dearly prized by the attentive (need I mention Philip Vincent?) had had the happy fortune of seeing, late in life, the dawn and then the full light of a higher criticism—an estimate in which, on the part of the public, there was something really of expiation. The edition in question, planned by a publisher of taste, was practically an act of high reparation; the wood-cuts with which it was to be enriched were the homage of English art to one of the most independent representatives of English letters. Major and Mrs. Monarch confessed to me that they had hoped I might be able to work *them* into my share of the enterprise. They knew I was to do the first of the books, "Rutland Ramsay," but I had to make clear to them that my participation in the rest of the affair—this first book was to be a test—was to depend on the satisfaction I should give. If this should be limited my employers would drop me without a scruple. It was therefore a crisis for me, and naturally I was making special preparations, looking about for new people, if they should be necessary, and securing the best types. I admitted however that I should like to settle down to two or three good models who would do for everything.

"Should we have often to—a—put on special clothes?" Mrs. Monarch timidly demanded.

"Dear, yes—that's half the business."

"And should we be expected to supply our own costumes?"

"Oh, no; I've got a lot of things. A painter's models put on—or put off—anything he likes."

"And do you mean—a—the same?"

"The same?"

Mrs. Monarch looked at her husband again.

"Oh, she was just wondering," he explained, "if the costumes are in *general* use." I had to confess that they were, and I mentioned further that some of them (I had a lot of genuine, greasy last-century things), had served their time, a hundred years ago, on living, world-stained men and women. "We'll put on anything that *fits*," said the Major.

"Oh, I arrange that—they fit in the pictures."

"I'm afraid I should do better for the modern books. I would come as you like," said Mrs. Monarch.

"She has got a lot of clothes at home: they might do for contemporary life," her husband continued.

"Oh, I can fancy scenes in which you'd be quite natural." And indeed I could see the slipshod rearrangements of stale properties—the stories I tried to produce pictures for without the exasperation of reading them—whose sandy tracts the good lady might help to people. But I had to return to the fact that for this sort of work—the daily mechanical grind—I was already equipped; the people I was working with were fully adequate.

"We only thought we might be more like *some* characters," said Mrs. Monarch mildly, getting up.

Her husband also rose; he stood looking at me with a dim wistfulness that was touching in so fine a man. "Wouldn't it be rather a pull sometimes to have—a—to have—?" He hung fire; he wanted me to help him by phrasing what he meant. But I couldn't—I didn't know. So he brought it out, awkwardly: "The *real* thing; a gentleman, you know, or a lady." I was quite ready to give a general assent—I admitted that there was a great deal in that. This encouraged Major Monarch to say, following up his appeal with an unacted gulp: "It's awfully hard—we've tried everything." The gulp was communicative; it proved too much for his wife. Before I knew it Mrs. Monarch had dropped again upon a divan and burst into tears. Her husband sat down beside her, holding one of her hands; whereupon she quickly dried her eyes with the other, while I felt embarrassed as she looked up at me. "There isn't a confounded job I haven't applied for—waited for—prayed for. You can fancy we'd be pretty bad first. Secretaryships and that sort of thing? You might as well ask for a peerage. I'd be *anything*—I'm strong; a messenger or a coalheaver. I'd put on a gold-laced cap and open carriage-doors in front of the haberdasher's; I'd hang about a station, to carry portmanteaus; I'd be a postman. But they won't *look* at you; there are thousands, as good as yourself, already on the ground. *Gentlemen*, poor beggars, who have drunk their wine, who have kept their hunters!"

I was as reassuring as I knew how to be, and my visitors were presently on their feet again while, for the experiment, we agreed on an hour. We were discussing it when the door opened and Miss Churm came in with a wet umbrella. Miss Churm had to take the omnibus to Maida Vale and then walk half-a-mile. She looked a trifle blowsy and slightly splashed. I scarcely ever saw her come in without thinking afresh how odd it was that, being so little in herself, she should yet be so much in others. She was a meagre little Miss Churm, but she was an ample heroine of romance. She was only a freckled cockney, but she could represent everything, from a fine lady to a shepherdess; she had the faculty, as she might have had a fine voice or long hair. She couldn't spell, and she loved beer, but she had two or three "points," and practice, and a knack, and mother-wit, and a kind of whimsical sensibility, and a love of the theatre, and seven sisters, and not an ounce of respect, especially for the *h*. The first thing my visitors saw was that her umbrella was wet, and in their spotless perfection they visibly winced at it. The rain had come on since their arrival.

"I'm all in a soak; there *was* a mess of people in the 'bus. I wish you lived near a stytion," said Miss Churm. I requested her to get ready as quickly as possible, and she passed into the room in which she always changed her dress. But before going out she asked me what she was to get into this time.

"It's the Russian princess, don't you know?" I answered; "the one with the 'golden eyes,' in black velvet, for the long thing in the *Cheapside*."

"Golden eyes? I *say!*" cried Miss Churm, while my companions watched her with intensity as she withdrew. She always arranged herself, when she was late, before I could turn round; and I kept my visitors a little, on purpose, so that they might get an idea, from seeing her, what would be expected of themselves. I mentioned that she was quite my notion of an excellent model–she was really very clever.

"Do you think she looks like a Russian princess?" Major Monarch asked, with lurking alarm.

"When I make her, yes."

"Oh, if you have to *make* her–!" he reasoned, acutely.

"That's the most you can ask. There are so many that are not makeable."

"Well now, *here's* a lady"–and with a persuasive smile he passed his arm into his wife's–"who's already made!"

"Oh, I'm not a Russian princess," Mrs. Monarch protested, a little coldly. I could see that she had known some and didn't like them. There, immediately, was a complication of a kind that I never had to fear with Miss Churm.

The young lady came back in black velvet–the gown was rather rusty and very low on her lean shoulders–and with a Japanese fan in her red hands. I reminded her that in the scene I was doing she had to look over someone's head. "I forgot whose it is; but it doesn't matter. Just look over a head."

"I'd rather look over a stove," said Miss Churm; and she took her station near the fire. She fell into position, settled herself into a tall attitude, gave a certain backward inclination to her head and a certain forward droop to her fan, and looked, at least to my prejudiced sense, distinguished and charming, foreign and dangerous. We left her looking so, while I went down-stairs with Major and Mrs. Monarch.

"I think I could come about as near it as that," said Mrs. Monarch.

"Oh, you think she's shabby, but you must allow for the alchemy of art."

However, they went off with an evident increase of comfort, founded on their demonstrable advantage in being the real thing. I could fancy them shuddering over Miss Churm. She was very droll about them when I went back, for I told her what they wanted.

"Well, if *she* can sit I'll tyke to bookkeeping," said my model.

"She's very lady-like," I replied, as an innocent form of aggravation.

"So much the worse for *you*. That means she can't turn round."

"She'll do for the fashionable novels."

"Oh yes, she'll *do* for them!" my model humorously declared. "Ain't they bad enough without her?" I had often sociably denounced them to Miss Churm.

III

It was for the elucidation of a mystery in one of these works that I first tried Mrs. Monarch. Her husband came with her, to be useful if necessary—it was sufficiently clear that as a general thing he would prefer to come with her. At first I wondered if this were for "propriety's" sake—if he were going to be jealous and meddling. The idea was too tiresome, and if it had been confirmed it would speedily have brought our acquaintance to a close. But I soon saw there was nothing in it and that if he accompanied Mrs. Monarch it was (in addition to the chance of being wanted), simply because he had nothing else to do. When she was away from him his occupation was gone—she never *had* been away from him. I judged, rightly, that in their awkward situation their close union was their main comfort and that this union had no weak spot. It was a real marriage, an encouragement to the hesitating, a nut for pessimists to crack. Their address was humble (I remember afterwards thinking it had been the only thing about them that was really professional), and I could fancy the lamentable lodgings in which the Major would have been left alone. He could bear them with his wife—he couldn't bear them without her.

He had too much tact to try and make himself agreeable when he couldn't be useful; so he simply sat and waited, when I was too absorbed in my work to talk. But I liked to make him talk—it made my work, when it didn't interrupt it, less sordid, less special. To listen to him was to combine the excitement of going out with the economy of staying at home. There was only one hindrance: that I seemed not to know any of the people he and his wife had known. I think he wondered extremely, during the term of our intercourse, whom the deuce I *did* know. He hadn't a stray sixpence of an idea to fumble for; so we didn't spin it very fine—we confined ourselves to questions of leather and even of liquor (saddlers and breeches-makers and how to get good claret cheap), and matters like "good trains" and the habits of small game. His lore on these last subjects was astonishing, he managed to interweave the station-master with the ornithologist. When he couldn't talk about greater things he could talk cheerfully about smaller, and since I couldn't accompany him into reminiscences of the fashionable world he could lower the conversation without a visible effort to my level.

So earnest a desire to please was touching in a man who could so easily have knocked one down. He looked after the fire and had an opinion on the draught of the stove, without my asking him, and I could see that he thought many of my arrangements not half clever enough. I remember telling him that if I were only rich I would offer him a salary to come and teach me how to live. Sometimes he gave a random sigh, of which the essence was: "Give me even such a bare old barrack as *this*, and I'd do something with it!" When I wanted to use him he came alone; which was an illustration of the superior courage of women. His wife could bear her solitary second floor, and she was in general more discreet; showing by various small reserves that she was alive to the propriety of keeping our relations markedly professional—not letting them slide into sociability. She wished it to remain clear that she and the Major were employed, not cultivated, and if she approved of me as a superior, who could be kept in his place, she never thought me quite good enough for an equal.

She sat with great intensity, giving the whole of her mind to it, and was capable of remaining for an hour almost as motionless as if she were before a photographer's lens. I could see she had been photographed often, but somehow the very habit that made her good for that purpose unfitted her for mine. At first I was extremely pleased with her lady-like air, and it was a satisfaction, on coming to follow her lines, to see how good they were and how far they could lead the pencil. But after a few times I began to find her too insurmountably stiff; do what I would with it my drawing looked like a photograph or a copy of a photograph. Her figure had no variety of expression—she herself had no sense of variety. You may say that this was my business, was only a question of placing her. I placed her in every conceivable position, but she managed to obliterate their differences. She was always a lady certainly, and into the bargain was always the same lady. She was the real thing, but always the same thing. There were moments when I was oppressed by the serenity of her confidence that she *was* the real thing. All her dealings with me and all her husband's were an implication that this was lucky for *me*. Meanwhile I found myself trying to invent types that approached her own, instead of making her own transform itself—in the clever way that was not impossible, for instance, to poor Miss Churm. Arrange as I would and take the precautions I would, she always, in my pictures, came out too tall—landing me in the dilemma of having represented a fascinating woman as seven feet high, which, out of respect perhaps to my own very much scantier inches, was far from my idea of such a personage.

The case was worse with the Major—nothing I could do would keep *him* down, so that he became useful only for the representation of brawny giants. I adored variety and range, I cherished human accidents, the illustrative note; I wanted to characterise closely, and the thing in the world I most hated was the danger of being ridden by a type. I had quarrelled with some of my friends about it—I had parted company with them for maintaining that one *had* to be, and that if the type was beautiful (witness Raphael and Leonardo), the servitude was only a gain. I was neither Leonardo nor Raphael; I might only be a presumptuous young modern searcher, but I held that everything was to be sacrificed sooner than character. When they averred that the haunting type in question could easily *be* character, I retorted, perhaps superficially: "Whose?" It couldn't be everybody's—it might end in being nobody's.

After I had drawn Mrs. Monarch a dozen times I perceived more clearly than before that the value of such a model as Miss Churm resided precisely in the fact that she had no positive stamp, combined of course with the other fact that what she did have was a curious and inexplicable talent for imitation. Her usual appearance was like a curtain which she could draw up at request for a capital performance. This performance was simply suggestive; but it was a word to the wise—it was vivid and pretty. Sometimes, even, I thought it, though she was plain herself, too insipidly pretty; I made it a reproach to her that the figures drawn from her were monotonously (*bêtement*, as we used to say) graceful. Nothing made her more angry: it was so much her pride to feel that she could sit for characters that had nothing in common with each other. She would accuse me at such moments of taking away her "reputytion."

It suffered a certain shrinkage, this queer quantity, from the repeated visits of my new friends. Miss Churm was greatly in demand, never in want of employment, so I had no scruple in putting her off occasionally, to try them more at my ease. It was certainly amusing at first to do the real thing—it was amusing to do Major Monarch's trousers. They *were* the real thing, even if he did come out colossal. It was amusing to do his wife's back hair (it was so mathematically neat,) and the particular "smart" tension of her tight stays. She lent herself especially to positions in which the face was somewhat averted or blurred; she abounded in lady-like back views and *profils perdus*. When she stood erect she took naturally one of the attitudes in which court-painters represent queens and princesses; so that I found myself wondering whether, to draw out this accomplishment, I couldn't get the editor of the *Cheapside* to publish a really royal romance, "A Tale of Buckingham Palace." Sometimes, however, the real thing and the make-believe came into contact; by which I mean that Miss Churm, keeping an appointment or coming to make one on days when I had much work in hand, encountered her invidious rivals. The encounter was not on their part, for they noticed her no more than if she had been the housemaid; not from intentional loftiness, but simply because, as yet, professionally, they didn't know how to fraternise, as I could guess that they would have liked—or at least that the Major would. They couldn't talk about the omnibus—they always walked; and they didn't know what else to try—she wasn't interested in good trains or cheap claret. Besides, they must have felt—in the air—that she was amused at them, secretly derisive of their ever knowing how. She was not a person to conceal her scepticism if she had had a chance to show it. On the other hand Mrs. Monarch didn't think her tidy; for why else did she take pains to say to me (it was going out of the way, for Mrs. Monarch), that she didn't like dirty women?

One day when my young lady happened to be present with my other sitters (she even dropped in, when it was convenient, for a chat), I asked her to be so good as to lend a hand in getting tea—a service with which she was familiar and which was one of a class that, living as I did in a small way, with slender domestic resources, I often appealed to my models to render. They liked to lay hands on my property, to break the sitting, and sometimes the china—I made them feel Bohemian. The next time I saw Miss Churm after this incident she surprised me greatly by making a scene about it—she accused me of having wished to humiliate her. She had not resented the outrage at the time, but had seemed obliging and amused, enjoying the comedy of asking Mrs. Monarch, who sat vague and silent, whether she would have cream and sugar, and putting an exaggerated simper into the question. She had tried intonations—as if she too wished to pass for the real thing; till I was afraid my other visitors would take offence.

Oh, *they* were determined not to do this; and their touching patience was the measure of their great need. They would sit by the hour, uncomplaining, till I was ready to use them; they would come back on the chance of being wanted and would walk away cheerfully if they were not. I used to go to the door with them to see in what magnificent order they retreated. I tried to find other employment for them—I introduced them to several artists. But they didn't "take," for reasons I could appreciate, and I became conscious, rather anxiously, that after such disappointments they fell back upon me with a heavier weight. They did me the honour to think that it was I who was most *their* form. They were not picturesque enough for the painters, and in those days there were not so many serious workers in black and white. Besides, they had an eye to the great job I had mentioned to them—they had secretly set their hearts on supplying the right essence for my pictorial vindication of our fine novelist. They knew that for this undertaking I should want no costume-effects, none of the frippery of past ages—that it was a case in which everything would be contemporary and satirical and, presumably, genteel. If I could work them into it their future would be assured, for the labour would of course be long and the occupation steady.

One day Mrs. Monarch came without her husband—she explained his absence by his having had to go to the City. While she sat there in her usual anxious stiffness there came, at the door, a knock which I immediately recognised as the subdued appeal of a model out of work. It was followed by the entrance of a young man whom I easily perceived to be a foreigner and who proved in fact an Italian acquainted with no English word but my name, which he uttered in a way that made it seem to include all others. I had not then visited his country, nor was I proficient in his tongue; but as he was not so meanly constituted—what Italian is?—as to depend only on that member for expression he conveyed to me, in familiar but graceful mimicry, that he was in search of exactly the employment in which the lady before me was engaged. I was not struck with him at first, and while I continued to draw I emitted rough sounds of discouragement and dismissal. He stood his ground, however, not importunately, but with a dumb, dog-like fidelity in his eyes which amounted to innocent impudence—the manner of a devoted servant (he might have been in the house for years), unjustly suspected.

Suddenly I saw that this very attitude and expression made a picture, whereupon I told him to sit down and wait till I should be free. There was another picture in the way he obeyed me, and I observed as I worked that there were others still in the way he looked wonderingly, with his head thrown back, about the high studio. He might have been crossing himself in St. Peter's. Before I finished I said to myself: "The fellow's a bankrupt orange-monger, but he's a treasure."

When Mrs. Monarch withdrew he passed across the room like a flash to open the door for her, standing there with the rapt, pure gaze of the young Dante spellbound by the young Beatrice. As I never insisted, in such situations, on the blankness of the British domestic, I reflected that he had the making of a servant (and I needed one, but couldn't pay him to be only that), as well as of a model; in short I made up my mind to adopt my bright adventurer if he would agree to officiate in the double capacity. He jumped at my offer, and in the event my rashness (for I had known nothing about him), was not brought home to me. He proved a sympathetic though a desultory ministrant, and had in a wonderful degree the *sentiment de la pose*. It was uncultivated, instinctive; a part of the happy instinct which had guided him to my door and helped him to spell out my name on the card nailed to it. He had had no other introduction to me than a guess, from the shape of my high north window, seen outside, that my place was a studio and that as a studio it would contain an artist. He had wandered to England in search of fortune, like other itinerants, and had embarked, with a partner and a small green hand-cart, on the sale of penny ices. The ices had melted away and the partner had dissolved in their train. My young man wore tight yellow trousers with reddish stripes and his name was Oronte. He was sallow but fair, and when I put him into some old clothes of my own he looked like an Englishman. He was as good as Miss Churm, who could look, when required, like an Italian.

IV

I thought Mrs. Monarch's face slightly convulsed when, on her coming back with her husband, she found Oronte installed. It was strange to have to recognise in a scrap of a lazzarone a competitor to her magnificent Major. It was she who scented danger first, for the Major was anecdotically unconscious. But Oronte gave us tea, with a hundred eager confusions (he had never seen such a queer process), and I think she thought better of me for having at last an "establishment." They saw a couple of drawings that I had made of the establishment, and Mrs. Monarch hinted that it never would have struck her that he had sat for them. "Now the drawings you make from *us*, they look exactly like us," she reminded me, smiling in triumph; and I recognised that this was indeed just their defect. When I drew the Monarchs I couldn't, somehow, get away from them—get into the character I wanted to represent; and I had not the least desire my model should be discoverable in my picture. Miss Churm never was, and Mrs. Monarch thought I hid her, very properly, because she was vulgar; whereas if she was lost it was only as the dead who go to heaven are lost—in the gain of an angel the more.

By this time I had got a certain start with "Rutland Ramsay," the first novel in the great projected series; that is I had produced a dozen drawings, several with the help of the Major and his wife, and I had sent them in for approval. My understanding with the publishers, as I have already hinted, had been that I was to be left to do my work, in this particular case, as I liked, with the whole book committed to me; but my connection with the rest of the series was only contingent. There were moments when, frankly, it *was* a comfort to have the real thing under one's hand; for there were characters in "Rutland Ramsay" that were very much like it. There were people presumably as straight as the Major and women of as good a fashion as Mrs. Monarch. There was a great deal of country-house life—treated, it is true, in a fine, fanciful, ironical, generalised way—and there was a considerable implication of knickerbockers and kilts. There were certain things I had to settle at the outset; such things for instance as the exact appearance of the hero, the particular bloom of the heroine. The author of course gave me a lead, but there was a margin for interpretation. I took the Monarchs into my confidence, I told them frankly what I was about, I mentioned my embarrassments and alternatives. "Oh, take *him!*" Mrs. Monarch murmured sweetly, looking at her husband; and "What could you want better than my wife?" the Major inquired, with the comfortable candour that now prevailed between us.

I was not obliged to answer these remarks—I was only obliged to place my sitters. I was not easy in mind, and I postponed, a little timidly perhaps, the solution of the question. The book was a large canvas, the other figures were numerous, and I worked off at first some of the episodes in which the hero and the heroine were not concerned. When once I had set *them* up I should have to stick to them—I couldn't make my young man seven feet high in one place and five feet nine in another. I inclined on the whole to the latter measurement, though the Major more than once reminded me that *he* looked about as young as anyone. It was indeed quite possible to arrange him, for the figure, so that it would have been difficult to detect his age. After the spontaneous Oronte had been with me a month, and after I had given him to understand several different times that his native exuberance would presently constitute an insurmountable barrier to our further intercourse, I waked to a sense of his heroic capacity. He was only five feet seven, but the remaining inches were latent. I tried him almost secretly at first, for I was really rather afraid of the judgment my other models would pass on such a choice. If they regarded Miss Churm as little better than a snare, what would they think of the representation by a person so little the real thing as an Italian street-vendor of a protagonist formed by a public school?

If I went a little in fear of them it was not because they bullied me, because they had got an oppressive foothold, but because in their really pathetic decorum and mysteriously permanent newness they counted on me so intensely. I was therefore very glad when Jack Hawley came home: he was always of such good counsel. He painted badly himself, but there was no one like him for putting his finger on the place. He had been absent from England for a year; he had been somewhere—I don't remember where—to get a fresh eye. I was in a good deal of dread of any such organ, but we were old friends; he had been away for months and a sense of emptiness was creeping into my life. I hadn't dodged a missile for a year.

He came back with a fresh eye, but with the same old black velvet blouse, and the first evening he spent in my studio we smoked cigarettes till the small hours. He had done no work himself, he had only got the eye; so the field was clear for the production of my little things. He wanted to see what I had done for the *Cheapside*, but he was disappointed in the exhibition. That at least seemed the meaning of two or three comprehensive groans which, as he lounged on my big divan, on a folded leg, looking at my latest drawings, issued from his lips with the smoke of the cigarette.

"What's the matter with you?" I asked.

"What's the matter with *you?*"

"Nothing save that I'm mystified."

"You are indeed. You're quite off the hinge. What's the meaning of this new fad?" And he tossed me, with visible irreverence, a drawing in which I happened to have depicted both my majestic models. I asked if he didn't think it good, and he replied that it struck him as execrable, given the sort of thing I had always represented myself to him as wishing to arrive at; but I let that pass, I was so anxious to see exactly what he meant. The two figures in the picture looked colossal, but I supposed this was *not* what he meant, inasmuch as, for aught he knew to the contrary, I might have been trying for that. I maintained that I was working exactly in the same way as when he last had done me the honour to commend me. "Well, there's a big hole somewhere," he answered; "wait a bit and I'll discover it." I depended upon him to do so; where else was the fresh eye? But he produced at last nothing more luminous than "I don't know—I don't like your types." This was lame, for a critic who had never consented to discuss with me anything but the question of execution, the direction of strokes and the mystery of values.

"In the drawings you've been looking at I think my types are very handsome."

"Oh, they won't do!"

"I've had a couple of new models."

"I see you have. *They* won't do."

"Are you very sure of that?"

"Absolutely—they're stupid."

"You mean *I* am—for I ought to get round that."

"You *can't*—with such people. Who are they?"

I told him, as far as was necessary, and he declared, heartlessly: "*Ce sont des gens qu'il faut mettre à la porte.*"

"You've never seen them; they're awfully good," I compassionately objected.

"Not seen them? Why, all this recent work of yours drops to pieces with them. It's all I want to see of them."

"No one else has said anything against it—the *Cheapside* people are pleased."

"Everyone else is an ass, and the *Cheapside* people the biggest asses of all. Come, don't pretend, at this time of day, to have pretty illusions about the public, especially about publishers and editors. It's not for *such* animals you work—it's for those who know, *coloro che sanno;* so keep straight for *me* if you can't keep straight for yourself. There's a certain sort of thing you tried for from the first—and a very good thing it is. But this twaddle isn't *in* it." When

I talked with Hawley later about "Rutland Ramsay" and its possible successors he declared that I must get back into my boat again or I would go to the bottom. His voice in short was the voice of warning.

I noted the warning, but I didn't turn my friends out of doors. They bored me a good deal; but the very fact that they bored me admonished me not to sacrifice them—if there was anything to be done with them—simply to irritation. As I look back at this phase they seem to me to have pervaded my life not a little. I have a vision of them as most of the time in my studio, seated, against the wall, on an old velvet bench to be out of the way, and looking like a pair of patient courtiers in a royal ante-chamber. I am convinced that during the coldest weeks of the winter they held their ground because it saved them fire. Their newness was losing its gloss, and it was impossible not to feel that they were objects of charity. Whenever Miss Churm arrived they went away, and after I was fairly launched in "Rutland Ramsay" Miss Churm arrived pretty often. They managed to express to me tacitly that they supposed I wanted her for the low life of the book, and I let them suppose it, since they had attempted to study the work—it was lying about the studio—without discovering that it dealt only with the highest circles. They had dipped into the most brilliant of our novelists without deciphering many passages. I still took an hour from them, now and again, in spite of Jack Hawley's warning: it would be time enough to dismiss them, if dismissal should be necessary, when the rigour of the season was over. Hawley had made their acquaintance—he had met them at my fireside—and thought them a ridiculous pair. Learning that he was a painter they tried to approach him, to show him too that they were the real thing; but he looked at them, across the big room, as if they were miles away: they were a compendium of everything that he most objected to in the social system of his country. Such people as that, all convention and patent-leather, with ejaculations that stopped conversation, had no business in a studio. A studio was a place to learn to see, and how could you see through a pair of feather beds?

The main inconvenience I suffered at their hands was that, at first, I was shy of letting them discover how my artful little servant had begun to sit to me for "Rutland Ramsay." They knew that I had been odd enough (they were prepared by this time to allow oddity to artists,) to pick a foreign vagabond out of the streets, when I might have had a person with whiskers and credentials; but it was some time before they learned how high I rated his accomplishments. They found him in an attitude more than once, but they never doubted I was doing him as an organ-grinder. There were several things they never guessed, and one of them was that for a striking scene in the novel, in which a footman briefly figured, it occurred to me to make use of Major Monarch as the menial. I kept putting this off, I didn't like to ask him to don the livery—besides the difficulty of finding a livery to fit him. At last, one day late in the winter, when I was at work on the despised Oronte (he caught one's idea in an instant), and was in the glow of feeling that I was going very straight, they came in, the Major and his wife, with their society laugh about nothing (there was less and less to laugh at), like country-callers—they always reminded me of that—who have walked across the park after church and are presently persuaded to stay to luncheon. Luncheon was over, but they could stay to tea—I knew they wanted it. The fit was on me, however, and I couldn't let my ardour cool and my work wait, with the fading daylight, while my model prepared it. So I asked Mrs. Monarch if she would mind laying it out—a request which, for an instant, brought all the blood to her face. Her eyes were on her husband's for a second, and some mute telegraphy passed between them. Their folly was over the next instant; his cheerful shrewdness put an end to it. So far from pitying their wounded pride, I must add, I was moved to give it as complete a lesson as I could. They bustled about together and got out the cups and saucers and made the kettle boil. I know they felt as if they were waiting on my servant, and when the tea was prepared I said: "He'll have a cup, please—he's tired." Mrs. Monarch brought him one where he stood, and he took it from her as if he had been a gentleman at a party, squeezing a crush-hat with an elbow.

Then it came over me that she had made a great effort for me—made it with a kind of nobleness—and that I owed her a compensation. Each time I saw her after this I wondered what the compensation could be. I couldn't go on doing the wrong thing to oblige them. Oh, it *was* the wrong thing, the stamp of the work for which they sat—Hawley was not the only person to say it now. I sent in a large number of the drawings I had made for "Rutland Ramsay," and I received a warning that was more to the point than Hawley's. The artistic adviser of the house for which I was working was of opinion that many of my illustrations were not what had been looked for. Most of these illustrations were the subjects in which the Monarchs had figured. Without going into the question of what *had* been looked for, I saw at this rate I shouldn't get the other books to do. I hurled myself in despair upon Miss Churm, I put her through all her paces. I not only adopted Oronte publicly as my hero, but one morning when the Major looked in to see if I didn't require him to finish a figure for the *Cheapside*, for which he had begun to sit the week before, I told him that I had changed my mind—I would do the drawing from my man. At this my visitor turned pale and stood looking at me. "Is *he* your idea of an English gentleman?" he asked.

I was disappointed, I was nervous, I wanted to get on with my work; so I replied with irritation: "Oh, my dear Major—I can't be ruined for *you!*"

He stood another moment; then, without a word, he quitted the studio. I drew a long breath when he was gone, for I said to myself that I shouldn't see him again. I had not told him definitely that I was in danger of having my work rejected, but I was vexed at his not having felt the catastrophe in the air, read with me the moral of our fruitless collaboration, the lesson that, in the deceptive atmosphere of art, even the highest respectability may fail of being plastic.

I didn't owe my friends money, but I did see them again. They re-appeared together, three days later, and under the circumstances there was something tragic in the fact. It was a proof to me that they could find nothing else in life to do. They had threshed the matter out in a dismal conference—they had digested the bad news that they were not in for the series. If they were not useful to me even for the *Cheapside* their function seemed difficult to determine, and I could only judge at first that they had come, forgivingly, decorously, to take a last leave. This made me rejoice in secret that I had little leisure for a scene; for I had placed both my other models in position together and I was pegging away at a drawing from which I hoped to derive glory. It had been suggested by the passage in which Rutland Ramsay, drawing up a chair to Artemisia's piano-stool, says extraordinary things to her while she ostensibly fingers out a difficult piece of music. I had done Miss Churm at the piano before—it was an attitude in which she knew how to take on an absolutely poetic grace. I wished the two figures to "compose" together, intensely, and my little Italian had entered perfectly into my conception. The pair were vividly before me, the piano had been pulled out; it was a charming picture of blended youth and murmured love, which I had only to catch and keep. My visitors stood and looked at it, and I was friendly to them over my shoulder.

They made no response, but I was used to silent company and went on with my work, only a little disconcerted (even though exhilarated by the sense that *this* was at least the ideal thing), at not having got rid of them after all. Presently I heard Mrs. Monarch's sweet voice beside, or rather above me: "I wish her hair was a little better done." I looked up and she was staring with a strange fixedness at Miss Churm, whose back was turned to her. "Do you mind my just touching it?" she went on—a question which made me spring up for an instant, as with the instinctive fear that she might do the young lady a harm. But she quieted me with a glance I shall never forget—I confess I should like to have been able to paint *that* —and went for a moment to my model. She spoke to her softly, laying a hand upon her shoulder and bending over her; and as the girl, understanding, gratefully assented, she disposed her rough curls, with a few quick passes, in such a way as to make Miss Churm's head twice as charming. It was one of the most heroic personal services I have ever seen rendered. Then Mrs. Monarch turned away with a low sigh and, looking about her as if for something to do, stooped to the floor with a noble humility and picked up a dirty rag that had dropped out of my paint-box.

The Major meanwhile had also been looking for something to do and, wandering to the other end of the studio, saw before him my breakfast things, neglected, unremoved. "I say, can't I be useful *here?*" he called out to me with an irrepressible quaver. I assented with a laugh that I fear was awkward and for the next ten minutes, while I worked, I heard the light clatter of china and the tinkle of spoons and glass. Mrs. Monarch assisted her husband—they washed up my crockery, they put it away. They wandered off into my little scullery, and I afterwards found that they had cleaned my knives and that my slender stock of plate had an unprecedented surface. When it came over me, the latent eloquence of what they were doing, I confess that my drawing was blurred for a moment—the picture swam. They had accepted their failure, but they couldn't accept their fate. They had bowed their heads in bewilderment to the perverse and cruel law in virtue of which the real thing could be so much less precious than the unreal; but they didn't want to starve. If my servants were my models, my models might be my servants. They would reverse the parts—the others would sit for the ladies and gentlemen, and *they* would do the work. They would still be in the studio—it was an intense dumb appeal to me not to turn them out. "Take us on," they wanted to say—"we'll do *anything*."

When all this hung before me the *afflatus* vanished—my pencil dropped from my hand. My sitting was spoiled and I got rid of my sitters, who were also evidently rather mystified and awestruck. Then, alone with the Major and his wife, I had a most uncomfortable moment. He put their prayer into a single sentence: "I say, you know—just let *us* do for you, can't you?" I couldn't—it was dreadful to see them emptying my slops; but I pretended I could, to oblige them, for about a week. Then I gave them a sum of money to go away; and I never saw them again. I obtained the remaining books, but my friend Hawley repeats that Major and Mrs. Monarch did me a permanent harm, got me into a second-rate trick. If it be true I am content to have paid the price—for the memory.

Questions

1. How does Mrs. Monarch's reference to photography reflect the layman's attitude toward art? What is the narrator's reaction to the photographic qualities of the Monarchs?
2. How does Miss Churm indicate the narrator's view of artistic reality? In the same sense, why is the name, Churm, appropriate? What does Oronte have to do with the narrator's changing attitude?
3. Why doesn't the narrator follow Jack Hawley's advice? Exactly what does Hawley mean when he calls the Monarchs stupid?
4. Do the Monarchs come to understand the artistic position? Explain.
5. Examine each of the narrator's remarks on the function and technique of art. How do these remarks fit into James's technique in the writing of this story?
6. What do you think the narrator means by his final remark?

Topics for Composition

1. In connection with your answer to question six, write an essay showing the humanizing influence on the narrator brought about by his contact with the Monarchs. Your essay, of course, will be a character study and should move from supported assumptions about the narrator's initial attitude toward people into the changes seen by his deepening relationship with the Monarchs.
2. Major and Mrs. Monarch are also apt subjects for a character study. Questions that need answers seem to be: Are they completely superficial? Can there be depth to their married relationships? Do they deserve their fate? Have they wronged themselves or are they products of a wrong society?

3. Both "Powerhouse" and "The Real Thing" deal with the search for artistic expression, but the points of view differ quite distinctly. Write an essay contrasting point of view in the two stories. An essay of this type should have a definite purpose in mind; therefore decide on a specific thesis which the contrast will support. You may use, for example, topics such as: Type of Characters Dictates Point of View; Time Span Dictates Point of View; Setting Dictates Point of View.

Poetry

SINCE about the end of the eighteenth century, poets especially have been preoccupied with the possibility of finding new modes of expression. They have been stimulated in their search by the fact that modern science and philosophy have raised difficult questions about the relation between the mind and "given" reality. In Alexander Pope's time it was still possible to think of reality, or "Nature," as an essentially unchanging arrangement of things and an essentially unchanging correspondence between things and ideas. Man's desires, themselves always basically the same, had to be accommodated to the way things are, and any exercise of the imagination that did not stay within the bounds of probability and common sense could not be permanently pleasurable. Pope therefore believed that the best modes of expression had long since been discovered—though he had to admit that language is subject to change and that a few geniuses had seemed able to express truths not clearly seen before.

Since the beginning of the Romantic period, however, there has been much excited poetic speculation about the idea that the mind or imagination partly creates reality. The general tendency has been to regard the mind and the world that it knows as being, by virtue of an all-pervasive process of symbolization, interdependent and interactive; reality flows, as it were, between symbols, things symbolized, and the mind that creates or perceives symbols. "Mind," in this view, includes emotion, or desire; pleasure, therefore, or beauty, is an important criterion of truth. Truth in its entirety—for science is only an abstraction—has thus become more elusive and at the same time seemingly more subject to desire. Expression has become more mysterious, and it has seemed that new modes of expression might bring a more satisfying sense of reality. It seemed possible, even, that only through *creative imagination* could one any longer see the world as having vital unity. The question of the limits of meaningful creativity and the question of the extent to which the creative process is controllable have been, to be sure, difficult and troublesome to modern poets; but also irresistibly challenging.

Thus Keats, as we see in "Ode on a Grecian Urn," is inclined to think and hope that art will always make men feel that somehow "Beauty is truth, truth beauty." Such a work of art as the Grecian urn gives us the sense of seeing things at moments when their true purpose and value are being realized, and so makes us feel closer than usual to reality; and this is true even though we cannot, as Keats admits, completely identify the artistic representation with our own experience of the things represented or even with the artist's.

Getting hold of truth of this kind, discovering effective symbols, in other words, is not easy, the poets tell us. Coleridge's famous "Kubla Khan" compares the poet to a magician, not only because his works, achieved single-handedly, are as monumental an edifice as the most powerful monarch could erect, but also because poetic power is so rare and difficult to invoke. Gerard Manley Hopkins, who is especially noted for his ability to convey a fresh sense of reality, also affirms, in "To R. B.," the mysterious nature of the poetic process; it is almost, he says, as if there were needed a mating with some superior intelligence in a moment of joy, followed by a kind of inevitable assimilation into an organic whole of various associations of the poet. W. B. Yeats's "Sailing to Byzantium" illuminates another side of the problem. The poet asserts the possibility of a life "out of nature"–of achieving a sense of immortality through identification with "monuments of unageing intellect"; yet it is apparent that neither the compulsive, thoughtless, transitory activities of the world of nature nor the rigid symmetries of the world of artifice can fully satisfy the drive toward reality, give a sense of human completeness.

Some modern poets have taken quite a modest view of the potentialities of art. A. E. Housman, for example, denies that imagination can change reality for the better; his gloomy poetry, he says, is merely intended to help people adapt themselves to the ills of life. Marianne Moore even admits that she finds much pretentiousness and triviality in poetry; she claims only that there is a place in it for "the genuine," and asks only for a fresh and honest emotional response. Perhaps in our times her claim is not so modest after all, or her request so small: Dylan Thomas, we perceive, feels that he may seem rather perverse because he does not labor for "ambition or bread / Or the strut and fret of charms / On the ivory stages," and Richard Wilbur deplores the current prevalence of "jerry-built things." Like Miss Moore, in any case, these poets ask only for the genuine, for a deep caring about essential values.

But the spirit of visionary romanticism in art is not dead by any means, though there is much disagreement about the way in which vision is to be attained. Stephen Spender believes that great art has always been the revelation of a spiritual reality that seems almost transcendent, yet is the essence of life. D. H. Lawrence repudiates such backward-looking, but feels that if we can escape the prison of our ideas, "vast realms of consciousness still undreamed of" will be opened to us. Taking still another approach, Wallace Stevens says that modern poetry must and can by an act of the mind create a shareable new order of values; and Archibald MacLeish boldly urges his fellow poets to stop guiltily manipulating dead symbols and "invent the age." Clearly, the search for new modes of expression is still a central concern of modern poetry—as it is, indeed, of most modern art.

An Essay on Criticism

ALEXANDER POPE

Part I

'Tis hard to say if greater want [1] of skill
Appear in writing or in judging ill;
But, of the two, less dangerous is the offence
To tire our patience, than mislead our sense.
Some few in that, but numbers err in this;
Ten censure [2] wrong for one who writes amiss;
A fool might once himself alone expose;
Now one in verse makes many more in prose.
'Tis with our judgments as our watches: none
Go just alike, yet each believes his own. *10*
In poets as true genius is but rare,
True taste as seldom is the critic's share;
Both must alike from heaven derive their light,
These born to judge, as well as those to write.
Let such teach others who themselves excel,
And censure freely who have written well.
Authors are partial to their wit, 'tis true,
But are not critics to their judgment too?
Yet if we look more closely, we shall find
Most have the seeds of judgment in their mind: *20*
Nature affords at least a glimmering light;
The lines, though touched but faintly, are drawn right.
But as the slightest sketch, if justly traced,
Is by ill-colouring but the more disgraced,
So by false learning is good sense defaced:
Some are bewildered in the maze of schools,
And some made coxcombs [3] nature meant but fools.
In search of wit these lose their common sense,

[1] *Lack.*
[2] *Judge.*
[3] *Conceited persons.*

And then turn critics in their own defence:
Each burns alike, who can, or cannot write,
Or with a rival's, or an eunuch's spite. 30
All fools have still an itching to deride,
And fain would be upon the laughing side.
If Mævius [4] scribble in Apollo's spite,
There are who judge still worse than he can write.
Some have at first for wits, then poets passed,
Turned critics next, and proved plain fools at last.
Some neither can for wits nor critics pass,
As heavy mules are neither horse nor ass.
Those half-learned witlings, numerous in our isle, 40
As half-formed insects on the banks of Nile;
Unfinished things, one knows not what to call,
Their generation's so equivocal;
To tell [5] 'em would a hundred tongues require,
Or one vain wit's, that might a hundred tire.
But you who seek to give and merit fame,
And justly bear a critic's noble name,
Be sure yourself and your own reach to know,
How far your genius, taste, and learning go;
Launch not beyond your depth, but be discreet, 50
And mark that point where sense and dulness meet.
Nature to all things fixed the limits fit,
And wisely curbed proud man's pretending wit.
As on the land while here the ocean gains,
In other parts it leaves wide sandy plains;
Thus in the soul while memory prevails,
The solid power of understanding fails;
Where beams of warm imagination play,
The memory's soft figures melt away.
One science only will one genius fit; 60
So vast is art, so narrow human wit–
Not only bounded to peculiar arts,
But oft in those confined to single parts.
Like kings we lose the conquests gained before,
By vain ambition still to make them more;
Each might his several province well command,
Would all but stoop to what they understand.
First follow nature, and your judgment frame
By her just standard, which is still the same:
Unerring nature, still divinely bright, 70
One clear, unchanged, and universal light,

[4] *An inferior Roman poet.*
[5] *Count.*

Life, force, and beauty, must to all impart,
At once the source, and end, and test of art.
Art from that fund each just supply provides,
Works without show, and without pomp presides;
In some fair body thus the informing soul
With spirits feeds, with vigour fills the whole,
Each motion guides, and every nerve sustains;
Itself unseen, but in the effects remains.
Some, to whom Heaven in wit has been profuse, *80*
Want as much more, to turn it to its use;
For wit and judgment often are at strife,
Though meant each other's aid, like man and wife
'Tis more to guide, than spur the muse's steed,
Restrain his fury, than provoke his speed;
The wingèd courser,[6] like a generous horse,
Shows most true mettle when you check his course.
Those rules of old discovered, not devised,
Are nature still, but nature methodised;
Nature, like liberty, is but restrained *90*
By the same laws which first herself ordained.
Hear how learned Greece her useful rules indites,
When to repress, and when indulge our flights:
High on Parnassus'[7] top her sons she showed,
And pointed out those arduous paths they trod;
Held from afar, aloft, the immortal prize,
And urged the rest by equal steps to rise.
Just precepts thus from great examples given,
She drew from them what they derived from heaven.
The generous critic fanned the poet's fire, *100*
And taught the world with reason to admire.
Then criticism the muses' handmaid proved,
To dress her charms, and make her more beloved:
But following wits from that intention strayed;
Who could not win the mistress, wooed the maid;
Against the poets their own arms they turned,
Sure to hate most the men from whom they learned.
So modern 'pothecaries, taught the art
By doctor's bills[8] to play the doctor's part,
Bold in the practice of mistaken rules, *110*
Prescribe, apply, and call their masters fools.
Some on the leaves of ancient authors prey,
Nor time nor moths e'er spoiled so much as they.
Some dryly plain, without invention's aid,

[6] *Pegasus, associated with poetic inspiration.*
[7] *A mountain in Greece sacred to Apollo and the Muses.*
[8] *Prescriptions.*

Write dull receipts how poems may be made.
These leave the sense, their learning to display,
And those explain the meaning quite away.
You then whose judgment the right course would steer,
Know well each ancient's proper character;
His fable,[9] subject, scope in every page; *120*
Religion, country, genius of his age:
Without all these at once before your eyes,
Cavil you may, but never criticise.
Be Homer's works your study and delight,
Read them by day, and meditate by night;
Thence form your judgment, thence your maxims bring,
And trace the muses upward to their spring.
Still with itself compared, his text peruse,
And let your comment be the Mantuan muse.
When first young Maro [10] in his boundless mind *130*
A work to outlast immortal Rome designed,
Perhaps he seemed above the critic's law,
And but from nature's fountains scorned to draw;
But when to examine every part he came,
Nature and Homer were, he found, the same.
Convinced, amazed, he checks the bold design;
And rules as strict his laboured work confine,
As if the Stagirite [11] o'erlooked each line.
Learn hence for ancient rules a just esteem;
To copy nature is to copy them. *140*
Some beauties yet no precepts can declare,
For there's a happiness [12] as well as care.
Music resembles poetry, in each
Are nameless graces which no methods teach,
And which a master-hand alone can reach.
If, where the rules not far enough extend,
(Since rules were made but to promote their end)
Some lucky licence answer to the full
The intent proposed, that licence is a rule.
Thus Pegasus, a nearer way to take, *150*
May boldly deviate from the common track;
From vulgar bounds with brave disorder part;
And snatch a grace beyond the reach of art,
Which without passing through the judgment, gains
The heart, and all its end at once attains.

[9] *Plot.*
[10] *Virgil, who was born near Mantua. He is also referred to as Maro.*
[11] *Aristotle, who was a native of Stagira. His* Poetics *was regarded as the supreme critical authority.*
[12] *Good luck.*

In prospects thus, some objects please our eyes,
Which out of nature's common order rise,
The shapeless rock, or hanging precipice.
Great wits sometimes may gloriously offend,
And rise to faults true critics dare not mend. *160*
But though the ancients thus their rules invade,
(As kings dispense with laws themselves have made)
Moderns, beware! or if you must offend
Against the precept, ne'er transgress its end;
Let it be seldom, and compelled by need;
And have, at least, their precedent to plead.
The critic else proceeds without remorse,
Seizes your fame, and puts his laws in force.
I know there are, to whose presumptuous thoughts
Those freer beauties, even in them, seem faults. *170*
Some figures monstrous and mis-shaped appear,
Considered singly, or beheld too near,
Which, but proportioned to their light, or place,
Due distance reconciles to form and grace.
A prudent chief not always must display
His powers in equal ranks, and fair array,
But with the occasion and the place comply,
Conceal his force, nay seem sometimes to fly.
Those oft are stratagems which error seem,
Nor is it Homer nods, but we that dream. *180*
Still green with bays [13] each ancient altar stands,
Above the reach of sacrilegious hands,
Secure from flames, from envy's fiercer rage,
Destructive war, and all-involving age.
See, from each clime the learned their incense bring!
Hear, in all tongues consenting pæans ring!
In praise so just let every voice be joined,
And fill the general chorus of mankind.
Hail, bards triumphant! born in happier days,
Immortal heirs of universal praise! *190*
Whose honours with increase of ages grow,
As streams roll down, enlarging as they flow;
Nations unborn your mighty names shall sound,
And worlds applaud that must not yet be found!
Oh, may some spark of your celestial fire,
The last, the meanest of your sons inspire,
(That on weak wings, from far, pursues your flights;
Glows while he reads, but trembles as he writes)
To teach vain wits a science little known,
To admire superior sense, and doubt their own! *200*

[13] *Garlands of laurel awarded for excellence.*

Part II

Of all the causes which conspire to blind
Man's erring judgment, and misguide the mind,
What the weak head with strongest bias rules
Is pride, the never-failing vice of fools.
Whatever nature has in worth denied,
She gives in large recruits [14] of needful pride;
For as in bodies, thus in souls, we find
What wants in blood and spirits, swelled with wind:
Pride, where wit fails, steps in to our defence,
And fills up all the mighty void of sense. *210*
If once right reason drives that cloud away,
Truth breaks upon us with resistless day.
Trust not yourself; but your defects to know,
Make use of every friend—and every foe.
A little learning is a dangerous thing;
Drink deep, or taste not the Pierian spring: [15]
There shallow draughts intoxicate the brain,
And drinking largely sobers us again.
Fired at first sight with what the muse imparts,
In fearless youth we tempt [16] the heights of arts, *220*
While from the bounded level of our mind
Short views we take, nor see the lengths behind;
But more advanced, behold with strange surprise
New distant scenes of endless science rise!
So pleased at first the towering Alps we try,
Mount o'er the vales, and seem to tread the sky;
The eternal snows appear already past,
And the first clouds and mountains seem the last;
But, those attained, we tremble to survey
The growing labours of the lengthened way; *230*
The increasing prospect tires our wandering eyes,
Hills peep o'er hills, and Alps on Alps arise!
A perfect judge will read each work of wit
With the same spirit that its author writ:
Survey the whole, nor seek slight faults to find
Where nature moves, and rapture warms the mind;
Nor lose, for that malignant dull delight,
The generous pleasure to be charmed with wit.
But in such lays as neither ebb, nor flow,
Correctly cold, and regularly low, *240*
That shunning faults, one quiet tenour keep,

[14] *Supplies.*
[15] *A spring on Mt. Olympus, sacred to the Muses.*
[16] *Attempt.*

We cannot blame indeed—but we may sleep.
In wit, as nature, what affects our hearts
Is not the exactness of peculiar parts;
'Tis not a lip, or eye, we beauty call,
But the joint force and full result of all.
Thus when we view some well-proportioned dome,[17]
(The world's just wonder, and even thine, O Rome!)
No single parts unequally surprise,
All comes united to the admiring eyes; *250*
No monstrous height, or breadth, or length appear;
The whole at once is bold, and regular.
Whoever thinks a faultless piece to see,
Thinks what ne'er was, nor is, nor e'er shall be.
In every work regard the writer's end,
Since none can compass more than they intend;
And if the means be just, the conduct true,
Applause, in spite of trivial faults, is due;
As men of breeding, sometimes men of wit,
To avoid great errors, must the less commit: *260*
Neglect the rules each verbal critic lays,
For not to know some trifles, is a praise.
Most critics, fond of some subservient art,
Still make the whole depend upon a part;
They talk of principles, but notions prize,
And all to one loved folly sacrifice.
Once on a time, La Mancha's knight,[18] they say,
A certain bard encountering on the way,
Discoursed in terms as just, with looks as sage,
As e'er could Dennis [19] of the Grecian stage; *270*
Concluding all were desperate sots and fools,
Who durst depart from Aristotle's rules.
Our author, happy in a judge so nice,
Produced his play, and begged the knight's advice;
Made him observe the subject, and the plot,
The manners, passions, unities—what not?
All which, exact to rule, were brought about,
Were but a combat in the lists left out.
"What! leave the combat out?" exclaims the knight;
"Yes, or we must renounce the Stagirite." *280*
"Not so by Heaven," he answers in a rage,
"Knights, squires, and steeds, must enter on the stage."
"So vast a throng the stage can ne'er contain."
"Then build a new, or act it in a plain."

[17] *The dome of St. Peter's in Rome, designed by Michelangelo.*
[18] *Don Quixote.*
[19] *John Dennis, a severe and rather pompous critic.*

Thus critics, of less judgment than caprice,
Curious [20] not knowing, not exact but nice,
Form short ideas, and offend in arts
(As most in manners) by a love to parts,
Some to conceit [21] alone their taste confine,
And glittering thoughts struck out at every line; *290*
Pleased with a work where nothing's just or fit,
One glaring chaos and wild heap of wit.
Poets like painters, thus, unskilled to trace
The naked nature and the living grace,
With gold and jewels cover every part,
And hide with ornaments their want of art.
True wit is nature to advantage dressed,
What oft was thought, but ne'er so well expressed;
Something, whose truth convinced at sight we find,
That gives us back the image of our mind. *300*
As shades more sweetly recommend the light,
So modest plainness sets off sprightly wit;
For works may have more wit than does 'em good,
As bodies perish through excess of blood.
Others for language all their care express,
And value books, as women men, for dress:
Their praise is still,—the style is excellent:
The sense, they humbly take upon content.[22]
Words are like leaves; and where they most abound,
Much fruit of sense beneath is rarely found: *310*
False eloquence, like the prismatic glass,
Its gaudy colours spreads on every place;
The face of nature we no more survey,
All glares alike, without distinction gay:
But true expression, like the unchanging sun,
Clears and improves whate'er it shines upon;
It gilds all objects, but it alters none.
Expression is the dress of thought, and still
Appears more decent as more suitable;
A vile conceit in pompous words expressed, *320*
Is like a clown [23] in regal purple dressed:
For different styles with different subjects sort,
As several garbs with country, town, and court.
Some by old words to fame have made pretence,
Ancients in phrase, mere moderns in their sense;

20 *Overscrupulous.*
21 *Elaborate wittiness.*
22 *Without questioning.*
23 *A rustic person.*

Such laboured nothings, in so strange a style,
Amaze the unlearned, and make the learned smile.
Unlucky, as Fungoso [24] in the play,
These sparks with awkward vanity display
What the fine gentleman wore yesterday; *330*
And but so mimic ancient wits at best,
As apes our grandsires, in their doublets dressed.
In words as fashions the same rule will hold;
Alike fantastic if too new or old:
Be not the first by whom the new are tried,
Nor yet the last to lay the old aside.
  But most by numbers [25] judge a poet's song;
And smooth or rough with them is right or wrong:
In the bright muse though thousand charms conspire,
Her voice is all these tuneful fools admire, *340*
Who haunt Parnassus but to please their ear,
Not mend their minds; as some to church repair,
Not for the doctrine, but the music there.
These equal syllables alone require,[26]
Though oft the ear the open vowels tire;
While expletives their feeble aid do join,
And ten low words oft creep in one dull line:
While they ring round the same unvaried chimes,
With sure returns of still expected rhymes;
Where'er you find "the cooling western breeze," *350*
In the next line, it "whispers through the trees";
If crystal streams "with pleasing murmurs creep,"
The reader's threatened (not in vain) with "sleep";
Then, at the last and only couplet fraught
With some unmeaning thing they call a thought,
A needless Alexandrine [27] ends the song
That, like a wounded snake, drags its slow length along.
Leave such to tune their own dull rhymes, and know
What's roundly smooth or languishingly slow;
And praise the easy vigour of a line, *360*
Where Denham's strength and Waller's sweetness join.[28]
True ease in writing comes from art, not chance,
As those move easiest who have learned to dance.
'Tis not enough no harshness gives offence;
The sound must seem an echo to the sense:

[24] *A character in Ben Jonson's* Every Man Out of His Humor.
[25] *Versification.*
[26] *Note that in lines 345–57 Pope's own style illustrates the faults he mentions.*
[27] *A line with six iambic feet, like the one following this one.*
[28] *Sir John Denham (1615–69) and Edmund Waller (1609–87).*

Soft is the strain when Zephyr gently blows,
And the smooth stream in smoother numbers flows;
But when loud surges lash the sounding shore,
The hoarse, rough verse should like the torrent roar:
When Ajax strives some rock's vast weight to throw, *370*
The line too labours, and the words move slow;
Not so, when swift Camilla scours the plain,
Flies o'er the unbending corn, and skims along the main.
Hear how Timotheus' varied lays surprise,[29]
And bid alternate passions fall and rise!
While, at each change, the son of Libyan Jove [30]
Now burns with glory, and then melts with love,
Now his fierce eyes with sparkling fury glow,
Now sighs steal out, and tears begin to flow:
Persians and Greeks like turns of nature found, *380*
And the world's victor stood subdued by sound!
The power of music all our hearts allow,
And what Timotheus was, is Dryden now.
  Avoid extremes, and shun the fault of such,
Who still are pleased too little or too much.
At every trifle scorn to take offence;
That always shows great pride or little sense;
Those heads, as stomachs, are not sure the best,
Which nauseate all, and nothing can digest.
Yet let not each gay turn thy rapture move; *390*
For fools admire, but men of sense approve:
As things seem large which we through mists descry,
Dulness is ever apt to magnify.
  Some foreign writers, some our own despise;
The ancients only, or the moderns prize.
Thus wit, like faith, by each man is applied
To one small sect, and all are damned beside.
Meanly they seek the blessing to confine,
And force that sun but on a part to shine,
Which not alone the southern wit sublimes, *400*
But ripens spirits in cold northern climes;
Which from the first has shone on ages past,
Enlights the present, and shall warm the last;
Though each may feel increases and decays,
And see now clearer and now darker days.
Regard not then if wit be old or new,
But blame the false, and value still the true.
  Some ne'er advance a judgment of their own,

[29] *See Dryden's "Alexander's Feast."*
[30] *Alexander the Great.*

But catch the spreading notion of the town;
They reason and conclude by precedent, *410*
And own stale nonsense which they ne'er invent.
Some judge of authors' names, not works, and then
Nor praise nor blame the writings, but the men.
Of all this servile herd the worst is he
That in proud dulness joins with quality;
A constant critic at the great man's board,
To fetch and carry nonsense for my lord.
What woeful stuff this madrigal would be,
In some starved hackney sonneteer, or me?
But let a lord once own the happy lines, *420*
How the wit brightens! how the style refines!
Before his sacred name flies every fault,
And each exalted stanza teems with thought!
The vulgar thus through imitation err;
As oft the learned by being singular;
So much they scorn the crowd, that if the throng
By chance go right, they purposely go wrong;
So schismatics the plain believers quit,
And are but damned for having too much wit.
Some praise at morning what they blame at night, *430*
But always think the last opinion right.
A muse by these is like a mistress used,
This hour she's idolised, the next abused;
While their weak heads, like towns unfortified,
'Twixt sense and nonsense daily change their side.
Ask them the cause; they're wiser still, they say;
And still to-morrow's wiser than to-day.
We think our fathers fools, so wise we grow;
Our wiser sons, no doubt, will think us so.
Once school-divines this zealous isle o'erspread; *440*
Who knew most sentences,[31] was deepest read;
Faith, gospel, all, seemed made to be disputed,
And none had sense enough to be confuted:
Scotists and Thomists now in peace remain,
Amidst their kindred cobwebs in Duck Lane.[32]
If faith itself has different dresses worn,
What wonder modes in wit should take their turn?
Oft, leaving what is natural and fit,
The current folly proves the ready wit;
And authors think their reputation safe, *450*
Which lives as long as fools are pleased to laugh.

[31] *An allusion to Peter Lombard's* Book of Sentences.
[32] *A street where secondhand books and publisher's leftover stocks were sold.*

Some, valuing those of their own side or mind,
Still make themselves the measure of mankind:
Fondly we think we honour merit then,
When we but praise ourselves in other men.
Parties in wit attend on those of state,
And public faction doubles private hate.
Pride, Malice, Folly, against Dryden rose,
In various shapes of parsons, critics, beaux;
But sense survived, when merry jests were past; *460*
For rising merit will buoy up at last.
Might he return, and bless once more our eyes,
New Blackmores[33] and new Milbournes must arise:
Nay, should great Homer lift his awful head,
Zoilus again would start up from the dead.
Envy will merit, as its shade, pursue;
But like a shadow, proves the substance true;
For envied wit, like Sol eclipsed, makes known
The opposing body's grossness, not its own.
When first that sun too powerful beams displays, *470*
It draws up vapours which obscure its rays;
But even those clouds at last adorn its way,
Reflect new glories, and augment the day.
Be thou the first true merit to befriend;
His praise is lost who stays till all commend.
Short is the date, alas, of modern rhymes,
And 'tis but just to let them live betimes.
No longer now that golden age appears,
When patriarch wits survived a thousand years:
Now length of fame (our second life) is lost, *480*
And bare threescore is all even that can boast;
Our sons their fathers' failing language see,
And such as Chaucer is, shall Dryden be.
So when the faithful pencil has designed
Some bright idea of the master's mind,
Where a new world leaps out at his command,
And ready nature waits upon his hand;
When the ripe colours soften and unite,
And sweetly melt into just shade and light;
When mellowing years their full perfection give, *490*
And each bold figure just begins to live,
The treacherous colours the fair art betray,
And all the bright creation fades away!
Unhappy wit, like most mistaken things,

[33] *Blackmore attacked Dryden for the immorality of his plays. Milbourne criticized his translation of Virgil.*

Atones not for that envy which it brings.
In youth alone its empty praise we boast,
But soon the short-lived vanity is lost:
Like some fair flower the early spring supplies,
That gaily blooms, but even in blooming dies.
What is this wit, which must our cares employ? *500*
The owner's wife, that other men enjoy;
Then most our trouble still when most admired,
And still the more we give, the more required;
Whose fame with pains we guard, but lose with ease,
Sure some to vex, but never all to please;
'Tis what the vicious fear, the virtuous shun;
By fools 'tis hated, and by knaves undone!
If wit so much from ignorance undergo,
Ah let not learning too commence its foe!
Of old, those met rewards who could excel, *510*
And such were praised who but endeavoured well;
Though triumphs were to generals only due,
Crowns were reserved to grace the soldiers too.
Now they who reach Parnassus' lofty crown
Employ their pains to spurn some others down;
And while self-love each jealous writer rules,
Contending wits become the sport of fools;
But still the worst with most regret commend,
For each ill author is as bad a friend.
To what base ends, and what abject ways, *520*
Are mortals urged through sacred lust of praise!
Ah, ne'er so dire a thirst of glory boast,
Nor in the critic let the man be lost.
Good nature and good sense must ever join;
To err is human; to forgive, divine.
But if in noble minds some dregs remain
Not yet purged off, of spleen and sour disdain,
Discharge that rage on more provoking crimes,
Nor fear a dearth in these flagitious times.
No pardon vile obscenity should find, *530*
Though wit and art conspire to move your mind;
But dulness with obscenity must prove
As shameful sure as impotence in love.
In the fat age of pleasure, wealth, and ease,
Sprung the rank weed, and thrived with large increase:
When love was all an easy monarch's [34] care;
Seldom at council, never in a war:
Jilts ruled the state, and statesmen farces writ;

[34] *The allusion is to Charles II.*

Nay wits had pensions, and young lords had wit:
The fair sate panting at a courtier's play, *540*
And not a mask [35] went unimproved away:
The modest fan was lifted up no more,
And virgins smiled at what they blushed before.
The following licence of a foreign reign [36]
Did all the dregs of bold Socinus [37] drain;
Then unbelieving priests reformed the nation,
And taught more pleasant methods of salvation;
Where Heaven's free subjects might their rights dispute,
Lest God himself should seem too absolute:
Pulpits their sacred satire learned to spare, *550*
And vice admired to find a flatterer there!
Encouraged thus, wit's Titans braved the skies,
And the press groaned with licensed blasphemies.
These monsters, critics! with your darts engage,
Here point your thunder, and exhaust your rage!
Yet shun their fault, who, scandalously nice,
Will needs mistake an author into vice;
All seems infected that the infected spy,
As all looks yellow to the jaundiced eye.

1711

[35] *Lady wearing a mask.*
[36] *An allusion to the fact that William III was a Dutchman.*
[37] *A sixteenth-century Italian theologian who denied the divinity of Jesus.*

Questions

1. Pope says that poets and critics alike need both good judgment and wit. The term "wit" is used elsewhere in another sense. See if you can distinguish between the two senses of the word. The dictionary will help you.
2. Is good judgment the same as "common sense" (line 28)? Is it the same as "understanding" (line 57)?
3. When Pope says (line 68), "First follow Nature," he does not mean nature in its visible forms, but rather what is natural in the sense of being normal. What is the best way of following Nature? Why?
4. Are all men capable of good judgment? What are the most general causes of disagreement in judgment?
5. What is the chief cause of men's failure to use the judgment they possess? How many common faults in criticism are mentioned in part 2?

Kubla Khan

SAMUEL TAYLOR COLERIDGE

In Xanadu did Kubla Khan [1]
  A stately pleasure-dome decree:
Where Alph, the sacred river, ran
Through caverns measureless to man
  Down to a sunless sea. *5*
So twice five miles of fertile ground
With walls and towers were girdled round:
And here were gardens bright with sinuous rills,
Where blossomed many an incense-bearing tree,
And here were forests ancient as the hills, *10*
Enfolding sunny spots of greenery.

But oh! that deep romantic chasm which slanted
Down the green hill athwart a cedarn cover!
A savage place; as holy and enchanted
As e'er beneath a waning moon was haunted *15*
By woman wailing for her demon-lover!
And from this chasm, with ceaseless turmoil seething,
As if this earth in fast thick pants were breathing,
A mighty fountain momently was forced,
Amid whose swift half-intermitted burst *20*
Huge fragments vaulted like rebounding hail,
Or chaffy grain beneath the thresher's flail:
And 'mid these dancing rocks at once and ever
It flung up momently the sacred river.
Five miles meandering with a mazy motion *25*
Through wood and dale the sacred river ran,
Then reached the caverns measureless to man,
And sank in tumult to a lifeless ocean:
And 'mid this tumult Kubla heard from far
Ancestral voices prophesying war! *30*

    The shadow of the dome of pleasure
    Floated midway on the waves;
    Where was heard the mingled measure
    From the fountain and the caves.
It was a miracle of rare device, *35*
A sunny pleasure-dome with caves of ice!

[1] *The historical Kubla Khan was the founder of the Mongol dynasty in China in the thirteenth century.*

A damsel with a dulcimer
In a vision once I saw:
It was an Abyssinian maid,
And on her dulcimer she played, 40
Singing of Mount Abora.
Could I revive within me
Her symphony and song,
To such a deep delight 'twould win me,
That with music loud and long, 45
I would build that dome in air,
That sunny dome! those caves of ice!
And all who heard should see them there,
And all should cry, Beware! Beware!
His flashing eyes, his floating hair! 50
Weave a circle round him thrice,
And close your eyes with holy dread,
For he on honey-dew hath fed,
And drunk the milk of Paradise.

1816 (Composed 1797)

Questions

1. Although the first part of "Kubla Khan" may be regarded as historical description, it may also be seen as a symbolic representation of basic human desires and fears. What, in this view, does the Khan himself symbolize? To what extent does he have control over his environment and destiny? What is his relation with the world of nature? With supernatural forces?
2. The second part of the poem is about poetic inspiration and poetic power. What does the damsel symbolize? What does the speaker mean by saying that he would "build that dome in air" if he could revive within himself the damsel's symphony and song? Is he being modest? What is the relation between the speaker and Kubla Khan?

Ode on a Grecian Urn

JOHN KEATS

I

Thou still unravished bride of quietness,
Thou foster-child of silence and slow time,
Sylvan [1] historian, who canst thus express

[1] *Pastoral.*

A flowery tale more sweetly than our rhyme:
What leaf-fringed legend [2] haunts about thy shape 5
Of deities or mortals, or of both,
In Tempe [3] or the dales of Arcady?
What men or gods are these? What maidens loth?
What mad pursuit? What struggle to escape?
What pipes and timbrels? What wild ecstasy? 10

II

Heard melodies are sweet, but those unheard
Are sweeter; therefore, ye soft pipes, play on;
Not to the sensual ear, but, more endeared,
Pipe to the spirit ditties of no tone: [4]
Fair youth, beneath the trees, thou canst not leave 15
Thy song, nor ever can those trees be bare;
Bold Lover, never, never canst thou kiss,
Though winning near the goal—yet, do not grieve;
She cannot fade, though thou hast not thy bliss,
For ever wilt thou love, and she be fair! 20

III

Ah, happy, happy boughs! that cannot shed
Your leaves, nor ever bid the Spring adieu;
And, happy melodist, unwearièd,
For ever piping songs for ever new;
More happy love! more happy, happy love! 25
For ever warm and still to be enjoyed,
For ever panting, and for ever young;
All breathing human passion far above,
That leaves a heart high-sorrowful and cloyed,
A burning forehead, and a parching tongue. 30

IV

Who are these coming to the sacrifice?
To what green altar, O mysterious priest,
Lead'st thou that heifer lowing at the skies,

[2] *The poet refers to pictures on the vase, carved in relief, that suggest a legend or history.*

[3] *Tempe is a beautiful valley in Greece. Arcadia, a Grecian state, is always regarded as the symbol of the pastoral ideal, i.e., the ideal of simple, carefree rural life.*

[4] *Lines 13–14 mean "Do not play for the senses, but rather pipe songs without tone for the spirit, and so be more endeared." The idea is that the songs must be imagined, and can be imagined to be sweeter than any actual tune.*

And all her silken flanks with garlands drest?
What little town by river or sea shore, *35*
Or mountain-built with peaceful citadel,
Is emptied of this folk, this pious morn?
And, little town, thy streets for evermore
Will silent be; and not a soul to tell
Why thou art desolate, can e'er return. *40*

V

O Attic [5] shape! Fair attitude! with brede [6]
Of marble men and maidens overwrought,
With forest branches and the trodden weed;
Thou, silent form, dost tease us out of thought
As doth eternity: Cold Pastoral! *45*
When old age shall this generation waste,
Thou shalt remain, in midst of other woe
Than ours, a friend to man, to whom thou say'st,
"Beauty is truth, truth beauty,"–that is all
Ye know on earth, and all ye need to know.[7] *50*

1820

[5] *Of Attica, the region in which Athens was located.*
[6] *Pattern.*
[7] *Since in one early published version of the poem there are no quotation marks, it is not certain whether the statement "that is all / Ye know on earth, and all ye need to know" is to be attributed to the urn or to the speaker of the poem; nor is the reference of "that" quite clear. The general idea, however, seems to be that the imaginative idealism of art will always provide man with a feeling that life, in spite of its misery and mystery, has some meaning and value.*

Questions

1. What is it about the urn that fascinates the poet? Is he mainly interested in it as a memento of an ancient civilization or as a work of art? Do the pictures on the urn give a realistic or an idealized representation of life? What is the significance of the question "What men or gods are these?" in line 8?
2. Does the urn become a symbol in the eyes of the poet? If so, what does it represent? Does the urn's message to mankind—"Beauty is truth, truth beauty"—help to suggest what it stands for?
3. What qualities of the urn are stressed most? Why does the poet ask so many questions? What is the relation between the "world" of the urn and the actual world?

To R. B.[1]

GERARD MANLEY HOPKINS

The fine delight that fathers thought; the strong
Spur, live and lancing like the blowpipe flame,
Breathes once and, quenchèd faster than it came,
Leaves yet the mind a mother of immortal song.
Nine months she then, nay years, nine years she long *5*
Within her wears, bears, cares and combs the same:
The widow of an insight lost she lives, with aim
Now known and hand at work now never wrong.
  Sweet fire the sire of muse, my soul needs this;
I want the one rapture of an inspiration. *10*
O then if in my lagging lines you miss
The roll, the rise, the carol, the creation,
My winter world, that scarcely breathes that bliss
Now, yields you, with some sighs, our explanation.

1918 (Composed 1889)

[1] *Robert Bridges, Hopkins' close friend and later his editor.*

Questions

1. What is the central metaphor in this sonnet about the composition of poetry? What three things are involved? Does the idea make sense to you? How can an insight that is lost produce a poem?
2. What seems to be the value of poetry to Hopkins?

Terence, This Is Stupid Stuff

A. E. HOUSMAN

'Terence, this is stupid stuff: [1]
You eat your victuals fast enough;
There can't be much amiss, 'tis clear,

[1] *The poet imagines that someone is complaining to him about his poetry.* The Poems of Terence Hearsay *was the title first intended for* The Shropshire Lad, *the collection from which this poem is taken. Throughout the collection the poet speaks as a young rustic.*

To see the rate you drink your beer.
But oh, good Lord, the verse you make,
It gives a chap the belly-ache.
The cow, the old cow, she is dead;
It sleeps well, the horned head:
We poor lads, 'tis our turn now
To hear such tunes as killed the cow. 10
Pretty friendship 'tis to rhyme
Your friends to death before their time
Moping melancholy mad:
Come, pipe a tune to dance to, lad.'

Why, if 'tis dancing you would be,
There's brisker pipes than poetry.
Say for what were hop-yards meant,
Or why was Burton built on Trent? [2]
Oh many a peer of England brews
Livelier liquor than the Muse, 20
And malt does more than Milton can
To justify God's ways to man.
Ale, man, ale's the stuff to drink
For fellows whom it hurts to think:
Look into the pewter pot
To see the world as the world's not.
And faith 'tis pleasant till 'tis past:
The mischief is that 'twill not last.
Oh I have been to Ludlow [3] fair
And left my necktie God knows where, 30
And carried halfway home, or near,
Pints and quarts of Ludlow beer:
Then the world seemed none so bad,
And I myself a sterling lad;
And down in lovely muck I've lain,
Happy till I woke again.
Then I saw the morning sky:
Heigho, the tale was all a lie;
The world it was the old world yet,
I was I, my things were wet, 40
And nothing now remained to do
But begin the game anew.

Therefore, since the world has still
Much good, but much less good than ill,

[2] *Burton-on-Trent is a famous English brewing town. In the next two lines Housman refers to the fact that some of the peers of England owed their titles to fortunes made in brewing.*
[3] *A market town.*

And while the sun and moon endure
Luck's a chance but trouble's sure,
I'd face it as a wise man would,
And train for ill and not for good.
'Tis true, the stuff I bring for sale
Is not so brisk a brew as ale: 50
Out of a stem that scored [4] the hand
I wrung it in a weary land.
But take it: if the smack is sour,
The better for the embittered hour;
It should do good to heart and head
When your soul is in my soul's stead;
And I will friend you, if I may,
In the dark and cloudy day.

There was a king reigned in the East:
There, when kings will sit to feast, 60
They get their fill before they think
With poisoned meat and poisoned drink.
He gathered all that springs to birth
From the many-venomed earth;
First a little, thence to more,
He sampled all her killing store;
And easy, smiling, seasoned sound,
Sate the king when healths went round.
They put arsenic in his meat
And stared aghast to watch him eat; 70
They poured strychnine in his cup
And shook to see him drink it up:
They shook, they stared as white's their shirt:
Them it was their poison hurt.
–I tell the tale that I heard told.
Mithridates,[5] he died old.

1896

[4] *Scratched.*
[5] *This story about Mithridates VI, king of Pontus, is told by Pliny in his* Natural History.

Questions

1. What would you suppose to be the subject matter of "Terence's" poetry?
2. What is the poet's opinion of religious faith? Of optimistic philosophy?
3. How does the poet justify his poetry? What would correspond to the effect of the small doses of poison upon Mithridates?

Sailing to Byzantium[1]

W. B. YEATS

1

That is no country for old men. The young
In one another's arms, birds in the trees
–Those dying generations–at their song,
The salmon-falls, the mackerel-crowded seas,
Fish, flesh, or fowl, commend all summer long *5*
Whatever is begotten, born, and dies.
Caught in that sensual music all neglect
Monuments of unageing intellect.

2

An aged man is but a paltry thing,
A tattered coat upon a stick, unless *10*
Soul clap its hands and sing, and louder sing
For every tatter in its mortal dress,
Nor is there singing school but studying
Monuments of its own magnificence;
And therefore I have sailed the seas and come *15*
To the holy city of Byzantium.

3

O sages standing in God's holy fire
As in the gold mosaic of a wall,[2]
Come from the holy fire, perne in a gyre,[3]
And be the singing-masters of my soul. *20*
Consume my heart away; sick with desire
And fastened to a dying animal
It knows not what it is; and gather me
Into the artifice of eternity.

4

Once out of nature I shall never take *25*
My bodily form from any natural thing,

[1] *Byzantium (modern Istanbul) was the "holy city" of Greek Orthodox Christianity and capital of the Eastern Roman Empire. It was, of course, a great center of culture. Speaking of its art in* A Vision, *Yeats said, "The painter, the mosaic worker, the illuminator of sacred books were almost impersonal, almost perhaps without the consciousness of individual design, absorbed in their subject matter and that the vision of a whole people."*

[2] *Yeats is thinking of the stylized figures in mosaic on the walls of the Church of Hagia Sophia ("Holy Wisdom") in Byzantium.*

[3] *"perne in a gyre": whirl downward in a spiral. Yeats often used the image of the spiral as a symbol of cyclic historical or spiritual development.*

But such a form as Grecian goldsmiths make
Of hammered gold and golden enamelling
To keep a drowsy Emperor awake;[4]
Or set upon a golden bough to sing *30*
To lords and ladies of Byzantium
Of what is past, or passing, or to come.

1927

[4] *Yeats wrote: "I have read someplace that in the Emperor's palace at Byzantium was a tree made of gold and silver, and artificial birds that sang."*

Questions

1. This poem uses a place metaphor. On the one hand, there is "that country," and on the other, Byzantium, to which the speaker proposes to go. Byzantium symbolizes the ideal life of the "intellect"; what, then, does "that country" stand for?
2. What is the general metaphor of the third stanza? Will the process he speaks of be painful? If so, why?
3. Why is the image of the bird in the last stanza particularly appropriate? Can you connect it with any metaphors used earlier? Is there any other mention of birds in the poem?

Terra Incognita[1]

D. H. LAWRENCE

There are vast realms of consciousness still undreamed of
vast ranges of experience, like the humming of unseen harps,
we know nothing of, within us.

Oh when man escaped from the barbed-wire entanglement
of his own ideas and his own mechanical devices *5*
there is a marvellous rich world of contact and sheer fluid beauty
and fearless face-to-face awareness of now-naked life
and me, and you, and other men and women
and grapes, and ghouls, and ghosts and green moonlight
and ruddy-orange limbs stirring the limbo *10*
of the unknown air, and eyes so soft
softer than the space between the stars.
And all things, and nothing, and being and not-being
alternately palpitant,
when at last we escape the barbed-wire enclosure *15*
of *Know Thyself*,[2] knowing we can never know,

[1] *The unknown land.*
[2] *The famous maxim of Socrates.*

we can but touch, and wonder, and ponder, and make our effort
and dangle in a last fastidious fine delight
as the fuchsia does, dangling her reckless drop
of purple after so much putting forth *20*
and slow mounting marvel of a little tree.

1929

Questions

1. What kind of ideas is Lawrence referring to in line 5? Does he have in mind conventional notions of beauty, or something more? What general terms or metaphors does he use to define the contrast between the world we know now and that which we might discover?
2. What is the general idea that the poet is trying to convey with the words "grapes, and ghouls and ghosts and green moonlight"? Can you think of another alliterative phrase that would in this context have essentially the same meaning?
3. How does Lawrence lead the reader toward the thought that "we can never know" (line 16)? Does this assertion contradict the statement in lines 6 and 7?
4. Consider carefully the comparison between human experience and the blooming of the fuchsia. Does Lawrence mean that we should live for pleasure? For beauty? That we should just be ourselves? That experience is its own end?

Hypocrite Auteur[1]

mon semblable, mon frère

ARCHIBALD MACLEISH

1

Our epoch takes a voluptuous satisfaction
In that perspective of the action
Which pictures us inhabiting the end
Of everything with death for only friend.

[1] *The title is taken from the last line of the prefatory poem, "Au Lecteur," in Baudelaire's* Fleurs du Mal: *"—Hypocrite lecteur,—mon semblable,—mon frère!" ("Hypocrite reader—my double—my brother!") In the poem Baudelaire singles out "l'Ennui" (boredom, emptiness) as the most hideous monster in the menagerie of mankind's enemies, and ends by telling the reader that he knows this monster well.*

Not that we love death, 5
Not truly, not the fluttering breath,
The obscene shudder of the finished act—
What the doe feels when the ultimate fact
Tears at her bowels with its jaws.
Our taste is for the opulent pause 10
Before the end comes. If the end is certain
All of us are players at the final curtain:
All of us, silence for a time deferred,
Find time before us for one sad last word.
Victim, rebel, convert, stoic— 15
Every role but the heroic—
We turn our tragic faces to the stalls
To wince our moment till the curtain falls.

2

A world ends when its metaphor has died.

An age become an age, all else beside, 20
When sensuous poets in their pride invent
Emblems for the soul's consent
That speak the meanings men will never know
But man-imagined images can show:
It perishes when those images, though seen, 25
No longer mean.

3

A world was ended when the womb
Where girl held God became the tomb
Where God lies buried in a man:
Botticelli's [2] image neither speaks nor can 30
To our kind. His star-guided stranger
Teaches no longer, by the child, the manger,
The meaning of the beckoning skies.

Sophocles, when his reverent actors rise
To play the king with bleeding eyes,[3] 35
No longer shows us on the stage advance
God's purpose in the terrible fatality of chance.

No woman living, when the girl and swan
Embrace in verses,[4] feels upon

[2] *A fifteenth-century Italian painter. The picture alluded to is his "Nativity."*
[3] *The allusion is to* Oedipus Rex.
[4] *According to Greek myth, Zeus visited Leda, the mother of Helen of Troy, in the form of a swan. Cf. W. B. Yeats's "Leda and the Swan."*

Her breast the awful thunder of that breast 40
Where God, made beast, is by the blood confessed.

Empty as conch shell by the water cast
The metaphor still sounds but cannot tell,
And we, like parasite crabs, put on the shell
And drag it at the sea's edge up and down. 45

This is the destiny we say we own.

4

But are we sure
The age that dies upon its metaphor
Among these Roman heads, these mediaeval towers,
Is ours?— 50
Or ours the ending of that story?

The meanings in a man that quarry
Images from blinded eyes
And white birds and the turning skies
To make a world of were not spent with these 55
Abandoned presences.

The journey of our history has not ceased:
Earth turns us still toward the rising east,
The metaphor still struggles in the stone,
The allegory of the flesh and bone 60
Still stares into the summer grass
That is its glass,
The ignorant blood
Still knocks at silence to be understood.

Poets, deserted by the world before, 65
Turn round into the actual air:
Invent the age! Invent the metaphor!

1952

Questions

1. Why does the poet say that we imagine that we are seeing the end of everything? Is it because of what we foresee or because of our attitude toward the past? Why is death regarded as our only friend? What are the "roles" played in our time? Why is the heroic lacking?

2. What are the "meanings men will never know" that the poet speaks of in the second section? Is he talking about divine purposes? Are these meanings invented, as well as the images that "show" them? Note that the poet uses the phrase "Emblems for the soul's consent." Does this imply that the man-invented images stand both for human feelings and for meanings that cannot be known? Or are the feelings and the meanings really the same? Is image wholly distinguishable from meaning?
3. Why have poets been deserted by the world? What does the advice "Turn round into the actual air" mean? What is the relation between the invented and the real?

Poetry

MARIANNE MOORE

I, too, dislike it: there are things that are important beyond all this
fiddle.
Reading it, however, with a perfect contempt for it, one discovers in
it after all, a place for the genuine.
Hands that can grasp, eyes
that can dilate, hair that can rise
if it must, these things are important not because a 5
high-sounding interpretation can be put upon them but because they are
useful. When they become so derivative as to become unintelligible,
the same thing may be said for all of us, that we
do not admire what 10
we cannot understand: the bat
holding on upside down or in quest of something to

eat, elephants pushing, a wild horse taking a roll, a tireless wolf under
a tree, the immovable critic twitching his skin like a horse
that feels a flea, the base- 15
ball fan, the statistician—
nor is it valid
to discriminate against "business documents and

school-books";[1] all these phenomena are important. One must make a
distinction
however: when dragged into prominence by half poets, the result
is not poetry, 20

[1] *In a note to this poem the author says that this quotation is derived from* The Diaries of Leo Tolstoy, *and that in lines 21–22 from W. B. Yeats's* Ideas of Good and Evil.

nor till the poets among us can be
"literalists of
the imagination"—above
insolence and triviality and can present
for inspection, "imaginary gardens with real toads in them," 25
shall we have
it. In the meantime, if you demand on the one hand,
the raw material of poetry in
all its rawness and
that which is on the other hand
genuine, you are interested in poetry.

1935

Questions

1. Why does the author say that "these things" (line 5) are useful? In what way might they be useful? Why does it matter whether they are useful or not?
2. Does the author object to the content of bad poetry or the manner of presentation—or both? Does she distinguish more than one kind of bad poetry?
3. The author demands "rawness" on the one hand and "the genuine" on the other. Can you tell what she means by these terms? Attempt a definition of them.

I Think Continually of Those

STEPHEN SPENDER

I think continually of those who were truly great.
Who, from the womb, remembered the soul's history
Through corridors of light where the hours are suns,
Endless and singing. Whose lovely ambition
Was that their lips, still touched with fire, 5
Should tell of the Spirit, clothed from head to foot in song.
And who hoarded from the Spring branches
The desires falling across their bodies like blossoms.

What is precious, is never to forget
The essential delight of the blood drawn from ageless springs 10
Breaking through rocks in worlds before our earth.
Never to deny its pleasure in the morning simple light

Nor its grave evening demand for love.
Never to allow gradually the traffic to smother
With noise and fog, the flowering of the Spirit. *15*

Near the snow, near the sun, in the highest fields,
See how these names are fêted by the waving grass
And by the streamers of white cloud
And whispers of wind in the listening sky.
The names of those who in their lives fought for life, *20*
Who wore at their hearts the fire's centre.
Born of the sun, they travelled a short while toward the sun,
And left the vivid air signed with their honour.

1934

Questions

1. What do you think the poet means by "the Spirit"? Is "the power of imagination" an adequate definition?
2. Is the idea of this poem comparable to that expressed in Wordsworth's "The World Is Too Much with Us"?
3. Explain the cause-and-effect relation that the poet has in mind when he says that the "truly great" are "fêted" by the waving grass.

In My Craft or Sullen Art

DYLAN THOMAS

In my craft or sullen[1] art
Exercised in the still night
When only the moon rages[2]
And the lovers lie abed
With all their griefs in their arms, *5*
I labour by singing light
Not for ambition or bread
Or the strut and trade of charms
On the ivory stages[3]
But for the common wages *10*
Of their most secret heart.

[1] *The meaning of "sullen" here probably includes the old sense of "lonely" or "solitary."*
[2] *Prevails uncontrollably.*
[3] *I.e. (conjecturally), not for a place in the world of "culture."*

Not for the proud man apart
From the raging moon I write
On these spindrift[4] pages
Nor for the towering dead[5] *15*
With their nightingales and psalms
But for the lovers, their arms
Round the griefs of the ages,
Who pay no praise or wages
Nor heed my craft or art. *20*

1939

[4] *Frail, short-lived, as if made of sea-spray.*
[5] *I.e., in emulation of the great poets of the past.*

Questions

1. The idea of the moon raging suggests, of course, a special kind of force or impulse, something different from that which is manifested in daytime activities. Does the rest of the poem help to define this influence?
2. Why would "the lovers" necessarily have griefs? Why does the poet use the term "the lovers" rather than just "lovers"?
3. Do lines 10–11 mean that the poet wants the lovers to reveal their hearts to him, or that he wants them to respond in their most secret hearts, or both?
4. Why do the lovers pay no heed to art?

Of Modern Poetry

WALLACE STEVENS

The poem of the mind in the act of finding
What will suffice. It has not always had
To find: the scene was set; it repeated what
Was in the script.
Then the theatre was changed *5*
To something else. Its past was a souvenir.
It has to be living, to learn the speech of the place.
It has to face the men of the time and to meet
The women of the time. It has to think about war
And it has to find what will suffice. It has *10*

To construct a new stage. It has to be on that stage
And, like an insatiable actor, slowly and
With meditation, speak words that in the ear,
In the delicatest ear of the mind, repeat,
Exactly, that which it wants to hear, at the sound *15*
Of which, an invisible audience listens,
Not to the play, but to itself, expressed
In an emotion as of two people, as of two
Emotions becoming one. The actor is
A metaphysician in the dark, twanging *20*
An instrument, twanging a wiry string that gives
Sounds passing through sudden rightnesses, wholly
Containing the mind, below which it cannot descend,
Beyond which it has no will to rise.
It must *25*
Be the finding of a satisfaction, and may
Be of a man skating, a woman dancing, a woman
Combing. The poem of the act of the mind.

1942

Questions

1. What does the phrase "finding what will suffice" mean? Suffice for what? Where does the poet explain what happens when the mind finds what it is looking for?
2. Once the mind did not have to find, the poet says, because the scene was set and a script was available; then, he goes on, "the theatre was changed." Does he mean that the world has changed? That attitudes are different from what they used to be? What does the "script" stand for?
3. Can you explain in your own words the unifying effect that the poet describes in lines 15–19?

Junk

RICHARD WILBUR

Huru Welandes
worc ne geswiceð
monna ænigum
ðara ðe Mimming can
heardne gehealdan.[1]

WALDERE

An axe angles
from my neighbor's ashcan;
It is hell's handiwork,
the wood not hickory,
The flow of the grain
not faithfully followed.
The shivered shaft
rises from a shellheap
Of plastic playthings,
paper plates,
And the sheer shards
of shattered tumblers
That were not annealed
for the time needful.
At the same curbside,
a cast-off cabinet
Of wavily-warped
unseasoned wood
Waits to be trundled
in the trash-man's truck.
Haul them off! Hide them!
The heart winces
For junk and gimcrack,
for jerrybuilt things
And the men who make them
for a little money,
Bartering pride
like the bought boxer
Who pulls his punches,
or the paid-off jockey
Who in the home stretch
holds in his horse.
Yet the things themselves
in thoughtless honor
Have kept composure,
like captives who would not
Talk under torture.
Tossed from a tailgate
Where the dump displays

[1] *"The epigraph, taken from a fragmentary Anglo-Saxon poem, concerns the legendary smith Wayland, and may be roughly translated: 'Truly, Wayland's handiwork—the sword Mimming which he made—will never fail any man who knows how to use it bravely.'" (Wilbur.)*

its random dolmens,[2]
Its black barrows[3]
and blazing valleys,
They shall waste in the weather
toward what they were.
The sun shall glory
in the glitter of glass-chips,
Foreseeing the salvage
of the prisoned sand,
And the blistering paint
peel off in patches,
That the good grain
be discovered again.
Then burnt, bulldozed,
they shall all be buried
To the depth of diamonds,
in the making dark
Where halt Hephaestus[4]
keeps his hammer
And Wayland's work
is worn away.

1957

[2] *Dolmens are prehistoric monuments, thought to be tombs.*
[3] *Burial mounds.*
[4] *Hephaestus is the god of fire and of metalworking. He was lame ("halt").*

Questions

1. In what sense or senses does Wilbur use the word "junk"?
2. Can you determine why the poet feels so strongly about poor workmanship? Is good workmanship connected in his mind with some sort of integrity? What does it have to do, if anything, with man's feeling for nature?

TOPICS FOR COMPOSITION

1. Present the main ideas of part 1 of "An Essay on Criticism" in a theme of about 500 words.
2. Analyze the general idea of beauty implicit in Keats's description of the Grecian urn.
3. Write a theme in which you describe the feelings or associations which certain lines in "Kubla Khan" have evoked in you.

4. Write your own interpretation of the symbolic meaning of any part of "Kubla Khan."
5. Do you consider Hopkins' analysis of artistic inspiration to be satisfactory? Present your answer, and your reasons for it, in a theme.
6. Why does Yeats deliberately exaggerate the difference between nature and art in "Sailing to Byzantium"? Does he have mixed feelings about leaving the country of the young for the "holy city"? If so, how is this ambivalence conveyed? Use these questions as a starting point for an analysis of the poet's treatment of the relation between art and nature.
7. Write on the subject of what poetry can or ought to express, according to one or more of the poets of this section.
8. Archibald MacLeish says that poets have been deserted by the world. Is that true? Is art of any kind very important nowadays? What is the most important art of our time? Present your own opinions about these matters in an essay.
9. Is it true that people have private symbols, perhaps without being aware of it? Are abstract or general terms like friendship, religion, success, death, and nature associated for you with images or pictures that might be called symbols? Write an essay on this subject.
10. Does the idea of a mountain have symbolic meaning for most people? An eagle? A rainbow? A spring or fountain? An H-bomb? Write an essay on common symbols.
11. Is there any evidence that D. H. Lawrence's desire for new realms of consciousness has been shared in recent years? If you think so, write an article on the subject.
12. Write an essay on the causes and effects of shoddy workmanship.
13. Critics have disagreed about the meaning of the phrase, "Beauty is truth, truth beauty," in Keats's "Ode on a Grecian Urn." Explain in an essay what you guess to be the meaning of the words in context.
14. Write an essay in which you work out Stevens' theater analogy.
15. Write a theme comparing or contrasting any two of the conceptions of poetry expressed in the poems of this unit.
16. Write an essay comparing two modes of expression, such as poetry and music, or the novel and the cinema.

PART SIX

In View of Death

Of all the wide range of man's experience, the inevitable fact of death necessarily remains the most mysterious. Hamlet spoke eloquently for all mankind in calling death "The undiscovered country, from whose bourn / No traveller returns. . . ." In view of death, man stands before a great mystery. He may confront it with the support of a religious faith which promises him a life after death, but he cannot postulate the lineaments of that other life. Whether he invests death with religious significance as the avenue to immortality, whether he chooses to reflect upon it morbidly with all the associations of the grave and the shroud and the body's dissolution, or whether he more objectively considers death merely a natural fact inherent in an order of physical law, man inevitably must view death as a culmination of life—a culmination which one way or another must give his life meaning. But whatever the kind of explanation or however varied the response, the awareness of death calls forth from writers their most eloquent declarations.

In an essay, "Despair is 'The Sickness Unto Death,'" Soren Kierkegaard takes a view of death that does not depend on death's physical manifestation, but, rather, questions the meaning of life. To illuminate Kierkegaard's discussion, we should agree that the single most important indication of life is embodied in the individual's ability to hope. If, then, hope denotes life, despair is, at the least, "the sickness unto death." At the most, despair is a death of a far worse kind, for where the simple fact of physical death may not negate hope, despair does. When all is negative, only nothingness remains. "Crito" is a dialogue between Socrates and his friend, in which Plato relates the argument by which Socrates patiently and logically teaches Crito the immortality of the just soul. In the same sense that death does not depend on physical being for its manifestation (Kierkegaard's despair), life does not depend on physical being for its continuance. Thus it is when Socrates is confronted with an even more dreadful danger than loss of life, he chooses death rather than destroy his immortal soul; hence, Socrates says, "not life, but a good life is to be chiefly valued."

Where Kierkegaard's essay treats the philosophy of despair, Ernest Hemingway's tightly written story, "A Clean, Well-Lighted Place," brings the reader directly into contact with despair. Furthermore, Hemingway confirms the everyday incidence of despair by centering his story around a commonplace situation and by characterizing a figure neither markedly wise nor markedly tragic. It is, consequently, the waiter's attitude toward life that gives the story force. If, indeed, the waiter is in despair and encounters nothingness (and we cannot minimize the depth of his profane indictment), his need for a clean, well-lighted place pathetically emphasizes the tragedy of despair. The other two short stories in this unit, John Cheever's "Torch Song" and Ambrose Bierce's "Parker Adderson, Philosopher," deal with the moment of physical death. Cheever's story probes the character of one who is obsessed with death, one literally in love with death. Bierce's story, like Plato's dialogue between Socrates and Crito, is, for the most part, a conversation between a man facing death and another for whom death is not as immediately imminent. Like Socrates, Parker Adderson postures a calm philosophical attitude toward his impending death. There, however, the similarities end.

Sophocles' Oedipus Rex, *considered narrowly, is not a play about death. However, Thebes is pervaded by a kind of mortal sickness. Death is in the air as Oedipus pursues his inevitable and tragic catastrophe. And by his farewell to the world, symbolized by his self-inflicted blindness and exile, Oedipus accepts a death-in-life that is far more dramatically appropriate than mere physical death.*

The Essay

KIERKEGAARD's discussion of despair is in one sense remarkable because of the intensity that he is able to sustain. An examination of his style shows:

1. Tight sentence transitions achieved mainly through the repetition of key words
2. Tight paragraph transitions achieved primarily by repeating a key idea from the preceding paragraph

Despair Is "The Sickness Unto Death"

SOREN KIERKEGAARD

The concept of the sickness unto death must be understood, however, in a peculiar sense. Literally it means a sickness the end and outcome of which is death. Thus one speaks of a mortal sickness as synonymous with a sickness unto death. In this sense despair cannot be called the sickness unto death. But in the Christian understanding of it death itself is a transition unto life. In view of this, there is from the Christian standpoint no earthly, bodily sickness unto death. For death is doubtless the last phase of the sickness, but death is not the last thing. If in the strictest sense we are to speak of a sickness unto death, it must be one in which the last thing is death, and death the last thing. And this precisely is despair.

Yet in another and still more definite sense despair is the sickness unto death. It is indeed very far from being true that, literally understood, one dies of this sickness, or that this sickness ends with bodily death. On the contrary, the torment of despair is precisely this, not to be able to die. So it has much in common with the situation of the moribund when he lies and struggles with death, and cannot die. So to be sick *unto* death is, not to be able to die—yet not as though there were hope of life; no, the hopelessness in this case is that even the last hope, death, is not available. When death is the greatest danger, one hopes for life; but when one becomes acquainted with an even more dreadful danger, one hopes for death. So when the danger is so great that death has become one's hope, despair is the disconsolateness of not being able to die.

It is in this last sense that despair is the sickness unto death, this agonizing contradiction, this sickness in the self, everlastingly to die, to die and yet not to die, to die the death. For dying means that it is all over, but dying the death means to live to experience death; and if for a single instant this experience is possible, it is tantamount to experiencing it forever. If one might die of despair as one dies of a sickness, then the eternal in him, the self, must be capable of dying in the same sense that the body dies of sickness. But this is an impossibility; the dying of despair transforms itself constantly into a living. The despairing man cannot die; no more than "the dagger can slay thoughts" can despair consume the eternal thing, the self, which is the ground of despair, whose worm dieth not, and whose fire is not quenched. Yet despair is precisely *self*-consuming, but it is an impotent self-consumption which is not able to do what it wills; and this impotence is a new form of self-consumption, in which again, however, the despairer is not able to do what he wills, namely, to consume himself. This is despair raised to a higher potency, or it is the law for the potentiation. This is the hot incitement, or the cold fire in despair, the gnawing canker whose movement is constantly inward, deeper and deeper, in impotent self-consumption. The fact that despair does not consume him is so far from being any comfort to the despairing man that it is precisely the opposite, this comfort is precisely the torment, it is precisely this that keeps the gnawing pain alive and keeps life in the pain. This precisely is the reason why he despairs—not to say despaired—because he cannot consume himself, cannot get rid of himself, cannot become nothing. This is the potentiated formula for despair, the rising of the fever in the sickness of the self.

A despairing man is in despair over *something*. So it seems for an instant, but only for an instant; that same instant the true despair manifests itself, or despair manifests itself in its true character. For in the fact that he despaired of *something*, he really despaired of himself, and now would be rid of himself. Thus when the ambitious man whose watchword was "Either Caesar or nothing" does not become Caesar, he is in despair thereat. But this signifies something else, namely, that precisely because he did not become Caesar he now cannot endure to be himself. So properly he is not in despair over the fact that he did not become Caesar, but he is in despair over himself for the fact that he did not become Caesar. This self which, had he become Caesar, would have been to him a sheer delight (though in another sense equally in despair), this self is now absolutely intolerable to him. In a profounder sense it is not the fact that he did not become Caesar which is intolerable to him, but the self which did not become Caesar is the thing that is intolerable; or, more correctly, what is intolerable to him is that he cannot get rid of himself. If he had become Caesar he would have been rid of himself in desperation, but now that he did not become Caesar he cannot in desperation get rid of himself. Essentially he is equally in despair in either case, for he does not possess himself, he is not himself. By becoming Caesar he would not after all have become himself but have got rid of himself, and by not becoming Caesar he falls into despair over the fact that he cannot get rid of himself. Hence it is a superficial view (which presumably has never seen a person in despair, not even one's own self) when it is said of a man in despair, "He is consuming himself." For precisely this it is he despairs of, and to his torment it is precisely this he cannot do, since by despair fire has entered into something that cannot burn, or cannot burn up, that is, into the self.

So to despair over something is not yet properly despair. It is the beginning, or it is as when the physician says of a sickness that it has not yet declared itself. The next step is the declared despair, despair over oneself. A young girl is in despair over love, and so she despairs over her lover, because he died, or because he was unfaithful to her. This is not a declared despair; no, she is in despair over herself. This self of hers, which, if it had become "his" beloved, she would have been rid of in the most blissful way, or would have lost, this self is now a torment to her when it has to be a self without "him"; this self which would have been to her her riches (though in another sense equally in despair) has now become to her a loathsome void, since "he" is dead, or it has become to her an abhorrence, since it reminds her of the fact that she was betrayed. Try it now, say to such a girl, "Thou art consuming thyself," and thou shalt hear her reply, "Oh, no, the torment is precisely this, that I cannot do it."

To despair over oneself, in despair to will to be rid of oneself, is the formula for all despair, and hence the second form of despair (in despair at willing to be oneself) can be followed back to the first (in despair at not willing to be oneself), just as in the foregoing we resolved the first into the second. A despairing man wants despairingly to be himself. But if he despairingly wants to be himself, he will not want to get rid of himself. Yes, so it seems; but if one inspects more closely, one perceives that after all the contradiction is the same. That self which he despairingly wills to be is a self which he is not (for to will to be that self which one truly is, is indeed the opposite of despair); what he really wills is to tear his self away from the Power which constituted it. But notwithstanding all his despair, this he is unable to do, notwithstanding all the efforts of despair, that Power is the stronger, and it compells him to be the self he does not will to be. But for all that he wills to be rid of himself, to be rid of the self which he is, in order to be the self he himself has chanced to choose. To be *self* as he wills to be would be his delight (though in another sense it would be equally in despair), but to be compelled to be *self* as he does not will to be is his torment, namely, that he cannot get rid of himself.

Socrates proved the immortality of the soul from the fact that the sickness of the soul (sin) does not consume it as sickness of the body consumes the body. So also we can demonstrate the eternal in man from the fact that despair cannot consume his self, that this precisely is the torment of contradiction in despair. If there were nothing eternal in a man, he could not despair; but if despair could consume his self, there would still be no despair.

Thus it is that despair, this sickness in the self, is the sickness unto death. The despairing man is mortally ill. In an entirely different sense than can appropriately be said of any disease, we may say that the sickness has attacked the noblest part; and yet the man cannot die. Death is not the last phase of the sickness, but death is continually the last. To be delivered from this sickness by death is an impossibility, for the sickness and its torment . . . and death consist in not being able to die.

This is the situation in despair. And however thoroughly it eludes the attention of the despairer, and however thoroughly the despairer may succeed (as in the case of that kind of despair which is characterized by unawareness of being in despair) in losing himself entirely, and losing himself in such a way that it is not noticed in the least—eternity nevertheless will make it manifest that his situation was despair, and it will so nail him to himself that the torment nevertheless remains that he cannot get rid of himself, and it becomes manifest that he was deluded in thinking that he succeeded. And thus it is eternity must act, because to have a self, to be a self, is the greatest concession made to man, but at the same time it is eternity's demand upon him.

Questions

1. What is the torment of despair? How does Kierkegaard develop this point as it relates to life? Explain the contradictions the author presents.
2. What is the contradiction in the statement, "it is said of a man in despair, 'He is consuming himself' "? How does the analogy about the man who wished to be Caesar support this contradiction?

3. What methods does Kierkegaard use in fashioning his definition of despair as "the sickness unto death"?
4. Granting that the topic is a difficult one, does the author sufficiently support his thesis? In other words, what more could he do to define his use of despair? Or, perhaps you feel that he has labored the point. If so, explain how he could shorten the essay and achieve his purpose.

Topics for Composition

1. This essay not only examines a philosophical concept but also illustrates the difficulty one may encounter when writing an extended definition of an abstract term such as "despair." However, the discipline of writing extended definitions can do much to eliminate "looseness" in both thought and structure, especially if the term to be defined is an abstract one. Keeping in mind the techniques illustrated by the essay, write an extended definition of an abstract term such as "hope," "faith," "charity," "love," etc. You might wish to qualify your approach, as does Kierkegaard; for example: "Hope is 'the breath of life.' "

ALTHOUGH this selection from Plato is not properly an essay, the dialogue as a form of teaching and persuasion is worthy of our attention. Note the way in which Socrates:

1. Allows Crito to state his position fully
2. Enlists Crito as a cothinker in solving the problem
3. Poses one specific point at a time from the overall problem
4. Encourages Crito to present opposing views
5. Systematically forces Crito to share in the refutation of each opposing idea

Crito

PLATO

Persons of the Dialogue

SOCRATES

CRITO

SCENE *The Prison of Socrates*

Socrates. Why have you come at this hour, Crito? it must be quite early?

Crito. Yes, certainly.

Socrates. What is the exact time?

Crito. The dawn is breaking.

Socrates. I wonder that the keeper of the prison would let you in.

Crito. He knows me, because I often come, Socrates; moreover, I have done him a kindness.

Socrates. And are you only just come?

Crito. No, I came some time ago.

Socrates. Then why did you sit and say nothing, instead of awakening me at once?

Crito. Why, indeed, Socrates, I myself would rather not have all this sleeplessness and sorrow. But I have been wondering at your peaceful slumbers, and that was the reason why I did not awaken you, because I wanted you to be out of pain. I have always thought you happy in the calmness of your temperament; but never did I see the like of the easy, cheerful way in which you bear this calamity.

Socrates. Why, Crito, when a man has reached my age he ought not to be repining at the prospect of death.

Crito. And yet other old men find themselves in similar misfortunes, and age does not prevent them from repining.

Socrates. That may be. But you have not told me why you come at this early hour.

Crito. I come to bring you a message which is sad and painful; not, as I believe, to yourself, but to all of us who are your friends, and saddest of all to me.

Socrates. What! I suppose that the ship has come from Delos, on the arrival of which I am to die?

Crito. No, the ship has not actually arrived, but she will probably be here to-day, as persons who have come from Sunium tell me that they left her there; and therefore to-morrow, Socrates, will be the last day of your life.

Socrates. Very well, Crito; if such is the will of God, I am willing; but my belief is that there will be a delay of a day.

Crito. Why do you say this?

Socrates. I will tell you. I am to die on the day after the arrival of the ship?

Crito. Yes; that is what the authorities say.

Socrates. But I do not think that the ship will be here until tomorrow; this I gather from a vision which I had last night, or rather only just now, when you fortunately allowed me to sleep.

Crito. And what was the nature of the vision?

Socrates. There came to me the likeness of a woman, fair and comely, clothed in white raiment, who called to me and said: O Socrates,

"The third day hence to Phthia shalt thou go."

Crito. What a singular dream, Socrates!

Socrates. There can be no doubt about the meaning, Crito, I think.

Crito. Yes; the meaning is only too clear. But, Oh! my beloved Socrates, let me entreat you once more to take my advice and escape. For if you die I shall not only lose a friend who can never be replaced, but there is another evil: people who do not know you and me will believe that I might have saved you if I had been willing to give money, but that I did not care. Now, can there be a worse disgrace than this—that I should be thought to value money more than the life of a friend? For the many will not be persuaded that I wanted you to escape, and that you refused.

Socrates. But why, my dear Crito, should we care about the opinion of the many? Good men, and they are the only persons who are worth considering, will think of these things truly as they happened.

Crito. But do you see, Socrates, that the opinion of the many must be regarded, as is evident in your own case, because they can do the very greatest evil to any one who has lost their good opinion.

Socrates. I only wish, Crito, that they could; for then they could also do the greatest good, and that would be well. But the truth is, that they can do neither good nor evil: they can not make a man wise or make him foolish; and whatever they do is the result of chance.

Crito. Well, I will not dispute about that; but please to tell me, Socrates, whether you are not acting out of regard to me and your other friends: are you not afraid that if you escape hence we may get into trouble with the informers for having stolen you away, and lose either the whole or a great part of our property; or that even a worse evil may happen to us? Now, if this is your fear, be at ease; for in order to save you, we ought surely to run this, or even a greater risk; be persuaded, then, and do as I say.

Socrates. Yes, Crito, that is one fear which you mention, but by no means the only one.

Crito. Fear not. There are persons who at no great cost are willing to save you and bring you out of prison; and as for the informers, you may observe that they are far from being exorbitant in their demands; a little money will satisfy them. My means, which, as I am sure, are ample, are at your service, and if you have a scruple about spending all mine, here are strangers who will give you the use of theirs; and one of them, Simmias the Theban, has brought a sum of money for this very purpose; and Cebes and many others are willing to spend their money too. I say therefore, do not on that account hesitate about making your escape, and do not say, as you did in the court, that you will have a difficulty in knowing what to do with yourself if you escape. For men will love you in other places to which you may go, and not in Athens only; there are friends of mine in Thessaly, if you like to go to them, who will value and protect you, and no Thessalian will give you any trouble. Nor can I think that you are justified, Socrates, in betraying your own life when you might be saved; this is playing into the hands of your enemies and destroyers; and moreover I should say that you were betraying your children; for you might bring them up and educate them; instead of which you go away and leave them, and they will have to take their chance; and if they do not meet with the usual fate of orphans, there will be small thanks to you. No man should bring children into the world who is unwilling to persevere to the end in their nurture and education. But you are choosing the easier part, as I think, not the better and manlier, which would rather have become one who professes virtue in all his actions, like yourself. And indeed, I am ashamed not only of you, but of us who are your friends, when I reflect that this entire business of yours will be attributed to our want of courage. The trial need never have come on, or might have been brought to another issue; and the end of all, which is the crowning absurdity, will seem to have been permitted by us, through cowardice and baseness, who might have saved you, as you might have saved yourself, if we had been good for anything (for there was no difficulty in escaping), and we did not see how disgraceful, Socrates, and also miserable all this will be to us as well as to you. Make your mind up then, or rather have your mind already made up, for the time of deliberation is over, and there is only one thing to be done, which must be done, if at all, this very night, and which any delay will render all but impossible; I beseech you therefore, Socrates, to be persuaded by me, and to do as I say.

Socrates. Dear Crito, your zeal is invaluable, if a right one; but if wrong, the greater the zeal the greater the evil; and therefore we ought to consider whether these things shall be done or not. For I am and always have been one of those natures who must be guided by reason, whatever the reason may be which upon reflection appears to me to be the best; and now that this fortune has come upon me, I can not put away the reasons which I have before given: the principles which I have hitherto honored and revered I still honor, and unless we can find other and better principles on the instant, I am certain not to agree with you; no, not even if the power of the multitude could inflict many more imprisonments, confiscations, deaths, frightening us like children with hobgoblin terrors. But what will be the fairest way of considering the question? Shall I return to your old argument about the opinions of men? some of which are to be regarded, and others, as we were saying, are not to be regarded. Now were we right in maintaining this before I was condemned? And has the argument which was once good now proved to be talk for the sake of talking;—in fact an amusement only, and altogether vanity? That is what I want to consider with your help, Crito:—whether, under my present circumstances, the argument appears to be in any way different or not; and is to be allowed by me or disallowed. That argument, which, as I believe, is maintained by many who assume to be authorities, was to the effect, as I was saying, that the opinions of some men are to be regarded, and of other men not to be regarded. Now you, Crito, are a disinterested person who are not going to die to-morrow—at least, there is no human probability of this, and you are therefore not liable to be deceived by the circumstances in which you are placed. Tell me then, whether I am right in saying that some opinions, and the opinions of some men only, are to be valued, and other opinions, and the opinions of other men, are not to be valued. I ask you whether I was right in maintaining this?

Crito. Certainly.

Socrates. The good are to be regarded, and not the bad?

Crito. Yes.

Socrates. And the opinions of the wise are good, and the opinions of the unwise are evil?

Crito. Certainly.

Socrates. And what was said about another matter? Was the disciple in gymnastics supposed to attend to the praise and blame and opinion of every man, or of one man only—his physician or trainer, whoever that was?

Crito. Of one man only.

Socrates. And he ought to fear the censure and welcome the praise of that one only, and not of the many?

Crito. That is clear.

Socrates. And he ought to live and train, and eat and drink in the way which seems good to his single master who has understanding, rather than according to the opinion of all other men put together?

Crito. True.

Socrates. And if he disobeys and disregards the opinion and approval of the one, and regards the opinion of the many who have no understanding, will he not suffer evil?

Crito. Certainly he will.

Socrates. And what will the evil be, whither tending and what affecting, in the disobedient person?

Crito. Clearly, affecting the body; that is what is destroyed by the evil.

Socrates. Very good; and is not this true, Crito, of other things which we need not separately enumerate? In the matter of just and unjust, fair and foul, good and evil, which are the subjects of our present consultation, ought we to follow the opinion of the many and to fear them; or the opinion of the one man who has understanding, and whom we ought to fear and reverence more than all the rest of the world: and whom deserting we shall destroy and injure that principle in us which may be assumed to be improved by justice and deteriorated by injustice;—is there not such a principle?

Crito. Certainly there is, Socrates.

Socrates. Take a parallel instance:—if, acting under the advice of men who have no understanding, we destroy that which is improvable by health and deteriorated by disease—when that has been destroyed, I say, would life be worth having? And that is—the body?

Crito. Yes.

Socrates. Could we live, having an evil and corrupted body?

Crito. Certainly not.

Socrates. And will life be worth having, if that higher part of man be depraved, which is improved by justice and deteriorated by injustice? Do we suppose that principle, whatever it may be in man, which has to do with justice and injustice, to be inferior to the body?

Crito. Certainly not.

Socrates. More honored, then?

Crito. Far more honored.

Socrates. Then, my friend, we must not regard what the many say of us: but what he, the one man who has understanding of just and unjust, will say, and what the truth will say. And therefore you begin in error when you suggest that we should regard the opinion of the many about just and unjust, good and evil, honorable and dishonorable.—Well, some one will say, "but the many can kill us."

Crito. Yes, Socrates; that will clearly be the answer.

Socrates. That is true: but still I find with surprise that the old argument is, as I conceive, unshaken as ever. And I should like to know whether I may say the same of another proposition—that not life, but a good life, is to be chiefly valued?

Crito. Yes, that also remains.

Socrates. And a good life is equivalent to a just and honorable one —that holds also?

Crito. Yes, that holds.

Socrates. From these premises I proceed to argue the question whether I ought or ought not to try and escape without the consent of the Athenians: and if I am clearly right in escaping, then I will make the attempt; but if not, I will abstain. The other considerations which you mention, of money and loss of character and the duty of educating children, are, as I fear, only the doctrines of the multitude, who would be as ready to call people to life, if they were able, as they are to put them to death—and with as little reason. But now, since the argument has thus far prevailed, the only question which remains to be considered is, whether we shall do rightly either in escaping or in suffering others to aid in our escape and paying them in money and thanks, or whether we shall not do rightly; and if the latter, then death or any other calamity which may ensue on my remaining here must not be allowed to enter into the calculation.

Crito. I think that you are right, Socrates; how then shall we proceed?

Socrates. Let us consider the matter together, and do you either refute me if you can, and I will be convinced; or else cease, my dear friend, from repeating to me that I ought to escape against the wishes of the Athenians: for I am extremely desirous to be persuaded by you, but not against my own better judgment. And now please to consider my first position, and do your best to answer me.

Crito. I will do my best.

Socrates. Are we to say that we are never intentionally to do wrong, or that in one way we ought and in another way we ought not to do wrong, or is doing wrong always evil and dishonorable, as I was just now saying, and as has been already acknowledged by us? Are all our former admissions which were made within a few days to be thrown away? And have we, at our age, been earnestly discoursing with one another all our life long only to discover that we are no better than children? Or are we to rest assured, in spite of the opinion of the many, and in spite of consequences whether better or worse, of the truth of what was then said, that injustice is always an evil and dishonor to him who acts unjustly? Shall we affirm that?

Crito. Yes.

Socrates. Then we must do no wrong?

Crito. Certainly not.

Socrates. Nor when injured injure in return, as the many imagine; for we must injure no one at all?

Crito. Clearly not.

Socrates. Again, Crito, may we do evil?

Crito. Surely not, Socrates.

Socrates. And what of doing evil in return for evil, which is the morality of the many—is that just or not?

Crito. Not just.

Socrates. For doing evil to another is the same as injuring him?

Crito. Very true.

Socrates. Then we ought not to retaliate or render evil for evil to any one, whatever evil we may have suffered from him. But I would have you consider, Crito, whether you really mean what you are saying. For this opinion has never been held, and never will be held, by any considerable number of persons; and those who are agreed and those who are not agreed upon this point have no common ground, and can only despise one another when they see how widely they differ. Tell me, then, whether you agree with and assent to my first principle, that neither injury nor retaliation nor warding off evil by evil is ever right. And shall that be the premiss of our argument? Or do you decline and dissent from this? For this has been of old and is still my opinion; but, if you are of another opinion, let me hear what you have to say. If, however, you remain of the same mind as formerly, I will proceed to the next step.

Crito. You may proceed, for I have not changed my mind.

Socrates. Then I will proceed to the next step, which may be put in the form of a question:—Ought a man to do what he admits to be right, or ought he to betray the right?

Crito. He ought to do what he thinks right.

Socrates. But if this is true, what is the application? In leaving the prison against the will of the Athenians, do I wrong any? or rather do I not wrong those whom I ought least to wrong? Do I not desert the principles which were acknowledged by us to be just? What do you say?

Crito. I can not tell, Socrates; for I do not know.

Socrates. Then consider the matter in this way:—Imagine that I am about to play truant (you may call the proceeding by any name which you like), and the laws and the government come and interrogate me: "Tell us, Socrates," they say; "what are you about? are you going by an act of yours to overturn us—the laws and the whole state, as far as in you lies? Do you imagine that a state can subsist and not be overthrown, in which the decisions of law have no power, but are set aside and overthrown by individuals?" What will be our answer, Crito, to these and the like words? Any one, and especially a clever rhetorician, will have a good deal to urge about the evil of setting aside the law which requires a sentence to be carried out; and we might reply, "Yes; but the state has injured us and given an unjust sentence." Suppose I say that?

Crito. Very good, Socrates.

Socrates. "And was that our agreement with you?" the law would say; "or were you to abide by the sentence of the state?" And if I were to express astonishment at their saying this, the law would probably add: "Answer, Socrates, instead of opening your eyes: you are in the habit of asking and answering questions. Tell us what complaint you have to make against us which justifies you in attempting to destroy us and the state? In the first place did we not bring you into existence? Your father married your mother by our aid and begat you. Say whether you have any objection to urge against those of us who regulate marriage?" None, I should reply. "Or against those of us who regulate the system of nurture and education of children in which you were trained? Were not the laws, who have the charge of this, right in commanding your father to train you in music and gymnastic?" Right, I should reply. "Well then, since you were brought into the world and nurtured and educated by us, can you deny in the first place that you are our child and slave, as your fathers were before you? And if this is true you are not on equal terms with us; nor can you think that you have a right to do to us what we are doing to you. Would you have any right to strike or revile or do any other evil to a father or to your master, if you had one, when you have been struck or reviled by him, or received some other evil at his hands? —you would not say this? And because we think right to destroy you, do you think that you have any right to destroy us in return, and your country as far as in you lies? And will you, O professor of true virtue, say that you are justified in this? Has a philosopher like you failed to discover that our country is more to be valued and higher and holier far than mother or father or any ancestor, and more to be regarded in the eyes of the gods and of men of understanding? also to be soothed, and gently and reverently entreated when angry, even more than a father, and if not persuaded, obeyed? And when we are punished by her, whether with imprisonment or stripes, the punishment is to be endured in silence; and if she lead us to wounds or death in battle, thither we follow as is right; neither may any one yield or retreat or leave his rank, but whether in battle or in a court of law, or in any other place, he must do what his city and his country order him; or he must change their view of what is just: and if he may do no violence to his father or mother, much less may he do violence to his country." What answer shall we make to this, Crito? Do the laws speak truly, or do they not?

Crito. I think that they do.

Socrates. Then the laws will say: "Consider, Socrates, if this is true, that in your present attempt you are going to do us wrong. For, after having brought you into the world, and nurtured and educated you, and given you and every other citizen a share in every good that we had to give, we further proclaim and give the right to every Athenian, that if he does not like us when he has come of age and has seen the ways of the city, and made our acquaintance, he may go where he pleases and take his goods with him; and none of us laws will forbid him or interfere with him. Any of you who does not like us and the city, and who wants to go to a colony or to any other city, may go where he likes, and take his goods with him. But he who has experience of the manner in which we order justice and administer the state, and still remains, has entered into an implied contract that he will do as we command him. And he who disobeys us is, as we maintain, thrice wrong; first, because in disobeying us he is disobeying his parents; secondly, because we are the authors of his education; thirdly, because he has made an agreement with us that he will duly obey our commands; and he neither obeys them nor convinces us that our commands are wrong; and we do not rudely impose them, but give them the alternative of obeying or convincing us;—that is what we offer, and he does neither. These are the sort of accusations to which, as we were saying, you, Socrates, will be exposed if you accomplish your intentions; you, above all other Athenians." Suppose I ask, why is this? they will justly retort upon me that I above all other men have acknowledged the agreement. "There is clear proof," they will say, "Socrates, that we and the city were not displeasing to you. Of all Athenians you have been the most constant resident in the city, which, as you never leave, you may be supposed to love. For you never went out of the city either to see the games, except once when you went to the Isthmus, or to any other place unless when you were on military service; nor did you travel as other men do. Nor had you any curiosity to know other states or their laws: your affections did not go beyond us and our state; we were your special favorites, and you acquiesced in our government of you; and this is the state in which you begat your children, which is a proof of your satisfaction. Moreover, you might, if you had liked, have fixed the penalty at banishment in the course of the trial—the state which refuses to let you go now would have let you go then. But you pretended that you preferred death to exile, and that you were not grieved at death. And now you have forgotten these fine sentiments, and pay no respect to us the laws, of whom you are the destroyer; and are doing what only a miserable slave would do, running away and turning your back upon the compacts and agreements which you made as a citizen. And first of all answer this very question: Are we right in saying that you agreed to be governed according to us in deed, and not in word only? Is that true or not?" How shall we answer that, Crito? Must we not agree?

Crito. There is no help, Socrates.

Socrates. Then will they not say: "You, Socrates, are breaking the covenants and agreements which you made with us at your leisure, not in any haste or under any compulsion or deception, but having had seventy years to think of them, during which time you were at liberty to leave the city, if we were not to your mind, or if our covenants appeared to you to be unfair. You had your choice, and might have gone either to Lacedaemon or Crete, which you often praise for their good government, or to some other Hellenic or foreign state. Whereas you, above all other Athenians, seemed to be so fond of the state, or, in other words, of us her laws (for who would like a state that has no laws), that you never stirred out of her; the halt, the blind, the maimed were not more stationary in her than you were. And now you run away and forsake your agreements. Not so, Socrates, if you will take our advice; do not make yourself ridiculous by escaping out of the city.

"For just consider, if you transgress and err in this sort of way, what good will you do either to yourself or to your friends? That your friends will be driven into exile and deprived of citizenship, or will lose their property, is tolerably certain; and you yourself, if you fly to one of the neighboring cities, as, for example, Thebes or Megara, both of which are well-governed cities, will come to them as an enemy, Socrates, and their government will be against you, and all patriotic citizens will cast an evil eye upon you as a subverter of the laws, and you will confirm in the minds of the judges the justice of their own condemnation of you. For he who is a corruptor of the laws is more than likely to be corruptor of the young and foolish portion of mankind. Will you then flee from well-ordered cities and virtuous men? and is existence worth having on these terms? Or will you go to them without shame, and talk to them, Socrates? And what will you say to them? What you say here about virtue and justice and institutions and laws being the best things among men. Would that be decent of you? Surely not. But if you go away from well-governed states to Crito's friends in Thessaly, where there is a great disorder and license, they will be charmed to have the tale of your escape from prison, set off with ludicrous particulars of the manner in which you were wrapped in a goatskin or some other disguise, and metamorphosed as the fashion of runaways is—that is very likely; but will there be no one to remind you that in your old age you violated the most sacred laws from a miserable desire of a little more life. Perhaps not, if you keep them in a good temper; but if they are out of temper you will hear many degrading things; you will live, but how?—as the flatterer of all men, and the servant of all men; and doing what?—eating and drinking in Thessaly, having gone abroad in order that you may get a dinner. And where will be your fine sentiments about justice and virtue then? Say that you wish to live for the sake of your children, that you may bring them up and educate them—will you take them into Thessaly and deprive them of Athenian citizenship? Is that the benefit which you would confer upon them? Or are you under the impression that they will be better cared for and educated here if you are still alive, although absent from them; for that your friends will take care of them? Do you fancy that if you are an inhabitant of Thessaly they will take care of them, and if you are an inhabitant of the other world they will not take care of them? Nay; but if they who call themselves friends are truly friends, they surely will.

"Listen, then, Socrates, to us who have brought you up. Think not of life and children first, and of justice afterwards, but of justice first, that you may be justified before the princes of the world below. For neither will you nor any that belong to you be happier or holier or juster in this life, or happier in another, if you do as Crito bids. Now you depart in innocence, a sufferer and not a doer of evil; a victim, not of the laws, but of men. But if you go forth, returning evil for evil, and injury for injury, breaking the covenants and agreements which you have made with us, and wronging those whom you ought least to wrong, that is to say, yourself, your friends, your country, and us, we shall be angry with you while you live, and our brethren, the laws in the world below, will receive you as an enemy; for they will know that you have done your best to destroy us. Listen, then, to us and not to Crito."

This is the voice which I seem to hear murmuring in my ears, like the sound of the flute in the ears of the mystic; that voice, I say, is humming in my ears, and prevents me from hearing any other. And I know that anything more which you may say will be vain. Yet speak, if you have anything to say.

Crito. I have nothing to say, Socrates.

Socrates. Then let me follow the intimations of the will of God.

Questions

1. Socrates' discussion with Crito shows the "Socratic method" at work. What are the major points in Crito's argument? How does Socrates impose his views on the will of Crito?

2. Socrates not only teaches Crito the immortality of the just soul, but also says much about the individual's allegiance to the state. What is Socrates' position in relation to allegiance to the state? Would you accept his position? Explain.
3. What is the warning concerning the preservation of law with which Socrates concludes his discussion?

Topics for Composition

1. Write an essay comparing and/or contrasting Socrates' reasons for accepting death, with the apparent reasons for protest-deaths in various parts of the world.
2. Either support or refute allegiance to the state as more important than personal freedom. Use Thoreau's "Civil Disobedience" as additional support for your argument.
3. If we accept the fact that Socrates was a great teacher and an intellectual leader among his people, we may decide that his position is a selfish one. Write an argument based on this view.

The Short Story

Hemingway's story is economically constructed, moving almost entirely through the terse conversation between the younger and the older waiter. We should note especially:

1. The lack of description except as implied by the remarks of the two waiters
2. The contrast in attitude toward life exhibited by the statements and tone employed by each waiter
3. The sense of isolation achieved by the older waiter's conversation with himself

A Clean, Well-Lighted Place

ERNEST HEMINGWAY

It was late and every one had left the café except an old man who sat in the shadow the leaves of the tree made against the electric light. In the daytime the street was dusty, but at night the dew settled the dust and the old man liked to sit late because he was deaf and now at night it was quiet and he felt the difference. The two waiters inside the café knew that the old man was a little drunk, and while he was a good client they knew that if he became too drunk he would leave without paying, so they kept watch on him.

"Last week he tried to commit suicide," one waiter said.

"Why?"

"He was in despair."

"What about?"

"Nothing."

"How do you know it was nothing?"

"He has plenty of money."

They sat together at a table that was close against the wall near the door of the café and looked at the terrace where the tables were all empty except where the old man sat in the shadow of the leaves of the tree that moved slightly in the wind. A girl and a soldier went by in the street. The street light shone on the brass number on his collar. The girl wore no head covering and hurried beside him.

"The guard will pick him up," one waiter said.

"What does it matter if he gets what he's after?"

"He had better get off the street now. The guard will get him. They went by five minutes ago."

The old man sitting in the shadow rapped on his saucer with his glass. The younger waiter went over to him.

"What do you want?"

The old man looked at him. "Another brandy," he said.

"You'll be drunk," the waiter said. The old man looked at him. The waiter went away.

"He'll stay all night," he said to his colleague. "I'm sleepy now. I never get into bed before three o'clock. He should have killed himself last week."

The waiter took the brandy bottle and another saucer from the counter inside the café and marched out to the old man's table. He put down the saucer and poured the glass full of brandy.

"You should have killed yourself last week," he said to the deaf man. The old man motioned with his finger. "A little more," he said. The waiter poured on into the glass so that the brandy slopped over and ran down the stem into the top saucer of the pile. "Thank you," the old man said. The waiter took the bottle back inside the café. He sat down at the table with his colleague again.

"He's drunk now," he said.

"He's drunk every night."

"What did he want to kill himself for?"

"How should I know."

"How did he do it?"

"He hung himself with a rope."

"Who cut him down?"

"His niece."

"Why did they do it?"

"Fear for his soul."

"How much money has he got?"

"He's got plenty."

"He must be eighty years old."

"Anyway I should say he was eighty."

"I wish he would go home. I never get to bed before three o'clock. What kind of hour is that to go to bed?"

"He stays up because he likes it."

"He's lonely. I'm not lonely. I have a wife waiting in bed for me."

"He had a wife once too."

"A wife would be no good to him now."

"You can't tell. He might be better with a wife."

"His niece looks after him."

"I know. You said she cut him down."

"I wouldn't want to be that old. An old man is a nasty thing."

"Not always. This old man is clean. He drinks without spilling. Even now, drunk. Look at him."

"I don't want to look at him. I wish he would go home. He has no regard for those who must work."

The old man looked from his glass across the square, then over at the waiters.

"Another brandy," he said, pointing to his glass. The waiter who was in a hurry came over.

"Finished," he said, speaking with that omission of syntax stupid people employ when talking to drunken people or foreigners. "No more tonight. Close now."

"Another," said the old man.

"No. Finished." The waiter wiped the edge of the table with a towel and shook his head.

The old man stood up, slowly counted the saucers, took a leather coin purse from his pocket and paid for the drinks, leaving half a peseta tip.

The waiter watched him go down the street, a very old man walking unsteadily but with dignity.

"Why didn't you let him stay and drink?" the unhurried waiter asked. They were putting up the shutters. "It is not half-past two."

I want to go home to bed."

"What is an hour?"

"More to me than to him."

"An hour is the same."

"You talk like an old man yourself. He can buy a bottle and drink at home."

"It's not the same."

"No, it is not," agreed the waiter with a wife. He did not wish to be unjust. He was only in a hurry.

"And you? You have no fear of going home before your usual hour?"

"Are you trying to insult me?"

"No, hombre, only to make a joke."

"No," the waiter who was in a hurry said, rising from pulling down the metal shutters. "I have confidence. I am all confidence."

"You have youth, confidence, and a job," the older waiter said. "You have everything."

"And what do you lack?"

"Everything but work."

"You have everything I have."

"No. I have never had confidence and I am not young."

"Come on. Stop talking nonsense and lock up."

"I am of those who like to stay late at the café," the older waiter said. "With all those who do not want to go to bed. With all those who need a light for the night."

"I want to go home and into bed."

"We are of two different kinds," the older waiter said. He was now dressed to go home. "It is not only a question of youth and confidence although those things are very beautiful. Each night I am reluctant to close up because there may be some one who needs the café."

"Hombre, there are bodegas open all night long."

"You do not understand. This is a clean and pleasant café. It is well lighted. The light is very good and also, now, there are shadows of the leaves."

"Good night," said the younger waiter.

"Good night," the other said. Turning off the electric light he continued the conversation with himself. It is the light of course but it is necessary that the place be clean and pleasant. You do not want music. Certainly you do not want music. Nor can you stand before a bar with dignity although that is all that is provided for these hours. What did he fear? It was not fear or dread. It was a nothing that he knew too well. It was all a nothing and a man was nothing too. It was only that and light was all it needed and a certain cleanness and order. Some lived in it and never felt it but he knew it all was nada y pues nada y nada y pues nada. Our nada who art in nada, nada be thy name thy kingdom nada thy will be nada in nada as it is in nada. Give us this nada our daily nada and nada us our nada as we nada our nadas and nada us not into nada but deliver us from nada; pues nada. Hail nothing full of nothing, nothing is with thee. He smiled and stood before a bar with a shining steam pressure coffee machine.

"What's yours?" asked the barman.

"Nada."

"Otro loco mas," said the barman and turned away.

"A little cup," said the waiter.

The barman poured it for him.

"The light is very bright and pleasant but the bar is unpolished," the waiter said.

The barman looked at him but did not answer. It was too late at night for conversation.

"You want another copita?" the barman asked.

"No, thank you," said the waiter and went out. He disliked bars and bodegas. A clean, well-lighted café was a very different thing. Now, without thinking further, he would go home to his room. He would lie in the bed and finally, with daylight, he would go to sleep. After all, he said to himself, it is probably only insomnia. Many must have it.

Questions

1. In this story, despair is visibly a mark of old age (the old man, the older waiter). What is it that the younger waiter has that wards off despair? What can we say, then, about the younger waiter, and the bartender's attitude toward the older waiter and the old man? Specifically, does youth understand age? Does age understand youth?
2. The place is clean and well-lighted. What other appeal does it have? For instance, is it attractive otherwise? Is it pervaded by warmth?
3. Do both the old man and the older waiter reveal Kierkegaard's "sickness unto death" to the same degree? Explain.
4. How does Hemingway's style (short sentences, terse conversation, limited description) complement the mood of the story?
5. Would you accept the statement that there is a magnificent dignity in despair in this story? How would you explain that dignity?

Topics for Composition

1. As we see by now, both Hemingway's story and Kierkegaard's essay present a "sickness" in modern society. Write an essay discussing man's attempts to remedy this "sickness." In other words, what have you observed in the behavior of those around you that fills the same need for them that the clean, well-lighted place fills for the waiter? In writing your essay, rely on specific observed behavior: avoid such abstract terms as "faith" and "hope."
2. Analyze Hemingway's story to show how his use of descriptive detail and motion complement the theme of despair. Keep in mind that the omission of description may in itself be a descriptive device.

CHEEVER's story turns on the ironical contrast between its title and its subject matter. Once we realize that a "torch song" is the sentimental, sweetly pathetic outpouring of unrequited love, we can see how Cheever's techniques complement the irony in his title. We should note the following:

1. The irony inherent in Cheever's reference to Joan Harris as "The Widow"
2. The sentiment attached to a period of mourning symbolized by Joan's insistence on wearing black
3. The long-suffering serenity with which Joan endures the loss of each love

Torch Song

JOHN CHEEVER

After Jack Lorey had known Joan Harris in New York for a few years, he began to think of her as The Widow. She always wore black, and he was always given the feeling, by a curious disorder in her apartment, that the undertakers had just left. This impression did not stem from malice on his part, for he was fond of Joan. They came from the same city in Ohio and had reached New York at about the same time in the middle thirties. They were the same age, and during their first summer in the city they used to meet after work and drink Martinis in places like the Brevoort and Charles', and have dinner and play checkers at the Lafayette.

Joan went to a school for models when she settled in the city, but it turned out that she photographed badly, so after spending six weeks learning how to walk with a book on her head she got a job as a hostess in a Longchamps. For the rest of the summer she stood by the hatrack, bathed in an intense pink light and the string music of heartbreak, swinging her mane of dark hair and her black skirt as she moved forward to greet the customers. She was then a big, handsome girl with a wonderful voice, and her face, her whole presence, always seemed infused with a gentle and healthy pleasure at her surroundings, whatever they were. She was innocently and incorrigibly convivial, and would get out of bed and dress at three in the morning if someone called her and asked her to come out for a drink, as Jack often did. In the fall, she got some kind of freshman executive job in a department store. They saw less and less of each other and then for quite a while stopped seeing each other altogether. Jack was living with a girl he had met at a party, and it never occurred to him to wonder what had become of Joan.

Jack's girl had some friends in Pennsylvania, and in the spring and summer of his second year in town he often went there with her for weekends. All of this—the shared apartment in the Village, the illicit relationship, the Friday-night train to a country house—were what he had imagined life in New York to be, and he was intensely happy. He was returning to New York with his girl one Sunday night on the Lehigh line. It was one of those trains that move slowly across the face of New Jersey, bringing back to the city hundreds of people, like the victims of an immense and strenuous picnic, whose faces are blazing and whose muscles are lame. Jack and his girl, like most of the other passengers, were overburdened with vegetables and flowers. When the train stopped in Pennsylvania Station, they moved with the crowd along the platform, toward the escalator. As they were passing the wide, lighted windows of the diner, Jack turned his head and saw Joan. It was the first time he had seen her since Thanksgiving, or since Christmas. He couldn't remember.

Joan was with a man who had obviously passed out. His head was in his arms on the table, and an overturned highball glass was near one of his elbows. Joan was shaking his shoulders gently and speaking to him. She seemed to be vaguely troubled, vaguely amused. The waiters had cleared off all the other tables and were standing around Joan, waiting for her to resurrect her escort. It troubled Jack to see in these straits a girl who reminded him of the trees and the lawns of his home town, but there was nothing he could do to help. Joan continued to shake the man's shoulders, and the crowd pressed Jack past one after another of the diner's windows, past the malodorous kitchen, and up the escalator.

He saw Joan again, later that summer, when he was having dinner in a Village restaurant. He was with a new girl, a Southerner. There were many Southern girls in the city that year. Jack and his belle had wandered into the restaurant because it was convenient, but the food was terrible and the place was lighted with candles. Halfway through dinner, Jack noticed Joan on the other side of the room, and when he had finished eating, he crossed the room and spoke to her. She was with a tall man who was wearing a monocle. He stood, bowed stiffly from the waist, and said to Jack, "We are very pleased to meet you." Then he excused himself and headed for the toilet. "He's a count, he's a Swedish count," Joan said. "He's on the radio, Friday afternoons at four-fifteen. Isn't it exciting?" She seemed to be delighted with the count and the terrible restaurant.

Sometime the next winter, Jack moved from the Village to an apartment in the East Thirties. He was crossing Park Avenue one cold morning on his way to the office when he noticed, in the crowd, a woman he had met a few times at Joan's apartment. He spoke to her and asked about his friend. "Haven't you heard?" she said. She pulled a long face. "Perhaps I'd better tell you. Perhaps you can help." She and Jack had breakfast in a drugstore on Madison Avenue and she unburdened herself of the story.

The count had a program called "The Song of the Fiords," or something like that, and he sang Swedish folk songs. Everyone suspected him of being a fake, but that didn't bother Joan. He had met her at a party and, sensing a soft touch, had moved in with her the following night. About a week later, he complained of pains in his back and said he must have some morphine. Then he needed morphine all the time. If he didn't get morphine, he was abusive and violent. Joan began to deal with those doctors and druggists who peddle dope, and when they wouldn't supply her, she went down to the bottom of the city. Her friends were afraid she would be found some morning stuffed in a drain. She got pregnant. She had an abortion. The count left her and moved to a flea bag near Times Square, but she was so impressed by then with his helplessness, so afraid that he would die without her, that she followed him there and shared his room and continued to buy his narcotics. He abandoned her again, and Joan waited a week for him to return before she went back to her place and her friends in the Village.

It shocked Jack to think of the innocent girl from Ohio having lived with a brutal dope addict and traded with criminals, and when he got to his office that morning, he telephoned her and made a date for dinner that night. He met her at Charles'. When she came into the bar, she seemed as wholesome and calm as ever. Her voice was sweet, and reminded him of elms, of lawns, of those glass arrangements that used to be hung from porch ceilings to tinkle in the summer wind. She told him about the count. She spoke of him charitably and with no trace of bitterness, as if her voice, her disposition, were incapable of registering anything beyond simple affection and pleasure. Her walk, when she moved ahead of him toward their table, was light and graceful. She ate a large dinner and talked enthusiastically about her job. They went to a movie and said goodbye in front of her apartment house.

That winter, Jack met a girl he decided to marry. Their engagement was announced in January and they planned to marry in July. In the spring, he received, in his office mail, an invitation to cocktails at Joan's. It was for a Saturday when his fiancée was going to Massachusetts to visit her parents, and when the time came and he had nothing better to do, he took a bus to the Village. Joan had the same apartment. It was a walkup. You rang the bell above the mailbox in the vestibule and were answered with a death rattle in the lock. Joan lived on the third floor. Her calling card was in a slot on the mailbox, and above her name was written the name of Hugh Bascomb.

Jack climbed the two flights of carpeted stairs, and when he reached Joan's apartment, she was standing by the open door in a black dress. After she greeted Jack, she took his arm and guided him across the room. "I want you to meet Hugh, Jack," she said.

Hugh was a big man with a red face and pale-blue eyes. His manner was courtly and his eyes were inflamed with drink. Jack talked with him for a little while and then went over to speak to someone he knew, who was standing by the mantelpiece. He noticed then, for the first time, the indescribable disorder of Joan's apartment. The books were in their shelves and the furniture was reasonably good, but the place was all wrong, somehow. It was as if things had been put in place without thought or real interest, and for the first time, too, he had the impression that there had been a death there recently.

As Jack moved around the room, he felt that he had met the ten or twelve guests at other parties. There was a woman executive with a fancy hat, a man who could imitate Roosevelt, a grim couple whose play was in rehearsal, and a newspaperman who kept turning on the radio for news of the Spanish Civil War. Jack drank Martinis and talked with the woman in the fancy hat. He looked out of the window at the back yards and the ailanthus trees and heard, in the distance, thunder exploding off the cliffs of the Hudson.

Hugh Bascomb got very drunk. He began to spill liquor, as if drinking, for him, were a kind of jolly slaughter and he enjoyed the bloodshed and the mess. He spilled whiskey from a bottle. He spilled a drink on his shirt and then tipped over someone else's drink. The party was not quiet, but Hugh's hoarse voice began to dominate the others. He attacked a photographer who was sitting in a corner explaining camera techniques to a homely woman. "What did you come to the party for if all you wanted to do was to sit there and stare at your shoes?" Hugh shouted. "What did you come for? Why don't you stay at home?"

The photographer didn't know what to say. He was not staring at his shoes. Joan moved lightly to Hugh's side. "Please don't get into a fight now, darling," she said. "Not this afternoon."

"Shut up," he said. "Let me alone. Mind your own business." He lost his balance, and in struggling to steady himself he tipped over a lamp.

"Oh, your lovely lamp, Joan," a woman sighed.

"Lamps!" Hugh roared. He threw his arms into the air and worked them around his head as if he were bludgeoning himself. "Lamps. Glasses. Cigarette boxes. Dishes. They're killing me. They're killing me, for Christ's sake. Let's all go up to the mountains, for Christ's sake. Let's all go up to the mountains and hunt and fish and live like men, for Christ's sake."

People were scattering as if a rain had begun to fall in the room. It had, as a matter of fact, begun to rain outside. Someone offered Jack a ride uptown, and he jumped at the chance. Joan stood at the door, saying goodbye to her routed friends. Her voice remained soft, and her manner, unlike that of those Christian women who in the face of disaster can summon new and formidable sources of composure, seemed genuinely simple. She appeared to be oblivious of the raging drunk at her back, who was pacing up and down, grinding glass into the rug, and haranguing one of the survivors of the party with a story of how he, Hugh, had once gone without food for three weeks.

In July, Jack was married in an orchard in Duxbury, and he and his wife went to West Chop for a few weeks. When they returned to town, their apartment was cluttered with presents, including a dozen after-dinner coffee cups from Joan. His wife sent her the required note, but they did nothing else.

Late in the summer, Joan telephoned Jack at his office and asked if he wouldn't bring his wife to see her; she named an evening the following week. He felt guilty about not having called her, and accepted the invitation. This made his wife angry. She was an ambitious girl who liked a social life that offered rewards, and she went unwillingly to Joan's Village apartment with him.

Written above Joan's name on the mailbox was the name Franz Denzel. Jack and his wife climbed the stairs and were met by Joan at the open door. They went into her apartment and found themselves among a group of people for whom Jack, at least, was unable to find any bearings.

Franz Denzel was a middle-aged German. His face was pinched with bitterness or illness. He greeted Jack and his wife with that elaborate and clever politeness that is intended to make guests feel that they have come too early or too late. He insisted sharply upon Jack's sitting in the chair in which he himself had been sitting, and then went and sat on a radiator. There were five other Germans sitting around the room, drinking coffee. In a corner was another American couple, who looked uncomfortable. Joan passed Jack and his wife small cups of coffee with whipped cream. "These cups belonged to Franz's mother," she said. "Aren't they lovely? They were the only things he took from Germany when he escaped from the Nazis."

Franz turned to Jack and said, "Perhaps you will give us your opinion on the American educational system. That is what we were discussing when you arrived."

Before Jack could speak, one of the German guests opened an attack on the American educational system. The other Germans joined in, and went on from there to describe every vulgarity that had impressed them in American life and to contrast German and American culture generally. Where, they asked one another passionately, could you find in America anything like the Mitropa dining cars, the Black Forest, the pictures in Munich, the music in Bayreuth? Franz and his friends began speaking in German. Neither Jack nor his wife nor Joan could understand German, and the other American couple had not opened their mouths since they were introduced. Joan went happily around the room, filling everyone's cup with coffee, as if the music of a foreign language were enough to make an evening for her.

Jack drank five cups of coffee. He was desperately uncomfortable. Joan went into the kitchen while the Germans were laughing at their German jokes, and he hoped she would return with some drinks, but when she came back, it was with a tray of ice cream and mulberries.

"Isn't this pleasant?" Franz asked, speaking in English again.

Joan collected the coffee cups, and as she was about to take them back to the kitchen, Franz stopped her.

"Isn't one of those cups chipped?"

"No, darling," Joan said. "I never let the maid touch them. I wash them myself."

"What's that?" he asked, pointing at the rim of one of the cups.

"That's the cup that's always been chipped, darling. It was chipped when you unpacked it. You noticed it then."

"These things were perfect when they arrived in this country," he said.

Joan went into the kitchen and he followed her.

Jack tried to make conversation with the Germans. From the kitchen there was the sound of a blow and a cry. Franz returned and began to eat his mulberries greedily. Joan came back with her dish of ice cream. Her voice was gentle. Her tears, if she had been crying, had dried as quickly as the tears of a child. Jack and his wife finished their ice cream and made their escape. The wasted and unnerving evening enraged Jack's wife, and he supposed that he would never see Joan again.

Jack's wife got pregnant early in the fall, and she seized on all the prerogatives of an expectant mother. She took long naps, ate canned peaches in the middle of the night, and talked about the rudimentary kidney. She chose to see only other couples who were expecting children, and the parties that she and Jack gave were temperate. The baby, a boy, was born in May, and Jack was very proud and happy. The first party he and his wife went to after her convalescence was the wedding of a girl whose family Jack had known in Ohio.

The wedding was at St. James', and afterward there was a big reception at the River Club. There was an orchestra dressed like Hungarians, and a lot of champagne and Scotch. Toward the end of the afternoon, Jack was walking down a dim corridor when he heard Joan's voice. "Please don't, darling," she was saying, "You'll break my arm. *Please* don't, darling." She was being pressed against the wall by a man who seemed to be twisting her arm. As soon as they saw Jack, the struggle stopped. All three of them were intensely embarrassed. Joan's face was wet and she made an effort to smile through her tears at Jack. He said hello and went on without stopping. When he returned, she and the man had disappeared.

When Jack's son was less than two years old, his wife flew with the baby to Nevada to get a divorce. Jack gave her the apartment and all its furnishings and took a room in a hotel near Grand Central. His wife got her decree in due course, and the story was in the newspapers. Jack had a telephone call from Joan a few days later.

"I'm awfully sorry to hear about your divorce, Jack," she said. "She seemed like *such* a nice girl. But that wasn't what I called you about. I want your help, and I wondered if you could come down to my place tonight around six. It's something I don't want to talk about over the phone."

He went obediently to the Village that night and climbed the stairs. Her apartment was a mess. The pictures and the curtains were down and the books were in boxes. "You moving, Joan?" he asked.

"That's what I wanted to see you about, Jack. First, I'll give you a drink." She made two Old-Fashioneds. "I'm being evicted, Jack," she said. "I'm being evicted because I'm an immoral woman. The couple who have the apartment downstairs—they're charming people, I've always thought—have told the real-estate agent that I'm a drunk and a prostitute and all kinds of things. Isn't that fantastic? This real-estate agent has always been so nice to me that I didn't think he'd believe them, but he's cancelled my lease, and if I make any trouble, he's threatened to take the matter up with the store, and I don't want to lose my job. This nice real-estate agent won't even talk with me any more. When I go over to the office, the receptionist leers at me, as if I were some kind of dreadful woman. Of course, there have been a lot of men here and we sometimes are noisy, but I can't be expected to go to bed at ten every night. Can I? Well, the agent who manages this building has apparently told all the other agents in the neighborhood that I'm an immoral and drunken woman, and none of them will give me an apartment. I went in to talk with one man—he seemed to be such a nice old gentleman—and he made me an indecent proposal. Isn't it fantastic? I have to be out of here on Thursday and I'm literally being turned out into the street."

Joan seemed as serene and innocent as ever while she described this scourge of agents and neighbors. Jack listened carefully for some sign of indignation or bitterness or even urgency in her recital, but there was none. He was reminded of a torch song, of one of those forlorn and touching ballads that had been sung neither for him nor for her but for their older brothers and sisters by Marion Harris. Joan seemed to be singing her wrongs.

"They've made my life miserable," she went on quietly. "If I keep the radio on after ten o'clock, they telephone the agent in the morning and tell him I had some kind of orgy here. One night when Phillip—I don't think you've met Phillip; he's in the Royal Air Force; he's gone back to England—one night when Phillip and some other people were here, they called the police. The police came bursting in the door and talked to me as if I were I don't know what and then looked in the bedroom. If they think there's a man up here after midnight, they call me on the telephone and say all kinds of disgusting things. Of course, I can put my furniture into storage and go to a hotel, I guess. I guess a hotel will take a woman with my kind of reputation, but I thought perhaps you might know of an apartment. I thought—"

It angered Jack to think of this big, splendid girl's being persecuted by her neighbors, and he said he would do what he could. He asked her to have dinner with him, but she said she was busy.

Having nothing better to do, Jack decided to walk uptown to his hotel. It was a hot night. The sky was overcast. On his way, he saw a parade in a dark side street off Broadway near Madison Square. All the buildings in the neighborhood were dark. It was so dark that he could not see the placards the marchers carried until he came to a street light. Their signs urged the entry of the United States into the war, and each platoon represented a nation that had been subjugated by the Axis powers. They marched up Broadway, as he watched, to no music, to no sound but their own steps on the rough cobbles. It was for the most part an army of elderly men and women —Poles, Norwegians, Danes, Jews, Chinese. A few idle people like himself lined the sidewalks, and the marchers passed between them with all the self-consciousness of enemy prisoners. There were children among them dressed in the costumes in which they had, for the newsreels, presented the Mayor with a package of tea, a petition, a protest, a constitution, a check, or a pair of tickets. They hobbled through the darkness of the loft neighborhood like a mortified and destroyed people, toward Greeley Square.

In the morning, Jack put the problem of finding an apartment for Joan up to his secretary. She started phoning real-estate agents, and by afternoon she had found a couple of available apartments in the West Twenties. Joan called Jack the next day to say that she had taken one of the apartments and to thank him.

Jack didn't see Joan again until the following summer. It was a Sunday evening; he had left a cocktail party in a Washington Square apartment and had decided to walk a few blocks up Fifth Avenue before he took a bus. As he was passing the Brevoort, Joan called to him. She was with a man at one of the tables on the sidewalk. She looked cool and fresh, and the man appeared to be respectable. His name, it turned out, was Pete Bristol. He invited Jack to sit down and join in a celebration. Germany had invaded Russia that weekend, and Joan and Pete were drinking champagne to celebrate Russia's changed position in the war. The three of them drank champagne until it got dark. They had dinner and drank champagne with their dinner. They drank more champagne afterward and then went over to the Lafayette and then to two or three other places.

Joan had always been tireless in her gentle way. She hated to see the night end, and it was after three o'clock when Jack stumbled into his apartment. The following morning he woke up haggard and sick, and with no recollection of the last hour or so of the previous evening. His suit was soiled and he had lost his hat. He didn't get to his office until eleven. Joan had already called him twice, and she called him again soon after he got in. There was no hoarseness at all in her voice. She said that she had to see him, and he agreed to meet her for lunch in a sea-food restaurant in the Fifties.

He was standing at the bar when she breezed in, looking as though she had taken no part in that calamitous night. The advice she wanted concerned selling her jewelry. Her grandmother had left her some jewelry, and she wanted to raise money on it but didn't know where to go. She took some rings and bracelets out of her purse and showed them to Jack. He said that he didn't know anything about jewelry but that he could lend her some money. "Oh, I couldn't borrow money from you, Jack," she said. "You see, I want to get the money for Pete. I want to help him. He wants to open an advertising agency, and he needs quite a lot to begin with." Jack didn't press her to accept his offer of a loan after that, and the project wasn't mentioned again during lunch.

He next heard from Joan from a young doctor who was a friend of theirs. "Have you seen Joan recently?" the doctor asked Jack one evening when they were having dinner together. He said no. "I gave her a checkup last week," the doctor said, "and while she's been through enough to kill the average mortal—and you'll never know what she's been through—she still has the constitution of a virtuous and healthy woman. Did you hear about the last one? She sold her jewelry to put him into some kind of business, and as soon as he got the money, he left her for another girl, who had a car—a convertible."

Jack was drafted into the Army in the spring of 1942. He was kept at Fort Dix for nearly a month, and during this time he came to New York in the evening whenever he could get permission. Those nights had for him the intense keenness of a reprieve, a sensation that was heightened by the fact that on the train in from Trenton women would often press upon him dog-eared copies of *Life* and half-eaten boxes of candy, as though the brown clothes he wore were surely cerements. He telephoned Joan from Pennsylvania Station one night. "Come right over, Jack," she said. "Come right over. I want you to meet Ralph."

She was living in that place in the West Twenties that Jack had found for her. The neighborhood was a slum. Ash cans stood in front of her house, and an old woman was there picking out bits of refuse and garbage and stuffing them into a perambulator. The house in which Joan's apartment was located was shabby, but the apartment itself seemed familiar. The furniture was the same. Joan was the same big, easy-going girl. "I'm so glad you called me," she said. "It's so good to see you. I'll make you a drink. I was having one myself. Ralph ought to be here by now. He promised to take me to dinner." Jack offered to take her to Cavanagh's, but she said that Ralph might come while she was out. "If he doesn't come by nine, I'm going to make myself a sandwich. I'm not really hungry."

Jack talked about the Army. She talked about the store. She had been working in the same place for—how long was it? He didn't know. He had never seen her at her desk and he couldn't imagine what she did. "I'm terribly sorry Ralph isn't here," she said. "I'm sure you'd like him. He's not a young man. He's a heart specialist who loves to play the viola." She turned on some lights, for the summer sky had got dark. "He has this dreadful wife on Riverside Drive and four ungrateful children. He—"

The noise of an air-raid siren, lugubrious and seeming to spring from pain, as if all the misery and indecision in the city had been given a voice, cut her off. Other sirens, in distant neighborhoods, sounded, until the dark air was full of their noise. "Let me fix you another drink before I have to turn out the lights," Joan said, and took his glass. She brought the drink back to him and snapped off the lights. They went to the windows, and, as children watched a thunderstorm, they watched the city darken. All the lights nearby went out but one. Air-raid wardens had begun to sound their whistles in the street. From a distant yard came a hoarse shriek of anger. "Put out your lights, you Fascists!" a woman screamed. "Put out your lights, you Nazi Fascist Germans. Turn out your lights. Turn out your lights." The last light went off. They went away from the window and sat in the lightless room.

In the darkness, Joan began to talk about her departed lovers, and from what she said Jack gathered that they had all had a hard time. Nils, the suspect count, was dead. Hugh Bascomb, the drunk, had joined the Merchant Marine and was missing in the North Atlantic. Franz, the German, had taken poison the night the Nazis bombed Warsaw. "We listened to the news on the radio," Joan said, "and then he went back to his hotel and took poison. The maid found him dead in the bathroom the next morning." When Jack asked her about the one who was going to open an advertising agency, she seemed at first to have forgotten him. "Oh, Pete," she said after a pause. "Well, he was always very sick, you know. He was supposed to go to Saranac, but he kept putting it off and putting it off and—" She stopped talking when she heard steps on the stairs, hoping, he supposed, that it was Ralph, but whoever it was turned at the landing and continued to the top of the house. "I wish Ralph would come," she said, with a sigh. "I want you to meet him." Jack asked her again to go out, but she refused, and when the all-clear sounded, he said goodbye.

Jack was shipped from Dix to an infantry training camp in the Carolinas and from there to an infantry division stationed in Georgia. He had been in Georgia three months when he married a girl from the Augusta boarding-house aristocracy. A year or so later, he crossed the continent in a day coach and thought sententiously that the last he might see of the country he loved was the desert towns like Barstow, that the last he might hear of it was the ringing of the trolleys on the Bay Bridge. He was sent into the Pacific and returned to the United States twenty months later, uninjured and apparently unchanged. As soon as he received his furlough, he went to Augusta. He presented his wife with the souvenirs he had brought from the islands, quarrelled violently with her and all her family, and, after making arrangements for her to get an Arkansas divorce, left for New York.

Jack was discharged from the Army at a camp in the East a few months later. He took a vacation and then went back to the job he had left in 1942. He seemed to have picked up his life at approximately the moment when it had been interrupted by the war. In time, everything came to look and feel the same. He saw most of his old friends. Only two of the men he knew had been killed in the war. He didn't call Joan, but he met her one winter afternoon on a crosstown bus.

Her fresh face, her black clothes, and her soft voice instantly destroyed the sense—if he had ever had such a sense—that anything had changed or intervened since their last meeting, three or four years ago. She asked him up for cocktails and he went to her apartment the next Saturday afternoon. Her room and her guests reminded him of the parties she had given when she had first come to New York. There was a woman with a fancy hat, an elderly doctor, and a man who stayed close to the radio, listening for news from the Balkans. Jack wondered which of the men belonged to Joan and decided on an Englishman who kept coughing into a handkerchief that he pulled out of his sleeve. Jack was right. "Isn't Stephen brilliant?" Joan asked him a little later, when they were alone in a corner. "He knows more about the Polynesians than anyone else in the world."

Jack had returned not only to his old job but to his old salary. Since living costs had doubled and since he was paying alimony to two wives, he had to draw on his savings. He took another job, which promised more money, but it didn't last long and he found himself out of work. This didn't bother him at all. He still had money in the bank, and anyhow it was easy to borrow from friends. His indifference was the consequence not of lassitude or despair but rather of an excess of hope. He had the feeling that he had only recently come to New York from Ohio. The sense that he was very young and that the best years of his life still lay before him was an illusion that he could not seem to escape. There was all the time in the world. He was living in hotels then, moving from one to another every five days.

In the spring, Jack moved to a furnished room in the badlands west of Central Park. He was running out of money. Then, when he began to feel that a job was a desperate necessity, he got sick. At first, he seemed to have only a bad cold, but he was unable to shake it and he began to run a fever and to cough blood. The fever kept him drowsy most of the time, but he roused himself occasionally and went out to a cafeteria for a meal. He felt sure that none of his friends knew where he was, and he was glad of this. He hadn't counted on Joan.

Late one morning, he heard her speaking in the hall with his landlady. A few moments later, she knocked on his door. He was lying on the bed in a pair of pants and a soiled pajama top, and he didn't answer. She knocked again and walked in. "I've been looking everywhere for you, Jack," she said. She spoke softly. "When I found out that you were in a place like this I thought you must be broke or sick. I stopped at the bank and got some money, in case you're broke. I've brought you some Scotch. I thought a little drink wouldn't do you any harm. Want a little drink?"

Joan's dress was black. Her voice was low and serene. She sat in a chair beside his bed as if she had been coming there every day to nurse him. Her features had coarsened, he thought, but there were still very few lines in her face. She was heavier. She was nearly fat.

She was wearing black cotton gloves. She got two glasses and poured Scotch into them. He drank his whiskey greedily. "I didn't get to bed until three last night," she said. Her voice had once before reminded him of a gentle and despairing song, but now, perhaps because he was sick, her mildness, the mourning she wore, her stealthy grace, made him uneasy. "It was one of those nights," she said. "We went to the theatre. Afterward, someone asked us up to his place. I don't know who he was. It was one of those places. They're so strange. There were some meat-eating plants and a collection of Chinese snuff bottles. Why do people collect Chinese snuff bottles? We all autographed a lampshade, as I remember, but I can't remember much."

Jack tried to sit up in bed, as if there were some need to defend himself, and then fell back again, against the pillows. "How did you find me, Joan?" he asked.

"It was simple," she said. "I called that hotel. The one you were staying in. They gave me this address. My secretary got the telephone number. Have another little drink."

"You know you've never come to a place of mine before—never," he said. "Why did you come now?"

"Why did I come, darling?" she asked. "What a question! I've known you for thirty years. You're the oldest friend I have in New York. Remember that night in the Village when it snowed and we stayed up until morning and drank whiskey sours for breakfast? That doesn't seem like twelve years ago. And that night—"

"I don't like to have you see me in a place like this," he said earnestly. He touched his face and felt his beard.

"And all the people who used to imitate Roosevelt," she said, as if she had not heard him, as if she were deaf. "And that place on Staten Island where we all used to go for dinner when Henry had a car. Poor Henry. He bought a place in Connecticut and went out there by himself, one weekend. He fell asleep with a lighted cigarette and the house, the barn, everything burned. Ethel took the children out to California." She poured more Scotch into his glass and handed it to him. She lighted a cigarette and put it between his lips. The intimacy of this gesture, which made it seem not only as if he were deathly ill but as if he were her lover, troubled him.

"As soon as I'm better," he said, "I'll take a room at a good hotel. I'll call you then. It was nice of you to come."

"Oh, don't be ashamed of this room, Jack," she said. "Rooms never bother me. It doesn't seem to matter to me where I am. Stanley had a filthy room in Chelsea. At least, other people told me it was filthy. I never noticed it. Rats used to eat the food I brought him. He used to have to hang the food from the ceiling, from the light chain."

"I'll call you as soon as I'm better," Jack said. "I think I can sleep now if I'm left alone. I seem to need a lot of sleep."

"You really *are* sick, darling," she said. "You must have a fever." She sat on the edge of his bed and put a hand on his forehead.

"How is that Englishman, Joan?" he asked. "Do you still see him?"

"What Englishman?" she said.

"You know. I met him at your house. He kept a handkerchief up his sleeve. He coughed all the time. You know the one I mean."

"You must be thinking of someone else," she said. "I haven't had an Englishman at my place since the war. Of course, I can't remember everyone." She turned and, taking one of his hands, linked her fingers in his.

"He's dead, isn't he?" Jack said. "That Englishman's dead." He pushed her off the bed, and got up himself. "Get out," he said.

"You're sick, darling," she said. "I can't leave you alone here."

"Get out," he said again, and when she didn't move, he shouted, "What kind of an obscenity are you that you can smell sickness and death the way you do?"

"You poor darling."

"Does it make you feel young to watch the dying?" he shouted. "Is that the lewdness that keeps you young? Is that why you dress like a crow? Oh, I know there's nothing I can say that will hurt you. I know there's nothing filthy or corrupt or depraved or brutish or base that the others haven't tried, but this time you're wrong. I'm not ready. My life isn't ending. My life's beginning. There are wonderful years ahead of me. There are, there are wonderful, wonderful, wonderful years ahead of me, and when they're over, when it's time, then I'll call you. Then, as an old friend, I'll call you and give you whatever dirty pleasure you take in watching the dying, but until then, you and your ugly and misshapen forms will leave me alone."

She finished her drink and looked at her watch. "I guess I'd better show up at the office," she said. "I'll see you later. I'll come back tonight. You'll feel better then, you poor darling." She closed the door after her, and he heard her light step on the stairs.

Jack emptied the whiskey bottle into the sink. He began to dress. He stuffed his dirty clothes into a bag. He was trembling and crying with sickness and fear. He could see the blue sky from his window, and in his fear it seemed miraculous that the sky should be blue, that the white clouds should remind him of snow, that from the sidewalk he could hear the shrill voices of children shrieking, "I'm the king of the mountain, I'm the king of the mountain, I'm the king of the mountain." He emptied the ashtray containing his nail pairings and cigarette butts into the toilet, and swept the floor with a shirt, so that there would be no trace of his life, of his body, when that lewd and searching shape of death came there to find him in the evening.

Questions

1. This story moves through a series of episodes involving both Jack Lorey and Joan Harris. How does each episode add to our understanding of Cheever's theme?
2. Are there parallels between Jack Lorey's fortunes and Joan Harris' affairs?
3. What is the unchanging characteristic in each of the men whom Joan adopts?
4. When do we begin to suspect that Joan Harris' motives are not entirely humanitarian? At that point, what earlier details are illuminated?

Topics for Composition

1. Cheever reveals the structure of his story in his second paragraph—the pink light, the black dress, the string music of heartbreak, the moving forward to greet the customers. Using these four devices as indicators of structure, write an essay showing the use of structure to reveal theme in "Torch Song."
2. Write an essay analyzing Joan Harris' characterization. Take the position that her obsession with death fulfills her need for love.

ONE of Bierce's major characteristics as a writer of short fiction is his ability to build to an unexpected climax which usually contrasts ironically with some other aspect of his story. Here, the contrast is evident in the word "philosopher" used in the title. We should consider the following:

1. Descriptive details that add reality to a scene that might otherwise seem fantastical
2. A sharp contrast in attitude between Adderson and the General

Parker Adderson, Philosopher

AMBROSE BIERCE

"Prisoner, what is your name?"

"As I am to lose it at daylight to-morrow morning it is hardly worth while concealing it. Parker Adderson."

"Your rank?"

"A somewhat humble one; commissioned officers are too precious to be risked in the perilous business of a spy. I am a sergeant."

"Of what regiment?"

"You must excuse me; my answer might, for anything I know, give you an idea of whose forces are in your front. Such knowledge as that is what I came into your lines to obtain, not to impart."

"You are not without wit."

"If you have the patience to wait you will find me dull enough to-morrow."

"How do you know that you are to die to-morrow morning?"

"Among spies captured by night that is the custom. It is one of the nice observances of the profession."

The general so far laid aside the dignity appropriate to a Confederate officer of high rank and wide renown as to smile. But no one in his power and out of his favor would have drawn any happy augury from that outward and visible sign of approval. It was neither genial nor infectious; it did not communicate itself to the other persons exposed to it—the caught spy who had provoked it and the armed guard who had brought him into the tent and now stood a little apart, watching his prisoner in the yellow candle-light. It was no part of that warrior's duty to smile; he had been detailed for another purpose. The conversation was resumed; it was in character a trial for a capital offense.

"You admit, then, that you are a spy—that you came into my camp, disguised as you are in the uniform of a Confederate soldier, to obtain information secretly regarding the numbers and disposition of my troops."

"Regarding, particularly, their numbers. Their disposition I already knew. It is morose."

The general brightened again; the guard, with a severer sense of his responsibility, accentuated the austerity of his expression and stood a trifle more erect than before. Twirling his gray slouch hat round and round upon his forefinger, the spy took a leisurely survey of his surroundings. They were simple enough. The tent was a common "wall tent," about eight feet by ten in dimensions, lighted by a single tallow candle stuck into the haft of a bayonet, which was itself stuck into a pine table at which the general sat, now busily writing and apparently forgetful of his unwilling guest. An old rag carpet covered the earthen floor; an older leather trunk, a second chair and a roll of blankets were about all else that the tent contained; in General Clavering's command Confederate simplicity and penury of "pomp and circumstance" had attained their highest development. On a large nail driven into the tent pole at the entrance was suspended a sword-belt supporting a long sabre, a pistol in its holster and, absurdly enough, a bowie-knife. Of that most unmilitary weapon it was the general's habit to explain that it was a souvenir of the peaceful days when he was a civilian.

It was a stormy night. The rain cascaded upon the canvas in torrents, with the dull, drum-like sound familiar to dwellers in tents. As the whooping blasts charged upon it the frail structure shook and swayed and strained at its confining stakes and ropes.

The general finished writing, folded the half-sheet of paper and spoke to the soldier guarding Adderson: "Here, Tassman, take that to the adjutant-general; then return."

"And the prisoner, General?" said the soldier, saluting, with an inquiring glance in the direction of that unfortunate.

"Do as I said," replied the officer, curtly.

The soldier took the note and ducked himself out of the tent. General Clavering turned his handsome face toward the Federal spy, looked him in the eyes, not unkindly, and said: "It is a bad night, my man."

"For me, yes."

"Do you guess what I have written?"

"Something worth reading, I dare say. And—perhaps it is my vanity—I venture to suppose that I am mentioned in it."

"Yes; it is a memorandum for an order to be read to the troops at *reveille* concerning your execution. Also some notes for the guidance of the provost-marshal in arranging the details of that event."

"I hope, General, the spectacle will be intelligently arranged, for I shall attend it myself."

"Have you any arrangements of your own that you wish to make? Do you wish to see a chaplain, for example?"

"I could hardly secure a longer rest for myself by depriving him of some of his."

"Good God, man! do you mean to go to your death with nothing but jokes upon your lips? Do you know that this is a serious matter?"

"How can I know that? I have never been dead in all my life. I have heard that death is a serious matter, but never from any of those who have experienced it."

The general was silent for a moment; the man interested, perhaps amused him—a type not previously encountered.

"Death," he said, "is at least a loss—a loss of such happiness as we have, and of opportunities for more."

"A loss of which we shall never be conscious can be borne with composure and therefore expected without apprehension. You must have observed, General, that of all the dead men with whom it is your soldierly pleasure to strew your path none shows signs of regret."

"If the being dead is not a regrettable condition, yet the becoming so—the act of dying—appears to be distinctly disagreeable to one who has not lost the power to feel."

"Pain is disagreeable, no doubt. I never suffer it without more or less discomfort. But he who lives longest is most exposed to it. What you call dying is simply the last pain—there is really no such thing as dying. Suppose, for illustration, that I attempt to escape. You lift the revolver that you are courteously concealing in your lap, and—"

The general blushed like a girl, then laughed softly, disclosing his brilliant teeth, made a slight inclination of his handsome head and said nothing. The spy continued: "You fire, and I have in my stomach what I did not swallow. I fall, but am not dead. After a half-hour of agony I am dead. But at any given instant of that half-hour I was either alive or dead. There is no transition period.

"When I am hanged to-morrow morning it will be quite the same; while conscious I shall be living; when dead, unconscious. Nature appears to have ordered the matter quite in my interest—the way that I should have ordered it myself. It is so simple," he added with a smile, "that it seems hardly worth while to be hanged at all."

At the finish of his remarks there was a long silence. The general sat impassive, looking into the man's face, but apparently not attentive to what had been said. It was as if his eyes had mounted guard over the prisoner while his mind concerned itself with other matters. Presently he drew a long, deep breath, shuddered, as one awakened from a dreadful dream, and exclaimed almost inaudibly: "Death is horrible!"—this man of death.

"It was horrible to our savage ancestors," said the spy, gravely, "because they had not enough intelligence to dissociate the idea of consciousness from the idea of the physical forms in which it is manifested—as an even lower order of intelligence, that of the monkey, for example, may be unable to imagine a house without inhabitants, and seeing a ruined hut fancies a suffering occupant. To us it is horrible because we have inherited the tendency to think it so, accounting for the notion by wild and fanciful theories of another world—as names of places give rise to legends explaining them and reasonless conduct to philosophies in justification. You can hang me, General, but there your power of evil ends; you cannot condemn me to heaven."

The general appeared not to have heard; the spy's talk had merely turned his thoughts into an unfamiliar channel, but there they pursued their will independently to conclusions of their own. The storm had ceased, and something of the solemn spirit of the night had imparted itself to his reflections, giving them the sombre tinge of a supernatural dread. Perhaps there was an element of prescience in it. "I should not like to die," he said—"not to-night."

He was interrupted—if, indeed, he had intended to speak further—by the entrance of an officer of his staff, Captain Hasterlick, the provost-marshal. This recalled him to himself; the absent look passed away from his face.

"Captain," he said, acknowledging the officer's salute, "this man is a Yankee spy captured inside our lines with incriminating papers on him. He has confessed. How is the weather?"

"The storm is over, sir, and the moon shining."

"Good; take a file of men, conduct him at once to the parade ground, and shoot him."

A sharp cry broke from the spy's lips. He threw himself forward, thrust out his neck, expanded his eyes, clenched his hands.

"Good God!" he cried hoarsely, almost inarticulately; "you do not mean that! You forget—I am not to die until morning."

"I have said nothing of morning," replied the general, coldly; "that was an assumption of your own. You die now."

"But, General, I beg—I implore you to remember; I am to hang! It will take some time to erect the gallows—two hours—an hour.

Spies are hanged; I have rights under military law. For Heaven's sake, General, consider how short—"

"Captain, observe my directions."

The officer drew his sword and fixing his eyes upon the prisoner pointed silently to the opening of the tent. The prisoner hesitated; the officer grasped him by the collar and pushed him gently forward. As he approached the tent pole the frantic man sprang to it and with cat-like agility seized the handle of the bowie-knife, plucked the weapon from the scabbard and thrusting the captain aside leaped upon the general with the fury of a madman, hurling him to the ground and falling headlong upon him as he lay. The table was overturned, the candle extinguished and they fought blindly in the darkness. The provost-marshal sprang to the assistance of his superior officer and was himself prostrated upon the struggling forms. Curses and inarticulate cries of rage and pain came from the welter of limbs and bodies; the tent came down upon them and beneath its hampering and enveloping folds the struggle went on. Private Tassman, returning from his errand and dimly conjecturing the situation, threw down his rifle and laying hold of the flouncing canvas at random vainly tried to drag it off the men under it; and the sentinel who paced up and down in front, not daring to leave his beat though the skies should fall, discharged his rifle. The report alarmed the camp; drums beat the long roll and bugles sounded the assembly, bringing swarms of half-clad men into the moonlight, dressing as they ran, and falling into line at the sharp commands of their officers. This was well; being in line the men were under control; they stood at arms while the general's staff and the men of his escort brought order out of confusion by lifting off the fallen tent and pulling apart the breathless and bleeding actors in that strange contention.

Breathless, indeed, was one: the captain was dead; the handle of the bowie-knife, protruding from his throat, was pressed back beneath his chin until the end had caught in the angle of the jaw and the hand that delivered the blow had been unable to remove the weapon. In the dead man's hand was his sword, clenched with a grip that defied the strength of the living. Its blade was streaked with red to the hilt.

Lifted to his feet, the general sank back to the earth with a moan and fainted. Besides his bruises he had two sword-thrusts—one through the thigh, the other through the shoulder.

The spy had suffered the least damage. Apart from a broken right arm, his wounds were such only as might have been incurred in an ordinary combat with nature's weapons. But he was dazed and seemed hardly to know what had occurred. He shrank away from those attending him, cowered upon the ground and uttered unintelligible remonstrances. His face, swollen by blows and stained with gouts of blood, nevertheless showed white beneath his disheveled hair—as white as that of a corpse.

"The man is not insane," said the surgeon, preparing bandages and replying to a question; "he is suffering from fright. Who and what is he?"

Private Tassman began to explain. It was the opportunity of his life; he omitted nothing that could in any way accentuate the importance of his own relation to the night's events. When he had finished his story and was ready to begin it again nobody gave him any attention.

The general had now recovered consciousness. He raised himself upon his elbow, looked about him, and, seeing the spy crouching by a camp-fire, guarded, said simply:

"Take that man to the parade ground and shoot him."

"The general's mind wanders," said an officer standing near.

"His mind does *not* wander," the adjutant-general said. "I have a memorandum from him about this business; he had given that same order to Hasterlick"—with a motion of the hand toward the dead provost-marshal—"and, by God! it shall be executed."

Ten minutes later Sergeant Parker Adderson, of the Federal army, philosopher and wit, kneeling in the moonlight and begging incoherently for his life, was shot to death by twenty men. As the volley rang out upon the keen air of the midnight, General Clavering, lying white and still in the red glow of the camp-fire, opened his big blue eyes, looked pleasantly upon those about him and said: "How silent it all is!"

The surgeon looked at the adjutant-general, gravely and significantly. The patient's eyes slowly closed, and thus he lay for a few moments; then, his face suffused with a smile of ineffable sweetness, he said, faintly: "I suppose this must be death," and so passed away.

Questions

1. What remarks made by Parker Adderson immediately arouse our interest in him?
2. Is General Clavering's attitude clearly developed in his dialogue with Adderson? What is the effect of the General's remark that he should

not like to die that night? In this sense, to whom is death a greater reality, Adderson or the General? Why?

3. How much good sense do Adderson's comments on death contain?
4. In what way does Bierce foreshadow events through his description of the General's tent?
5. Why does Adderson react as he does to the command for his immediate death? Does his action seem realistic, or can we pass judgment on his reaction? What previous statement by Adderson is particularly ironic at this point in the story?
6. How do Adderson's "philosophy" and subsequent reactions combine to indicate Bierce's theme? How clearly can you state the theme of this story?

Topics for Composition

1. To an extent, Bierce seems to say that bravery is predicated on ignorance. Write an essay supporting or rejecting this idea.
2. Write an essay expanding the view that General Clavering knows more of death than Parker Adderson.
3. Contrast the method and logic of Adderson's and Socrates' arguments.

Drama

THE rigid conventions of Greek tragedy may at first strike the twentieth-century reader as unnecessarily forbidding and starkly artificial. But Sophocles is consciously giving *form* to the mythical articulation of a human dilemma—how to balance individual, clearly perceived desires against the apparently ambiguous but nevertheless immutable demands of a moral order. Oedipus is really a spokesman for "free will," although he pays lip service to the sovereignty of the gods. He believes in his own invincibility, but the cosmic order, represented in this play by the reports of Apollo's commands relayed through the oracle of Delphi, must teach Oedipus the limitations of man. Thus, the exchanges between characters and chorus operate to synthesize and, by accretion, to expand man's acceptance of his life's meaning and his ultimate accountability. Several features of the play should be kept in mind as one reads:

1. The choruses, speaking for bewildered mankind, typically question and comment upon the strange, unsettling communal events of the narrative.
2. Oedipus, in his ignorance, utters his own sentence; but after he recognizes that the gods, rather than "Luck," control the destinies of man, he remains a kingly figure as he carries out his self-sentence.
3. The language, especially the verse, enhances the grandeur of the tragedy by lifting into universality events of time and place.

Oedipus Rex

SOPHOCLES

An English Version by Dudley Fitts and Robert Fitzgerald

Prologue [Oedipus, Suppliants, Priest, Creon]
Párodos [Chorus]
Scene I [Oedipus, Choragos, Teiresias]
Ode I [Chorus]
Scene II [Creon, Choragos, Oedipus, Iocastê]
Ode II [Chorus]
Scene III [Iocastê, Messenger, Oedipus, Choragos]
Ode III [Chorus]

Scene IV [Oedipus, Choragos, Messenger, Shepherd]
Ode IV [Chorus]
Éxodos [Second Messenger, Choragos, Oedipus, Creon, Antigonê, Ismenê]

Persons Represented:

OEDIPUS
A PRIEST
CREON
TEIRESIAS
IOCASTE
MESSENGER
SHEPHERD OF LAÏOS
SECOND MESSENGER
CHORUS OF THEBAN ELDERS

THE SCENE. *Before the palace of Oedipus, King of Thebes. A central door and two lateral doors open onto a platform which runs the length of the façade. On the platform, right and left, are altars; and three steps lead down into the* "orchestra," *or chorus-ground. At the beginning of the action these steps are crowded by suppliants who have brought branches and chaplets of olive leaves and who lie in various attitudes of despair.* Oedipus *enters.*

PROLOGUE

Oedipus. My children, generations of the living
In the line of Kadmos, nursed at his ancient hearth:
Why have you strewn yourselves before these altars
In supplication, with your boughs and garlands?
The breath of incense rises from the city
With a sound of prayer and lamentation.

Children,

I would not have you speak through messengers,
And therefore I have come myself to hear you—
I, Oedipus, who bear the famous name.

[*To a* Priest:

You, there, since you are eldest in the company,
Speak for them all, tell me what preys upon you,
Whether you come in dread, or crave some blessing:
Tell me, and never doubt that I will help you
In every way I can; I should be heartless
Were I not moved to find you suppliant here.

Priest. Great Oedipus, O powerful King of Thebes!
You see how all the ages of our people
Cling to your altar steps: here are boys
Who can barely stand alone, and here are priests
By weight of age, as I am a priest of God,
And young men chosen from those yet unmarried;
As for the others, all that multitude,
They wait with olive chaplets in the squares,
At the two shrines of Pallas, and where Apollo
Speaks in the glowing embers.
Your own eyes
Must tell you: Thebes is tossed on a murdering sea
And can not lift her head from the death surge.
A rust consumes the buds and fruits of the earth;
The herds are sick; children die unborn,
And labor is vain. The god of plague and pyre
Raids like detestable lightning through the city,
And all the house of Kadmos is laid waste,
All emptied, and all darkened: Death alone
Battens upon the misery of Thebes.

You are not one of the immortal gods, we know;
Yet we have come to you to make our prayer
As to the man surest in mortal ways
And wisest in the ways of God. You saved us
From the Sphinx, that flinty singer, and the tribute
We paid to her so long; yet you were never
Better informed than we, nor could we teach you:
It was some god breathed in you to set us free.

Therefore, O mighty King, we turn to you:
Find us our safety, find us a remedy,
Whether by counsel of the gods or men.
A king of wisdom tested in the past
Can act in a time of troubles, and act well.
Noblest of men, restore
Life to your city! Think how all men call you
Liberator for your triumph long ago;
Ah, when your years of kingship are remembered,
Let them not say *We rose, but later fell*—
Keep the State from going down in the storm!

Once, years ago, with happy augury,
You brought us fortune; be the same again!
No man questions your power to rule the land:
But rule over men, not over a dead city!
Ships are only hulls, citadels are nothing,
When no life moves in the empty passageways.

Oedipus. Poor children! You may be sure I know
All that you longed for in your coming here.
I know that you are deathly sick; and yet,
Sick as you are, not one is as sick as I.
Each of you suffers in himself alone
His anguish, not another's; but my spirit
Groans for the city, for myself, for you.

I was not sleeping, you are not waking me.
No, I have been in tears for a long while
And in my restless thought walked many ways.
In all my search, I found one helpful course,
And that I have taken: I have sent Creon,
Son of Menoikeus, brother of the Queen,
To Delphi, Apollo's place of revelation,
To learn there, if he can,
What act or pledge of mine may save the city.
I have counted the days, and now, this very day,
I am troubled, for he has overstayed his time.
What is he doing? He has been gone too long.
Yet whenever he comes back, I should do ill
To scant whatever duty God reveals.

Priest. It is a timely promise. At this instant
They tell me Creon is here.

Oedipus. O Lord Apollo!
May his news be fair as his face is radiant!

Priest. It could not be otherwise: he is crowned with bay,
The chaplet is thick with berries.

Oedipus. We shall soon know;
He is near enough to hear us now.

[*Enter* Creon

O Prince:
Brother: son of Menoikeus:
What answer do you bring us from the god?

Creon. A strong one. I can tell you, great afflictions
Will turn out well, if they are taken well.
Oedipus. What was the oracle? These vague words
Leave me still hanging between hope and fear.
Creon. Is it your pleasure to hear me with all these
Gathered around us? I am prepared to speak,
But should we not go in?
Oedipus. Let them all hear it.
It is for them I suffer, more than for myself.
Creon. Then I will tell you what I heard at Delphi.

In plain words
The god commands us to expel from the land of Thebes
An old defilement we are sheltering.
It is a deathly thing, beyond cure;
We must not let it feed upon us longer.
Oedipus. What defilement? How shall we rid ourselves of it?
Creon. By exile or death, blood for blood. It was
Murder that brought the plague-wind on the city.
Oedipus. Murder of whom? Surely the god has named him?
Creon. My lord: long ago Laïos was our king,
Before you came to govern us.
Oedipus. I know;
I learned of him from others; I never saw him.
Creon. He was murdered; and Apollo commands us now
To take revenge upon whoever killed him.
Oedipus. Upon whom? Where are they? Where shall we find a clue
To solve that crime, after so many years?
Creon. Here in this land, he said.
If we make enquiry,
We may touch things that otherwise escape us.
Oedipus. Tell me: Was Laïos murdered in his house,
Or in the fields, or in some foreign country?
Creon. He said he planned to make a pilgrimage.
He did not come home again.
Oedipus. And was there no one,
No witness, no companion, to tell what happened?
Creon. They were all killed but one, and he got away
So frightened that he could remember one thing only.
Oedipus. What was that one thing? One may be the key

To everything, if we resolve to use it.

Creon. He said that a band of highwaymen attacked them,
Outnumbered them, and overwhelmed the King.

Oedipus. Strange, that a highwayman should be so daring—
Unless some faction here bribed him to do it.

Creon. We thought of that. But after Laïos' death
New troubles arose and we had no avenger.

Oedipus. What troubles could prevent your hunting down the killers?

Creon. The riddling Sphinx's song
Made us deaf to all mysteries but her own.

Oedipus. Then once more I must bring what is dark to light.
It is most fitting that Apollo shows,
As you do, this compunction for the dead.
You shall see how I stand by you, as I should,
To avenge the city and the city's god,
And not as though it were for some distant friend,
But for my own sake, to be rid of evil.
Whoever killed King Laïos might—who knows?—
Decide at any moment to kill me as well.
By avenging the murdered king I protect myself.

Come, then, my children: leave the altar steps,
Lift up your olive boughs!
One of you go
And summon the people of Kadmos to gather here.
I will do all that I can; you may tell them that.

[*Exit a* Page

So, with the help of God,
We shall be saved—or else indeed we are lost.

Priest. Let us rise, children. It was for this we came,
And now the King has promised it himself.
Phoibos has sent us an oracle; may he descend
Himself to save us and drive out the plague.

[*Exeunt* Oedipus *and* Creon *into the palace by the central door. The* Priest *and the* Suppliants *disperse R and L. After a short pause the* Chorus *enters the* orchestra.

PÁRODOS

[Strophe 1

Chorus. What is God singing in his profound
Delphi of gold and shadow?
What oracle for Thebes, the sunwhipped city?

Fear unjoints me, the roots of my heart tremble.

Now I remember, O Healer, your power, and wonder:
Will you send doom like a sudden cloud, or weave it
Like nightfall of the past?

Speak, speak to us, issue of holy sound:
Dearest to our expectancy: be tender!

[Antistrophe 1

Let me pray to Athenê, the immortal daughter of Zeus,
And to Artemis her sister
Who keeps her famous throne in the market ring,
And to Apollo, bowman at the far butts of heaven—

O gods, descend! Like three streams leap against
The fires of our grief, the fires of darkness;
Be swift to bring us rest!

As in the old time from the brilliant house
Of air you stepped to save us, come again!

[Strophe 2

Now our afflictions have no end,
Now all our stricken host lies down
And no man fights off death with his mind;

The noble plowland bears no grain,
And groaning mothers can not bear—

See, how our lives like birds take wing,
Like sparks that fly when a fire soars,
To the shore of the god of evening.

[Antistrophe 2

The plague burns on, it is pitiless,
Though pallid children laden with death
Lie unwept in the stony ways.

And old gray women by every path

Flock to the strand about the altars

There to strike their breasts and cry
Worship of Phoibos in wailing prayers:
Be kind, God's golden child!

There are no swords in this attack by fire, [Strophe 3
No shields, but we are ringed with cries.
Send the besieger plunging from our homes
Into the vast sea-room of the Atlantic
Or into the waves that foam eastward of Thrace–

For the day ravages what the night spares–

Destroy our enemy, lord of the thunder!
Let him be riven by lightning from heaven!

Phoibos Apollo, stretch the sun's bowstring, [Antistrophe 3
That golden cord, until it sing for us,
Flashing arrows in heaven!
Artemis, Huntress,
Race with flaring lights upon our mountains!

O scarlet god, O golden-banded brow,
O Theban Bacchos in a storm of Maenads,

[*Enter* Oedipus, C.

Whirl upon Death, that all the Undying hate!
Come with blinding torches, come in joy!

SCENE I

Oedipus. Is this your prayer? It may be answered. Come,
Listen to me, act as the crisis demands,
And you shall have relief from all these evils.

Until now I was a stranger to this tale,
As I had been a stranger to the crime.
Could I track down the murderer without a clue?
But now, friends,
As one who became a citizen after the murder,
I make this proclamation to all Thebans:
If any man knows by whose hand Laïos, son of Labdakos,

Met his death, I direct that man to tell me everything,
No matter what he fears for having so long withheld it.
Let it stand as promised that no further trouble
Will come to him, but he may leave the land in safety.

Moreover: If anyone knows the murderer to be foreign,
Let him not keep silent: he shall have his reward from me.
However, if he does conceal it; if any man
Fearing for his friend or for himself disobeys this edict,
Hear what I propose to do:

I solemnly forbid the people of this country,
Where power and throne are mine, ever to receive that man
Or speak to him, no matter who he is, or let him
Join in sacrifice, lustration, or in prayer.
I decree that he be driven from every house,
Being, as he is, corruption itself to us: the Delphic
Voice of Zeus has pronounced this revelation.
Thus I associate myself with the oracle
And take the side of the murdered king.

As for the criminal, I pray to God–
Whether it be a lurking thief, or one of a number–
I pray that that man's life be consumed in evil and wretchedness.
And as for me, this curse applies no less
If it should turn out that the culprit is my guest here,
Sharing my hearth.

You have heard the penalty.
I lay it on you now to attend to this
For my sake, for Apollo's, for the sick
Sterile city that heaven has abandoned.
Suppose the oracle had given you no command:
Should this defilement go uncleansed for ever?
You should have found the murderer: your king,
A noble king, had been destroyed!

Now I,
Having the power that he held before me,
Having his bed, begetting children there
Upon his wife, as he would have, had he lived–
Their son would have been my children's brother,
If Laïos had had luck in fatherhood!
(But surely ill luck rushed upon his reign)–

I say I take the son's part, just as though
I were his son, to press the fight for him
And see it won! I'll find the hand that brought
Death to Labdakos' and Polydoros' child,
Heir of Kadmos' and Agenor's line.
And as for those who fail me,
May the gods deny them the fruit of the earth,
Fruit of the womb, and may they rot utterly!
Let them be wretched as we are wretched, and worse!

For you, for loyal Thebans, and for all
Who find my actions right, I pray the favor
Of justice, and of all the immortal gods.

Choragos. Since I am under oath, my lord, I swear
I did not do the murder, I can not name
The murderer. Might not the oracle
That has ordained the search tell where to find him?
Oedipus. An honest question. But no man in the world
Can make the gods do more than the gods will.
Choragos. There is one last expedient—
Oedipus. Tell me what it is.
Though it seem slight, you must not hold it back.
Choragos. A lord clairvoyant to the lord Apollo,
As we all know, is the skilled Teiresias.
One might learn much about this from him, Oedipus.
Oedipus. I am not wasting time:
Creon spoke of this, and I have sent for him—
Twice, in fact; it is strange that he is not here.
Choragos. The other matter—that old report—seems useless.
Oedipus. Tell me. I am interested in all reports.
Choragos. The king was said to have been killed by highwaymen.
Oedipus. I know. But we have no witnesses to that.
Choragos. If the killer can feel a particle of dread,
Your curse will bring him out of hiding!
Oedipus. No.
The man who dared that act will fear no curse.

[*Enter the blind seer* Teiresias, *led by a* Page

Choragos. But there is one man who may detect the criminal.
This is Teiresias, this is the holy prophet
In whom, alone of all men, truth was born.

Oedipus. Teiresias: seer: student of mysteries,
Of all that's taught and all that no man tells,
Secrets of Heaven and secrets of the earth:
Blind though you are, you know the city lies
Sick with plague; and from this plague, my lord,
We find that you alone can guard or save us.

Possibly you did not hear the messengers?
Apollo, when we sent to him,
Sent us back word that this great pestilence
Would lift, but only if we established clearly
The identity of those who murdered Laïos.
They must be killed or exiled.
Can you use
Birdflight or any art of divination
To purify yourself, and Thebes, and me
From this contagion? We are in your hands.
There is no fairer duty
Than that of helping others in distress.
Teiresias. How dreadful knowledge of the truth can be
When there's no help in truth! I knew this well,
But made myself forget. I should not have come.
Oedipus. What is troubling you? Why are your eyes so cold?
Teiresias. Let me go home. Bear your own fate, and I'll
Bear mine. It is better so: trust what I say.
Oedipus. What you say is ungracious and unhelpful
To your native country. Do not refuse to speak.
Teiresias. When it comes to speech, your own is neither temperate
Nor opportune. I wish to be more prudent.
Oedipus. In God's name, we all beg you—
Teiresias. You are all ignorant.
No; I will never tell you what I know.
Now it is my misery; then, it would be yours.
Oedipus. What! You do know something, and will not tell us?
You would betray us all and wreck the State?
Teiresias. I do not intend to torture myself, or you.
Why persist in asking? You will not persuade me.
Oedipus. What a wicked old man you are! You'd try a stone's
Patience! Out with it! Have you no feeling at all?
Teiresias. You call me unfeeling. If you could only see
The nature of your own feelings . . .

Oedipus. Why,
Who would not feel as I do? Who could endure
Your arrogance toward the city?
Teiresias. What does it matter!
Whether I speak or not, it is bound to come.
Oedipus. Then, if "it" is bound to come, you are bound to tell me.
Teiresias. No, I will not go on. Rage as you please.
Oedipus. Rage? Why not!
And I'll tell you what I think:
You planned it, you had it done, you all but
Killed him with your own hands: if you had eyes,
I'd say the crime was yours, and yours alone.
Teiresias. So? I charge you, then,
Abide by the proclamation you have made:
From this day forth
Never speak again to these men or to me;
You yourself are the pollution of this country.
Oedipus. You dare say that! Can you possibly think you have
Some way of going free, after such insolence?
Teiresias. I have gone free. It is the truth sustains me.
Oedipus. Who taught you shamelessness? It was not your craft.
Teiresias. You did. You made me speak. I did not want to.
Oedipus. Speak what? Let me hear it again more clearly.
Teiresias. Was it not clear before? Are you tempting me?
Oedipus. I did not understand it. Say it again.
Teiresias. I say that you are the murderer whom you seek.
Oedipus. Now twice you have spat out infamy. You'll pay for it!
Teiresias. Would you care for more? Do you wish to be really angry?
Oedipus. Say what you will. Whatever you say is worthless.
Teiresias. I say you live in hideous shame with those
Most dear to you. You can not see the evil.
Oedipus. It seems you can go on mouthing like this for ever.
Teiresias. I can, if there is power in truth.
Oedipus. There is:
But not for you, not for you,
You sightless, witless, senseless, mad old man!
Teiresias. You are the madman. There is no one here
Who will not curse you soon, as you curse me.
Oedipus. You child of endless night! You can not hurt me
Or any other man who sees the sun.

Teiresias. True: it is not from me your fate will come.
That lies within Apollo's competence,
As it is his concern.
Oedipus. Tell me:
Are you speaking for Creon, or for yourself?
Teiresias. Creon is no threat. You weave your own doom.
Oedipus. Wealth, power, craft of statesmanship!
Kingly position, everywhere admired!
What savage envy is stored up against these,
If Creon, whom I trusted, Creon my friend,
For this great office which the city once
Put in my hands unsought—if for this power
Creon desires in secret to destroy me!

He has bought this decrepit fortune-teller, this
Collector of dirty pennies, this prophet fraud—
Why, he is no more clairvoyant than I am!
Tell us:
Has your mystic mummery ever approached the truth?
When that hellcat the Sphinx was performing here,
What help were you to these people?
Her magic was not for the first man who came along:
It demanded a real exorcist. Your birds—
What good were they? or the gods, for the matter of that?
But I came by,
Oedipus, the simple man, who knows nothing—
I thought it out for myself, no birds helped me!
And this is the man you think you can destroy,
That you may be close to Creon when he's king!
Well, you and your friend Creon, it seems to me,
Will suffer most. If you were not an old man,
You would have paid already for your plot.
Choragos. We can not see that his words or yours
Have been spoken except in anger, Oedipus,
And of anger we have no need. How can God's will
Be accomplished best? That is what most concerns us.
Teiresias. You are a king. But where argument's concerned
I am your man, as much a king as you.
I am not your servant, but Apollo's.
I have no need of Creon to speak for me.

Listen to me. You mock my blindness, do you?

But I say that you, with both your eyes, are blind:
You can not see the wretchedness of your life,
Nor in whose house you live, no, nor with whom.
Who are your father and mother? Can you tell me?
You do not even know the blind wrongs
That you have done them, on earth and in the world below.
But the double lash of your parents' curse will whip you
Out of this land some day, with only night
Upon your precious eyes.
Your cries then—where will they not be heard?
What fastness of Kithairon will not echo them?
And that bridal-descant of yours—you'll know it then,
The song they sang when you came here to Thebes
And found your misguided berthing.
All this, and more, that you can not guess at now,
Will bring you to yourself among your children.

Be angry, then. Curse Creon. Curse my words.
I tell you, no man that walks upon the earth
Shall be rooted out more horribly than you.

Oedipus. Am I to bear this from him?—Damnation
Take you! Out of this place! Out of my sight!

Teiresias. I would not have come at all if you had not asked me.

Oedipus. Could I have told that you'd talk nonsense, that
You'd come here to make a fool of yourself, and of me?

Teiresias. A fool? Your parents thought me sane enough.

Oedipus. My parents again!—Wait: who were my parents?

Teiresias. This day will give you a father, and break your heart.

Oedipus. Your infantile riddles! Your damned abracadabra!

Teiresias. You were a great man once at solving riddles.

Oedipus. Mock me with that if you like; you will find it true.

Teiresias. It was true enough. It brought about your ruin.

Oedipus. But if it saved this town?

Teiresias. [*To the* Page:
Boy, give me your hand.

Oedipus. Yes, boy; lead him away.
—While you are here
We can do nothing. Go; leave us in peace.

Teiresias. I will go when I have said what I have to say.
How can you hurt me? And I tell you again:
The man you have been looking for all this time,

The damned man, the murderer of Laïos,
That man is in Thebes. To your mind he is foreign-born,
But it will soon be shown that he is a Theban,
A revelation that will fail to please.
A blind man,
Who has his eyes now; a penniless man, who is rich now;
And he will go tapping the strange earth with his staff
To the children with whom he lives now he will be
Brother and father—the very same; to her
Who bore him, son and husband—the very same
Who came to his father's bed, wet with his father's blood.

Enough. Go think that over.
If later you find error in what I have said,
You may say that I have no skill in prophecy.
[*Exit* Teiresias, *led by his* Page. Oedipus *goes into the palace.*

ODE I

Chorus. The Delphic stone of prophecies [Strophe 1
Remembers ancient regicide
And a still bloody hand.
That killer's hour of flight has come.
He must be stronger than riderless
Coursers of untiring wind,
For the son of Zeus armed with his father's thunder
Leaps in lightning after him;
And the Furies follow him, the sad Furies.

Holy Parnassos' peak of snow [Antistrophe 1
Flashes and blinds that secret man,
That all shall hunt him down:
Though he may roam the forest shade
Like a bull gone wild from pasture
To rage through glooms of stone.
Doom comes down on him; flight will not avail him;
For the world's heart calls him desolate,
And the immortal Furies follow, for ever follow.

But now a wilder thing is heard [Strophe 2
From the old man skilled at hearing Fate in the wingbeat of a bird.

Bewildered as a blown bird, my soul hovers and can not find
Foothold in this debate, or any reason or rest of mind.
But no man ever brought—none can bring
Proof of strife between Thebes' royal house,
Labdakos' line, and the son of Polybos;
And never until now has any man brought word
Of Laïos' dark death staining Oedipus the King.

Divine Zeus and Apollo hold [Antistrophe 2
Perfect intelligence alone of all tales ever told;
And well though this diviner works, he works in his own night;
No man can judge that rough unknown or trust in second sight,
For wisdom changes hands among the wise.
Shall I believe my great lord criminal
At a raging word that a blind old man let fall?
I saw him, when the carrion woman faced him of old,
Prove his heroic mind! These evil words are lies.

SCENE II

Creon. Men of Thebes:
I am told that heavy accusations
Have been brought against me by King Oedipus.

I am not the kind of man to bear this tamely.

If in these present difficulties
He holds me accountable for any harm to him
Through anything I have said or done—why, then,
I do not value life in this dishonor.
It is not as though this rumor touched upon
Some private indiscretion. The matter is grave.
The fact is that I am being called disloyal
To the State, to my fellow citizens, to my friends.
Choragos. He may have spoken in anger, not from his mind.
Creon. But did you not hear him say I was the one
Who seduced the old prophet into lying?
Choragos. The thing was said; I do not know how seriously.
Creon. But you were watching him! Were his eyes steady?
Did he look like a man in his right mind?
Choragos. I do not know.

I can not judge the behavior of great men.
But here is the King himself.

[*Enter* Oedipus

Oedipus. So you dared come back
Why? How brazen of you to come to my house,
You murderer!
Do you think I do not know
That you plotted to kill me, plotted to steal my throne?
Tell me, in God's name: am I coward, a fool,
That you should dream you could accomplish this?
A fool who could not see your slippery game?
A coward, not to fight back when I saw it?
You are the fool, Creon, are you not? hoping
Without support or friends to get a throne?
Thrones may be won or bought: you could do neither.
Creon. Now listen to me. You have talked; let me talk, too.
You can not judge unless you know the facts.
Oedipus. You speak well: there is one fact; but I find it hard
To learn from the deadliest enemy I have.
Creon. That above all I must dispute with you.
Oedipus. That above all I will not hear you deny.
Creon. If you think there is anything good in being stubborn
Against all reason, then I say you are wrong.
Oedipus. If you think a man can sin against his own kind
And not be punished for it, I say you are mad.
Creon. I agree. But tell me: what have I done to you?
Oedipus. You advised me to send for that wizard, did you not?
Creon. I did. I should do it again.
Oedipus. Very well. Now tell me:
How long has it been since Laïos—
Creon. What of Laïos?
Oedipus. Since he vanished in that onset by the road?
Creon. It was long ago, a long time.
Oedipus. And this prophet,
Was he practicing here then?
Creon. He was; and with honor, as now.
Oedipus. Did he speak of me at that time?
Creon. He never did;
At least, not when I was present.

Oedipus. But . . . the enquiry?
I suppose you held one?
Creon. We did, but we learned nothing.
Oedipus. Why did the prophet not speak against me then?
Creon. I do not know; and I am the kind of man
Who holds his tongue when he has no facts to go on.
Oedipus. There's one fact that you know, and you could tell it.
Creon. What fact is that? If I know it, you shall have it.
Oedipus. If he were not involved with you, he could not say
That it was I who murdered Laïos.
Creon. If he says that, you are the one that knows it!—
But now it is my turn to question you.
Oedipus. Put your questions. I am no murderer.
Creon. First, then: You married my sister?
Oedipus. I married your sister.
Creon. And you rule the kingdom equally with her?
Oedipus. Everything that she wants she has from me.
Creon. And I am the third, equal to both of you?
Oedipus. That is why I call you a bad friend.
Creon. No. Reason it out, as I have done.
Think of this first: Would any sane man prefer
Power, with all a king's anxieties,
To that same power and the grace of sleep?
Certainly not I.
I have never longed for the king's power—only his rights.
Would any wise man differ from me in this?
As matters stand, I have my way in everything
With your consent, and no responsibilities.
If I were king, I should be a slave to policy.

How could I desire a scepter more
Than what is now mine—untroubled influence?
No, I have not gone mad; I need no honors,
Except those with the perquisites I have now.
I am welcome everywhere; every man salutes me,
And those who want your favor seek my ear,
Since I know how to manage what they ask.
Should I exchange this ease for that anxiety?
Besides, no sober mind is treasonable.
I hate anarchy
And never would deal with any man who likes it.

Test what I have said. Go to the priestess
At Delphi, ask if I quoted her correctly.
And as for this other thing: if I am found
Guilty of treason with Teiresias,
Then sentence me to death! You have my word
It is a sentence I should cast my vote for–
But not without evidence!

You do wrong
When you take good men for bad, bad men for good.
A true friend thrown aside–why, life itself
Is not more precious!

In time you will know this well:
For time, and time alone, will show the just man,
Though scoundrels are discovered in a day.

Choragos. This is well said, and a prudent man would ponder it.
Judgments too quickly formed are dangerous.

Oedipus. But is he not quick in his duplicity?
And shall I not be quick to parry him?
Would you have me stand still, hold my peace, and let
This man win everything, through my inaction?

Creon. And you want–what is it, then? To banish me?

Oedipus. No, not exile. It is your death I want,
So that all the world may see what treason means.

Creon. You will persist, then? You will not believe me?

Oedipus. How can I believe you?

Creon. Then you are a fool.

Oedipus. To save myself?

Creon. In justice, think of me.

Oedipus. You are evil incarnate.

Creon. But suppose that you are wrong?

Oedipus. Still I must rule.

Creon. But not if you rule badly.

Oedipus. O city, city!

Creon. It is my city, too!

Choragos. Now, my lords, be still. I see the Queen,
Iocastê, coming from her palace chambers;
And it is time she came, for the sake of you both.
This dreadful quarrel can be resolved through her.

[*Enter* Iocastê

Iocastê. Poor foolish men, what wicked din is this?

With Thebes sick to death, is it not shameful
That you should rake some private quarrel up?

[*To* Oedipus:

Come into the house.

—And you, Creon, go now:

Let us have no more of this tumult over nothing.

Creon. Nothing? No, sister: what your husband plans for me
Is one of two great evils: exile or death.

Oedipus. He is right.

Why, woman I have caught him squarely
Plotting against my life.

Creon. No! Let me die
Accurst if ever I have wished you harm!

Iocastê. Ah, believe it, Oedipus!
In the name of the gods, respect this oath of his
For my sake, for the sake of these people here!

[Strophe 1

Choragos. Open your mind to her, my lord. Be ruled by her, I beg you!

Oedipus. What would you have me do?

Choragos. Respect Creon's word. He has never spoken like a fool,
And now he has sworn an oath.

Oedipus. You know what you ask?

Choragos. I do.

Oedipus. Speak on, then.

Choragos. A friend so sworn should not be baited so,
In blind malice, and without final proof.

Oedipus. You are aware, I hope, that what you say
Means death for me, or exile at the least.

Choragos. No, I swear by Helios, first in Heaven! [Strophe 2
May I die friendless and accurst,
The worst of deaths, if ever I meant that!
It is the withering fields
That hurt my sick heart:
Must we bear all these ills,
And now your bad blood as well?

Oedipus. Then let him go. And let me die, if I must,
Or be driven by him in shame from the land of Thebes.
It is your unhappiness, and not his talk,

That touches me.
As for him—
Wherever he goes, hatred will follow him.
Creon. Ugly in yielding, as you were ugly in rage!
Natures like yours chiefly torment themselves.
Oedipus. Can you not go? Can you not leave me?
Creon. I can.
You do not know me; but the city knows me,
And in its eyes I am just, if not in yours.

[*Exit* Creon

[Antistrophe 1

Choragos. Lady Iocastê, did you not ask the King to go to his Chambers?
Iocastê. First tell me what has happened.
Choragos. There was suspicion without evidence; yet it rankled
As even false charges will.
Iocastê. On both sides?
Choragos. On both.
Iocastê. But what was said?
Choragos. Oh let it rest, let it be done with!
Have we not suffered enough?
Oedipus. You see to what your decency has brought you:
You have made difficulties where my heart saw none.

[Antistrophe 2

Choragos. Oedipus, it is not once only I have told you—
You must know I should count myself unwise
To the point of madness, should I now forsake you—
You, under whose hand,
In the storm of another time,
Our dear land sailed out free.
But now stand fast at the helm!
Iocastê. In God's name, Oedipus, inform your wife as well:
Why are you so set in this hard anger?
Oedipus. I will tell you, for none of these men deserves
My confidence as you do. It is Creon's work,
His treachery, his plotting against me.
Iocastê. Go on, if you can make this clear to me.
Oedipus. He charges me with the murder of Laïos.

Iocastê. Has he some knowledge? Or does he speak from hearsay?
Oedipus. He would not commit himself to such a charge,
But he has brought in that damnable soothsayer
To tell his story.
Iocastê. Set your mind at rest.
If it is a question of soothsayers, I tell you
That you will find no man whose craft gives knowledge
Of the unknowable.

Here is my proof:

An oracle was reported to Laïos once
(I will not say from Phoibos himself, but from
His appointed ministers, at any rate)
That his doom would be death at the hands of his own son—
His son, born of his flesh and of mine!

Now, you remember the story: Laïos was killed
By marauding strangers where three highways meet;
But his child had not been three days in this world
Before the King had pierced the baby's ankles
And left him to die on a lonely mountainside.

Thus, Apollo never caused that child
To kill his father, and it was not Laïos' fate
To die at the hands of his son, as he had feared.
This is what prophets and prophecies are worth!
Have no dread of them.
It is God himself
Who can show us what he wills, in his own way.
Oedipus. How strange a shadowy memory crossed my mind,
Just now while you were speaking; it chilled my heart.
Iocastê. What do you mean? What memory do you speak of?
Oedipus. If I understand you, Laïos was killed
At a place where three roads meet.
Iocastê. So it was said;
We have no later story.
Oedipus. Where did it happen?
Iocastê. Phokis, it is called: at a place where the Theban Way
Divides into the roads toward Delphi and Daulia.
Oedipus. When?
Iocastê. We had the news not long before you came
And proved the right to your succession here.

Oedipus. Ah, what net has God been weaving for me?
Iocastê. Oedipus! Why does this trouble you?
Oedipus. Do not ask me yet.
First, tell me how Laïos looked, and tell me
How old he was.
Iocastê. He was tall, his hair just touched
With white; his form was not unlike your own.
Oedipus. I think that I myself may be accurst
By my own ignorant edict.
Iocastê. You speak strangely.
It makes me tremble to look at you, my King.
Oedipus. I am not sure that the blind man can not see.
But I should know better if you were to tell me—
Iocastê. Anything—though I dread to hear you ask it.
Oedipus. Was the King lightly escorted, or did he ride
With a large company, as a ruler should?
Iocastê. There were five men with him in all: one was a herald,
And a single chariot, which he was driving.
Oedipus. Alas, that makes it plain enough!
But who—
Who told you how it happened?
Iocastê. A household servant,
The only one to escape.
Oedipus. And is he still
A servant of ours?
Iocastê. No; for when he came back at last
And found you enthroned in the place of the dead king,
He came to me, touched my hand with his, and begged
That I would send him away to the frontier district
Where only the shepherds go—
As far away from the city as I could send him.
I granted his prayer; for although the man was a slave,
He had earned more than this favor at my hands.
Oedipus. Can he be called back quickly?
Iocastê. Easily.
But why?
Oedipus. I have taken too much upon myself
Without enquiry; therefore I wish to consult him.
Iocastê. Then he shall come.
But am I not one also
To whom you might confide these fears of yours?
Oedipus. That is your right; it will not be denied you,

Now least of all; for I have reached a pitch
Of wild foreboding. Is there anyone
To whom I should sooner speak?

Polybos of Corinth is my father.
My mother is a Dorian: Meropê.
I grew up chief among the men of Corinth
Until a strange thing happened—
Not worth my passion, it may be, but strange.

At a feast, a drunken man maundering in his cups
Cries out that I am not my father's son!

I contained myself that night, though I felt anger
And a sinking heart. The next day I visited
My father and mother, and questioned them. They stormed,
Calling it all the slanderous rant of a fool;
And this relieved me. Yet the suspicion
Remained always aching in my mind;
I knew there was talk; I could not rest;
And finally, saying nothing to my parents,
I went to the shrine at Delphi.
The god dismissed my question without reply;
He spoke of other things.

Some were clear,
Full of wretchedness, dreadful, unbearable:
As, that I should lie with my own mother, breed
Children from whom all men would turn their eyes;
And that I should be my father's murderer.

I heard all this, and fled. And from that day
Corinth to me was only in the stars
Descending in that quarter of the sky,
As I wandered farther and farther on my way
To a land where I should never see the evil
Sung by the oracle. And I came to this country
Where, so you say, King Laïos was killed.

I will tell you all that happened there, my lady.

There were three highways
Coming together at a place I passed;
And there a herald came towards me, and a chariot
Drawn by horses, with a man such as you describe
Seated in it. The groom leading the horses
Forced me off the road at his lord's command;

But as this charioteer lurched over towards me
I struck him in my rage. The old man saw me
And brought his double goad down upon my head
As I came abreast.
He was paid back, and more!
Swinging my club in this right hand I knocked him
Out of his car, and he rolled on the ground.
I killed him.

I killed them all.
Now if that stranger and Laïos were—kin,
Where is a man more miserable than I?
More hated by the gods? Citizen and alien alike
Must never shelter me or speak to me—
I must be shunned by all.
And I myself
Pronounced this malediction upon myself!

Think of it: I have touched you with these hands,
These hands that killed your husband. What defilement!

Am I all evil, then? It must be so,
Since I must flee from Thebes, yet never again
See my own countrymen, my own country,
For fear of joining my mother in marriage
And killing Polybos, my father.
Ah,
If I was created so, born to this fate,
Who could deny the savagery of God?

O holy majesty of heavenly powers!
May I never see that day! Never!
Rather let me vanish from the race of men
Than know the abomination destined me!

Choragos. We too, my lord, have felt dismay at this.
But there is hope: you have yet to hear the shepherd.

Oedipus. Indeed, I fear no other hope is left me.

Iocastê. What do you hope from him when he comes?

Oedipus. This much:
If his account of the murder tallies with yours,
Then I am cleared.

Iocastê. What was it that I said
Of such importance?

Oedipus. Why, "marauders," you said,
Killed the King, according to this man's story.
If he maintains that still, if there were several,
Clearly the guilt is not mine: I was alone.
But if he says one man, singlehanded, did it,
Then the evidence all points to me.

Iocastê. You may be sure that he said there were several;
And can he call back that story now? He can not.
The whole city heard it as plainly as I.
But suppose he alters some detail of it:
He can not ever show that Laïos' death
Fulfilled the oracle: for Apollo said
My child was doomed to kill him; and my child—
Poor baby!—it was my child that died first.

No. From now on, where oracles are concerned,
I would not waste a second thought on any.

Oedipus. You may be right.
But come: let someone go
For the shepherd at once. This matter must be settled.

Iocastê. I will send for him.
I would not wish to cross you in anything,
And surely not in this.—Let us go in.

[*Exeunt into the palace*

ODE II

Chorus. Let me be reverent in the ways of right, [Strophe 1
Lowly the paths I journey on;
Let all my words and actions keep
The laws of the pure universe
From highest Heaven handed down.
For Heaven is their bright nurse,
Those generations of the realms of light;
Ah, never of mortal kind were they begot,
Nor are they slaves of memory, lost in sleep:
Their Father is greater than Time, and ages not.

The tyrant is a child of Pride [Antistrophe 1
Who drinks from his great sickening cup
Recklessness and vanity,

Until from his high crest headlong
He plummets to the dust of hope.
That strong man is not strong.
But let no fair ambition be denied;
May God protect the wrestler for the State
In government, in comely policy,
Who will fear God, and on His ordinance wait.

Haughtiness and the high hand of disdain [Strophe 2
Tempt and outrage God's holy law;
And any mortal who dares hold
No immortal Power in awe
Will be caught up in a net of pain:
The price for which his levity is sold.
Let each man take due earnings, then,
And keep his hands from holy things,
And from blasphemy stand apart—
Else the crackling blast of heaven
Blows on his head, and on his desperate heart;
Though fools will honor impious men,
In their cities no tragic poet sings.

Shall we lose faith in Delphi's obscurities, [Antistrophe 2
We who have heard the world's core
Discredited, and the sacred wood
Of Zeus at Elis praised no more?
The deeds and the strange prophecies
Must make a pattern yet to be understood.
Zeus, if indeed you are lord of all,
Throned in light over night and day,
Mirror this in your endless mind:
Our masters call the oracle
Words on the wind, and the Delphic vision blind!
Their hearts no longer know Apollo,
And reverence for the gods has died away.

SCENE III

[*Enter Iocastê*

Iocastê. Princes of Thebes, it has occurred to me
To visit the altars of the gods, bearing

These branches as a suppliant, and this incense.
Our King is not himself: his noble soul
Is overwrought with fantasies of dread,
Else he would consider
The new prophecies in the light of the old.
He will listen to any voice that speaks disaster,
And my advice goes for nothing.

[*She approaches the altar, R.*

To you, then, Apollo,
Lycean lord, since you are nearest, I turn in prayer.
Receive these offerings, and grant us deliverance
From defilement. Our hearts are heavy with fear
When we see our leader distracted, as helpless sailors
Are terrified by the confusion of their helmsman.

[*Enter Messenger*

Messenger. Friends, no doubt you can direct me:
Where shall I find the house of Oedipus,
Or, better still, where is the King himself?
Choragos. It is this very place, stranger; he is inside.
This is his wife and mother of his children.
Messenger. I wish her happiness in a happy house,
Best in all the fulfillment of her marriage.
Iocastê. I wish as much for you: your courtesy
Deserves a like good fortune. But now, tell me:
Why have you come? What have you to say to us?
Messenger. Good news, my lady, for your house and your husband.
Iocastê. What news? Who sent you here?
Messenger. I am from Corinth.
The news I bring ought to mean joy for you,
Though it may be you will find some grief in it.
Iocastê. What is it? How can it touch us in both ways?
Messenger. The word is that the people of the Isthmus
Intend to call Oedipus to be their king.
Iocastê. But old King Polybos—is he not reigning still?
Messenger. No. Death holds him in his sepulchre.
Iocastê. What are you saying? Polybos is dead?
Messenger. If I am not telling the truth, may I die myself.

Iocastê. [*To a* Maidservant:
Go in, go quickly; tell this to your master.

O riddlers of God's will, where are you now!
This was the man whom Oedipus, long ago,
Feared so, fled so, in dread of destroying him—
But it was another fate by which he died. [*Enter* Oedipus, C.

Oedipus. Dearest Iocastê, why have you sent for me?

Iocastê. Listen to what this man says, and then tell me
What has become of the solemn prophecies.

Oedipus. Who is this man? What is his news for me?

Iocastê. He has come from Corinth to announce your father's death!

Oedipus. Is it true, stranger? Tell me in your own words.

Messenger. I can not say it more clearly: the King is dead.

Oedipus. Was it by treason? Or by an attack of illness?

Messenger. A little thing brings old men to their rest.

Oedipus. It was sickness, then?

Messenger. Yes, and his many years.

Oedipus. Ah!
Why should a man respect the Pythian hearth, or
Give heed to the birds that jangle above his head?
They prophesied that I should kill Polybos,
Kill my own father; but he is dead and buried,
And I am here—I never touched him, never,
Unless he died of grief for my departure,
And thus, in a sense, through me. No. Polybos
Has packed the oracles off with him underground.
They are empty words.

Iocastê. Had I not told you so?

Oedipus. You had; it was my faint heart that betrayed me.

Iocastê. From now on never think of those things again.

Oedipus. And yet—must I not fear my mother's bed?

Iocastê. Why should anyone in this world be afraid,
Since Fate rules us and nothing can be foreseen?
A man should live only for the present day.

Have no more fear of sleeping with your mother:
How many men, in dreams, have lain with their mothers!
No reasonable man is troubled by such things.

Oedipus. That is true; only—
If only my mother were not still alive!
But she is alive. I can not help my dread.

Iocastê. Yet this news of your father's death is wonderful.

Oedipus. Wonderful. But I fear the living woman.

Messenger. Tell me, who is this woman that you fear?
Oedipus. It is Meropê, man; the wife of King Polybos.
Messenger. Meropê? Why should you be afraid of her?
Oedipus. An oracle of the gods, a dreadful saying.
Messenger. Can you tell me about it or are you sworn to silence?
Oedipus. I can tell you, and I will.
Apollo said through his prophet that I was the man
Who should marry his own mother, shed his father's blood
With his own hands. And so, for all these years
I have kept clear of Corinth, and no harm has come—
Though it would have been sweet to see my parents again.
Messenger. And is this the fear that drove you out of Corinth?
Oedipus. Would you have me kill my father?
Messenger. As for that
You must be reassured by the news I gave you.
Oedipus. If you could reassure me, I would reward you.
Messenger. I had that in mind, I will confess: I thought
I could count on you when you returned to Corinth.
Oedipus. No: I will never go near my parents again.
Messenger. Ah, son, you still do not know what you are doing—
Oedipus. What do you mean? In the name of God tell me!
Messenger. —If these are your reasons for not going home.
Oedipus. I tell you, I fear the oracle may come true.
Messenger. And guilt may come upon you through your parents?
Oedipus. That is the dread that is always in my heart.
Messenger. Can you not see that all your fears are groundless?
Oedipus. How can you say that? They are my parents, surely?
Messenger. Polybos was not your father.
Oedipus. Not my father?
Messenger. No more your father than the man speaking to you.
Oedipus. But you are nothing to me!
Messenger. Neither was he.
Oedipus. Then why did he call me son?
Messenger. I will tell you:
Long ago he had you from my hands, as a gift.
Oedipus. Then how could he love me so, if I was not his?
Messenger. He had no children, and his heart turned to you.
Oedipus. What of you? Did you buy me? Did you find me by chance?
Messenger. I came upon you in the crooked pass of Kithairon.
Oedipus. And what were you doing there?

Messenger. Tending my flocks.
Oedipus. A wandering shepherd?
Messenger. But your savior, son, that day.
Oedipus. From what did you save me?
Messenger. Your ankles should tell you that.
Oedipus. Ah, stranger, why do you speak of that childhood pain?
Messenger. I cut the bonds that tied your ankles together.
Oedipus. I have had the mark as long as I can remember.
Messenger. That was why you were given the name you bear.
Oedipus. God! Was it my father and my mother who did it?
Tell me!
Messenger. I do not know. The man who gave you to me
can tell you better than I.
Oedipus. It was not you that found me, but another?
Messenger. It was another shepherd gave you to me.
Oedipus. Who was he? Can you tell me who he was?
Messenger. I think he was said to be one of Laïos' people.
Oedipus. You mean the Laïos who was king here years ago?
Messenger. Yes; King Laïos; and the man was one of his herdsmen.
Oedipus. Is he still alive? Can I see him?
Messenger. These men here
Know best about such things.
Oedipus. Does anyone here
Know this shepherd that he is talking about?
Have you seen him in the fields, or in the town?
If you have, tell me. It is time things were made plain.
Choragos. I think the man he means is that same shepherd
You have already asked to see. Iocastê perhaps
Could tell you something.
Oedipus. Do you know anything
About him, Lady? Is he the man we have summoned?
Is that the man this shepherd means?
Iocastê. Why think of him?
Forget this herdsman. Forget it all.
This talk is a waste of time.
Oedipus. How can you say that,
When the clues to my true birth are in my hands?
Iocastê. For God's love, let us have no more questioning!
Is your life nothing to you?
My own is pain enough for me to bear.
Oedipus. You need not worry. Suppose my mother a slave,

And born of slaves: no baseness can touch you.
Iocastê. Listen to me, I beg you: do not do this thing!
Oedipus. I will not listen; the truth must be made known.
Iocastê. Everything that I say is for your own good!
Oedipus. My own good
Snaps my patience, then; I want none of it.
Iocastê. You are fatally wrong! May you never learn who you are!
Oedipus. Go, one of you, and bring the shepherd here.
Let us leave this woman to brag of her royal name.
Iocastê. Ah, miserable!
That is the only word I have for you now.
That is the only word I can ever have.

[*Exit into the palace*

Choragos. Why has she left us, Oedipus? Why has she gone
In such a passion of sorrow? I fear this silence;
Something dreadful may come of it.
Oedipus. Let it come!
However base my birth, I must know about it.
The Queen, like a woman, is perhaps ashamed
To think of my low origin. But I
Am a child of Luck; I can not be dishonored.
Luck is my mother; the passing months, my brothers,
Have seen me rich and poor.
If this is so,
How could I wish that I were someone else?
How could I not be glad to know my birth?

ODE III

Chorus. If ever the coming time were known [Strophe
To my heart's pondering,
Kithairon, now by Heaven I see the torches
At the festival of the next full moon,
And see the dance, and hear the choir sing
A grace to your gentle shade:
Mountain where Oedipus was found,
O mountain guard of a noble race!
May the god who heals us lend his aid,
And let that glory come to pass
For our king's cradling-ground.

Of the nymphs that flower beyond the years, [Antistrophe
Who bore you, royal child,
To Pan of the hills or the timberline Apollo,
Cold in delight where the upland clears,
Or Hermês for whom Kyllenê's heights are piled?
Or flushed as evening cloud,
Great Dionysos, roamer of mountains,
He—was it he who found you there,
And caught you up in his own proud
Arms from the sweet god-ravisher
Who laughed by the Muses' fountains?

SCENE IV

Oedipus. Sirs: though I do not know the man,
I think I see him coming, this shepherd we want:
He is old, like our friend here, and the men
Bringing him seem to be servants of my house.
But you can tell, if you have ever seen him.

[*Enter* Shepherd *escorted by servants*

Choragos. I know him, he was Laïos' man. You can trust him.
Oedipus. Tell me first, you from Corinth: is this the shepherd
We were discussing?
Messenger. This is the very man.
Oedipus. [*To* Shepherd
Come here. No, look at me. You must answer
Everything I ask.—You belonged to Laïos?
Shepherd. Yes: born his slave, brought up in his house.
Oepidus. Tell me: what kind of work did you do for him?
Shepherd. I was a shepherd of his, most of my life.
Oedipus. Where mainly did you go for pasturage?
Shepherd. Sometimes Kithairon, sometimes the hills near-by.
Oedipus. Do you remember ever seeing this man out there?
Shepherd. What would he be doing there? This man?
Oedipus. This man standing here. Have you ever seen him before?
Shepherd. No. At least, not to my recollection.
Messenger. And that is not strange, my lord. But I'll refresh
His memory: he must remember when we two
Spent three whole seasons together, March to September,
On Kithairon or thereabouts. He had two flocks;

I had one. Each autumn I'd drive mine home
And he would go back with his to Laïos' sheepfold.—
Is this not true, just as I have described it?

Shepherd. True, yes; but it was all so long ago.

Messenger. Well, then: do you remember, back in those days
That you gave me a baby boy to bring up as my own?

Shepherd. What if I did? What are you trying to say?

Messenger. King Oedipus was once that little child.

Shepherd. Damn you, hold your tongue!

Oedipus. No more of that!
It is your tongue needs watching, not this man's.

Shepherd. My King, my Master, what is it I have done wrong?

Oedipus. You have not answered his question about the boy.

Shepherd. He does not know . . . He is only making trouble . . .

Oedipus. Come, speak plainly, or it will go hard with you.

Shepherd. In God's name, do not torture an old man!

Oedipus. Come here, one of you; bind his arms behind him.

Shepherd. Unhappy king! What more do you wish to learn?

Oedipus. Did you give this man the child he speaks of?

Shepherd. I did.
And I would to God I had died that very day.

Oedipus. You will die now unless you speak the truth.

Shepherd. Yet if I speak the truth, I am worse than dead.

Oedipus. Very well; since you insist upon delaying—

Shepherd. No! I have told you already that I gave him the boy.

Oedipus. Where did you get him? From your house? From somewhere else?

Shepherd. Not from mine, no. A man gave him to me.

Oedipus. Is that man here? Do you know whose slave he was?

Shepherd. For God's love, my King, do not ask me any more!

Oedipus. You are a dead man if I have to ask you again.

Shepherd. Then . . . Then the child was from the palace of Laïos.

Oedipus. A slave child? or a child of his own line?

Shepherd. Ah, I am on the brink of dreadful speech!

Oedipus. And I of dreadful hearing. Yet I must hear.

Shepherd. If you must be told, then . . .
They said it was Laïos' child;
But it is your wife who can tell you about that.

Oedipus. My wife!—Did she give it to you?

Shepherd. My lord, she did.

Oedipus. Do you know why?

Shepherd. I was told to get rid of it.
Oedipus. An unspeakable mother!
Shepherd. There had been prophecies . . .
Oedipus. Tell me.
Shepherd. It was said that the boy would kill his own father.
Oedipus. Then why did you give him over to this old man?
Shepherd. I pitied the baby, my King,
And I thought that this man would take him far away
To his own country.
He saved him—but for what a fate!
For if you are what this man says you are,
No man living is more wretched than Oedipus.
Oedipus. Ah God!
It was true!
All the prophecies!
—Now,
O light, may I look on you for the last time!
I, Oedipus,
Oedipus, damned in his birth, in his marriage damned,
Damned in the blood he shed with his own hand!

[*He rushes into the palace*

ODE IV

Chorus. Alas for the seed of men. [Strophe 1

What measure shall I give these generations
That breathe on the void and are void
And exist and do not exist?

Who bears more weight of joy
Than mass of sunlight shifting in images,
Or who shall make his thought stay on
That down time drifts away?

Your splendor is all fallen.

O naked brow of wrath and tears,
O change of Oedipus!
I who saw your days call no man blest—
Your great days like ghósts góne.

That mind was a strong bow. [Antistrophe 1

Deep, how deep you drew it then, hard archer,
At a dim fearful range,
And brought dear glory down!

You overcame the stranger—
The virgin with her hooking lion claws—
And though death sang, stood like a tower
To make pale Thebes take heart.

Fortress against our sorrow!

True king, giver of laws,
Majestic Oedipus!
No prince in Thebes had ever such renown,
No prince won such grace of power.

And now of all men ever known [Strophe 2
Most pitiful is this man's story:
His fortunes are most changed, his state
Fallen to a low slave's
Ground under bitter fate.

O Oedipus, most royal one!
The great door that expelled you to the light
Gave at night—ah, gave night to your glory:
As to the father, to the fathering son.

All understood too late.

How could that queen whom Laïos won,
The garden that he harrowed at his height,
Be silent when that act was done?

But all eyes fail before time's eye, [Antistrophe 2
All actions come to justice there.
Though never willed, though far down the deep past,
Your bed, your dread sirings,
Are brought to book at last.
Child by Laïos doomed to die,
Then doomed to lose that fortunate little death,
Would God you never took breath in this air
That with my wailing lips I take to cry:

For I weep the world's outcast.

I was blind, and now I can tell why:

Asleep, for you had given ease of breath
To Thebes, while the false years went by.

ÉXODOS

[*Enter, from the palace,* Second Messenger

Second Messenger. Elders of Thebes, most honored in this land,
What horrors are yours to see and hear, what weight
Of sorrow to be endured, if, true to your birth,
You venerate the line of Labdakos!
I think neither Istros nor Phasis, those great rivers,
Could purify this place of the corruption
It shelters now, or soon must bring to light—
Evil not done unconsciously, but willed.

The greatest griefs are those we cause ourselves.

Choragos. Surely, friend, we have grief enough already;
What new sorrow do you mean?
Second Messenger. The Queen is dead.
Choragos. Iocastê? Dead? But at whose hand?
Second Messenger. Her own.
The full horror of what happened you can not know,
For you did not see it; but I, who did, will tell you
As clearly as I can how she met her death.

When she had left us,
In passionate silence, passing through the court,
She ran to her apartment in the house,
Her hair clutched by the fingers of both hands.
She closed the doors behind her; then, by that bed
Where long ago the fatal son was conceived—
That son who should bring about his father's death—
We heard her call upon Laïos, dead so many years,
And heard her wail for the double fruit of her marriage,
A husband by her husband, children by her child.

Exactly how she died I do not know:
For Oedipus burst in moaning and would not let us
Keep vigil to the end: it was by him
As he stormed about the room that our eyes were caught.
From one to another of us he went, begging a sword,

Cursing the wife who was not his wife, the mother
Whose womb had carried his own children and himself.
I do not know: it was none of us aided him,
But surely one of the gods was in control!
For with a dreadful cry
He hurled his weight, as though wrenched out of himself,
At the twin doors: the bolts gave, and he rushed in.
And there we saw her hanging, her body swaying
From the cruel cord she had noosed about her neck.
A great sob broke from him, heartbreaking to hear,
As he loosed the rope and lowered her to the ground.

I would blot out from my mind what happened next!
For the King ripped from her gown the golden brooches
That were her ornament, and raised them, and plunged them down
Straight into his own eyeballs, crying, "No more,
No more shall you look on the misery about me,
The horrors of my own doing! Too long you have known
The faces of those whom I should never have seen,
Too long been blind to those for whom I was searching!
From this hour, go in darkness!" And as he spoke
He struck at his eyes—not once, but many times;
And the blood spattered his beard,
Bursting from his ruined sockets like red hail.

So from the unhappiness of two this evil has sprung,
A curse on the man and woman alike. The old
Happiness of the house of Labdakos
Was happiness enough: where is it today?
It is all wailing and ruin, disgrace, death—all
The misery of mankind that has a name—
And it is wholly and for ever theirs.

Choragos. Is he in agony still? Is there no rest for him?

Second Messenger. He is calling for someone to lead him to the gates
So that all the children of Kadmos may look upon
His father's murderer, his mother's—no,
I can not say it!
And then he will leave Thebes,
Self-exiled, in order that the curse
Which he himself pronounced may depart from the house.
He is weak, and there is none to lead him,

So terrible is his suffering.
But you will see:
Look, the doors are opening; in a moment
You will see a thing that would crush a heart of stone.

[*The central door is opened;* Oedipus, *blinded, is led in*

Choragos. Dreadful indeed for men to see.
Never have my own eyes
Looked on a sight so full of fear.

Oedipus!
What madness came upon you, what daemon
Leaped on your life with heavier
Punishment than a mortal man can bear?
No: I can not even
Look at you, poor ruined one.
And I would speak, question, ponder,
If I were able. No.
You make me shudder.
Oedipus. God. God.
Is there a sorrow greater?
Where shall I find harbor in this world?
My voice is hurled far on a dark wind.
What has God done to me?
Choragos. Too terrible to think of, or to see.

Oedipus. O cloud of night, [Strophe 1
Never to be turned away: night coming on,
I can not tell how: night like a shroud!

My fair winds brought me here.
O God. Again
The pain of the spikes where I had sight,
The flooding pain
Of memory never to be gouged out.
Choragos. This is not strange.
You suffer it all twice over, remorse in pain,
Pain in remorse.

Oedipus. Ah dear friend [Antistrophe 1
Are you faithful even yet, you alone?
Are you still standing near me, will you stay here,

Patient, to care for the blind?
The blind man!
Yet even blind I know who it is attends me,
By the voice's tone—
Though my new darkness hide the comforter.
Choragos. Oh fearful act!
What god was it drove you to rake black
Night across your eyes?

Oedipus. Apollo. Apollo. Dear [Strophe 2
Children, the god was Apollo.
He brought my sick, sick fate upon me.
But the blinding hand was my own!
How could I bear to see
When all my sight was horror everywhere?
Choragos. Everywhere; that is true.
Oedipus. And now what is left?
Images? Love? A greeting even,
Sweet to the senses? Is there anything?
Ah, no, friends: lead me away.
Lead me away from Thebes.
Lead the great wreck
And hell of Oedipus, whom the gods hate.
Choragos. Your fate is clear, you are not blind to that.
Would God you had never found it out!

Oedipus. Death take the man who unbound [Antistrophe 2
My feet on that hillside
And delivered me from death to life! What life?
If only I had died,
This weight of monstrous doom
Could not have dragged me and my darlings down.
Choragos. I would have wished the same.
Oedipus. Oh never to have come here
With my father's blood upon me! Never
To have been the man they call his mother's husband!
Oh accurst! Oh child of evil,
To have entered that wretched bed—
the selfsame one!
More primal than sin itself, this fell to me.
Choragos. I do not know how I can answer you.

You were better dead than alive and blind.
Oedipus. Do not counsel me any more. This punishment
That I have laid upon myself is just.
If I had eyes,
I do not know how I could bear the sight
Of my father, when I came to the house of Death,
Or my mother: for I have sinned against them both
So vilely that I could not make my peace
By strangling my own life.
Or do you think my children,
Born as they were born, would be sweet to my eyes?
Ah never, never! Nor this town with its high walls,
Nor the holy images of the gods.
For I,
Thrice miserable!—Oedipus, noblest of all the line
Of Kadmos, have condemned myself to enjoy
These things no more, by my own malediction
Expelling that man whom the gods declared
To be a defilement in the house of Laïos.
After exposing the rankness of my own guilt,
How could I look men frankly in the eyes?
No, I swear it,
If I could have stifled my hearing at its source,
I would have done it and made all this body
A tight cell of misery, blank to light and sound:
So I should have been safe in a dark agony
Beyond all recollection.
Ah Kithairon!
Why did you shelter me? When I was cast upon you,
Why did I not die? Then I should never
Have shown the world my execrable birth.

Ah Polybos! Corinth, city that I believed
The ancient seat of my ancestors: how fair
I seemed, your child! And all the while this evil
Was cancerous within me!
For I am sick
In my daily life, sick in my origin.

O three roads, dark ravine, woodland and way
Where three roads met: you, drinking my father's blood,
My own blood, spilled by my own hand: can you remember
The unspeakable things I did there, and the things

I went on from there to do?
O marriage, marriage!
The act that engendered me, and again the act
Performed by the son in the same bed—
Ah, the net
Of incest, mingling fathers, brothers, sons,
With brides, wives, mothers: the last evil
That can be known by men: no tongue can say
How evil!
No. For the love of God, conceal me
Somewhere far from Thebes; or kill me; or hurl me
Into the sea, away from men's eyes for ever.

Come, lead me. You need not fear to touch me.
Of all men, I alone can bear this guilt.

[*Enter* Creon

Choragos. We are not the ones to decide; but Creon here
May fitly judge of what you ask. He only
Is left to protect the city in your place.
Oedipus. Alas, how can I speak to him? What right have I
To beg his courtesy whom I have deeply wronged?
Creon. I have not come to mock you, Oedipus,
Or to reproach you, either.
[*To* Attendants:
—You, standing there:
If you have lost all respect for man's dignity,
At least respect the flame of Lord Helios:
Do not allow this pollution to show itself
Openly here, an affront to the earth
And Heaven's rain and the light of day. No, take him
Into the house as quickly as you can.
For it is proper
That only the close kindred see his grief.
Oedipus. I pray you in God's name, since your courtesy
Ignores my dark expectation, visiting
With mercy this man of all men most execrable:
Give me what I ask—for your good, not for mine.
Creon. And what is it that you would have me do?
Oedipus. Drive me out of this country as quickly as may be
To a place where no human voice can ever greet me.
Creon. I should have done that before now—only,

God's will had not been wholly revealed to me.
Oedipus. But his command is plain: the parricide
Must be destroyed. I am that evil man.
Creon. That is the sense of it, yes; but as things are,
We had best discover clearly what is to be done.
Oedipus. You would learn more about a man like me?
Creon. You are ready now to listen to the god.
Oedipus. I will listen. But it is to you
That I must turn for help. I beg you, hear me.

The woman in there–
Give her whatever funeral you think proper:
She is your sister.
–But let me go, Creon!
Let me purge my father's Thebes of the pollution
Of my living here, and go out to the wild hills,
To Kithairon, that has won such fame with me,
The tomb my mother and father appointed for me,
And let me die there, as they willed I should.
And yet I know
Death will not ever come to me through sickness
Or in any natural way: I have been preserved
For some unthinkable fate. But let that be.

As for my sons, you need not care for them.
They are men, they will find some way to live.
But my poor daughters, who have shared my table,
Who never before have been parted from their father–
Take care of them, Creon; do this for me.
And will you let me touch them with my hands
A last time, and let us weep together?
Be kind, my lord,
Great prince, be kind!
Could I but touch them,
They would be mine again, as when I had my eyes.

[*Enter* Antigonê *and* Ismenê, *attended*

Ah, God!
Is it my dearest children I hear weeping?
Has Creon pitied me and sent my daughters?
Creon. Yes, Oedipus: I knew that they were dear to you
In the old days, and know you must love them still.

Oedipus. May God bless you for this—and be a friendlier
Guardian to you than he has been to me!

Children, where are you?
Come quickly to my hands: they are your brother's—
Hands that have brought your father's once clear eyes
To this way of seeing—
Ah dearest ones,
I had neither sight nor knowledge then, your father
By the woman who was the source of his own life!
And I weep for you—having no strength to see you—,
I weep for you when I think of the bitterness
That men will visit upon you all your lives.
What homes, what festivals can you attend
Without being forced to depart again in tears?
And when you come to marriageable age,
Where is the man, my daughters, who would dare
Risk the bane that lies on all my children?
Is there any evil wanting? Your father killed
His father; sowed the womb of her who bore him;
Engendered you at the fount of his own existence!
That is what they will say of you.

Then, whom
Can you every marry? There are no bridegrooms for you,
And your lives must wither away in sterile dreaming.

O Creon, son of Menoikeus!
You are the only father my daughters have,
Since we, their parents, are both of us gone for ever.
They are your own blood: you will not let them
Fall into beggary and loneliness;
You will keep them from the miseries that are mine!
Take pity on them; see, they are only children,
Friendless except for you. Promise me this,
Great Prince, and give me your hand in token of it.

[Creon *clasps his right hand*

Children:
I could say much, if you could understand me,
But as it is, I have only this prayer for you:

Live where you can, be as happy as you can—
Happier, please God, than God has made your father!

Creon. Enough. You have wept enough. Now go within.

Oedipus. I must; but it is hard.

Creon. Time eases all things.

Oedipus. But you must promise—

Creon. Say what you desire.

Oedipus. Send me from Thebes!

Creon. God grant that I may!

Oedipus. But since God hates me . . .

Creon. No, he will grant your wish.

Oedipus. You promise?

Creon. I can not speak beyond my knowledge.

Oedipus. Then lead me in.

Creon. Come now, and leave your children.

Oedipus. No! Do not take them from me!

Creon. Think no longer
That you are in command here, but rather think
How, when you were, you served your own destruction.

[*Exeunt into the house all but the* Chorus; *the* Choragos *chants directly to the audience:*

Choragos. Men of Thebes: look upon Oedipus.

This is the king who solved the famous riddle
And towered up, most powerful of men.
No mortal eyes but looked on him with envy,
Yet in the end ruin swept over him.

Let every man in mankind's frailty
Consider his last day; and let none
Presume on his good fortune until he find
Life, at his death, a memory without pain.

Questions

1. In the Prologue, Oedipus appears supremely confident of his ability to alleviate the sufferings of the people of Thebes. Does the Priest contribute to the overweening confidence of the King? Although the Priest admits that Oedipus is "not one of the immortal gods," does his later suggestion imply that man (at least a king) can control his destiny and even the history of the state? What is the irony of the state-

ment by Oedipus to the people that, "Sick as you are, not one is as sick as I"?

2. Aristotle defines the tragic hero as "the man who occupies the mean between saintliness and depravity. He is not extraordinary in virtue and righteousness, and yet does not fall into bad fortune because of evil and wickedness, but because of some error of the kind found in men of high reputation and good fortune. . . ." Do you think Oedipus fulfills these requirements?
3. Do the outbursts of impatience and rage from Oedipus suggest that he believes a simple, rational solution can be found for every human problem? Do you think that he attempts to solve the problem of the sickness of Thebes in much the same way that he achieved the leadership of the state?
4. Why is Teiresias reluctant to reveal to Oedipus the truth about the cause of the pollution of Thebes, especially when he asserts, "It is the truth sustains me"? Does Teiresias give to "truth" here a meaning that Oedipus is not ready to understand?
5. The Chorus often seems to sympathize with Oedipus, and as often passes harsh judgment upon him. What does this apparent change in viewpoint add to the richness of the plot?

Topics for Composition

1. Compare and contrast Creon and Oedipus from the standpoint of their temperaments, their attachment to "facts" as the basis for action, their commitment to royal prerogative and responsibility, and their sense of the greatness and limitation of man. Be sure to cite passages or phrases, even single words, of dialogue that reveal the likenesses or distinctions between the two men.
2. Analyze the position represented by Iocastê's judgment of the prophecy. Does she seem to argue for a meaningless existence when she says (in scene ii), "From now on, where oracles are concerned, / I would not waste a second thought on any"? Does her position seem attractive to Oedipus? In your paper, you may wish to trace the steps by which she develops her suspicion of and contempt for oracles.
3. Classify the associations developed by the words "see," "eyes," "sight," "blind," and related words in the play. In Milton's **Samson Agonistes,** the blind Samson's heroic destruction of his enemies is described thus by the Chorus: "But he though blind of sight, / Despis'd and thought extinguish't quite, / With inward eyes illuminated / His fierie vertue rouz'd / From under ashes into sudden flame . . . ." In **King Lear,** after Gloucester has been blinded and is told by the Old Man, "You cannot see your way," Gloucester comments on the remarkable inability of mankind to see with the eyes: "I have no way and therefore want no eyes; / I stumbled when I saw." (IV, i, 17–19.) Do these echoes of other great tragedies blend with the hints in **Oedipus** of the hero's inability to see significantly into the heart of the human condition until he has destroyed his own eyesight?

Poetry

EVERY common attitude toward death has found vital expression in poetry. The poems of this section, while they do not by any means represent adequately the whole range of significantly varying views, illustrate some of the most notable differences of opinion about the subject. At the same time, there are enough resemblances among them to make possible a kind of classification which may be of some use in analysis. We can begin with the reflection that just as the fact of death affects in some way everyone's attitude toward life, so do our general responses to life shape our views of death. For example, people who have found life richly rewarding may be able, as Robert Louis Stevenson's "Requiem" suggests, to accept death without complaint and without much questioning; those who have found life harrowing or frustrating, on the other hand, may be inclined, like the speaker in Swinburne's "The Garden of Proserpine," to look to death as a means of escape. Both of these poets think of death as a sleep; but while Stevenson uses the analogy as an expression of fulfillment, Swinburne is asserting, it seems, the ultimate futility of life. Robert Frost's "After Apple-Picking," although it offers a more complex and ambiguous statement, may be compared with "Requiem" in the respect that the reflections on death that it suggests are related to a sense of satisfaction with the efforts and achievements of a lifetime: having worked hard and faithfully, the speaker of this poem is ready for the sleep of death; and he knows that his dreams, if he has any, will embody, not unpleasantly, the essence of his feeling about his work. John Keats's "To Autumn" expresses, more subtly, the same general attitude, the feeling that "ripeness is all." With Swinburne's poem we may tentatively place Thomas Hardy's "Channel Firing"; at any rate, Hardy's poem poses the question whether the best fate for men generally would not be just eternal sleep.

In very different ways, then, either satisfaction with life or disappointment may reconcile reflective men to the idea of death as a sleep, even a dreamless sleep. Most men, however, find just enough of good and of evil in life to make them hope for something better beyond. Such an attitude appears in Wordsworth's "Ode: Intimations of Immortality." Although the poet has found growing up to involve an increasing sense of vulnerability and restriction, he has experienced enough beauty and love to be able to trust and cherish certain childhood intimations of immortality. A more confident expression of embattled faith is to be found in Browning's well-known "Prospice." For one who has rejoiced in the battle of life, it is easy, the poem asserts, to regard the fearfulness of death as a challenge, rewarding to the brave. But the greatest triumphs of the sense of moral value over the sense of natural evil have been achieved with the support of traditional religion; and poetry has offered no more eloquent testimony of that fact than such poems as John Donne's subtle and powerful "Death, Be Not Proud," Henry Vaughan's poignant "They Are All Gone into the World of Light," Milton's great elegy "Lycidas," and Gerard Manley Hopkins' sweetly thoughtful "The Caged Skylark."

There is another attitude toward death that may be said to reflect a general attitude toward life: we may be, and perhaps usually are, so involved with life's manifold pursuits that we can scarcely even believe in death. Such an attitude is most likely to be revealed by our responses to the death of others. Some of the poems that follow—"Musée des Beaux Arts," "Bells for John Whiteside's Daughter," and "Tract"—show that when it strikes others death often seems an incongruity, a cruel hoax, an embarrassment, or even a piece of irrelevance, depending upon how close it comes to us.

The method of classifying concepts of death by relating them to attitudes toward life is really useful only insofar as it leads, through careful comparison, to increased understanding of the possibilities of meaning and the sources of appeal of particular poems. It should certainly be tested, both by closer analysis of the works mentioned above, and by application to the other poems that appear in this section.

From *The Tempest*[1]

WILLIAM SHAKESPEARE

Our revels now are ended. These our actors,
As I foretold you, were all spirits, and
Are melted into air, into thin air; *150*
And, like the baseless fabric [2] of this vision,
The cloud-capp'd towers, the gorgeous palaces,
The solemn temples, the great globe itself,

[1] *Act IV, i, 148–58. Prospero, a magician, has summoned up spirits in the form of reapers and nymphs to perform a dance for the entertainment of his guests.*
[2] *Unsubstantial material.*

Yea, all which it inherit, shall dissolve
And, like this insubstantial pageant faded, *155*
Leave not a rack [3] behind. We are such stuff
As dreams are made on, and our little life
Is rounded [4] with a sleep.

1623

[3] *Cloud.*
[4] *Surrounded, framed.*

Death, Be Not Proud

JOHN DONNE

Death, be not proud, though some have called thee
Mighty and dreadful, for thou are not so;
For those whom thou think'st thou dost overthrow
Die not, poor Death; nor yet canst thou kill me.
From rest and sleep, which but thy picture be, *5*
Much pleasure; then from thee much more must flow;
And soonest our best men with thee do go—
Rest of their bones and souls' delivery!
Thou'rt slave to fate, chance, kings, and desperate men,
And dost with poison, war, and sickness dwell; *10*
And poppy [1] or charms can make us sleep as well
And better than thy stroke. Why swell'st thou then? [2]
One short sleep past, we wake eternally,
And Death shall be no more: Death, thou shalt die.

1633

[1] *Opiates.*
[2] *I.e., with pride.*

Questions

1. In addressing himself to death, the poet uses the device of personification. What does this contribute to the emotional content of the poem?
2. What arguments are used to refute the claim that death is mighty and dreadful? Are they convincing? Does the statement made in the last

two lines necessarily follow from the preceding statements? Is the poet really concerned about making a case, or is he more interested in expressing an attitude? If the latter is the important thing, of what use is the argument?

Hymn to God, My God, in My Sickness

JOHN DONNE

Since I am coming to that holy room,
Where, with thy choir of saints for evermore,
I shall be made thy music; as I come
I tune the instrument here at the door,
And what I must do then, think here before. *5*

Whilst my physicians by their love are grown
Cosmographers, and I their map, who lie
Flat on this bed, that by them may be shown
That this is my south-west discovery [1]
Per fretum febris,[2] by these straits to die, *10*

I joy, that in these straits, I see my west; [3]
For though their currents yield return to none,
What shall my west hurt me? As west and east
In all flat maps (and I am one) are one,
So death doth touch the Resurrection. *15*

Is the Pacific Sea my home? Or are
The eastern riches? Is Jerusalem?
Anyan,[4] and Magellan, and Gibraltar,
All straits, and none but straits, are ways to them,
Whether where Japhet dwelt, or Cham, or Shem.[5] *20*

We think that Paradise and Calvary,
Christ's cross, and Adam's tree, stood in one place;
Look, Lord, and find both Adams [6] met in me;
As the first Adam's sweat surrounds my face,
May the last Adam's blood my soul embrace. *25*

[1] *The reference is to the discovery of the Straits of Magellan.*
[2] *Through the straits of fever.*
[3] *I.e., the end of his life—and his own realm of discovery.*
[4] *The Bering Straits.*
[5] *The sons of Noah. The descendants of Japhet inhabited Europe, those of Ham, Africa, and those of Shem, Asia. See Genesis 10.*
[6] *Christ is the "last Adam."*

So, in his purple [7] wrapp'd, receive me, Lord,
By these his thorns [8] give me his other crown;
And as to others' souls I preach'd thy word,
Be this my text, my sermon to mine own,
Therefore that he may raise, the Lord throws down. 30

1635

[7] *I.e., in Christ's blood. Purple is also the color of royalty.*
[8] *Donne refers to the suffering caused by his illness.*

Questions

1. What is the point of resemblance between physicians and cosmographers that Donne has in mind?
2. With what is the discovery of new lands equated?
3. Why is it appropriate to compare sailing through straits with the experience of dying?
4. Is the wittiness of Donne's metaphors in keeping with the seriousness of the theme? How would you describe the poet's attitude toward his imminent death?

Lycidas[1]

JOHN MILTON

Yet once more, O ye laurels, and once more
Ye myrtles brown, with ivy never-sere,
I come to pluck your berries [2] harsh and crude; [3]
And, with forc'd fingers rude,
Shatter your leaves before the mellowing year. 5
Bitter constraint, and sad occasion dear,[4]
Compels me to disturb your season due:
For Lycidas is dead, dead ere his prime,
Young Lycidas, and hath not left his peer:

[1] *Lycidas is Milton's pastoral name for Edward King, his friend and fellow student at Cambridge, who was drowned in 1637. In keeping with the convention of pastoral poetry, Milton represents himself and his friend as being shepherds. Their piping and singing represent the writing of poetry. King had gone into the church, but he was also a poet.*
[2] *The first five lines mean that the speaker will attempt once more to write serious poetry even though the time is not ripe for him to do so. The laurel, myrtle, and ivy are all associated with poetic inspiration.*
[3] *Unripe.*
[4] *Sorely felt.*

Who would not sing for Lycidas? He knew *10*
Himself to sing, and build the lofty rhyme.
He must not float upon his watery bier
Unwept, and welter to the parching wind,
Without the mead [5] of some melodious tear.
Begin then, Sisters of the sacred well,[6] *15*
That from beneath the seat of Jove doth spring;
Begin, and somewhat loudly sweep the string.
Hence with denial vain, and coy excuse:
So may some gentle Muse
With lucky words favour my destin'd urn; [7] *20*
And, as he passes, turn,
And bid fair peace be to my sable shroud.
For we were nurs'd upon the self-same hill,
Fed the same flock by fountain, shade, and rill.
Together both, ere the high lawns appear'd *25*
Under the opening eye-lids of the morn,
We drove afield, and both together heard
What time the grey-fly winds her sultry horn,
Battening our flocks with the fresh dews of night,
Oft, till the star, that rose, at evening, bright, *30*
Toward heaven's descent had slop'd his westering wheel.
Meanwhile the rural ditties were not mute,
Temper'd to the oaten flute;
Rough Satyrs danc'd, and Fauns with cloven heel
From the glad sound would not be absent long; *35*
And old Damœtas [8] lov'd to hear our song.
But, O the heavy change, now thou art gone,
Now thou art gone, and never must return!
Thee, Shepherd, thee the woods, and desert caves
With wild thyme and the gadding vine o'ergrown, *40*
And all their echoes mourn:
The willows, and the hazel copses green,
Shall now no more be seen
Fanning their joyous leaves to thy soft lays.
As killing as the canker to the rose, *45*
Or taint-worm to the weanling herds that graze,
Or frost to flowers, that their gay wardrobe wear,
When first the white-thorn blows; [9]
Such, Lycidas, thy loss to shepherd's ear.

[5] *Reward.*
[6] *The Muses.*
[7] *I.e., burial urn.*
[8] *A typical pastoral name. Milton may refer to a tutor of theirs at Cambridge.*
[9] *Blossoms.*

Where were ye, Nymphs,[10] when the remorseless deep 50
Clos'd o'er the head of your lov'd Lycidas?
For neither were ye playing on the steep,[11]
Where your old Bards, the famous Druids, lie,
Nor on the shaggy top of Mona high,
Nor yet where Deva spreads her wizard stream: 55
Ay me! I fondly dream!
Had ye been there–for what could that have done?
What could the Muse [12] herself that Orpheus bore,
The Muse herself, for her enchanting son,
Whom universal Nature did lament. 60
When, by the rout that made the hideous roar,[13]
His gory visage down the stream was sent,
Down the swift Hebrus to the Lesbian shore?
Alas! what boots [14] it with incessant care
To tend the homely, slighted shepherd's trade, 65
And strictly meditate the thankless Muse?
Were it not better done, as others use,
To sport with Amaryllis [15] in the shade,
Or with the tangles of Neæra's hair?
Fame is the spur that the clear spirit doth raise 70
(That last infirmity of noble mind)
To scorn delights, and live laborious days;
But the fair guerdon [16] when we hope to find,
And think to burst out into sudden blaze,
Comes the blind Fury [17] with the abhorred shears, 75
And slits the thin-spun life. 'But not the praise',
Phœbus [18] replied, and touch'd my trembling ears;
'Fame is no plant that grows on mortal soil,
Nor in the glistering foil
Set off to the world, nor in broad rumour lies; 80
But lives and spreads aloft by those pure eyes,
And perfect witness of all-judging Jove;
As he pronounces lastly on each deed,

[10] *Nature deities.*
[11] *Ancient Celtic poet-priests. "Mona," the island of Anglesey, and "Deva," the river Dee, are near the place where his friend drowned.*
[12] *Calliope, Muse of epic poetry, was the mother of Orpheus, the famous musician.*
[13] *Orpheus was torn to pieces by a mob ("rout") of frenzied Maenads, female worshipers of Bacchus. They threw his head into the river Hebrus, down which it floated, still singing, and out to Lesbos.*
[14] *Profits.*
[15] *Some pretty nymph.*
[16] *Reward.*
[17] *Milton refers to Atropos, actually one of the three Fates. It is she who cuts the thread of life.*
[18] *Phoebus Apollo, the god of poetic inspiration.*

Of so much fame in heaven expect thy meed.'
O fountain Arethuse [19] and thou honour'd flood, *85*
Smooth-sliding Mincius, crown'd with vocal reeds.
That strain I heard was of a higher mood:
But now my oat proceeds,
And listens to the herald of the sea [20]
That came in Neptune's plea; *90*
He ask'd the waves, and ask'd the felon winds,
What hard mishap hath doom'd this gentle swain?
And question'd every gust of rugged wings
That blows from off each beaked promontory:
They knew not of his story; *95*
And sage Hippotades [21] their answer brings,
That not a blast was from his dungeon stray'd;
The air was calm, and on the level brine
Sleek Panope [22] with all her sisters play'd.
It was that fatal and perfidious bark, *100*
Built in the eclipse,[23] and rigg'd with curses dark,
That sunk so low that sacred head of thine.
Next Camus,[24] reverend sire, went footing slow,
His mantle hairy, and his bonnet sedge,
Inwrought with figures dim, and on the edge *105*
Like to that sanguine flower [25] inscrib'd with woe.
'Ah! Who hath reft (quoth he) my dearest pledge?'
Last came, and last did go,
The pilot of the Galilean lake; [26]
Two massy keys he bore of metals twain, *110*
(The golden opes, the iron shuts amain),
He shook his mitred [27] locks, and stern bespake:
'How well could I have spar'd for thee, young swain,
Enow of such, as for their bellies' sake,
Creep, and intrude, and climb into the fold! [28] *115*

19 *Arethusa, a fountain in Sicily, is associated with the pastoral poetry of Theocritus; Mincius, a river in Lombardy, with that of Virgil.*
20 *Triton.*
21 *Aeolus, the god of the winds, was the son of Hippotas.*
22 *The leader of the Nereids, or sea nymphs.*
23 *A most unpropitious time.*
24 *God of the river Cam.*
25 *I.e., like the hyacinth, on which the words of woe AI AI are found. The hyacinth was supposed to have sprung from the blood of a young man accidentally killed by Apollo.*
26 *St. Peter, originally a fisherman of Galilee, keeper of the keys of heaven.*
27 *He wears the bishop's miter because he was the founder and first bishop of the Christian church. It should be remembered that Milton's friend was a young clergyman.*
28 *I.e., the church.*

Of other care they little reckoning make,
Than how to scramble at the shearers' feast
And shove away the worthy bidden guest;
Blind mouths! that scarce themselves know how to hold
A sheep-hook,[29] or have learn'd aught else the least *120*
That to the faithful herdman's art belongs!
What recks it them? [30] What need they? They are sped;
And when they list, their lean and flashy songs
Grate on their scrannel [31] pipes of wretched straw;
The hungry sheep look up, and are not fed, *125*
But, swoln with wind and the rank mist they draw,
Rot inwardly, and foul contagion spread:
Besides what the grim wolf [32] with privy paw
Daily devours apace, and nothing said:
But that two-handed engine at the door [33] *130*
Stands ready to smite once, and smite no more.'
  Return Alpheus,[34] the dread voice is past,
That shrunk thy streams; return, Sicilian Muse,
And call the vales, and bid them hither cast
Their bells, and flowerets of a thousand hues. *135*
Ye valleys low, where the mild whispers use
Of shades, and wanton winds, and gushing brooks,
On whose fresh lap the swart star sparely looks; [35]
Throw hither all your quaint enamell'd eyes,
That on the green turf suck the honied showers, *140*
And purple all the ground with vernal flowers.
Bring the rathe [36] primrose that forsaken dies,
The tufted crow-toe, and pale jessamine,
The white pink, and the pansy freak'd with jet,
The glowing violet, *145*
The musk-rose, and the well-attir'd woodbine,
With cowslips wan that hang the pensive head,
And every flower that sad embroidery wears:
Bid Amaranthus [37] all his beauty shed,
And daffodillies fill their cups with tears, *150*
To strew the laureat herse [38] where Lycid lies.
For, so to interpose a little ease,

[29] *It should be noted that these men are pastors, properly keepers of flocks. The bishop's staff is made in the form of a shepherd's crook.*
[30] *What do they care? "They are sped": they have prospered.*
[31] *Harsh.*
[32] *The allusion is to Roman Catholicism.*
[33] *Perhaps the sword of St. Peter.*
[34] *A river in Sicily. The poet returns now to the pastoral vein.*
[35] *"the swart star sparely looks": the Dog Star looks witheringly.*
[36] *Early.*
[37] *The amaranth is a mythical flower that was supposed never to fade.*
[38] *The bier covered with laurels.*

Let our frail thoughts dally with false surmise;[39]
Ay me! Whilst thee the shores and sounding seas
Wash far away, where'er thy bones are hurl'd, *155*
Whether beyond the stormy Hebrides,[40]
Where thou perhaps, under the whelming tide,
Visit'st the bottom of the monstrous world;
Or whether thou, to our moist vows denied,
Sleep'st by the fable of Bellerus[41] old, *160*
Where the great Vision of the guarded Mount[42]
Looks towards Namancos and Bayona's hold;
Look homeward, Angel, now, and melt with ruth:[43]
And, O ye dolphins, waft the hapless youth.[44]
  Weep no more, woful Shepherds, weep no more, *165*
For Lycidas your sorrow is not dead,
Sunk though he be beneath the watery floor;
So sinks the day-star[45] in the ocean bed,
And yet anon repairs his drooping head,
And tricks[46] his beams, and with new-spangled ore *170*
Flames in the forehead of the morning sky:
So Lycidas sunk low, but mounted high,
Through the dear might of Him that walk'd the waves;
Where, other groves and other streams along,
With nectar pure his oozy locks he laves,[47] *175*
And hears the unexpressive nuptial song,[48]
In the blest kingdoms meek of joy and love.
There entertain him all the saints above,
In solemn troops, and sweet societies,
That sing, and, singing, in their glory move, *180*
And wipe the tears for ever from his eyes.
Now, Lycidas, the shepherds weep no more;
Henceforth thou art the Genius[49] of the shore,
In thy large recompense, and shalt be good
To all that wander in that perilous flood. *185*

39 *False because Lycidas' body had not been recovered from the sea.*
40 *Islands off Scotland that mark the northern limit of the Irish Sea.*
41 *I.e., by Land's End in Cornwall, where the giant Bellerus is supposed to have been buried.*
42 *St. Michael's mount in Cornwall. Milton imagines the archangel to be looking southward across the Atlantic to Bayona and Namancos in northern Spain, stronghold of Roman Catholicism, against which he stands guard.*
43 *Pity.*
44 *In Greek myth, dolphins carried Arion ashore because they loved his verses.*
45 *The sun.*
46 *Dresses.*
47 *Bathes.*
48 *The inexpressible song sung at "the marriage supper of the Lamb" (Revelation 19).*
49 *Local spirit.*

Thus sang the uncouth swain [50] to the oaks and rills,
While the still morn went out with sandals grey;
He touch'd the tender stops of various quills,
With eager thought warbling his Doric [51] lay:
And now the sun had stretch'd out all the hills, *190*
And now was dropt into the western bay:
At last he rose, and twitch'd his mantle blue:
To-morrow to fresh woods, and pastures new.

1637

[50] *Uneducated shepherd.*
[51] *Rustic.*

Questions

1. What, in the most general terms, is the subject of the fifth paragraph?
2. What is the connection between the thought of the sixth paragraph and that of the fifth?
3. Are lines 112–131 relevant to the central theme of the poem?
4. What is the effect of the poem's many allusions to legendary or historical places, persons, and events?

They Are All Gone into the World of Light!

HENRY VAUGHAN

They are all gone into the world of light!
  And I alone sit lingering here;
Their very memory is fair and bright,
  And my sad thoughts doth clear.[1]

It glows and glitters in my cloudy breast *5*
  Like stars upon some gloomy grove,
Or those faint beams in which this hill is dressed
  After the sun's remove.

I see them walking in an air of glory,
  Whose light doth trample on my days; *10*
My days, which are at best but dull and hoary,
  Mere glimmering and decays.

O holy hope, and high humility,

[1] *I.e., the memory of them brightens my thoughts.*

High as the heavens above!
These are your walks, and you have showed them me *15*
To kindle my cold love.

Dear, beauteous death! the jewel of the just,
Shining nowhere but in the dark;
What mysteries do lie beyond thy dust,
Could man outlook that mark! [2] *20*

He that hath found some fledged bird's nest may know
At first sight if the bird be flown;
But what fair well [3] or grove he sings in now,
That is to him unknown.

And yet, as angels in some brighter dreams *25*
Call to the soul when man doth sleep,
So some strange thoughts transcend our wonted [4] themes,
And into glory peep.

If a star were confined into a tomb,
Her captive flames must needs burn there; *30*
But when the hand that locked her up gives room,
She'll shine through all the sphere.

O Father of eternal life, and all
Created glories under Thee!
Resume Thy spirit from this world of thrall [5] *35*
Into true liberty!

Either disperse these mists, which blot and fill
My perspective [6] still as they pass;
Or else remove me hence unto that hill [7]
Where I shall need no glass. *40*

1655

[2] *I.e., see beyond that limit.*
[3] *Spring.*
[4] *Usual.*
[5] *I.e., reclaim the spirit, which is yours because created by you, from the captivity of earthly life.*
[6] *Telescope, i.e., the power to see far into the future.*
[7] *The allusion is to Zion Hill.*

Questions

1. Where is the speaker? What time of day is it?
2. How many metaphors involving light or vision or both are there in this poem?

Dirge

JAMES SHIRLEY

The glories of our blood and state
  Are shadows, not substantial things;
There is no armor against fate;
  Death lays his icy hand on kings:
    Scepter and crown *5*
    Must tumble down,
And in the dust be equal made
With the poor crooked scythe and spade.

Some men with swords may reap the field,
  And plant fresh laurels where they kill; *10*
But their strong nerves at last must yield;
  They tame but one another still:
    Early or late,
    They stoop to fate,
And must give up their murmuring breath, *15*
When they, pale captives, creep to death.

The garlands wither on your brow,
  Then boast no more your mighty deeds;
Upon Death's purple altar now,
  See where the victor-victim bleeds: *20*
    Your heads must come
    To the cold tomb;
Only the actions of the just
Smell sweet and blossom in their dust.

1658

Questions

1. What are the glories of "blood"? Of "state"?
2. What class of men is Shirley talking about in the second stanza? What does "plant fresh laurels" mean?
3. Why is the glory achieved through killing unimpressive when viewed in the right perspective?
4. Do you think that men would behave differently if they had a stronger sense of the imminence of death?

Ode: Intimations of Immortality from Recollections of Early Childhood

WILLIAM WORDSWORTH

The Child is Father of the man;
And I could wish my days to be
Bound each to each by natural piety.[1]

1

There was a time when meadow, grove, and stream,
The earth, and every common sight,
To me did seem
Appareled in celestial light,
The glory and the freshness of a dream.[2] *5*
It is not now as it hath been of yore;–
Turn whereso'er I may,
By night or day,
The things which I have seen I now can see no more.

2

The rainbow comes and goes, *10*
And lovely is the rose,
The moon doth with delight
Look round her when the heavens are bare,
Waters on a starry night
Are beautiful and fair; *15*
The sunshine is a glorious birth;
But yet I know, where'er I go,
That there hath passed away a glory from the earth.

3

Now, while the birds thus sing a joyous song,
And while the young lambs bound *20*
As to the tabor's[3] sound,
To me alone there came a thought of grief;

[1] *These are the concluding lines of Wordsworth's "My Heart Leaps Up."*
[2] *In a commentary on this poem Wordsworth wrote: "To that dreamlike vividness and splendor which invest objects of sight in childhood, everyone, I believe, if he would look back, could bear testimony. . . ."*
[3] *Small drum.*

A timely utterance gave that thought relief,
And I again am strong:
The cataracts blow their trumpets from the steep; 25
No more shall grief of mine the season wrong;
I hear the echoes through the mountains throng,
The winds come to me from the fields of sleep,[4]
And all the earth is gay;
Land and sea 30
Give themselves up to jollity
And with the heart of May
Doth every beast keep holiday;–
Thou child of joy,
Shout round me, let me hear thy shouts, thou happy shepherd boy. 35

4

Ye blessed Creatures, I have heard the call
Ye to each other make; I see
The heavens laugh with you in your jubilee;
My heart is at your festival,
My head hath its coronal, 40
The fullness of your bliss, I feel–I feel it all.
Oh evil day! if I were sullen
While Earth herself is adorning,
This sweet May-morning,
And the children are culling 45
On every side,
In a thousand valleys far and wide,
Fresh flowers; while the sun shines warm,
And the babe leaps up on his mother's arm:–
I hear, I hear, with joy I hear! 50
–But there's a tree, of many, one,
A single field which I have looked upon,
Both of them speak of something that is gone:
The pansy at my feet
Doth the same tale repeat: 55
Whither is fled the visionary gleam?
Where is it now, the glory and the dream?

5

Our birth is but a sleep and a forgetting:
The soul that rises with us, our life's star,
Hath had elsewhere its setting, 60
And cometh from afar;
Not in entire forgetfulness,
And not in utter nakedness,

[4] *I.e. (conjecturally), from dreamland.*

But trailing clouds of glory do we come
From God, who is our home. 65
Heaven lies about us in our infancy;
Shades of the prison-house begin to close
Upon the growing boy,
But he beholds the light, and whence it flows.
He sees it in his joy; 70
The youth, who daily farther from the east
Must travel, still is Nature's priest,
And by the vision splendid
Is on his way attended;
At length the man perceives it die away, 75
And fade into the light of common day.

6

Earth fills her lap with pleasures of her own;
Yearnings she hath in her own natural kind,
And, even with something of a mother's mind,
And no unworthy aim, 80
The homely [5] nurse doth all she can
To make her foster-child, her inmate man,
Forget the glories he hath known,
And that imperial palace whence he came.

7

Behold the child among his newborn blisses, 85
A six years' darling of a pygmy size!
See, where 'mid work of his own hand he lies,
Fretted [6] by sallies of his mother's kisses,
With light upon him from his father's eyes!
See, at his feet, some little plan or chart, 90
Some fragment from his dream of human life,
Shaped by himself with newly learned art;
A wedding or a festival,
A mourning or a funeral;
And this hath now his heart, 95
And unto this he frames his song:
Then will he fit his tongue
To dialogues of business, love, or strife;
But it will not be long
Ere this be thrown aside, 100
And with new joy and pride
The little actor cons another part;

[5] *Kindly.*
[6] *Imprinted.*

Filling from time to time his "humorous stage" [7]
With all the persons, down to palsied age,
That life brings with her in her equipage; *105*
As if his whole vocation
Were endless imitation.

8

Thou, whose exterior semblance doth belie
Thy soul's immensity;
Thou best philosopher, who yet dost keep *110*
Thy heritage, thou eye among the blind,
That, deaf and silent, read'st the eternal deep,
Haunted forever by the eternal mind–
Mighty prophet! seer blest!
On whom those truths do rest, *115*
Which we are toiling all our lives to find,
In darkness lost, the darkness of the grave;
Thou, over whom thy immortality
Broods like the day, a master o'er a slave,
A presence which is not to be put by; *120*
Thou little Child, yet glorious in the might
Of heaven-born freedom on thy being's height,
Why with such earnest pains dost thou provoke
The years to bring the inevitable yoke,
Thus blindly with thy blessedness at strife? *125*
Full soon thy Soul shall have her earthly freight,
And custom lie upon thee with a weight,
Heavy as frost, and deep almost as life!

9

O joy! that in our embers
Is something that doth live, *130*
That nature yet remembers
What was so fugitive!
The thought of our past years in me doth breed
Perpetual benediction: not indeed
For that which is most worthy to be blest– *135*
Delight and liberty, the simple creed
Of childhood, whether busy or at rest,
With new-fledged hope still fluttering in his breast:–
Not for these I raise
The song of thanks and praise; *140*
But for those obstinate questionings
Of sense and outward things,

[7] *The quotation is from a sonnet by Samuel Daniel, the Elizabethan poet. "Humorous" means "whimsical."*

Falling from us, vanishings; [8]
Blank misgivings of a creature
Moving about in worlds not realized,[9] *145*
High instincts before which our mortal nature
Did tremble like a guilty thing surprised: [10]
But for those first affections,
Those shadowy recollections,
Which, be they what they may, *150*
Are yet the fountain-light of all our day,
Are yet a master-light of all our seeing;
Uphold us, cherish, and have power to make
Our noisy years seem moments in the being
Of the eternal silence: truths that wake, *155*
To perish never;
Which neither listlessness, nor mad endeavor,
Nor man nor boy,
Nor all that is at enmity with joy,
Can utterly abolish or destroy! *160*
Hence in a season of calm weather,
Though inland far we be,
Our souls have sight of that immortal sea
Which brought us hither,
Can in a moment travel thither, *165*
And see the children sport upon the shore,
And hear the mighty waters rolling evermore.

10

Then sing, ye birds! sing, sing a joyous song!
And let the young lambs bound
As to the tabor's sound! *170*
We in thought will join your throng,
Ye that pipe and ye that play,
Ye that through your hearts today
Feel the gladness of the May!

[8] *Wordsworth wrote: ". . . I was often unable to think of external things as having external existence, and I communed with all that I saw as something not apart from, but inherent in, my own immaterial nature. Many times while going to school I have grasped at a wall or tree to recall myself from this abyss of idealism to the reality. At that time I was afraid of such processes. In later periods of life I have deplored, as we have all reason to do, a subjugation of an opposite character, and have rejoiced over the remembrances, as expressed in the lines—*

Obstinate questionings
Of sense and outward things,
Fallings from us, vanishings, etc."

[9] *Not become real.*

[10] *An allusion to the Ghost in Hamlet, which "started like a guilty thing" upon hearing the cock crow.*

What though the radiance which was once so bright *175*
Be now forever taken from my sight,
    Though nothing can bring back the hour
Of splendor in the grass, or glory in the flower;
        We will grieve not, rather find
        Strength in what remains behind; *180*
        In the primal sympathy [11]
        Which having been must ever be;
        In the soothing thoughts that spring
        Out of human suffering;
        In the faith that looks through death, *185*
In years that bring the philosophic mind.

11

And oh, ye fountains, meadows, hills, and groves,
Forbode not any severing of our loves!
Yet in my heart of hearts I feel your might;
I only have relinquished one delight *190*
To live beneath your more habitual sway.
I love the brooks which down their channels fret,
Even more than when I tripped lightly as they;
The innocent brightness of a new-born day
        Is lovely yet; *195*
The clouds that gather round the setting sun
Do take a sober coloring from an eye
That hath kept watch o'er man's mortality;
Another race hath been, and other palms are won.
Thanks to the human heart by which we live, *200*
Thanks to its tenderness, its joys and fears,
To me the meanest flower that blows can give
Thoughts that do often lie too deep for tears.

1807

[11] *The basic sympathy between the mind and nature that gives a sense of the unity of existence.*

Questions

1. What is the relation between the child's sense of his own being and his sense of the glory of nature?
2. Why is growing up, as it is described here, like a process of imprisonment?
3. What does the poet mean by "the soothing thoughts that spring / Out of human suffering" (lines 183–184)?
4. Explain the meaning of the last two lines of the poem.

Thanatopsis[1]

WILLIAM CULLEN BRYANT

To him who in the love of Nature holds
Communion with her visible forms, she speaks
A various language: for his gayer hours
She has a voice of gladness, and a smile
And eloquence of beauty; and she glides *5*
Into his darker musings with a mild
And healing sympathy that steals away
Their sharpness ere he is aware. When thoughts
Of the last bitter hour come like a blight
Over thy spirit, and sad images *10*
Of the stern agony and shroud and pall
And breathless darkness and the narrow house
Make thee to shudder and grow sick at heart,
Go forth under the open sky and list
To Nature's teachings, while from all around – *15*
Earth and her waters and the depths of air –
Comes a still voice:
Yet a few days, and thee
The all-beholding sun shall see no more
In all his course; nor yet in the cold ground,
Where thy pale form was laid with many tears, *20*
Nor in the embrace of ocean, shall exist
Thy image. Earth, that nourished thee shall claim
Thy growth, to be resolved to earth again
And, lost each human trace, surrendering up
Thine individual being, shalt thou go *25*
To mix for ever with the elements,
To be a brother to the insensible rock
And to the sluggish clod, which the rude swain
Turns with his share and treads upon; the oak
Shall send his roots abroad and pierce thy mould. *30*

Yet not to thine eternal resting-place
Shalt thou retire alone, nor couldst thou wish
Couch more magnificent. Thou shalt lie down
With patriarchs of the infant world, with kings,
The powerful of the earth, the wise, the good, *35*
Fair forms, and hoary seers of ages past,
All in one mighty sepulchre. The hills
Rock-ribbed and ancient as the sun; the vales

[1] *Derived from Greek words meaning "view of death."*

Stretching in pensive quietness between;
The venerable woods, rivers that move *40*
In majesty, and the complaining brooks
That make the meadows green; and, poured round all,
Old Ocean's gray and melancholy waste, –
Are but the solemn decorations all
Of the great tomb of man. The golden sun, *45*
The planets, all the infinite host of heaven,
Are shining on the sad abodes of death,
Through the still lapse of ages. All that tread
The globe are but a handful to the tribes
That slumber in its bosom. Take the wings *50*
Of morning, pierce the Barcan wilderness,
Or lose thyself in the continuous woods
Where rolls the Oregon, and hears no sound
Save his own dashings; yet the dead are there,
And millions in those solitudes, since first *55*
The flight of years began, have laid them down
In their last sleep: the dead reign there alone.
So shalt thou rest; and what if thou withdraw
In silence from the living, and no friend
Take note of thy departure? All that breathe *60*
Will share thy destiny. The gay will laugh
When thou art gone, the solemn brood of care
Plod on, and each one as before will chase
His favorite phantom; yet all these shall leave
Their mirth and their employments, and shall come *65*
And make their bed with thee. As the long train
Of ages glide away, the sons of men –
The youth in life's green spring, and he who goes
In the full strength of years, matron and maid,
The speechless babe, and the gray-headed man – *70*
Shall one by one be gathered to thy side
By those who in their turn shall follow them.

So live that when thy summons comes to join
The innumerable caravan which moves
To that mysterious realm where each shall take *75*
His chamber in the silent halls of death,
Thou go not, like the quarry-slave at night,
Scourged to his dungeon, but, sustained and soothed
By an unfaltering trust, approach thy grave
Like one who wraps the drapery of his couch *80*
About him and lies down to pleasant dreams.

1817

Questions

1. Nature, personified, begins to speak at line 17. How far does this speech extend?
2. What are the main points in the utterance attributed to Nature?
3. Define the conception of nature presented here.
4. Do you think that sufficient basis has been supplied for the "unfaltering trust" recommended in line 79?

To Autumn

JOHN KEATS

Season of mists and mellow fruitfulness,
Close bosom-friend of the maturing sun;
Conspiring with him how to load and bless
With fruit the vines that round the thatch-eaves run; *5*
To bend with apples the mossed cottage-trees,
And fill all fruit with ripeness to the core;
To swell the gourd, and plump the hazel shells
With a sweet kernel; to set budding more,
And still more, later flowers for the bees,
Until they think warm days will never cease, *10*
For summer has o'er-brimmed their clammy cells.

II

Who hath not seen thee oft amid thy store?
Sometimes whoever seeks abroad may find
Thee sitting careless on a granary floor,
Thy hair soft-lifted by the winnowing wind; *15*
Or on a half-reaped furrow sound asleep,
Drowsed with the fume of poppies, while thy hook [1]
Spares the next swath and all its twined flowers:
And sometime like a gleaner thou dost keep
Steady thy laden head across a brook; *20*
Or by a cider-press, with patient look,
Thou watchest the last oozings hours by hours.

III

Where are the songs of Spring? Ay, where are they?
Think not of them, thou hast thy music too,—
While barred clouds bloom the soft-dying day, *25*
And touch the stubble-plains with rosy hue;
Then in a wailful choir the small gnats mourn

[1] *Scythe.*

Among the river sallows,[2] borne aloft
Or sinking as the light wind lives or dies;
And full-grown lambs loud bleat from hilly bourn; *30*
Hedge-crickets sing; and now with treble soft
The red-breast whistles from a garden-croft; [3]
And gathering swallows twitter in the skies.

1820

[2] *Willows.*
[3] *A croft is a small, enclosed piece of land.*

Questions

1. How would you justify the inclusion of this poem in a group of poems having to do with death? Is the passing of time mentioned?
2. The poet makes much of the fact that the movement of time seems to be suspended. With what frame of mind, attitude, or emotional state is this idea connected?

Prospice[1]

ROBERT BROWNING

Fear death?—to feel the fog in my throat,
The mist in my face,
When the snows begin, and the blasts denote
I am nearing the place,
The power of the night, the press of the storm,
The post of the foe;
Where he stands, the Arch Fear in a visible form,
Yet the strong man must go:
For the journey is done and the summit attained,
And the barriers fall, *10*
Though a battle's to fight ere the guerdon be gained,
The reward of it all.
I was ever a fighter, so—one fight more,
The best and the last!
I would hate that death bandaged my eyes, and forebore,
And bade me creep past.
No! let me taste the whole of it, fare like my peers
The heroes of old,
Bear the brunt, in a minute pay glad life's arrears

[1] *"Prospice" means "look forward." This poem was written shortly after the death of the poet's wife.*

Of pain, darkness and cold. *20*
For sudden the worst turns the best to the brave,
The black minute's at end,
And the elements' rage, the fiend-voices that rave,
Shall dwindle, shell blend,
Shall change, shall become first a peace out of pain,
Then a light, then thy breast,
O thou soul of my soul! I shall clasp thee again,
And with God be the rest!

1864

Questions

1. Why does the poet want to be fully aware of the approach of death? Does he expect the experience to be pleasant?
2. Does the poet's conception of "the reward of it all" suggest that he regards life merely as a trial, a means to an end?

The Garden of Proserpine[1]

A. C. SWINBURNE

Here, where the world is quiet;
Here, where all trouble seems
Dead winds' and spent waves' riot
In doubtful dreams of dreams;
I watch the green field growing
For reaping folk and sowing,
For harvest-time and mowing,
A sleepy world of streams.

I am tired of tears and laughter,
And men that laugh and weep; *10*
Of what may come hereafter
For men that sow to reap:
I am weary of days and hours,
Blown buds of barren flowers,
Desires and dreams and powers
And everything but sleep.

Here life has death for a neighbour,

[1] *Proserpine, in ancient myth, is queen of the underworld. Thus her garden is the dwelling-place of the dead.*

And far from eye or ear
Wan waves and wet winds labour,
Weak ships and spirits steer; *20*
They drive adrift, and whither
They wot not who make thither;
But no such winds blow hither,
And no such things grow here.

No growth of moor or coppice,
No heather-flower or vine,
But bloomless buds of poppies,
Green grapes of Proserpine,
Pale beds of blowing rushes
Where no leaf blooms or blushes *30*
Save this whereout she crushes
For dead men deadly wine.

Pale, without name or number,
In fruitless fields of corn,
They bow themselves and slumber
All night till light is born;
And like a soul belated,
In hell and heaven unmated,
By cloud and mist abated
Comes out of darkness morn. *40*

Though one were strong as seven,
He too with death shall dwell,
Nor wake with wings in heaven,
Nor weep for pains in hell;
Though one were fair as roses,
His beauty clouds and closes,
And well though love reposes,
In the end it is not well.

Pale, beyond porch and portal,
Crowned with calm leaves, she stands *50*
Who gathers all things mortal
With cold immortal hands;
Her languid lips are sweeter
Than love's who fears to greet her
To men that mix and meet her
From many times and lands.

She waits for each and other,
She waits for all men born;
Forgets the earth her mother,
The life of fruits and corn; *60*
And spring and seed and swallow

Take wing for her and follow
Where summer song rings hollow
  And flowers are put to scorn.

There go the loves that wither,
  The old loves with wearier wings;
And all dead years draw thither,
  And all disastrous things;
Dead dreams of days forsaken,
Blind buds that snows have shaken, *70*
Wild leaves that winds have taken
  Red strays of ruined springs.

We are not sure of sorrow,
  And joy was never sure;
To-day will die to-morrow;
  Time stoops to no man's lure;
And love, grown faint and fretful,
With lips but half regretful
Sighs, and with eyes forgetful
  Weeps that no loves endure. *80*

From too much love of living,
  From hope and fear set free,
We thank with brief thanksgiving
  Whatever gods may be
That no life lives for ever;
That dead men rise up never;
That even the weariest river
  Winds somewhere safe to sea.

Then star nor sun shall waken,
  Nor any change of light: *90*
Nor sound of waters shaken,
  Nor any sound or sight:
Nor wintry leaves nor vernal,
Nor days nor things diurnal;
Only the sleep eternal
  In an eternal night.

1866

Questions

1. By means of the garden metaphor the poet describes a state of mind in which the thought of becoming extinct is more than acceptable. If you were asked to explain this state of mind in more ordinary terms,

what facts would you emphasize? Does the speaker, for example, make any distinctions in speaking of human ambitions and desires? Does he think that moral desires matter more than others? Does he feel that he is different from other people? What has brought him to his present state of mind?

2. Do you find the rhyme scheme appropriate? Explain the effect that it has on you.

Requiem

ROBERT LOUIS STEVENSON

Under the wide and starry sky
Dig the grave and let me lie:
Glad did I live and gladly die,
And I laid me down with a will.

This be the verse you grave for me:
Here he lies where he long'd to be;
Home is the sailor, home from the sea,
And the hunter home from the hill.

1887

Questions

1. What does the poet mean by the line "Here he lies where he long'd to be"? In what sense is he "home"? Can you imagine any resemblance between the feelings of a sailor returning home from the sea and those of a man nearing the end of the whole adventure of life?
2. "Home," it seems, is anywhere under the "wide and starry" sky. What does this suggest about the speaker's attitude toward life? What does the word "starry" add to the meaning or effect?

The Caged Skylark

GERARD MANLEY HOPKINS

As a dare-gale skylark scanted in a dull cage
Man's mounting spirit in his bone-house,[1] mean house, dwells —

[1] *The body.*

That bird beyond the remembering his free fells;
This in drudgery, day-labouring-out life's age.

Thou aloft on turf [2] or perch or poor low stage, 5
Both sing sometímes the sweetest, sweetest spells,
Yet both droop deadly sómetimes in their cells
Or wring their barriers in bursts of fear or rage.

Not that the sweet-fowl, song-fowl, needs no rest –
Why, hear him, hear him babble and drop down to his nest, 10
But his own nest, wild nest, no prison.

Man's spirit will be flesh-bound when found at best,
But uncumbered: [3] meadow-down is not distressed
For a rainbow footing it nor he for his bónes rísen.

1918 (Composed 1877)

[2] *A mound of turf is usually put inside a lark's cage. "Poor low state" may refer both to a shelf in a cage and any human situation.*
[3] *Hopkins is referring to the Catholic doctrine which states that the resurrected body is immortal and not subject to physical limitations.*

Questions

1. What precisely are the implications of the analogy between an uncaged skylark and the condition of man after resurrection?
2. Do you think that in comparing the spirit in its earthly condition with a caged bird, the poet is thinking only of the limitations of the body? Explain.

Channel Firing

THOMAS HARDY

That night your great guns, unawares,
Shook all our coffins as we lay,
And broke the chancel window-squares,
We thought it was the Judgment-day

And sat upright. While drearisome 5
Arose the howl of wakened hounds:
The mouse let fall the altar-crumb,
The worms drew back into the mounds,

The glebe [1] cow drooled. Till God called, "No;
It's gunnery practice out at sea *10*
Just as before you went below;
The world is as it used to be:

"All nations striving strong to make
Red war yet redder. Mad as hatters
They do no more for Christés [2] sake *15*
Than you who are helpless in such matters.

"That this is not the judgment-hour
For some of them's a blessed thing,
For if it were they'd have to scour
Hell's floor for so much threatening . . . *20*

"Ha, ha. It will be warmer when
I blow the trumpet (if indeed
I ever do; for you are men,
And rest eternal sorely need)."

So down we lay again. "I wonder, *25*
Will the world ever saner be,"
Said one, "than when He sent us under
In our indifferent century!"

And many a skeleton shook his head.
"Instead of preaching forty year," *30*
My neighbor Parson Thirdly said,
"I wish I had stuck to pipes and beer."

Again the guns disturbed the hour,
Roaring their readiness to avenge,
As far inland as Stourton [3] Tower, *35*
And Camelot, and starlit Stonehenge.

1914

[1] *A "glebe" is a small field.*
[2] *The archaic spelling suggests the old ballads and their sad, fatalistic tone.*
[3] *A town some distance away. Camelot, of course, is the legendary capital of King Arthur's realm, Stonehenge the famous prehistoric circle of stones in Salisbury plain.*

Questions

1. Does the poet seem to find the thought of the dead rising from their graves exciting? Is he being ironic in suggesting the possibility? Would it be appropriate to associate this imagined incident with such a phrase as "enough racket to wake the dead"?

2. Can you detect a change of tone in the utterance ascribed to God? Which part of the speech best fits the conventional conception of God? What is the point of introducing a different conception?
3. Is there a significant connection between the phrase "Roaring their readiness to avenge" (line 34) and the threat uttered in lines 19–20?
4. What relationship does the poet see between the channel firing and Camelot or "starlit Stonehenge"?

Tract

WILLIAM CARLOS WILLIAMS

I will teach you my townspeople
how to perform a funeral–
for you have it over a troop
of artists–
unless one should scour the world– *5*
you have the ground sense necessary.

See! the hearse leads.
I begin with a design for a hearse.
For Christ's sake not black–
nor white either–and not polished! *10*
Let it be weathered–like a farm wagon–
with gilt wheels (this could be
applied fresh at small expense)
or no wheels at all:
a rough dray to drag over the ground. *15*

Knock the glass out!
My God–glass, my townspeople!
For what purpose? Is it for the dead
to look out or for us to see
how well he is housed or to see *20*
the flowers or the lack of them–
or what?
To keep the rain and snow from him?
He will have a heavier rain soon:
pebbles and dirt and what not. *25*
Let there be no glass–
and no upholstery phew!
and no little brass rollers
and small easy wheels on the bottom–
my townspeople what are you thinking of? *30*

A rough plain hearse then
with gilt wheels and no top at all.
On this the coffin lies
by its own weight.
                    No wreaths please— 35
especially no hot house flowers.
Some common memento is better,
something he prized and is known by:
his old clothes—a few books perhaps—
God knows what! You realize 40
how we are about these things
my townspeople—
something will be found—anything
even flowers if he had come to that.
So much for the hearse. 45

For heaven's sake though see to the driver!
Take off the silk hat! In fact
that's no place at all for him—
up there unceremoniously
dragging our friend out to his own dignity! 50
Bring him down—bring him down!
Low and inconspicuous! I'd not have him ride
on the wagon at all—damn him—
the undertaker's understrapper!
Let him hold the reins 55
and walk at the side
and inconspicuously too!

Then briefly as to yourselves:
Walk behind—as they do in France,
seventh class, or if you ride 60
Hell take curtains! Go with some show
of inconvenience; sit openly—
to the weather as to grief.
Or do you think you can shut grief in?
What—from us? We who have perhaps 65
nothing to lose? Share with us
share with us—it will be money
in your pockets.
                    Go now
I think you are ready. 70

1917

Questions

1. Why does the poet want the hearse to be weathered? How would the effect of a weathered vehicle differ from that of one painted entirely in black or white? If the poet does not want the vehicle painted, why should he suggest gilt wheels?
2. The poet explains why he does not want glass in the hearse. Does he object to upholstery for the same reason? Why does he find "small easy wheels" almost unthinkable?
3. Is the poet being snobbish in calling the driver the "undertaker's understrapper"? What is his point in using a snobbish phrase with such vehemence?
4. Explain the phrase, "We who have perhaps / nothing to lose." Nothing to lose by what? What is the tone of the phrase, "money in your pockets"?
5. What is the general attitude toward death that the poet is objecting to?

Bells for John Whiteside's Daughter

JOHN CROWE RANSOM

There was such speed in her little body,
And such lightness in her footfall,
It is no wonder that her brown study [1]
Astonishes us all.

Her wars were bruited [2] in our high window. 5
We looked among orchard trees and beyond,
Where she took arms against her shadow,
Or harried unto the pond

The lazy geese, like a snow cloud
Dripping their snow on the green grass, 10
Tricking and stopping, sleepy and proud,
Who cried in goose, Alas,

For the tireless heart within the little
Lady with rod that made them rise
From their noon apple dreams, and scuttle 15
Goose-fashion under the skies!

But now go the bells, and we are ready;
In one house we are sternly stopped
To say we are vexed at her brown study,
Lying so primly propped. 20

1927

[1] *Withdrawn, meditative look.*
[2] *Reported.*

Questions

1. Why does the poet devote so much space to the description of the little girl driving the geese into the pond? Is the image symbolic? What elements in the description make us think of the coming death of the child? Is there irony in the implications of the description? What is the tone of the passage?
2. What is the effect of the bells on the mourners? Are the mourners really ready?

After Apple-Picking

ROBERT FROST

My long two-pointed ladder's sticking through a tree
Toward heaven still,
And there's a barrel that I didn't fill
Beside it, and there may be two or three
Apples I didn't pick upon some bough. *5*
But I am done with apple-picking now.
Essence of winter sleep is on the night,
The scent of apples: I am drowsing off.
I cannot rub the strangeness from my sight
I got from looking through a pane of glass *10*
I skimmed this morning from the drinking trough
And held against the world of hoary grass.
It melted, and I let it fall and break.
But I was well
Upon my way to sleep before it fell, *15*
And I could tell
What form my dreaming was about to take.
Magnified apples appear and disappear,
Stem end and blossom end,
And every fleck of russet showing clear. *20*
My instep arch not only keeps the ache,
It keeps the pressure of a ladder-round.
I feel the ladder sway as the boughs bend.
And I keep hearing from the cellar bin
The rumbling sound *25*

Of load on load of apples coming in.
For I have had too much
Of apple-picking: I am overtired
Of the great harvest I myself desired.
There were ten thousand thousand fruit to touch, *30*
Cherish in hand, lift down, and not let fall.
For all
That struck the earth,
No matter if not bruised or spiked with stubble,
Went surely to the cider-apple heap *35*
As of no worth.
One can see what will trouble
This sleep of mine, whatever sleep it is.
Were he not gone,
The woodchuck could say whether it's like his *40*
Long sleep, as I describe its coming on,
Or just some human sleep.

1930

Questions

1. How do we know that the poet is not talking just about the experience of apple-picking and ordinary drowsiness? How would you "translate" the following lines: "There were ten thousand thousand fruit to touch, / Cherish in hand, lift down, and not let fall"?
2. Pick out the words or phrases in this poem that suggest a sense of the ideal.
3. Why does the poet use such an ordinary experience as apple-picking to symbolize all of his aspirations and achievements?
4. What is the point of the last four lines?

Musée des Beaux Arts[1]

W. H. AUDEN

About suffering they were never wrong,
The Old Masters: how well they understood
Its human position; how it takes place

[1] *Museum of Fine Arts.*

While someone else is eating or opening a window or just walking
dully along;
How, when the aged are reverently, passionately waiting 5
For the miraculous birth, there always must be
Children who did not specially want it to happen, skating
On a pond at the edge of the wood:
They never forgot
That even the dreadful martyrdom must run its course 10
Anyhow in a corner, some untidy spot
Where the dogs go on with their doggy life and the torturer's horse
Scratches its innocent behind on a tree.
In Brueghel's *Icarus*,[2] for instance; how everything turns away
Quite leisurely from the disaster; the ploughman may 15
Have heard the splash, the forsaken cry,
But for him it was not an important failure; the sun shone
As it had to on the white legs disappearing into the green
Water; and the expensive delicate ship that must have seen
Something amazing, a boy falling out of the sky, 20
Had somewhere to get to and sailed calmly on.

1940

[2] *Icarus was the son of Daedalus, the legendary craftsman. The father and son escaped from the Cretan labyrinth by flying with artificial wings fastened to their shoulders with wax. Icarus, disregarding his father's warning, flew too near the sun; the wax which held his wings melted, and he fell into the sea. In the painting "Landscape with the Fall of Icarus" by Pieter Brueghel (c. 1520–1569), Icarus is shown disappearing into the sea. Only his legs are visible in the distance. The rest of the picture has nothing to do with him.*

Questions

1. Define the theme of this poem as precisely as you can. It is about suffering, of course, including the suffering that attends the facing of death. What else? Does the phrase, "the forsaken cry" pinpoint the matter?
2. Are there Christian allusions in the poem? What is their effect?
3. Does the poem have a "moral"? Does it have more meaning, would you say, than the painting by Brueghel?

TOPICS FOR COMPOSITION

1. Write an essay on the subject of coping with the fear of death, using one or more of the following poems for illustration: "Death, Be Not Proud"; "Thanatopsis"; "Prospice."

2. Analyze the use of the analogy between death and sleep in one or more of the poems in this unit.
3. Write an essay on the topic "Love of Nature and the Question of Death," using one or more of the following poems for illustration: "Ode: Intimations of Immortality"; "Thanatopsis"; "To Autumn"; "After Apple-Picking"; "Hurt Hawks" (see Part Two).
4. Defend the opinion that men can live good and happy lives without believing in life after death.
5. Defend the opinion that traditional moral ideals are meaningless without belief in an afterlife.
6. Analyze Thomas Hardy's view of the traditional conception of divine judgment of the dead.
7. Compare the spirit of Swinburne's "The Garden of Prosperpine" with that of Browning's "Prospice."
8. In recent years there has been considerable protest against current funeral practices. Following William Carlos Williams' example, write on the subject of what is or is not appropriate at funerals.
9. If you have access to Brueghel's "Icarus," write your own impressionistic description of the scene portrayed in that painting.
10. Do you agree or disagree with Wordsworth's statement that growing up is a process of imprisonment? If you agree, explain his idea more fully. If you disagree, write a refutation of his argument.
11. Write an analysis of the handling of tone in any one of the poems of this section.
12. Write an essay on the topic, "The Poetic Idea of Heaven."
13. Write an analysis of the use of imagery in any of the poems in this unit.

Index of Authors, Titles, First Lines of Poems